THUNDER AND FLAMES

Modern War Studies

Theodore A. Wilson
General Editor

Raymond Callahan
J. Garry Clifford
Jacob W. Kipp
Allan R. Millett
Carol Reardon
Dennis Showalter
David R. Stone
Series Editors

Thunder and Flames

Americans in the Crucible of Combat, 1917–1918

EDWARD G. LENGEL

University Press of Kansas

© 2015 by the University Press of Kansas
First paperback edition published in 2023.
All rights reserved

Published by the University Press of Kansas (Lawrence, Kansas 66045), which was organized by the Kansas Board of Regents and is operated and funded by Emporia State University, Fort Hays State University, Kansas State University, Pittsburg State University, the University of Kansas, and Wichita State University

Library of Congress Cataloging-in-Publication Data

Lengel, Edward G.
Thunder and flames : Americans in the crucible of combat, 1917–1918 / Edward G. Lengel.
pages cm. — (Modern war studies)
Includes bibliographical references and index.
ISBN 978-0-7006-2084-5 (cloth : alk. paper)
ISBN 978-0-7006-2783-7 (paperback)
ISBN 978-0-7006-2085-2 (ebook)
1. World War, 1914–1918—United States. 2. United States. Army—History—World War, 1914–1918. 3. United States. Army. American Expeditionary Forces. 4. World War, 1914–1918—Campaigns—Western Front. I. Title.
D570.L46 2015
940.4′1273—dc23
2014048867

British Library Cataloguing-in-Publication Data is available.

Printed in the United States of America

10 9 8 7 6 5 4 3 2 1

The paper used in this publication is acid free and meets the minimum requirements of the American National Standard for Permanence of Paper for Printed Library Materials Z39.48-1992.

CONTENTS

Preface, *vii*

A Note on Maps, *xi*

Introduction: Approaches to Study of the AEF at War, 1917–1918, *1*

1 Setting the Stage, *10*

2 Into the Line: November 1917–April 1918, *26*

3 Cantigny: May 1918, *44*

4 Château-Thierry: May 1918, *63*

5 The 2d Division Enters the Lines: May 31–June 5, 1918, *74*

6 Into the Woods: June 6, 1918, *98*

7 "Sporting Soldiers": Belleau Wood, June 7–8, 1918, *124*

8 "We Want the Damn Woods": Belleau Wood, June 9–10, 1918, *136*

9 "No Idea of Tactical Principles": Belleau Wood, June 11–12, 1918, *142*

10 Gas and Exhaustion: Belleau Wood, June 13–15, 1918, *163*

11 Enter the US Army: Belleau Wood, June 16–21, 1918, *173*

12 Finishing the Job: June 22–July 2, 1918, *188*

13 Rock of the Marne: The Marne River Defense, July 15–17, 1918, *207*

14 "Deal the Enemy a Crushing Blow": Soissons, July 18–22, 1918, *242*

15 Reducing the Marne Salient: US Troops in the Aisne-Marne Campaign, July 18–August 6, 1918, *302*

16 Tragedy at Fismette: Travails of the 28th Division, August 1918, *338*

Conclusion: The Road to Saint-Mihiel, September 1918, *368*

Notes, *377*

Bibliography, *427*

Index, *435*

An illustration gallery follows page 155.

PREFACE

Writing about American military participation in World War I is rewarding but never easy. It is rewarding not only because of the subject's importance and inherent interest but also because so much of it has not been studied in any detail before. It is challenging because the choice of approach is not straightforward. No one will dispute that, in the United States, World War I is both poorly understood by the general public and understudied in the academy. From the outset, then, the historian has choices to make. One possibility is to take a "popular" approach, seeking to make a seemingly unattractive subject palatable to general readers by emphasizing the doughboys' personal experiences. Another is to write an academic monograph exploring subjects such as the foibles of high command, the challenges of strategy and tactics, the problems of administration and supply, or even culture and memory. The advantages and disadvantages of either approach are not necessarily clear-cut.

"Popular" books on America in the First World War typically make ample use of letters, diaries, memoirs, and other firsthand testimonies. The advantages of these are obvious. They make events come alive as no dry, official reports can do. They also remind us that, while generals were making decisions at the 30,000-foot level and lines were shifting on maps, individuals were making decisions and enduring or enjoying an infinite variety of experiences on the ground. Because the doughboys' stories have so rarely been told, and because (as this author can attest) the demand by veterans' descendants for these stories is great, there is a strong argument in favor of popular studies, regardless of how much academics may decry them. There are, however, dangers. First and foremost, memory is unreliable. Any comparison of personal and official accounts of any given military engagement reveals how much the former suffers from confusion, forgetfulness, rear-area gossip, or even deceit. Because each individual soldier's experience is unique, every story presents a different perspective. Which does the historian choose? No matter what the popular historian does, critics will inevitably chastise him or her for either glamorizing tragedies or trampling on the doughboys' dignity by emphasizing their misery and neglecting their heroism.

Academic studies (the good ones, anyway), by contrast, rely largely on official sources, with a few personal accounts thrown in as window dressing to loosen up the narrative. Here too the advantages are obvious. Official records are, of course, more accurate than personal accounts. Staff and field officers typically prepared these records on the basis of military documents and maps, along with eyewitness testimony. Intended for purposes of professional evaluation, such reports are often profoundly detailed and sometimes exceptionally dry. Although they are indispensable and, in the aggregate, truer to the actual events than (say) a memoir written fifty years after the war ended, official records do not tell the whole story or necessarily even the correct story, and they should not be considered in isolation. Many American after-action reports are based on poor and inaccurate information and even hearsay. Official records are replete with battle accounts that are wholly misleading, reflecting the optimism or pessimism of staff and field officers rather than what the soldiers were actually experiencing. In that sense, at least, there is strong justification not only for perusing official documents but also for considering the personal impressions of men and women remembering what it was like to be there—not a topic of concern for the compilers of official accounts. Although military officials studied the official records to greater or lesser degrees, personal experiences—rightly or wrongly—resonated with both the fighting men and the civilian society to which they would have to readjust.

This book attempts to strike a balance between the official and the personal, if not between the academic and the popular. In recounting and analyzing the combat experiences of the American Expeditionary Forces (AEF) between November 1917 and August 1918—many of which have never been chronicled before—it makes extensive use of American official records and some use of German and French official records. These records are extensive, and although they have been considered here in great depth, no single author can claim to have done more than scratch their surface. To do them justice would require a team of scholars working many years to compile an official history of the AEF in World War I—something that, alas, has never been undertaken. At the same time, this book seeks to integrate official records with a broad but by no means comprehensive variety of firsthand accounts, especially those that pertain to specific personal memories rather than to general recollections of what supposedly happened.

As with any balancing act, this one is bound to disappoint, in some fashion, both those looking for a "pure" operational study and those looking for a fast-paced narrative of thrill and adventure. No single volume can justly claim to have taken into consideration all the source material necessary to understand all aspects of such a broad sweep of events (ten months is practically an eternity in modern military history). My hope, however, is that it takes academic and general readers a step or two closer to understanding both the nature and the scale of American military participation in World War I. The tale is compelling, but it will take many more storytellers—and dedicated researchers—before it can be told with the accuracy and thoroughness it deserves.

Many individuals and institutions provided invaluable assistance in the preparation of this work. All scholars of the United States in the First World War are indebted to Dr. Timothy Nenninger, chief of the Textual Records staff at the US National Archives and Records Administration (NARA) in College Park, Maryland. In the absence of an official history of the AEF, historians must attempt (and for any individual, it can only be an attempt) a broad and deep perusal of the vast collection of records held at NARA. Dr. Nenninger is both the gatekeeper and the foremost expert on these records, and he and his staff extend a kind and actively helpful welcome to researchers. He was particularly helpful in directing me toward G-3 and G-5 files relating to Franco-American relations. This book could not have been completed without his assistance and expertise.

The US Army Heritage and Education Center in Carlisle, Pennsylvania, is rightfully considered a mecca for researchers on practically every topic in US military history. That reputation emerges not only from the vastness of its invaluable collections but also from the courtesy and professionalism of its staff. Dr. Richard J. Sommers, now emeritus but still welcoming visitors to the center on a regular basis, set the standard that has allowed it to become a model research facility. The collections there played a large role in this work.

Paul B. Barron, director of library and archives at the George C. Marshall Foundation in Lexington, Virginia, provided an invaluable entrée to the foundation's superb collection of materials relating to Marshall and the 1st Division. Dr. Paul H. Herbert, executive director of the First Division Museum at Cantigny, provided support and advice. Dr. Elizabeth Greenhalgh of the University of New South Wales was instrumental in helping me understand French military records. Alex Gregorio performed invaluable work as a student research assistant in 2013–2014. My gratitude is also extended to Dr. Mark E. Grotelueschen of the US Air Force Academy, Dr. Steven Trout of the University of South Alabama, Dr. Richard S. Faulkner of the US Army Command and General Staff College, Dr. Michael Neiberg of the US Army War College, and Dr. Jennifer Keene of Chapman University. Financial support for research was provided from a fund managed by the dean of the College of Arts and Sciences and the vice president for research and graduate studies at the University of Virginia.

Of course, all mistakes are my own.

A NOTE ON MAPS

Military history readers rightfully demand plentiful and accurate maps. The perception may be that military historians are unaccountably ignorant of this fact, but the truth is more prosaic. Works focusing solely on high-level strategy can usually narrate within the limits of a few large-scale maps. Tactical-level works face greater challenges, but as long as their scope is not too broad in terms of time, space, or units covered, providing adequate maps remains within the realm of possibility. Unfortunately, works presenting large battles—or a series of large battles—thoroughly and on a tactical level face almost insuperable cartographic obstacles. Custom-drawn maps may cost several hundred dollars apiece, so doing cartographic justice to complex military maneuvers often transcends the limited financial resources of authors and publishers.

This book presents multiple military encounters in detail from the corps level down to the squad level, over a period of ten months, and across broad swaths of eastern France. Visually depicting all the actions described would have entailed the preparation of at least a dozen custom maps (a conservative estimate), preferably of the foldout variety. This author has chosen not to "dumb down" the narrative just to remain within the limited confines of the official maps capable of being reproduced in this volume. Doing so would have meant, for example, neglecting the full story of the fight for Belleau Wood or discarding never-before-told stories of the Marne River defensive and the Aisne-Marne offensive. This would have robbed the narrative of its value.

The maps reproduced in this volume derive from two previously published sources: *American Armies and Battlefields in Europe* by the American Battle Monuments Commission, originally published in 1938 and reprinted by the US Army Center of Military History in 1992, and the seventeen-volume *United States Army in the World War*, published by the Center for Military History in 1988–1992. Others are taken from originals in the National Archives at College Park, Maryland. It is hoped that these will suffice for the general reader.

Readers interested in perusing the full details of the tactical events covered in this volume are referred to the superb and exceptionally detailed foldout maps published in the divisional *Summary of Operations* pamphlets by the American Battle Monuments Commission in 1944. Fortunately for readers and military historians, the maps from these paper-bound volumes (which are available in many university libraries) have been reproduced online by the University of Alabama. They are available at: http://alabamamaps.ua.edu/historicalmaps/worldwarI/OperationsintheWarIndex.htm.

Introduction

Approaches to Study of the AEF at War,
1917–1918

General Robert L. Bullard remembered the little French town of Fismette as the site of "the only accident of my military career." His men called the place Hell, partly because they had to pass through "Flames" to get there. "Flames" was doughboy jargon for the village of Fismes, on the south bank of the Vesle River. Situated in a broad, open valley, it was under constant enemy observation in August 1918, and the more the Americans reinforced it, the more the Germans saturated it with high explosives and poison gas. After moving up through Fismes—as thousands of doughboys of the 28th Division had to do that dreary August—the men could either race across a half-ruined stone bridge or pick their way over an adjacent shell-torn and jerry-rigged footbridge to reach Fismette on the river's north bank. This place, Bullard and other American and French generals insisted, must be held.[1]

Lieutenant Hervey Allen was one of those unfortunate enough to be ordered to cross the Vesle. He tried the stone bridge, but it was under bombardment, and "only a fool would have dashed out." So he found a drainage ditch, crawled down it, and eventually reached the riverside and the damaged footbridge:

> It took me about half an hour to crawl to the river. I had to put my mask on at the last, as the mustard gas was strong in the little hollow in which I lay. My hands were smarting. Some of the shells brought my heart into my mouth; lying there waiting for them was intolerable. I was sure I was going to be blown to pieces. The river was very nearly in flood and so there was no bank, the field gradually getting soggy and

swampy till it sloped out into the water. There was a lot of submerged barbed wire that made going ahead very painful and slow. I had, of course, to throw away my mask as it got full of water. My pistol went also. It was too heavy to risk.

When he reached the footbridge, the way across proved more difficult than it first looked:

Once in the water, I worked along under the single board of the footbridge, shifting along hand over hand, which took me halfway across. There I struck out, plunging in a few strokes to the other side and working through the wire. Swimming with shoes was not so difficult as I had thought, but the cold water seemed to take all my courage, which was what I needed more than ever. Our own machine guns were playing along the railroad track. . . . After getting across, it seemed for a while that I would be caught between the two fires. I lay there in the river for a minute and gave up. When you do that something dies inside.[2]

Allen survived. In Fismette, however, conditions were much worse than along the river. That tiny village formed a glorified "bridgehead" across the Vesle. The doughboys were supposed to hold it and expand it, if possible, with a view to launching an all-out offensive at a later date. At most, however, the place could hold two companies of men, and all they could do was hold on. From time to time, officers in Fismes or further back—no one above the rank of captain ever made it into Fismette, and the garrison was usually commanded by junior lieutenants—would order patrols, but these were typically shot down as soon as they left the shelter of a stone wall running along the village's northern rim. And the men had to be vigilant at all hours. As often as the Americans sent out patrols, the Germans attempted to wipe out the bridgehead with soldiers wielding bayonets, grenades, and flamethrowers.

One day, Allen's good friend Lieutenant Frank Whelton was commanding a small Chauchat (light machine gun) post in a shell hole in Fismette with a few men and his Italian "striker," Nick de Saza: According to Whelton:

We sat there and waited but nothing more happened and it became too quiet. Nick saw that I was fidgety and started to tell me about his little girl, "joosta eighteen year old, joosta right," and told of the wonderful wedding he'd put on when he got home. He said he'd been through war before and there wasn't a bullet made that could touch him. . . . then he got something off his chest that must have been rankling him for some time. It was the attitude of the other men in the company toward him. He thought that because they called him a "dog-robber" and a few of those other pet names, that they figured he wasn't much of a soldier. All he wanted was a chance to show up a few of the rest camp heroes, when things started to hum.

While they were talking, the Germans attacked. It began with a barrage that caved in the walls of the shell hole and covered Whelton's little squad with dirt.

I could hear that barrage in my dreams for many years and I don't think I'll ever forget it. Our own artillery joined in and it looked as though the curtain was about to ring down for us. To make matters still worse, another machine gun strafing commenced. Bullets bounced off the edge of our post and crashed into the wall behind us. I knew that something was about to happen and got the gun ready. Nick laid along side of me on my right to feed the magazines while Jeffery lay on Nick's right to do the observing if I had to fire.

As the shelling stopped and the machine gun fire intensified, Whelton knew an attack was imminent. He was correct.

Finally, by popping up heads for half a second at a time, Nick saw them coming down the river bank. The ground sloped at that point and gave them some cover. I got the gun over the edge and gave them a full magazine. Nick slapped another in its place and I threw the single shot lever in order to conserve ammunition. For about ten long minutes it became a game of hide and seek and then a series of explosions took place very close to us. There was no screech of a shell and I knew then that they must have worked through the ruins in front of us, so I poured a few in that general direction. When I did this, Jeffery called that they were again trying to come down the river. Another explosion at this point occurred just in front of the gun and piled us back into the trench. I remember crying out, "Come on you dirty (and very unprintable language for one who thought he was about to kick in) so-and-so!" and we got the old gun back into position. Nick had just placed a new magazine and I was drawing the handle back to throw in the first cartridge when there came a flash, a terrific roar and I seemed to float back and drop off to sleep. There was no pain. This feeling couldn't have lasted more than a couple of seconds because when I opened my eyes again, I could see the barrel of the Chauchat bent in the shape of an "L," the magazine bent and twisted directly in front of me and from both of them rose a blue flame something like alcohol burning. I stared at it fascinated and it gradually died away. I looked down and saw that I was buried waist-deep in dirt. Then I turned to my right and saw Nick.

There followed one of those moments that every soldier dreads:

He was buried to his waist the same as I, his body erect, helmet off, eyes wide open as if watching over me. I spoke to him, but he never moved. I shook him and he fell back staring up at the sky. Then I saw that the whole right side of his upper body was gone. There was no red blood—just dirty, muddy liquid. I looked beyond him and saw Jeffery's body. His head was on the edge of the trench, facing forward about three yards away. His left leg was entirely gone but his rifle was still in position near his shoulder. I reached for my forty-five and prepared for what I was sure would come, but nothing happened. Then I laid my head on my arms in the dirt and cried like a fool. This must have relieved my nerves a little because I freed myself from the dirt and crawled back into the protection of the ruins.

It took only a few moments before the remaining doughboys in Fismette were essentially leaderless. Their lieutenants were killed, wounded, or fighting for survival like the rest of their men. Fismes was entirely cut off from them. No officers of any kind were available to issue commands. And yet—somehow, incredibly—the garrison held, fighting the Germans hand to hand and finally driving them out. As the fighting died down, Allen appeared, found Whelton lying stunned with a group of wounded, and ordered him back across the river with those who could walk. "Although I tried to put on a front when you told me to go back with the wounded who could walk," Whelton wrote to Allen almost twenty years later, "I'll confess to you that I was just a horribly scared kid and I prayed all the way back that I might have a chance to pull through safely."[3]

Whelton and Allen were among the lucky ones. On August 27, 1918, less than two weeks after they departed Fismette, the Germans—members of the battered but elite 4th Guards Division—stormed the bridgehead and wiped it out. A few dozen of the more than 200 men in the garrison, made up of two companies of the 112th Regiment, managed to swim across the river to safety; the rest were killed or captured. While they recovered, Bullard and his officers, including 28th Division commander Major General Charles H. Muir and 112th Regiment commander Colonel George Rickards, tried to determine what had gone wrong. Some pointed to one cause; some to another: the troops had not deployed properly, they were tired, they were poorly led, their equipment was insufficient, the Germans were just too strong. For Bullard, however, the blame for this military "accident" and the tragic loss of American lives lay entirely with the French. And his accusing finger was only one of many pointed in the same direction for all manner of mistakes great and small.

Popular conceptions of America in the First World War—so far as they exist at all—are laden with stereotypes. Some depict the war as a miserable slugfest from top to bottom, with no lessons to convey. Others dismiss American participation as fleeting and insignificant. More optimistic interpretations, especially popular in the ten years after 1918 but still common today, portray the doughboys as the saviors of France who physically stopped the German army on the road to Paris and then thrashed the kaiser's minions until they surrendered; or they claim that the doughboys provided the confidence in victory that allowed the beleaguered British and French to fight on. Whereas European writers commonly ignore or undervalue the American contribution, many American writers like to portray soldiers of the Entente powers—especially France—as beaten men or even craven cowards who were unable to stand up to Germany until the doughboys arrived on the scene. Unfortunately, World War I scholarship has yet to reach a critical mass sufficient to explode many of these misconceptions for good.

Scholarship on the American Expeditionary Forces (AEF) in combat during World War I includes some works of high quality, but coverage is spotty. Moreover, most scholarly studies have been written from the perspective of military and political administration rather than at the company to regimental level. Discounting general studies, two important recent works examine US training, leadership, and combat performance: Mark E. Grotelueschen's *The AEF Way of War: The American Army and Combat in World War I* (2007) and Richard S. Faulkner's *The School of Hard Knocks: Combat Leadership in the American Expeditionary Forces* (2012). These works are foundational texts in modern AEF scholarship because of the clarity with which they set the context of poor or nonexistent training, "hard knocks," and eventual improvement in the field. Thorough narrative and analytical accounts of individual actions, however, are few and far between.

Excluding unit histories, significant book-length works on battles occurring before the Meuse-Argonne (September 26–November 11, 1918) can be summed up in a single paragraph. Detailed works on early actions such as Bathelémont (November 1917) and Seicheprey (April 1918) have yet to be written. For Cantigny, there is Allan R. Millett's *Well Planned, Splendidly Executed: The Battle of Cantigny, May 28–31, 1918* (2010). Nothing has been published about the action of the US 3d Division at Château-Thierry at the end of May 1918—admittedly, only an interlude. For Belleau Wood, there is Robert Asprey, *At Belleau Wood* (1996), some general work on the US Marine Corps in World War I by George B. Clark, and a host of lesser works. For other actions by US Army units during the first half of July—from the capture of Vaux to the Marne defensive of July 15–18—nothing of scholarly importance has been published since shortly after the war. For the Soissons offensive of July 18–22, there is Douglas V. Johnson and Rolfe L. Hillman Jr.'s *Soissons 1918* (1999). Nothing of note has been published on American forces in the Aisne-Marne or Oise-Aisne offensives lasting from July 18 until September. Mitchell Yockelson, *Borrowed Soldiers: Americans under British Command, 1918* (2008), examines American actions in Flanders, while Robert J. Dalessandro's *American Lions: The 332nd Infantry Regiment in Italy in World War I* (2010) is the only thorough book on its subject. Finally, for Saint-Mihiel, there is James H. Hallas, *Squandered Victory: The American First Army at St. Mihiel* (1995). In almost every case, these works portray their subjects from the command (AEF, army, corps, or division) level.

One result of this paucity of scholarship is that our knowledge of the AEF before September 26, 1918, takes the form of a series of vignettes rather than a totality of knowledge. In contrast, our knowledge of AEF operational concepts and training—thanks in large part to Grotelueschen and Faulkner, among others—is quite strong. We are also aware, thanks to works by Edward Coffman and David Trask, of the outlines of the amalgamation controversy that plagued John J. Pershing's relations with Generalissimo Ferdinand Foch and Field Marshal Douglas Haig. But after that, we venture into largely uncharted territory. We know (or think we know) that after experiencing a couple of embarrassing German raids, the AEF went on the offensive in late May when the 1st Division took Cantigny. Simultaneously, Ludendorff launched a major offensive along the Chemin des Dames on May 27 and shattered the French army before the US 3d and 2d Divisions helped stem the tide. After that, the marines attacked Belleau Wood and took it after suffering terrible casualties. There followed a series of lesser actions before the 3d Division—known as the Rock of the Marne—helped halt the final German offensive of July 15. Three days later, the US 1st and 2d Divisions went on the offensive at Soissons, forcing the puncture that eventually deflated the Marne salient. Thereafter, American forces operated in a kind of haze before the opening of the Saint-Mihiel offensive on September 12—the first action of the war by an independent American army. Through it all, the doughboys trained, gained combat experience, and prepared for the big battles to come in the autumn.

Providing some sense of narrative cohesion to this series of events is one of the goals of this volume. The combat development of the AEF from November 1917 to September 1918 was a process that took place neither episodically nor entirely at the command level. For instance, the 1st Division developed with changes in leadership and the application of new command priorities during events occurring both at and behind the front. Regiments, battalions, companies, and squads developed for better or worse as they accrued positive and negative experiences, weeded out or appointed officers, and gained or lost unit cohesion. Episodes such as Cantigny defined certain units at certain points in time, whereas long, grueling experiences at Fismette would help define the 28th Division and its constituent units. No one narrative can bring every experience equally to the fore. Sometimes this is because of a lack of adequate source material, and other times it reflects the simple fact that not every American division participated in operations of equal significance (though admittedly, they were all significant to the men doing the fighting). Much more needs to be written before American military operations in this period are fully understood. However, a unified narrative can provide a broader and deeper understanding of how the AEF developed between its landing in France and the opening of the Saint-Mihiel offensive.

That being said, it is important to recognize that the history of the AEF in this period resists broad generalizations. Some outlines are clear. American officers and men lacked training, and they paid the price for it in France. Although every division suffered unnecessary casualties on its introduction to hard fighting, for nearly inexplicable reasons, some performed well almost from the outset (42d Division), while others (26th Division) did not. The reasons for these divergences cannot be attributed to differences in tactical doctrine or command and control. Often, they simply depended on circumstances. And though the maxim that experience begets competence generally applies, the arc is not always easy to trace. The 2d Division, for example, plunged into Belleau Wood employing outmoded tactics that resulted in tremendous slaughter. In the unique combat conditions in those woods, which often left the men out of touch with officers above the squad level, marines and soldiers quickly learned to overcome through improvisation—ironically, the individual initiative championed by Pershing. On the very different battlefield of Soissons a month later, however, the lessons learned in Belleau Wood would have a largely negative impact on the conduct of operations.

Nowhere is the importance of avoiding generalizations more important than in the case of Franco-American relations. Many American works portray this relationship as almost uniformly poor. The bitter controversy over amalgamation, resulting in verbal battles and even near fisticuffs between Foch and Pershing, is well known. So are the images of fleeing French soldiers crying *"la guerre est fini"* while hardy marines and doughboys hurried to take their places in the line. In the many Francophobic American works on the war, men such as General Jean-Marie Degoutte—a longtime American bête noir—appear alternately as craven cowards (at Château-Thierry) and fanatically bloodthirsty butchers (at Fismette). Robert B. Bruce, in *A Fraternity of Arms: America and France in the Great War* (2003), has provided a useful corrective to some of these more extreme accounts. The research presented here, however, suggests a more nuanced view. At some levels and in some places, Franco-American relations were quite good; in many others, they were generally tense. And in a few cases—particularly with regard to the US 2d and 3d Divisions—Franco-American relations were dismal to the point of costing lives. At the tactical level—which is my primary focus—American and French soldiers cooperated effectively in some cases and failed to do so in others. In almost every instance, however, the temptation to blame the French for every setback suffered by American forces proved too strong to resist.

Part of the reason for the skewed perspective in many American accounts of the war is a strange unwillingness to consider French and German points of view. Thus, there is a tendency to take for granted sometimes slanderous and usually secondhand reports that French units fled or "did not advance" or that German units resisted stoutly or surrendered spontaneously for no discernible reason. This is true despite the availability, either digitally or in print, of extensive French and German records. Although providing French and German perspectives on the events of November 1917–September 1918 was not the original intent of this book—which aimed to focus on Americans rather than provide a multinational study of the operations themselves—some operations and relationships are impossible to understand without a perusal of French and German primary source materials. This book emphasizes military operations that took place before the American

First Army came into its own at Saint-Mihiel; it does not cover American operations under British command or those in Italy (admirably handled by Yockelson and Dalessandro, cited above). As such, this book can rightly be considered a study of AEF operations under French command. Readers should not assume, however, that this book provides the last word on the French and the Germans. Vast troves of unexplored archival materials continue to beckon intrepid researchers.

European records will have to be studied much more thoroughly before any reliable conclusions can be reached about the military impact of American intervention on the western front in 1918. Without a doubt, American formations packed a punch. They were large, moderately well supplied, and always aggressive. Enough anecdotal evidence exists in French and German records to suggest that the Americans boosted the allies' morale and discouraged the kaiser's men.[4] Just as it is currently impossible to fully quantify the military impact of American forces in 1918, anecdotes cannot prove whether French forces fought more strongly or more ineffectually because of the appearance of American forces nearby. In broad outlines, this book suggests that French forces fighting alongside Americans performed much more effectively than they have been given credit for; however, Franco-American command and tactical dysfunction frequently precluded operational success.

More humbly, this book tells some of the stories of those who fought. Such an objective is not as unscholarly as it might seem, for World War I was a peculiar war. Technological advances in weaponry such as artillery, machine guns, and poison gas, combined with technological deficiencies in communications, practically ensured that most men fought beyond the command reach of officers above the battalion level (and often below it as well). It was a common characteristic of military operations that major generals, brigadier generals, and even colonels and majors often lost touch with operations after they began and restored contact only after they had concluded. In this context, generals often appear in this narrative as distant figures—not from any inherent bias but because that was how the war was fought. In Belleau Wood, for example, no American officers ever figured out exactly how the main German position was finally broken—for the simple reason that a few marines spontaneously decided to follow an uncharted streambed and break through an unidentified unit boundary into the German rear, making all the difference. Yet many other stories remain to be told. And although this book takes us some steps—hopefully, many steps—toward a better understanding of American military operations in World War I, it also points out how much remains to be learned.

I

Setting the Stage

War preparedness cannot be accurately assessed solely by numbers of troops mobilized and quantities of military equipment. When the United States entered World War I in April 1917, it possessed a far-flung Regular Army of 121,000 men, a Marine Corps of 13,000 men and 462 officers, and a National Guard with 80,000 men under arms.[1] The tally was small but certainly not unprecedented for a Western democracy entering a major war. In 1914 Great Britain's first expeditionary force to France consisted of only 100,000 soldiers—famously derided by Kaiser Wilhelm II as a "contemptible little army." Like the American Expeditionary Forces (AEF) three years later, the British Expeditionary Force (BEF) was in many respects unprepared to fight a major war. Deficient in large-caliber artillery, machine guns, and ammunition, its troops also lacked widespread combat experience. Although many British officers and soldiers had participated in colonial conflicts such as the Boer War, no one, from Commander in Chief Sir John French down to the lowliest private, had any wartime experience on the scale they were about to encounter on the western front.

Contrary to the stereotypical image of an imperial, horse-fancying, and hidebound British military establishment, Sir John French's contemptible little army was a sleek, modern affair by the standards of the time. The Haldane Reforms of 1907 had thoroughly overhauled the British army from top to bottom, introducing innovations and adaptations that included an up-to-date Imperial General Staff, a seven-division overseas expeditionary force, a fourteen-division territorial force, and an efficiently operating reserve. Wedded to the time-honored British regimental system, these reforms established the foundations for a military organization capable of either fighting colonial wars in Africa and Asia or expanding to almost unlimited proportions for war on the European continent. Anticipating the possibility of a major war before it occurred, British military planners insisted on regular field exercises and practice mobilization. Of course, it helped that they had to navigate only the English Channel to deploy to Europe.

The US Army of 1917 was comparable to the British army of 1914 at some levels. It had also been recently reformed, albeit not so thoroughly, during the tenure of Secretary of War Elihu Root (1899–1904). In addition, American staff and field officers in 1917 were not necessarily less combat experienced than their British counterparts had been in 1914. In the Indian Wars, the Spanish-American War, the Philippine insurrection, the Mexican expedition, and numerous smaller conflicts, Americans such as John J. Pershing had gained experience comparable to that of the veterans of Great Britain's imperial wars. Fifty years earlier, the United States had experienced conflict on a scale not seen in Europe for a century or more. Most important, in 1917 the United States enjoyed the advantage—at least in theory—of being able to observe the Great War's military developments from the sidelines and learn from its protagonists' missteps. No such opportunity had availed itself—with the dubious exception of the Russo-Japanese War of 1904–1905—to military observers from any of the European belligerents before they marched off to war in 1914. That Pershing and many of his generals and staff officers did not adequately learn from the mistakes of others constitutes one of the war's many tragedies.

The United States was not even remotely ready for armed conflict on a large scale. In 1917 its armed forces were deficient in both military equipage and combat doctrine—as the British had been three years earlier. The AEF had a good rifle—the Springfield—but there were insufficient quantities to supply an army of millions. It also lacked adequate machine guns and artillery and was almost bereft of mortars, grenades, automatic rifles, tanks, and aircraft. Doctrinally, as Mark Grotelueschen has pointed out, the American army of 1917 remained fixated on fighting conflicts like those it had engaged in against decrepit Spanish colonial forces or Filipino and Mexican guerrillas. Emphasis was placed—rightly, in that context—on mobility, initiative, and light infantry weapons.[2] In neither respect had the British in 1914 been very different.

The fundamental difference between the British in 1914 and the Americans in 1917 was this: whereas the former had long viewed their involvement in a major conflict as a strong possibility, the latter continued to believe, almost up to the last moment, that they would be able to steer clear of large-scale war. Unlike the British, the Americans lacked a well-defined military infrastructure or apparatus for rapid organizational expansion. With no military organization in 1917 above the regimental level (and very little even at that level), and with no coherent plan to expand training or to organize on a scale sufficient for modern warfare, the United States' armed forces were critically handicapped from the start. Therein lay the basic contrast between Great Britain in 1914 and the United States in 1917. The BEF had an immediate, tangible impact on the fighting in France and Belgium despite its puny size, inadequate equipment and munitions, and conceptual unpreparedness for modern war. The AEF took much longer to make its presence felt after arriving in Europe, even though the Americans' weaponry and supplies of basic necessities were not much worse than the BEF's had been three years earlier. True, the war in 1917 was far different from the war in 1914; however, the Americans enjoyed the advantage of easing into the conflict over a period of months against a still potent but already half-beaten adversary, whereas the British had been hurled into war against enemy forces that were confident, fresh, far better equipped, and up to ten times larger.

Many American officers and men were simply not up to the task of combat—and they and the men they commanded often paid with their lives. In 1918 American staff and field officers endured the same painful process of weeding out incompetents that the British, French, and Germans had undergone long ago. Looked at broadly, however—and keeping in mind that most Americans stubbornly resisted the military wisdom proffered by their cobelligerents—the ability of American officers and men to tackle the steep learning curve of combat was surprising. In 1917 many seasoned British, French, and German generals were still repeating the same mistakes they had made at the war's outset—and on a large scale. Overall, the Americans seemed more adaptable, as evidenced by the tactics employed by the marines in Belleau Wood between June 6 and 24, 1918. Unfortunately, despite efforts by Pershing's general headquarters (GHQ) and staff officers at other levels to incorporate these lessons and transmit them to the AEF, for a variety of reasons, each green unit entering combat had to relearn the principles its predecessors had imbibed in blood. As Richard S. Faulkner has rightly argued, "the ill-coordinated and costly frontal attacks that continued to characterize American infantry operations from Soissons through much of the Meuse-Argonne seem to belie the assertions that the skills of the AEF improved over time."[3] Yet units engaged in lengthy combat *did* improve over time, albeit haltingly. For instance, the 28th Division, a callow, unwieldy division in July 1918, had become an effective and tactically proficient formation three months later. Despite their short if intense experience of combat, the veteran American forces deployed in Europe were among the most potent anywhere in the world by the time of the armistice. The story of how that transformation came about is one of the more compelling dramas in American military history.

The deficiency of the training offered to American volunteers and conscripts in 1917–1918 is the stuff of legend. Overseen by generals and staff struggling to create an expeditionary force from scratch, and commanded by field officers who often knew less about military matters than they did, the bewildered doughboys stumbled through basic training. They had few weapons of any kind—not even rifles. Marching out of slapdash training camps hastily constructed across the country, they engaged in close-order drill, endless route hikes, and some rifle and bayonet training, but little else. Tactical regulations, studied assiduously by historians and lambasted for their shortcomings, were poorly understood at the regimental, battalion, company, and platoon levels. As events would show, what little instruction was received by officers and men had little time to sink in. Under trials of combat, they followed the book for a relatively short time before tossing it aside and proceeding by instinct.

Officer training, as Faulkner has demonstrated, was dismal on the whole and negatively affected performance in the field. Of the 200,000 officers required for the wartime army of some 4 million men, only 18,000 were already serving in the Regular Army and National Guard in April 1917. Of the 182,000 new officers required, some would come from the reserve, be commissioned from the ranks, or attain commissions by other venues; about half received their commissions from officers' training camps. Most of these young men were recent or soon-to-be college graduates, and their courses of instruction must have reminded them of cramming for final exams. Time was at a premium, and there was much to learn. Aside from the obligatory drill and marching, officer candidates learned the rudiments of tactics and the military arts. However, these courses were taught by inexperienced instructors who were often trying desperately to get themselves up to snuff. As one instructor put it, "It was a case of the blind leading the blind." Like students overdosed on information, officer candidates took their exams and then promptly forgot much of what they had learned. As a result, during their first weeks in the field, junior officers needed a lot of hand-holding, and the quality of their performance generally reflected the amount of real-time tutelage they had received. When they lost contact with headquarters (as frequently happened under battle conditions), junior officers did what they thought best at the moment, often without regard to the training they had received in camp. Others whose Stateside training was deemed inadequate by their superiors or themselves spent extra time training in France, and as a result, they never made it into the field before the war ended.[4]

This is not to say, of course, that the tactical theories expounded by Pershing and his staff were irrelevant. Pershing's notorious belief in the primacy of mobility and the rifle and bayonet over trenches and heavy weapons was widely expounded and generally understood. Despite horror stories of new recruits and conscripts who were sent to the front without knowing how to operate weapons of any kind, once they entered combat, most doughboys were familiar with their rifles and knew how to use them effectively. American troops were aggressive, as Pershing demanded, and they demonstrated a distinct preference for open warfare over trench warfare. American-built trenches in France were few and far between, making the phrase "over the top" something of a misnomer when applied to attacking American troops. In the field, French observers frequently pointed out Americans' tendency to rely excessively on their rifles, advance too quickly without regard to their flanks, and fail to dig in effectively.

But there were contradictions. While Pershing expounded the concept of the "self-reliant" infantryman in the context of strong "individual and group initiative, resourcefulness, and tactical judgment," he also cultivated a culture of strict obedience to orders throughout the AEF. Although trench warfare was treated as a degenerate and aberrant form of warfare, most US troops received some form of training in trench warfare, especially in France. Despite the long battle against amalgamation conducted by the Wilson administration along with Pershing and his staff, most of the US troops who participated in fighting through August 1918 did so under French or British command. As a result, French and British officers had opportunities to impart lessons of their own to the doughboys under their care. Even the rifle was not sacrosanct. From the beginning, AEF doctrine emphasized light over heavy weapons, but men like Colonel (later General) Charles P. Summerall and Lieutenant Colonel John H. Parker lobbied aggressively for a greater emphasis on artillery and machine guns. And although their efforts were unsuccessful at first, it did not take long for the AEF in France to appreciate the utility of both types of weapons and to use them in quantity.[5]

There was, then, an inherent though largely inadvertent flexibility in AEF tactics in practice, if not in doctrine. Men were taught doctrines based on Pershing's ideas and the Field Service Regulations of 1914 (updated to 1917), emphasizing initiative, rapid maneuver, mobility, flexible (not massed) assault tactics, rifle fire superiority, fire and maneuver, and close-quarters combat. The understanding of these doctrines among field officers, noncommissioned officers (NCOs), and men, however, was often shallow at best. In combat, what Pershing understood as "self-reliance"—independence from artillery and other supporting arms—was easily translated into independence from camp doctrine and the chain of command. Improvisation was often atavistic, as officers habitually opted for the thick linear formations that Pershing's open-warfare doctrines were intended to replace. Thus, as Douglas Johnson remarked, US training initially produced "infantry that attacked in linear formations of the decades gone by . . . that only knew how to attack straight ahead . . . [that was] unfamiliar with its normal supporting arms . . . [and that was] willing to be killed in straight-ahead attacks because it knew no better."[6]

Grotelueschen has suggested that the units that "rose above" these backward concepts did so "despite official AEF doctrine [rather] than because of it," but this is not necessarily true. In many instances, official AEF doctrine was actually helpful—such as inside Belleau Wood, where individual initiative and facility with rifle and bayonet were primary, and supporting weapons such as artillery and mortars were largely ineffective. In other cases, ineffective training ironically facilitated either the flexible interpretation of certain dicta—even (heaven and Pershing forbid) incorporating French and British advice—or their abandonment altogether. This was especially the case when combat conditions required quick decision making outside the orbit of headquarters staff. Remembering the principles of obedience propounded in camp, officers and men at first floundered in such conditions, but then they learned how to make up their own minds. Wasn't this what Pershing called "resourcefulness"? British captain Alexander Stewart, an officer in the prewar army, commented on one aspect of this phenomenon, noting the difference between the old "Regular Army" British officers of 1914 and their "New Army" replacements of 1916 and afterward:

> I think that all the regular officers, anyhow all those I met up to and including the rank of Major, were splendid fellows; but nevertheless speaking generally I soon came to the very definite opinion that the new "war officers" were infinitely more capable, led their men better and did their job better than the old pre-war regulars with whom I came into contact. The old regular was frightened of doing anything

that was not quite according to Cocker, and to my mind went far too much on the assumption, "theirs not to reason why"; very fine and very brave, but if God has given you a brain why not use it? There were of course very many exceptions but, again speaking generally, it seemed to me that the longer a man had been in the army the less intelligent he was.[7]

This was, after all, one definition of an army of citizen-soldiers, and it may help explain why the AEF was able to adapt so quickly.

At the battalion level and above, officers were more hidebound and took longer to learn. In part, this was the inevitable result of their distance from the battlefield and the generally poor apparatus for transmitting knowledge from below. In Belleau Wood, for example, General James Harbord's slowness to understand the nature of the fighting resulted partially from his subordinates' inability to supply him with accurate intelligence—a state of affairs he found exceedingly troublesome. Eventually, however, they adapted, at least at the division level. As Grotelueschen has pointed out in his case studies of the 1st, 2d, 26th, and 77th Divisions:

> Commanders at various levels opened up infantry attack formations and made them more flexible; they stressed the importance of communication up and down the chain of command, as well as with neighboring units, during battle; they increasingly appreciated the benefits of comprehensive attack plans designed to take and hold relatively small portions of enemy defensive positions (and eliminate the defending troops within those limited areas); and, perhaps most important, they began to see firepower as the sine qua non of battlefield success.[8]

Yet the progression was not linear, and it often failed to take changing circumstances into account. General Robert Bullard's experiences and lessons learned with the 1st Division in early 1918, for example, did not translate well to the Vesle in August 1918, where his overly aggressive stance would harm units (e.g., 28th Division) under his command in III Corps. Moreover, an increasingly adversarial attitude toward the French by Bullard, Harbord, 1st Division commander General Charles P. Summerall, and 3d Division commander General Joseph T. Dickman would significantly hinder their ability and willingness to apply what should have been easy lessons—such as the need for well-paced attacks.

★ ★ ★

Three Regular Army divisions, the 1st, 3d, and 4th (along with the 3d Brigade of the 2d Division) participated significantly in US military efforts in the spring and summer of 1918. In theory, these divisions formed from prewar regiments were better prepared for combat than the formations that would follow. But they were not comparable to the "regular" divisions of the old BEF that went to war in 1914—much to the surprise of the French and British officers who received the Americans during their initial period of training in Europe. When the United States entered the war, the old Regular Army regiments were, for the most part, dismantled to form new unit cadres and then received a mass infusion of wholly green officers, NCOs, and men. The 1st Division, for example, "was almost as much a new creation of inexperienced officers and soldiers as the other divisions that followed." Training for the Regular Army was on roughly the same level as that for officers in the National Guard—that is, quite poor. The difference was that Regular Army officers at the battalion level and above were more likely to have had long terms of military service.[9]

The War Department set aside division numerals 26–75 for National Guard formations. Of these, only the 26th, 28th, 32d, and 42d Divisions were ready in time to see significant combat in the spring and summer of 1918. The perception was widespread, especially at Pershing's GHQ, that National Guard formations as a whole were less experienced, more poorly trained, and less efficient than their counterparts in the Regular Army. That impression was misleading. Although the training of National Guard officers and men was poor overall, it was no worse than in the Regular Army. Many National Guard officers and men had seen prewar combat, and their esprit de corps was often quite strong. And although both Regular Army and National Guard officers were perniciously affected by some of the principles foisted on them in camp, the latter "were less likely to be dogmatically committed to the anachronistic elements of prewar U.S. Army doctrine." Nevertheless, like many other rivalries in the AEF, rivalries between Regular Army and National Guard officers hindered combat efficiency in France. Army–National Guard distrust long predated the war and had been exacerbated by the 1916 National Defense Act, which enhanced National Guard autonomy over the objections of many in the army establishment.[10]

In the context of the AEF as a whole, the Marine Corps was unique. And, of course, the marines thought of themselves that way. When the United States entered the war, Marine Corps commander Major General George Barnett determined that his men would play a leading role in the conflict. But despite their subsequent status as elite troops in the United States' arsenal, Barnett's task of securing recognition and support for his marines was not an easy one. The US Army accepted the services of the 5th Marine Regiment—at the time of its formation, one of the only truly veteran units in the country—only reluctantly. Barnett formed the second regiment, the 6th, at his own initiative, and his attempt to build up two more regiments into another brigade that could constitute an all-marine division came to naught. Instead, the 5th and 6th Regiments would eventually form the 4th Brigade of the US 2d Division, along with the 3d Brigade of US Army troops.[11]

Marine training was much more intensive than that undergone by US Army or National Guard formations. The primary marine boot camps were at Parris Island, South Carolina, and Mare Island, California. There, the all-volunteer recruits completed eight-week courses in physical training, drill, close-quarters combat, and marksmanship. Private Melvin Krulewitch described a typical day's first exercise after reveille at 0500 hours:

> "Standby for Swedish" would be the next command, and we would then begin our physical drill under arms—the Marine Corps had adopted the Swedish system as part of the training and hardening process. Exercising with the nine-pound Springfield included vertical and horizontal swings, side and forward lunges, rifle twists, and most difficult of all, the torturing front sweep—you held the rifle overhead with hands on the stock and the muzzle, and lowered your arms at full length to touch your toes without bending your knees. . . . Again and again we did this, pushing our limits.[12]

The physical training was tougher than any of them had imagined, but unlike the endless route hikes endured by most army recruits, it was training with a purpose. And it gave them a hardness they would need in France. Rifle training was also intensive, as described by another recruit:

> You shoot from three positions: prone, kneeling, and sitting. We shoot from 200, 300, 400, 500, and 600 yards. From the latter distance, those bull's-eyes look like pin-heads. Rapid fire you shoot ten shots in one minute. It's real exciting when you are actually shooting. The things sound like a cannon. They shoot a bullet as long as your index finger. All rapid fire is done, not at a bull's-eye, but at a silhouette of a man's head and shoulders, the bottom of which is 36 inches.[13]

This too would prove valuable in places like Belleau Wood.

After boot camp, the marines were sent to advanced training at a camp in Quantico, Virginia, which had been established in May 1917. There, the men underwent more drill and marksmanship training and learned about infantry weapons and trench warfare. Some (but not all) junior officers received instruction in command and tactics—though it was not always suited to the realities in France. Second Lieutenant James McBrayer Sellers of the 2/6th Marines remembered that "practically all we did at Quantico was drill and dig trenches. We did not have any real combat training, map reading, or other obligatory requirements for survival in the field. And our trenches were anything but standard. We just dug wherever we were and whatever the contour of the ground would call for."[14]

In aggregate, then, marine training did not impart a great deal of knowledge, but it did inculcate courage, toughness, and esprit de corps. The marines—both veterans (who already had some field experience) and new recruits—displayed a special kind of arrogance that set them apart from other troops. They were the best, and they knew it. The marines' disdain for other services—and allies—sometimes made them difficult to work with. They were perfectly willing to go it alone, and they often did. Nevertheless, as a fighting force, the Marine Brigade towered over its contemporaries in 1917 and had the potential to become even better—elite in every respect of the word—in 1918.

The hopes and travails of the American Expeditionary Forces were evident as the doughboys began to arrive in France. At the time (and even today), Pershing was one of the United States' more controversial top military commanders. Seemingly inscrutable, he was a complex man possessed of indomitable willpower and a fierce determination to achieve victory. His confidence in his troops was embodied in his unyielding belief in their innate superiority over their war-wizened European cobelligerents. This attitude permeated the AEF staff and officer corps, resulting in an often irrational stubbornness when it came to collaborating with or learning from the British and French and a driving desire to prove that American troops could win the war single-handed. Yet Pershing was a detached commander; he was much more absorbed in problems of politics and grand military administration than in studying American performance in the field and determining how to develop and improve it.

Pershing's staff was an equally complex mixture of talent and hidebound prejudice. And for much of the war, it was in flux. Pershing had begun assembling his GHQ in May 1917 in close collaboration with his first chief of staff, Colonel (later General) James G. Harbord. Born in Illinois in 1866,

Harbord had served in the army since 1889 and was energetic and amiable. But aside from a brief stint with Pershing pursuing Pancho Villa, Harbord had never seen combat, and his understanding of field tactics was purely by the book. Events would prove him a better administrator than a field commander. In assembling their staff, he and Pershing favored men with credentials from the Army Staff College and the Leavenworth School of the Line. Many of the officers they selected were exceptionally talented, but none of them were visionaries.

The GHQ structure was laid out in General Orders No. 8 on July 5, 1917, and updated in General Orders No. 31 on February 16, 1918. It established the component general staff and technical staff, with the former divided into "G" sections for administration, intelligence, and so on. The GHQ staff members who would have the greatest practical impact on operations in 1918 were the chief of intelligence (G-2), Major (later Brigadier General) Dennis E. Nolan, and the chief of operations (G-3), Colonel (later Brigadier General) Fox Conner. Conner in particular would play an important role in evaluating and comparing American and French (he was fluent in that language) combat operations. Significantly, the GHQ staff system was ordered to be replicated at the corps and division levels. Thus, each army, corps, and division commander had a chief of staff who wielded strong authority, including the ability to issue orders in the commander's absence. This sometimes created competing chains of authority, and it caused problems with the French, who expressed particular frustration over working with divisional chiefs of staff.[15]

On the whole, though, the AEF staff arrangements worked effectively enough at all levels. This was fortunate, because the administrative challenges were overwhelming. The logistical problems of assembling and training the AEF in the United States were daunting enough, but those involved in shipping the AEF to Europe, organizing it into a coherent whole, and preparing it for combat were even more so. The organization of the so-called blockbuster or square divisions, containing up to 28,000 men in four regiments and two brigades, exponentially increased the organizational challenges. In theory, such large divisions would be able to absorb substantial punishment without losing steam and thus be capable of serving longer terms at the front; in practice, however, they stretched the already rudimentary American staff, administration, and supply mechanisms to the limit. As a consequence, divisions took longer to organize, train, equip, and deploy, and as experience would prove, there was no concomitant benefit in terms of their durability at the front. Indeed, squeezing such large formations into narrow frontages designed for European divisions would promote administrative confusion and clog the lines of supply. Ironically, this increased the temptation, in the summer of 1918, to break up these divisions and introduce them to the front in brigade-size units or smaller.

Shipping such large formations to Europe was, of course, challenging. The first organized military unit to make the journey to France was the 1st Division in June 1917, with the 5th Marine Regiment (a sometimes unwelcome appendage) accompanying it on separate ships. Elements of the 2d Division (which would be assembled in Europe) and the 3d, 26th, 28th, 32d, and 42d Divisions followed later in 1917 and in the spring of 1918. Logistical support for these formations was initially provided through the formation of the Line of Communications in the summer of 1917, which shanghaied the unfortunate marines to reinforce its inadequate personnel. This would later become the far better-staffed and (under Harbord) better-managed Services of Supply. Early arrivals benefited from the presence of constituent artillery, engineer, and machine gun units, but by the spring of 1918, the emphasis on shipping only infantry to France meant that the American divisions were only partially formed and had to rely on French support and supply units. Heavy equipment was typically of British or French manufacture, and aside from a limited number of American squadrons, tank and air support was entirely European.

In France, Pershing and his generals came face-to-face with the problem of how to negotiate the relationship with their cobelligerents (hereafter referred to as allies). The story of the amalgamation controversy has often been told. Foch and Haig, along with Clemenceau and Lloyd George, believed that the best way to use the Americans in the short term was to integrate them into French and British military units at some level. In some forms, the argument for "amalgamation," as it came to be called, encompassed the radical suggestion that the Americans don their allies' uniforms and fight as full-fledged members of their armies. It is doubtful that the French (fighting a war of survival and thus profoundly invested in victory) and the British actually expected the Americans to accept this proposal. Amalgamation did, however, serve as a bargaining ploy. At a minimum, the French and British sought to establish and maintain the arrangement that prevailed in the spring and summer of 1918, whereby distinct American units from brigade to platoon level would be incorporated into larger European formations.

Any such arrangement would not have endured for long. Pershing had been instructed by Secretary of War Newton D. Baker to work toward the establishment of a "separate and distinct" American army on the western front. More important, Pershing himself was inclined that way. In this, as Donald Smythe has pointed out, Pershing was like any other general worth the uniform he wore: "In preserving American troops under his own command (which many think was the great Pershing achievement), he was simply following a national tradition and the natural inclination of any commander." Although they expected that an American army would form eventually, the French and British were determined to delay that day as long as possible—hopefully, long enough to ensure that France was out of immediate danger and that any mistakes made by the Americans would not ruin the cause altogether.[16]

The battle between Pershing and his European associates over amalgamation grew increasingly bitter as the war progressed. For Harbord, the Americans' predicament at the hands of their allies amounted to a kind of martyrdom. He wrote in his diary:

> Our Allies hate each other and disagree on many subjects but they are a unit when it comes to casting lots for our raiment. They seem to look on America as a common resource, and while loudly proclaiming their wish to see America on the firing line as a National Unit, resort to all manner of subterfuge to defeat and delay that eventuality to which we look forward with such hope.[17]

The ongoing disputes between Pershing and his British and French counterparts were closely monitored throughout the AEF. Of course, the great majority were rooting for Black Jack to triumph and get the long-cherished American field army formed as soon as possible.

The amalgamation dispute would continue to hover—menacing and tangible—over every American combat deployment through the summer of 1918. In practice, American units were amalgamated, albeit temporarily, with French (and British) units from the division level all the way down to the platoon level. Born of necessity, this arrangement produced dangerous tensions. On French sectors of the front, American and French military observers watched every deployment closely, with an eye toward determining whether American troops fought more effectively under European officers or American officers and whose tactics, whose morale, and whose raw human material was superior. Each party had a vested interest in ensuring that the evidence from the field enhanced their own point of view. As such, the process of assessment—a vital component of any military endeavor—was skewed from the start. Objectivity was impossible.

Upon the Americans' arrival for training in France, tensions were evident immediately and at all levels. Language barriers and cultural differences caused trouble between the doughboys and French civilians. "We had the feeling that we were over there to help them," complained Private William P. Carson, "yet all that concerned them was getting paid for damages." Among common soldiers, NCOs, and junior officers, differences seemed to be ironed out fairly quickly, and a sense of mutual respect developed. At staff and command levels, however, resentments often increased over time. Some officers were afraid the Yanks were taking their French instructors too seriously, to the detriment of their effectiveness and the overarching objective of forming an independent American army that could say it had won the war on its own merits.[18]

Of all the American divisions that would experience combat in the spring and summer of 1918, the 1st, 2d, 26th, and 42d came the closest to completing the standard three-month training program advocated by Pershing. In many respects, this gave them an advantage over the divisions that followed later in the spring of 1918, when the constantly changing situation at the front forced the adoption of more ad hoc training plans. Yet, as the guinea pigs, these early arrivals had to overcome the many challenges of learning from the French. On October 8, 1917, 1st Division's commander, Major General William S. Sibert, sent a memo to Pershing outlining some of the disjunctions his officers were already beginning to face and the measures he had adopted to solve them. "Much trouble has been experienced with interpreters," he wrote. "It is particularly difficult to secure an interpreter who will convey the full meaning of one's remark to the person addressed. It is also hard to be certain that the interpreter understands what you mean." He continued:

> Training in conjunction with French troops is slow and we have found that after one or two demonstrations by French organizations it is difficult to keep our soldiers interested. . . . Our officers are not sufficiently familiar with trench warfare conditions to draft good problems and both the officers and men fail to visualize the possible effects of hostile artillery and trench mortar fire. Consequently dispositions of troops, liaison arrangements, etcetera, which seem satisfactory to us frequently meet with severe and absolute[ly] correct criticism from French officers observing the exercises. They will quickly explain to our satisfaction how impossible or dangerous the dispositions, liaison arrangements, etcetera, would be under battle conditions.
>
> We have made the most rapid progress since adopting the following arrangement:
>
> French officers prepare a series of company, battalion and regimen-

tal problems involving all the various phases of trench warfare and give a setting on the "Centers of resistance" which each regiment has prepared (entrenchments, barbed wire, etc.). Our officers take these problems, state them in American fashion, if necessary, and proceed to prepare the necessary orders. The problem is then gone over on the map, rehearsed on the ground, and corrected, and finally the unit or units carry out the orders on the ground. French officers observe the work of the troops and are called upon in the critique to criticize all mistakes observed. The problem, with the orders and a summary of the critique attached, is then forwarded to Div. Hdqrs., and a general summary of all the mistakes noted during the week is prepared by selected officers.

Problems in training with the French persisted at all levels, however, provoking another memo from Sibert to Pershing on November 27, in which the division commander pointed out major difficulties with liaison, especially at the battalion level.[19]

The 26th Division, organized from New England National Guard formations and dubbed the "Yankee" Division, received more extensive training in European trench warfare tactics than any other American division. This was partly due to the fact that its commander, Major General Clarence Edwards, had spent a month in the autumn of 1917 with British and French divisions in service on the western front. He was therefore more open than many of his counterparts to European methods, such as reliance on artillery and machine guns, and his troops were trained primarily by the French in their own manner. French army commander General Henri-Philippe Pétain suggested taking this a step further in a letter to Pershing dated December 28, 1917. Pétain recommended breaking up the 26th Division into its four constituent regiments, each of which would train for two months at the front with a different French division. After that time, the division would be reassembled and sent to the front as an intact unit that could eventually help form an American sector.[20]

The suggestion was not well received at GHQ. Colonel Paul B. Malone, then a member of the AEF general staff's training section, wrote a memorandum for Harbord on January 3, 1918, in which he stated that training for both trench and open warfare would be beneficial, but the Americans would learn only trench warfare from the French—something they could do just as well on their own. "If not at the same time trained in open warfare," Malone wrote, "these regiments will, in the event of a successful assault from the trenches, be incapable of successful action in the open." He therefore recommended against Pétain's proposal and believed that American regiments should not train with French divisions. On the same day, Colonel Fox Conner wrote to Harbord suggesting that the French proposal was indicative of their weak "moral state" and reflected "sentiments as to the coming German offensive which bodes no good to the allied resistance. . . . The Allied morale in high quarters must be nursed in order that the war may continue until such time as our forces can turn the balance in our favor, i.e. 1919." Conner was willing to countenance Pétain's proposal—under strict American supervision—but only with the 26th, 2d, and 42d Divisions. In the event, only the 26th Division received such a Francocentric course of training, giving GHQ and Pershing—who already had problems with Edwards—an incentive to demonstrate that the Yankee Division performed less proficiently under fire than did other units trained according to more strictly American methods.[21]

Even as the first stages of training moved forward, doughboys were receiving their first small tastes of combat on the western front. Those portions would rapidly increase.

2

Into the Line
November 1917–April 1918

By the autumn of 1917, the western front had settled into a pattern of stalemate in an atmosphere of tense anticipation. In April the French had launched the catastrophic Nivelle offensive, leading to mutinies in the French army and the appointment of Pétain. He was able to hold the army together in part by inculcating a spirit of quiet determination tempered by caution. The French would continue to fight, but no longer would they heedlessly squander lives by the thousand. The British launched the year's final major offensive, Third Ypres or Passchendaele, on July 31, but it made insignificant progress and finally ground to a miserable halt on November 6. Germany, meanwhile, was administering the final blows to Russia in the east and making obvious preparations to launch a final offensive on the western front, with the intention of ending the war. When and where it would fall, of course, none of the allies knew, but they hoped the Americans would act in time to stem it. It was under these circumstances that American troops were first deployed to quiet sections of the front.

Private Charles Abels of the US 1st Division's 18th Regiment later complained that "Pershing had very little regard for the troops under his command, or at least he showed no regard for the First Division." Pershing would have been shocked to hear this—insofar as he showed any emotion at all—as the 1st Division was clearly his favorite. But Sibert, its commander, did not inspire much confidence either at GHQ or among his troops. Though a high-ranking West Point graduate, he was a career engineer with only theoretical knowledge of infantry or artillery tactics. By early October, the division's four regiments—the 16th, 18th, 26th, and 28th—had received a haphazard course of training that was American in theory but heavily influenced by the French instructors who carried it out. The resulting sense of ambivalence and uncertainty would color the division's first experiences at the front.[1]

On October 6 the 1st Division was ordered to make arrangements with the French 18th Division of French IX Corps for a ten-day tour of the front lines in the Sommerviller sector of Lorraine, about ten kilometers southeast of Nancy. Each infantry and artillery battalion would participate to some extent. The first elements of the division entered the sector on October 20, and three days later the Americans officially entered the front lines in relief of some French units. Like many of his fellow officers, Colonel Beaumont Bonaparte Buck, commanding the 28th Regiment, was eager to see what the French could do. But his first observation of a French raid near Verdun on October 20 left him feeling "greatly disappointed." The French attack, he griped, "appeared a farce. I felt that we could fight like this for 20 years and accomplish but little, and it was with an exultant feeling that I recalled it was General Pershing's purpose, as soon as the American force in France should be strong enough, to push the enemy out of the trenches and force the fighting into the open. It was my opinion . . . that in no other way could the war be won." So long as they occupied the trenches, though, open-warfare concepts would remain just a dream. Practically speaking, the American officers and men learned how the French did things and little else.[2]

The Germans taught them some lessons, too. On the night of November 2–3, Company F of the 2/16th occupied trenches rimming a treeless hill overlooking the Rhine-Marne canal in front of the town of Bathelémont. Three platoons fronted the position—essentially a salient—with one in support. The whole company was under the command of Lieutenant Willis E. Comfort, with a French lieutenant serving as liaison officer. It was a vulnerable position despite the French machine guns posted in support, and the Germans chose to test it. At about 0250 on the morning of November 3, a German barrage slammed down, stunning the defenders. "I saw a wall of fire rear itself in the fog and darkness," remembered Sergeant Ed Halyburton. "Extending to right and left a couple of hundred yards, it moved upon us with a roar, above which I could not hear my own voice. The earth shuddered. The mist rolled and danced. Sections of the trench began to give way. Then the explosives were falling all around me. The air was filled with mud, water, pieces of duckboard and shell splinters." A shell blast knocked Halyburton to the ground, scorching his back and shattering his rifle. The commander of the most exposed platoon, Lieutenant McLaughlin, tried to pull his men back to support trenches, but they were unable to penetrate the heavy German shelling to their rear. He and his men dove into dugouts. So did the men of the other two front-line platoons, leaving sentries posted at the entrance to each dugout.[3]

As soon as he saw the barrage fall, Lieutenant Comfort attempted to contact the supporting artillery to initiate a counterbarrage, only to be frustrated by a "French telephone operator" who could not speak English. That left signal rockets. When one of his men attempted to fire a rocket, however, the French liaison officer stopped him. Comfort then tried to fire a rocket on his own, but the Frenchman rushed over and stopped him, "saying it was just a bombardment [and he] thought he knew his business." Minutes later it became clear that a German raid was under way, and the French lieutenant allowed the Americans to fire off a signal. Unfortunately, the major commanding the supporting French artillery "saw the signal but did not respond," as he "did not believe a raid was coming." When he finally did open fire, the Germans' barrage had already lifted, and their infantry was gone. When Comfort later confronted the French major, he "said he was Very sorry, but he knew that the Germans could not capture the Position, so he only put on a petite Barrage."[4]

While Comfort frantically sought artillery support, soldiers of the 7th Bavarian Landwehr Regiment blew up the protective wire surrounding the American position with Bangalore torpedoes. As their box barrage cut off the hill from American reinforcement, the German infantry rushed forward. Ten minutes after the bombardment began, they were in the American trenches. A weaponless Halyburton, stumbling around and looking for shelter, thought "hundreds of little lights blinked as the Boches switched on the electric lamps fastened to their breasts." The Germans swooped down on the wrecked American trenches, deftly employing pistols and grenades. One of them knocked Halyburton out with a blow to the head. When he regained consciousness, two Germans had him pinioned, while a third searched his pockets. A German officer stood nearby, "smoking a cigar and viewing the operations of the raiders with satisfaction."[5]

Most of the defenders never emerged from their dugouts. The men in McLaughlin's platoon "were Demoralized by the Barrage to a large extent and were spread over quite a little ground and in some cases got excited and beyond control," Comfort would later report. "In one dugout the men were not awakened during Bombardment." McLaughlin stayed put in his dugout, where Corporal James B. Gresham was posted as a sentry. Gresham peered through the smoke and fog, trying to identify the men he saw moving outside—and made the wrong decision. Recalled one of the enlisted men in the dugout: "Three men that they thought were Americans, passed along—Gresham called don't shoot I am an American. The man replied in English that is the man I am looking for—and Shot him. Lieut McLachlan sprang out calling Halt, when a high explosive Shell [more likely a grenade] exploded above him [and] made him unconscious." Elsewhere, five doughboys emerged from their holes together. They saw a group of men pass and thought, at first, that they were American. A minute later they realized that the men were German and opened fire in the fog, but the doughboys were scattered after a brief firefight. "Several mistakes were made by our men taking the Germans for American Troops in the darkness and smoke," Comfort admitted. When he visited the front line later on, Comfort found McLaughlin so dazed that he was not sure whether the Germans had been there or not.[6]

The raiders departed after just a few minutes, taking with them a dozen prisoners and leaving behind five wounded and three dead Americans. One soldier (Gresham) was killed, "shot by a revolver as he stepped to the door of his dugout"; another "had his head crushed in—whether by a club or piece of shell fragment" was not apparent; and the third was found lying on top of a parapet with his throat cut—possibly a sentry that the Germans had silenced during their initial approach. German losses were insignificant, with just one soldier wounded by his own artillery barrage. In all, the raid was a complete success for the Germans—who immediately publicized their catch—and a minor disaster for the Americans. Its aftermath would put Franco-American relations to the test.[7]

The next morning at about 0730, Captain George C. Marshall, the division's operations officer, prepared to set out from division headquarters to inspect the troops in the line. He was not yet aware of the raid. When the commander of the French 18th Division, General Paul Bordeaux, ordered Marshall's staff car stopped before it could leave headquarters, the American assumed that he had irritated the Frenchman in some way. But then the general appeared and told Marshall he had reports of *les premiers Americains sont tués*—the first American fatalities. At 0800 the two left for the front.

After chafing under some French-imposed delays, Marshall finally arrived at American battalion headquarters in a stone quarry at Einville. The 2/16th battalion commander, evidently confused, knew no details of the raid and declined to accompany Marshall to the front. Marshall visited some other posts and found Lieutenant Comfort dazed with what he took to be shell shock; he then decided to visit the trenches that had been attacked. Accompanied by his interpreter–liaison officer and General Bordeaux, Marshall raced along a communications trench. After dodging enemy sniper fire, which Marshall phlegmatically characterized as "beautiful target shooting," they arrived at the front-line trench. Marshall followed the trench until he came to a place where it had caved in:

> I remember climbing up on top of the trench. Everything was very quiet. No Man's Land was about half a mile wide there and I got up on top and here down below me, just a little to my right front, was the blasted gap in the wire which was about sixty yards wide there. The white tape to guide the raiding party that night through the wire leading up to the front trench—here was the scene of the raid—no question about it now. We had a hard time to get up to the part of the trench which this tape came in and where the defenders had been surprised. And we went down into this dugout—where there was quite a bit of blood about—where some had been killed or wounded—and then we came up and found the dead on the ground and the wounded had gone back.[8]

Among the men he found was Lieutenant McLaughlin, who was "slightly wounded in the face, his helmet bent by a shell fragment and he himself very much shaken by the bombardment he had experienced." Afterward, while Marshall was questioning some of the wounded, his interpreter hissed in his ear that the French general was questioning whether the Americans had "showed fight." Furious, Marshall turned to the general and declared:

> General, I understand you are trying to find whether the Americans showed fight or not. I don't think there is any necessity for your questioning that—they had been surprised and they probably put up a disordered fight. Most of them were trapped in a dugout. But I don't think that is the thing to investigate. I think it would be very much more to the point if you look into the fact that you forbade the Americans to go beyond the wire in any reconnaissance and now they are surprised by the assault right through the wire. I think General Pershing is going to be very much interested in that reaction of a French commander to American troops.

The upstart captain's feisty tirade silenced the general, who became "very stiff." Annoyed that the French were apparently itching to blame the Americans, Marshall decided to submit his report to the French corps commander in addition to his own boss, Major General Sibert. Alerted to Marshall's plan, Bordeaux summoned Marshall to his headquarters and told him not to proceed. "You are a very young officer," he chided, "and this is a very serious matter." But Marshall wouldn't back down; he barked, "That's the reason I am going there [to the French commander]. It is a very serious matter and I am representing the division commander." When the French corps chief of staff arrived, he was visibly upset and asked Marshall "not to embarrass the corps commander at this particular moment." Marshall relented but said he "would have to go ahead and report this to General Sibert . . . because it is a very, very serious matter and I don't have to be a general to see that. I said I wish you would tell your corps commander so he can interest himself in it right away." "We had," Marshall remembered, "quite a scene there."[9]

The official ceremony memorializing the dead helped paper over these differences. The three dead soldiers—the first Americans killed by hostile action after the United States officially entered the war—were Corporal James B. Gresham, Private Thomas F. Enright, and Private Merle D. Hay. They were buried, with full honors, the next day in Bathelémont, which Marshall described as "just a crossroad and a manure pile" with "a haystack or two around." To Marshall's surprise, General Bordeaux gave "a very beautiful talk," calling for their graves to lie under a permanent monument. Marshall was so delighted with the general's words that he thanked him personally and had the speech transcribed and widely published. Pershing, likewise impressed, opined that "this joint homage to our dead, there under the fire of the guns, seemed to symbolize the common sacrifices our two peoples were to make in the same great cause." Rumor had it that one of the dead American soldiers had been a Protestant and was therefore buried just outside the churchyard of the Catholic cemetery. That night, villagers broke down the cemetery fence so "the American boy was no longer lonesome as he lay sleeping in foreign soil." Thus the appearance of Franco-American comity was restored.[10]

Public protestations of fellowship notwithstanding, this minor affair exacerbated simmering tensions that had emerged during 1st Division's training program with the French. General Bordeaux's speech had mollified Marshall, whose report to Sibert led to a thorough investigation of safety precautions against raids but provoked no blow-up with the French. Publicly, Bordeaux reported—falsely, as the Americans well knew—that the assaulted American battalion had "offered the utmost possible resistance." He backed this up with an official report to Sibert's headquarters stating that the "attitude of the garrison" had been "very honorable" and concluding that "everything shows that after having undergone an extremely violent bombardment, the American N.C.O. and men fought with an enemy much stronger in number. The killed and wounded were struck by grenade fragments, pistol bullets, rifle bullets and knife." Conversely, Marshall's own report indicated that four of the five wounded had been injured by enemy shell fire and that, aside from the dead, almost all the Americans had remained in their dugouts. Bordeaux's report to the IX Corps commander also stated that the Americans had fought "with courage," and he refrained from any recriminations except to ask for more thorough postengagement reports. Bordeaux's orders to his division on November 14 cited the Americans who had perished "bravely in a hand to hand fight" and declared that the Germans had been driven off with energetic resistance after taking only "a few prisoners."[11]

The Americans, who later captured the German officer who had led the raid, consoled themselves with Bordeaux's remark that the doughboys had performed well in hand-to-hand fighting. But privately there was embarrassment and more than a little griping about the French. A board of officers convened on November 14 severely castigated the 2/16th for not actively patrolling, a precaution that would have uncovered German preparations: "certainly when their presence became evident, strong patrols should have been sent to drive them off instead of resting content with a little firing." The board also criticized defenses that were "careless" and too dispersed; the lieutenants' orders to retreat to the dugouts, which left their men "helpless"; and a general impression that "everyone concerned had fallen into a sense of false security and the disbelief that the Germans had any intention of strenuous action." However, the board pointed out that "the division of authority in the battalion sector between French and American officers led to conflicting ideas and indecisive action." Others picked up on the criticism of the French emanating from Comfort and others. On January 7, 1918, Fox Conner wrote to Colonel LeRoy Eltinge, who served on the general staff of the American Mission at French GHQ, "When the 1st Division was in the trenches for instruction and suffered the trench raid the authorities in Washington received their first news of the raid from the Germans. This was due to the fact that we received no reports except through the French [who were dilatory]. We are not willing to have it possible that such a thing may again occur." Shortly after the raid, Major Theodore Roosevelt Jr. of the 26th Regiment (who had been seriously gassed during an earlier German raid but refused to be evacuated) and his brother Lieutenant Archie Roosevelt attempted to lead a retaliatory raid against the Germans. The raid went forward despite initial French opposition, but Archie and his French adviser began to argue as soon as they left the trenches. Their dispute soon became "quite acrimonious," and they had to turn back. "What

Theodore said to me at this time about the French," Marshall remembered, "will not bear repeating."[12]

After its brief and not altogether pleasant experiences at Bathelémont, the 1st Division withdrew to Gondrecourt to resume training from November 20, 1917, to January 5, 1918. Despite Pershing's stated emphasis on open-warfare training, application was uneven. In practice, the division received a combination of both trench and open-warfare training that left both officers and troops confused. The frequent disappearance of trained officers who were transferred or sent on special assignment caused additional disruption as their inexperienced replacements struggled to adapt. But not all the changes were detrimental. On December 14 General Robert Lee Bullard replaced Sibert as division commander. Bullard then placed General Charles P. Summerall in command of the 1st Field Artillery Brigade. Neither man was without flaw, but they were vigorous leaders. Bullard demanded a change in attitude in the form of frequent and aggressive patrols. He also showed a moderate degree of flexibility in his willingness to learn tactical lessons from the French. Summerall possessed a firm understanding of the importance of massed artillery firepower and infantry-artillery liaison.[13]

The 1st Division was assigned to the French XXXII Corps on January 5, and ten days later it began to move up toward the Ansauville sector in Lorraine—on the eastern side of the Saint-Mihiel salient north of Toul. Elements of the division began to enter the front lines on January 20, and the Americans took command of the sector on February 5. They would remain there until April 3. Ansauville was another "quiet" sector, but there were many more lessons to be learned. The division occupied a front measuring about 7.5 kilometers long, from Seicheprey to Bouconville. Much of the line was under German observation from Montsec, and in some places, the opposing lines were only fifty yards apart. The weather was miserable, with frequent heavy rain, snow, and sleet.

General Bullard's insistence on an aggressive posture toward the enemy meant that patrols, raids, and artillery duels were common enough to keep the troops on their toes. He was right to do so in light of what had happened at Bathelémont under his predecessor. Around the end of February he proudly reported, "In doing these things we have inevitably lost men but gained heart and made the enemy feel us as is shown by his increased circumspection." Staff memorandums were plentiful as officers attempted to learn the proper lessons from front-line experiences. An attempted German raid on March 1 against troops of the 18th Infantry was smartly repelled, as "on their arrival in front of our lines they were met by a strong fire from our infantry, who stood up before the enemy without flinching, refraining from going into the dugouts and holding their trenches with rifle fire and hand grenades." The Americans lost four prisoners but also took four German prisoners. The doughboys were "very high spirited over [the] result of the attack," while the "Boche seems to be pretty nervous ever since the attack." Of course, mistakes were made, but the men and officers continued to learn.[14]

Some of the most jarring experiences in the Ansauville sector took place not in the front lines but in the rear, where American artillery and support troops were exposed to enemy gas attacks on a large scale for the first time. These became particularly intense during the frequent raids and patrols by both sides, exposing deficiencies in American training and equipment. Although instructions had been issued during training at Gondrecourt and elsewhere, lack of equipment hindered the efficacy of drills, and at the front, observance was lax. Thousands of soldiers entered the lines in February without gas respirators of any kind, and others badly neglected their equipment. Despite admonitions that gas attacks would separate "the quick and the dead," men inured to drills ignored the real thing—to their detriment. Heavy saturations of German gas sometimes neutralized entire artillery batteries, leaving front-line troops weakly supported. There were also episodes of panic when enemy gas attacks caught the Americans by surprise. Of the 549 casualties suffered by the division during its stay in the Ansauville sector, well over half—70 percent of them artillerymen—were victims of mustard gas and other types of German gas.[15]

On March 21 the first German spring offensive slammed into British positions along a forty-mile front from Arras to La Fère. Enemy activity increased in the Ansauville sector as well, in the form of intensified artillery and gas bombardments. Gas continued to have a heavy impact, as the Americans were slow to implement defensive preparations. Massive gas attacks in the last days of March continued to catch dozens of Americans without their masks. The painful self-examination necessary for improvement seems to have dissipated in the larger atmosphere of self-congratulation as doughboys of the 1st Division received their first field decorations—including the Croix de Guerre given out by Clemenceau—and listened to a string of morale-boosting proclamations by French and American commanders.[16]

Ludendorff had made his decision to launch the German spring offensive—code-named Michael—on January 21. The primary objective was to defeat the British in northern France and Flanders through an immediate infiltration and penetration of the enemy front, followed by a sweep across the British rear. In the longer run, Ludendorff hoped that a series of operations would capture the English Channel ports, force Great Britain out of the war, and destroy the remaining French forces at leisure. It was not, in other words, the beginning of a no-holds-barred drive on Paris. In the first two weeks of the offensive, however, the Germans achieved startling successes, capturing 90,000 allied prisoners and 1,300 guns, overrunning 1,200 square miles of territory, and penetrating allied lines up to sixty kilometers. The lack of a decisive strategic victory was not immediately apparent to the allies, who began to fear that the war would end before the Americans could make their mark felt.[17]

By this time, the United States had been in the war for almost a year and had about 287,000 troops in France; however, the AEF played no role in combating Operation Michael. With the exception of the brief and accidental involvement of the US 3d Division's 6th Engineers in British defensive efforts at Amiens, Pershing's divisions continued to serve only as temporary relief in quiet sectors. His desire to form a US corps and then a distinct US army remained the overarching objective. And he stuck to that plan doggedly, despite the annoyance of the French and British, who pointed out (truthfully) that the Americans barely had the administrative and supply capacity to keep individual divisions in the field, let alone corps or armies.

The issuance of Joint Note No. 18 on March 27 by the military representatives at Versailles illustrated the chasm between the Americans and their cobelligerents. This note, which General Tasker Bliss endorsed, proposed that American troops be temporarily assigned to active British and French sectors to help stem the crisis and that only American infantry and machine gun units be shipped overseas. Although Secretary Baker cautiously endorsed the note, on the condition that Pershing maintain sole control over when, where, and for how long to assign his troops, Pershing remained firmly opposed to any concessions. German successes in March and April appeared to vindicate his conviction in the bankruptcy of British and French military thinking, and he had no desire for Americans to be swept up in the disaster. Publicly he proclaimed to Foch, "I have come to tell you that the American people would consider it a great honor for our troops to be engaged in the present battle. I ask you for this in their name and my own. At this moment there are no other questions but of fighting." Behind closed doors, however, relations remained tense, and nothing immediate transpired from either Joint Note No. 18 or Pershing's declaration. American troops remained only in quiet sectors.[18]

Foch was appointed supreme commander over allied and American forces in France on April 3, although for practical purposes, his powers remained limited. On April 9 Ludendorff opened the next stage of his series of offensives—this one in Flanders and code-named Georgette. Once again, the initial gains were spectacular, and on April 12 Haig issued his famous "backs to the wall" order. The same day, Pershing offered the 1st Division for service at the front (tiny American elements, including engineers, gas warfare men, and fliers, had already participated in the fighting in Flanders). Within a few days, however, the German offensive had lost steam, and the immediate need had passed. The offensive ended on April 29 after inflicting some 112,000 casualties but without making any decisive gains—it was an "operational failure."[19]

While the allies were fighting off the Germans in Flanders without any noticeable American help, the AEF was enduring a humiliating and public drubbing farther south at Seicheprey. The 1st Division had been withdrawn from the Ansauville sector on April 5 in preparation for its transfer to Picardy. Its replacement, the 26th Division, was a different sort of formation. It had been federalized on July 25, 1917, consolidated from various New England units in what division historian Michael E. Shay labeled a "traumatic" process. Dubbed the Yankee Division, the 26th had been shipped to France in September–October 1917, where it received training in trench warfare, thanks in part to the predilections of its controversial commander, Major General Clarence Edwards.[20]

Like most senior officers of the division, Edwards was a graduate of West Point (in his case, the class of 1883), and like most generals in the AEF, he had seen limited military service in the Philippines. He took command of the 26th Division on August 22, 1917. Edwards was the quintessential soldier's general. He got along well with his staff, and his officers and men believed that he was looking out for their welfare. Edwards's relationship with Pershing, the AEF staff, and his fellow generals was another story. Supporters of the Yankee Division commander accused Pershing and his generals of being jealous of Edwards's popularity and of discriminating against him because he commanded a National Guard division with many National Guard officers. For his part, Edwards displayed a Jekyll-and-Hyde personality when it came to dealing with his own staff and with outside authorities. With his subordinates, he was all sunshine and smiles, and he could be depended on to defend them even when they were clearly in the wrong. With members of the AEF, army, corps, and other divisional staffs, by contrast, he could be haughty and overbearing, and such behavior made him more than a few enemies. Worse, Edwards apparently had a proclivity for gossip and backbiting at the expense of other officers. "This habit of loose comment of other officers," Chief of Staff Harbord scolded Edwards in March 1918, "is especially harmful from a General Officer of the Regular Army commanding a National Guard unit. Criticism of officers outside your command, especially in the presence of junior officers, is inexcusable and must cease." Edwards refused to admit wrongdoing, insisting that his "heart" was "pure," but the damage had been done. Pershing doubted that General Hunter Liggett, who held administrative and training authority over the 26th Division as a unit of US I Corps, "could succeed in making anything out of Edwards." Liggett had serious reservations about Edwards as well—reservations that would increase as the war progressed.[21]

The Yankee Division took an unusually rapid path to front-line service. After landing in France in the autumn of 1917, it trained with the French near Neufchâteau until it was assigned to French XI Corps of French Sixth Army in early February 1918. The division moved by rail toward the Chemin des Dames sector, northeast of Soissons; it then proceeded on foot from the railheads to the front. It was the first National Guard division to see service at the front. The Chemin des Dames sector was hilly, with dugouts and caves perforating the chalk and limestone. Installed in deep dugouts, the Americans had their first taste of intermittent shell fire and occasional gas alarms. The soldiers also found some unusual pets there—rats "as tame as kittens, the reason being that they had been fed and protected by previous tenants, because they were a safeguard against gas attacks. These rats could detect the slightest scent of gas, and their subsequent squealing would warn us in time to protect ourselves."[22]

French officers shepherded the doughboys gently into the front-line trenches, first by platoons and then by companies. They provided hands-on instruction in the routines of trench warfare and the tricks of the trade of modern soldiering. By all accounts, the French and the Americans got along quite well, partly because the French provided their new friends with much-needed equipment that the inexperienced Americans had failed to procure or left behind. Training, which included some short patrols, proceeded largely without a hitch, even though the division's first casualty was a victim of friendly fire. On March 18 the division was withdrawn for further training at Rimaucourt.[23]

Late in March the 26th Division was ordered to relieve the much-ballyhooed 1st Division in the Ansauville sector, thus joining French Eighth Army and its XXXII Corps. The relief took place in the first days of April and did not go well. As might be expected, the inexperienced Americans became confused during nighttime movements. Units became intermingled and made enough of a racket to alert the Germans, who sent over barrages that inflicted hundreds of casualties on both divisions. Nor was the relief amicable. Edwards and his officers complained about the condition of the trenches left behind by the 1st Division soldiers, thus offending Bullard and his staff. Already partially isolated, Edwards succeeded in making new enemies he could ill afford.[24]

It was a miserably squalid sector. The 1st Division had done little to improve it, although the defenses had been somewhat strengthened. The low-lying ground was frequently flooded. German artillery and gas attacks—fostered by observation from Montsec—made life a misery. Edwards thought the sector defenses were dangerously weak, and he futilely protested the French army commander's insistence that he simultaneously defend eighteen kilometers of frontage with his units crammed into the front lines rather than defending in depth. But Edwards and his officers had little time to improve the defenses before the first large-scale German raids began. On April 10 the Germans launched a tentative attack on the 3/104th that was broken up by artillery before it could get going—convincing the Americans that they had inflicted an unlikely 90 percent casualty rate on the attackers. Another series of attacks against the 2/104th and adjoining French units on April 12 was likewise repelled, albeit with more difficulty. Neither could compare, however, to the devastating German assault at Seicheprey on April 20.[25]

Responsibility for the portion of the division's front around the ruined village of Seicheprey was delegated to the 102d Regiment under Colonel John H. "Machine Gun" Parker, renowned as one of the army's experts on that weapon. The colonel's men did not altogether admire him; some even suspected Parker of insanity. When Private Philip Hammersmith of the Yankee Division's 101st Machine Gun Battalion arrived in France, he witnessed a remarkable scene in which Parker ordered his troops to fire over his car as the colonel drove past. When they finished, Parker's car came to a screeching halt and he leaped up, yelling, "I've brought you over here to get killed, and that's what I'm going to do!" According to Hammersmith, Parker "was always cheering the boys up like that." Later, as his troops marched by on their way to the front, Parker flashed that "crazy grin of his" and yelled, "Go get 'em boys! Give 'em hell, boys!"[26]

Parker's assigned positions were precarious. Between Seicheprey and the German lines, which jutted forward in a sharp salient, snaked a network of battered, half-ruined trenches. The primary trenches were dubbed Sibille and Remières, the latter of which connected Seicheprey with strongpoints in Remières Wood, about 1,650 yards to the right. Further in that direction lay the French 162d Division in Jury Wood. Regimental headquarters was located a mile further back in Beaumont, along a highway paralleling the Yankee Division's designated main line of resistance. Parker later claimed that he objected to initial French orders directing him to place a substantial number of troops in the forward positions. But although General Peter E. Traub (51st Brigade commander) gave him some leeway to redeploy, the arrangements remained substantially unchanged on the night of April 19–20.[27]

On that cold and misty night, the 1/102d Infantry moved up to the vicinity of Seicheprey to relieve the 3/102d. Battalion commander Major J. George Rau, who established his headquarters in the ruined village, was aware of intelligence reports that warned of German troops gathering in the vicinity. German artillery had also registered on American positions, in obvious preparation for a raid later on. Nevertheless, few serious precautions were taken against an enemy attack. At 0300, German artillery placed a heavy barrage on Seicheprey, Beaumont, and the surrounding trench systems. Two hours later this morphed into a box barrage around positions held by Companies C and D of the 1/102d, cutting lines of communication with regimental and divisional headquarters. Simultaneously, under cover of a rolling barrage and a heavy mist, about 1,000 highly trained German *Stosstruppen* of the 258th and 259th Regiments of the 78th Reserve Division moved against the American positions. The Germans had dubbed their operation *Kirschblüte*, or Cherry Blossom. "Those chaps from the other side of the Big Pond," said a German participant, "should learn about real war." The German objectives were simple: bloody the Americans, take as many prisoners as possible, wreck enemy installations in and around Seicheprey, and withdraw as quickly as possible.[28]

The Germans executed their attack with exemplary efficiency. One combat group penetrated a gap on the American left, while another followed a poorly defended ravine between Remières and Jury Wood. These two penetrating forces linked at Seicheprey and cut off American companies in the front lines, which then came under direct assault. "Commands in English are shouted," recalled P. C. Ettighoffer, an NCO with the assaulting Germans, and "hand grenades are thrown":

> The enemy gives ground at last, fighting back desperately. Nothing but dead or wounded he leaves behind, all of them big, athletic physiques in wonderful uniforms and rubber boots. A party which begins to yield during close-combat is lost and we begin to feel superiority. . . . The Americans withdraw to the next cluster of dugouts. We fol-

low closely, sloshing through mud, passing by tins, woolen blankets and various booty. . . . We believe the enemy to have escaped, when suddenly, just around a trench shoulder, we face them nose to nose. Strong, healthy men, the flat steel helmets worn obliquely over angular, beardless faces. There they stand, preparing two machine guns. "Hands up, you bloody fools," the Stellmacher shouts at them, bringing up his dagger to a nearby officer's throat. The officer haltingly lifts his hands, but his men turn around a machine gun and start firing. We throw our stick grenades. Fountains of mud splash around, covering both adversaries over and over, leaving us almost unrecognizable. Stones, clumps of dirt and splinters fly in all directions. Again we push forward and suddenly those big buggers start to grin merrily, offering hands, remarking "This damn bloody war is now finished for us!" Real sportsmen against us landsknechte![29]

In Seicheprey the Germans captured much of the village and the regimental aid station, but they faced determined resistance from clerks, aides, staff officers, and other headquarters personnel. Small-unit combat was scattered through the village and surrounding area and then centered in the cemetery before the Germans withdrew. In the trenches, meanwhile, the *Stosstruppen* encountered doughboys still huddled in dugouts, taking shelter from the barrage—just as the Americans at Bathelémont had done back in November. Those who did not surrender immediately were bombed or burned out with grenades and flamethrowers. Some Americans fought to the end, while others attempted to flee. Prisoners were divested of their boots and sent to the rear.[30]

The German raid moved too rapidly for the Americans to react effectively. Indeed, for several hours, the atmosphere at regimental, brigade, and divisional headquarters verged on the delusional. After 0900, with Seicheprey in German hands and dozens of bootless doughboys filing to the rear, Parker phoned Traub to report that he was "confident and can handle situation." Traub then called Edwards at 0956 to say that the line had been entirely reestablished and that 300 Germans had been killed by the defenders of Seicheprey. At 1135 Traub told Edwards that he had refused Parker's request for an immediate counterattack, and at last he confessed that his troops had been "overwhelmed by superiority of numbers but fought to a finish."[31]

Traub marshaled his reserves that morning and afternoon, but he did not seriously consider implementing any countermeasures until nightfall. "Our aviators observe long trains at the ramps of Toul detraining troops to be transported further towards the front by lorry and on foot," noted Ettighoffer. Traub phoned Edwards and then contacted the XXXII Corps commander, General Fénelon Passaga, who ordered that a counterattack be launched at 1900 that evening. But Traub demurred. The German dispositions remained uncertain, and his reserves were both disorganized and ill trained for offensive action. Traub picked up the phone and called Edwards to express his doubts. As the two generals spoke, two mischievous Germans "cut in on the wire, brazenly calling themselves two crooks and frankly said they were 'in the game.'" Whether afraid that the enemy had discovered their plans or in deference to Traub's doubts, Edwards and Passaga agreed to defer the counterattack until 0445 the next morning in four-company strength. But by then, it was too late. "What an effort," said Ettighoffer, "and all because of our small band of men, who are waiting to withdraw quietly by nightfall anyway."[32]

The brigade commander was not the only one with doubts. Traub placed Major John J. Gallant in charge of organizing and leading the counterattack, which the French would support. But Gallant refused, pointing out that the enemy infantry was dug in too well and would slaughter the attackers. Traub repeated his orders until Gallant refused to obey them point-blank; the major was promptly relieved and court-martialed. As it turned out, Gallant ruined his army career for nothing. When the attack went forward the next day, the Americans found that all the Germans were gone and the trenches were empty, except for dozens of dead Americans.[33]

German propaganda trumpeted the American defeat at Seicheprey for all it was worth. The *Stosstruppen* had killed or wounded about 300 Americans and had captured 5 officers and 178 men, plus two dozen machine guns and other materiel. German casualties are uncertain, with tallies varying from 600 to nearly 3,000. Even the lowest estimate suggests that they paid a heavy price for their victory, but the Germans left few corpses behind for inspection. The Americans put their own spin on the affair as officers sought to protect their reputations and counter German propaganda. Traub claimed in his initial reports to Edwards that most of the Americans reported as missing were actually dead and "buried in the ruins of Seicheprey." The demoralized Germans, he insisted, had suffered staggering casualties and fled before the counterattackers could come to grips with them, leaving behind "immense" piles of abandoned supplies in their wake.[34]

The first patrols on the morning of April 21 seemed to bear out Traub's narrative. Lieutenant A. F. Oberlin wandered around the ruins and discovered quantities of light German equipment lying about, including grenades, a machine gun, a grenade thrower, and small piles of ammunition.

Oberlin also discovered a few German corpses. From such detritus, he concluded that "their intention must have been to hold ... if possible. It is quite evident, though, from the amount of material scattered about that their retreat was made in some haste."[35] Edwards backed up this interpretation, haranguing a bemused Pierpont L. Stackpole on April 23 with an "incoherent account" of how his men had "found the lines deserted by the Boche when they went up to them later, but full of grenades and rapid-fire pistols and helmets in regular rows along trenches and parapets, indicating that the Boche was thoroughly prepared to resist an attack if it had been made and that the artillery had killed all those whose helmets were lying around, the bodies themselves having been taken away by the Boche." "Bunk!" Stackpole wryly concluded.[36]

Lieutenant Colonel W. S. Grant, conducting a separate investigation for G-3 on April 24, was not so sanguine. Referring contemptuously to claims that the Germans had fled in haste, he said the real reason they had left material behind was that "the German soldier is quite as human as the American soldier and will often abandon ammunition and munitions rather than gather it together and take it back." Parker boasted to Grant that the regiment's internal and external liaison during the raid had been "perfect," but the French did not agree, and neither did Grant. Contrary to reports from the division, Grant estimated that up to 200 American prisoners may have been taken.[37]

Parker, Traub, and Edwards conspired rather amateurishly to cover up the scale of the defeat. Writing in 1919, US Third Army's chief of staff, Brigadier General Malin Craig (who had served in Liggett's I Corps at the time of the German attack), told Brigadier General LeRoy Eltinge that Edwards and his staff had "denied very strenuously that they had lost prisoners, this denial being made to me over the 'phone several times by General Edwards and the Chief of Staff, who at that time was Col. Dowell ... nor was there ever any admission of loss of prisoners made to me until I sent the Division Commander a photographic copy of an edition of the 'Ardennes Gazette' giving the names of 183 prisoners." Parker backed up the division commander's assertions, and he and Edwards vigorously denounced German claims to the contrary as mere propaganda. At the same time, their "extravagant" after-action reports estimated up to 1,500 German casualties. Such obfuscation was especially foolish because, as Edwards must have known, GHQ had sources of its own. These sources reported to Fox Conner that the German claims were essentially correct. No one admitted as much in public, but Pershing viewed Edwards's evasions with growing disdain. In a memorandum dated April 30 that did not specifically name Edwards, Pershing denounced the practice of keeping excessive forces in forward positions, without saying who was to blame for it. He added that "to sit quietly in trenches during a heavy fog and allow a surprise attack to be sprung on men who are unprepared is, to my mind, inexcusable and will not be tolerated in this command." The Yankee Division's general was becoming a marked man.[38]

The French did their part to support the official "spin" on Seicheprey, soothing the Yankee Division's feelings by decorating the 104th Regiment's flag for earlier fighting at Apremont. This was the first time, newspapers reported, that such an award had been given to a US flag by a foreign power. A young American fainted as he was about to receive a French medal from General Passaga in the ceremony that followed. As bystanders helped the boy to his feet, French officers flatteringly commented that "it is usually a savage fighter who gets stage fright and goes faint when he is decorated for bravery."[39]

Such praise was not always accepted in the spirit in which it was offered. Pershing was infuriated by the Seicheprey affair and prepared some sort of disciplinary action, possibly against Edwards. But Passaga's well-intentioned rewards and words of praise sheltered Edwards and his officers from punishment. Conner conveyed the general's annoyance in a letter to Harbord on April 29, complaining that the "excessive liberality of the French" in giving decorations to undeserving units such as the 26th Division had resulted in a "cheapening" of American decorations and had made it harder for commanders to point out mistakes. He recommended that the French be told not to give decorations to American units without the permission of GHQ. Edwards and Traub, meanwhile, complained loudly that the "French plan of disposition," which forced the strong manning of front lines allegedly imposed by XXXII Corps and French Eighth Army, along with Passaga's refusal to let the Americans root out "spies . . . operating in large numbers through all the villages," had been to blame for the casualties that Edwards and Traub strenuously denied having suffered.[40]

In reality, American propaganda fooled no one. Privately, the Europeans were more critical. German after-action reports noted both the bravery of the doughboys and the cluelessness of their commanders. And British prime minister Lloyd George remarked that such apparent disasters were "bound to occur on an enormous scale if a large amateur United States Army is built up without the guidance of more experienced General Officers."[41]

3

Cantigny
May 1918

On April 19, even as the 26th Division was enduring its trial by fire at Seicheprey, Secretary Baker provided the British with a memorandum agreeing in principle to their earlier proposal to ship 120,000 American infantrymen and machine gunners to Europe each month on British and American vessels. Five days later Pershing, who was negotiating separately in London and had no knowledge of the Baker memorandum, signed a much narrower accord promising to send men for six US divisions for training with the British. These divisions, and any sent to the front, would be employed at Pershing's sole discretion and with a view to the eventual formation of an American army. Learning of the contradictory agreements, Baker and Wilson decided to endorse Pershing's agreement and give him full control over future negotiations on such matters. Knowing the general's stubbornness, the British and French were not amused.[1]

The Abbeville agreement of May 1–2 among Foch, Haig, and Pershing confirmed the program of shipping American infantry to Europe quickly and employing them with the British and French at Pershing's discretion; the emphasis was still on the eventual formation of an American army. But the agreement left a legacy of bitter feelings on all sides, and Haig privately dismissed Pershing's yearning for an American army as "ridiculous." Meanwhile, the travails of American units training with the British and French left the latter disgusted with the Yanks. At the command and staff levels, the Americans seemed incapable of efficient organization and stubbornly unwilling to learn; the troops lacked facility with weaponry and elementary tactics. Taken in conjunction with Seicheprey,

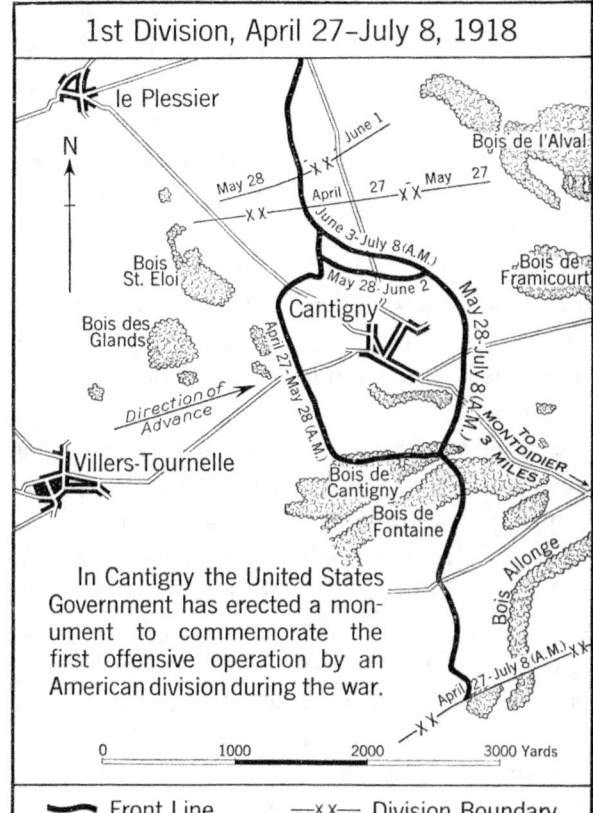

The 1st Division at Cantigny, May 28, 1918. (*American Armies and Battlefields in Europe*, 415)

In Cantigny the United States Government has erected a monument to commemorate the first offensive operation by an American division during the war.

these shortcomings seemed to confirm that without some form of amalgamation, the Americans would provide no help at all during 1918.[2]

It was in this context that the first noticeable American contribution at the front would be engineered—a joint Franco-American production. From the French point of view, it would reassure friends and warn the enemy that the Americans were combat ready and could operate effectively under French corps command. From the American point of view, it would prove that the Yanks could fight—better and more aggressively than their cobelligerents—and that they would soon be ready to go it alone. Pershing's beloved 1st Division was selected to take the test.

After being relieved by the 26th Division, the 1st Division had moved back to Gisors, northwest of Paris, to receive further training. Although some of its experiences at Ansauville had been painful, Pershing had reported to Foch on April 12 that the division was ready for service "wherever you desire to place it." Afterward he gave a stirring speech to the division in anticipation of immediate combat. A week later the division concentrated southwest of Montdidier, where it came under the command of French VI Corps of the French First Army (French X Corps would take over the sector on May 5). On the night of April 24–25 the division entered the front lines between the French 45th and 162d Divisions on the left and right, respectively, and opposite the village of Cantigny. The sector was placed under American command on April 27.[3]

Conditions in the front-line trenches disgusted Private Charles Abels. They were "dug through a cracked chalk formation that was actually alive with lice which would crawl out of the cracks in the trench and attach themselves to humans," he complained. Others found only crumbling foxholes that they labored to extend into a rudimentary trench system. Despite these complaints, the division was well supported by both French and American artillery, and Bullard directed his troops to launch frequent patrols and raids even as they worked to improve their positions. Special attention was also given to establishing firm liaison with the neighboring French forces; the division's liaison officer to French VI Corps, Major Robert H. Lewis, made a lengthy visit to the front on May 2 to ensure that everything was operating efficiently. At the juncture of the American and French fronts, he noted with satisfaction that a "mixed post" had been established consisting of a French squad and NCO and an American squad and NCO.[4]

In his aggressiveness, however, Bullard violated the terms of the "live and let live" system that had previously prevailed in this largely inactive sector. Before the Americans arrived, French artillery in the Cantigny area had fired an average of 2,000 shells per day against German positions. After the 1st Division entered the trenches, daily averages increased to 5,000, 8,000, and finally 12,000 rounds per day on May 2–3. This uptick in shelling, in combination with aggressive American patrols and raids, irritated the Germans and perhaps indicated to them that a large-scale attack was imminent. Retaliation was not slow in coming. In early May, German artillery began pummeling the American positions with increasingly high concentrations of both high explosives and gas. Unfazed, Bullard thought his raids were "regularly successful" and that his artillery quickly got the "upper hand" over the enemy because of the Americans' "zest" compared with the Germans' "staleness." Further behind the lines, Pershing worried about the effectiveness of the German bombardments, noting that they caused Bullard's troops "great difficulty" as they prepared for possible offensive action against Cantigny.[5]

The German bombardments reached a crescendo on May 3–4, primarily against positions held by a battalion of the 18th Infantry in Villers-Tournelle.

During a three-and-a-half-hour period beginning at 0830 on May 4, American observers estimated that 15,000 high-explosive shells and mustard gas canisters fell on their positions. In fact, less than a third of that number actually hit the Americans, but the observers apparently based their estimates on the bombardment's disproportionate impact on the defending troops. The 18th Infantry suffered more than 850 casualties in less than twenty-four hours, mostly from gas. Bullard's chief of staff, Lieutenant Colonel Campbell King, wrote bitterly on May 8, "American losses are from two to four times as great as those of the French. There is but one conclusion; it is that our men, either from ignorance or carelessness, are not taking cover." The French at VI Corps headquarters, Lewis reported, were "quite worked up" about the level of casualties and expressed "doubts as to the quality of the gas discipline in the division." Adding to the humiliation, doughboys in mustard-splashed uniforms had to beg for replacements from their French neighbors.[6]

Numerous factors were to blame for this fiasco. To be fair, the available protective equipment was less than ideal. The standard-issue AEF gas mask was the small box respirator (SBR), which the British had designed two years earlier. This device featured a face piece resembling a shapeless canvas bag; beneath it, a nose clip cut off nasal inhalation while the wearer breathed through a tube held in the mouth. A canister filtered out poison gas from the air supplied through the tube. Although this mask was advertised as effective for up to twenty hours, most soldiers found it intolerable to wear for more than six to eight hours. Frustrated doughboys therefore sought alternatives. Some used the far more comfortable French M-2 mask, but it was effective for only a few hours and easily damaged; even heavy rain rendered it useless. Others, especially officers, donned the *appareil respiratoire spéciale* (ARS), which the French had copied from the German snout mask early in 1918. This exceptionally effective mask was expensive to manufacture and therefore typically issued only to assault troops, but American officers pulled strings to get ARS masks for themselves. The AEF GHQ banned the M-2 and ARS in early June 1918—the former because it was ineffective, and the latter because it caused jealousy among those who did not have it and destroyed their confidence in the standard-issue SBR. Many officers continued to use the ARS anyway. Bullard ordered his officers and men to stop complaining about the SBR, but privately he admitted that it was impossible to wear.[7]

The primary problem, though, was the weakness—or entire absence—of American gas discipline. The night of May 3–4 was dark and cloudy, creating poor visibility that frustrated the nervous officers and men. Despite warnings of possible gas attacks, many officers removed their masks, and the men followed their example. Even after the gas bombardment began, troops removed their masks, ignorant of the deadliness of even low concentrations of mustard. Rainy conditions on May 5 incited the French to evacuate some of their positions because experience had shown that rain allowed gas pockets to endure for longer periods without dissipating. When the French returned, they discovered an entire company of Americans, along with headquarters staff, stationed in the positions they had abandoned. Some of the doughboys even loitered in gas-saturated trenches. The French ordered the Americans out immediately, but not before many doughboys became casualties. "Shell holes," recalled one doughboy, "were frequently used by the soldiers as latrines. Many of the soldiers lost their testicles from the mustard gas in the holes."[8]

Almost as soon as the 1st Division entered this sector, French and American officers set their sights on the village of Cantigny, northwest of Montdidier. Militarily, the village was worthless. Captured by the Germans earlier that spring, it had been blasted by artillery week after week until only the church tower remained standing—and even that collapsed into ruins two weeks after the Yanks arrived opposite the town. The village lay within a small salient 1,000 meters deep and 1,500 meters wide, and it was situated below the southern end of a German-held ridge. South of the town lay a shallow ravine. Troops of the German 82d Reserve Division had occupied Cantigny and fortified it to some extent, but they took no special pains in this regard because they knew the only nearby terrain worth fighting for was the ridge above the village, designated Hill 104 on maps. Capturing *that* would require a major operation.[9]

Whatever its value, Cantigny seemed ripe for the picking, so plans were conceived for a "prestige operation" to capture it. Initially these plans formed one component of a larger Franco-American offensive to recapture Montdidier. In this version, proposed by Major General Marie-Eugène Debeney of French First Army and Major General Charles A. Vandenberg of French X Corps, the entire corps would drive forward to capture the plateaus of Cantigny and Mesnil–St. Georges. French units to 1st Division's right would carry out the primary task of capturing Montdidier and Framicourt, while the Americans assaulted Cantigny. When rumors of renewed German offensives led Foch to cancel any major attacks, Vandenberg and Bullard put their heads together and conceived a smaller operation against Cantigny that would be "analogous to a powerful raid," Vandenberg wrote in a letter to Debeney on May 12. It would not drain the 1st Division of its offensive capacity in the near future, but it would do much to boost American morale. "We have the right to count on a complete and easy success," Vandenberg wrote, "susceptible of having great moral effect . . . and in particular to confirm the confidence of the staff of the 1st Inf. Div." Pershing concurred—although his sense of the "moral effect" differed somewhat from that envisioned by the French—and Debeney approved the plan on May 15. The attack was originally scheduled for May 25, but at Bullard's request—and partly because a portion of the 18th Infantry had been devastated by gas earlier that month—D-day was postponed to May 28.[10]

Writers seeking to justify the attack on Cantigny—Pershing among them—later claimed that it had been conceived with the intention of capturing "high ground which jutted out into the line held by the Allies, observing and menacing the trenches occupied by our First American Division." Lieutenant Colonel Jennings C. Wise claimed that German-held high ground at Cantigny and Grivesnes (three kilometers to the northwest) had long made movement in the sector difficult, resulting in gas and artillery casualties for the 1st Division. This has led some historians to surmise that the assault possessed "some tactical and operational justification" beyond its obvious symbolic purpose. Yet the Cantigny attack did nothing to interrupt German observation—if anything, it only provided the enemy with better and closer targets. The only valuable terrain in the area—the ridge above the village from which the Germans could view the surrounding region—could be neither taken nor held without at least a corps-sized operation. So long as the ridge remained in enemy hands, Cantigny would remain under direct German observation—rendering it not only tactically worthless but also a firetrap. This truth was no secret to Pershing, Bullard, or anyone else. Their rationale for taking Cantigny was entirely symbolic. Although a successful operation would show the Germans that the Americans were prepared for offensive action (as the French hoped it would), it would also constitute an argument against amalgamation by demonstrating to Foch and his colleagues that, in Pershing's words, "we could best help the Allies by using our troops in larger units instead of adopting their plan of building up their forces."[11]

Bullard delegated responsibility for planning the assault on Cantigny to his G-3, Lieutenant Colonel George C. Marshall; Brigadier General Charles Summerall, commanding the 1st Artillery Brigade, planned the artillery support. The product of Marshall's labors, issued on May 20, was Field Order 18, "Operation against Cantigny." Marshall assigned the attack to the 2,800-strong 28th Infantry Regiment, commanded by Colonel Hanson

Ely. Competent but no military genius, Ely "was hard to like, gruff, pugnacious, heavy, a complainer, humorless, overbearing." After a brief but violent preparatory barrage from French and American artillery and then a rolling and finally a "box" barrage, three battalions of the 28th with attached machine gun and infantry support units would advance on Cantigny side by side. The center battalion, supported by twelve French Schneider tanks (5th Groupe Char d'Assaut Schneider), French sappers with "mobile charges," and French engineers wielding flamethrowers, would advance straight through the village from the west and north. Their objective was to take and hold Cantigny—nothing more. The high ground above the village would remain in enemy hands. In essence, the assault was traditional and in the European style, but on a minor scale.[12]

On May 22–24 the 28th Regiment was withdrawn to an area around Maisoncelle-Tuillerie and St. Eusoye, about twenty-five kilometers southwest of Cantigny. There the regiment spent two days rehearsing the attack, using trenches and strongpoints that had been constructed to replicate the German positions, based on information provided by aerial reconnaissance photographs and ground patrols. Soldiers drilled and were trained down to the platoon level, and they were instructed how to root out the Germans by eliminating machine gun nests and bombing shelters. Soldiers also received much-needed training in how to cooperate with tanks and planes, while signalers learned the basics of laying cables, conducting repairs, and, where necessary, relaying information on foot. At the front, meanwhile, the 1st Engineers constructed two trenches—one of them an actual jumping-off line, and the other a "dummy to deceive the enemy."[13]

As D-day approached and the 28th Regiment moved back toward the front in preparation to relieve the 18th Regiment and commence the attack, the Germans launched strong local attacks of their own. On the night of May 26–27 German artillery directed a strong phosgene and mustard gas bombardment against American artillery and infantry positions. The Yanks were not caught entirely off guard, as they had been earlier in the month, but they still suffered more than 300 casualties. The bombardment also forced already fatigued infantrymen to spend another sleepless night panting in their gas masks. Worse, the infantry began to show signs of shakiness. During the bombardment on May 26, Company H of the 28th Infantry, composed in large part of poorly trained immigrants, showed signs that it was preparing to flee the lines. Only the intervention of a level-headed French officer who soothed the frightened men kept the company in line.[14]

On May 27 Ludendorff launched the next major phase of his spring offensive against the French at Chemin des Dames. Simultaneously, the German 18th Army conducted a series of strong raids, code-named Manfred, against the 1st Division and adjacent French units to convince them that major attacks would take place in their sector. In the Cantigny area, the German 82d and 25th Reserve Divisions conducted raids code-named Tarnopol and Tannenberg, respectively, south and north of Cantigny. "No special practice was given" for the raids, said a German officer, "and the men were told that it would be easy as they had only the Americans up against them."[15]

Under a sky specked with scudding clouds and whipped by gusty spring winds, German raiders surged forward under strong artillery cover and penetrated 1st Division lines at multiple points. Unlike on some previous occasions, the Americans put up what German reports characterized as a "stout and bitter resistance," inflicting some 200 casualties on the attackers. Still, the Germans managed to capture several American prisoners, along with a few machine guns. Fear gripped Bullard's headquarters that the captives would divulge information about the coming attack, but the general need not have worried—at least two of the American prisoners were killed by their own artillery on their way back to the German lines, and the others evidently kept their mouths shut.[16]

As the raids subsided, the 28th Regiment moved toward jumping-off positions and past a large array of weaponry gathered in support: 386 French artillery pieces and almost 150,000 stacked rounds of high-explosive, gas, and smoke shells; American and French trench mortar batteries; and dozens of machine guns. German artillery had been somewhat successful in disrupting these formations over the previous two days, but they were still formidable. Tanks and flamethrower specialists had also assembled, and dressing stations and ambulances were prepared to receive casualties. German infantry opposition would not be formidable. The positions in and around Cantigny were held primarily by the German 82d Reserve Division, forming part of the XXVI Reserve Corps on the left of Von Hutier's Eighteenth Army. The 82d Reserve Division had served primarily on the eastern front, where it had been completely gutted in the 1915 offensive. Its ranks had been filled with "healed veterans, young recruits, dismounted cavalry, overage *landwehr* men, and railway guards." The division had been removed from the east as Russia collapsed in November 1917, and it was subsequently retrained; however, it remained an inferior formation that was intended only for defensive purposes. The division's 271st Reserve Regiment held Cantigny and the area to the south, while the 272d Reserve Regiment held the area to the north. Each regiment had one battalion in front-line positions—one within supporting distance in woods to the rear, and another up to twelve kilometers further in the rear. The 25th Reserve Division, also an inferior formation, provided support. Because the Germans did not expect an attack in this sector, entrenchments and earthworks were decidedly weak.[17]

The night was clear but cool; by dawn, a blanket of haze had settled over the area. The artillery, gas, and machine gun barrage began on schedule at 0545. For many Americans, it was their first experience of a preattack bombardment. "It was a remarkable sight," said one witness, "great clouds of smoke rolling up from the shelled districts, against which the flashes of bursting shells stood out." Private Dan Edwards described how "Cantigny just began to boil up. And it kept on boiling. In a short time we couldn't see it at all, we couldn't see the ground anywheres. The air was full of trees, stones, timber, equipment, bodies, everything you can imagine, all smashed up and whirling around with the dirt. The shells kept right on going overhead in one steady screeching yowl, without a let-up." An hour later the rolling barrage commenced at a rate of fifty meters per minute, and the infantry rose up to follow.[18]

The attack took place on a frontage of 2,200 meters and would reach a maximum depth of 1,600 meters. The 3/28th (Companies K, L, and M, from left to right) moved forward on the left, with the 2/28th (Companies F, E, and H) in the center and the 1/28th (Companies D, B, and A) on the right. French infantry from the neighboring 152d Division supported the Americans with machine gun and rifle fire. French planes flew overhead, looking for enemy counterfire and directing their artillery to silence the German guns. Tanks of the 5th Groupe Char d'Assaut Schneider joined the infantry in the first wave. Lieutenant Daniel Sargent of the 5th Field Artillery watched as "the tanks were coming out of the woods, escorted by the infantrymen. Nothing could have been less romantic seeming. The tanks looked like haycarts (horseless); the infantry looked like haymakers that carried rifles instead of pitchforks." In front of them walked a dapper French officer, merrily twirling his walking stick, but the tanks' overall commander, Captain Emile Noscereau, followed the advance in his special command tank. French-speaking American runners trotted alongside to maintain liaison among the tank groups and with the infantry; a French liaison officer was mortally wounded during the attack. Some of the tanks broke down or were disabled, but their presence had a tangible effect on the defenders as the vehicles veered north and wiped out several German machine gun nests, materially assisting the infantry. The French tank group commander reported after the action:

The cooperation of the Tanks and Infantry was accomplished in a manner beyond expectations. Aside from the evidence of spirit and courage which aroused admiration on the part of all members of Tank Battalion 5, the American Infantry showed a remarkable knowledge of how to use Tank assistance, following them closely without allowing themselves to be held up by them, and sticking close to their barrage. The advantages of this cooperation were appreciable.

The tanks returned on schedule after the infantry captured its objectives—in the process, tearing up phone lines the American signalers had laid.[19]

The attack on Cantigny took its German defenders by surprise. Some of the Americans were not observed until they had entered the village, where the defenders—some of whom had arrived only that morning—"lost their heads somewhat," according to the German postmortem. Field officers who survived the initial bombardment performed poorly overall, and the commander of the 271st Regiment collapsed with a nervous breakdown. Nevertheless, German infantry initially showed some fight, even though their numerous signal flares for artillery support were ignored—perhaps because they were obscured by fog. As the doughboys moved out, recalled Dan Edwards:

> The enemy popped up behind [the barrage] and began pelting hell out of us. They had been hid down in deep dugouts, and they came up with plenty of reserve guns and ammunition. They had machine guns and one-pounders, and they gave us the merry devil. They'd rip into us, and down we'd go, flat. We'd lay there until a lull in the firing and then those left of us would get up and make another dash and then down again.

Overall, though, the German defensive performance was uncharacteristically poor. In Cantigny the Americans engaged in some close-quarters fighting, but they also found dozens of demoralized Germans hunkered down in their dugouts—a nice reversal of fortune. Those Germans who did not surrender immediately met a grim fate at the hands of French troops wielding flamethrowers. Edwards described his advance behind one of the Frenchmen:

> This French bimbo was about fifty years old, with a bushy black beard. The weather was hotter than billy-be-damned, but he had on the reg-

ulation French army overcoat with its bottom buttoned back to the knees on each side. On his back he had two long tanks, each with a nozzle, and he had a big sack full of grenades swung on each side of him. He was loaded down.

Well, you'd have thought he was hoeing a garden, the way he worked. Just before we started out he lighted up his pipe, and he was still puffing away at it the last I saw of him. He was just as calm and cool as if he was working on a farm. Placid and methodical, he walked along smoking his pipe and looking around for dugouts. When he spotted one, over he'd go. Just as he got to the entrance he'd unlimber the nozzle of his canned flame and yell:

"*Raus mit ihm!*" in a tone of voice that meant: "Get the hell out of there!"

As he yelled, he trained the nozzle down into the dugout and let her rip. Then he'd take out a grenade, tap it on his tin hat, and toss it in. Then he'd fall flat and take a long comfortable draw on his pipe, tamping down the tobacco with his forefinger.

After the bang down in the dugout he'd look it over carefully to make sure it was on fire. He didn't give them a chance to "*Raus mit ihm.*"[20]

All three of the American battalions made steady progress toward their objectives, although the flank battalions took casualties from German machine guns stationed to the right and left. In the process, the Americans captured 230 German soldiers and officers who, according to an eyewitness, were "80% boys and 70% hollow-cheeked, wan and underfed looking." The 1/28th cleared out the southern rim of the village, the ravine, and the area to the southeast, although Ely had to reinforce it with a company of the 18th Regiment. The 2/28th lost its commander, Lieutenant Colonel Robert Maxey, who was mortally wounded by an enemy shell at 0830; still, it pushed through the village quickly and reached its objective, despite encountering serious resistance from the high ground to the east. The 3/28th moved forward rapidly to its objective but suffered some disorganization in the advance as it was raked by enemy fire. Once at its objective, heavy artillery and machine gun fire from the left flank forced Company K to abandon two trenches it had captured there. Company I, previously held in reserve, moved up to fill the gap. Overall, the operation proceeded smoothly, with all units achieving their objectives by 0730. Vandenberg was thrilled, calling it an "excellent operation from every point of view," even though the inexperienced Americans had made some mistakes, such as moving about "in the captured village as though they were out of sight and out of enemy reach."[21]

The victorious Americans now turned to the task of establishing a defensive perimeter. Men from Company D of the 1st Engineers established previously designated strongpoints with "hasty emplacements" for American and captured German machine guns in a cemetery north of Cantigny, in woods to the north and northeast, and 200 meters beyond a château east of town. Supporting troops dug trenches and laid wire, connecting and protecting the strongpoints, and established outposts. Anticipating a German counterbarrage, very few men were stationed in the ruins of the village itself. It all seemed to be efficiently laid out, and Ely felt confident of his ability to take on all comers. He seemed to be unaware that he had in fact entered into a newly formed, dangerous salient under direct enemy observation. On the flanks, the 1/28th and 3/28th had suffered some confusion during the advance and did not consolidate their positions as effectively as they should have. That was doubly unfortunate, as they would have to bear the main brunt of enemy flanking fire and eventual counterattacks.[22]

At first, French and American artillery lent support to these defensive arrangements by laying heavy barrages of high explosives and smoke around Cantigny. However, pressure from the German offensive on the Chemin des Dames that began on May 27 led to the quick withdrawal of French artillery support. This left the American gunners on their own, and they lacked the firepower—or perhaps the organization—to maintain effective support. At the same time, the German artillery, dormant during the actual assault, woke up. Expecting the Americans to resume their attack, the Germans directed both gas and high explosives in withering "annihilation fire," combining with machine guns to make life miserable for the doughboys. By noon, the German barrage reached full intensity, and by then, half the American companies in the American sector, especially on the left, had incurred 30 percent casualties. This intense fire would continue for another forty-eight hours.[23]

The German response was slow in coming, thanks to ongoing command confusion. For much of the day, German corps and army headquarters persisted in the belief that the attack at Cantigny had been carried out primarily by French troops, with supporting American formations being "repulsed with heavy losses." Counterattacks, coming from tired, disorganized troops who had been unceremoniously tumbled out of the rest quarters they had just entered, were poorly coordinated. The first feeble attacks, coming just after daylight from the Bois de Fontaine to the southeast, achieved nothing except to increase the German casualty count. Pressure increased throughout the day, however, and by late afternoon, the Germans were obviously preparing for a full-scale infantry assault. German artillery hit so hard that all wired communications between the 28th Regiment and 2d Brigade were cut from 1600 to 1800, forcing the use of brave-hearted runners. Just after 1700, attack teams from the 82d and 25th Reserve Divisions assaulted Cantigny from three directions: from the Bois de Framicourt to the northeast, from Hill 104 directly above the village, and from along the Cantigny-Fontaine Road to the southeast. German artillery—directed by aerial spotters who went largely unchallenged—supported the late-afternoon assaults, which got inside the 28th Regiment's barrage line before the American artillery could react.[24]

The defense of Cantigny was a close-run thing. Private Dan Edwards, manning a machine gun east of the village, described one episode in a fanciful retelling by Lowell Thomas: "When they came out of that woods in double ranks it looked like the trees were moving on us. They came right on, solid, the files pressing back to breast all along the line. What a target!" Officers had ordered that fire be withheld until the Germans were within 300 yards, however, so Edwards waited nervously as the enemy infantry entered a draw and then emerged seemingly right before his eyes. He opened fire, and his gun spurted what seemed like 15,000 rounds. Germans tumbled down, but those who did not fall doggedly kept coming. Edwards was so focused on his targets that he did not notice his flank guards had been killed until a German soldier bearing a "haggle-tooth bayonet," with a face "all lit up and shining with joy," rose up before him. The German lunged, badly gashing Edwards, who nevertheless managed to draw his .45 and shoot the enemy soldier in the chest. "He kneeled down slowly on the edge of the pit," Edwards recalled, "and a mighty change came over his face. All the pleasure left it. He looked surprised, and then disappointed, and then, just as he keeled over, he looked completely hopeless."[25]

Had the final German assaults been better coordinated and pressed more aggressively, they might have succeeded in bundling the Americans out of Cantigny. Ely already had concerns before the attacks began. That afternoon, he had warned Bullard that enemy artillery was pummeling his positions so thoroughly that by morning, casualties would be "serious." He also complained that friendly aircraft "are not and have not been active enough." Fortunately for the Americans, German officers rushed their exhausted infantry into position for their counterattacks and failed to coordinate them properly. Timed to proceed simultaneously and concentrically, the counterattacks instead went forward at different moments, substantially simplifying matters for the defenders. Even so, the Germans pressed Ely's defensive perimeter to the breaking point. At 1800 division headquarters thought its "first line [was] probably lost," but it hoped to "retake [it] with [an] artillery barrage."[26]

German artillery significantly disorganized the American perimeter. Unseasoned troops—in essence, the 1st Division remained a green formation—grew skittish under the enemy barrage as it continued through the afternoon. And as the German infantry pressed home their attacks, some American companies, especially those in relatively exposed positions on the flanks, lost cohesion. Junior officers struggled to manage men who froze, fled, or hunkered down in bunkers and fieldworks. At 1745 Ely passed on reports that troops of the 1/28th and 3/28th on the flanks were "falling back under heavy fire artillery and M.G. [machine guns]." He demanded support: "Unless heavy artillery can give us support," he claimed, "it will [be] necessary to withdraw for entire front line is battered to pieces with artillery." Company commanders sent similar messages.[27]

Unfortunately for the infantry, American artillery support—already feeble—further slackened under the pressure of German counterfire. Lieutenant Daniel Sargent of the 5th Field Artillery, deployed to support Cantigny, described how he and another lieutenant experienced the German bombardment side by side:

Lieutenant L. C. and I were lying on the ground side by side, squirming now and then to the right or left as if thereby to evade a shell that we heard screaming towards us. While engaged in this futility, Lieutenant L. C. began what seemed to me an inappropriate social conversation. "Lieutenant Sargent," he began. "Do you remember the date of your commission as first lieutenant?" I answered, "September 1917." "But," he said, "my commission was dated August 1917, which makes me your senior, in which case I suppose this foxhole falls to me." At this he ensconced himself in a three-foot foxhole, protruding from it like a jack-in-the-box with a broken spring. A French captain heard our conversation and he had turned and seen Lieutenant L. C. insert himself into the foxhole and was staring at him not with contempt nor commiseration—but in sheer amazement. In all his war experience, he had never seen the likes of it.[28]

An hour after the German evening attacks began, Ely relayed reports that three of his flank companies, L, M, and K, had completely fallen out and were "headed off." He committed his last reserve company and asked that the 18th Regiment be sent in to relieve his "entire line" because of "very heavy losses" around Cantigny. By this time, the Germans had reached positions within 200 meters north and 500 meters southeast of Cantigny, but their attempts to drive through the center and seize the village failed; they did, however, manage to seize part of the manor park. Bullard and the new brigade commander, Brigadier General Beaumont Buck, remained levelheaded in the face of Ely's desperate pleas for relief or withdrawal, which they denied, despite sending forward three companies of the 18th Regiment as reinforcements. "Position must be held," Bullard instructed Buck to tell Ely at 2027, "Commander in Chief expects it." Bullard's instincts that the enemy attacks would peter out were correct. Although they had achieved local success in some places, the Germans were too exhausted to take advantage of the company-sized gaps that had appeared in the American lines. German artillery had effectively disorganized the Americans at first, but because the German infantry was sometimes too slow to follow up the barrage, the Americans had time to emerge from their bunkers and man their machine guns. As a result, the German infantry sustained heavy losses. American artillery—including four batteries of heavy 155s—also recovered from its initial disorganization, pounding German machine guns and infantry staging areas and driving the enemy entirely out of the Bois de Fontaine. Although the 1st Division had shown some disquieting signs of shakiness, Cantigny held.[29]

German pressure did not let up. Overnight, German infantry carried out strong patrols and small raids against the Cantigny perimeter. Though these were unsuccessful, they kept the already tired doughboys from sleeping. German "annihilation" artillery fire and gas remained relentless, as it would all the next day too. At sunrise on May 29—a beautiful, clear day with blustery winds—the Germans launched two small attacks. These were beaten back, but additional attacks that afternoon were not so easy to repulse. American artillery managed to partially break up the enemy infantry formations but failed to drive them back, while planes from both sides buzzed angrily overhead. By late afternoon, German concentric attacks were in full swing against elements of the 18th, 26th, and 28th Regiments. Some field reports even claimed that the Germans had tanks.[30]

Even though the attacks were anticipated, the Americans were not fully prepared to meet them. This was because getting reinforcements to Ely's front lines had proved difficult under enemy fire. Captain S. D. Campbell of Company E, 18th Regiment, watched in horror as two platoons of the 28th

Regiment, which were attempting to reinforce the front at 1630, just before the full-scale German attack began, were caught by German machine guns and dissolved before his eyes: "Four enemy Machine Guns were squirting death into their ranks like a hose squirting water and we were under the necessity of retaining our position and seeing them drop like flies as there was nothing we could do to help them." Again, some men fled. At 1600 Campbell had to stop and arrest sixteen men "who had broken and run from the front line during a counter attack." Campbell gave their officer the option of returning under arrest or returning to the front lines with a warning "that we would shoot to kill if any of his men stopped enroute." The officer returned to the front with his men, and later on, Campbell's company was also sent to reinforce the front.[31]

North of Cantigny, the German attacks drove the Americans back "several hundred meters," and for a time it looked as if the entire perimeter would collapse. Portions of the 2/28th and 3/28th also fell back under German fire—sometimes even without infantry pressure—before being shepherded back into line. The Germans—who were also skittish—interpreted American attempts to regain their positions as full-scale attacks, and alert German gunners blasted them. At 2045, claimed a German regimental war diary, the Americans "attacked along their entire front in dense waves" but were slaughtered by German artillery. By evening, some American companies were reporting 60 to 70 percent casualties. At 2055 Ely reported to the brigade that his "front line was pounded to hell and gone," and he warned that the "entire front line must be relieved tomorrow night or he would not be responsible."[32]

Again, however, the Germans lacked the strength to press their advantage, and the American perimeter around Cantigny resisted collapse. Further attacks would come, but the crisis had passed. The final German assaults came early on the morning of the thirtieth. After these were repulsed—this time with ease—German artillery satisfied itself with pummeling the sector and showing the Americans the disadvantages of holding ground under their direct observation. The "cheerful" weather was obscured by billowing clouds of gas and smoke that enveloped the shattered village and its environs. Under its cover, Ely finally got his wish as the remnants of the 28th and supporting units were relieved by the 16th Regiment, which consolidated positions over the following days through the yawning shell holes and imploded strongpoints that served as a "line." Still unhappy about being pushed out of Cantigny by a bunch of Americans, the Germans planned a full-scale attack for June 3, to be carried out by the 270th

Reserve Regiment and half of another regiment supported by flamethrowers. Given the state of the American defenses, such an assault may well have succeeded, but the Germans called it off two days before it was supposed to move forward.[33]

German losses in the Cantigny affair were significant, with 300 reported casualties on May 28 and 1,667 through May 31. The loss of officers was particularly heavy. American casualties during the same period were 1,067, almost entirely from the 28th Regiment. Of these, about 200 had been gassed. By the measure of casualties alone, Cantigny was an American success. Over the duration of its presence in this front-line sector, however, from April 23 to June 16, the 1st Division took some 6,519 casualties, just under half of them from gas. This steep price was attributable in large part to the effectiveness of German artillery and gas and the ineffectiveness of American defensive measures. Once again, gas discipline was dismal, despite painful earlier experiences. Many gas casualties were the result of masks being worn improperly or men pulling them down to see where they were going. At least one analysis attributed the 28th Regiment's "near failure" to hold off German counterattacks at Cantigny to "prolonged gassing and gas mask fatigue." There were more worrisome signs, too. Doctors determined that many men had deliberately gassed themselves slightly in order to malinger, and divisional psychiatric reports later indicated that up to half the gas cases at Cantigny were in fact "neuropsychiatric."[34]

For Bullard, Cantigny proved that "Americans will both fight and stick." Pershing proclaimed it "a matter of pride to the whole A.E.F. that the troops of this division, in their first battle . . . displayed the fortitude and courage of veterans, held their gains, and denied to the enemy the slightest advantage." It also demonstrated, as he put it, "the importance of organizing our own divisions and higher units as soon as circumstances permit. It is my firm conviction that our troops are the best in Europe and our staffs are the equals of any." Public announcements and press releases presented the battle similarly, as a test that had proved the doughboys' mettle and promised greater things to come. Modern analysts have advanced similar interpretations, with Grotelueschen writing that Cantigny "was proof that at least some AEF units, even early in their combat experience, possessed the ability to carry out the limited, firepower-centered attacks that were the apex of trench-warfare methods"—in notable contrast to the open-warfare methods the American units were supposed to adopt. Precise planning, generally fluid execution, and effective fire support all contributed to the success of the initial attack, as did support from French artillery, tanks, engineers, and aircraft and the weakness and inefficiency of the German units defending the sector.³⁵

While Cantigny certainly provided a significant boost to AEF morale at all echelons, it also gave cause for private concern. The heavy casualties taken by the 1st Division in its occupation of the Cantigny sector and its shaky defense of the village on May 28–30 worried Pershing, Bullard, and their staffs. Pershing placed oblique blame on the French by suggesting that the withdrawal of French resources to meet the German attacks along the Chemin des Dames on May 27–28 had placed undue and unexpected pressure on the 28th Regiment at Cantigny. If anything, however, complaints about the French withdrawal only highlighted the Americans' dependence on them in many respects. Without direct French support after the capture of Cantigny, the barely blooded 1st Division had struggled to fend off poorly coordinated counterattacks from an exhausted, third-rate German division. After the battle, one German battalion commander reported "that the power of resistance of the Americans was slight, and that the success of our counterattack would have been certain had it been undertaken in close cooperation with the artillery and carried forward simultaneously along the entire front."³⁶

German observers were aware that "the moral element, of the success obtained by the enemy, must also not be underrated," although they thought the French would benefit most from the sense that *les Americains* were in the fight. In practical terms, however, the battle provided next to no value for the lives lost. As an astute postwar American analysis put it, "as a topographical conquest, Cantigny was admittedly worthless. What had been a salient in the French lines was now a salient in the German lines." The Germans initially assumed that the goal of the attack was to capture Hill 104 east of Cantigny, which would have provided command of the Dom valley. Early in the battle, panicky German field communiqués had brought their worst fears to life by reporting that the Yanks were driving on Hill 104 and even "entrenching" there. In reality, if any Americans ever reached the hill, they were only stray patrols. To the Germans' surprise, the Americans made no effort to take Hill 104—perhaps prudently in hindsight, given their trouble in holding Cantigny. Without the heights, though, "the ruins of Cantigny had no military value whatever." And by clinging to this dubious prize, the 1st Division infantry suffered terribly in the weeks to come from enemy artillery and gas, driving the formation almost to exhaustion by the beginning of July, when it was finally relieved by French units.³⁷

On the whole, however, Cantigny helped erase the unsettling memories of Bathelémont and Seicheprey, and it generated an encouraging sense that the Americans were at long last making their presence felt in the west. This came none too soon, for even as the 1st Division seized Cantigny and struggled to hold on to it, far more significant German attacks elsewhere forced the war's final allied crisis on the western front. Within days, that crisis would envelop American forces in fighting on a scale not seen before.

4

Château-Thierry
May 1918

The German offensives of March 21 (Michael) and April 9 (Georgette) came close to defeating the British in Flanders but ultimately failed. In the process, they attracted substantial French reserves to Flanders to back up the British. Ludendorff nevertheless remained focused on defeating the BEF first and conceived a new offensive farther south—code-named Blücher—to pummel the French and hoodwink them into drawing their reserves away from Flanders. The goal of this attack was never to take Paris but to push twelve to thirteen miles to the Vesle River and thus convince the French they were facing a crisis on that front. Once their forces had been withdrawn from Flanders, Ludendorff intended to direct the final, killing blow against the British.[1]

The new offensive, launched on May 27 along the Chemin des Dames, seemed likely to accomplish everything Ludendorff intended. The Germans met their primary objective—the Vesle River—on the offensive's first day, shattering the French defenders and throwing Paris into a panic. Pétain responded as the Germans had hoped by directing sixteen divisions to stop the Germans in a line anchored on the town of Château-Thierry, through which the primary road to Paris ran. Foch, however, called Ludendorff's bluff and blocked the reallocation of reserves from Flanders. As he saw it, the axis of the German advance took it across terrain favorable to defense and unfavorable to the attackers' supply routes, making an advance on Paris unlikely. This left Ludendorff no choice but to continue his attack beyond the initial objectives—not to take Paris but in the desperate hope that the French would finally call their reserves down from Flanders.[2]

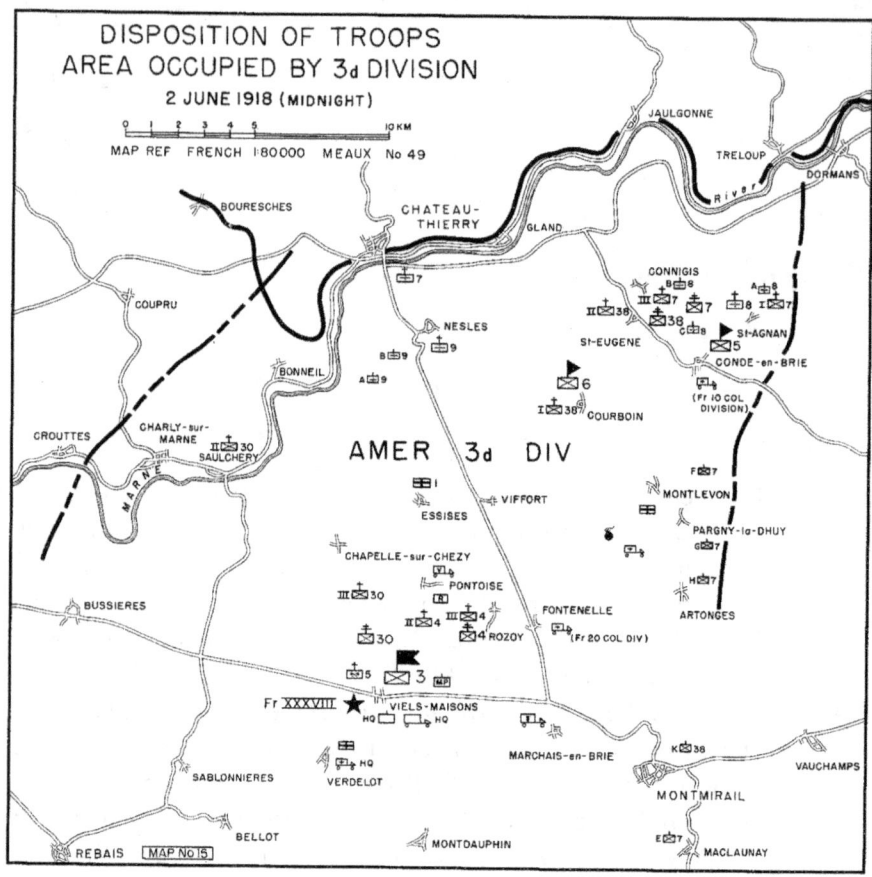

The 3d Division on the Marne, May–June 1918. (*United States Army in the World War*, 4:196)

Foch and Haig both assigned available American divisions to quiet sectors of the front, allowing them to release their own veteran formations for more important service. This time, however, some Americans would be sent to the front. Before the French called on their forces in Flanders, they had other options closer at hand—including the American 2d and 3d Divisions. On May 30, while the 1st Division engaged the Germans at Cantigny, Foch ordered elements of the 2d and 3d Divisions to the front to shore up the allied lines. They would deploy in the vicinity of Château-Thierry, on the direct route the Germans would have to take if they wanted (as it seemed) to reach Paris. By then, however, the German axis of advance in this offensive—which remained diversionary—had shifted to the west. There, the German VII Corps captured Soissons on May 29 and continued to push southwest, with the objective of capturing Compiègne and securing a vital rail supply route. Twenty-five miles to the southeast, the German IV Reserve Corps advanced toward the Marne at Château-Thierry, but only with the goal of securing the left flank of VII Corps' line of advance.[3]

The American 2d and 3d Divisions, then, would face the IV Reserve Corps at Château-Thierry—ostensibly to protect Paris, but in reality to hold the Germans in a subsidiary sector of a diversionary offensive meant to distract the French from Flanders. Unfortunately, the American divisions initially deployed not in their entirety but in segments. And although propagandists would present their move forward as a heroic march, with fresh doughboys sauntering forward past dejected Frenchmen lurching rearward, the French harbored serious concerns about whether either American division was prepared for battle.

The 3d Division was considered suspect. It had been organized in November 1917 from Regular Army formations scattered across the country but had not been assembled as a full division in the United States. Instead, its various components had trained separately, been buttressed with generous helpings of feckless draftees, and been shipped over to France and Britain in March–April 1918. It was then assembled for training in France. Except for the 6th Engineers, which had been assembled and sent to France in December 1917 and had helped the British in Flanders, many units of the division received barely three to four weeks of training in France before being sent to the front. It is no wonder, then, that the French had concerns about the division's readiness for combat. In a "Special Memorandum Relating to the Guarding of the Marne Crossings" dated May 29, Pétain's chief of staff, Major General François Paul Anthoine, indicated that the 3d Division needed an infusion of French backbone:

> [The American infantrymen] have absolutely no experience and should therefore be used with judgment.... The duties of the detachments assigned to guarding the Marne crossings, consist of maintaining order on the approaches to these crossings, and in case of need to defend them against possible incursions by light enemy detachments. [They will be provided specific detailed orders on their duties.] In order to prevent any mistakes, especially at night, American detachments will be reenforced whenever possible by a French unit. This French unit will maintain supervision sufficiently in advance of the crossing being guarded and will challenge troops or individuals approaching the crossing. Liaison between these French units and the American detachments should be carefully organized.[4]

The division's commander, General Joseph T. Dickman, was a cavalryman with more combat experience than just about any other American officer of his rank. Born in Ohio in 1857, he had graduated from West Point in 1881 and had seen action in Indian fighting, Mexican border operations (twice), the Spanish-American War, the Philippine insurgency, and even the Chinese Boxer Rebellion, when he was chief of staff to General Adna Chaffee. Since then he had served on the Army General Staff and was generally regarded as both an able leader and a tactician. He was placed in command of the 3d Division upon its organization in November 1917 and seems to have been well liked by the men he commanded during the war. Relations with the French would be a different matter, however; by the war's end, the 3d Division would have the dubious distinction of being something of a lightning rod in the Franco-American partnership.

The start of the German offensive on May 27 found the 3d Division in the Châteauvillain Training Area, about 160 kilometers southeast of Château-Thierry. Colonel Fox Conner phoned Dickman's headquarters the following day and passed on Pershing's instructions that the division should prepare to entrain on May 31 for an unnamed destination. On May 29, however, Conner issued a memo to the division indicating that plans had changed; the formation should "hold all units now in the divisional area in readiness to move this afternoon or tonight by motor truck or train to the north for the purpose of furnishing bridge guards for the bridge across the Marne." Dickman simultaneously learned of the arrival of ten French officers who would be attached to his battalions to help ready them for combat and provide battlefield consultation.[5]

The division began to move on May 30 as the infantry brigades, less artillery and engineers, headed out by train and foot northwest toward Provins. General Franchet d'Espèrey assigned the division to the French Sixth Army, part of the Groupe d'Armées du Nord. The division's 7th, 8th, and 9th Machine Gun Battalions, which had their own motor transport and could move quickly, rushed forward via Condé-en-Brie to the Marne River, where they were ordered to support French and colonial infantry guarding the river crossings from Château-Thierry east to Dormans. The 7th Battalion, with 395 officers and men and twenty-four guns under Major James Taylor, left La Ferté-sur-Aube at 1455 in Ford Model T trucks driven by greenhorns who bounced them recklessly over the pothole-pocked roads. Breakdowns and gas shortages caused some straggling, but seventeen machine gun squads arrived at Château-Thierry at 1800 on May 31 and were assigned to the French 10th Colonial Division of the French XXXVIII Corps.[6]

The arrival of the 7th Machine Gun Battalion at Château-Thierry would be magnified into legend, replete with the usual bedraggled, defeatist Frenchmen and the cheery doughboys eager to sock it to the Huns. Future Medal of Honor recipient Jack Barkley of the 3d Division's 4th Regiment described fleeing crowds of French soldiers: "They were completely disorganized. Many of them were in their shirt-sleeves, and most of them had thrown away their rifles. Those who weren't wounded were half carrying those who were. They were staggering, drunk with exhaustion. They didn't even look at us as they passed."[7] Surely there *were* many French stragglers, since the German attack had broken through at several points and shattered some of Pétain's tired formations. To the green American troops who had never seen such scenes before (despite their commonness in any rear sector when the front lines were being pushed back), all signs pointed to a total French rout. However, the sameness of the many alleged American "eyewitness" accounts, as well as the almost total absence of reference to the many French formations that continued to stubbornly resist the German advance, indicates that collective impressions of French weakness were being spread by word of mouth rather than by direct experience. After all, these conjured images inevitably boosted American self-regard. To Jennings C. Wise, the men of the 3d Division arrived at the front like the proverbial cinematic US Cavalry:

> As the column formed by the two motorized companies of the battalion approached Château-Thierry a great cloud of dust signaled its arrival. Before the head of the column reached the stone bridge spanning the Marne and leading into the town, the wild cheering of the throng of French soldiery through which it passed on the southern bank of the river gave further notice that the Americans were coming. . . . On the stone bridge stood the celebrated General Marchand of Fashoda fame, commanding the 10th Colonial Division, surrounded by a group of anxious staff officers. When through the dust, which obscured their identity for a time, he perceived that American troops were at last arriving he waved aloft his cap in greeting, followed by his staff, who vied with their commander in the enthusiasm of their welcome. Already the hostile artillery was firing on Château-Thierry.[8]

Château-Thierry stood in the middle of a shallow valley about 80 kilometers from Paris. It was a significant railway junction and crossroads, and the Germans were as determined to take it as the French were to defend it. Containing roughly 7,000 inhabitants in peacetime, the town straddled the Marne, with the greater part situated north of the river on an east-west axis. Buildings and streets constructed parallel to the river rose upward like terraces to heights of 150 meters. The Marne, which flowed westward, was about 70 meters wide at this point but too deep to ford. West of town it widened and bent sharply southward, away from an eminence on the north bank dubbed Hill 204—the site of much future fighting. Two bridges crossed the river: the central, stone bridge entered just below the ruined château from which the town took its name, and there was a combination wagon and railroad bridge about 500 meters farther east.[9]

As the Americans arrived, the town was already under attack from advance elements of the German 231st Division, which were pushing forward at the apex of a steadily growing salient. Shells fell steadily on Château-Thierry and on both banks of the river as General Jean-Baptiste Marchand, a former African explorer, deployed the Americans along the south bank of the river. A French machine gun officer attached to the battalion, Lieutenant Georges Wackerine, carefully helped the Americans site their guns. He would be an exceptionally active adviser to the gun crews in the action to come. Most of Company A established nests in houses overlooking the stone bridge, while Company B deployed in a sugar refinery and along a tree-lined road with clear views of the railroad bridge. From these positions, which contained seventeen guns in all and were fully established by 0400 on June 1, the American gunners could both support the French colonial infantry preparing to defend the town and cover the two bridges, which had been prepared for demolition. A single section of Company A, consisting of twelve men and two machine guns under First Lieutenant John T. Bissell, was sent across the central bridge into Château-Thierry. His orders were to take positions about 300 meters northeast of that bridge alongside the French colonials. Bissell and his men acted primarily as scouts, with the duty of keeping their captain, Charles H. Houghton, informed of developments. If attacked, Bissell was to fight a brief delaying action before withdrawing.[10]

Ordered to seize Château-Thierry with its bridges intact and cross the river to establish a bridgehead for further advances later on, the German 231st Division attacked at 1610 on May 31, with support from the German 10th Division. The Germans made steady progress, reaching the ridgeline above the town at 2100. There, however, they were halted by stern resistance from the Senegalese infantry, as well as by "stubborn" French machine gun fire. To the allied left, the German 442d Regiment reached the foot of Hill 204 that evening and seized it by direct assault at 0100 on June 1. To the allied right, the German 444th Regiment reached the eastern edge of Château-Thierry, and patrols of the 304th Pioneer Company managed to reconnoiter the railroad bridge. They discovered it still intact and usable, despite a small hole where the French had tried to blow it up earlier. According to the German divisional war diary, "Since this patrol as well as the foremost infantry squads received intense machine gun fire from the south bank of the Marne and from the houses in the north part of the city as well, they could not hold their ground and had to withdraw." Because the American guns on the south bank of the Marne were not in position until approximately 0345 on June 1—and were initially ordered to maintain silence to keep their positions concealed—credit for halting the German thrust on May 31 must go entirely to the French colonials.[11]

By the morning of June 1, the remaining American machine gun battalions and the body of the 3d Division arrived at the Marne and started deploying along a thirty-kilometer front. General Jean de Montdésir, commanding the XXXVIII Corps, assigned the division's 38th Regiment to the area between Nesles-la-Montagne and Courboin, several kilometers southeast of Château-Thierry; he assigned the 7th Regiment east of that, to the sector between Monthurel and St. Agnan. The 4th and 30th Regiments remained in reserve. The 38th and 7th Regiments were intermingled with French units and remained under French divisional control; only the reserve regiments reported directly to 3d Division headquarters, which was established at Viels-Maisons. Only the machine gun battalions, particularly the 7th, were in direct contact with the enemy. Dickman considered his troops "tired and weary but intensely earnest and anxious to participate in the actual fight."[12]

The Americans engaged in scattered fire with German troops across the river during the day, but the fight did not resume in earnest until that evening, when the 231st attacked at 1900. This time, three infantry battalions assaulted Château-Thierry from the west and one from the north; the exhausted 444th Regiment to the east remained idle. Advancing against fierce Senegalese resistance in buildings and from behind barricades of wreckage and overturned wagons, the three western battalions reached the edge of town by 2030, but the battalion advancing from the north again failed to make headway against French and American machine gun fire. The Germans resumed the advance after dark, and by 2215 they had captured the château in the center of town, opposite the stone bridge. Captain Wilhelmy of the 442d then led two lieutenants and a small party of men toward the bridge to see if they could seize it before the French blew it up.[13]

Lieutenant Bissell, meanwhile, decided that his mission in Château-Thierry had ended. His two guns had been firing actively on the enemy since the previous evening, but as the Germans pushed farther into town, his orders to withdraw under significant pressure became operable. Sometime around midnight on June 1–2 he pulled out his guns and, with a French machine gun unit, attempted to make his way toward the stone bridge. Near the bridge, however, his detachment came under heavy machine gun fire, and his men took cover or scattered. Thinking his detachment had been wiped out, Bissell made his way back toward the railroad bridge, picking up a few stragglers on the way. In fact, almost his entire detachment had made it out alive, although they lost their guns and ammunition in the process.[14]

At around the same time, Captain Wilhelmy and his men dashed across the stone bridge—unhindered by Company A's guns, which remained silent to avoid hitting the numerous French soldiers still fighting for the bridge—only to run smack into an occupied French barricade on the south end. The French immediately detonated a charge, but it misfired, injuring the German captain. Realizing that another charge would detonate in seconds, Wilhelmy and his men turned and fled frantically. The captain and some of his men made it across just as the bridge exploded behind them, blowing several Germans sky high. A few days later General Marchand described how "a terrific explosion destroyed the entire central portion and threw into space some Boche corpses. Several Boches, who had already crossed, were captured on the south bank." The French had thus halted the first of two German attempts to storm across the Marne. It was 2230.[15]

With heavy gunfire all around him, Bissell apparently did not hear the bridge blow. If he had, a near disaster might have been averted more easily. Reaching the railroad bridge, the young lieutenant attempted to cross, only to come under fire from vigilant American gunners of Company B on the south bank. Bissell slipped down the embankment and thought of swimming across the Marne but soon rejected that idea. Instead, he climbed back up to the north end of the bridge and just kept yelling across the river to his comrades until they ceased fire. Another American lieutenant came across from the south bank to escort Bissell and his band of stragglers to safety.[16]

As he reached the south bank, the exhausted Bissell stopped to talk briefly with the Company B commander, Captain John R. Mendenhall. Neither of them knew the French had blown the central bridge, and Bissell relayed to the captain his belief—reinforced by information received from a French officer in Château-Thierry—that the bridge was in German hands. Moreover, Bissell thought that Company A, which defended the bridge's south bank, had been defeated (it had merely taken some casualties from German fire during the attempt to storm the bridge). If he "expected to escape capture," Bissell told Mendenhall, he had better pack up his company and move to the rear as quickly as possible.[17]

To Mendenhall, by his own account, "the situation appeared desperate." Runners he had sent to the battalion command post had failed to return, and he considered the possibility that the rest of the battalion had withdrawn without him. The captain therefore decided to get out—and quickly. He gave verbal, not written, instructions to his runners to inform two platoons to withdraw immediately while the third, which he "hoped was still commanding the bridge," covered the withdrawal. Whether this explanation was true or not, the message received by all three platoons was, in the words of one of the platoon commanders, "nothing less than to 'beat it.'" And so they did, leaving a vital bridge across the Marne guarded by only a handful of French infantrymen that the Americans did not deign to consult.[18]

In the dark, Mendenhall happened upon the battalion command post that he thought had moved. There he learned that the stone bridge had been blown and that Company B's original positions were in no danger—except from Germans attacking directly across the railroad bridge. Shamefacedly, Mendenhall ran back to the bridge with a handful of headquarters clerks and a few reserve machine guns he had managed to pick up. It is unclear whether he informed Major Taylor of the fiasco. Mendenhall subsequently claimed, alternately, that he either assisted a few French infantrymen in driving back preparations for a German assault across the east bridge or led his reserve section in driving back several hundred Germans who had already crossed the river. In truth, there is no record of the Germans either preparing to cross or actually crossing the east bridge—for the simple reason that they were not yet aware of its existence![19]

Meanwhile, after sitting in reserve positions for some time, two of Mendenhall's platoon leaders decided on their own initiative to bring their units back to the bridge, despite receiving no intelligence from their company commander. They led their guns back to the bridge, only to discover that the Germans had not reached the south bank of the Marne. The two lieutenants then went to the battalion command post to ask a harassed Major Taylor why they had been told to pull out. "The major denied any knowledge of our retreat," one of them reported later, "and showed no interest in the matter. He didn't seem to give a darn what we had done or might do."[20]

This comedy of errors, which might have ended in disaster if the Germans had made any forceful attempt to take the railroad bridge, detracted from what was otherwise a solid performance by the green 7th Machine Gun Battalion in its first action. Firing mostly at night and with only limited vision, the men of the 7th played a role in slowing the German attack. Their fire, but especially the "mad house to house fighting" conducted by the doughty Senegalese, inflicted grievous losses on the Germans. The Germans later admitted to a growing feeling of "complete hopelessness," especially as French artillery began to take its toll on the town.[21]

Not yet prepared to give up their hope of crossing the Marne, the Germans launched one final grand effort on June 2. French and Senegalese infantry and machine guns remained throughout the town, especially in the north and east, and they were still scrappy. German infantry fought all day to clear up the last pockets of enemy resistance in Château-Thierry and managed to capture seventy prisoners and several machine guns. American guns covered some of those who managed to withdraw. Even then, however, individual Senegalese held out for days, sniping at the Germans from ruined buildings that were still occupied by many terrified civilians. That evening the Germans discovered—too late by twenty-four hours—the existence of the railroad bridge. A brief attempt to rush it failed, thanks in part to firm resistance from Mendenhall's Company B, and the Germans gave up. They were, at this point, totally exhausted. The heroic resistance of the Senegalese, backed up by the eager American machine gunners, left the 231st Division incapable of further offensive effort. On June 3, with French artillery bludgeoning Château-Thierry and the first troubling signs of influenza appearing—incapacitating an entire battalion of the 442d Regiment—the 231st Division reverted to the defensive. At that moment, the last stages of Ludendorff's failed offensive were taking place farther west, including in the zone where the US 2d Division had taken up positions opposite Belleau Wood.[22]

Relief orders arrived on June 4. The doughboys of the 7th Machine Gun Battalion felt tired but satisfied, having lost one man missing, five killed, and thirty-two wounded in the fight for Château-Thierry. Mendenhall's temporary withdrawal notwithstanding, the battalion had performed quite creditably and played an important supporting role—though pride of place went to the Senegalese—in blunting the German attempt to seize Château-Thierry and cross the Marne. But time would blow the American contribution out of proportion. An after-action report compiled for Dickman on June 12 determined that the men of the 7th Battalion had "performed their mission in a creditable manner," but it made no claims to any decisive impact on the battle for Château-Thierry. A divisional operations report compiled on June 23, however, proclaimed that the battalion had turned back a "fierce attack and attempt to cross the Marne" and thus had been "a very great factor in the final arrest of the German advance." The official postwar divisional history would assert that the battalion had, "by its stubborn resistance, prevented the crossing of the Marne at this point, inflicting losses on the enemy which were out of proportion to the losses sustained by the small, but resolute, defending Battalion." More recently, marine historian George B. Clark claimed that "the Americans and French slammed the door shut" on the German advance at Château-Thierry—giving almost all the credit to the 7th Machine Gun Battalion. Such hyperbole aside, the doughboys had good reason to feel pleased. They had seen the enemy and stood firm. As General Marchand reported on June 3, he and his officers thought the Americans had displayed "extraordinary sang-froid."[23]

5

The 2d Division Enters the Lines
May 31–June 5, 1918

While leading elements of the 3d Division saw their first action at Château-Thierry, the 2d Division moved into line a short distance to the west and prepared for the first major US military engagement of the war. Expectations for this division were almost as high as for the 1st Division. Journalists loved it and would continue to give it substantial coverage throughout the war, especially its marine contingent. But the 2d Division had a Frankenstein-like character, in that it was a fusion of US Army (3d Brigade, 9th and 23d Regiments) and US Marine Corps (4th Brigade, 5th and 6th Marine Regiments) components. Legend has it that placing the army and marine regiments side by side worked to the benefit of both, since it made each fight harder to maintain bragging rights in the rivalry. Events would prove otherwise. In terms of potential, though, the 2d Division was second to none. Soldiers and marines had received uneven training, but they were as enthusiastic as any men in the AEF and better led than most. They were also well equipped. The division included a machine gun battalion consisting of four companies, plus one machine gun company per infantry regiment—making sixteen companies in all. They were equipped with French Hotchkiss air-cooled machine guns.[1]

The 5th Marines—comprising the contingent offered for service by Marine Corps commandant Major General George Barnett when the war began—sailed to France with the 1st Division in June 1917. This regiment was "largely veteran; old-timers with all the campaign ribbons and rows of hash-marks." Its training for modern warfare in France was neglected, however, as Pershing ordered the regiment and its officers dispersed for the next several months

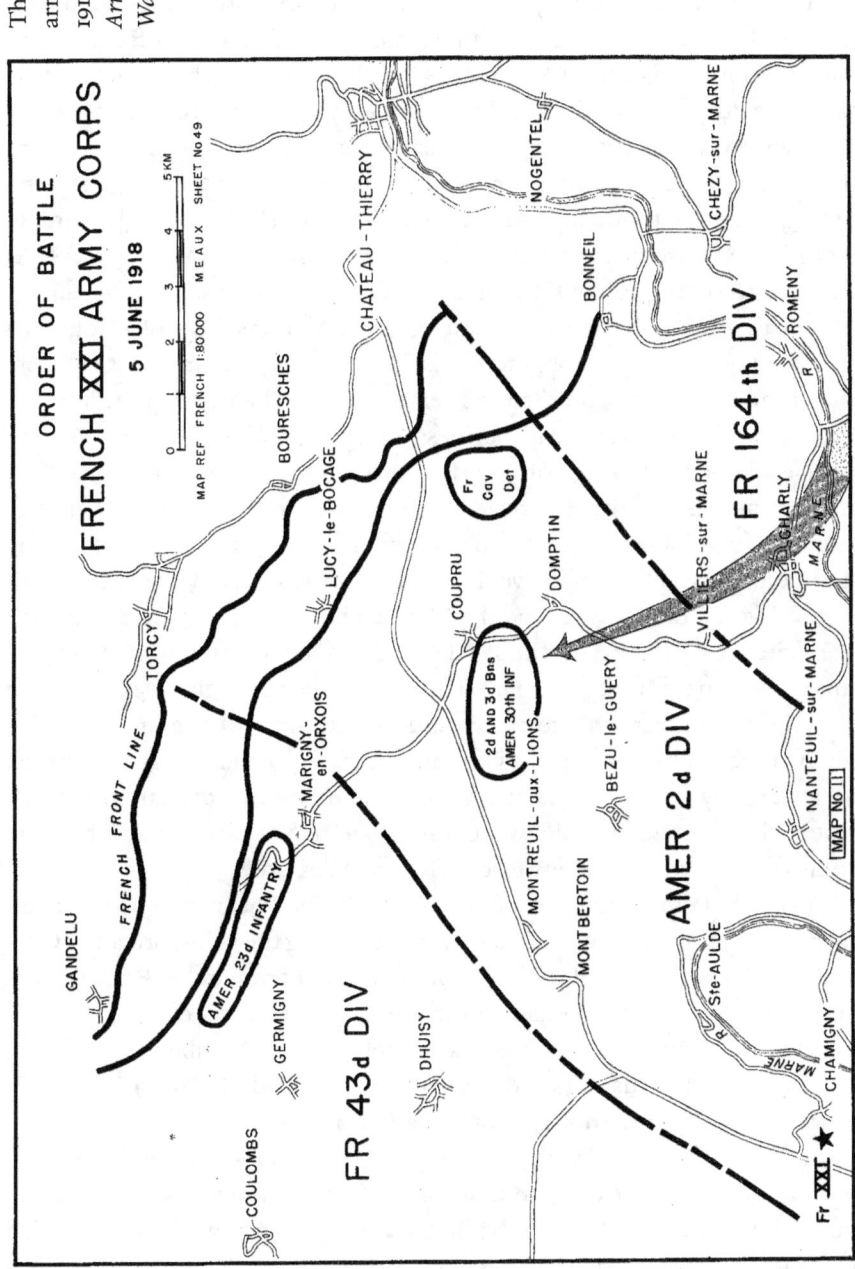

The 2d Division arrives, June 1–5, 1918. (*United States Army in the World War*, 4:144)

on communications, provost, and other support duty. The 6th Marines, meanwhile, was assembled at Quantico from new volunteers with a leavening of old-timers. These regiments made up the 4th Brigade, which was formed officially in September 1917 and shipped to France over the next six months. There, the 6th Regiment's marines assumed the same inglorious support duties as their comrades in the 5th, to the detriment of both training and morale. Not until March 1918 did the marines get a small taste of front-line duty near Verdun, and not until May 14—just three weeks before the division would enter major combat—did they participate in an intensive course of "open warfare training." The division's other brigade—the 3d Brigade, with its 9th and 23d Regiments—also lacked thorough training. Indeed, the entire division was not assembled as a unit until May 1918. As a result, according to division historian John W. Thomason Jr., "of all the American regular divisions, the training of the 2nd was the most haphazard and sketchy, and its assembly the most delayed. It got many of its officers and some of its 'non-coms' to the service schools before it went into the line, but actually, it learned its business under fire."[2]

There was no shortage of colorful personalities in command of the 2d Division and its constituent brigades and regiments. Ironically, the division's commander, Major General Omar Bundy of the US Army, was among the least colorful and least effective. Born in 1861 in Indiana, he had seen combat during the Indian Wars and the Mexican border expedition, and he had been cited for gallantry at the Battle of El Caney in Cuba in 1898. He assumed command of the 2d Division on October 26, 1917. Despite being a thoughtful officer who correctly understood some of the limitations of the American blockbuster divisions and Pershing's open-warfare doctrine, he apparently lacked confidence as a division commander and, as events would show, tended to follow the lead of more forceful men, such as the commander of his Marine Brigade, General Harbord.[3]

Formerly Pershing's chief of staff, Harbord had been assigned to command the Marine Brigade on May 7, 1918, replacing the ailing Brigadier General Charles A. Doyen. "I can give you no better command in France," said Pershing. Harbord was initially intimidated by the prospect of commanding two regimental commanders, Colonel Wendell Neville (5th Marines) and Colonel Albertus Catlin (6th Marines), who held Medals of Honor for bravery at Vera Cruz in 1914. Doyen had been a marine, but Harbord was army. Yet Harbord—a "boyish, friendly extrovert, polished, and with an air of aplomb"—evidently hoped that some of the marines' luster would rub off on him. Halfway through the Belleau Wood campaign, Neville handed Harbord a pair of Marine Corps collar devices, saying, "Here, we think it is about time you put these on." Harbord later wrote, "I wore those Marine Corps Devices until after I became a Major General, and I still cherish them as among my most valued possessions. I think no officer can fail to understand what that little recognition meant to me, an Army officer commanding troops of a sister service in battle." Harbord's admiration for the marines contrasted starkly with his utter contempt for the French—an attitude that emerges clearly from his diary and subsequent writings. Among the general's milder remarks about his allies was the expostulation in his diary on June 23: "It will be a wonder if we do not feel as much like fighting them as we do the Germans before the war is over, for our alliance tries human patience—American patience—almost to the limit." During the fighting to come, Harbord would lose no opportunity to ignore French successes and trumpet their failures, while pointing out that it was the Americans, after all, who did all the real fighting, even when their allies abandoned them. His interpretation of events, which Bundy made no effort to contradict, would color subsequent American narratives of Belleau Wood.[4]

The 3d Brigade was commanded by Brigadier General Edward M. Lewis. Born in Indiana in 1863, he had graduated from West Point in 1886 (along with Pershing) and seen action in the Spanish-American War and the Philippine insurrection. Since then, he had served as an instructor at the University of California and in an administrative capacity during the Vera Cruz expedition. Though a Pershing favorite—he would go on to command the 30th Division—Lewis would play little direct role in the Belleau Wood campaign, perhaps partly because of Harbord's greater proclivity to lobby with Bundy at division headquarters. Lewis's regimental commanders, Colonel Leroy Upton (9th Regiment) and Colonel Paul Malone (23d Regiment)—both solid, experienced officers—were also fated to fade into the shadows cast by their highly decorated counterparts in the Marine Brigade.

The 2d Division had not yet been substantially blooded at the end of May 1918, although some elements had seen front-line action and encountered or conducted small raids. One of the most significant actions occurred on the night of April 13–14, when the Germans raided the 3/9th Battalion near Maizey. Although supposedly a quiet sector where the Americans could learn at their own pace, the French had assigned the 3/9th to hold a vulnerable salient that their own infantry was allegedly afraid to hold; there was a river to its rear, and it was overlooked entirely by enemy artillery, offering easy routes for an enemy approach. After pummeling the 3/9th for three days, the Germans laid a ninety-minute box barrage on the battalion before attacking in strength just after midnight on April 14. The Americans stepped out of their dugouts just as the barrage ended, only to find their trenches bouncing with 650 German *Stosstruppen* of the 82d Reserve Division's 272d Reserve Regiment, whose commanding officer had motivated them with extra rations of food and a stirring quotation from Schiller.

The attack was extremely well rehearsed and well executed. Self-justifying American reports later claimed that the Germans had made such quick entry by virtue of dirty tricks. According to one account, thirty Germans dressed as French surgeons and sporting Red Cross armbands had approached the lines. When challenged, they said they were treating the wounded from a French patrol. How they managed to do so during an intense box barrage without being killed or arousing suspicion is not stated, but the faux Frenchmen supposedly overpowered the American sentries and cut lanes through the wire for their storm troopers to follow. More likely, superb coordination and discipline allowed the Germans to follow their own barrage and enter the trenches before the Americans could react.

However it was done, the German attack caught the 3/9th unprepared. Germans penetrated the lines at four points and at one place broke into the rear areas. Companies L and I bore the brunt of the attack from both front and rear, and intense hand-to-hand fighting ensued. During the fighting, the Germans spread confusion by yelling that they were French or by shouting "Gas!" in English to get the doughboys to fumble for their gas masks. Despite this, the Americans defended themselves savagely. At 0200 the Germans began to withdraw with a number of prisoners and some equipment. But events now began to go wrong for the attackers. Enraged and undefeated, many Americans chased the withdrawing Germans and butchered them in No-Man's-Land, where they hesitated before a wall of steel thrown down by the American counterbarrage. Caught with bayonets at their backs and high explosives to their front, dozens of Germans perished before the remainder managed to escape, leaving behind some of their prisoners. According to the Americans, in all, the 3/9th lost seven killed, thirty-nine wounded, and twenty-six captured; the Germans lost fifty-nine dead (including some of those who had dressed as Frenchmen and were executed with hand grenades) and eleven prisoners.[5]

Despite their casualties, the Germans considered their raid a success because of the number of prisoners captured. They interrogated these men, partly with a view to assessing the qualities of the American soldier. After these interrogations the Germans decided that the typical doughboy possessed a fine physique and was a doughty fighter but was "not concerned . . . with anything that does not approach his personal comfort." As for the 2d Division, the Germans regarded its evident poor training and discipline with contempt. It was, they concluded, "excellent military material, with which much might be done; but as yet the 2nd American Division was not ready for important combat."[6]

Not much had changed for the 2d Division—on paper, at least—by the time the German offensive began on May 27. On that date the division lay at Chaumont-en-Vexin, northwest of Paris, as part of the French Group of Armies of the Reserve. The division was preparing to move toward the front on May 30 when instructions arrived assigning it to the French Sixth Army, part of the French Group of Armies of the North. Its destination would be in the vicinity of Meaux on the Marne River, about forty kilometers west of where the 3d Division was about to enter combat at Château-Thierry. The 2d Division's infantrymen climbed into dozens of French trucks—"big, powerful motor trucks . . . with seats at the sides and with canvas covers like those of prairie schooners"—while the tired Indochinese drivers watched bleary-eyed from the cabs. It took fifty trucks to carry a battalion with about thirty soldiers and marines per truck. American and French officers escorted the trucks in staff cars, but this did not prevent some of the exhausted Indochinese, who had been hauling troops for days, from falling asleep at the wheel and running their trucks off the road. Other, more fortunate support and auxiliary units took slower but more reliable trains.[7]

Leading elements of the 2d Division arrived near Meaux at 1400 on May 31, where they learned of their assignment to French VII Corps and then XXI Corps. The latter formation, commanded by Major General Jean-Marie Degoutte (who would later command French Sixth Army), consisted of the French 43d and 164th Divisions, which had been badly knocked about in the recent fighting but continued to resist stubbornly. According to Major General Hunter Liggett, who later worked with him closely, Degoutte was "a forceful character, a great driver and an optimist both by nature and policy." He was also an efficient commander and a seasoned warrior who had seen extensive action in France's colonial wars and in this war. As a veteran military man, Degoutte was openly skeptical of American abilities. Colonel Upton ran into Degoutte on his way to the front and unadvisedly commented on the amount of time his troops had been marching. "I don't suppose," the general needled the American, "you will be able to do anything until you have had a rest." Upton responded that his regiment "can do anything you want done," and Degoutte brusquely ordered him forward.[8]

In a conference with Degoutte beside the road near Coupru that evening, General Bundy and his chief of staff Colonel Preston Brown discussed how to deploy the 2d Division. Ever aggressive, Degoutte proposed sending the Americans forward to attack the Germans immediately—which would have meant, given the strung-out status of the division, attacking in small packets. Bundy and Brown rightly refused to consent to this plan. Instead, they proposed assembling the intact division a few kilometers behind the front and allowing the retreating French to filter through it—a sensible suggestion that would give the Americans time to organize and the French an opportunity to withdraw in good order and recuperate. Degoutte consented to that proposal but—evidently still hoping to get a rise out of the Americans—expressed doubt that the 2d Division would be able to hold. It was a sly taunt, but Bundy, Brown, and other Americans who heard about it afterward interpreted it as timidity: the French—who were "on the run," as Catlin put it—really thought the Germans were invincible and that Paris was lost. In response, Brown proudly proclaimed: "Gen. Degoutte, these are American regulars. In one hundred and fifty years they have never been beaten. They will hold." This huffy retort would eventually attain some measure of immortality, being quoted in almost every American account of the war.[9]

Degoutte's questioning of the 2d Division's mettle no doubt reminded Bundy and Brown of the remarks they had been hearing from French civilians and soldiers pulling back from the front. As they moved forward on the evening of May 31 and in the early hours of June 1, the Yanks had encountered scenes of fear and dejection, the standard detritus of war that accompanied every German push in 1914 as well as 1918. Pitiable French civilian refugees clogged the roads. With them came French army stragglers who seemed to take special pleasure in looking miserable, crying *"la guerre est fini,"* and making throat-cutting gestures to the wide-eyed Americans. Such men accompanied every army engaged in major fighting during this war, but the Americans had never encountered them before—although some of them had read of such things in books. Harbord thought the stragglers represented "that motley array which we read characterizes the rear of a routed army." To Private Warren Jackson of the 1/6th Marines, the French "reminded one more of hunted beasts than human beings"; one of them told him that Paris would fall in eight days. For Catlin, contemplating the Germans "flushed with victory" versus the "defeat and demoralization" of the French, the marines' march was both heroic and poignant. He recalled:

> [The Americans had approached] one of the most dangerous points on the whole front . . . the emergency was acute. The Second Division of the American Army was thrown in in a final effort to defend the Metz-to-Paris road and save the city. The Germans, who had become

accustomed to the weakening resistance of the French, did not know what to make of it at first. But they soon learned the taste of American mettle and metal. They were stopped in their overwhelming rush, and stopped for good.

Regarding the French, Catlin said, "Pity swelled our hearts as we watched them stagger back to the rear, a bruised and broken remnant, with utter despair written on their war-weary faces. To them the war was lost, life held no hope. We wanted to take them by the hand and say, 'Brother, at last we have come.'" In reality, such scenes were little different from later episodes when bedraggled American veterans, on their way to the rear after being relieved from front-line duty, taunted their fresh-faced replacements with remarks about the hellish experiences awaiting them. Thus it always was and always will be with veterans and newcomers. But here, of course, the French poilus—sly and cynical as a rule—were the veterans, and the Americans were the greenhorns. The cynical humor was not appreciated.[10]

Stragglers notwithstanding, the truth was that Degoutte's exhausted men were still resisting the enemy. Bundy understood this, writing that "with fine courage [Degoutte's] corps had fought against greatly superior numbers for five days. He had retreated, it is true, but the retreat had been an orderly one." By contrast, most of Bundy's officers and men took the appearance of French stragglers as evidence of a wider rout—the stories of French cowardice would grow more lurid over time—and convinced themselves that the Americans had come to save the day. Ironically, the reverse was also true: the French were unconvinced that the Americans were ready or even willing to fight. On June 3 Degoutte would write to General Denis Duchêsne, the commander of Sixth Army:

> A staff officer of the 1st Army asked me yesterday if there was any truth in the rumor which was being circulated in regard to an evidence of hesitation on the part of the 2nd U.S. Infantry Division in coming into the battle line. I cannot comprehend how such a rumor was started . . . the 2nd American Division on joining us evidenced a knowledge of the situation, a cheerful enthusiasm and a keenness which has gained for it the admiration of all the troops and all the members of the staff.

Suggestions to the contrary, he said, had likely been "spread by the Boche or defeatists." More likely, they reflected the taunts hurled by the poilus at their untested new comrades, who knew nothing of war.[11]

★ ★ ★

The troops of the 2d Division proceeded on a forced march overnight, and leading elements arrived at Montreuil-aux-Lions just after daybreak on June 1. Elements of the division deployed that morning at varying rates of speed, depending on conditions, and formed the semblance of an organized line of defense. The 4th Brigade's 6th Machine Gun Battalion, commanded by Major Edward Cole, took positions between Champillon and Lucy-le-Bocage. The 6th Marines, led by the 2d Battalion under Major Thomas Holcomb, took point in front of the Paris–Château-Thierry road, from Lucy-le-Bocage to Triangle and along the east edge of the Bois de Clerembauts. These units were assigned to the French 43d Division. From there, the line continued in a southeasterly direction, with the 9th Regiment, attached to the French 164th Division, holding positions from Le Thiolet and along the north edge of the Bois de la Morette toward Bonneil. The 2d Division's other regiments organized in reserve. For the Americans, the air was pregnant with the anticipation of great events. Levi Hemrick's 2/6th Marines was assembled by the side of the road and ready to move when "someone in the line near me raised the question, 'Where do we go from here?' Our sergeant answered in these words, 'For all we know we are on our way to hell.'" Soldiers and marines believed that the kaiser was driving on Paris and it was up to them to stop him.[12]

In reality, German objectives in this sector were modest and did not include a drive on Paris. The German Seventh Army under General Hans von Böhn was directing its main effort westward toward Compiègne. The left flank of that advance would be covered by the Seventh Army's 4th Reserve Corps (referred to as Corps Conta after its commander, General Richard Von Conta) as it drove generally southwest between Château-Thierry and Belleau Wood. In orders issued at 2330 on May 31, Von Conta specified that "the [Seventh] Army will continue the attack until the enemy's resistance breaks between Soissons and Villers Cotterete [the push directed ultimately at Compiègne]." Corps Conta, meanwhile, was "covering the left flank of the Army by advancing as far as the line Gandelu–Château-Thierry." From left to right, Von Conta's right wing consisted of the 197th, 237th, 10th, and 231st Divisions, with the 5th Guards and 28th Division in support. The 197th, 237th, and 10th Divisions—the first two "trench divisions" unsuited for protracted offensive action—attacked with the objective of reaching "the line Gandelu-Marigny-Bouresches-Vaux." Meanwhile, the 231st Division pushed forward at Château-Thierry with the goal of establishing lightly held bridgeheads over the Marne. Attaining these objectives would not entail significant advances in the area assigned to the 2d Division, although after

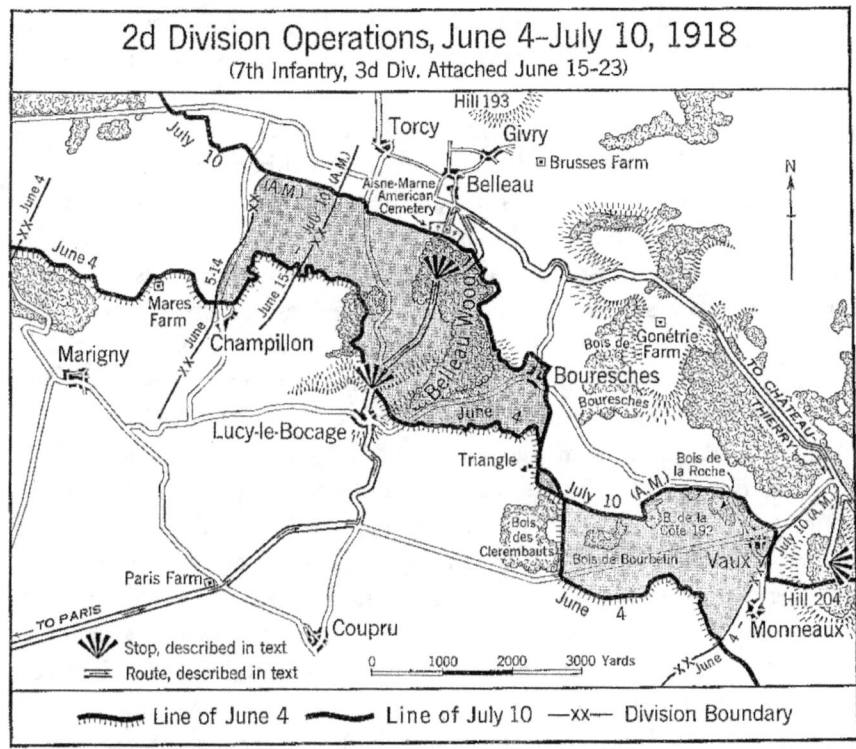

The 2d Division at Belleau Wood, June 4–July 10, 1918. (*American Armies and Battlefields in Europe*, 45)

June 2, French units and elements of the 23d Regiment and the 5th Marines would be responsible for holding the Germans back from Marigny.[13]

The French, allegedly amounting to no more than "bruised and broken remnants, with despair written on their war-weary faces," continued to fight heroically, giving the Americans crucial time to organize their defenses. "The enemy has been forced back step by step, altho tenaciously defending the ground," Corps Conta announced in its 2330 report. The resistance continued, with the 197th Division war diary chronicling frustratingly stiff opposition from French artillery, machine guns, and infantry. But instead of incurring terrible casualties as the American presence increased, German casualties steeply declined over the first days of June as the French gradually pulled back and their offensive ground to a halt. German morale was in steep decline over the same period, as Von Conta himself observed: "The horse play, which I saw much to my surprise, of the men of a division on the march when they put on straw hats, plug hats (toppers), women's apparel, etc., and decorated themselves with flags, and ribbons must be countered by all means possible as through these things discipline is slackened."[14]

By early on the morning of June 2, the French 43d Division had been attacked at multiple points along its line but had been pushed back only slightly. Yet concern about pressure on the left flank of that division north of Marigny, thanks to a French command error that inadvertently created a gap in the line that the Germans exploited, led to the establishment of a support line consisting of Colonel Paul Malone's 23d Regiment, the 1st Battalion of Colonel Wendell Neville's 5th Marines, two companies of the 5th Machine Gun Battalion, and a company of the 2d Engineers. From the left, the westernmost portion of the American sector would be held by the 23d Regiment, stationed from the vicinity of Brumetz west of Gandelu and to the southeast along the Ruisseau de Boulard. The 1/5th Marines, under Major Julius Turrill, continued the line eastward from Prémont through the Bois de Vaurichart. Major Frederic Wise's 2/5th Marines deployed from the north edges of the Bois de Vaurichart and the Bois de Veuilly, just north of Marigny, to the vicinity of Les Mares Farm and Hill 142 on the right, just north of Champillon. Here the 2/5th was supposed to link up with the 6th Machine Gun Battalion and the left sector of the 1/6th Marines, but this area would remain in flux for some time, with numerous gaps. To the east, Holcomb's 2/6th remained deployed from Lucy-le-Bocage to Triangle.[15]

A primary flash point in this line would be occupied by the 55th Company of the 2/5th Marines. Lieutenant Lemuel Shepherd of that company later remembered hordes of apparently beaten poilus shouting, *"Retournez, retournez! La guerre est finie! Retournez, retournez—La Boche est victorieuse!"* as he approached the front on June 2. Supposedly all these soldiers "immediately fell asleep on the ground" as soon as the American lines were safely behind them. The company commander, Captain John Blanchfield, chose to deploy his men in a patch of woods northwest of Champillon, around Les Mares Farm and across the road to the south of the Bois des Mares. As eventually established, his company's line ran half a mile from Les Mares Farm on the left (partly surrounded by a stone wall, and on a prominent rise) to the Champillon-Bussiares road to the right. There, the 55th Company linked securely with the 51st Company above Champillon, but to the left was a 600-yard gap across waist-high wheat fields from the farm to the Bois de Veuilly, where the 43d and 18th Marine Companies of Major Turrill's 1/5th Marines deployed with some guns from the battalion's 8th Machine Gun Company. French troops in that vicinity promised to cover the gap, but just in case, Shepherd—who acted as his company's second in command—placed sharpshooters in a barn to watch the area as well. Retreating French soldiers coming down the road reported that the Germans were just behind them, and the 18th Company reported that the sector to their front was swarming with Germans. The position was tenuous, and Shepherd knew it.[16]

At 0830 on the morning of June 2, Major Holcomb of the 2/6th Marines sent a nervous report to Harbord, commanding the 4th Brigade. German infantry, he said, had approached to within 1,200 yards of his positions below Bouresches and Bouresches Wood. Although Holcomb didn't know it yet, the troops approaching him consisted of elements of the German 10th Division. But he would not have to fight them directly—yet. French 43d Division infantry and artillery beat the Germans back from Bouresches and Bouresches Wood while two companies of the US 6th Machine Gun Battalion engaged the Germans at long range. Thrown back on their heels, the enemy troops advanced no farther. The 6th Machine Gun Battalion's war diary covering these actions cites mostly routine covering fire for troop deployments, along with some firing by the "right group guns" (77th and 81st Companies) in support of French infantry.[17]

The machine gun support was undoubtedly welcomed by the hard-pressed French, but its significance loomed even larger to the Americans. General Harbord inflated the gunners' action into a major defensive victory, proudly reporting to Bundy that "two attacks were made over in front of our right and were stopped principally by the fire of my M.G. Bn." Relaying flattering reports from his French liaison officer, Harbord claimed that his men had left "piles" of German dead and that "French morale has been greatly stiffened by the presence of our men." Harbord did not credit the French infantry with any role in stopping the German attacks, but he worried about his marines. At 1440 that afternoon, the French 43d Division was still battling the Germans vigorously from Bussiares to Belleau Wood and Bouresches. Unaware that the French were still holding firm, and hearing an erroneous report (likely of French origin) that the Germans had driven back the 2/6th Marines, Harbord ordered Holcomb to "stiffen your lines." This prompted Holcomb to retort, "When this outfit runs it will be in the other direction. Nothing doing in the fall-back business."[18]

German records place the American effort on June 2 in a broader context. To the west, the 197th Division noticed heavy machine gun fire into its left flank from around Champillon; this was one ingredient in a French defensive effort that slowed the Germans down at multiple points. The Germans also faced "constantly strengthening resistance" from hard-fighting French soldiers who were backed by flanking fire from French machine guns at Hill

126, about three kilometers northeast of Champillon between Bussiares and Torcy, and possibly by fire from American guns around Hill 142. Against such resistance, the 197th Division managed to push as far as Clignon Creek but was unable to take Hill 165 or penetrate beyond the Bussiares-Torcy road. Farther east, the German 237th Division captured Belleau and pushed as far as the Belleau-Bouresches road, while the 10th Division edged forward between Bouresches (captured at 1900 hours) and Vaux. The French deliberately abandoned Belleau Wood and Torcy at 2200 that night. The "piles" of dead that Harbord's gunners supposedly inflicted on the 237th and 10th Divisions are not mentioned in German operational journals or casualty rolls. By the evening of June 2, the Germans were still, on average, two to three kilometers from the American front line, which the slowly withdrawing French infantry and dismounted cavalry continued to mask.[19]

By the morning of June 3, the American line had gained definition from the left flank of the 23d Regiment near Brumetz to the right of the 9th Regiment in the Bois de la Morette. Important gaps remained, however, especially in the center, where the 2/5th Marines and 1/6th Marines struggled to sort out the confusion over who was responsible for Hill 142. Attempts to close this gap were unsuccessful, and the Germans would eventually occupy the hill's northern slopes, from which they would be ejected on June 6 at great cost. The Americans were also having problems with aspects of command and control, and they were enduring the painful but necessary weeding-out process that affects all green formations entering battle for the first time. A battalion commander of the 9th Regiment was relieved by his commanding officer "because of his inability to read a map & give directions on a map." Taking such confusion into consideration, had the Germans been close enough to apply pressure on the American line on June 3, the results might have been disastrous. Fortunately, however, the 2d Division was able to report that "no important German activity against our lines occurred during the day." The sorely needed respite occurred thanks to the continuing feistiness of nearby French troops. At daybreak the French 43d Division, which had abandoned Belleau Wood the previous evening, launched a forceful counterattack that managed to "reconquer" the woods as far as Hill 169. The French would battle the Germans therein all morning and evening until the poilus finally withdrew that night under heavy German pressure.[20]

German corps orders for June 3 set the 197th Division's main effort on the Franco-American center-left, from Veuilly-la-Poterie (in front of the 23d Regiment) to the Bussiares-Marigny road toward Marigny. The latter axis of advance would take the Germans from Bussiares and Hill 126 to Hill 165 and the Bois des Mares—all held by French troops. The 23d Regiment's positions were not tested; the commanding officer of the 3/23d reported that the Germans in his area had apparently outrun their artillery and had made no attempt to seek combat with the Americans. To reach Marigny, though, the 197th would have to breach American positions held by the 5th Marines from the Bois de Veuilly and Les Mares Farm to Champillon and Hill 142—just the spot where the 2d Division's positions were most tenuous. Farther east, the German 237th Division aimed to complete the capture of Belleau Wood and push toward Lucy in front of the 6th Marines, while the German 10th Division made minor advances between Bouresches and Vaux. The 10th Division would then hunker down for "passive defense," to be followed shortly by the 237th and 197th Divisions.[21]

The German advance on June 3 was frustratingly slow—again, thanks primarily to stout French resistance. To the east, the 237th Division pushed slowly through Belleau Wood, consolidating it by 2100; however, French forces fought bitterly for possession of Bussiares and Hill 126. After the 237th and 197th Divisions combined to dislodge the French from these positions, the French 43d Division infantry in the Bois des Mares launched a strong counterattack—derided by George B. Clark as "little more than a gallant gesture" or an "ego trip" that "came to nothing" and even "put a heavier burden on the 2d Division than before the attempt was made." Far from being an exercise in futility, however, this counterattack succeeded in halting the German advance at this point and giving the 2d Division more time to prepare for its first engagement. The 197th Division's war diary explained its failure to advance any further. It cited:

> The strong [French] artillery effectiveness which could not be neutralized, and . . . the fire from the [French and American] machine gun nests in the ravine and patches of woods near Les Mares Ferme. . . . In the patches of woods southwest of Bussiares the fighting see-sawed for a long time without a decision. Coming from Hills 165 and 183 the [French] made several counter attacks into patches of woods organized in waves and great depth, which after being scattered by our artillery fire, were time and again assembled anew and led forward.

These French counterattacks are given little to no credit in American sources, which almost uniformly present the poilus as broken and on the run; however, they undoubtedly played a central role in halting the German advance. Late that evening the Germans renewed their assault. Germans of the 1/28th Ersatz Infantry wrested Veuilly-la-Poterie from the French after a severe struggle, while the 26th Reserve Jäger Battalion occupied Hill 165—which the French had abandoned, as planned—and pushed to within fifty meters of the Americans at Les Mares Farm.[22]

By this point, Von Conta's advance was nearly over. Thanks to the courageous delaying action of French infantry between Veuilly-la-Poterie and Bussiares, the Germans had been stopped well short of their final objective around Marigny. Contrary to subsequent histories in which the Americans were credited with holding back the Germans from June 1, Lieutenant Colonel W. S. Grant of G-3 reported to Fox Conner on June 4, "It should be understood that in front of our line . . . there has been until today, a French line engaged with the enemy from which advanced line small groups of French have been gradually filtering back." That is, their tasks completed to perfection, the poilus withdrew in good order and according to plan. As Grant continued, "Upon the adjustment of Gen. Bundy's sector today [June 4], this French line is to be wholly withdrawn and its elements regrouped in rear." In other words, the French had fought a strong delaying action, falling back "gradually" until Bundy's 2d Division had a chance to organize its own positions. Only then, beginning on June 4, did the whole body of the French advance forces pull back —a planned withdrawal that some American observers and historians have presented as a rout. German troops of the 197th Division followed up the French withdrawal, and patrols probed at various points, including toward Les Mares Farm, to assess the extent of the French withdrawal and prospects for the morrow. In the process, they would finally encounter the Americans face-to-face.[23]

As the French pulled back that afternoon, a French major—disagreeing, as field officers are entitled to do, about the suitability of the American position—apparently handed Captain William O. Corbin, adjutant of the 51st Company above Champillon, written orders to pull back. American accounts have generally interpreted these orders (which cannot be found) as a simple demand for the marines to flee for their lives. Corbin reported the order to his commanding officer, Captain Lloyd Williams, who countermanded it—expostulating, according to legend, "Retreat? Hell! I just got here." Setting aside subsequent reports that portrayed the French troops as "dispirited" and "ashamed" and described the "breathless" French major as "stumbl[ing]" from the front, the order was probably given because the positions around Les Mares Farm were thought to be too exposed to maintain for long. For the marines, though, the encounter conveniently encapsulated an interpretation of events that juxtaposed alleged French cowardice with American heroism. Later that day, Harbord sent Catlin a message of congratulations for defying his French allies. Soon the story was making the rounds—with the response being attributed to Wise, Harbord, or even Bundy. This led marine sergeant Daniel Morgan to gripe: "I do not like to alter the phraseology of a general, but what he should have said is, 'Retreat? Hell! *They* just got there.' The general was always back in a bomb proof dugout, while the Suicide Squad was out on the firing line."[24]

As fighting raged on the afternoon of June 3 between Bussiares and the Bois des Mares, Lieutenant Lemuel Shepherd of the 55th Company nervously scanned his positions around Les Mares Farm. Noting a small knoll about 300 yards in front, along the road from Bussiares and Hill 165 to Marigny, he detailed ten men to set up a post there with a Chauchat. He ordered them to observe the approach from Hill 165 and open fire on any advancing enemy troops before withdrawing. The advance warning would give his company time to prepare to engage the enemy. Unfortunately, even as he established this advance post, French troops in the vulnerable gap to the left of the 55th Company withdrew, forcing Captain Blanchfield to withdraw a platoon from his right flank to cover it. French troops withdrawing from Hill 165 then passed through the American lines, warning that the Germans were right behind them.[25]

The German advance from Hill 165 toward Les Mares Farm, following up the withdrawing French, began in the early afternoon. According to Catlin, the Germans were "loafing on the job" because they had had everything "so easy" up to this point. Actually, they were advancing with an abundance of caution because of the drubbing they had received from the French. By 1320, according to the 197th Division's war diary, there was an "Attack under way against les Mares Fme." This "attack" was apparently directed against French rear guards rather than the Americans, for twenty minutes later, the Germans found their hands full with yet another French counterattack from the direction of the farm. This attack is not mentioned (needless to say) in any American sources, but it likely significantly blunted the German advance before it reached the marines' positions around 1700.[26]

As German shell fire against Les Mares Farm steadily increased over the course of the afternoon, Shepherd asked for a counterbarrage, but no artillery was in place to deliver it. His company commander, Captain Blanchfield, ordered the marines to spread out thinly and "form as skirmishers to withstand attacks." Impatient, Shepherd asked Blanchfield, "Don't you think I'd better go back and look after that outpost?" Receiving a brief affirmative reply, he trotted forward toward the knoll. It was around 1700, and the enemy attack had already begun. The German soldiers were approaching "in a very open formation, preceded by scouts." Shepherd made it a hundred yards before a dud shell landed six feet away, showered him with dirt, and "scared the hell out of me." Stunned, he paused for a moment and then tottered onward.[27]

Shepherd later provided contradictory versions of what happened next. He told one interviewer that as he paused on his way to the outpost to lean against a tree, another shell landed and a fragment tore into his neck. He told Robert Asprey that after he made it to the outpost, a bullet from the first enemy machine gun burst caught him in the neck. Others, writing soon after the war and presumably after speaking to Shepherd, thought he had remained at the outpost, directing fire. Reconciling these contradictory accounts is impossible now. At some point, though, Shepherd was bandaged and evacuated to a field hospital.[28]

Meanwhile, the Germans were attacking, "and we're knocking the hell out of them with rifle fire." Such aptitude with the rifle—as advocated by Pershing—allegedly stunned the Germans. "We could actually hear them yelling about it," said Shepherd. What really happened during the German attack is unclear. Separate accounts have the advance party on the knoll temporarily stopping the German attack and pulling back at leisure or withdrawing under fire. In any event, German infantry then assaulted the farm complex proper. Catlin, commanding the adjacent 6th Marines, claimed that he witnessed what followed from his command post at La Voie du Châtel a few kilometers to the south. In his dramatic, oft-quoted, but hopelessly garbled account—misdated June 2—the Germans came on in two columns, "steady as machines. To me as a military man it was a beautiful sight. I could not but admire the precision and steadiness of those waves of men in grey with the sun glinting on their helmets. On they came, never wavering, never faltering, apparently irresistible." French infantry, said Catlin, conducted a fighting retreat through the wheat fields until the pressure became too much and they broke in headlong retreat. Cue the marines, who opened up on the Germans with everything they had—rifles, machine guns, and mortars—at 300 yards. Three (not two) times the Germans came on, and three times their assault was broken amidst "terrible slaughter" before they too "broke and ran for cover." "The French told us that they had never seen such marksmanship practiced in the heat of battle," said Catlin, but it made no difference; the French, as he portrayed them, continued to flee, leaving the marines alone to face the "hordes of Attila."[29]

Catlin went on to quote other unnamed marines who had allegedly participated in fighting off Germans who had, for some reason, reverted to the tactics of 1914. "The Boches tore out of the woods," said one, "a machine gun to every ten of them. A rain of good American lead from good American riflemen met them. We saw them stop. Surprised? Why, they never dreamed of anything like it. We kept pounding and they turned and raced for the wood. . . . We lay in the open, digging in with bayonets and firing while the Boche was frantically passing back word that a cog in the wheel had slipped." An unnamed machine gunner—a "Toledo boy"—said:

> I estimated them at about 500 and they were in fairly compact masses. We waited until they got close, oh, very close. In fact, we let them think they were going to have a leadpipe cinch. Oh, it was too easy; just like a bunch of cattle coming to slaughter. . . . Curiously the infantry, which had been steady up to this time, paused as though waiting for us of the "devil's snare drums" to take up the great work. And we did! Rat-tat-tat-tat full into them, and low down, oh! But it was good to jam down the trigger, to feel her kick, to look out ahead, hand on the controlling wheel, and see the Heinies fall like wheat under the mower. . . . The poor devils didn't know they were facing the Marines—Americans.[30]

George B. Clark and David Bonk provide significantly more detailed but uncited accounts that portray two German infantry battalions attacking the 55th Company with fixed bayonets. They advanced through green wheat fields in four or five extended lines twenty-five yards apart, with six paces between each man. "The devils are coming on," Blanchfield told his men. "You have been waiting for them for a year; now go get them." Stymied by "those terrible rifles"—which they had allegedly never encountered before and were far more effective than artillery or machine guns—the Germans dove for the ground. They attempted to renew the advance several times, seeking unsuccessfully to flank the Americans and suffering inconceivable slaughter before finally retiring "more rapidly than they had advanced."[31]

It is impossible to say whether the attack on Les Mares Farm on the evening of June 3 really happened as described by American accounts. Some narratives, like Catlin's, are clearly exaggerated and unreliable. And the slight mention the event receives in official German and even American records indicates that the scale of the engagement was far below the prominence it attained in the retelling. Indeed, were it not for the near-legendary status the action later attained, it would hardly be worth mentioning in any comprehensive account of the 2d Division's deployment in the Belleau Wood sector. Garbled accounts of the incident circulated almost immediately after it took place. Tales making the rounds at French Sixth Army headquarters inaccurately placed the action in the "northern edge of Veuilly Wood," where somebody reported that a German attack "directed against an American Battalion failed completely. The Battalion, which behaved valiantly, lost more than 200 men." But in time, the varying tales of Les Mares Farm would all boil down to one thing: the Germans had been turned back from their relentless drive on Paris—which several French divisions had been unable to halt—by a mere handful of marines.[32]

By that evening and early the next morning, infantry and machine gun reinforcements had arrived from regimental headquarters, the 1/5th Marines, and the 6th Machine Gun Battalion. The American 2d Field Artillery Brigade also arrived in position behind the lines with 75mm and 155mm guns, although it did not fire "effectively" for several more days. As Corporal Amos Wilder moved into position with his battery of the 17th Field Artillery, he heard worrisome rumors that the German "superiority in numbers is very great," but a Frenchman reassured him that "the morale of the German troops was poor." At 0800 on June 4, the 2d Division officially took command of the sector. French units had entirely withdrawn from in front of the division, although a force of dismounted cavalry remained in the Bois de la Morette on the far right flank. Otherwise, the division was on its own, following a readjusted line roughly from the Bois de Veuilly on the left, where the 23d Regiment met the French 43d Division (which had pulled back to hold a shortened front but was still fit enough to hold a portion of the lines), to La Nouette Farm on the right, south of the Bois de la Morette, where the 9th Regiment met the French 10th Colonial Division. Desultory German shelling continued throughout the day.[33]

German probing around Les Mares Farm continued all day on June 4. The nature of these attacks varied, depending on the source. The few American "eyewitness" accounts, most of which were published during or shortly after the war, portray the German probes as massed attacks that collapsed in blood and gore under the "superb rifle fire of the marines." Sergeant Martin Gus Gulberg of the 75th Company, 6th Marines, included an account of the morning attack in his memoir:

> I don't remember the exact time, but before noon on the third day they made a few calls. They came out of the wood opposite our position in close formation. They came on as steadily as if they were on parade. We opened up on them with a slashing barrage of rifles, automatics and machine guns. They halted, withdrew a space and then came on again. They were brave men—we had to grant them that. They had a good artillery barrage in front of them, but it didn't keep us down. Three times they tried to break through, but our fire was too accurate and too heavy for them. It was terrible in its effective-

ness. They fell by the scores, there among the poppies and the wheat. Then they broke and ran for cover. We expected them to try again, but they stayed in the woods. This was the "Belleau Woods."

Official sources describe the German attacks as "local" and resulting in relatively minor casualties. According to the 4th Brigade's war diary, "During the early hours of the morning the Germans made a violent attack on the portions of the sector held by the 2nd Bn. 5th Regiment and two companies of the 3rd Bn. of the 6th Regiment. This attack was successfully repulsed, inflicting losses on the enemy." The German 197th Division's war diary indicates that "during the early morning hours the 26th Res Jager Bn attempted to seize les Mares Ferme through a coup, but without success." The attack was not pressed aggressively, as attested by the mere 117 casualties suffered by the entire 197th Division over the course of the day.[34]

Further skirmishing took place that afternoon, including a "small enemy attack against Hill 142, held by our troops, [that] broke down under artillery fire." However, some marines grew tired of defensive combat and decided to take matters into their own hands. Annoyed by reports of a German machine gun near Les Mares Farm, a twelve-man patrol from the 6th Marines under Corporal Francis J. Dockx deftly wrecked the enemy nest, capturing two Germans with their gun and killing six.[35] Dockx was also killed in the attack. And with that, the Marine Brigade's direct role in halting the German offensive came to an end.

The nature, extent, and consequences of the Marine Brigade's defensive actions on June 1–5 are impossible to determine for certain, but the fact that the brigade incurred a total of seventy-four battle deaths during that period helps establish perspective. The haze of self-serving braggadocio and propaganda surrounding these events, combined with the paucity of official sources, exponentially increases the difficulty of teasing out the truth. As we have seen, Lemuel Shepherd's and Albertus Catlin's postwar reminiscences are self-justifying and often mutually contradictory. Blanchfield was killed at Belleau Wood and never told his own story. No other reliable eyewitness accounts exist. As a result, historians have often made uncritical use of articles published shortly after the war ended. Major Edwin N. McClellan, chief of the Marine Corps Historical Section, published articles in 1920 in the *Marine Corps Gazette* in which he called Les Mares Farm a "historic" engagement whereby "the Germans reached the nearest point to Paris." This provided the basis for much of the mythology, as did an article by William E. Moore titled "The 'Bloody Angle' of the A.E.F.," published in the *American Legion Weekly* in 1922. Articles in the *Marine Corps Gazette* and *Leatherneck* in subsequent years repeated the same stories. Presumably based on interviews with survivors, but short on detail and largely unattributed, these accounts credited the marines with turning back the German tide. John W. Thomason's much more modest and thoroughly researched account of the division's actions, prepared in 1927 but abandoned because it evidently ran afoul of the Marine Corps hierarchy, remained unpublished until 2006.[36]

If the marines really did turn back the German drive on Paris, it had to occur at Les Mares Farm on June 3. Nowhere else did the marines and the Germans come into direct contact until June 6, by which time the German advance had definitely ground to a halt. And on the whole, postwar accounts concur that this is what happened. The German attack at Les Mares Farm was the "tip of the spear," says Shepherd's biographer Tom FitzPatrick, and the "last effort the Germans made to proceed towards Paris [was] through the Les Mares Farm locale." *American Armies and Battlefields in Europe* asserts that "a determined assault against the left of the 2d Division position was repulsed with heavy losses . . . and on that day the advance of the German forces in this region was definitely stopped." A 1963 article in the *Marine Corps Gazette* bluntly claims that the marines' resistance spelled "the end of the German drive for Paris." George B. Clark writes:

> The first few days of the continued German assault during early June were most murderous for the Boche as the 2d Division's Doughboys and marines took careful aim and shot down the enemy in windrows as they crossed the wheat fields. Sustained, well-aimed rifle fire will stop any army, no matter how good that army is. Flesh and blood can stand just so much before even the most courageous soldier gives way. What happened, of course, was that the Germans took up defensive positions and then it was the Marine Brigade's turn.

Alan Axelrod claims that "the marines had been instrumental in mauling the right wing of Corps Conta, an achievement that did prevent a German breakthrough, right then and there, west and toward Paris." David Bonk presents the somewhat more nuanced—if unproved—argument that Von Conta and Ludendorff probably interpreted the Germans' repulse at Les Mares Farm as a "hardening" of enemy defenses, which meant the German offensive should be called to a halt.[37]

In German records, however, the fighting at Les Mares Farm—which, according to some American accounts, left behind mountainous heaps of German dead—is barely mentioned. The initial attempt to seize the farm was apparently made at the regimental level on June 3 and continued in a desultory fashion over the next eighteen to twenty-four hours at the battalion or even company level. Further up the chain of command, Von Conta had issued the following corps orders at midnight on June 3–4:

> The attack by the right flank of the 7th Army will be continued. Group Conta will be responsible for the flank protection of this attack. To accomplish this, the corps will fight for a position that is especially suited for defense. Such a position lies in the line: Veuilly–Marigny–La Vois du Chatel–Hill 201, about 1 kilometer southeast of Montgivrault–Le Thiolet–Hill 204 about 1 kilometer west of Château-Thierry.

Corps orders for June 4 had the German 5th Guards Division, which was moving up behind the 197th and would soon relieve it, attacking the heights of Veuilly and proceeding from the northwest to the Marigny heights. This advance probably would have hit the 23d Regiment, but it never got under way. Farther east, the 197th Division was to proceed along the road from Bussiares over Hill 165 to take Les Mares Farm and capture La Voie du Châtel. This advance was never pressed aggressively and was apparently turned back by the 2/5th Marines holding the farm complex. Whether it would have proceeded anyway, given the failure of the 237th, 28th, 231st, and 10th Divisions to advance toward Lucy-le-Bocage, Triangle, and Le Thiolet against the right flank of the 6th Marines and the 9th Regiment, is open to question.[38]

On a grander scale, Operation Blücher had already ended by June 5—in dismal failure. German Army Group Prince Wilhelm had sent Ludendorff a message on June 3 recommending that the offensive be called off. And although it continued for a little while longer, Von Conta continued to emphasize, in corps orders issued later on June 4, that his corps sought only to achieve suitable defensive positions that it could hold to protect the army's flank:

> Corps Conta, which is charged with the protection of the left flank of the 7th Army during the attack of the 7th Army right flank, is compelled to temporarily assume the defensive, after positions most suitable for this purpose are captured. . . . The offensive spirit must be

maintained even though a temporary lull in the attack seems to exist. We are the victors and will remain on the offensive. . . . Besides this organization for defense, the main task of the commanders for the present is to reorganize their units, and commanders to regain strict control of their troops again, and replace the shortages of officers, men and equipment.

Such brave talk notwithstanding, there was no real prospect of continuing the offensive after it was officially called off on June 5—for reasons that had little if anything to do with Les Mares Farm. On that date, the German Seventh Army officially ended the offensive, and Von Conta "ordered the consolidation of the main line of resistance." Plans to resume the attack were promised by June 8, and units were ordered to be ready to restart their forward movement on forty-eight hours' notice. This was to be in support of Operation Gneisenau, launched on June 9 and continued through June 13 in a futile last-gasp effort to reach Compiègne. By then, however, the total exhaustion of Von Conta's troops and the Franco-American counterattack at and around Belleau Wood made further advance by the 4th Reserve Corps impossible. "Though we told ourselves and our men, 'On to Paris,'" wrote Von Conta's chief of staff, "we knew this was not to be. . . . In truth the brilliant offensive had petered out."[39]

The Americans' appearance also had less immediately tangible effects that even the Germans observed. In a summary of prisoner interrogations carried out by Von Conta's officers from May 27 through June 6, the high quality of the French 10th Colonial Division around Château-Thierry was noted, along with the "highest patriotism" of the French officers, who often defiantly harked back to the First Battle of the Marne in 1914. German interrogators also noted—no doubt with considerable amusement—how much the French despised the British. The appearance of the American 2d Division, however, pointed to a hardening of enemy defenses—not just because the marines were tough but also because the French were reorganizing. "The employment of Americans on the Corps Front," stated the report, "as was verified during the last few days indicates—not counting the political reaction—an increasing clearing up and reorganization of the hostile units." French knowledge that the Americans had arrived made a tangible difference in their morale. Whereas French prisoners captured at the beginning of the offensive around May 27 had been suitably dejected, those captured later "gave a self-confident impression and believed that the panacea for all their woes lay in the spirit of the Americans. The momentary setback had no decisive meaning to them." Such an attitude, ironically, might have made the French both stiffer in defense and more cautious in the attack. The Americans had stood by for almost three years while France fought for its life. Now that they were finally here, the French feeling was: let them do the dirty work. In Belleau Wood, that is exactly what they would do.[40]

6

Into the Woods
June 6, 1918

Von Conta's drive to establish defensive positions in the vicinity of Belleau Wood and Château-Thierry petered out without seriously testing the 2d Division. Though tired from their hurried approach to the front and still trying to straighten out a confused deployment, the Americans were relatively fresh and eager to enter the fight. Despite the fact that every American division suffered from inadequate training and other deficiencies in the spring of 1918, Degoutte and Bundy still wielded a powerful instrument of war. Used properly, the 2d Division had the potential to deliver the Germans a significant blow, and given the time to acclimate itself to front-line conditions and learn the tricks of the trade, the division could attain elite status—on the level of the Canadians or the Australians—fairly quickly. Whether the division would ever reach its full potential would depend on men like Degoutte, Bundy, and Harbord.

On June 5 the 2d Division faced little more than "local attacks," incurring "slight" losses. For the artillery, though, the fight continued. Artillery sergeant Joseph J. Gleeson noted in his diary: "Our part of the fight to stop Boche and save Paris. . . . Hundreds of batteries were firing and such a roar, indescribable." Meanwhile, at Degoutte's orders, the American and French infantry spent the morning, day, and evening readjusting their locations, with a view to establishing positions "indispensable to the effective defense against renewed attacks by the enemy." The overall effect for the Americans was a short sidestep to the right. To the left, the French 167th Division entered the line, taking over from the French 43d Division and relieving American positions west of Champillon, including the area around Les Mares Farm. There, the French 116th Infantry Regiment linked up with the 4th Brigade, consisting of the 5th Marines with the 1st and 3d Battalions in line left to right, and the 6th Marines with the 2d and 3d Battalions in line left to right. This placed the 3/5th Marines to the west of Belleau Wood and the 2/6th Marines south of the woods. The 2/5th and 1/6th Marines remained in brigade and corps reserve, respectively. Next came the 3d Brigade, with the 23d and 9th Regiments in line left to right. In all, the division's frontage ran about 20 kilometers, from a point on the road about 800 meters north of Champillon, through the southern edge of Hill 142, Lucy-le-Bocage, Triangle, the Bois de Clerembauts, and the southeast corner of the Bois de la Morette. Opposite, the Germans occupied a line running roughly from Bouresches through the southern edge of Belleau Wood (which they worked furiously to consolidate), Torcy, and Bussiares.[1]

For most of the marines and soldiers deployed with the 2d Division, this was not a time of nail-biting crisis but one of line adjustment, digging in, and attempting to scope out enemy dispositions, despite their lack of adequate maps. Unfortunately, many of them had to do so with scant supplies of food and drink. Private Warren Jackson of the 1/6th Marines remembered:

> The rations that did come consisted of French hard bread and French corned beef, known as monkey meat. The hard bread was the size of a biscuit, well browned and with a smooth, glossy top. When dipped in coffee for a moment the biscuit attained a mushy softness almost instantly. Without this immersion it had the physical characteristics of a brick. "Rain barred, a fort made of this hardtack would be impregnable, joking aside." The cans of beef held about as much as a teacup. Had water not been so scarce, this meat would have done very well as a substitute for something to eat, but it was salty as brine. When a fellow ate this monkey meat he was ravenously thirsty. . . . While in this position little else did we have to do but count our miseries.

Others made the acquaintance of nearby French soldiers, who could relax now that the Americans were in the line and the German offensive had obviously come to a halt. Second Lieutenant Robert Kean of the 15th Field Artillery encountered a group of French soldiers calmly enjoying their noonday meal near Bonneil, opposite German-held Hill 204. Happily bidding the Americans welcome, the French shared their ample wine provision. "I was amazed to see what fine trenches these French had already built in their couple of days there," Kean recalled. "Our American soldiers would not have built such good trenches in a week, but the French from their long experience knew the value of deep trenches and they had already something there which would protect them well if necessary."[2]

Idleness was not an acceptable state of affairs for Degoutte. Although he is generally lambasted by American writers for his alleged timidity at the end of May, the French general was in fact an almost uniformly aggressive commander for whom the presence of Americans apparently acted as an incentive to undertake offensive operations. Degoutte demonstrated this native aggressiveness on June 5 by demanding that the American and French troops under his command launch a counterattack. His stated objective was to deny the Germans the woods and valleys west of Bussiares and south of Clignon Creek as assembly points for future attacks. Degoutte wanted this accomplished as quickly as possible, before the Germans had time to bring up their artillery in force and consolidate their lines. This news was most welcome to Bundy and his officers and men. Pershing, visiting Harbord's headquarters on the afternoon of June 4, had "expressed his satisfaction of the work of the Marine brigade." The time had come to show what they could do in the attack.[3]

On the afternoon of June 5 Degoutte decided that the French 167th Division would play the primary initial role in the upcoming attack. It would jump off at 0345 on June 6, attacking from the Bois de Vaurichart and the Bois de Veuilly on the left to Champillon on the right. During their advance, the French would take Veuilly-la-Poterie, Hill 165, and the Bois des Mares and occupy the edge of the hills overlooking Clignon Creek from the south. To their right, Degoutte ordered the 2d Division to "maintain liaison" with the French advance by moving forward on Hill 142 to objectives that Bundy would determine. Degoutte ordered that "as soon as possible after the execution of the first [French] operation," probably that afternoon, "an analogous operation will be executed by the American 2d Division, for the purpose of seizing the Bois de Belleau and the long crest (southeast-northwest), which immediately dominates Torcy and Belleau." By standards of terrain and distance, neither operation—stretching no more than a few kilometers at its greatest extent—could be qualified as major, although they would turn out that way.[4]

At 2225 on June 5, Harbord set his brigade's objectives for the following day. The primary initial advance would be by Turrill's 1/5th Marines, which would move in conjunction with the French and push down the German-held northern slopes of Hill 142 to occupy patches of woods southeast of Bussiares. The 3/5th Marines would advance to their left slightly to support this attack. Machine guns and artillery would support the advance. Once the objective was taken, it would be held and organized for defense against counterattack with the help of tools brought forward by the 2d Engineers. After these objectives had been attained, Berry's 3/5th Marines would shift direction and attack east into the northern portion of Belleau Wood. To their right, Sibley's 3/6th Marines would seize the southern portion of the woods and then take Bouresches. Holcomb's 2/6th would support Sibley's right and maintain liaison with the 23d Regiment.[5]

Execution of the American plan proved difficult, thanks in part to slipshod staff work. Much of the blame must be laid at Harbord's door. His troops carried out no thorough reconnaissance of the terrain over which they would have to advance, either because Harbord did not specifically order them to do so (a charge he later denied) or because his officers were dilatory. Whoever was to blame for this omission, his officers had to rely on inaccurate French maps of the terrain, with unfortunate results. Moreover, late-night reshuffling of some units in the line, as directed by Harbord, caused additional confusion in the predawn darkness, leaving Turrill's troops struggling to reach their jumping-off positions in time. Two companies never made it. Artillery support was also poorly organized. Harbord wanted to limit the barrage to maintain the element of surprise—a typically open-warfare doctrine the infantry would come to rue—and no attention was given to specific planning for the second-phase attack against Belleau Wood that afternoon. Most damaging of all was Harbord's mishandling of the tactics to be employed by the 1/5th Marines in their initial attack. In a conversation at 1500 on June 5, Harbord agreed with his chief of staff, Colonel Preston Brown, that "the infantry will attack by infiltration rather than by waves." Harbord neglected to ensure that this tactical prescription was passed down to his officers, however. As a consequence, the marines would move forward in dense waves, with disastrous results.[6]

The task before Major Turrill's 1/5th Marines did not involve the conquest of a lot of territory, but it would be difficult nonetheless. Finger-shaped Hill 142 pointed north-northeast toward a road and a ravine roughly midway between Bussiares to the west and Torcy to the east. To reach the hill's crest and northern slopes, the marines would first have to cross some 300 yards of wheat fields. Beyond the wheat rose a patch of woods strongly occupied by German infantry with machine guns. On the other side of the woods the terrain opened out again. If the flanks were secured by the time the marines reached this point, Hill 142 would provide a useful vantage point for observation and future operations; if not, the marines would find themselves in an exposed salient open to enemy fire from three sides. Ultimately, securing the left flank would depend on the French. The right could not be entirely cleared until the afternoon's operations drove the enemy out of Belleau Wood (assuming all went well). During their morning advance, however, the 1/5th Marines would be responsible for covering shallow ravines that paralleled the hill on either side. One advantage operating in the marines' favor was that Hill 142 marked a divisional boundary between the German 197th Division to the west and the 237th Division to the east. This would play an important role on June 6.[7]

The predawn hours of June 6 found French and American artillery laying a dense preparatory barrage over the area to be assaulted at 0345. "No sleep for third night," Sergeant Gleeson wrote in his diary. "When it comes to having it rough this can't be beaten. Most of boys are deaf from roar of guns." The infantrymen were tired and hungry too—they had received no regular rations for days. For the attack, they shed their backpacks and carried only the essentials—rifles, grenades, gas masks, and ammunition. As the barrage reached a crescendo, the sun broke over the horizon, auguring a glorious day despite the puffs of mist and smoke that continued to drift over the landscape. So began what marine historian George B. Clark has called the "most catastrophic day in Marine Corps history."[8]

Two companies of Turrill's 1/5th Marines were designated to lead the attack. On the left, First Lieutenant Orlando Crowther's 67th Company would push north while keeping its flank along the western ravine and maintaining contact with the French. On the right, Captain George Hamilton's 49th Company was tasked with taking the hill's eastern slope and capturing its northern crest. Never having been informed of Harbord's supposed prescription for infiltration tactics that would allow rapid movement and minimize casualties, Crowther and Hamilton prepared to move forward in the standard, dense wave formations they had been taught over the preceding weeks. Nor did Harbord provide any instructions for American machine guns to provide fire support. The 17th and 66th Companies, which were supposed to support the attack, remained out of position due to some administrative foul-up and were missing when the assault began. Their absence worsened the problem of maintaining contact with flanking units.[9]

The American barrage was supported by guns of the 15th Company of the 6th Machine Gun Battalion, despite the lack of clear instructions from the brigade. Initially, this sufficed to keep the defenders—three companies of the German 460th Infantry Regiment, 237th Division—under cover. As NCOs blew their whistles and the men moved forward in platoon waves through the wheat, the German guns remained silent at first. But there was no rolling barrage to keep them down. Before the marines had gone fifty yards, the thin, bone-tired men in field gray on Hill 142 and the surrounding terrain hurried to their guns and opened fire.

On the left, Crowther's company was hit almost immediately by heavy machine gun fire from the front and to the left across the ravine. The marines took awful casualties but ignored them and pushed forward. Some threw themselves to the ground under strong bursts of enemy fire but then stood up and lurched on, again and again. Individual marines such as Private Joseph M. Baker (who would receive the Distinguished Service Cross) took it upon themselves to flank and eliminate German machine gun nests. Others just plunged forward until they either fell or reached the woods, where they came to grips with the enemy hand-to-hand. According to one battle story, a group of marines under a Corporal Geer stormed a Maxim nest pell-mell. One man grabbed the machine gun by the muzzle even as it was firing and upended it, wrecking the gun but losing his hand in the process. Four of the company's five officers, including Crowther, fell. On their own, individual marines followed their instincts—and met their objectives. The remnants of the 67th Company, "commanded" by Geer, burst through the woods in a brawling melee of brown and field gray and surged over the hill's northern and western slopes.[10]

On the right, the 49th Company had an equally challenging morning. Hit by machine guns just after they entered the wheat, most of the marines dove to the ground. Hamilton "had to run along the whole line and get each man (almost individually) on his feet to rush that wood." Supported by American machine guns that Turrill goaded into pouring fire on the German-held woods, the marines rose up and bulled ahead. In the woods, Americans and Germans engaged in such a frenzy of hand-to-hand fighting that Hamilton had no clear recollection of what happened there—only glimpses of wild shooting, darting figures, shouts to his men to hurry faster, and ripping the Iron Cross off a vanquished German officer. Beyond, Hamilton and his marines ran across an open field dotted with red poppies, taking more casualties from enemy machine guns before plunging into another patch of woods on the hill's northeast slope.[11]

It was about 0630, and both companies had reached their objectives. Hamilton, however, was engrossed in a frenzy of combat. Even though the Germans seemed "pretty well on the run," he was not ready to stop. Continuing ahead with a platoon, he left the woods and entered a field swept by enemy machine guns. "What saved me from getting hit I don't know," he remembered, but several of his men fell. Grabbing an automatic rifle team, he continued northeast toward a road leading to Torcy, not noticing that most of his platoon had abandoned him and moved west to take care of some enemy machine guns. Seeing an entire German company ahead preparing to counterattack, Hamilton realized he had gone too far and turned back. For his tiny party, "it was a case of every man for himself. I crawled back through a drainage ditch filled with cold water and shiny reeds. Machine gun bullets were just grazing my back and our own artillery were dropping close." Fortunately, he made it back to Hill 142 in time to organize the defense, for the Germans were coming.[12]

Further back, Colonel Neville phoned brigade headquarters at 0701 to tell Harbord that Turrill's men had reached their objective, despite the evidently slow advance of the French 167th Division on the left. In fact, the French had advanced aggressively, reaching the cemetery in Veuilly-la-Poterie and the Bois des Mares, but they had been held back by *"les nombreuses mitrailleuses"*—plentiful German machine guns—in the villages and woods, especially north of Clignon Creek. Believing that his own operation had been "an entire success," Harbord was "as happy as a clam even though he has about 10 batteries so close to his P.C. [post of command] that it sounds as if the guns were all in his bedroom." His adjutant phoned corps headquarters a few minutes later to relay the good news. Harbord got on the phone himself at 1019 to report that he had seen "all" the American wounded and that "they show a fine spirit and are very cocky. Most of the wounds are slight—result of machine gun fire." German morale, he said, was "low." Crowning the glory, marines who were not yet in the fight had passed around just-arrived French newspapers announcing that, as one of the Americans commented, "you-all saved their capital. Our chest stuck out a little further after that."[13]

While Harbord celebrated, Turrill fretted about his men on Hill 142. The French on his left had yet to advance significantly, so far as he could tell; to the right, the 45th Company of the 3/5th Marines had managed to advance only half the distance necessary to maintain contact in that direction. It was obvious to Turrill that the marines on the hill would be in a difficult place once the inevitable German counterattack developed. Fortunately, some reinforcements had arrived in the form of the 17th and 66th Companies. The major sent them forward, along with some machine gun squads and engineers, to anchor the line on Hill 142. As they moved forward, these reinforcements probably encountered and cleared out the numerous Germans who had been left behind in the woods in the marines' initial surge over the hill. Another company, the 51st, helped cover the gap opened by the slow progress of the French on the left.[14]

Meanwhile, the Germans counterattacked. A company of the 460th Regiment (237th Division) came from Torcy (which Hamilton had seen forming), and the 26th Jäger Battalion of the 273d Regiment (197th Division)—the same outfit that had clashed with the marines at Les Mares Farm—attacked from Bussiares. Worn out but employing the tactics drilled into them by their few remaining officers, the Germans advanced in small groups by infiltration, attempting to avoid Hamilton's strongpoints and work through the ravines around his flanks. The marines countered aggressively, however, resulting in bitter hand-to-hand fighting. Hamilton recalled "five nasty" counterattacks "that came near to driving us back off our hill—but—we hung on." He continued:

> One especially came near getting me. There were heavy bushes all over the hill, and the first thing I knew hand grenades began dropping near. One grenade threw a rock which caught me behind the ear and made me dizzy for a few minutes. But I quickly recovered my senses when I saw one of my gunnery sergeants [Gunnery Sergeant Charles F. Hoffman, who would receive the Medal of Honor] jump toward the bushes with a yell and start shooting to beat the devil. Not twenty feet from us, was a line of about fifteen German helmets and five light machine guns just coming into action. It was hand-to-hand work for several strenuous minutes, and then all was over.

At 0950 Hamilton reported to Turrill that his men, occupying the northern tip of a "salient" with insufficient support, were struggling to maintain their positions. "Our casualties are *very* heavy," he relayed. "We need medical aid badly. . . . All my officers are gone." At 1210 he reported that his men were running desperately short of ammunition and water and needed flare pistols. Half an hour later, Turrill sensed that Hamilton's position was growing desperate as shell-shocked marines began filtering to the rear, spreading tales of panic and confusion. Turrill reported to Neville that he would have to abandon Hill 142 unless Berry's 3/5th Marines came into position on the right. Unfortunately, Berry was unable to come up, but just at that moment, relief appeared: the French troops on the left finally arrived at their objectives, just after 1300.[15]

American accounts of the fight for Hill 142 were apt to blame the French for their slow advance on the left, which left the 1/5th Marines' left flank open and resulted in heavy casualties. No efforts were made to take into account either the strong resistance faced by the French or the Americans' impetuous advance. It was an early example of what would happen often when American and French units fought side by side: the Americans would surge ahead with speed, almost regardless of casualties, while the savvy, war-weary French, anxious to avoid useless casualties, would advance at a measured, cautious—some might say timid—pace. Later on, Americans would report that the French had been shelled by their own artillery that morning and that their attack consequently "fell apart," but there is no evidence of this.[16] German and French records show that the French attacked Veuilly-la-Poterie immediately and in force, but the Germans threw them out with counterattacks that inflicted heavy losses. Nevertheless, the French made steady progress in the center from Les Mares Farm over Hill 165 toward Bussiares. There, the German 273d Regiment hurled its only remaining reserve—a weak company—against the French, but it shattered against strong French opposition. The Germans then evacuated most of Veuilly-la-Poterie. The French arrival abreast of Hill 142 at about 1300 was roughly on schedule; unfortunately, the Americans had moved much too quickly. Fortunately for all, German artillery had been "particularly feeble" during the day, increasing in volume only after the morning's objectives had been met—bearing out Degoutte's belief that the attack had to be carried out before the enemy artillery could fully establish its presence.[17]

The battle for Hill 142 had been much bloodier than expected, with casualties amounting to roughly 90 percent of the 1/5th's officers and 50 percent of its men. In all, the 1/5th lost 8 officers and 325 men, including a few prisoners; the German 273d Regiment lost 13 officers and 405 men, including 273 captured. Despite the heavy casualties and a few missteps, the marines had performed magnificently in both attack and defense. Now, aside from fending off persistent German efforts to infiltrate the ravine to the west, Turrill's battalion could rest for a few hours. The primary scene of action had shifted to the east—in Belleau Wood.[18]

No one—not Bundy or Harbord, their staff and field officers, or the lowly army and marine privates—had any way of knowing the size or duration of the challenge facing them in Belleau Wood. Catlin, writing a year later, recalled that the "baleful" wood "loomed up before us like a heavy, menacing frown in the landscape." But on June 6 there was nothing to indicate—certainly not to Harbord, who did not anticipate strong resistance—that the woods would be difficult to take. Catlin continued:

> It was a typical piece of well kept French woodland, which the foresters had thinned and cared for so that the timber was of fairly uniform

size and the underbrush fairly well cleaned out inside. At the edges there was some undergrowth and smaller trees and saplings. The timber was not large but grew very thickly. The trees were rather tall. I should say that they would not average more than five or six inches in diameter, but they were set so closely that when our men got in they found they could not see more than fifteen or twenty feet through the wood, except where ax or shell fire had made small clearings. Belleau Wood stood on high, rocky ground and hid innumerable gullies and boulder heaps. We were nearer to the woods on the south than on the west, and on both sides open wheat fields lay between our lines and the forest. From without it appeared almost impenetrable, and there were those open spaces to cross. Behind us lay the smaller woods where our own reserves were waiting.[19]

The wood was roughly rectangular in shape—two kilometers north to south, and one kilometer east to west—with a chunk seemingly bitten out of its lower left side. To the south, the 3/6th and 2/6th Marines occupied a strip of woods below a road that ran from (American-held) Lucy-le-Bocage to the southwest and (German-held) Bouresches to the northeast. Sibley's 3/6th Marines on the left had a reasonably quick and partially covered avenue of approach from Lucy-le-Bocage into the southwestern tip of Belleau Wood. To Sibley's left, Berry's 3/5th Marines faced a considerably more daunting prospect. They had to traverse about a kilometer of open wheat fields on rolling terrain leading into the woods' western edge and toward its narrow "waist." German-held Hill 169 looked directly over their line of advance from the north. Enemy machine guns in the woods to Berry's front and right also enjoyed a clear field of fire. "There was," as Thomason succinctly put it, "no cover anywhere." The 3/5th had no choice but to push straight ahead through converging fire from three sides.[20]

Whether or not the Germans held the woods in strength, the complexity of the operation demanded careful planning and time. The marines got neither. Degoutte, Bundy, and Harbord were all raring to go. Accordingly, Degoutte ordered the 2d Division to capture Belleau Wood and the ridge to the northwest—connecting it to Hill 142—on the evening of June 6. Harbord issued Field Order 2, detailing the attack, at 1405. Phase one would begin at 1700, in conjunction with a French attack farther west. At that time, the 3/5th Marines (less 45th Company) would attack into the northern two-thirds of the woods, approaching Hill 133 on the left, at the woods' northern tip, and Hill 181 on the right, at the lower end of the woods' waist. On the right, the 3/6th Marines would drive from the southwest to capture the woods' southern portion below the waist, while the 2/6th provided flank protection on the right. Catlin would command this phase.

Phase two would follow immediately afterward. On the left, Turrill's 1/5th Marines plus a company from the 2/5th and Berry's 45th Company would surge northeast from the vicinity of Hill 142 to take the ridgeline between the hill and Belleau Wood. This would take Turrill's men from Hill 126 on the left to Hill 133 (exclusive) on the right, directly facing Torcy and the village of Belleau. In the center, the 3/5th would take Hill 133 on the left and push to the edge of the wood facing a railroad bridge north of Bouresches on the right. On the right, the 3/6th Marines would surge beyond the southeastern edge of Belleau Wood to take Bouresches and its railroad station, which was occupied by a reinforced company of German infantry. Catlin would continue to command Berry's and Sibley's men, while Lieutenant Colonel Logan Feland of the 5th Marines took responsibility for Turrill. Both phases would receive support from the 3/5th Battalion's 77th Machine Gun Company and limited support from the 2d Field Artillery Brigade.[21]

Though clear enough in conception, this plan took no account of the 1/5th's experiences that morning and little account of the realities on the ground. Once again, Harbord made no effort to correct the parade-ground tactics used that morning in favor of the "infiltration" he had agreed to the night before. And just as he had in the morning's attack, Harbord hoped to maintain the element of surprise by limiting preassault support from the 2d Field Artillery Brigade—a ludicrous concept, given that the Germans had already been alerted by the attack on Hill 142. In essence, the marines would be flung headlong across open ground against poorly reconnoitered positions with obvious advantages for the defense. Marines on the ground knew that the Germans held the opposite tree line in force—they had already experienced some of their fire firsthand. Catlin, for one, cringed at what Berry's 3/5th Marines were about to face. Harbord, though, remained oblivious, choosing to believe reports—which he later blamed on the French—that the woods were all but empty of the enemy.[22]

Although Harbord specifically put Catlin in command of phase one, Catlin did not receive his orders until 1545. That was when Harbord's aide, puttering along on his motorcycle, finally arrived, having taken about ninety minutes to cover the three kilometers separating Harbord's headquarters from Catlin's. Catlin summoned his battalion commanders to discuss the plans, but only Holcomb and Sibley arrived. Catlin later claimed that he tried to phone Berry, only to discover that the latter was off rambling in the woods about a mile away from his battalion. Runners sent to find Berry did not reach him until 1645. By this time, according to Catlin, Berry had already received his orders from 5th Marines headquarters, but the major acted as if he had not and made some flustered last-second dispositions. Berry chose to take Captain Peter Conachy's 45th Company with him instead of leaving it behind for Turrill, and he also ignored Harbord's order to place himself under Catlin's command. In any case, it was too late for Berry to seek out Catlin, who had elected to watch the attack from a hedge-covered knoll—probably Hill 200, just northwest of Lucy-le-Bocage. "I did not," Catlin recalled, "believe [Berry] could ever reach the woods."[23]

The German defenders, by contrast, were quite well prepared, despite the short time they had to dig in. Major Josef Bischoff, a veteran of the war in East Africa who had commanded a Turkish camel regiment in 1916, exercised overall command of the 1,169 men of the 237th Division's 461st Infantry Regiment in Belleau Wood. His troops were supported by some 200 machine guns (each manned by one NCO and six men) and plentiful trench mortars. With his local commander, Major Hans von Hartlieb, Bischoff had established three lines of defense in the woods. Each made maximum use of the terrain's advantages, which included "many rock formations with large boulders offering good cover and retreats for machine guns," and was protected by barbed wire. Contrary to the methods employed by some other German units, however, Bischoff and Hartlieb elected not to echelon in depth. Instead, they placed their main line of resistance at the woods' edge, buttressed by rifle pits and strongpoints with machine guns. At the woods' western edge they placed two heavy machine guns to cover the Torcy-Lucy road, over which Berry's men would have to attack. They positioned the bulk of their infantry reserves close to the main line of resistance. Believing that it was essential to maintain direct command control, Hartlieb—who would prove his physical bravery in the days that followed—generally commanded from no more than 200 meters behind the point where the action was hottest, and he demanded that his junior officers remain in firm and direct control of their units at all times.[24]

Artillery fired for about half an hour before the attack, "but there was no artillery preparation in the proper sense of the term," Catlin recalled. "They had no definite locations and were obliged to shell at random in a sort of hit-or-miss fire. It must have been largely miss." In fact, though, the shelling did have an impact on the Germans, who were not yet fully dug in and suffered badly from large-caliber shells that splintered trees. Had Harbord permitted more severe shelling along the woods' edge, the results for the defenders might have been catastrophic. The constant, close presence of their leaders helped the Germans withstand the bombardment. German counterfire was more effective, thanks in part to clear observation of marine concentrations from their observation balloons. Just before the Americans jumped off, shell fire caused them significant disorganization. It would get worse.[25]

At 1700 the attack began, with Catlin's battalions moving forward once again in dense waves, giving enemy machine guns and artillery clear targets. Sergeant Merwin Silverthorn of the 20th Company described their tactics:

> We started off in trench warfare formation, the only formation we knew, which consisted of four waves with the first wave and all waves holding their rifles at what is called high port, not even aiming or firing or hip firing or anything like that. And the first wave, consisting of riflemen and hand grenadiers that were supposed to throw hand grenades to protect the riflemen; the second wave consisting of rifle grenadiers, people who had rifle grenades and riflemen; and then the third wave duplicating the first wave, and the fourth wave duplicating the second wave—with 75 meters between the first wave and the second wave—and then actually the third and fourth waves are replacements for the first and second wave. . . . We moved towards Belleau Woods, which we could see at this high point, nobody firing a shot. Bayonets fixed, moving at a low steady cadence that we had been taught to move, because theoretically a barrage is shooting in front of you and you don't want to go too fast or you'll walk into your own barrage.

Of course, there was no need to worry about running into a rolling barrage, because none existed. The German defenders were stunned by the clumsiness of the American tactics, which compared unfavorably with those employed by adjoining French units that day:

> The Americans were obliged to come down from the heights they were occupying before the eyes of the Germans. They did this in thick lines of skirmishers, supported by columns following immediately behind. The Germans could not have desired better targets; such a spectacle was entirely unfamiliar to them. Under similar conditions, German troops would have advanced in thin lines of skirmishers following one another like waves, or in small, separate units of shock troops, moving forward in rows with their light machine guns, utilizing whatever shelter was offered by the terrain until they were in

a position to open fire. It was thus that the French had advanced the same day, through the grain fields, until they had crept close to the German defenders.

Berry's men entered a perfect storm of enemy fire as they moved downslope through the green wheat fields. "They had us enfiladed," recalled Sergeant Silverthorn. "They were to our left front; and as we got out far enough, we were perfectly enfiladed from them. So it was absolutely like a shooting gallery and not a single Marine of ours firing a shot. We weren't trained that way. We went on."[26]

War correspondent Floyd Gibbons of the *Chicago Tribune* accompanied Berry and later wrote that the attack was heralded by an "old gunnery sergeant" who leaped up and shouted, "Come on, you sons-o' bitches! Do you want to live forever?" True or false, Gibbons's colorful imagery—resented by soldiers as a product of the marines' publicity machine—gave an air of glory to what was in reality a pointless bloodbath. Most of the attackers had no chance. From left to right, the 45th, 20th, and 47th Companies were all hit hard as German machine guns tore into them from multiple directions. Some survived by virtue of instinct; a veteran marine in the 47th recalled "spreading out in the wheat and taking the old formations we had used so many times in the cane fields of Santo Domingo." On the left and in the center, the men in the first wave got nowhere, and those who survived turned back. So did the 16th Company, designated for support but hit by German artillery and machine guns as it attempted to move forward. Only on the right did one platoon of the 20th Company and some fragments of the 47th manage to veer right into the southwestern edge of the woods, where they joined the marines of the 3/6th.[27]

At 1810 Berry reported to Harbord, "What is left of battalion is in woods close by. Do not know whether will be able to stand or not." Berry next reported at 1922 that he had entered the woods to find his men and was gaining the impression that "his casualties are heavy." He was accompanied by a party of fifteen men, including Gibbons. Some distance within the woods, the group entered a "V-shaped oat field." Berry led the group across the field, but German machine guns opened up and pinned them down halfway across. Gibbons recalled:

> I was busily engaged flattening myself on the ground. Then I heard a shout in front of me. It came from Major Berry. I lifted my head cautiously and looked forward. The Major was making an effort to get to his feet. With his right hand he was savagely grasping his left wrist.

"My hand's gone," he shouted. One of the streams of lead from the left had found him. A ball had entered his left arm at the elbow, had travelled down the side of the bone, tearing away muscles and nerves of the forearm and lodging itself in the palm of his hand. His pain was excruciating.

Gibbons shouted, sensibly, for the major to get down, and Berry obeyed. The correspondent then tried to crawl to him through the oats. One bullet grazed Gibbons in the arm and another in the shoulder, but he kept crawling. Then he was hit a third time:

> Then there came a crash. It sounded to me like some one had dropped a glass bottle into a porcelain bathtub. A barrel of whitewash tipped over and it seemed that everything in the world turned white. That was the sensation. . . . I did not know yet where I had been hit or what the bullet had done. I knew that I was still knowing things. I did not know whether I was alive or dead but I did know that my mind was still working. . . . I did not know then, as I know now, that a bullet striking the ground immediately under my left cheek bone, had ricocheted upward, going completely through the left eye and then crashing out through my forehead, leaving the eyeball and upper eyelid completely halved, the lower eyelid torn away, and a compound fracture of the skull.

Berry jumped up and ran to shelter, while Gibbons waited until after dark before crawling to safety. Both were destined for long hospital stays.[28]

Sibley's 3/6th Battalion had it a little easier. On the left, the 82d and 83d Companies were supposed to advance into the woods, while on the right, the 84th and 97th Companies would be moving along the road from Lucy-le-Bocage toward Bouresches. The marines moved off silently in waves, "as if," said Catlin, "on parade." The 82d and 83d Companies were able to take advantage of orchards and small patches of woods that provided cover on their way toward Belleau Wood, but German machine guns still took a heavy toll. The 82d Company was entirely pinned down for a time, but the 83d managed to reach the tree line and pull the other company along with it. Inside, the marines broke into combat teams, wiping out some German machine gun and mortar nests and capturing unoccupied Hill 181. In this fashion they cleared the southwestern arm of Belleau Wood, advancing several hundred yards before halting in front of the German main line of resistance along a rocky slope that was "so securely placed that direct hits from heavy artillery would have been necessary to dislodge it." The disorganized marines had no chance of capturing this position. On the right, the 84th and 97th Companies had advanced steadily northeast along the road and a ditch that paralleled the woods' southern edge, but they were pinned down in the wheat fields in front of Bouresches.[29]

To Private Levi Hemrick, the ditch along the south edge of Belleau Wood was reminiscent "of the sunken road that played a part in the battle of Fredericksburg during the Confederate War. The sides of this ditch were lined with wounded men who had been shot down when they had charged up the wooded hill just a few yards at the other side of a narrow strip of growing wheat." There he encountered Major Sibley, furious at his men's inability to clear the rocky slope and at the casualties his battalion had incurred. For some reason, the major found it convenient to blame the French for the mess the marines found themselves in:

> We were greeted by a hatless, jacketless, well-built Major [Sibley] who had his sleeves rolled above his elbows. He was literally in a rage. He had been ordered to take the hill, presumably at the request of the French Command, who hadn't as yet left all our local movements in the control of our on the spot officers. This hill contained a large number of boulders with German machine gun barrels sticking out from their almost impregnable position. Such an attack, to be successful, required special preparation and munitions that had not been given the Major and he was "dam mad about it." . . . Thus, the enraged Major, popping his fist in the palm of his hand, walked up and down the gully, yelling his explosive language. . . . He was hard boiled, he was a man's man, and really did care for his men and their welfare. He was not putting on a make believe show. He was in his own words, "ordered to send men to hell," and he did not like it and wanted us to know it.[30]

By this point—about 2030—Catlin had long been hors de combat. He had chosen his position on the knoll north of Lucy-le-Bocage ostensibly to keep an eye on Berry, but in fact, the colonel kept his field glasses trained on Sibley. Nearby, some of Cole's machine guns maintained a steady barrage of cover fire, but the Germans responded in kind. Just as Sibley's men began entering the woods at 1737, a German bullet slammed into Catlin's chest, perforating his lung. Spinning around and slamming to the ground, he felt like he had been hit with a sledge. His entire right side went numb. Catlin's French liaison officer grabbed the American and dragged him to a nearby trench, where he would wait another ninety minutes before being evacuated.[31]

Holcomb's 2/6th was tasked with maintaining contact and moving forward in conjunction with Sibley, who was supposed to take Bouresches. But it didn't quite work out that way. The 96th Company, commanded by Captain Donald Duncan and followed by Captain Randolph T. Zane's 79th Company, moved up to the northern edge of the Bois de Triangle, which was bisected by La Cense Ravine, snaking 600 yards north toward Bouresches. Duncan "had on his best suit, [was] carrying a swagger stick, and [was] smoking a straight-stem pipe"; he was "the coolest man on the field, always giving orders and smiling all the time." The marines couldn't see Sibley from this spot and essentially "didn't know where we were going," but they advanced anyway after 1700 and immediately took heavy fire from Bouresches and the heights above the village. Duncan was hit, and a German shell soon finished him off, along with his stretcher bearers.[32]

Command devolved on First Lieutenant James F. Robertson as the marines went to ground, pinned down in the wheat field. After holding out for almost an hour, Robertson finally shouted, "Come on, let's go!" He formed his men into a skirmish line and drove them forward, firing as they advanced. There was no way back, so on they went, some moving through the partial shelter offered by the ravine. Just twenty-one men made it into the village, where they inflicted some losses on the withdrawing Germans of the 398th Regiment. That regiment's war diary contradicted American claims that they had advanced in an open skirmish line, but it agreed with the horrendous casualties inflicted:

> The enemy riflemen, who advanced in dense lines, were taken under an effective machine gun and infantry rifle fire. . . . The enemy, who again and again launched new masses, worked themselves closely against the southeast exit of Bouresches. . . . They succeeded in forcing their way into Bouresches with considerable forces by following a creek depression and slipping thru our barrage, the danger of a possibility of cutting off our weak outguard posts arose. Therefore, the 7th and 8th companies withdrew, as per order, into the main line of resistance along the railroad embankment.

The defending infantrymen had used up every bullet they possessed and would need an emergency resupply.[33]

With the majority of the 96th Company lying dead or wounded in the fields below Bouresches, Robertson put First Lieutenant Clifton B. Cates in charge of the village and left to seek reinforcements. Even though his uniform was soaking wet—a marine had unceremoniously poured a bottle of champagne on his head to revive him after a bullet hit his helmet and knocked him woozy—Cates methodically directed the elimination of enemy snipers and prepared to receive a counterattack. The remainder of the 79th Company and a company of engineers arrived to reinforce Cates that evening. The village would hold, although the marines never managed to snatch the railway station north of the village.[34]

Holcomb's success in Bouresches—which was not clearly reported until much later that evening—did not outweigh the American failures elsewhere. With Berry's attack broken down entirely and Sibley's stalled, Catlin's replacement, Lieutenant Colonel Harry Lee, declined to push the attack further. The reason for the halt seemed inconceivable at division and 4th Brigade headquarters, where rosy reports of the attack's progress had been filtering in all evening. Half an hour after the attack began, Harbord's adjutant, Major Harry Lay, told chief of staff Colonel Preston Brown that the "men went over the top in fine shape, proper deployment around the edges of the Bois de Belleau—and no casualties." At about the same time, Major Cole phoned Harbord to report that the "troops started out in beautiful deployment in beautiful line and entered into woods to the attack as far as he could see with absolutely no loss. . . . Things are going fine." As of 1910, the consensus at division and brigade headquarters was that the "attack went very well indeed, even beyond our most sanguine expectations. . . . Casualties have been light. . . . Messages come in to the effect that the artillery fire was most successful and delivered exactly at the right time." Word was that the marines had captured not only Bouresches but Torcy too. Delighted, Bundy went to the 12th Field Artillery headquarters to congratulate Colonel McCloskey.[35]

The truth filtered in only gradually. Berry's worried reports about his battalion either did not reach Harbord or did not impress him. At 2007 Harbord phoned Brown to say, "So far as I know, we have the station at Bouresches. We have the east edge of the Bois de Belleau." The only note of frustration was that the French troops supposedly tasked to take Triangle Woods below Bouresches on Holcomb's right had "met with machine-gun fire and gave it up." Reports from Turrill that the 1/5th had not been able to advance on the left because the French had not advanced on his left increased Harbord's irritation with his allies. But in fact, the French 167th Division had met all its objectives in the evening attack, despite taking heavy enemy artillery and machine gun fire. During the day it had advanced two kilometers and captured 290 enemy prisoners from the German 197th Division, along with a couple of machine guns. At 2015 Harbord learned that Sibley was not advancing as quickly as desired; half an hour later Sibley reported by phone that his casualties were "heavy" and his battalion was "unable to advance." Furious at these indications that the advance had stalled—and that Bouresches had not been captured—Harbord could not understand why Lee seemed unwilling to move his men forward and undertake phase two. The general therefore composed an angry message that he sent to Lee at 2055 via motorcycle courier. "I am not satisfied with the way you have conducted your engagement this afternoon," Harbord stated. "I want you to take charge and push this attack with vigor. Carry the attack through the woods from Hill 133, south along the Bouresches-Torcy Road and send Sibley to take Bouresches." The isolated machine gun nests that were reportedly holding up the attack were to be contained and bypassed.[36]

Harbord's berating of Lee indicated how far out of touch with reality the brigade commander was. Berry's battalion, in effect, no longer existed. Sibley's left-hand companies in the woods had taken serious casualties and were badly disorganized and thus incapable of moving forward. As for Bouresches, it had already been taken. A grossly misleading message at 2145 from Cole, who had just returned from visiting Sibley in the woods, reinforced Harbord's misperceptions. Sibley's "whole outfit," Cole reported, "was held up in the north [sic] edge of the wood by [a single] machine gun nest." Cole had obligingly gone to look at this single nest, which had supposedly held up two battalions, and learned that Sibley intended to encircle it. But the Americans were "at the north edge of the woods," Cole reiterated, with some wounded "but not as bad as it was this morning." Fragmentary reports arriving thereafter began to hint at the scale of the difficulties and the hopelessness of opening phase two. At 2150 5th Marines commander Colonel Neville reported to Harbord that when the attack began, Berry's battalion had "started to advance across the open square. The line advanced about half way across. Machine guns got busy. Larsen says he does not think many of them left." Berry—badly wounded but attempting to stay and do his duty—reported that only nine men remained out of three platoons of the 45th Company.[37]

Not until later that evening did Harbord begin to glimpse the truth, and he officially called off phase two and ordered the consolidation of whatever ground his brigade had managed to capture. That amounted to Hill 142, the southwestern portion of Belleau Wood, and Bouresches. In almost every respect, the day had been a disaster. The Marine Brigade had suffered 1,087 casualties—outnumbering all the battle casualties the marines had suffered in history before 1918, and second only to the first day of the Battle of Tarawa in 1943. The 1/5th Marines had been severely bloodied while capturing Hill 142, the 3/5th Marines had been all but wiped out, the 3/6th Marines had taken serious losses, and the 96th Company of the 2/6th Marines had been effectively destroyed. In his report for June 6, written on the morning of the following day, Harbord conceded that the 3/5th "appear[s] to have encountered machine-gun fire in crossing open country west of the north half of the Bois de Belleau and have suffered very severely." Overall, he admitted that his losses were "known to be heavy. . . . The brigade can hold its present position, but is not able to advance at present." He could not conclude, however, without chiding the French for failing to provide "satisfactory liaison" and blaming "French sources" for the inaccurate information he had received during the day.[38]

Despite their heavy losses, the Americans made a definite impression on their enemies. Although prisoners told the Germans that "the attack was made by a brigade, consisting of Americans, French, and English," the defenders knew the Americans had played the leading role. The war diary of the German 237th Division, which had begun the day defending territory from the eastern slopes of Hill 142 to eastern Belleau Wood (but not Bouresches), indicated that it had been hard-pressed. Although not losing any territory of note (the Germans claimed they retook most of Belleau Wood in a counterattack and captured a number of American prisoners), the division commander had been forced to dispatch scarce reserves to hold the front. As for Bouresches, the German 10th Division did not consider it much of a loss. Only a company had been posted to hold the village because, according to orders issued on June 3, "being located in a hollow, [it] possesses no vital importance for the defense." Under attack, the company had followed orders—inflicting maximum casualties and then withdrawing to the main line of defense along the railroad embankment to the north. German machine guns overlooking the village from the northeast would pour fire into it for many days to come. What the Germans failed to consider, and what the marines did not yet realize, was that from Bouresches, American machine guns had a clear field of fire into the eastern boundaries of Belleau Wood and could break up any attempts to reinforce that sector from the east during the day. This would play an important role in the attack of June 11.[39]

In Belleau Wood, Major Bischoff—a dedicated military man with an analytical mind but not always accurate information about his enemies—meditated on the quality of the marines' performance in his report on the day's events. The Americans "demonstrated skill," he mused, "especially in advantageous use of cover":

It may be that the 6th Regiment, coming from Virginia, had drafted reinforcements that were naturally adapted to this method of combat. But here too, our infantry was superior to the enemy. The counterattacks were always successful, but they had to be carried out with hand grenades, for it was impossible to dislodge the enemy from their positions merely by shooting at them with rifles. They displayed unusual calmness and self-assurance while firing from under their covers. They did not know how to utilize advantages once gained. . . . The human material is physically well developed, the average man fights stubbornly and with valour, possesses a natural resourcefulness and is well adapted for Guerrilla warfare whereby an excellent training in the handling and firing of the rifle gives him a decided advantage. The tactical training of the men could be classified as inferior, junior commanders as well as some of the higher leaders failed in critical moments. In several instances hostile artillery ceased while the infantry was in the act of carrying the attack forward; this gave the impression of insufficient cooperation between the artillery and the infantry.

Hartlieb was somewhat less complimentary about his opponents' tactics. Far from achieving surprise, the Americans' desultory artillery and machine gun barrages had alerted the defenders. The marines then attacked "in a mob," the major later reported. They did not use their rifles effectively, and when flanked, they withdrew in dense masses and ran for their lines, suffering heavy losses in the process. In the woods, American officers gave commands in loud voices, "and several men—in the nature of amateurs—clumsily left cover and showed themselves."[40]

The best that could be said of the tactics employed by the marines that day was that they improved once they left the wheat fields and entered the woods. Although they continued to show their inexperience, as Bischoff and Hartlieb pointed out, the necessity of improvising on the spot put them in their element. And while the marines' almost fanatical aggressiveness cost them casualties as they outran the French—who met their objectives against heavy resistance but with far fewer casualties—their boldness had tremendous shock value in the woods on Hill 142 and in the southwestern portion of Belleau Wood. These two qualities of adaptability and courage would serve them well over the following weeks.

Contrary to the popular impression, the marines were not the only Americans to go into action on June 6. Southeast of Bouresches and Triangle

Wood, the 1st and 3d Battalions of the 23d Infantry, commanded by Colonel Paul B. Malone, had orders to protect the marines' flank by advancing a short distance from Triangle village and the edge of the Bois des Clerembauts toward the Bouresches-Vaux road. Like the marines, their advance lay almost entirely over open ground, and while they protected the marines' flank, their own right flank would be exposed to enemy fire from Vaux and Hill 204. The soldiers were not supposed to move, however, until the advance of the 3/6th and 2/6th Marines on the left clearly made it advisable to do so "where necessary to prevent a reentrant angle in the line near Triangle Farm."[41]

Opposing them were elements of two regiments of the German 10th Division. The 398th Regiment defended territory from Bouresches to a road fork north of Hill 192, where the 47th Regiment held the ground east to Vaux. Fortunately for Malone, the once-proud 10th Division was a basket case. Battalions were at company strength, and some companies consisted of only a few dozen men and no officers. Speaking of his men, the 398th Regiment's commander reported on June 4 that "their nerves are run down to such an extent as to make it impossible for them to withstand another prolonged and severe artillery bombardment." The 47th Regiment's commander reported on the same day that "the eagerness to attack, with which the troops were originally imbued, has given way to a certain indifference and apathy." Both regiments lacked adequate teams to man their machine guns. But their guns were well sited, and despite their exhaustion, the men remained willing to fight.[42]

Though short of stature, Malone was as eager to fight as any marine. After the war he would write a series of juvenile books about a West Point cadet, and in 1940 he expanded the series into a fictional account, titled *Barbed Wire Entanglements*, of his hero's command of a regiment in World War I. He may have been storing away ideas for his later work as he watched the marines advancing toward Belleau Wood at 1700 on June 6. They advanced "in splendid order," Malone told Bundy in a bald-faced attempt at flattery that evening. "The spectacle was inspiring." Malone's orders were to wait until the advance of the marines dictated his own advance, at which time the 1/23d on the left, under Major Edmund C. Waddill, and the 3/23d on the right, under Major Charles B. Elliott, would move forward only "slightly" to a "very limited objective" marked on a map by Malone—no more than half a kilometer, and not including Hill 192 on the right.[43]

What happened next would provoke a controversy that lasted beyond the war. After explaining—clearly, he thought—the orders to Waddill and Elliott, Malone left for brigade headquarters in response to what he interpreted as an "urgent" summons. Because the marines on Waddill's immediate left did not move, neither did the 1/23d. The 3/23d, however, advanced at 1715, making it necessary for Waddill's battalion to move forward at 1900 to protect Elliott's flank. According to Malone, this was a breach of orders, but Elliott later claimed that Malone had given him "peremptory" orders: "you attack at 5:00 p.m.," specifically designating his objective as Hill 192. The 3d Brigade commander, Brigadier General Edward M. Lewis, also implicated Malone, reporting that when the colonel saw the "splendid" advance of the marines—presumably, the 96th Company attacking Bouresches, although this company was not on Malone's immediate left—he ordered his own troops to advance. The colonel then went to brigade headquarters, where Lewis pointed out that "the brigade order did not contemplate his advance until it was necessary to do so to prevent a reentrant angle." Lewis then ordered the advance to halt, but by that time, it was too late—both battalions were already engaged with the enemy.[44]

Whoever was to blame, the consequences were disastrous. As they advanced impetuously toward Hill 192—without artillery support—the leading K and M Companies were exposed to devastating machine gun and artillery fire from three directions. The "excellently located" German guns "inflicted heavy losses on the ranks of the enemy who partly advanced in march columns," and many of them "streamed back in confusion," exulted the 47th Regiment's war diary. Elliott's soldiers, reported Malone, "either did not recognize their objective or were carried by enthusiasm and by the desire for combat far beyond it, to a position which could not possibly be sustained in view of the position occupied by the rest of the division." Incredibly, though, the two companies managed to take the hill and a small sector of the woods to the northeast, pushing back portions of a German company that feared it was about to be outflanked. The Americans tried to hold on for some time, despite the fact that both their flanks were in the air. Elliott desperately called for aid, and after 1900 the 1/23d came forward on his left, while the 9th Regiment and the French made some small advances further but not immediately to his right. This move did the two companies on Hill 192 little good, as they continued to take heavy fire and grievous casualties. A runner arrived at Elliott's command post at 2055 with a message from a lieutenant near Hill 192, who complained that "my objective [was] never definitely given me." He reported that his troops were being fired on by their own machine guns—which were probably German guns filtering in to their rear. "Rush us assistance," Elliott begged Malone at the same time, adding that the commander of Company K "just reports he can't find a soul." Malone responded by ordering Elliott to withdraw to his original positions and "restore the situation," but once again, it was a case of too little too late.[45]

American accounts present what happened next as a withdrawal. German records describe it as a rout with an especially harrowing aftermath. After dark, the firing around Hill 192 increased. Officers struggled to make sense of confused reports on the status of Elliott's companies. At 2225 Lewis phoned division headquarters to report that the Germans had attacked Elliott's right and broken through, forcing Lewis to call up two companies from the brigade reserve to plug the gap. But at 2300 the general phoned again to say that the report was false and had been spread by some mixed-up engineers. Malone told Bundy after the encounter that reports of the two companies being broken were "grossly exaggerated," and they had withdrawn according to orders.[46]

According to the 47th Regiment's war diary, however, after dark the Germans brought up a number of machine guns that opened a converging fire on the Americans from concealed positions. Infantry then hit the Americans in the right and rear, forcing many to flee west, where they were captured by the 398th Regiment. Lieutenant Glückert, the wounded commander of the German 4th Company, summoned the few doughboys holding on to Hill 192 to surrender, but they took him prisoner instead. German infantry then surged over the hill and wiped out what remained of Elliott's two companies. Afterward, said the 47th's war diary, "numerous killed and wounded Americans, some of whom begged for water in the German language, covered the field in front of our lines." They would remain there for days. On June 8 the 398th Regiment's war diary recorded that the Germans sent out stretcher parties to recover those wounded Americans who were still alive, but they had to withdraw when Malone's machine guns opened fire on them.[47]

Both companies were wiped out. Malone admitted to losing the "entire personnel" of Company M and most of Company K, against which he noted the capture of "one German officer" with "some very valuable papers." German records admitted to only four killed and thirty wounded in the 47th Regiment and twenty wounded in the 398th, not counting casualties from enemy artillery. Malone, who successfully avoided disciplinary action for his role in this fiasco, chalked it up as an important learning experience for his green troops. "It is highly undesirable to check the fine spirit of fight in the troops," he told Bundy. "Experience will instill caution rapidly enough." For Corporal Frank L. Faulkner of the 23d Regiment's Company B, however, this was a case of soldiers sacrificing their lives for marines who received all the publicity. The soldiers were "pretty sore," recalled Faulkner after the war. In accounts of Belleau Wood:

Only the marines are mentioned, never the less the 9th and 23rd were there and they did just as deserving work for they were sacrificed that the Marines might win their objective. I was on a point of a hill [on June 6] where I could see both the Marines and the "Doughboys" and if there was any difference the Marines had the best protection and they had an artillery barrage. We had neither, the 9th and 23rd advanced about 300 yds across an absolutely open field and without a barrage except the hot one that the Germans put over against them, they drove the Germans out of the woods before them only to find that it was not the purpose of the command to hold the position so costly gained, it was merely that the Marines could gain theirs.[48]

At the end of the day on June 6, Degoutte conceded that the 2d Division's attack had failed. He ordered that the line be held to prepare for defense in anticipation of the likely German counterattacks the next day. The American 4th and 3d Brigades had made little progress, although east of the 23d Regiment, the 2/9th had pushed as far as a stream running east from Bourbelin in support of the French 10th Colonial Division, which had managed to get a toehold on the lower slopes of Hill 204. The French 167th Division on the left had also met its objectives, seizing most of Veuilly-la-Poterie and pushing methodically toward Clignon Creek. Indeed, the staying power of this formation would be remarkable, as it would remain fighting in the line until well into July. The operations of both French divisions would stand in stark contrast to those of the Americans over the following weeks.[49]

There was no reason why June 6 had to turn out as it did. Although Degoutte had ordered—with the Americans' enthusiastic endorsement—an immediate attack that morning, the timing of the afternoon assault on Belleau Wood was left to Bundy's discretion, and there was no reason to do so right away. Given time, Bundy and Harbord might have evaluated the lessons of the bloody assault on Hill 142 and adapted their tactics accordingly. Artillery might have been employed, and the effect likely would have been devastating if the barrage had been directed on the crowded and insufficiently entrenched German positions along the woods' edge. With patience, the 2d Division might have been eased into battle, gained potency with experience, and captured Belleau Wood just as quickly as it actually did. Instead, Bundy, Harbord, and, to a lesser degree, Lewis treated their men like so much cannon fodder. Why they did so will probably always remain something of a mystery. The absence of artillery support, as Grotelueschen has pointed out, "appears to have been intentional, a product of the official AEF doctrine that minimized its importance and exaggerated the capabilities of a 'self-reliant infantry.'" The clumsy infantry tactics employed, despite the divisional chief of staff's recommendation of an advance by infiltration, seem to have been the product of haste, carelessness, and lack of direction at the brigade and division level, rather than the conscious application of any specific military doctrine. In the absence of clear planning or oversight, regimental and battalion commanders formed up their men and sent them forward in waves and by the book; however, company and platoon officers and NCOs quickly abandoned these prescriptions—albeit after taking heavy casualties—in favor of a more freewheeling style as they entered the woods. Although the Marine Brigade was severely bloodied, German losses were light to moderate. Of the two main divisions facing the Americans, the German 237th Division lost 78 killed, 228 wounded, and 95 missing, and the 10th Division lost 24 killed, 101 wounded, and 26 missing. The two divisions also captured 47 American prisoners. At this pace, the Americans would grind themselves into powder before producing any tangible effects on the enemy.[50]

7

"Sporting Soldiers"
Belleau Wood, June 7–8, 1918

For the Americans, June 7 was a day of licking wounds, taking stock, and making plans for the morrow. No German attacks took place during the night, except for cleanup operations around Hill 192. German artillery pounded the American positions, though, and at 0400 German infantry attacked from Torcy east of Hill 142. Wise's 2/5th Marines, which had moved up to relieve the remnants of Berry's 3/5th and had suffered heavily from German machine guns in the process, beat back the attack and later pushed on to expand their grip on the woods adjacent to Hill 142. Farther down the line to the east, the 2/23d replaced Elliott's battered 3/23d at La Thiolet that evening, after supplying the latter with hot food and coffee on Malone's orders. Late-night German probing assaults against the 3/6th Marines and the 23d and 9th Regiments were also repulsed.[1]

The Americans expected and intended to continue their attacks, despite the horrendous losses of the previous day. In orders issued at 2020, Degoutte nevertheless instructed the 2d Division to proceed more cautiously, making "every effort to reach the Clignon River between Lucy-Clignon and Bouresches. In view of the strength of the hostile points of support in that area, this advance will be conducted methodically, by means of successive minor operations, making the utmost use of artillery and reducing the employment of infantry to the minimum necessary." The prescription for the advance to be "conducted methodically" seems pointed, although it would do little good. As he made plans, Harbord was still receiving intelligence that led him to believe that German resistance would be minimal. At 0800 that morning, a French aerial observer flew low over Belleau Wood. Some machine guns fired at the plane from the north edge of the woods, but the observer determined that Bouresches was quiet and the village of Belleau empty. A four-horse wagon that he took to be American trundled peacefully on a road leading to Torcy. Digesting this and other aerial reports, the captain in charge of the air units attached to the 2d Division opined that it was "possible" that the enemy present in Belleau Wood was "merely an isolated party and that the remainder of the enemy immediately in rear of this point have been driven back." At 1500 Harbord told Bundy he thought there were "18 machine guns and some infantry in the wood."[2]

While Harbord rotated fresh units into the line and pondered how he would take Belleau Wood, the Germans received a first-class mauling at the hands of the French. Early on the morning of June 7 the German 197th Division encountered "densely massed enemy attacks" by French forces to the west of the Americans between Vinly and Veuilly-la-Poterie. The French—elements of the 73d and 167th Divisions—conducted their assault with vigor and efficiency. A heavy preparatory barrage caught Germans in the middle of a relief, with devastating effect. French infantry followed quickly on the barrage at 0410, closed with the Germans in furious hand-to-hand fighting, captured the remainder of Veuilly-la-Poterie, and hustled the enemy eastward as far as Heloup in a series of enveloping attacks. These attacks bent back the Germans' line on the right, threatening Hautevesnes and significantly reducing the pressure on the marines defending Hill 142. German counterattacks against the French failed utterly as their reserves of ammunition—and morale—disappeared. The 197th was a total loss. "All three regiments had suffered severely and were no longer capable of fighting," indicated the division's war diary. "After using up all of its reserves the division had nothing left with which to oppose a renewed enemy attack." That night it would be relieved in the territory between Heloup and Hill 142 by the German 5th Guards Division, which was tasked "to prevent any further hostile advance by way of Hautevesnes and to force him [the enemy] back over the Clignon creek by attacking him in the flank from Bussiares"— in other words, to concern itself solely with the French, even though it also faced the marines at Hill 142.[3]

East of the positions now being assumed by the 5th Guards, the German 237th Division had defended Hill 142 through Belleau Wood to the Bouresches railway station, where it joined the 10th Division. By new dispositions effected on June 7–8, in the teeth of the American drive, the 237th Division shortened its front. Incredibly—and despite the lessons that should have been learned on June 6, when the boundary between the 197th and

237th Divisions bisecting Hill 142 had created problems for the Germans—Von Conta decided to establish a new divisional boundary in Belleau Wood.

Major Bischoff's 461st Regiment—confident, well reinforced, and amply supplied with well-sited heavy and light machine guns—had successfully defended the whole of Belleau Wood on June 6–7. Now, on the evening of June 7–8, Bischoff was ordered to pull back his left and make room for the 40th Fusilier Regiment of the 28th Division, which was moving into line to replace the weary 10th Division. Bischoff's front now ran from just east of Torcy on the right, through the north and west faces of Belleau Wood to around Hill 181. There, the 461st joined with the 40th Fusilier Regiment, which deployed its second battalion in the southern and central portions of the woods facing the 3/6th Marines, and its third battalion at the railway station above Bouresches. From there, the 28th Division's 109th Grenadier Regiment defended the railway embankment and high ground stretching to the southeast, facing the 23d and 9th US Regiments. Farther east, the 231st Division defended Hill 204 and Château-Thierry.

This new deployment was undertaken at the behest of the 28th Division commander, General Gustav Böhm, who had taken over on June 4. He, unlike Bischoff, preferred to deploy in depth rather than pack the front line; he also expected the axis of any renewed American attack on the woods to take place from Bouresches in an attempt to outflank the German positions. This assumption made it appear more reasonable to deploy elements of the 40th Fusiliers farther back in the central, northern, and eastern portions of the woods rather than crowding the woods' southern rim. His divisional relief orders on June 7 specified:

> The 40th and 109th Infantry Regiments will distribute their light and heavy machine guns in checkerboard formation. . . . The 40th Infantry Regiment will, in addition, be charged with the task of covering with enfilading fire the south edge of the Bois de Belleau. M.G.'s will be placed around Belleau in a semi-circle and distributed in depth. The 109th Regiment will provide the flanking of the south edge of Bouresches and the wooded areas southwest of this village. . . . The regiments will be strongly distributed in depth, men will avoid concentrations at certain points, special care will be taken to avoid a strong occupation of the railroad embankment [to avoid heavy casualties from enemy mortars and artillery].

Contact between the 40th and 461st would be maintained only by means of patrols. Böhm considered this arrangement "absolutely dependable."[4]

Both Lieutenant General Von Jacobi, commanding the 237th Division, and Bischoff protested their new neighbor's deployment in Belleau Wood. They did so not just because of the new divisional boundary running through the woods above Hill 181 but also because the 40th Regiment was disregarding previous, effective defensive dispositions in the woods' southern rim. The 461st Regiment had held that portion of the woods with six infantry companies with reserves and six heavy machine guns in close support. Bischoff had also placed four heavy machine guns to pour a constant stream of lead into Bouresches. The 40th, by contrast, placed only two companies and two heavy machine guns in or near the front line, with reserves far to the rear in the northern woods and above the railway embankment. In all, the newly arriving regiment would occupy three lines in the western-southern, central, and eastern portions of the woods.

During the relief, Jacobi warned a staff officer of the 28th Division "of the danger of a weaker occupation, because in such a densely wooded terrain, once the enemy broke thru, it would only be possible to expel him thru counter-attacks provided the assault troops were held closely behind the front lines." The staff officer brushed off the warning, so Jacobi "ordered that the 461st Infantry Regiment organize a switch position with its remaining weak forces in the direction of the 28th Infantry Division." This was a poor remedy, and Jacobi knew it. Had the 237th been left in control of the woods, he later complained to Von Conta, Bischoff could have beaten back all attacks. For his part, Bischoff thought his neighbor's dispositions were slipshod in general; he strenuously sought the 40th Regiment's commander, hoping to point out the error of his ways, but that individual stayed incognito until the new deployment was complete. Major General Georg Pohlmann, commanding the 244th Brigade of which Bischoff's regiment was a part, found and confronted a captain of the 40th Regiment, but the latter rebuffed him in a speech that ended with a recitation of "the achievements of the 28th Infantry Division." Further protests at brigade, division, and corps levels were likewise unavailing.[5]

The impact of the German shift, which was not completed until the evening of June 8, would not be immediately apparent. The 40th Fusiliers and 109th Grenadiers were relatively fresh regiments, vigorously led and with a strong divisional esprit de corps. The 28th Division, formed in Baden, had seen all the western front's major battles, including the Somme and Verdun; although it retained only a smattering of old hands, its officers were well seasoned and tough. Exhorting his troops as they entered the line on June 8, General Böhm said, "We do not belong to any sort of unit at random but . . . we belong to a division that enjoys a special reputation in this Army and of whom may be expected unusual accomplishments even after particularly critical days." Over the following weeks, the Americans would come to respect the Badeners as formidable adversaries. But just like any army, the German Imperial Army had its share of jealousies and rivalries. In Belleau Wood it swiftly became apparent that the 461st Regiment (237th Division) and 40th Fusiliers (28th Division) despised each other and worked together only reluctantly. In the days to come, each regiment's officers would blame their neighbors when things went wrong. Given experience and a chance to employ their instinctive individual initiative to its fullest potential, the Americans would exploit this German weakness—albeit unwittingly—to achieve victory.[6]

While the 2d Division underwent its trial in and around Belleau Wood, farther east the 3d Division's 30th Regiment participated in attacks by the French 10th Colonial Division (French XXXVIII Corps) on Hill 204. The Germans had captured this important piece of terrain during their drive on Château-Thierry at the end of May. Standing just east of the boundary between the US 2d Division and the French 10th Colonial Division, Hill 204 dominated both Château-Thierry to the east and the positions of the US 23d and 9th Regiments around Hill 192 to the west. Indeed, the destruction of the two American companies at Hill 192 on the evening of June 6 had resulted in part from German fire directed from the western slopes of Hill 204. The hill thus formed an anchor in Corps Conta's line of defense and would have to be taken to ensure the viability of future offensive operations.

Roughly pear shaped, with its base to the south, Hill 204 had wide-open slopes and a wooded crest. And it was steep. To Lieutenant Bob Hoffman of the US 28th Division's 111th Regiment, which would later see action there, the hill seemed like a "young Alps." The southern tree line was partially bisected by a small clearing. To the southwest, the hill was bordered by the village of Monneaux, and the village of Vaux was nestled at the base of its northwestern slope. From Vaux, a road ran west in front of positions held by the US 9th Regiment and through their lines to the American-held village of La Thiolet. On June 5–6 the 9th Regiment had advanced its right sector to positions just southwest of Vaux, while the French, assisted by a pioneer platoon of the 30th Regiment's headquarters company, captured Monneaux and began infiltrating up the southern slopes of Hill 204.[7]

The tactics employed by the French against Hill 204 contrasted starkly with the set-piece attacks conducted by the marines against Hill 142 and

Belleau Wood farther west. Indeed, the Germans did not even realize they were under attack until a ration-carrying party ambling over the top of Hill 204 at dawn on June 7 surprised and captured two American soldiers. Nearby, and at about the same time, a routine relief of the German 2/442d Battalion stumbled upon French and American troops who had worked their way uphill overnight and established positions in the woods along the wedge-shaped clearing on the southern crest. The Germans immediately attacked, only to bog down in thick underbrush swept by well-sited French and American machine guns. After a popular German lieutenant fell mortally wounded before the defenders' guns, demoralizing his men, the Germans withdrew, still uncertain what they were facing—a full but patiently deployed assault, or just a patrol?

That afternoon, reinforcements of French and American troops, including E and F Companies of the 30th Regiment, infiltrated further into the woods and along a ravine on the west side of Hill 204 between Monneaux and Vaux. Instead of rushing forward impetuously, they advanced short distances and then dug in, anticipating German counterattacks. That afternoon, German artillery bombarded suspected enemy positions; French artillery replied in kind. One of the two Americans captured that morning confessed at 2110 that about thirty of his comrades had entered the southeastern edge of the woods, unbeknownst to the Germans. Utilizing this knowledge, infantry of the 3/442d Battalion crawled through thick underbrush toward the woods at 2200, edging the clearing under cover of another artillery barrage, which was largely inaccurate. They found the French and Americans alert and waiting for them. Machine guns once again took a heavy toll on the attackers, who tried but failed to outflank the defenders. Those Germans who did not withdraw quickly enough fell "into the hands of Americans who speak German." At the cost of almost no casualties of their own, the French and American infantry, working together, had made "decided gains" against an enemy strongpoint and inflicted stinging defeats on enemy counterattacks.[8]

The effectiveness of the ongoing conquest of Hill 204 reflected the high quality of the French 10th Colonial Division's officers and proved the advantages of an arrangement that allowed the Americans to learn under their tutelage (although General Dickman and his staff would hardly credit the French for the learning experience). At Belleau Wood, Degoutte and Harbord impatiently flung the marines into headlong attacks against prepared enemy positions, even though the tactical situation did not demand undue haste. At Hill 204, by contrast, officers of the 10th Colonial Division successfully wed American bravery and individual initiative to their own greater experience and sense of caution. Counseling patience, French officers directed a step-by-step assault by infiltration that might have worked with equal effectiveness against Belleau Wood—despite the differences in topography—and, ironically, with quicker results. A more cautious approach certainly would have saved the lives of more than a few marines.

June 8 witnessed a renewal of the struggle for Belleau Wood. The Germans reopened the contest just after midnight with artillery barrages followed by a series of small probing attacks against the 9th Regiment's left, the 23d Regiment's front, and positions held by the 2/6th Marines around Triangle and Bouresches. These were all repulsed, with few casualties on either side. Marine and US Army forces then tried to follow up with attacks of their own; these were similarly repulsed but "with heavy losses," thanks in part to "opportune artillery support."[9]

At daylight, Sibley's 3/6th attacked in force, following a mortar barrage on German emplacements on and around the rocky ridge in the southeast corner of the woods. This time, the marines advanced in skirmish lines, with the 83d Company on the left, the 82d Company on the right, and elements of the 80th Company and some engineers in support. Holcomb's 2/6th at and around Bouresches fired on the woods in support. Early reports to brigade headquarters were mixed. Sibley, after interrogating some wounded marines who had filtered back to his command post, phoned his regimental commander early on to report that the enemy was "mowing our men down pretty fast," but "good progress" was being made in spots. Neville, in turn, contacted Harbord at 0610 to say that "Sibley's advance has been checked at points and they are finding many more M.G.'s [machine guns] than expected." Fifteen minutes later, Harbord phoned Bundy to say that the attack was going "very well," despite some troublesome machine guns; "we think it will be all right," he reported. From his post in Bouresches, Captain Randolph T. Zane of the 2/6th phoned the brigade at 0658 to report that the attack seemed to be making good progress. The marines were still in fine fettle, at least, since the captain had distinctly heard someone in the woods shout, "Get that Son of a Bitch!"[10]

In fact, Sibley's men had made little progress. Pushing forward about 200 meters, they discovered that the mortar barrage had had no impact whatsoever on the now well-entrenched German positions. The marines pressed on regardless and managed to take some machine guns from the German 461st Regiment, which had not yet been relieved by the 40th Fusiliers in this part of the woods. They managed to take out three machine gun nests, but for each one silenced, two more seemed to open up a converging fire on them. The attack had bogged down by 0800; at 1027 Sibley finally reported:

> They are too strong for us. Soon as we take one M.G., the losses are so heavy. . . . All the officers of the 82d Co. wounded or missing. . . . These machine guns are too strong for our infantry. . . . We did not take the hill, but did take some of the guns on it. There are three hills, they went up and surrounded the one hill and we went up and have taken some of the guns on the second.[11]

In short, the morning's results had been disastrous for the Americans. "The enemy was thrown back by our infantry in bitter hand-to-hand clashes, even grenade and bayonet charges," noted the 237th Division's war diary; the Americans managed to penetrate the 461st Regiment's left but were "enfiladed" by German machine guns and left "large clusters" of dead behind. It got worse. As Sibley's troops withdrew under orders but in haste and confusion, the marines lost cohesion and became easy prey for an alert enemy. Swooping in to take advantage of Sibley's "hasty withdrawal," the Germans "inflicted still heavier casualties" that included as many as forty prisoners. The Germans lost 51 killed, 136 wounded, and 2 missing.[12]

Resigning himself to the fact that the German positions could not simply be taken by storm, Harbord ordered Sibley at 1230 to pull out of the woods entirely and shelter in the ravine to the south. "Let your men rest," he advised, while artillery—which he had come to appreciate the value of, but too late—pounded the woods. Sibley responded at 1355 that he would complete the operation by 1500, adding (just in case Harbord had any second thoughts), "officers and men too much exhausted for further attack on strong resistance until after several hours rest." The marines pulled out, and American and French artillery opened up. That night Sibley's shattered 3/6th was relieved by the 1/6th Marines under Major John Hughes, which moved up from reserve. Meanwhile, the severely wounded Major Berry relinquished command of what remained of the 3/5th to Major Maurice Shearer.[13]

Contemplating his rapidly withering command, Harbord took time out that evening to vent some of his frustration on his regimental, battalion, and company commanders. Sloppy field reports had been submitted that did not indicate the time of dispatch or specify map coordinates for unit positions. They also abounded with vague phrases such as "losses are heavy." In combat, officers had failed to maintain firm control of their units and had wasted reserve assets. "Dispersion of troops," Harbord lectured, "is the fault of beginners . . . and has in our brigade, with the length of our line, deprived us of the necessary echelons in depth." Moreover, "Officers given a task must plan to execute it with forces at their own command, and not count on reinforcements which may not be available. Only a grave emergency not apparent when the task is begun will justify requests for help. Supports have been thrown in during this first week at a rate not to be expected thereafter." Harbord then moved on to the grievously heavy casualties—both officers and men—his marines had suffered. In explaining them, he accepted no blame but sought silver linings in his officers' bravery and their men's fearsome reputation with the enemy. "The heavy losses of officers compared to those among the men," he stated, "are most eloquent as to the gallantry of our officers, and correspond nearly to the proportions suffered by both the Allies and the enemy in 1914–15"—the latter being an ironic compliment, if it was intended as such. But, he continued, "Officers of experience are a most valuable asset and must not be wasted." As for the casualties suffered by the men, Harbord chose not to credit the enemy's bravery but to cite the Germans' fear of being given no quarter. "The enemy have been told that Americans do not take prisoners," he speculated, "which makes their men fight to the death rather than surrender when they think they will be given no quarter. This idea that we do not take prisoners undoubtedly costs us many lives."[14]

Whether Harbord took note of the effectiveness of Franco-American operations on Hill 204, a short distance to the east, is impossible to say for certain. There, French and American troops continued to inch forward cautiously through the woods on the hill's crest, while intrepid patrols from the US 30th Regiment's Company E managed to penetrate Vaux. As intended, these advances drew counterattacks from the German 231st Division, all of which collapsed in bloody futility. At only a small cost to themselves, the French and Americans were progressively gaining ground and wearing down the enemy. The 231st Division's war diary reported in frustration that the enemy had resisted counterattacks "stubbornly. He had been underestimated, had many machine guns and probably had also received reinforcements during the night." The encroachment on Hill 204 also sucked in German reserves as the 231st Division prepared to renew its assaults over the following days.[15]

Rather than modeling a new approach to Belleau Wood on the tactics being employed by the French on Hill 204, Harbord prescribed more artillery (which was some concession, at least) and more men. He had begun to envisage a "set piece" rather than a helter-skelter attack and thus "was going to rely on the trench-warfare methods the division spent so much of its training period learning," but he undertook no serious reappraisal of infantry tactics. Despite all the evidence of the past two days, division and brigade generals and staff continued to underestimate German powers of resistance. A division intelligence report prepared on the afternoon of June 8 concluded that the Germans were arrayed for offense, not defense. "Further [German] counterattacks or an offensive presumably planned," the intelligence officer reported. "From statements of prisoners, there is apparently little work being done to entrench the present enemy positions nor do the aeroplane photographs indicate more than machine-gun emplacements and shallow trenches in certain localities." Such intelligence encouraged Harbord—despite conflicting reports that the Germans held the woods in strength and were well dug in—to imagine that a strong and prolonged artillery bombardment of the sort he had eschewed before Sibley's failed June 8 attack would suffice to wipe out the Germans. "At dawn tomorrow morning," he informed Neville at 2145, "an artillery preparation will begin on the Bois de Belleau which by the late afternoon is expected to obliterate any enemy organizations in that wood."[16]

For their part, the Germans did not yet take the Americans very seriously. On June 8 a war correspondent boasted:

> The enemy has been bleeding himself to death with wild counterattacks [resulting in] ghastly losses. . . . Sportsman like, as if participating in a track meet, they came on a run, in three consecutive rows, crowding elbow to elbow with entire body exposed above the undergrowth. . . . In long rows and in places rolled in heaps lay the dead Americans in front of Belleau Woods. [American prisoners] are erect fellows, very unmilitary, and happy to be out of an affair, the purpose of which, they do not understand. From the distance they view the war as a sporting event—but up close it seemed very unsympathetic as they have learned that valor alone avails nothing and that experience must also be had. "They have much to learn, even more than the British had to learn in their days, before they become fullfledged warriors, [said an officer returning from the front]. At the present time they are Sporting soldiers. And this will prove very expensive."[17]

General Böhm, commanding the 28th Division, shared this assessment. While moving into Belleau Wood on the afternoon and evening of June 8, he saw "no signs that the enemy has serious attack intentions." After the brutal losses of June 6–7, he thought the 2d Division was "probably no longer very efficient" and was incapable of sustaining prolonged attacks.

Instead, he thought, they would probably undertake only "partial attacks" aimed at immobilizing the Germans and making local line improvements. He said of such minor attacks:

> [They will] give the Americans—as he supposes—the opportunity for cheap successes. These are then to be headlines in the newspapers. It will be said that one American division had been sufficient to stop the German attack without difficulty. . . . Should the Americans on our front gain the upper hand only temporarily, this may have the most unfavorable influence on the morale of the Entente and on the continuation of the war. In the fighting that faces us it is therefore not a matter of the possession or non-possession of a village or wood of indifferent value in itself, but the question of whether the English-American publicity will succeed in representing the American Army as one equal to the German Army or as actually superior troops.

Böhm amended this report at 2130 to state that an American attempt to take the southern portion of Belleau Wood "can be counted on with certainty." But he still did not expect the effort to amount to anything worthy of his notice. Indeed, on June 8, possibly in response to Ludendorff's admonition that "American units appearing on the front should be hit particularly hard in order to render difficult the formation of an American Army," Böhm began planning for a strong raid against the marines from Bouresches to the west and southwest. Code-named Baden, the assault was planned for June 10, with unlimited artillery support. It was "designed to depreciate (belittle) and prevent a utilization of the success of the Americans obtained at this point which, most likely, is now being magnified to exaggerated proportions." But just like Harbord, Böhm underestimated his opponent. When the Americans renewed their own assault in force, the Germans' raid would be canceled.[18]

Von Conta was charged with broader responsibilities. At 1530 on June 8 he ordered, "I expect that, during the hostile attacks that are now taking place, the main lines of resistance as were chosen by the Divisions will positively be held or, as the case may be, recaptured. . . . Should the enemy penetrate the outpost zone or even the main line of resistance, the counterattack will be launched automatically." But the attacks of the French 167th Division toward Hautevesnes worried him much more than the American drive on Belleau Wood. That was why he placed his best division, the 5th Guards, in that sector, with the objective of hurling the French back across

Clignon Creek. The 237th Division to its east was charged not with opposing the Americans but with supporting the 5th Guards against the French. It "will organize Hill 126 and the Bois de Belleau," Von Conta ordered, "as a flank position against the enemy opposing the 5th Guard Inf. Div. It will be able to give invaluable support to the 5th Guard Inf. Div. by means of this flanking position thru its flanking observation possibilities." Böhm's 28th Division was to "organize the south edge of the Bois de Belleau as a strong point, in order to keep Bouresches under continuous good observation and under flanking rifle and machine gun fire in case it is not desirable to move the main line of resistance as far forward as Triangle." Finally, the 231st "will organize Vaux and the Hill 204 west of Château-Thierry into a strong point in order to flank our own lines. The Marne front and Château-Thierry must be protected by flank fire from the artillery."[19]

Essentially, then, even though Ludendorff admonished his generals to seek opportunities to punish the Americans, Von Conta chose to take the defensive against them in Belleau Wood and against the French 10th Colonial Division and the Americans at Hill 204 and Château-Thierry, while pushing back vigorously against the French 167th Division between Hautevesnes and Veuilly-la-Poterie. The more aggressive Böhm looked to knock the marines about with a strong raid, but of course, he could not order a major offensive on his own authority; thus, he remained primarily on the defensive as well. Across the lines, Degoutte's XXI Corps and Montdésir's XXXVIII Corps sought to advance methodically against the Germans toward Hautevesnes on the left and Hill 204 on the right; while in the middle, they permitted Bundy's 2d Division to continue to hurl itself desperately against Belleau Wood. This would remain the center of the action for many days to come.

8

"We Want the Damn Woods"
Belleau Wood, June 9–10, 1918

On June 9, while the 2d Division continued to batter itself to pieces in Belleau Wood, Ludendorff launched the next stage of his offensive: Operation Gneisenau, aimed at the Montdidier-Noyon sector, which included the 1st Division zone at Cantigny. Over the next two days his forces would manage to drive a tight salient six miles deep into the French lines. Just a week earlier, the Supreme War Council had completed a testy and nearly explosive meeting at Versailles, where Pershing had bluntly rebuffed desperate Anglo-French efforts to get American troops to the front more quickly. Although a new agreement was ratified on the shipment of US troops to Europe—they would now include desperately needed support and supply personnel—Foch and Haig were still furious at the ongoing delays. And even though the new German offensive failed dismally, thanks to stout French counterattacks beginning on June 11 (the American contribution was minor), it only increased Entente pressure on Pershing. Unfortunately, it also bolstered his determination to act as the guardian of American national pride. In that context, the need for a glorious victory in Belleau Wood became more important.[1]

Pershing telegraphed Bundy and Harbord on June 9, congratulating the generals for the "magnificent example of American courage and dash" their troops had shown in and around Belleau Wood. Bundy duly relayed this praise to his men. But Harbord wanted to accomplish far more. He had initially hoped that after allowing his artillery to pulverize Belleau Wood for about eighteen hours, he would be able to resume the attack on the morning of June 9, but he soon moved it back to the afternoon. At 2115 on June

8 he informed Holcomb, "About 50 batteries will play on that wood all day tomorrow and we will probably occupy the far edge in the afternoon." However, attempts to get the troops back into position in time for an afternoon attack failed. At about 0500 on June 9, some marines "advanced some distance into the southern end of the woods but were again held up by machine gun fire from nests and rocks," incurring what the Germans routinely recorded as heavy losses. Meanwhile, elements of the 1/6th—relieving Sibley's 3/6th—took a wrong turn while moving up the line and were then pinned down after daybreak by German artillery. These difficulties, and the evident ineffectiveness of his artillery, forced Harbord to push back his schedule even further. At 1830 on June 9 he ordered the 1/6th Marines to disentangle themselves and move up again after dark. They were instructed to prepare for an assault against Belleau Wood at 0430 on June 10, supported by the 2/5th on the left and the 3/5th (relieving Holcomb's 2/6th at Bouresches) on the right. The battalion's objective was now somewhat more modest: halfway through the woods, rather than all the way to its northern rim.[2]

The French, meanwhile, continued their well-paced advances on both flanks, with notable success. To the west, the 167th Division hit the 5th Guards early on the morning of June 9, just as it was relieving the shattered 197th Division. The momentum of the French assault hurled back the vaunted guards and opened a dangerous gap between that unit and the 237th Division holding the line north of Hill 142. The French rushed through the gap to capture the hamlets of Heloup and Montecouve. In a "furious attack" followed by a "violent house-to-house fight," the French then took "the rectangular woods to the southwest of Bussiares and pushed on into that village, capturing additional prisoners." In all, the French captured 7 German officers and 217 men, plus several machine guns. Frantic German counterattacks failed at first, opening the possibility that the French would unhinge the entire line and force Von Conta to abandon Belleau Wood and perhaps even Vaux and Hill 204. Fortunately for him, the 237th Division's 1/460th Battalion moved into the gap in the nick of time and, with some help from elements of the 5th Guards, pushed the French back out of Bussiares and Heloup by about 2000 hours. It had been a close call. As evening fell, French troops continued to infiltrate aggressively eastward along the valley of Clignon Creek, forcing the Germans to reinforce this position with the 2/462d Battalion and maintain their vigilance, lest they lose their entire line of defense. This—not Belleau Wood—was the critical point.[3]

Farther east, the German 231st Division continued to be frustrated in its attempt to halt Franco-American progress up Hill 204. Well-led Franco-

American patrols infiltrated the lines of the German 2/442d Battalion on the hill at numerous points during the day. Ragged holes began to appear in the German lines as their forward posts and sentries were forced apart. Faced by what they grudgingly acknowledged as the enemy's "enterprising spirit," the 231st Division was forced to rush stronger forces to its front lines, contradicting Von Conta's prescription for defense in depth and making the Germans more vulnerable to casualties from raids, artillery, and other arms. The Germans managed to capture two American prisoners from the 30th Regiment, and although the Yanks were chatty enough, they claimed to know nothing of their officers' intentions and instead "gave an impertinent and unsuspecting impression."[4]

For the US 2d Division, the objectives were more straightforward. Said Sergeant Gleeson on June 10: "We want the damn woods." Earlier projections of taking the entire woods in one gulp, however, had been abandoned. Now, Harbord's plan was for Hughes's 1/6th Battalion to capture the lower woods and advance about halfway across its waist—"approximately an east and west line through Hill 169." Following a preparatory barrage that Hughes thought "blew the wood all to hell" and then a rolling barrage, the marines attacked on schedule at 0430. "Major Hughes—more familiarly known as 'Johnnie the Hard,' tall, imposing figure that he was—led the way quietly, serenely," recalled Private Warren Jackson. "The line followed to the right and left, walking with bayonets fixed." Supported for the first time by massed American machine guns in Bouresches, and taking advantage of the 40th Fusiliers' loose dispositions in the lower woods, thanks to Böhm's mistaken assumption that an attack would come from the direction of Bouresches, the marines made what appeared to be steady progress. Hughes and his men thought they had reached their objective by 0510, capturing some *minenwerfers* and machine guns; by 0520, the intelligence officer of the 6th Marines was able to report, "Action in woods deemed finished."[5]

Hughes was badly mistaken. Instead of reaching his objective, he had only managed to recapture the ground held by Sibley on the morning of June 8, making no dent in the primary German defenses. The war diary of the 28th Division's 40th Fusiliers in Belleau Wood reported that the Americans had been "completely repulsed" after hand-to-hand fighting, with the marines unable "to wrest more than a foot's breadth of ground from the defenders of the wood." Nevertheless, at 0545 the 6th Marines' interim commander, Lieutenant Colonel Harry Lee, relayed a report from his 20th

Company commander to Harbord: "he thinks the Bois de Belleau has been cleared of M.G." Messages from Lee over the next few hours, however, reported (with apparent puzzlement) the appearance of enemy mortars and machine guns in portions of the woods he thought had been cleared. Casualties rose too, although Hughes assured Harbord at 0712 that things were going "quite nicely." At 0756 Hughes reported that Major Cole, commanding the 6th Machine Gun Battalion, had been severely (and mortally, as it turned out) wounded in the right hand, left arm, both legs, and right eye.[6]

These troubling reports of German resistance in portions of the woods that were supposed to be cleared did not register with Harbord, who seemed to have a facility for believing what he wanted to believe. Thinking that Hughes was 800 yards further ahead than he really was, and tantalized by the prospect of taking the whole woods once and for all, Harbord sent an urgent message to Hughes by motorcycle at 1002: "Very important that you give me your judgment on what is north of you in the Bois de Belleau. Push your reconnaissance and let me know at the earliest possible moment whether you think it possible to take part of the wood north of your present position." If Hughes did not think he could take the rest of the woods alone, Harbord wanted to know how many additional troops and what level of artillery support would be necessary. In view of the apparent disappearance of German resistance (at least by dint of early reports), Harbord imagined that the French and American guns had blown them out of existence. "My judgment is that the action of the artillery has very effectually silenced serious opposition in that part of the wood," he told Hughes, making it possible to renew the attack soon.[7]

No positive response from Hughes was immediately forthcoming, so consideration turned to how to complete the conquest of the woods on June 11. The only certainty was that Wise's 2/5th Marines, now in position on Hughes's left, would have primary responsibility for carrying out the attack. Wise later claimed that Harbord gave him "carte blanche" to prepare the next assault as he wished, and he hoped to do so in an original manner:

> I didn't see any use following the same line of attack which had failed with the Sixth Marines, as the Germans evidently had their lines of defense worked out to receive attacks from that direction. It was common sense to hit them where they weren't looking for it. So I determined to risk everything on the unexpected and attack them from their rear. Thus I would get in between them and their lines of sup-

port, which were along the railroad in the northern edge of the Bois de Belleau.

Harbord's Field Order No. 4, issued at 1745, specified that the 2/5th would capture the entire Belleau Wood all the way to Hill 133 on the northeastern edge. Though based on the erroneous assumption—still held by Harbord at the time—that the 1/6th controlled the lower half of the woods, the order could have been interpreted to allow for Wise's northern angle of attack above the woods' waist, where the approach was easier. Wise gathered his company commanders together under a tree, told them his plans, and ordered them to prepare accordingly.[8]

Böhm still had his sights set on Bouresches to the southeast, and he was not expecting an attack such as the one envisioned by Wise's scheme. Neither was Bischoff. In truth, though, the Germans were not arrayed to fend off attacks from any specific direction. No unified German scheme existed for the defense of Belleau Wood, thanks to the jealousy and distrust between the 237th Division's 461st Regiment and the 28th Division's 40th Fusiliers. Though ordered to coordinate, in practice, their commanders had little to do with each other and defended their portions of the woods as they saw fit. Their poor liaison would ultimately prove fatal. Still, they were far from impotent. Set-piece attacks from any direction were bound to suffer heavily from German machine guns.

Whatever its ultimate prospects for success, Wise's plan was rendered moot by fresh orders from Harbord that the major received at midnight. Wise was flabbergasted:

> My battalion was ordered to attack the Bois de Belleau FROM THE SOUTHERN EDGE at four o'clock that morning, behind a rolling barrage.... I was dumbfounded. All my plans were up in the air. I knew that piece of paper I held in my hand meant the needless death of most of my battalion. Some of them would have died in the attack I had planned. But now, instead of hitting the Germans from the rear, I had to take that battalion to a frontal attack against a prepared position.

What Harbord intended, evidently, was for Wise to attack just as Berry's men had on June 6: directly across the open ground toward the waist of Belleau Wood, exposed all the way to converging fire from three directions. Harbord's reason for this correction of the angle of attack is hard to fathom, and it certainly resulted in far heavier casualties. Whether Wise's alternative plan held the key to success, as he claimed vociferously after the war, is impossible to say. In the event, the angle of attack would conform to neither Wise's nor Harbord's plan.⁹

For all the ink spilled in American accounts over the change of direction in Wise's attack, the question remains whether the attack was necessary at all. Von Conta was still having serious problems with his flanks—problems overshadowed by Harbord's fixation on Belleau Wood. On his right, continuing pressure from the French 167th Division forced Von Conta to order, at 1730, a partial withdrawal of the left sector of the 5th Guards Division and the right sector of the 237th Division behind Clignon Creek. Farther east on Hill 204, meanwhile, the Germans found themselves in a situation that was exactly the reverse of that in Belleau Wood. Again and again, the German 231st Division's 1/444th Battalion attacked against well-sited French and American machine guns that denied flank approaches and forced the German infantry to attack frontally, leading to "unimportant" gains and disastrous casualties. By the end of the day, the 231st Division had used up all its reserves and was utterly exhausted. It would be withdrawn from the lines on June 19 and replaced by the 201st Division. According to the author of one of the 231st Division's regimental war diaries, the French and Americans missed an opportunity on Hill 204 by not driving aggressively forward, which might have netted them the rest of the hill and perhaps Château-Thierry. The fact remains, however, that the methodical Franco-American advance won much of the hill's crest—effectively neutralizing it as a German machine gun and mortar emplacement and observation post—and it destroyed one of Von Conta's divisions at practically no cost. With Von Conta's vital flanks weakened and under threat, the Americans at Belleau Wood still insisted on pushing head-on at the tip of a growing German salient.¹⁰

9

"No Idea of Tactical Principles"
Belleau Wood, June 11–12, 1918

Harbord's set-piece attack on Belleau Wood erupted on schedule at 0430 on June 11, after an hour's artillery preparation. Wise deployed four companies, with the 43d and 51st Companies forming the assault wave on the left and right, and the 18th and 55th Companies following in support. The evening before, Wise had assured his company and platoon leaders that "there probably aren't any Boche in those woods at all. That means we will simply have to walk over and take the place"—a senseless assertion, in light of the colonel's belief that taking the woods depended on adopting a well-covered avenue of attack. At first, though, it appeared that Wise might be right. Heavy mist covered the American advance, and as they passed over fields soaked by the blood of Berry's marines, the German guns remained silent. First Lieutenant Elliot D. Cooke, a platoon leader in the 18th Company, turned to the commander of his reserve platoon and said, "The Old Man must have been right after all. . . . There don't seem to be any more Dutchmen around."[1]

But Wise was wrong; there were plenty of Germans in the woods, and as soon as the marines entered the center of the killing ground between Hills 169 and 181, they opened fire from three directions. "Through the mist the forest ahead loomed up as a grim shadow," recalled Cooke. "We entered a deep indentation of the woods and the shadows moved to surround us. Without the slightest warning those shadows suddenly were split apart by chattering, stabbing flames. A crackling sheath of machine-gun bullets encased our battalion, closing on us fiercely." The slaughter was almost as bad as it had been on June 6. "The battalion went on" as

Wise watched with a sinking feeling, "men dropping, men dropping, men dropping." Thanks to the heavy mist that covered their initial approach, however, the marines had somewhat less ground to cover under fire than their comrades had previously. Demonstrating intrepidity that must have startled the Germans, the marines dove for the tree line and made it; the assault companies were all but destroyed, but the support companies were still partially intact.[2]

So far, the marines had attacked according to Harbord's plan and suffered grievously for it. In the woods, the bulk of the battalion fortuitously hit directly at the junction of the 1/461st and 2/40th Fusilier Battalions. The 51st and 55th Companies then angled right (southeastward), toward where they had been told the 1/6th Battalion would be. There, they found no Americans but plenty of Germans—more men of the 40th Fusiliers, only recently arrived in the woods. The 43d and 18th Companies, meanwhile, fanned out to the east and northeast, pressing Bischoff's 461st Regiment and the junction of the two regiments. Most important, elements of Major Shearer's 3/5th Marines in Bouresches maintained heavy fire on the eastern and southeastern sectors of the woods, distracting the 40th Fusiliers and 109th Grenadiers, who had been told to expect an attack from that direction, and hindering the deployment of reserves.[3]

The events that followed transpired at the platoon level, or more often at the level of individual German soldiers and US marines. The Germans had the advantage of good defensive terrain, prepared positions, and carefully sited machine guns with interlocking fields of fire. The Americans, though, were improving their tactics in an environment that demanded individual initiative, quick decision making, and above all bravery. Junior officers such as Cooke had a hand in keeping the men going. As the marines paused under heavy fire:

> For the first time since the battle began I actually shucked off fear like an old coat. Duty, responsibility, and something like rage took command of my thoughts. Those damn Boche couldn't go shooting up our whole outfit and get away with it like that. I stood up in plain sight and blew a blast on my whistle. From holes, furrows, and clods of dirt, faces looked up. Eyes, thankful to see someone in authority, watched expectantly. I pointed at the woods to our right front. Parker, Brown and I walked forward.

And the marines followed—not silently, as they had on June 6, but "firing from the hip."[4]

The fury of the marines' onslaught shocked the defenders, as an impressionistic account left behind by a German survivor indicates:

> Gangs of 10 to 20 men. Dashing conduct. Alcohol. Some of the wounded kept on in the attack. Our men threw hand grenades into these gangs, were simply ignored by the enemy. No idea of tactical principles. Fired while walking, with rifle under the arm. They carried light machine guns with them. No hand grenades, but knives, revolvers, rifle butts, and bayonet. All big fellows, powerful (Rowdys). No sort of leadership. German bugle signals.

Bischoff still thought the Americans, though dashing and energetic, "lacked skill in open and in group attacks. They exposed dense skirmish lines and columns in rear that suffered most severe casualties from our machine gun fire." Their officers sometimes seemed confused. Yet the marines had also learned how to improvise—even when it meant employing the so-called dirty tricks that, up to now, the Germans had been the sole masters of. For instance, during the attack, some marines played the German retreat signal on bugles or called out commands in German, such as "orders from the left, do not shoot"—tactics that Bischoff and other officers admitted were effective. The marines also called for their adversaries to surrender—to disabuse them, Wise later claimed, of the rumor that marines took no prisoners, but more likely just to bewilder the defenders. More important, the marines fanned out upon entering the woods, hitting the Germans simultaneously at multiple points and forging on relentlessly, regardless of casualties. Inevitably, they found weak spots.[5]

In the long contest for Belleau Wood, German records are perhaps most thorough for the morning of June 11. That is because both regiments defending the woods sought to blame the other for what ensued. According to the records of the 461st Regiment, defending the woods' northwest quadrant, the Americans failed in their initial assault and left at least fifty dead bodies behind. At around 0600, however, the marines attacked again. Bischoff heard firing off to his left, and then the Americans appeared like gangbusters, having "apparently squeezed in there" and shattered the 2/40th Fusiliers. They drove in on the left flank and rear of the 1/461st Battalion before Bischoff could react, surrounding two German companies that had to cut their way out in "savage hand-to-hand combat." The local commander, Major Von Hartlieb, brought up his reserves and two companies of the 2/462d; he then "built up a switch barrier and . . . advanced rapidly in a counterattack." The energetic major led the counterattack from the front, "carrying along those who were somewhat unnerved by the heavy daily attacks." By noon, he had managed to restore the German lines in the northern sector of the woods after incurring 231 casualties.[6]

The 40th Fusiliers recounted the events of that morning differently. In their sector, too, the initial marine attack was considered repulsed. The Americans pushed aggressively into the woods, however, and hit the fusiliers at multiple points. According to survivors, some of the marines "were German-Americans who tried to mislead our men by German calls 'Where is the 40th Regiment?'" The fusiliers were also pressured by the 1/6th Marines still lurking in the lower woods, the American machine guns firing aggressively into the woods from Bouresches, and the well-directed American artillery bombardments that broke up reserves as they formed, throwing them back in "great disorder." Two companies of the 2/40th, the 7th and 8th, took the brunt of the American assault in the woods, but they managed to hold their ground with the support of the 5th Company, brought up from reserve. However, "the very dense fog prevented the signal flares [from] penetrat[ing] the haze; as a result, our own artillery fire did not commence." Subsequently, heavy rifle and machine gun fire was heard on the battalion's right, in the gap between it and the 1/461st Battalion, along a dry ravine or creek bed that bisected the woods.[7]

The Germans believed—probably erroneously—that the preassault bombardment had deliberately targeted this ravine, "opening up a lane about 70 to 80 meters in width." In any event, it was almost entirely bereft of German defenders. A trench mortar section of the 2/40th Battalion was deployed there to secure that flank, but as soon as the Germans opened fire, the Americans surged out of the ravine and broke in on them "like a mob." The marines immediately fell on the trench mortar section and the 5th Company from the flank and rear, engaging them in their emplacements in frantic bayonet and hand-to-hand fighting. Two German lieutenants attempted to rally their comrades but failed, and the marines swarmed through to attack the 7th and 8th Companies "in the rear and surrounded them completely. Only a handful of men succeeded in fighting their way to the rear, the majority were killed during the combat." The 1/6th Marines then hit the 2/40th Fusiliers in front just as Wise's men broke in on the German right, shattering the entire battalion and driving it from the woods. Large groups of Germans surrendered to the exultant marines or were shot down as they tried to escape.[8]

Taking both the German records and the American records (which are far less thorough) into account, it appears that an unnamed and unheralded group of marines discovered and aggressively exploited the primary and perhaps only vulnerable spot—the ravine that formed the weakly patrolled boundary between the two defending regiments. Other men might have waited for direction or slavishly followed orders that made no allowance for such an opportunity, but the marines simply drove along the ravine and slammed with unstoppable momentum into the enemy flank and rear. Just like a flood hitting a dike will inevitably breach the tiniest weak point, the broad-based and aggressively pursued marine attack penetrated, pried apart, and finally broke the German defensive perimeter.

If the Germans were stunned by the ferocity of the American assault, Wise and Harbord were almost equally amazed by their victory. Some 400 German prisoners had been captured, and contact was finally established between the 2/5th and the 1/6th Marines, bringing the entire central and southern portions of the woods—but not the north—firmly under American control. Harbord confidently—and erroneously—reported to Bundy at 0700 that "the northern half of the Bois de Belleau belongs to 5th Marines." He followed this up with another message to Bundy at 0925 declaring that, "in my judgment, the capture of the Bois de Belleau is the most important event that has taken place for the Allies holding in this vicinity. I do not believe there would be any advance in this region without first an attempt to dislodge us from the Bois de Belleau." Losses, Harbord thought, were "probably quite light," although he added that "the physical exhaustion of the brigade . . . approximates complete physical exhaustion."[9]

Half an hour earlier, Wise had reported that his casualties were "quite heavy," and he was beginning to worry about his flanks in the face of German counterattacks. Troubled by reports from his company commanders that they were holding on with only the thinnest of forces, Wise warned Harbord at 1125, "My left flank is rather weak. The Germans are massing in our front. I can hardly spare any men. They could very easily filter through tonight for counterattack." Part of Wise's problem—and one reason for Harbord's mistaken impression that the entire woods had been taken—was that the colonel thought he had reached the northern edge of the woods, when in fact he was at the eastern edge. Wise was so convinced of this false belief that when his intelligence officer, Lieutenant Bill Hughes, tried to convince him otherwise, Wise shouted, "You goddamned young bonehead, you don't know what you're talking about!" Not until around noon did he realize that the "bonehead" was right. By then, the Germans were back, hitting Wise in the left flank.[10]

At 1130 Böhm had been forced to admit that the "enemy has apparently captured the greater part of the Bois de Belleau." He ordered an immediate counterattack by the 1/40th Fusiliers and 2/110th Grenadiers, and they initially made "good progress," hustling back some of Wise's northern outposts and recovering some of the positions lost that morning. But Böhm's Germans were unable to restore communications with Bischoff's 461st Regiment. Bischoff sent a message to the 40th Fusiliers at 1220, reporting that his left flank was "in the air" and he had no more reserves. It was "absolutely necessary," he demanded, that the gap be closed. Hartlieb followed this up with another message at 1415, reporting that the 1/461st "has held intact and entirely the position still in our possession yesterday," and "reinforcements have moved into such portions of the positions in which gaps have arisen as a result of losses"; he demanded again that the gap be closed. The 1/40th and 2/110th Battalions tried their best, managing to push about 400 meters into the woods, but no further. The tables were turned, and as Wise reconfigured his lines to face north, the marines inflicted heavy casualties on the attacking Germans. By 2000 the Germans were entirely exhausted and had to halt for the night. Small patrols that attempted to maintain contact between the regiments, still about 400 meters apart, were killed or captured.[11]

Wise's position, now reinforced by the 2d Engineers (which had helped the marines dig in), included Hill 181 and ran roughly across the middle of the woods' waist; Hill 169 was at least partially under American control. The 1/6th Marines came up to anchor the line to the east against potential German pressure from north of Bouresches. Harbord reassured Wise at 1400 that artillery was "very watchful on your left flank, you need have no fear for it. . . . Your affair today was certainly well handled and is the biggest thing in prisoners that the A.E.F. has yet pulled off. We are delighted." By then, compliments and congratulations were flying thick and fast. Bundy ambled over to 4th Brigade headquarters to applaud the troops late that morning, and Harbord relayed the praise to Wise: "Hearty congratulations to you and your gallant men. He says the task could not have been performed any better. The objectives of the Brigade have been attained everywhere after days of fighting which the Division Commander has never known to be excelled." At 1255 Bundy telegrammed Pershing to say that "reports indicate that attack has reached the northern and eastern limits of the woods and that our troops have occupied the eastern edge . . . our casualties comparatively light considering the nature of the operation." Officers charged with the interrogation of prisoners even fished for compliments from the Germans. An adjutant of the 6th Marines reported to Harbord at 1410 that a "German officer complained that they had been up against Canadians and British but that they had found us a bit worse." Until late in the day, division and brigade headquarters remained under the impression that the entire woods was under American control; only "late in the afternoon" was it discovered that "a part of the woods was still held by some Germans with machine guns." Several "small enemy groups [had] managed to conceal themselves in the thick wood and rocky formations. These small groups were apparently concealed in the western end of the Bois de Belleau on the top of Hill 169."[12]

There remained, therefore, a good deal of unfinished business. Initial impressions to the contrary, Belleau Wood had only partially fallen into American hands. And by the evening of June 11, Harbord had not yet devised a plan to complete the job. The 2/5th Battalion, which had taken 182 casualties during the day, was exhausted. The marines had finally gotten the Germans' attention, but at a heavy cost. The marines' facility in hand-to-hand combat particularly impressed Lieutenant Colonel Ernst Otto, who wrote an account of the battle ten years later. The Germans, he said, had always prided themselves on the "Furor Teutonicus" that allegedly gave them the upper hand over the French and the Russians, but this was only to be expected: "The marked superiority of the German race over the Roman and Slavic races in hand-to-hand fighting impressed itself throughout the hardest battles of the World War. If the sport-loving English, and the powerful Canadians and Australians, proved to [be] the equals of the Germans in hand-to-hand combat, it must be remembered that like ourselves, they are of Germanic blood." The Americans had the double advantage of hard fighting ability—no doubt due in part, from Otto's perspective, to their "German blood"—and superior numbers, for "the rifle strength of an American company at this time was about equal to that of a German battalion."[13]

For Böhm, the immediate task was to regain at least some of his positions in the southern reaches of Belleau Wood, and he proposed to do so first thing in the morning on June 12. Von Conta had bigger ambitions. At 1830 on June 11 he issued an order for the preparation of a major attack—date to be determined—aimed at advancing as far as Hill 181 in Belleau Wood, Hill 211 a kilometer south of Le Thiolet, and the southern edge of the Bois de Loup. To accomplish the two latter objectives—which he proposed to do with the 28th Division and the newly arrived 195th and 36th Divisions—he would have to plow through General Lewis's 3d Brigade southeast of Bouresches and the French 10th Colonial Division, with elements of the US 30th Regiment, on Hill 204. "The purpose of this attack," he declared, "is to improve our positions and to place at a disadvantage the Americans in position opposite this sector."[14]

If launched, Von Conta's attack would hit a relatively fresh portion of the American line. Harbord's brigade had bloodied itself at Belleau Wood, but over at 3d Brigade, the primary concern at the moment was the commander's sensitive eardrums. "Motorcycles and automobiles must be particular not to open mufflers near Brigade Hdqrs. as the noise is particularly irritable to General Lewis," brigade staff ordered. The French 10th Colonial Division and US 30th Regiment also remained fairly solid, despite the fighting of recent days. In the same time it had taken the French and Americans on Hill 204 to gut the already badly weakened German 231st Division, however, the Germans in Belleau Wood had practically brought the Marine Brigade to its knees. Lieutenant Cooke thought the marines had paid a "bitter price" on June 11 "for a piece of woods that stank of high explosives, crushed shrubbery, and scattered human flesh. Dead men littered the ground and lay hidden in every thicket and rocky cleft. Even the living walked about in a sort of shell-shocked daze."[15]

Harbord, usually stubbornly optimistic and detached, was growing increasingly aware of his brigade's exhaustion and depletion. "Officers and men are now at a state scarcely less than complete physical exhaustion," he reported to Bundy at 0800. "Men fall asleep under bombardment, and the physical exhaustion and the heavy losses are a combination calculated to damage morale. . . . I cannot too strongly urge that immediate arrangements be made for its relief, to enable us to rest and reorganize." Bundy heard the message from his brigade commander but hesitated to ask for relief. Telegraphing from his new headquarters at Genevois, where he had moved from Montreuil-aux-Lions, Bundy told Pershing that his marines had been fighting continuously since May 30 with no relief. He did not, however, ask for the brigade to be pulled out of the line; instead, he proudly demanded that his men be allowed to continue to hold what they had taken rather than turn it over to other Americans or—God forbid—the French. "It is highly desirable," he said, "that the ground gained and held by American troops be maintained by American troops." In response, Fox Conner duly asked Paul H. Clark, the chief of staff of the French Mission, to place the American 42d Division on the 2d Division's left to shorten its line or to lend the 2d Division a brigade from the 4th Division. But relief would not be forthcoming for a very long time.[16]

June 12 dawned overcast, heralding the rain that would swoop in the following day. In Belleau Wood the first major German counterattack had already begun. Detachment Mencke, consisting of the 2/110th Grenadiers with elements of the 1/110th and 1/40th Battalions, advanced under cover of darkness to avoid the machine guns in Bouresches and entered the woods to attack through the gap between the remnants of the 2/40th Battalion and Bischoff's 461st Regiment. Resisted fiercely by the marines and engineers, the Germans made little progress and suffered some sixty casualties. By 0500, Detachment Mencke had ground to a halt with both flanks open. The German line was extremely porous, and the soldiers who defended it were tired, hungry, and thirsty. Many of them shook with the beginnings of fever—"an epidemic," reported the 237th Division's war diary that morning, "apparently of the nature of influenza, [that] has caused considerable losses to the troop units." Field reports throughout the morning and afternoon from officers of the 40th and 110th Regiments indicate that they had no expectation of being able to resist an American attack in their sector of the woods unless Böhm sent them major reinforcements, which were not forthcoming. Had the marines been prepared to attack, they might have found the remainder of Belleau Wood ripe for the taking.[17]

But the marines were unprepared to exploit this vulnerability to the fullest. They had incurred devastating casualties over the past few days and were entirely worn out from lack of food and sleep. German artillery punished them mercilessly. "Never had I undergone anything that would compare with the horrifying shellfire that fell unrelentingly on the twelfth day of June 1918," recalled Private Warren R. Jackson:

> I crouched under a rock six or eight feet high and on the German side. Shell after shell screeched by with awful sounds, many of the shells seeming to go only inches above the rock. But one of those shells had to come a bit lower to strike the edge of the rock above me to explode and blow me to pieces. So fast did they come that many times the sounds of different shells were not discernable. One deadly explosive after another passed over, or fell nearby, with a rapidity that stifled the senses, and brought upon us almost frenzying madness.

"Men in fine shape and line is holding but getting thinner," Wise reported to Harbord at 1000 hours. "Heavy shelling and some gas. About out of officers. Request barrage immediately. Are getting hell shelled out of us now." Unshaven and filthy, the marines were more in a mood to receive attacks than to deliver them. "Many a time," remembered Private William A. Francis, "when the Germans were attacking us, we would pray for them to come into the trench and either kill us or we would kill them, for the attacks we [delivered] were worse than death." Harbord's artillery support, both French and American, was ample, though, and it struck back at the Germans in Belleau Wood until the marines were ready to go at 1700.[18]

Wise, who that morning had feared his men would be unable to hold against a German counterattack, had recovered his confidence by the afternoon. He felt certain that his battalion could clear out the remainder of the woods on its own. "I studied the northeastern point of the woods carefully," he recalled. "It didn't look like a very hard nut to crack. It was slightly higher ground than the rest of the Bois de Belleau—the same tall trees; the same thick underbrush; the same bowlders. I made up my mind we'd attack it that afternoon whether reinforcements came up or not." He shifted his battalion to the left slightly, expecting Hughes's 1/6th to advance along the woods' edge to his right, and then he attacked the woods frontally.[19]

Although Wise had requested and received an extensive preparatory artillery barrage, including a delay in H-hour to give the guns more time, it didn't have the impact he had hoped. Even so, the marines—tired and hungry though they were—applied the lessons they had learned over the past few days and moved forward in small groups to quickly penetrate the German positions. The defenders paid them the compliment of observing that "the methods of attack employed by the Americans . . . could well be classified as assault tactics." Hartlieb marveled that they had learned so quickly to employ what he thought were snipers and sharpshooters or men with rifle grenades. These marines fired on anything that moved, causing serious losses and having a "most disturbing" effect on the defenders. As before, German Americans called out company commands in German, which severely confused the enemy. Overall, Hartlieb thought, the marines "were mostly husky young fellows who were well armed and had an abundance of self-confidence and otherwise gave a good impression." Also, "their uniform of a dark-brown color proves very advantageous, especially in the woods, as it is hardly possible to recognize them even at the shortest distance."[20]

The marines were definitely improving, and fast. But in many respects, the Germans remained their own worst enemies. Once again—inadvertently, it seemed—the Americans took advantage of the poorly coordinated defensive dispositions. Elements of three German regiments were now deployed in the woods—the 461st (237th Division) on the German right, and the 110th and 40th (28th Division) on the left. All three regiments performed well at first, as the commander of the German 55th Brigade warned the commander of the 40th Regiment—numbering some 600 men—that he would be held "personally responsible [to ensure] that the enemy obtains no successes at this point!" Shortly afterward, however, Wise's 2/5th Marines broke through the jointure of the two divisions. The marines slammed into the left flank and rear of the 1/461st Battalion—supported by elements of the 2/462d Battalion—and attacked the 110th and 40th Regiments on the right and rear while Hughes's 1/6th Marines pressed them on the left. "Extravagantly using rifle grenades," and "in squad columns, deployed in depth, he came on against our lines of machine guns and rifle men and forced them to retreat," reported the 110th Regiment's war diary. Actually, these regiments had to cut their way out. All but broken, and leaving their heavy machine guns and other weapons behind, German troops of the 28th Division fled the woods "in a panic," reported Bischoff, with "hosts of weaponless malingerers . . . in full flight." Following this "fiasco," the 40th and 110th Regiments took up what they claimed were positions along the Belleau-Bouresches road to the east but were actually along the Torcy–Château-Thierry road much farther northeast. The 461st Regiment was likewise bundled back into the northwestern corner of the woods. Despite incurring serious casualties, the marines managed to push through the northeastern woods and capture a hunting lodge (pavilion) that had previously served as Bischoff's headquarters, along with several Germans. During their advance they angled east, however, and Bischoff's men maintained pressure on Wise's left, which was eventually anchored on a rocky knoll called the Hook. Wise also bent back his right flank to maintain contact—with limited success—with Hughes's slower-moving 1/6th. Gaps opened behind both of Wise's flanks as he advanced, while only 300 bone-tired marines held his front. It was about 1800.[21]

As German artillery opened a murderous fire on the marine positions, a captured and mortally wounded enemy officer warned that his comrades would be back. Wise already anticipated an enemy counterattack. "Lost a great many men," he reported to Colonel Neville at 2040. "We are getting a devil of a shelling and quite accurate. . . . Everything running smooth and men in fine shape, but as I put in my report I am afraid of the reaction. . . . This is a different outfit from the one of yesterday." Private Warren Jackson of Hughes's 1/6th Marines, which endured the shelling along with Wise's outfit, had "never . . . undergone anything that would compare with the horrifying shellfire that fell unrelentingly" that evening. Wise therefore decided to pull back his positions and secure his flanks. Germans of the 461st Regiment followed up aggressively, regaining most of the ground they had lost, including the hunting lodge, and establishing a new line along a rocky knoll to the south. "Too much ground had to be occupied," Wise explained to Bundy a few days later, "and they filtered in again and we received the heaviest bombardment that I have heard in France that night. June 13th. Was convinced that we did not hold entire north and eastern edge of woods and that the enemy still had re-occupied some strong positions, but did not have sufficient men to drive them out." Even with his lines retracted, the 2/5th Marines remained shaky, despite Wise's defiant cry that his men were in "full spirits." Harbord ordered Holcomb's 2/6th to be prepared to move up in support.[22]

Burgeoning animosity between Wise and Hughes boded ill for the Americans' ability to hold what they had gained. Wise was furious with Hughes's tardy show of support on June 11 and with the 1/6th Marines' slow advance in the woods' eastern edge on June 12, and he showed it. Hughes and his battalion intelligence officer made their way forward to Wise's command post and attempted to point out enemy defensive dispositions, but "the conference as usual resulted in nothing." Hughes then went to reconnoiter the connection between the two battalions and determined that they were "exactly where they showed on the map" and quite secure. But when he returned to the 2/5th Marines' command post to share this information, Hughes "found everybody shooting. I stayed there 15 minutes but Col. Wise wouldn't notice me," so he left.[23]

Mixed signals as to the division's status further complicated the situation. On June 11 Harbord had dispatched signals that the marines had reached the end of their tether, but on June 12 Lieutenant Colonel W. S. Grant of G-3 prepared a conflicting memorandum for GHQ based on his experiences with the division from June 6 to 10 (thus, by the time the memorandum reached Pershing, it was already two days out of date). Grant reported that although the marines had incurred significant casualties and had especially "lost heavily in officers," the morale of the division was "excellent," and twice he emphasized that "nothing was said to me or in my hearing about the necessity of relieving the Marine brigade." At the same time, Harbord's chief of staff, Colonel Preston Brown, reported to Pershing that the June 12 attack had been a "complete success," and "it is now believed that the Bois de Belleau has been completely cleaned out of enemy detachments." Such reports, implying that the Germans had been defeated and that the marines were bloodied but defiant, seemed to obviate any need for immediate relief. American divisions had specifically been built to last, and the colossal wastage of Harbord's repeated frontal assaults on Belleau Wood was as yet poorly understood at GHQ.[24]

At 1745 on June 12, however, Major Robert C. Richardson, the American liaison officer with Degoutte's XXI Corps, phoned Colonel Fox Conner with more direct and up-to-date information on the Marine Brigade. It was not encouraging. Harbord was "emphatic," said Richardson, "that if they have another attack, which they think they will have, he does not believe they would stand it." Richardson agreed that although the 3d Brigade "could stand" a serious German attack, the marines could not. Yet what were the alternatives? The US 4th Division was unprepared to enter the line because of a lack of training and equipment, and the French had allocated the US 28th Division to another section of the front. Richardson thought it "would be better to relieve the entire [2d] division for a couple of weeks," but the prospect of asking the French to complete a task—the conquest of Belleau Wood—the marines had been unable to finish was too humiliating to contemplate. Anyway, Bundy had already stated that the American troops should hold on to what they had taken. For now, at least, the marines would stay.[25]

Having bludgeoned each other to a state of mutual prostration, the Americans and Germans now faced the question of what to do next. Although Malone congratulated Harbord on securing a "victory" that would "inspire all Americans," the 4th Brigade commander was well aware that his victory remained incomplete so long as the Germans held any portion of Belleau Wood. Yet the position was not one of profound tactical or strategic importance. Degoutte's orders set the overall objective for the French XXI Corps as "continuing the impression on the enemy that he is being threatened by an attack on our part and thus compelling him to engage, as heretofore, fresh units needed for battle"—the sort of mission that had already been performed to perfection by the French 10th Colonial Division supported by the US 30th Regiment on Hill 204. On his left, Degoutte ordered the French 167th Division to occupy Bussiares (it managed to take the railway station there by June 14, as the German 5th Guards Division withdrew its main line of resistance to the north of Clignon Creek). The US 2d Division, meanwhile, would straighten out its line and secure advantageous points of observation by pushing forward from Triangle and the Bois de Clerembauts to Hill 192 and Vaux—in other words, action would be conducted entirely in the sector of the 3d Brigade. These positions were to be taken by means of "a series of successive minor attacks, well prepared by artillery." There was therefore no need for haste, and the 4th Brigade was under no orders to advance at all.[26]

Von Conta considered the "wildly-fought-for Bois de Belleau" as much as lost, but he was still determined to retake it if possible. Böhm in particular maintained an offensive mind-set, despite his troops' poor showing so far and their total eviction from Belleau Wood. Flattered by a loquacious prisoner from the American 23d Regiment who provided detailed descriptions of his comrades' defensive dispositions and noted "that the German troops opposite the American front are said to belong to the best divisions in the German army," Böhm still hoped to retake at least a portion of the woods.

The best defense, he thought, would be a good offense. His division's current "position cannot be held in its present trace for any considerable time," he declared. "Enemy can at any time break forward in a surprise move from the parts of the Bois de Belleau and Bouresches occupied by him. To ward off this attack will cause more casualties than an attack on our part carried through with dash. It can be accepted as certain that the enemy intends to capture Bois de Belleau." The Germans would attack.[27]

French instructors training US marines how to throw hand grenades in the European fashion, 1917. (Courtesy National Archives)

US marines endure gas mask training with French instructors, 1917. (Courtesy National Archives)

Funeral for three US 1st Division soldiers killed in the German raid at Bathelémont, November 19, 1917. (Courtesy National Archives)

General John J. Pershing (left foreground) and General Robert Bullard (right foreground) inspect 1st Division troops, June 1918. (Courtesy National Archives)

Aerial photograph, taken from 500 meters, of the 1st Division's assault on Cantigny, 0700, May 28, 1918. (Courtesy National Archives)

General James G. Harbord sporting the helmet of a French brigadier general—his standard headgear as commander of the Marine Brigade in Belleau Wood. (Courtesy National Archives)

A private in the 6th Marines' Medical Detachment wearing a rubber outfit used during the treatment of mustard gas cases, summer 1918. (Courtesy National Archives)

General Joseph T. Dickman, commander of the US 3d Division during the spring and summer of 1918. (Courtesy National Archives)

German infantry (foreground) face an attack by French infantry near Soissons, 1918. (Courtesy National Archives)

General Charles H. Muir (right), commander of the US 28th Division, confers at headquarters, 1918. (Courtesy National Archives)

US infantry at a captured German street barricade in Fismes, August 1918. (Courtesy National Archives)

The footbridge over the Vesle River at Fismes-Fismette, August 1918. (Courtesy National Archives)

German machine gun crew in Fismette, August–September 1918. (Courtesy National Archives)

Dead Germans with a flamethrower in Fismes or Fismette, August–September 1918. (Courtesy National Archives)

10

Gas and Exhaustion
Belleau Wood, June 13–15, 1918

Much has been written—and rightly so—about the courage and audacity of US marines and soldiers in the protracted fight for Belleau Wood. The bravery and sheer endurance of the German soldiers who opposed them were equally astonishing. Major Hartlieb of the 461st Regiment thought it nothing less than "superhuman." A lieutenant in that regiment wrote in his diary:

> He who escaped being wounded during the days around here may surely boast of exceptionally good fortune. But there was no time to worry about that; we were too exhausted. What our men did here can only be judged by one who was on the scene himself. How feeble and sick we were, with fever (the influenza), and diarrhea, all of us without exception, and yet we held out! Here we had a good example of the influence of a leader. Major Bischoff, the veteran African fighter, said to his men: "I know you are all sick. Any physician would have you put on the sick list. But will you allow the successes won with our blood to be jeopardized or even lost? A man can endure anything so long as he has the will to do so. Clench your teeth, then! Pull yourselves together! When we get out of this place we will have time to recuperate." Not a man reported himself sick.

By June 13, the troops of the 237th and 28th Divisions—proud but hardly elite formations—had long passed the limits of what ordinary infantry was supposed to experience. Like the Americans, they had been fighting for the woods for days—both attacking and defending—but they had been in the thick of combat for many weeks, months, and years. Exhausted, racked with hunger and influenza, well below strength, short of officers, and knowing full well that their country was staring defeat in the face, they chose to fight on. On June 13 the 28th Division—taken over that day by the aptly named General Emil Hell—rated the combat value of the 40th and 110th Regiments (the latter struggling to recover from a direct hit by an artillery shell on its headquarters at Étrépilly) as "extremely low." General Hell threw them into the attack anyway, and the men obeyed.[1]

The attack began before dawn, at about 0315, after an artillery bombardment that included significant quantities of gas. From the eastern fringe of Belleau Wood to Bouresches, the 28th Division, backed up by elements of the 5th Guards Division (the 237th declined to join the attack), surged forward. But the American sentries were alert, and artillery and machine guns quickly opened fire on the enemy. The Germans struck most aggressively toward Bouresches, which was vulnerable to quick encroachment from the north and northeast. "In accordance with orders," a company of the 109th Grenadiers under Lieutenant Von Mach "forced entrance into the village from the south as far as the church, where they were fired on by infantry and machine guns from cellars so that further advance was impossible. One other platoon pushed forward from the east of the village to a strongly defended barricade; a platoon of the 2d Company sent forward in support was not able to carry the attack further since it had not been possible to force the withdrawal of the enemy northwest of the village." Here, the Germans held on for some time, hoping that the 40th Fusiliers would make enough progress from the northwest to force the Americans entirely out of the village.[2]

The conduct of the defenders—including elements of the 1/6th Marines and the 1/23d—was "magnificent," according to their officers. A lieutenant of the 1/23d panicked as the Germans entered the village, however, and dispatched a runner who arrived at Harbord's headquarters at 0448 with news that Bouresches had been lost. General Hell's headquarters thought the same, based on signal flares fired by the 109th Regiment. Harbord relayed the bad news up the chain, and at a request from 2d Division headquarters, American artillery obligingly opened fire on the village. But the runner's report was false. Fortunately, the American artillery was called off before it could do much damage, and the German company "withdrew to its line of departure, taking along a prisoner." The Germans had suffered a couple dozen casualties. Elsewhere, the attackers also withdrew, having incurred severe casualties to no purpose. German bodies lay scattered in town and through the wheat fields to the north.[3]

For once, Belleau Wood had not been the scene of major fighting. Marines hunted down and disposed of Germans who had been left behind by their regiments and had thus far managed to evade detection. They also probed Bischoff's positions in the woods' northwestern corner and then fell back with—in the obligatory language of German war diaries—"heavy losses." Had they been capable of doing more, they might have bundled out the 461st Regiment with relative ease. Writing at 1800 from the cellar of a shell-rattled château in Belleau, Bischoff reported to his brigade commander:

> I am unable to guarantee the successful warding off of another strong hostile attack. The bloody losses among the men have been increased by an epidemic of fever which . . . carries with it the possibility of growing into a high fever which subsequently exhausts the men mentally and physically. Of the few officers still doing duty, a large percentage are only able to carry on by exerting their last bit of energy. All company commanders report that their men are completely apathetic and many are suffering from neurasthenia due to overexertion.

Von Conta ordered his 87th Division up from reserve to replace the 237th, but in any realistic estimation, such relief was too little too late. Had the American "blockbuster" divisions lived up to their reputations—or been handled more carefully—the story of Belleau Wood might have ended there, if not earlier.[4]

But the 2d Division was like a vehicle without wheels—unable to either advance or withdraw. Harbord once again erroneously reported to Degoutte on June 13 that "it is now believed that the Bois-de-Belleau has been completely cleaned out of enemy detachments," and he desperately wanted to make that happen. Every battalion of his brigade was in shambles, however, and no American replacements were at hand. Even the 3d Brigade was out of the picture, given that Degoutte had designated that formation for an advance in its own sector. A French reserve division was in easy reach, but pride kept the Americans from calling on it. To Lieutenant Colonel W. S. Grant, who stayed with the 2d Division to evaluate its performance and relay any requests to GHQ, Bundy offered only a lukewarm request for relief. He preferred that "another American division be brought in in his rear to alternate with his division in the line."[5]

With such reassurances, Grant concluded that although the 3d Brigade could ease the marines' predicament by expanding its sector of the front to include Bouresches—certainly a humiliating proposal from the marines' point of view—the division's withdrawal was "not essential though it is desirable, provided there are enough divisions available to permit it." But calling on the French was a last resort. Conner, who received Grant's report, reinforced that point in a phone call to Major Richardson at 1800. French relief could be accepted, but only if they proposed it; under no circumstances were the marines permitted to ask the French for help. The matter of relief must be left "entirely to the French," Conner ordered. "Do not insist on any relief. The reports that we have show that conditions are not very bad. Do nothing further in the matter. . . . Tell them [the French] that [it] is entirely in their hands and that we think anything they do in that way is right." That evening, the 23d Regiment took over responsibility for Bouresches from Shearer's 3/5th Marines.[6]

Just after midnight on June 14, the sound of gas shells plopping throughout Belleau Wood heralded a new kind of misery for the beleaguered marines. On the previous day, Von Conta had released an army order announcing "the conclusion of the great offensive begun by the Seventh Army on May 27." However, Von Conta still held on to the hope of launching the attack between Bouresches and Hill 204 that he had announced on June 11. Before doing so, the 28th Division would need to make at least some progress in Belleau Wood. General Hell's troops were too tired and disorganized to launch another major attack, though, and the neighboring 237th Division was preparing for relief by the 87th Division. In the meantime, the German artillery took a hand in softening up the Americans by firing a concentration of mustard gas that the battered Marine Brigade had never encountered before.[7]

Like the other American divisions, the 2d Division had some experience of gas at the front. The first large-scale German gas attack had hit the 1/6th Marines while in reserve near Bonchamp on the morning of April 13, in the form of more than 3,000 chlorine and mustard gas shells. During this bombardment, one 105mm shell filled with mustard made a direct hit on a shack where sixty marines slept, with devastating results. Official reports of this attack claimed 277 casualties, with most "only slightly gassed." As the corps gas officer pointed out, however, being "slightly gassed" could entail tremendous suffering that put men out of commission for weeks: "Of these all suffered from conjunctivitis, many having infected lungs and several are badly blistered, especially between the legs." More than 40 of them subsequently died. Moreover, the officer continued, "practically all" of the "inexcusably large" number of gas casualties were "caused by the ignorance of the officers concerning the persistence of this gas, and the consequent premature removal of masks (half an hour after the bombardment) and the failure to promptly evacuate the camp." Attempts were made to improve gas training in the division, but as events would prove, both marines and soldiers remained poorly prepared by the beginning of June to cope with a large-scale gas attack.[8]

The Germans used poison gas only intermittently in Belleau Wood in the week following the initial marine attack. French artillery fired gas shells from time to time, but the American artillery lacked gas shells in any quantity. All that changed after midnight on June 14, when German artillery saturated the area between Lucy-le-Bocage and Belleau Wood with 6,000 to 7,000 rounds of mustard gas. The stated intention of this "drenching" bombardment was to "cut off the territory likely to be used in advancing against Belleau Wood." In that, it succeeded. A section of the 3/6th Marines moving from Lucy to the woods at 0345 reported that the gassing was "*very serious*," forcing the men to wear their respirators for hours. The bombardment also caught elements of the 23d Infantry moving into Bouresches and—worst of all—the 2/6th Marines moving up to relieve their comrades of the 2/5th Marines in Belleau Wood. The 2/6th Marines were hit simultaneously by both high-explosive and gas shells. Dozens of marines removed their masks to attend to their injuries, only to breathe in lungfuls of mustard gas. They were hit so badly that the regimental surgeon reported at 1040 that "practically [the] entire battalion [is] physically unfit due to gas."[9]

Soldiers and marines and their field officers were not the only ones to underestimate the destructive power of poison gas used in quantity. Lieutenant Colonel Grant complacently reported to GHQ on June 15 that the night of June 13–14 had "passed quietly. Troops were able to get some rest. Gen. Bundy, Colonel Brown and General Harbord all seemed to feel better, and need of relief did not seem so great as it had 48 or even 24 hours before." Grant then noted that gas shelling had inflicted a whopping 700 to 800 casualties from gas, "mostly burns with some severe cases. Medical officer reported that practically none of the gassed would be available for duty for at least two weeks." How the marines would be able to "get some rest" in such circumstances remained unclear. And the gassing continued.[10]

All through the day, the Germans continued to fire gas shells intermittently, and they laid yet another "drenching" gas attack in and around Belleau Wood from 2130 to 0030 on June 14–15. Men who had worn their masks for several hours became desperate to remove them, regardless of the circumstances. At 0130 on June 15, for example, three companies of the 23d Regiment approaching Belleau Wood were hit by a shower of gas shells as they moved through the ravine bordering the lower woods. Two of the companies pulled out of the ravine, where the gas settled in dank clouds.

The third company, however, encountered a marine officer who told the soldiers that they could safely remove their masks. Nearly the entire company had to be evacuated as gas casualties later that day.[11]

In the woods, the marines could take no more. Wise, who had hoped for relief by the 2/6th Marines, was appalled by the gas-soaked remnants of his battalion—a mere 150 men—that showed up early in the morning. He reported to Harbord at 0605 on June 14 that because Holcomb's battalion was so "badly broken up," he had no choice but to absorb them into his own outfit and continue to hold the line as best he could. Wise reported that his men were "physically unable to make another attack," and he warned that his "present line unsafe unless whole woods are in our possession and not enough troops on hand and if those woods are taken there must be enough troops to hold them, or it will be the same story again: that is they will filter in. The woods are larger than shown [on the map]." He requested permission to withdraw, at least slightly.[12]

Harbord recognized that much more than a slight withdrawal would be necessary if he was to save his brigade. Even his battalion officers were failing. Major Shearer of the 3/5th Marines, just pulled out of Bouresches, was under the care of a physician for exhaustion. Major Hughes, commanding the 1/6th in the woods, gamely told a concerned gas officer that "his orders are to stick," so stick he would; however, the gas officer reported that Hughes was "showing effects" from the constant gassing and advised that the whole battalion be pulled out as quickly as possible. At 1650 Harbord told Bundy that he would hold the east edge of the woods with a "very thin line" of machine guns, while the bulk of his troops pulled back to the vicinity of Hills 169 and 181. The northeast portion of the woods, not yet heavily gassed because of the proximity of German troops to the northwest, would continue to be held with such forces as Wise could muster. Ten minutes later, Harbord passed on the order to Colonel Neville of the 5th Marines:

> On account of the mustard gas in the south half of the Bois de Belleau, the following is ordered: Leave not to exceed one company of the 1st Bn., 6th, on the east edge of the Bois de Belleau. These men can with care get far enough into the open to strike sunlight and be out of the gas which remains in the woods. Withdraw the rest of the command to the neighborhood of 181 and 169, sheltering them as best you can. The enemy is not liable to attack within several days a wood which he has filled with yperite gas. It is necessary that this be done with the utmost expedition. . . . Pending information as to the area of yperite gas in north half of the woods, it will be held as at present.

Such a move could not be carried out immediately, however, and in the event it was not completed until about 0800 on June 15. In the meantime, Harbord reported to Bundy that although "the spirit of the brigade remains unshaken . . . morale under such conditions is on pure nerve and is liable to snap." In other words, the Marine Brigade—and possibly the entire division—had reached the breaking point.[13]

Although the German gas attacks of June 13–15 lacked the intensity of the offensives against the British and French earlier that year, to the untried, poorly trained, and exhausted Americans, they were devastating. "This sector is hell on earth," Sergeant Gleeson reported in his diary on June 13. "Shrapnel, high explosive and then the damn gas. It's terrible." On the following day, he reported succinctly: "Tired and sick and don't care what happens." Cases of shell shock reached nearly epidemic proportions. The continued presence of numerous dead marines scattered through the woods days and even weeks after they fell (as repeatedly noted by those who entered the woods later that summer) indicates how low morale had plummeted.[14]

In all, from June 1 to 12, the entire division had suffered 3,279 killed and wounded, including from gas. Now, in just over twenty-four hours, they suffered in excess of 800 more casualties from gas alone. By June 16, Bundy reported that his division had incurred a total of 4,301 casualties. And although 2,740 replacements had been received in the same period, Bundy observed, "They are only partly trained, are unknown to their officers and noncommissioned officers, and are without experience in war. In the case of the Marine brigade it was unfortunately necessary to send some of the replacements to the fighting line. The natural result was confusion." So debilitated was the division that, as noted by gas warfare historian Rexmond Cochrane, "For a period of three or four days following the gas attack of 14–15 June, a determined effort by the German forces opposite might well have shattered the entire front of the 2nd Division and opened the way to Meaux and Paris." Fortunately, Von Conta's preparations for an offensive were delayed by the exhaustion and weakness of his own troops—but of course, the Americans were unaware of this. So far as they knew, an attack could come at any time.[15]

In such circumstances, it was clear that half measures—such as shifting the 23d Regiment into Bouresches—were not enough. Few other options were available, however, given Bundy's refusal to countenance relief of his division by the French. Pershing had asked Brigadier General Camille M. Rageneau, chief of the French Military Mission with the AEF, to relay to Foch his desire that the Marine Brigade be relieved "without too much delay" by other American troops. Foch replied through Rageneau on June 14 that it was not feasible to do so with any unit other than the US 42d Division, which meant that, "under these conditions, the relief could not be effected before the 25th instant at the earliest." Colonel Preston Brown urged GHQ to move the 42d Division forward as quickly as possible, but in any event, it would clearly arrive far too late. Swallowing their pride—at least to some extent—Bundy and Brown went to corps headquarters on the evening of June 14 and asked Degoutte to lend them a nearby American regiment—the 3d Division's 7th Infantry, held in reserve behind Château-Thierry to the east—to bolster the marines in Belleau Wood. Degoutte and his soon-to-be replacement, General Stanislaus Naulin, agreed, apparently after some dispute with Bundy. In addition, "for the purpose of enabling the American 2d Division to gain the necessary rest and to reorganize its units which have been engaged in the Bois de Belleau," Degoutte ordered the French 167th Division—which had been engaged in combat in this sector for as long as the 2d Division—to take over the area north of Hill 142 and west of Belleau Wood from the 3/6th and 1/5th Marines.[16]

Despite the gas, Americans and Germans continued to spar at various points on June 14–15. At 0300 on the fourteenth, some of Wise's marines made a probing attack against Hartlieb's positions in the northwest woods. Although some of the Americans donned German helmets and called out orders to retreat in German as they advanced, those tricks had become stale, and they were driven back. Near a stone bridge at Bouresches at about 0800, a patrol of the 23d Infantry attempted to sneak up on a German officers' post of the 109th Grenadiers and storm it with grenades. Although they succeeded in wounding four of the Germans, an alert sentry "picked off" one of the Americans with his rifle, and the rest were driven back before they could recover the body. When not conducting or fending off raids or donning masks in the midst of wafting clouds of gas, other Americans busied themselves with hunting down spies. Some of them found a "Russian prisoner" loafing near the 5th Marines' regimental headquarters, accused him of "tapping their lines," and dispatched him under guard to division headquarters.[17]

For all the constant probing and the "dirty tricks" regularly employed by both sides, the "rules of war"—and possibly a sense of mutual respect—were beginning to settle around Belleau Wood. General Hell's divisional orders noted that the Americans had shown "that they respect the Red Cross flag." German stretcher bearers were generally permitted to rescue their wounded unmolested, and the Germans reciprocated by not firing on American ambulances going into Bouresches. "This tacit agreement is to be respected by all commands," Hell ordered. And although the recent gas shelling by the Germans was considered worthy of reprisal, the Americans had little with which to deliver a counterblow. French artillery requested and then hoarded mustard shells of their own, ostensibly to avenge their American comrades, but they did not actually use them until the attack on Vaux early the next month. American divisional artillery had to make do with whatever gas shells they could scratch together to fire back at the Germans, but they reportedly managed to inflict some 400 casualties.[18]

On the morning of June 15, most of the marines in the southern woods pulled out according to Harbord's orders. Wise held on in the north, awaiting relief from the 7th Regiment, which was to commence that evening and continue through the following day. To unify command in the woods—and partly to allay the difficulties between Wise and Hughes—Harbord had given Lieutenant Colonel Logan Feland responsibility for that area on June 14, and Feland arrived at Wise's command post that evening. That night and the following morning, he scouted German positions in the woods' northwestern corner and concluded that they would be difficult to uproot. "The topography is so difficult and the woods so dense in the north half of the Bois de Belleau," Harbord reported to Bundy at 2000 hours, "that the troops that have occupied it have been unable to entirely clear it of the enemy. There is a small knoll in the western half of the north end of the wood on which there are an estimated number of 40 or 60 Germans with several machine guns." Attempts to outflank and surround this knoll had so far been unsuccessful.[19]

Partly to exert pressure on this knoll and to secure Wise's left, Feland directed the 17th Company to enter the woods from the southwest. Captain Roswell Winans did so at about 0715 on June 15, supported by guns of the 1/5th Battalion's 8th Machine Gun Company and elements of the 49th and 66th Companies. They succeeded in pushing back Hartlieb's outer sentries and establishing contact with Wise, but the Germans immediately counterattacked with infantry, accompanied by both heavy and light machine guns. By 0820, the 17th Company had been pushed out of the woods, and Wise's flank was back in the air. Fortunately, although the Germans followed up with some probing attacks of their own that evening, they made no attempt to press the marines very hard. That night, the German 87th Division began its relief of the 237th Division—a process slated for completion by June 19. Under the new arrangement, the 87th took full responsibility for Belleau Wood, while the 28th Division shifted directly to the east—its 109th and 110th Grenadier Regiments in the line, and the battered 40th Fusiliers in reserve.[20]

The untried US 7th Regiment approached the dreaded "hell wood" that evening, with orders to complete its relief of the marines by the night of June 16–17. It was to remain under the command of the 2d Division until June 22, when it would be pulled out. "While the American 7th Infantry is holding the front," ordered General Stanislaus Naulin, the newly appointed commander of the French XXI Corps (Degoutte having been promoted to command the French Sixth Army), "the 4th Brigade of Marines will be given the maximum of rest. Its only duty will be to hold its least tired battalions as reserves, ready in case of need, either to occupy the support line or to be used on any part of the front that may be attacked." As for the 7th Regiment, Brown told its commander, Colonel Thomas M. Anderson Jr., that it was entering the lines only "for purposes of trench relief." Anderson and his soldiers were willing, but they would soon find that they had been assigned a thankless task.[21]

11

Enter the US Army
Belleau Wood, June 16–21, 1918

Relief of the marines in Belleau Wood, led at first by soldiers of the US 1/7th Battalion, 3d Division, commanded by Lieutenant Colonel John P. Adams, was completed during the night and morning of June 15–16. Wise, eager for relief, "cursed the hell" out of the soldiers as they arrived. "Don't you God-damned fools know there's a war on?" he shouted. The soldiers marched forward under direct observation of German artillery, and Wise ordered their officers to take cover and hurry up their men. The soldiers nevertheless managed to deploy with few casualties. The 1/7th Battalion placed four companies in positions vacated by the 2/5th, 2/6th, and 1/6th Marines. Farther back, the 2/7th Battalion was assigned the gruesome task of cleanup. This entailed burial details for the numerous dead marines who had been left behind by their comrades, along with dead Germans, wrecked machine gun nests, mortars, and discarded equipment. As the woods were still polluted by mustard gas, this was no easy chore, but it was probably a useful introduction to what the soldiers could expect during their week in the line. On the following night the 3/7th Battalion would move into position to the left rear, along the Lucy-Torcy road. Despite the changeover in personnel, Colonel Neville remained in command of the divisional sector, and Lieutenant Colonel Feland maintained overall responsibility for the woods. Colonel Anderson reported to them, and they had the final say on how the 7th Regiment would be employed.[1]

Wise knew that relief had not come too soon as he watched his men depart: "Two weeks' growth of beard bristled on their faces. Deep lines showed, even beneath beard and dirt. Their eyes

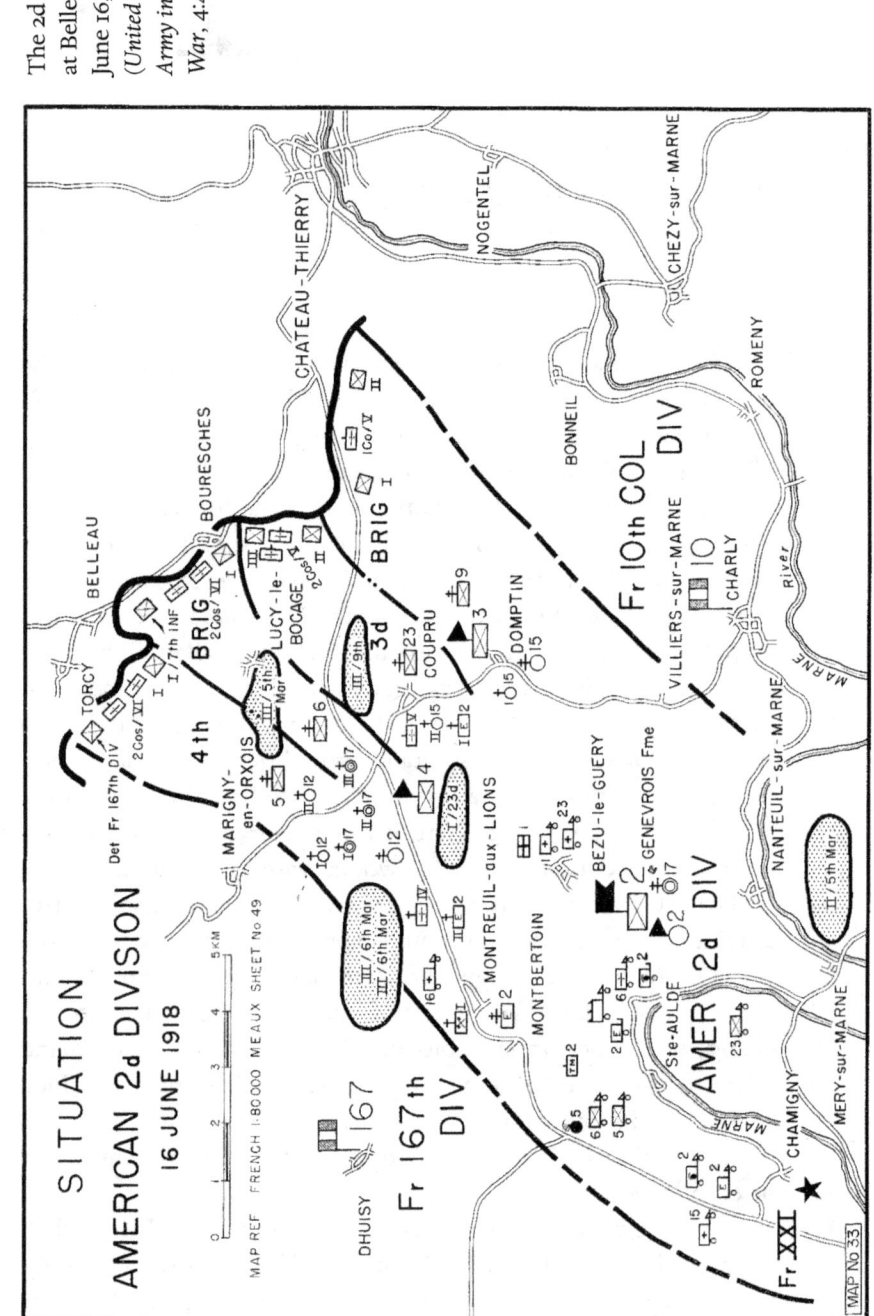

The 2d Division at Belleau Wood, June 16, 1918. (*United States Army in the World War*, 4:496)

were red around the rims, bloodshot, burnt out. They were grimed with earth. Their cartridge belts were almost empty. They were damned near exhausted. Past physical limits. Travelling on their naked nerve. But every one of them was cocky—full of fight."[2]

As his battalion entered the reserve two miles back, Wise reported to Neville on the lessons the marines had learned during their days in the woods: "We were continually fighting for two weeks," said Wise, "and during that time, the men did not have even a hot cup of coffee and lived entirely on cold food, and at times water was scarce, and from June 11 were without packs. I have never seen such a spirit as existed in the men in regard to every task that was given them and their losses seemed to inspire fresh courage, and at all times were eager for the attack." Wise's tactical lessons included the advice that "automatic and rifle fire from the hip was the only kind that could be used in thick cover and it was found very effective." Rifle and hand grenades proved useful, but artillery was unable to drive enemy machine guns out of the woods; for that, it took "the personal contact of the bayonet." Moreover, "in open warfare and when the lines are under 1000 yards, sniping was very successful as they had no idea we could kill at that range." For their part, the Germans used the same weapons, along with 37mm, 47mm, and even 77mm artillery, at point-blank range against marine positions.

The employment of deception—dirty tricks—had become a standard part of both the American and the German repertoires. Wise advocated the use of German-speaking men to call on the enemy to surrender, which was cheaper for both sides than "killing all in sight"; however, as advances progressed, "it is a safe method to bayonet all men on the ground as some are not wounded." Likewise, for safety's sake, it was essential to disable enemy machine guns as soon as they were captured; otherwise, the Germans could be counted on to slip back in and use them again. At bay, Wise found that the Germans were "only too willing to surrender," and when captured, they "were more than willing to tell everything they knew and, in fact, to assist you, as the ones I saw were dead tired of the war." To exploit the knowledge obtained from prisoners, Wise urged that intelligence sections maintain expert interrogators near the front, so they could glean information quickly from captured Germans; likewise, staff officers should be present to process such information quickly. The Germans' pleasure at captivity and their willingness to talk were enhanced by their surprise at not being killed immediately, since Germans soldiers had been told that marines took no prisoners. Nevertheless, the marines had found it expedient to use captured Germans as human shields to approach enemy machine gun nests, "as they would not shoot on their own men."

Wise spoke with the authority of a combat veteran who had made mistakes and learned from them. Among his mistakes, as he freely admitted, was dispatching untrained replacements directly into the lines, where they often proved to be more of a danger to themselves and their comrades than to the enemy. Thanks in part to these painful lessons, Wise had lost a good two-thirds of his command: his battalion, which had entered the woods with 965 men and 26 officers, lost 615 men and 19 officers before it departed. "I can also state with pride," he concluded, "that we may have overrun ground, but not one inch of it that was ever taken up was given after consolidation." Whether the 7th Regiment would be able to learn these lessons—which Wise evidently did not bother to communicate—and perform to the same standards remained to be seen. As the soldiers probably realized, however, their inevitable errors would be viewed with scant tolerance by the battle-tested marines.[3]

For that matter, the Germans would be even less tolerant of the soldiers' mistakes. They too had learned lessons in those brutal woods, and they had carefully studied the tactics employed by their enemies. On June 17–18 a German IV Reserve Corps intelligence officer—one Lieutenant Von Buy—presented a detailed evaluation of the US 2d Division based on field experiences and interrogations of American prisoners. American attack tactics, based on what the Germans had encountered since June 6, seemed to consist of the following:

> 3 to 4 skirmish lines with about 30 to 50 paces distance between lines, fairly close behind these came separate attack groups in platoon column formation. They were well equipped with rapid-fire weapons and hand grenades. The attack groups worked their machine guns to the front and had instructions to penetrate the German positions at some weak position, then veer to the flanks and attack the stronger sectors from the rear.

Overall, "the American 2d Division may be rated as a very good division, if not even as an attack unit," Von Buy reported. He continued:

> The various attacks by both of the Marine regiments were carried out with vigor and regardless of losses. The moral effect of our firearms did not materially check the advance of the infantry. The nerves of the Americans are still unshaken. . . . The personnel may be considered excellent. They are healthy, strong and physically well-developed men from 18–20 years old who, at present, lack only the necessary training

to make them a very worthy opponent. The spirit of the troops is fresh and one of careless confidence. A characteristic expression of one of the prisoners is "we kill or get killed." . . . In general, the prisoners made a wide-awake, agreeable impression; but they seem entirely disinterested in military matters. They were intentionally kept ignorant of certain things by their superiors, for instance, most of them have never seen a map. . . . For the time being, they still view the war from the standpoint of the "Big brother" who is coming to the aid of his distressed brothers and sisters, and who is being received everywhere with a friendly welcome. However, a certain moral basis is not lacking; the majority of the prisoners stated with obvious unconcern that they had come to Europe to defend their fatherland. Only a few of the men are genuine Americans by ancestry, the majority is of German, Dutch, or Italian parentage; but these half-Americans who, with few exceptions, were born in America, and who never before had been in Europe, consider themselves unhesitatingly as genuine sons of America.[4]

The same evaluation process for the 3d Division would result in the following observations on June 21:

The men appear to be in good health and are strong; they carried out their raid in the Bois de Belleau [on June 20] with much valor but somewhat awkwardly. The division may be accepted as a good average division whose combat value is apt to increase with a little more war experience. These men are not, as is the case with the 2d American Division, mostly volunteers, but have been drafted.[5]

Whereas the marines were rated a "very good" division in the German estimation, the soldiers were rated a "good average" division.

Now opposite the Americans in Belleau Wood was the 87th Division, designated by them a "fourth class unit." The unit it had replaced—the 237th Division, with its 461st Regiment commanded by Major Bischoff—had given a good account of itself in the woods. The same could not be said for the 28th Division, which remained in line to the east of the woods. Although his available tools were hardly keen-edged, Von Conta took an aggressive stance toward the Americans. The commander of the 87th Division requested permission to abandon the woods altogether and withdraw to Belleau and the reverse slope of Torcy to create a clear field of fire against possible future attacks, but Von Conta would have none of it.

Both divisions, he ordered at 2000 hours on June 16, must continue to make strong "assault raids" on Belleau Wood and Bouresches. These, along with coordinated high-explosive and gas barrages, would be aimed at inflicting "the heaviest casualties possible" on the Americans, including prisoners, and keeping them off balance.[6]

These aggressive patrols and raids took place as soon as the 7th Regiment moved in and continued unabated for the next few days. German patrols made almost constant attempts to infiltrate American positions by slipping between their outposts and establishing machine gun nests deeper in the woods, and they sometimes launched attacks against the 7th Regiment and the 3d Brigade. At 0200 on June 19, for example, a nine-man patrol from the 1/109th Grenadiers, led by a corporal, approached an American sentry post at the northeastern edge of Bouresches. Their mission was to capture the sentry for the purpose of determining his unit—the Germans were particularly interested in whether the Americans still held the village or whether the French had moved in. At 0300 the raiders arrived near the post, under a "ball-shaped tree." The corporal signaled, and four of his men sprang forward to capture the sentry. Startled but alert, the sentry cried out—just in time. A nearby American machine gun opened fire, and several other American soldiers darted out of a nearby house, firing rifles and throwing grenades. The Germans fled, leaving behind three wounded, who lay there all night, groaning and calling for aid. The Americans brought them in later, securing prisoners of their own. Other raids were more successful, and German shelling caused a hundred casualties per day.[7]

The Americans' ability to respond was limited by the resources available to them. As ill luck would have it, the French chose this moment to limit the expenditure of ammunition by 2d Division artillery, which had lavishly supported marine operations after the ill-advised restraint ordered by Harbord on June 6–7. American artillery "activity is often limited by the number of shells supplied by the French, who frequently report that the expenditure of ammunition by the American artillery is excessive," reported the 2d Division's journal of operations on June 16. "In order to reduce the expenditure they fix a daily supply, which, in the opinion of our artillery officers, is often inadequate." In addition, against the "very marked" activity of enemy aircraft, the French cut back their aircraft deployments in response.[8]

The soldiers were nevertheless eager to test their mettle. On June 17 Naulin ordered the French 167th Division and US 2d Division to "accentuate along the entire front the offensive activity necessary to maintain our ascendancy over the enemy and to improve our positions." The 167th Division was to drive toward Hautevesnes, and the 3d Brigade was to advance (as Degoutte had ordered a few days earlier) to a line from Triangle to Hills 182 and 192 and Vaux. Meanwhile, the 4th Brigade was to study prospects for an advance to a line between Hill 142 and "the summit north of Bois de Belleau, with a view to shortening the front between these two points and to effect thereby a greater economy of forces." In other words, the eventual capture of the remainder of Belleau Wood was still an objective. Toward this end, and to maintain an active stance toward the enemy, Harbord directed the 1/7th to begin operations against the enemy in Belleau Wood on June 18–19.[9]

Unlike its predecessors in the 237th Division, the 87th Division elected to distribute its forces in the woods in depth, with elements of its 347th Regiment facing the 1/7th Battalion. Although this contradicted the methods Bischoff had employed, the deployment in depth proved effective at first. The Americans, unlike their comrades of the 30th Regiment on Hill 204, lacked veteran tutelage from either the French or the marines, so they carried out their first offensive operations by the book. Nor did Harbord or Feland make any effort to transmit to the soldiers the tactical lessons the marines had learned over the preceding days. The results were not pretty. On the evening of the June 18, B Company of the 1/7th Battalion attacked the Germans arrayed along the rocky knoll without artillery support, but with light machine guns and grenades. They were repulsed, with twenty-one casualties. Early the next morning, C Company tried again and reached a trench atop the knoll, but it was also repulsed—bloodily—with sixty-three casualties.[10]

The soldiers launched another attempt on June 20. Elements of three companies took part, and once again, there was no artillery support. They advanced, said the Germans, "in strong . . . skirmish lines"—and were mown down, leaving behind sixty to seventy dead "within a small area." A German postaction evaluation presumed that the Americans had attacked to disable some machine guns that "were quite troublesome" and observed: "The distribution for the attack was carried out so as to allow a strong line of riflemen, followed up by several assault detachments in the strength of about ten men, abundantly armed with hand grenades." Though defeated, the Americans had, according to their enemies, fought bravely.[11]

Harbord was not only unsympathetic to the 1/7th Battalion's struggles—he was contemptuous. Despite everything that had gone before, and despite reports from recent marine and army patrols indicating that German positions in the northwestern portion of Belleau Wood remained strongly held, he had decided that only one or two German machine guns in the woods were holding the Americans back. And as the case two weeks before had proved, it would take a lot to disabuse the general of an idea he had convinced himself was true. After speaking with Bundy, who expressed his dissatisfaction with the army battalion, Harbord shot off a curt message to Lieutenant Colonel Adams: "Your battalion will be relieved tomorrow night. Tomorrow morning is its only chance to redeem the failure made this morning. If you clear the northern half of the Bois de Belleau, the credit will belong to the 1st Battalion, 7th Infantry, and will be freely given. The battalion cannot afford to fail again." The soldiers had been held back, the general thought, by a "little machine-gun nest," and they had "failed because, after slight casualties, the companies of the 7th Inf., failed to go forward." The general seemed to have no memories of his own grave misunderstanding of the nature of German resistance in the woods on June 6–7, or of the struggles his marines had endured in those early days.[12]

Adams, of course, had no choice but to follow orders. But before beginning the attack, set for 0315 on June 21, he gutsily (and rightly) told Harbord that it would be "absolutely necessary" for his battalion to receive ample supplies of hand and rifle grenades (which the marines had lacked during their first days in the woods), mortar and artillery support (hitherto denied, despite the bloody lessons of June 6–7), and food so that the attacking company "may have supper before beginning fight." In a postscript, Adams added that the Germans had managed to infiltrate a number of machine guns into his rear. He warned: "Under the conditions noted I do not believe any attack without a heavy artillery fire preceding can move the [German] guns from the woods. They are all emplaced and strongly held. The woods is almost a thicket and the throwing of troops into the woods is filtering away men with nothing gained." After reiterating the essential need for substantial artillery support, Adams continued: "I can assure you that the orders to attack will stand as given but it cannot succeed. This is only my individual expression and has not reached the ears of any one else."

Adams concluded by noting a curious anomaly in his dispositions, which had presumably been set by Feland and Neville. "The line held by Co. B," he pointed out, "can be crushed at any time and it leaves the woods open. Please consider this. It is serious and requires immediate action, for I can assure you that it is only made after careful consideration and earnest thought." To Harbord, this objection must have seemed odd, as both he and the regimental commander, Colonel Anderson, believed that Company B was supposed to be on the battalion's left front, with its left resting on the western edge of the woods and its right in liaison with Company A. As the events of the following morning would reveal, however, Company B had its right on the western edge of the woods and its left bent back to the south in liaison with the 3/7th Battalion to the rear. A gap therefore existed between the right of Company B and the left of Company A, and the Germans had apparently already infiltrated machine guns into that gap. As Wise's earlier experiences had shown, it was easy to lose direction in the woods, but because Adams did not clarify the nature of his dispositions, Harbord ignored the warning. After agreeing to artillery support—which he treated as a major concession, when it should have been a sine qua non—the general gave Adams a simple order: "Your troops will attack at 3:15 and capture or destroy the enemy."[13]

During the night of June 20–21, the 1/7th Battalion withdrew about 200 meters to allow the artillery to shell German positions in the northern woods; this was supposed to consist of light to moderate shelling from midnight until 0200, after which "all the artillery" would engage "in an endeavor to crush the enemy" until the attack began at 0315. Although the official 3d Division history claims that the preparatory bombardment "failed to materialize," Harbord recorded on the day of the battle that it "proceeded as planned," and German records indicate that they were indeed subjected to a strong bombardment. Then the Germans retaliated. Alerted by the American barrage or by some other means, German artillery opened up a damaging and accurate counterfire on the 1/7th Battalion's positions just after the advance began.[14]

The attack was doomed from the start. Company B, facing in the wrong direction, advanced into empty space and never engaged the enemy. Company A, with Company C in support, advanced straight into the teeth of the German counterbarrage and was torn to pieces by shell fire just as the enemy machine guns opened up. The company reeled back, "practically stunned," and suffered about 150 casualties. Harbord recounted the claims of Captain Helms, the company commander:

> That something, a hand grenade he thinks, struck close to him and stunned him. That when he recovered consciousness he saw sixteen or seventeen men of his company running back toward their former position. That he tried to rally them, but could not. That he stopped to attend to a wounded man, and then got lost, and reported at the P.C. of the 3d Bn. This officer has no marks of any kind on himself or his clothing. The P.C. at which he reported is a full kilometer west of where he claims to have been stunned, and in the opposite direction from his company.[15]

The imputation of cowardice was crystal clear.

If some soldiers and even officers fled, however, others pushed ahead.

Company C advanced and, sweeping up the remnants of Company A, engaged the enemy to within "four paces" of the German 2/347th Battalion's main line of resistance. The fighting was bitter for a time, and there was a moment when it appeared that the Americans had broken through. But the green Yanks were no match for the ingenuity of the defenders, who had apparently learned some tricks from their predecessors of the 461st Regiment. As Colonel Anderson later reported to Harbord:

> The officers and several enlisted men questioned by me all said that the enemy they saw were in groups of from 6 to 10 to 12, manipulating machine guns and rifles, and were dressed in American uniforms; that certain of them mixed with our troops and attempted to interfere with the plan of attack, saying that the line should not advance as our own people were up there and we should not kill our own people. At one point in the attack, when the line had engaged the enemy, a German in American uniform approached Lieut. Paysley of Co. A saying to him: "My God, you are not going to fire on your own men out there in front of you; you are not going to kill your own men." It being so apparent to Lt. Paysley that this officer was an enemy in our own uniform, that he immediately shot and killed him, in the excitement of the moment not obtaining insignia or identification from the body. It is quite apparent that the enemy so dressed tried to influence the movements in this attack.

The attack failed. Company C incurred about thirty casualties, Company A shattered, and Company B sent panicky but false messages that the Germans had broken through to its right rear. The 1/7th Battalion thus fell back to its previous positions under a cloud of ignominy. The entire regiment was due to be relieved by the marines on the following day, and Harbord would not be sorry to see it go. Overall, he concluded that the regiment was "unreliable" because of the "inefficiency" of its officers and the poor training of its men. Among its battalions, the 1/7th was "untrustworthy for first line work"; the 2/7th had performed acceptably, but "nothing but watching was required of it"; and the 3/7th had shown "no enterprise" in sending out patrols, and those it had sent out "accomplished nothing."[16]

The 7th Regiment had unquestionably shown poor initiative. Its inexperienced officers and men were understandably intimidated by the situation, and instead of patrolling aggressively, they had hunkered down in their posts and allowed the Germans to infiltrate their flanks and rear. Captain

P. J. Hurley, commanding the 2/7th Battalion, subsequently reported that although the men were eager to fight, "platoon leaders as a rule are not equal to their task. They are willing enough, but ignorant. During excitement, they take orders from anyone who ranks them, whether they belong to their units or not, regardless of what previous explicit orders had been given them. In attacks this is going to be a serious menace."[17]

Unsurprisingly, the soldiers' understanding of tactics was rudimentary. They had little concept of fire and maneuver or the use of supporting arms. Nor had the soldiers employed any snipers, an essential element of combat under these conditions. Harbord therefore sent out specific instructions to the marines who were about to reenter the woods (which he had failed to do for the soldiers) that they should use snipers to "reduce the German positions without much expenditure of men. These men should be provided with canteens of water, with some rations and crawl out toward the German position exerting every effort, exercising the patience of Indians and waiting for shots without exposing themselves." Sent out in pairs from all sides, these snipers would also be able to help stop German infiltration.[18]

Arguably, the 7th Regiment had been set up to fail. When the regiment arrived in Belleau Wood, Harbord insisted that Neville and Feland retain full authority over its activities and dispositions. Anderson and his battalion commanders were given no leeway for initiative of any kind. At the same time, Neville and Feland—to say nothing of Harbord—apparently provided no tutelage to the army officers or men. Marine battalion commanders such as Wise and other field officers were just a little more helpful, providing only the barest instructions to their successors on June 16 before hightailing it out of the woods as quickly as they could—and leaving behind many dead marines for the soldiers to bury. As Captain Hurley reported:

> As far as getting any information was concerned, the whole movement [into the woods] was attended by chaos. The company commanders and myself were taken to brigade headquarters, then walking to 5th Marine Hqs., then to 6th Marine Hqs., and finally to the woods, arriving there at 5 o'clock. At none of these places, except brigade headquarters [where Harbord remained out of touch with the true situation] did we receive any information.

The contrast with the 30th Regiment, which received close and constant guidance from the French on Hill 204, is stark.[19]

Moreover, Harbord imposed on the 7th Regiment what would later be denoted "mission creep." The regiment entered the woods with the stated objective of doing no more than holding the lines for a week so the marines could rest, and the soldiers deployed accordingly. Told only to hold on, they had no incentive to take any initiative against the enemy. "General Harbord said, 'Your mission is to hold the line' and we held it," reported Captain Hurley. "That was all the information or orders I received." After a few days, however, Harbord demanded that the regiment attack and attempt to clear the enemy out of the remainder of Belleau Wood, employing the same open-warfare tactics that had been discredited on June 6–7 and dismissing enemy opposition as no more than a "little machine gun nest." That the soldiers failed should have come as no surprise, but Harbord made no apology for his or the marines' role in their failure. Instead of offering advice, Harbord tossed the 7th Regiment into Belleau Wood with the injunction to sink or swim. When it sank, he turned away in contempt. He treated the marines with far greater indulgence.[20]

Harbord's obvious favoritism for the marines—which the ineffectual Bundy shared—created serious resentment within and without the division, especially when combined with the overblown praise the marines received from the American publicity machine. The 3d Division commander, General Dickman, was furious at glaring headlines claiming, "With the help of God and a few Marines we stopped the Germans at Château-Thierry." The press gave no credit to the soldiers who had engaged the enemy first. Dickman also resented criticism of his 7th Regiment, which had failed because of incomplete training, inexperience, unfamiliarity with the territory, and lack of artillery support up to June 21. The Germans, he proudly noted, had at least credited his soldiers with "audacity"—praise that was not forthcoming from Harbord or the marines.[21]

Colonel Malone, commanding the 23d Regiment, responded to reports of the 7th Regiment's struggles by saying, "We have to accept small knocks and smile. Better luck next time." But he and his battalion commander had problems of their own with the marines and with divisional administration. Since the missteps of June 6 during the advance to Hill 192—which some soldiers believed they had undertaken in support of the marines, and for which they had received ample blame but no credit—the army regiments of the 3d Brigade had played a decidedly unglamorous supporting role. Only after the marines had utterly exhausted themselves around Belleau Wood was the 3/23d Battalion shifted into Bouresches and closer to the action. But there the soldiers found themselves short of supplies, under constant German observation and fire, and still treated as an afterthought by divisional command, which seemed to be interested only in the marines.[22]

Malone brought the simmering problems in Bouresches to the attention of Colonel Preston Brown on the afternoon of June 16. "Our men," said Malone, "are beginning to sicken at the French canned meat and in general do not like the French ration. Some diarrhea is beginning to appear. Can we not get fresh meat and if not all at least a portion of the American ration?" His officers reported that the cans of beans and stew that arrived at night were often spoiled and had to be thrown away. Malone attempted to address the supply troubles by requisitioning a Ford truck from a machine gun unit to carry rations to Bouresches, but Major Elliott, commanding the 3/23d Battalion, complained that the food they received was still spoiled and that "canned alcohol" was running short.[23]

But nothing changed, and the men in Bouresches grew increasingly sick of their predicament. On June 20 Captain Charles E. Moore of I Company contacted Elliott regarding the temporary relief of his company by K Company. Moore claimed that Captain Valentine, the commander of K Company, "has absolutely no confidence in his men as they are," for they were poorly organized and distinctly "nervous" about entering the lines. "I am tired and my men are tired but it's the kind of state, that nothing will help a great deal unless we get entirely out of it," Moore continued. "When I leave this place I want to keep on going until I get entirely out of it and never see it again."[24]

On the same day, Elliott relayed to Malone his own frustrations with the ridiculous orders filtering down from the regimental staff (which relayed orders from higher up):

> As some of the requests, orders, and reports of some of the staff are so absurd, ludicrous, and in many cases impossible, I request that the [regimental gas, intelligence, signals, and medical] officers visit my C.P. [command post] as soon as possible to see situations for themselves.... To receive instructions that no one will sleep within 1200 yds. of the front line unless in a gas-proof dugout and with gas sentries over each dugout, would keep us awake all of the time.... Another is that a man who is exposed to mustard gas should have a warm bath with soap and change of clothing, when as a matter of fact, we don't get enough water to wash regularly and some are about to fall through their clothes even though requisitions were submitted some time ago.... When we are doing all in our power... it becomes

exasperating to receive so many orders and requests which someone had "doped" out of a book and from the maps. Another thing they should remember is that the actual defense of this position must be considered and that it takes some time each day.[25]

While no military formation has ever been immune to griping, a sense of neglect and resentment was clearly brewing in the 3d Brigade.

Word of the soldiers' increasing disquiet reached Bundy, who relayed through Malone his approval of the 3/23d Battalion's "splendid work" in Bouresches. But Moore and Elliott were unimpressed. Despite Malone's complaints, the ration situation remained dismal. The soldiers in Bouresches had slaughtered some cows out of desperation, but they had no salt and, for the most part, had to make do with some old canned French "monkey meat" left behind by the marines and some half-rotten potatoes they found in cellars. Hearing it said that they were "nicely situated" in Bouresches, Moore's frustration boiled over in a communication to Elliott on June 22: "Please extend my invitation to any one at Hdqrs. who feels so inclined, to pay a little visit." Moore continued:

> If they consider, having a town completely demolished over head, suffering 12 to 15% casualties, not having sufficient food, previously having 100 to 500 shells dropped on you every day and night, having to *sneak* and gum-shoe wherever you go running here and there across spaces open to observation, being sniped at constantly, having to remain under cover, when not actually on post, in places that are not shell proof, to be covered with lice and fleas and to be under the mental and physical strain that the men are under, if they call that "nicely situated" I would like some of them to try a shift at it, I don't believe there are a great many companies which could have stood what this company has and but for the emergency they wouldn't have done it and I want the men to get every bit of credit that is justly theirs.

Malone tried to calm Moore by saying that the phrase "nicely situated" referred to the deployment of his machine guns, and he praised Moore effusively. "God bless you, and will never forget what you have done," he concluded.[26]

Words could temporarily placate, but they could not heal such resentments. Rather than addressing the army regiments' sense of neglect directly, Bundy elected to push them to the sidelines. The marines were coming back into the lines and would be relieving the 23d Regiment in

Bouresches. The 3/5th Marines would replace the 1/7th Battalion in northern Belleau Wood, the 3/6th Marines would replace the 2/7th Battalion in the southern woods, and the 2/5th Marines would replace the 3/7th Battalion in the western end of the sector. It would be up to them, and them alone, to defeat the Germans and claim the final glory for the conquest of Belleau Wood.

12

Finishing the Job
June 22–July 2, 1918

The Marine Brigade returned to Belleau Wood between June 22 and 24, still tired and below strength. Its mission remained unclear, if only because Harbord still did not know exactly where his front lines were located or what sort of opposition the enemy could muster. For weeks, the general had seen fit to release regular reports—avidly consumed by the media—that the woods had been completely or almost taken, and he had blustered about the 7th Regiment's inability to finish the job by clearing out a "little" machine gun nest. Reports to the contrary were regularly submitted by marine and army officers on the ground, but Harbord either ignored them at the outset or forgot about them hours later in favor of more optimistic reports that better fit his preconceived ideas.

Now, however, Harbord suddenly admitted to himself and others that the Germans still held part of the woods in strength. "The statement made by a German deserter that the German line runs through the northern part of the Bois-de-Belleau is practically true," he told Bundy on June 22. "Reconnaissance made shows that the Germans hold a small fraction of the northern part of this woods." This "small fraction," which Harbord thought consisted of about 200 meters of the woods' northwestern edge, was not an isolated pocket but an integral part of the enemy line into which the Germans had long been "free to come and go." Rather than fessing up to his own ignorance of the situation on the ground and his refusal to credit reports of enemy dispositions, the general took this opportunity to throw his subordinates—both marine and army—under the bus. "The undersigned has been misled as to affairs in that end of the woods," he fretted, "either consciously or

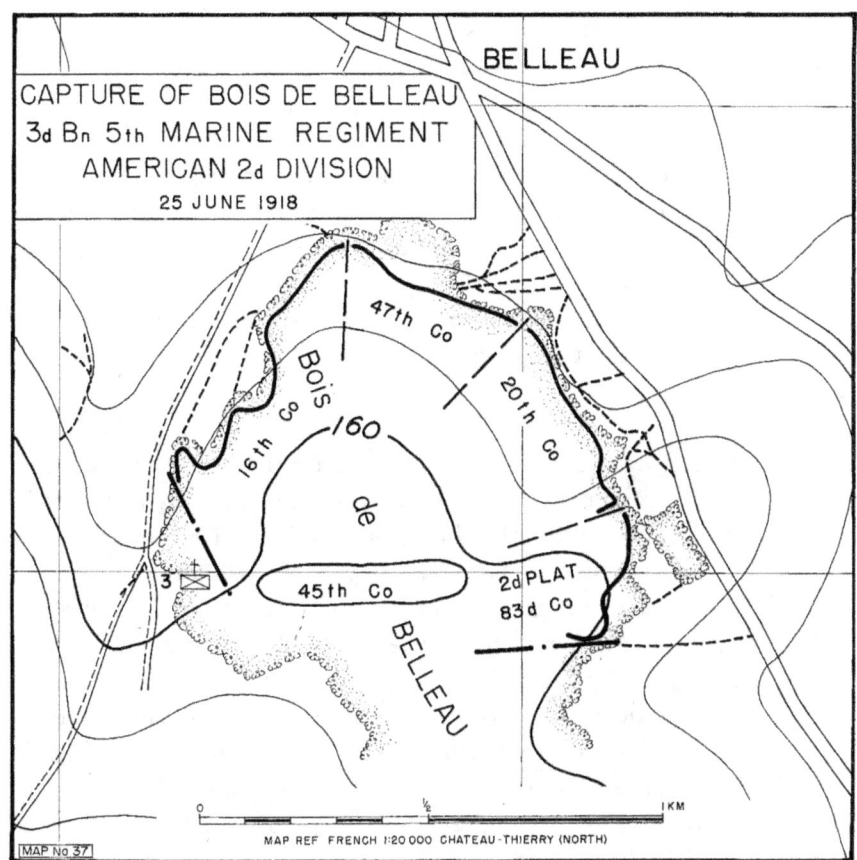

Completing the capture of Belleau Wood, June 25, 1918. (*United States Army in the World War*, 4:562)

unconsciously, ever since its first occupation by the battalion under command of Lieutenant Colonel Wise and later by the battalion of the 7th Infantry." Harbord relieved Wise because of this, and he gave command of the 2/5th to Major Ralph S. Keyser.[1]

Dubbing the continuing German occupation of part of Belleau Wood "intolerable," Harbord commanded Shearer, whose 3/5th now occupied the section of the northern woods possessed by the marines, to drive the enemy out of the remainder by 2200 on June 23. There would be no additional artillery preparation. Instead, the marines would make ample use of snipers—as Harbord had separately prescribed—mortars, and rifle and hand grenades. Even as the attack was under way, however, Harbord reverted to characterizing it as an operation "against the machine-gun nest in the northern part of the Bois de Belleau."[2]

FINISHING THE JOB [189]

At 1900 hours the 3/5th Marines, led by the 16th and 20th Companies, assaulted the German positions defended by elements of the 347th and 3d Ersatz Regiments. At first the marines appeared to make good progress, and the Germans realized immediately that these were no greenhorns. "The enemy during these attacks sneaked up cautiously and had disguised themselves by fastening green tufts of twigs on their helmets," read a German report. In addition, it claimed, "Alongside the Americans, were also recognized the presence of French Soldiers." The official report of the German 1/347th expounded at length on American tactics, which included the full repertoire of deception that journalists preferred to attribute solely to the dastardly Germans:

> While the enemy approached the clearing on the right flank, dashing forward in rather small groups of from 4 to 8 men, he advanced against the rest of the front in a line of skirmishers with about 2 pace intervals. 1 or 2 light lines of skirmishers appeared to follow in the rear. Received with machine gun and infantry fire, the Americans threw themselves to the ground. In this they showed an astounding tenaciousness, repeatedly spurred themselves on by calling to each other to advance. It required an hour by assaults on our part to subdue the last Americans who had not fallen, who had concealed themselves behind tree trunks and in the thicket, and put them to flight. Summoned by call from two places to come close, two or one men would raise themselves with lifted hands and when our men were about to make them prisoners would throw themselves into the brush. Other Americans behind them fired over them and wounded several of ours. The men who did this were shot by us.

Of course, the Germans did the same whenever they got chance, and eventually, neither side was in the mood to take prisoners. According to Private Frank Jacobs, when he and his fellow marines encountered German machine gun crews shouting *Kamerad*, "we shot down the majority, for we knew if we gave them a chance they would pump us full of machine gun bullets. When we came close to them, they would jump out of their holes and attempt to be friendly. We took a few prisoners for the purpose of getting identification from them."[3]

As Harbord had ordered, the Americans employed grenades in quantity, although Shearer later related that they had insufficient supplies of them. The Germans quickly withdrew from their machine gun nests, but they took both their guns and their dead with them. After the marines had advanced almost 200 meters—according to Harbord, the remaining forest that was still in German hands—they ran into the main enemy line of resistance along the rocky knoll, which was still well within the woods' northern limits. What Harbord had labeled "the machine gun nest" now materialized into an estimated sixteen heavy and thirty-five light enemy machine guns on the 16th Company's front alone. After absorbing about 130 casualties, the marines had to pull back to their original positions.

Neville reported to Harbord at 0105 on June 24: "Things are rather bad. One company almost wiped out." Shearer extrapolated the next morning: "The enemy seems to have unlimited alternate gun positions and many guns. Each gun position covered by others. I know of no other way of attacking these positions with chance of success than one attempted and am of opinion that infantry alone cannot dislodge enemy guns. Water is difficult to obtain and rations scarce. Men and officers very tired, but retain their spirit." This was no idle boast. Despite their defeat, marine patrols prowled the woods all night and through the day to engage the Germans in small firefights. They also actively recovered their own wounded and dead—which had not always been the case in earlier actions—by "creeping up to them with most extreme care." The Germans managed to isolate and surround a few marines, but they refused to surrender and instead "protected themselves with the revolver and had to be shot."[4]

Despite the increasingly elite fighting qualities of his men, Harbord was not satisfied. He had once again been caught red-faced after prematurely announcing success. At 2205 he had reported: "We have captured 5 machine guns and made satisfactory progress. Have suffered some losses." A short time later, however, he had to confess, "Latest reports indicated this was an error. No machine guns were taken, and the lines held are practically the same as those prior to the attack." But nobody bothered to correct Bundy, who telegrammed Pershing on June 24 that the marines had captured five machine guns and "made considerable progress," even as Harbord wrote in the operations report that the attack had been an outright "failure." Forced to admit that the Germans held far more than 200 meters of shattered forest, the general angrily castigated the departing 7th Regiment for misreporting its positions, and he blasted his own marines for not moving ahead forcefully enough when they relieved the soldiers.[5]

Skirmishing continued in the woods all day on June 24, while German artillery saturated the lines of the 9th and 23d Regiments with mustard gas. Despite the detailed "Orders for Gas Defense" issued by the division a week earlier, the Americans responded poorly. As always, the biggest problem was that, after wearing gas masks for hours on end, the men grew frustrated and took them off too soon. Sometimes they even took off their masks before flopping down in gas-poisoned shell holes or trenches to go to sleep. The regiments suffered some 500 casualties.[6]

The battle for Belleau Wood had seemingly reached an impasse. But behind the scenes, the tables were definitely turning. Mentally, the Germans were growing increasingly aware of their own miseries, even as they became more and more bedazzled by their adversaries. Regardless of whether the unsubstantiated legend that the Germans labeled the marines in Belleau Wood *Teufelhunde*—Devil Dogs—is accurate, by the end of June, their interest in the Americans was approaching the level of fascination. On June 24 German VIII Corps headquarters sent out a message to all other army headquarters, the German general staff officers' school in Sedan, and all intelligence officers that included an exceptionally detailed history of the US Marine Corps, as provided by prisoners. The report contained this observation:

> The prisoners are mostly members of the better class, many of them artisans and they consider their membership to the Marine Corps as something of an honour. They proudly resent any attempts to place their Regiments on a par with other Infantry Regiments; call themselves "Soldiers of the Land and the Sea" and are well informed as far as the glorious history of their Regiments during the period of the Revolutionary War is concerned.[7]

German reports about themselves made for depressing reading. The 28th Division commander, General Hell, warned his superiors, "I despair whether the division in its present condition is capable of repelling a strong hostile attack." A June 19 report on the state of his 40th Fusilier Regiment concluded: "Especially the recent fighting in Belleau Woods has greatly weakened the morale and power of resistance of the personnel. In addition the uniforms have suffered; the boots and breeches are badly torn, overcoats and blankets were dropped before the offensive and the personnel are all suffering from colds." The troops suffered particularly from the "appearance of a disease which has the nature of grippe." For the same reason, the 110th Regiment reported on June 23, "The health condition of the troops is poor." Similar conditions prevailed in the 5th Guards, 87th, 201st, and 4th Ersatz Divisions, which together formed Corps Schoeler (VII Corps), now that Corps Conta had been disbanded.[8]

In the close conditions of Belleau Wood, influenza easily skipped the lines. Moore reported on June 24 that "a very large percentage of the Co is suffering from bad colds. It seems to be an epidemic." For the most part, however, the impact of influenza was not as widely recognized among the Americans as it was among the Germans—or it might have been confused with the symptoms of gas poisoning. However tired or sick they were, the marines had become inured to the expectation that they would keep attacking until the whole of Belleau Wood was theirs.[9]

On June 24 Harbord ordered the 3/5th Battalion to withdraw its present lines before 0300 on the following morning. Artillery, including eighteen batteries of French light and heavy guns, would then bombard the woods' northern tip until the fire reached "maximum intensity" at 1700. The marines would then renew their attack. The bombardment was indeed heavy, and this time it was quite effective. At least 2,300 artillery rounds dropped between 0300 and 1700, inflicting what the Germans admitted was "the heaviest kind of losses," as projectiles burst among the trees. Then the marines attacked.[10]

The combat was fierce and protracted. Once again, Shearer's 3/5th Marines led the attack, with the 2/5th Battalion to the west extending its right flank in liaison. Marksman Stabenau of the defending 1/347th Battalion's 2d Machine Gun Company later described rushing from post to post in the woods as the Americans knocked out machine gun nests one by one. The marines were as tough as they come. "The Americans called out: 'German soldiers, surrender!'" remembered Stabenau, who was traumatized by the image of Americans who "smoked cigarettes while they fired with rifles." The Americans were ruthless too. In addition to calling out in German, they paid back the enemy in their own coin by wearing German uniforms. According to the 1/347th Battalion's war diary, "a reliable officer, who came back wounded," reported that "part of the Americans wore German uniforms with the insignia of the 109th Body Gren Regt and sought to create confusion among our men by calling them in German."[11]

The marines' bearing conveyed the certainty that they would not be denied. But the defenders fought bravely. Shearer's men took many casualties, and as officers and NCOs fell, individual marines had to proceed on their own. It didn't slow them down at all. By 1830, the German line was beginning to waver, but reserves rushed into the line at 1912 and restored it within the hour. Some Americans were captured. French and American artillery resumed the bombardment at 2030, however, and within minutes, the marines were back. Within two hours, the Germans had lost all their officers, and only a few remnants were left. Dozens of Germans surrendered, even as their former comrades shot some of them down. Then, suddenly, the defenders broke and fled, abandoning their guns and all their American prisoners. It was 2215. The 1/347th Battalion was utterly wiped out, with only 66 survivors from it and supporting units—all of them wounded—and 440 more killed or captured.[12]

The American victory did not sink in at first. Harbord, contrary to his usual exuberance, cautiously reported to division, "Things are going O.K." Shearer called for reinforcements and warned that "any counterattack by enemy would be fatal to us in present condition." At division headquarters, much of the afternoon had been spent fretting over a report of a possible spy: an old woman who lived on a nearby hill had seen a suspicious character in white corduroy trousers and a funny hat skulking about. By 2300, however, word was beginning to leak out concerning the marines' victory. "Your Shearer battalion has done splendid work," Harbord told Neville at 2320. "I have no fear of a counterattack by the Germans tonight." A few minutes later, a message arrived from the French III Corps, congratulating the Americans on their "splendid success." At 0140 on June 26, 4th Brigade headquarters reported, "A message from the front lines by runner issued at 12:55 stated that the action so far as the Americans are concerned, is over." And for once, they were right.[13]

Even so, Harbord and Bundy were reluctant to declare Belleau Wood entirely theirs. They had done so many times before and been wrong. Colonel Preston Brown's report of operations for June 25 claimed only that the American lines "have been pushed forward but the exact location has not yet been definitely reported," and the division's journal of operations said the marines had advanced "practically to the northern edge." Bundy's telegram to Pershing on operations from June 25 to 26 said only that his division had made a successful attack on German positions "south of Torcy" and that its lines were "slightly advanced in the western part of our sector"; it said nothing about conquering Belleau Wood. For once, it was the Germans who were in denial. To General Hell, the marines' attack meant only that the Americans were still seeking "'newspaper successes' by delivering small raids against our lines."[14]

In the aftermath of the Belleau Wood saga, the 2d Division's army regiments finally received a tidbit they could call their own. On June 12, as noted earlier, Degoutte had conceived the idea of an advance of the 3d Brigade and adjoining units from Triangle to Vaux in a series of "minor attacks." So far, none of these attacks had taken place, although the gradual advance of the French 10th Colonial Division with the US 30th Infantry Regiment to the crest of Hill 204 on the right was a necessary preliminary to the capture of Vaux on the hill's western slopes. On June 25 the French III Corps issued formal orders for the capture of this territory, with an emphasis on the Bois de la Roche (just northwest of Vaux), the village of Vaux, and the remainder of Hill 204. The capture of Hill 204 would be the responsibility of the French 39th Division, which was now under III Corps and would be moving in to replace the doughty 10th Colonial Division on June 26–27. The US 3d Brigade would capture Vaux and all the relevant territory to the west. This was not intended to be a full-scale infantry assault; instead, the commanders of the two divisions would "use such forces as they may consider necessary for this operation, having in mind the desirability of keeping the use of infantry to the minimum." French heavy artillery, including a battalion of 155mm howitzers, would be lent to the Americans for the assault.[15]

Officers and men in the 3d Brigade were eager for the operation to begin. Malone's 23d Regiment, occupying the line from Bouresches to Triangle on the left, had been embarrassed on June 6 and had participated in the defense of Bouresches after the relief of the Marine Brigade, but it had few accomplishments to its credit. Colonel Leroy Upton's 9th Regiment on the right, extending as far as the base of Hill 204 between Monneaux and Vaux, had seen no action at all and was anxious to prove its worth. Fortunately for them, some lessons had been learned at Bundy's headquarters. Days before the proposed attack, divisional intelligence officer Colonel Arthur Conger prepared a thorough intelligence report on Vaux and the German defenses there, based on information gleaned from aerial photographs, prisoners, and a local stonemason. A detailed map of the village and its eighty-two stone houses was made available before the attack. The defending German 201st Division had placed its 402d Regiment and supporting units in and around Vaux, for a total force of about 2,100 men.[16]

Unlike the marines who had been thrown at Belleau Wood without preparation on June 6, the 3d Brigade had time to organize for this operation. Not until 0900 on June 30 did orders arrive setting the attack for 1800 on the following day. French and American artillery began a twenty-four-hour barrage at 1800 on June 30, giving Brigadier General Edward M. Lewis time to confer and peruse intelligence reports and maps at length with Upton and Malone. The 3/23d Battalion would lead the attack on the left, while the 2/9th captured Vaux on the right in liaison with French forces advancing over Hill 204 (those forces no longer included the US 30th Regiment, which had been redeployed east of Château-Thierry on June 10; however, they did include some untested companies of the US 28th Division). The attack orders for the 23d and 9th Regiments were models of thoroughness, specifying dispositions down to the last detail. The 3/23d would advance with three companies in line, and the 2/9th with two.[17]

The artillery barrage, which had been carefully planned, was effective, inflicting severe casualties on the defenders, who were (by their own admission) poorly dug in. The waiting American infantry watched the bombardment with interest, "with most of the men smoking cigarettes" as H-hour approached. When the American and French troops moved forward at 1800, they followed a rolling barrage that was also "very good, [with] no blank spaces." And for once, aircraft worked in close and effective liaison with the American infantry and artillery. Second Lieutenant Robert Kean of the 15th Field Artillery remembered: "On that afternoon . . . there suddenly was a roar from behind our lines and there appeared over the front a score of planes with the Allied insignia. This was very heartening. But this short period was the only time during my stay in the front line when the Allies had control of the air." So far, the operation had been a model of precision.[18]

The infantry assault also went like clockwork. As the soldiers moved forward behind the rolling barrage, German counterfire was insignificant. The 2/9th found Vaux a "wreck," and although many Germans surrendered "with broad grins on their faces," others retreated into deep dugouts. Fortunately, "the plan for cleaning had been rehearsed and was thoroughly carried out." Private William Brown of the 2/9th threw a grenade into the first cellar he encountered, with the following results:

> After the smoke cleared away out came the "Fritzies" with their hands up—and they kept a-coming and a-coming until I thought I'd captured the whole German army. There were twenty altogether and I called out, gun leveled, you know—"Anyone in this bunch speak English?" and one fellow said, "Sure, I'm from Milwaukee" and I said, "Well, tell your friends to keep their hands up and march and do it d--- quick"—and they marched, believe me, and I took them to camp and that's all I did. . . . The poor geeks were half starved. One of them had a loaf of the worst black bread I ever saw and he held on to it—hands up—until we got to camp. . . . And that is how I won my Croix de Guerre.

The 3/23d experienced some flanking fire for a short time but moved forward to take all its objectives on schedule. Together, the two American battalions killed and wounded about 400 Germans and captured some 500 prisoners, at the cost of only 46 killed and 270 wounded and missing.[19]

★ ★ ★

On the right, however, the French, along with two platoons of the US 28th Division's 111th Regiment, were unable to capture the remainder of Hill 204. The failure did not result from any absence of enthusiasm on the Americans' part, although the French approached the operation with a somewhat different mind-set. Lieutenant Bob Hoffman of the 1/111th Battalion's Company A participated in the attack—his first action—and was surprised at the sober attitude of his French comrades. "I went around to talk to them and found them not feeling much like conversation," he remembered. "Some were telling the beads of their rosaries and offering prayers; while still others sat grimly and waited." By contrast, many of Hoffman's American comrades laughed delightedly as the bombardment began: "What must the French have thought of these crazy Americans!" Hoffman studied a book on tactics as H-hour approached. Fortunately, a nineteen-year-old French lieutenant instructed Hoffman on the terrain and the nature of the enemy defenses, disabusing him and the other green Americans of some rear-area legends, such as the one that the Germans had a number of feisty female "Amazons" fighting among them. But not everything the veteran lieutenant told his understudies sank in. Recalled Hoffman, "In the action he was to rush over to me and tell us to slow up, that we were going too fast. But his advice was soon forgotten in the heat of battle."[20]

When the attack on Hill 204 began at 1800 and the bullets began flying, Hoffman forgot everything he had studied in his book on tactics, and he and his men acted by instinct and by whatever "experience" they had gained in life:

> We fought just as our ancestors had always fought—instinctive rushing forward, stopping to shoot, rushing again, and shooting again.... We were advancing, remembering only the moving pictures we had seen of the soldiers fighting in the Civil War, and fighting the Indians in the old pioneer days.... The entire action was like a gigantic Indian fight; pausing to fire, at one time one of our men complained that I had fired my gun too close to his ear. We sniped, rushed forward where we could, crawled through the grass over the more exposed portions; rapid fire, running forward, and soon the Germans would run back, with us getting some of them as they ran.

Hoffman paused to crawl under a raspberry bush and gorge himself on the fruit before reentering the battle. He had no idea what was happening, except that hand-to-hand combat was taking place everywhere. "We kept going on, giving no thought to the manner in which we were overrunning our objective, or our failure to keep contact with the French troops to right and left of us." Hoffman had just finished dispatching a number of Germans in a trench with a Chauchat he had picked up from the ground when he looked behind him and saw that the French had pulled back—"so far back that they were hardly more than specks. I saw tiny men in blue digging in." Eventually, the Americans did too. Such was the "individual initiative" as practiced by Americans entering battle for the first time—a complete free-for-all that must have bewildered the French.[21]

In truth, the operation at Vaux and Hill 204 had not been much of a test. In Vaux, the defending German regiment had simply fallen apart. After a brief and unsuccessful counterattack, the 201st Division abandoned any idea of retaking lost ground, "since . . . it would have led to no advantage, and our infantry in the compact Village of Vaux (shell-shattered) would have been needlessly exposed to heavy bombardment involving many casualties." The capture of Vaux and adjoining territory nevertheless provided a useful experience for the army regiments and a sorely needed boost to their pride. "I consider the manner in which the company officers and all men performed their duties to have been perfect," reported the 2/9th's commander, Major A. E. Bouton. Even occasional acts of indiscipline, born of aggressiveness, appeared in a positive light:

> Practically all officers and men whose duty required their presence in rear of the assaulting companies had to be restrained to prevent them from joining the assaulting troops; in fact, some of them begged so strongly to accompany the assault that, where their presence could be spared, they were allowed to join the attack, and did most excellent work. Some men even went forward without authority and also did excellent work, but I know not of a single case of anyone attempting to go to the rear.

Even the obligatory postbattle German mustard gas attack was well handled. When the drenching bombardment arrived, Malone urged his company officers to "keep masks on all night if necessary, dispose your troops to avoid results." The troops obeyed—the masks stayed on. As a result, the type of gas attack that had caused several hundred casualties in the past inflicted only eighty-six casualties on the night of July 1–2. Unfortunately, an opportunity to launch another well-planned and well-prepared set-piece operation of the sort carried out by the 3d Brigade at Vaux would not come again for a long time.[22]

★ ★ ★

On January 14, 1919, the General Staff's Historical Section presented to Pershing a classified report titled "The American Military Factor in the War." It established, quite unapologetically, the "spin" to be placed on the activities of the 2d Division around Belleau Wood in June 1918. The report set out "the argumentative points put in the most concise and irrefutable form possible, for the use either of diplomats in argument or possibly of our press agents." At the beginning of June, the narrative began, the French were fleeing in disorder before a relentless German advance:

> Finally, when the French retreat had reached the neighbourhood of Château-Thierry, there was nothing left on the line save a weak string of small detachments. Behind these, for many miles, disbanded French troops were pillaging their own country. The news had reached Paris. Profound discouragement had seized both the Army and the public; and, indeed, there seemed to be very little hope left. It was at this moment that the 2nd U.S. Division was rushed to the front [the report did not credit the 3d Division] . . . [and] it would be very difficult indeed to exaggerate the important results that were the outcome of an incident of such apparently small scale. The impression on the broken French troops of seeing our men go into position, the impression on French public opinion of knowing that an American division as a unit had been thrown into a vital part of the line, had a steadying effect. It gave France, so to speak, time to take a breath and to come back once more to the old hope that perhaps after all the United States might prove to be her salvation and the deciding factor in the war. . . . [The 2d Division] had fought superbly, it had by its example improved the French troops in its neighbourhood to an incalculable extent; and it had, partly through the errors of the German High Command, succeeded in stopping the gaping hole through which Paris already thought it saw the advance of the German columns.

The report did not single out the marines, but as they had done the majority of the 2d Division's fighting in June, the lion's share of the credit obviously belonged to them. Here, at least, the army made no effort to sideline the marines. The primary objective was not to score points in an interservice rivalry but to ensure that American military efforts were respected at the Versailles peace conference. After surveying subsequent engagements, the report concluded with a blast at "Anti-American Propaganda" that sought to minimize the US war effort, when in fact "there is every ground for stating that the United States has played the decisive part in the war."[23]

The report's slanderous imputations of French cowardice contradicted facts that were well known to Pershing and other American officers: the French had conducted a phased, fighting withdrawal (by agreement with Bundy and his staff) in front of the 2d Division at the beginning of June, and the French 167th and 10th Colonial Divisions had continued to fight effectively on either flank of the 2d Division throughout the month. Likewise misleading was the reference to French "pillaging," which was apparently based on a few minor instances that the Americans chose to blow out of proportion (and which often appear in American accounts alongside humorous depictions of marines and doughboys raiding abandoned French farms for chickens, pigs, provisions, and other items). No one refuted the report, however, and the images it promoted would stick. Instead of crediting the French as they deserved, American military leaders and commentators, particularly marines, trumpeted their own qualities at their erstwhile comrades' expense. Harbord's diary abounds with Francophobic commentary, and he wrote there in mid-June that from May 27 until the marines arrived, "No unit along their [the French's] entire front had stood against the foe. . . . The first unit to stand . . . was the Marine Brigade." In marked contrast, with the exception of a few snarky remarks by Clemenceau and others, French military officials and journalists went out of their way to praise the Americans' intrepidity, even thanking them for their role in saving Paris—while stopping short, for obvious reasons, of crediting them with winning the war single-handedly.[24]

This refusal to credit the French clearly resulted in part from an unwillingness to admit the utility of their tactics. Pershing and others had decided beforehand that the French and British had grown demoralized by trench warfare, and if the evidence suggested otherwise, then the evidence must be wrong. No effort was expended at GHQ to compare the performance of the US 2d Division at Belleau Wood with that of the French units on its flanks (one of which, the 167th Division, remained in the line long after the marines had departed). Instead, staff officers continued to fret about training programs that infected American officers and men with French methods. On July 5 Colonel Harold B. Fiske, assistant chief of staff in G-5, issued a memo to AEF training officers based on field and training experiences in June. According to Fiske, the French were still trying to "impregnate the American units with French methods and doctrine." He continued:

> In view of these memoranda, I desire to point out the present unsatisfactory situation so far as training is concerned. . . . The offensive spirit of the French and British Armies has largely disappeared as a

result of their severe losses. Close association with beaten forces lowers the morale of the best troops. . . . In many respects, the tactics and technique of our Allies are not suited to American characteristics or the American mission in this war. The French do not like the rifle, do not know how to use it, and their infantry is consequently too entirely dependent upon a powerful artillery support. Their infantry lacks aggressiveness and discipline. The British infantry lacks initiative and resource. The junior officers of both allied services, with whom our junior officers are most closely associated, are not professional soldiers, know little of the general characteristics of war, and their experience is almost entirely limited to the special phases of war in the trenches. [British and French training] has hindered the development of responsibility and self reliance [by American officers]. The assistance of our Allies has become not an asset but a serious handicap in the training of our troops. Berlin can not be taken by the French or the British Armies or by both of them. It can only be taken by a thoroughly trained, entirely homogenous American Army. . . . I strongly recommend that the earliest practicable opportunity be taken to secure our emancipation from Allied supervision.

So far as learning was concerned, it was as if Belleau Wood had not happened at all.[25]

Ironically, the bus that ran over the French also inflicted collateral damage on the reputation of the US Army. Marines thought of Belleau Wood and the saving of Paris as their victory, and they had no intention of sharing the credit with the army. After the battle, Degoutte announced that Belleau Wood would be renamed "Bois de la Brigade de la Marine." It was a fitting tribute, and it was in keeping with strenuous French efforts to credit their American friends and thus strengthen their (unofficial) alliance. Apparently prompted by resentful army generals such as Dickman and Bullard, Pershing reputedly tried (and failed) to cancel Degoutte's gesture. Harbord denounced this move as "pettiness," and so did historian Robert Asprey, who treated the army protest as a simple case of sour grapes: "It is a great pity that these and other envious senior army officers failed to recognize the true symbol of the wood in preference to petty trees, that they failed to appreciate and respect the manner in which accidental participants lived up to the highest traditions of American arms." According to marine historian George B. Clark, "The AEF leaders and those of the Second Division didn't accept the fact that the Marines had made a superb reputation for themselves, and many frankly hated the Marines because of it." Yet army resentment went beyond mere envy. Many army men had good reason to be unhappy: the American publicity machine glorified the marines or even attributed army contributions, such as the defense of Château-Thierry, to them; the 3d Brigade was relegated to second-class status throughout the contest for Belleau Wood; the 7th Infantry Regiment was misused from June 16 to 21; and Bundy and Harbord were often openly contemptuous of army officers and the men under their command, despite the fact that they were army officers themselves.[26]

In a speech to the Detroit Bond Club on February 22, 1928, Harbord—still enamored with his old Marine Brigade, despite his primary role in its practical destruction—perpetuated the standard interpretation of "the stopping of the Germans on the high road to Paris." "No unit along that whole front," he claimed, "had stood against the foe. The first unit to stand, and it not only stood but went forward, was the Second Division—the Marine Brigade of which, for nearly a month, was conspicuously active in the Bois de Belleau." In the process, said Harbord, "the Marine Brigade used up four German divisions." And the legend lives on. "This battle was the most important one fought by American troops in the war," Clark asserts. "It was that which stopped the Germans from any further advance into France. . . . None were so effective in proving the will and ability of the Americans to stay and fight and their determination to win—one month and the Americans not only stayed the rout but beat the mightiest army then in existence." Popular historian Richard Rubin, writing in the *New York Times* in 2014, goes even further. In panegyrics worthy of any journalist writing in 1918, he argues that had the 2d Division "not attacked and taken those woods from the Germans, many [unidentified] historians believe, Germany would have won the war that month." Before the battle began, he explains, the "only hope" of saving Paris had been "to drive the Germans out of Belleau Wood somehow," but as the French were "panicked" and thus "dreaded the prospect" of attacking the horrible woods themselves, they asked the Americans to do it for them. And it was fortunate that they did, for the Americans rejected needlessly complex tactics in favor of the simplest and most effective method of all: charging the enemy. Rubin concludes that "the course of the greatest war the world had ever seen was determined by a charge of men on foot, the oldest maneuver there is."[27]

Any balanced assessment of the 2d Division's performance in the Belleau Wood sector from June 1 to July 1 must move beyond the popular mythology that has held sway since 1918. To begin with, it is clear that the Americans never stopped a German drive on Paris. Paris was not the objective of the offensive that began on May 27. Corps Conta's role in that offensive was subsidiary, and that corps had practically ground to a halt in the face of stout French resistance by the time the 2d Division began entering the lines at the beginning of June. By then, Corps Conta's only objective was to secure positions advantageous for the defense. Moreover, the lion's share of the credit for shutting down the vestige of German momentum that remained should go to the French. From June 1 to 4, French infantry, mostly elements of the 43d Division between Veuilly-la-Poterie and Château-Thierry, conducted a classic and quite successful fighting withdrawal. In the process, the poilus severely bloodied the Germans (as German records make abundantly clear) and gave the Americans precious time to organize their defenses before the expected storm hit. The marines' role in the defense of Les Mares Farm on June 3–4, however bravely conducted, was negligible in the overall strategic scheme and played no significant part in stopping the already exhausted Germans.

The impact of the 2d Division's arrival on French morale is harder to assess. Historian Robert Bruce has asserted that "the valor and rugged determination the Americans exhibited throughout this engagement made a profound impression on the French units operating on their flanks and in support of the operation." There is some primary evidence to support this argument. In mid-June 1918 Major P. H. Clark, the American liaison officer at French GHQ, supplied Pershing with a collection of excerpted quotations by French officers suggesting that the American troops had injected vigor into the French simply by virtue of their freshness and willingness to fight. Other anecdotal evidence, much of it cited by Bruce, also suggests that this is true. Therefore, it is not unreasonable to deduce that the French troops in this sector fought more effectively because they knew the Americans had their backs (although, ironically, numerous American accounts suggest that the French ran away faster because they expected the Yanks to save Paris for them). Also, it is undeniable that the 2d Division had a tangible impact on the overall military situation by freeing French units to rest or to fight elsewhere.[28]

About the next phase of the contest there is little dispute: the attack of the Marine Brigade into Belleau Wood on June 6 and the several days that followed was nothing short of catastrophic. American tactics and battle performance will be discussed shortly, but first, one must ask: was their attack even necessary? In throwing the Americans into the battle on June 6, General Degoutte was guilty of an all-too-common French failing in 1918: exploiting the Americans' eagerness by tossing them casually into battle with scant preparation, resulting in the needless loss of lives. This was not the first or the last time this would happen. After June 6, however, neither Degoutte nor his successor expressed any urgency about the capture of Belleau Wood. Bundy and Harbord were free to proceed essentially as they wished, which might have meant working toward the woods' occupation incrementally (as the French 10th Colonial Division did on Hill 204) or even canceling the operation altogether.[29]

General Böhm maintained that the American decision to launch all-out attacks on Belleau Wood was motivated by the desire to secure "newspaper successes," and he was not entirely wrong. In and of itself, the wood had no particular military value, except locally. Von Conta was much more concerned by the advances of the French 167th Division (which he opposed with his best division, the 5th Guards) and the French 10th Colonial Division with elements of the US 30th Regiment. For Bundy and Harbord, however, the conquest of Belleau Wood quickly became a matter of personal and Marine Brigade reputation and pride. The two generals had prematurely trumpeted their conquest of the woods and been quoted in the American press so many times that they had no choice but to continue until they won the woods in fact. The refusal to allow the French to relieve the marines or to give comparatively well-rested army regiments an opportunity to finish the job can be explained only as an attempt to protect Bundy's and Harbord's reputations and secure glory for the marines. The American generals also sought to impress their allies and secure an independent AEF command. Harbord wrote in his diary in mid-June that he hoped the marines' performance would give the French "High Command a confidence in American troops that will contribute powerfully to the early establishment of an American sector in the Western front where our troops shall operate under their own staff and no longer be step-mothered by the French or British."[30]

The bloody and wasteful attacks that followed cannot be blamed purely on American inexperience. Though unaccustomed to battle conditions on the western front, the marines possessed an almost unimaginable bravery and a willingness to adapt. The soldiers were good men too. A measured approach to the conquest of Belleau Wood would have eased the marines into combat, giving them time to discover their many good qualities. Such an approach also would have inflicted far greater casualties on the aggressive (and proud) Germans, particularly those of the 28th Division and its generals, Böhm and Hell, who were always eager to attack the Americans. Belleau Wood might not have been captured any more quickly, but because of its limited inherent tactical value, that hardly mattered.

Instead of emerging from the battle seasoned and ready for bigger challenges, the 2d Division was so badly handled in Belleau Wood that it never really recovered. Not until Blanc Mont in October did it begin to find its feet and develop the fearsome reputation it deserved. Blame must begin at the top. Bundy was a disengaged division commander who was more concerned with trumpeting the Marine Brigade's achievements—to the detriment of 3d Brigade morale—than with providing direction or control. Harbord's faults were legion. More than any other officer, he was responsible for wrecking the Marine Brigade. His slipshod management of the assault of June 6 resulted in magnificent troops being treated like cannon fodder, at the cost of many lives; the countless attacks he ordered thereafter demonstrated an almost total lack of creativity and vision. He belatedly came around and developed a respect for artillery and well-planned set-piece attacks, but when the US 7th Regiment arrived in the woods in mid-June, he flung these lessons out the window and had the green soldiers attack just as the marines had on June 6. Throughout the contest for Belleau Wood, he remained out of touch with conditions on the ground, but that did not stop him from relentlessly bullying subordinates who failed to overcome what Harbord considered trivial opposition. Lewis's abilities as commander of the 3d Brigade were never fully tested.

Regimental and battalion commanders were a mixed bag. Though they were undoubtedly courageous men, Neville and Lee, commanding the 5th and 6th Marines, respectively (Catlin had been wounded early on), are notable more for their absence as active players in the official records than for anything they accomplished. For the most part, they remained at headquarters, largely out of touch with affairs in the woods. Indeed, the very nature of the fighting excluded anyone who did not physically enter Belleau Wood from impacting the course of events. After June 14, Neville, as sector commander, and Lieutenant Colonel Feland, as commander in Belleau Wood, were partly responsible for leaving the 7th Regiment in the dark, and they were apparently nonfactors in directing the fighting that followed. Battalion commanders played a much larger role, and judged by courage alone, they left nothing to be desired. Berry led from the front and was wounded as he checked on his men. Wise—outspoken and stubborn as a mule—became disoriented in the woods, but so did many others; he fought side by side with his marines. Harbord scapegoated Wise, relieving the colonel for misreporting his position (something every officer in those woods was guilty of) when in fact the general was to blame for misassessing or ignoring intelligence reports. Sibley was a constantly visible inspiration to his men. The other battalion commanders, including Holcomb, Shearer, Keyser, and

Hughes, were generally effective if not notably brilliant, although the last-named commander seems to have shown some dilatoriness (according to Wise, at least) in commanding the 1/6th Marines. Again, the army regiment and battalion commanders were barely tested, although they performed efficiently enough at Vaux.

From company commander down to private, the dross burned off quickly in the battle's first days. Those who deserted or were relieved for incompetence were no loss. Unfortunately, some of the bravest and most talented men became casualties or unwilling captives—particularly, as Harbord noted, the field-grade officers. The survivors, however, were pure gold. In the battle's first days, the marines were exceptionally courageous, but their tactics were clumsy. By the end, though, they had become formidable adversaries—still brave, but also seasoned, wily, and tough. German records testify to the vast improvement in marine tactics by late June, and to how intimidating the marines had become. Unfortunately, they were also much fewer in number and largely exhausted. Army officers and soldiers did not make a good showing at first, from the 23d Regiment's premature advance and subsequent drubbing on June 6 to the 7th Regiment's shaky performance in the woods from June 16 to 21. But they too fought bravely, and the attack on Vaux was a model of military efficiency.

In the end, of course, the 2d Division did capture Belleau Wood. It also gutted the already weak German 28th and 237th Divisions and inflicted damage on the German 10th and 87th Divisions. These formations fought bravely on the whole, although their officers (with the notable exceptions of Majors Bischoff and Hartlieb) hardly demonstrated brilliance. Von Conta's proclivity for establishing unit borders at sensitive points of the line was particularly ill advised. Put baldly, the Americans won and the Germans lost. In the process of achieving this victory, however, Degoutte, Bundy, and Harbord failed a splendid group of marines and soldiers. If Degoutte had eased the Americans into battle, and if Bundy and Harbord had demonstrated patience, planned carefully, and exercised control—for haste was never a necessity—the 2d Division would have captured Belleau Wood, gained vital experience, and avoided the horrendous casualties and exhaustion. By July, it would have been well on its way to becoming one of the premier elite divisions on the western front, instead of being a punch-drunk prizefighter just trying to recover.

13

Rock of the Marne
The Marne River Defense, July 15–17, 1918

With the capture of Belleau Wood, the Holy Grail—the formation of an American army on the western front—seemed to be within reach. In mid-June worrying signs that suggested the French might be close to buckling under German pressure led Pershing to two decisions. First, he accepted the principle of American divisions, brigades, and even smaller units operating further in active sectors under French and British command—albeit always with a view to seasoning them for deployment in a solely American sector later on. Second, Pershing decided that the American army or armies eventually deployed on the western front would have to be much larger than he had originally envisaged. He now spoke of 100 divisions and 5 million men. On July 10 Pershing met with Foch at Bombon and got him to agree in principle to the formation of an American army in the near future.[1]

Ludendorff, meanwhile, began preparations for an offensive code-named Operation Marneschutz-Reims. Since the start of the German offensives in March, Ludendorff had believed that the ultimate decision would take place against the British in Flanders. That belief had not changed. To divert attention and hopefully substantial reserves away from Flanders, as well as to better secure the Marne salient, Ludendorff elected to launch a dual offensive against French, American, and Italian forces on either side of Reims. Three German armies—from west to east the Seventh, First, and Third—would conduct the attack beginning on July 15. While the First Army fixed the front above Reims, the Seventh and Third Armies would drive south-southeast and south-southwest, respectively,

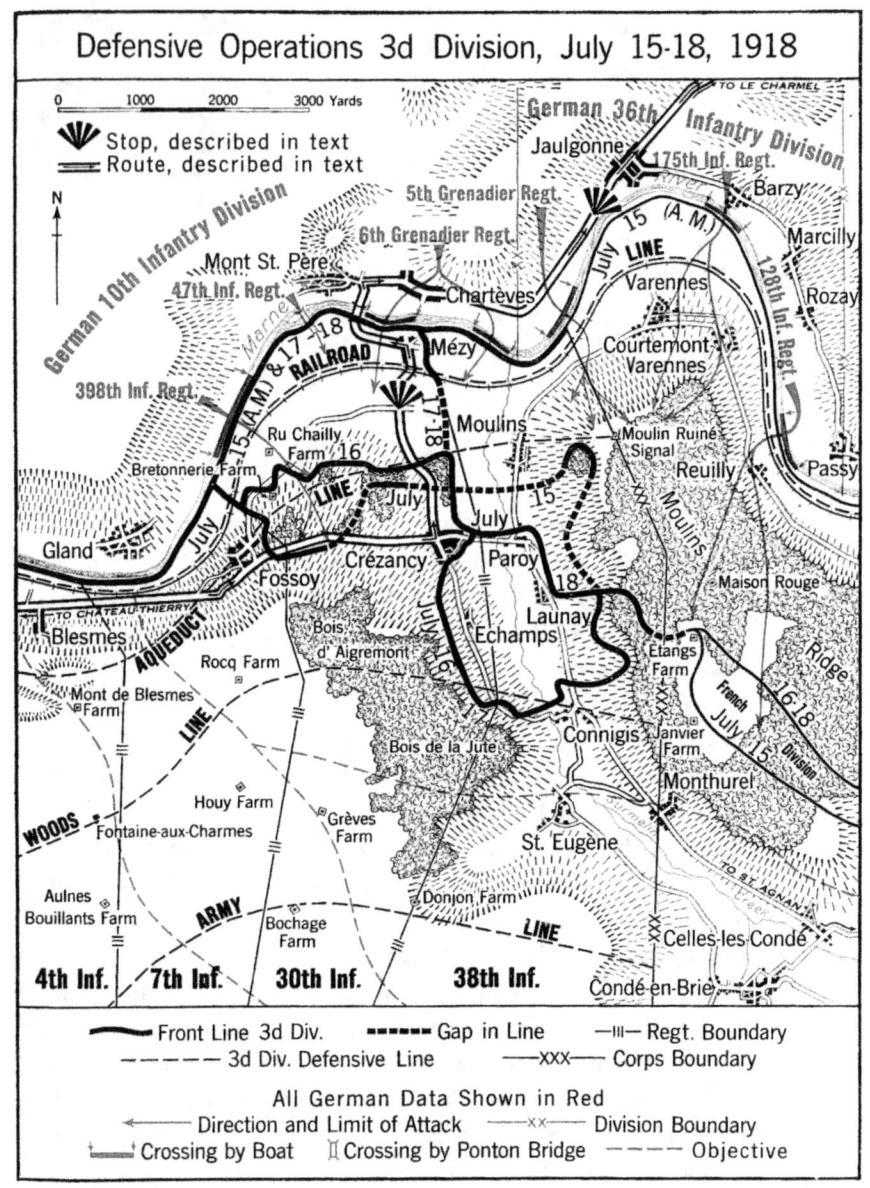

Defensive dispositions of the 3d Division, July 15, 1918. (*American Armies and Battlefields in Europe*, 61)

to converge near Bisseuil on the Marne. In so doing, they would divide the French armies and possibly cut off the Reims salient.[2]

In developing such an ambitious plan—which Crown Prince Wilhelm, commanding the army group tasked with carrying out the offensive, viewed with less than optimism—Ludendorff clearly had in mind the growing power of the American Expeditionary Forces in France. German intelligence had noted the courage and energy of the American soldiers, as well as the poor training of their officers. The key was to achieve some sort of decision on the western front before the Yanks learned the ropes and truly made their presence felt. Unfortunately for Ludendorff, German morale at the front was declining at a frighteningly rapid pace. Although German military and political leaders strenuously sought to shield their soldiers from the ugly realities of their country's sinking fortunes, the truth was obvious. Front-line soldiers endured abysmal rations and poor sanitary conditions, and they lacked basic necessities such as clothing and medicine. Moreover, the German casualty count in recent months—138,574 in May and 163,348 in June—had generated no tangible military advantage. Although most troops would continue to fight hard, they did so with receding confidence in ultimate victory.[3]

The French received information about the proposed German strike as early as June. At first, Foch and Pétain refused to credit reports that this would constitute a major, as opposed to a secondary or diversionary, German attack. By the end of the first week of July, however, they realized that something big was brewing, and Pétain transferred five French divisions to the sector. He also reorganized the primary defending formations into the Central Army Group under General Franchet d'Espèrey, with the Sixth (Degoutte), Fifth (Henri-Mathias Berthelot), and Fourth (Henri Gouraud) Armies from left to right. By July 10–12, Foch and Pétain accepted that they were about to face a significant German offensive in the vicinity of Reims.

By then, they had also started planning for a massive counterstroke to follow the German attack. After the enemy offensive had spent its force (the plans for accomplishing this are discussed presently), Foch proposed to launch a massive counteroffensive against the western shoulder of the Marne salient, toward Soissons. This plan, which he had been mulling since May, was well developed by July. The primary attack would be carried out by General Charles Mangin's Tenth Army on the west face of the salient, assisted by its right-hand neighbor, Degoutte's Sixth Army. It would go forward on July 18. If all went well, Pétain was prepared to include additional attacks by the Fifth and Fourth Armies against the southern and eastern faces of the salient. Foch had no expectation that this counterstroke would end the war in 1918 or even end the threat to Paris, but he hoped to set the Germans back on their heels and give himself breathing space to muster allied strength for a final victory offensive in 1919.[4]

First, though, there was the German offensive to be disposed of. American participation in what would be known as the Marne Defensive would take place primarily in the area immediately east of Château-Thierry (the US 42d Division and the 369th Regiment, which formed part of the Fourth Army, are considered separately). Here, the westernmost elements of the German Seventh Army's XXIII Reserve Corps under General Hugo von Kathen—renowned as a "specialist in open warfare"—would attack the French Sixth Army's XXXVIII and III Corps east of Gland, with the objective of advancing as far as seven kilometers along the Surmelin River toward St. Eugène and Condé-en-Brie. In doing so, the Germans would serve as flank guards for the far more important operations taking place farther east.[5]

The two French corps defending this sector included significant, if unhappy, American components. The French XXXVIII Corps under General Jean de Montdésir was deployed between Vaux and the bend of the Marne above Moulins. It consisted of the French 39th Division (including the US 28th Division's 56th Brigade) and the US 3d Division, but only the latter division would face the German assault. To Montdésir's right, the French III Corps under General Lebrun defended the Marne to a point east of Verneuil, where the front lines moved north of the river. This corps consisted of (after July 8) the French 125th Division (including the US 28th Division's 55th Brigade) and the French 51st Division. The latter division's right boundary marked the left flank of the French Fifth Army, and to that army's right stood the French Fourth Army. The Fourth Army's center corps, the French XXI Corps under General Naulin, included the US 42d Division in the second line of defense.

The terrain that would be defended by XXXVIII and III Corps was, on the whole, strong. The 3d Division defended a frontage of about twelve kilometers along the Marne, which flowed three to four meters deep and was forty to seventy meters wide in that area. There were no bridges, except for a ruined one near Mézy. The German-held north bank was steep; the south bank, less so. On both banks, heavy woods alternating with ripe wheat fields and stone-built farms and villages offered strong defensive terrain. Along the south bank, a double-track railroad embankment offered shelter for defenders and helped create a natural killing ground for attackers caught in the open ground between the railroad and the riverbank. Here, at least, the ground seemed well suited for a defensive deployment based on throwing the enemy back across the river immediately. The French 125th Division and its US 28th Division components had to defend the salient created by the Jaulgonne Bend of the Marne, but there was a bluff on which to anchor its infantry.[6]

Although the south bank of the Marne was strong, the manner of conducting its defense was the subject of debate at French and American army, corps, and division headquarters. The war's first four years had shown that even ideal defensive terrain offered only limited protection against well-laid artillery. Among the various branches of the German armed forces, the artillery remained by far the most efficient in 1918. Expertly commanded, thoroughly seasoned, and, for the most part, well equipped and well supplied, the German gunners maintained a high level of morale. Granted, the officer-starved German infantry was not as adept at coordinating with the artillery as it had been earlier in the war, but an effective barrage—including mustard gas, which the Germans possessed in ample quantities—was certain to inflict casualties on the defenders and make the attacking infantry's job that much easier. The central question facing the French and the Americans was whether to meet the Germans head-on from a strongly defended front line—risking casualties from artillery, but hitting the enemy infantry before it could fully deploy—or to establish a soft front line—avoiding the German barrage, but giving the enemy infantry time to build momentum for its attack. It was the same issue the Germans had faced in Belleau Wood: every man to the front line, or defense in depth?

Back on January 24, 1918, Pétain had issued his Directive No. 4, prescribing the formation of the main combat zone in any defensive deployment several kilometers behind the front—"a perfect encapsulation," writes historian Michael S. Neiberg, "of the theory of the defense in depth." Yet Pétain's instructions to his generals on July 5, 1918, specified that the "enemy effort must be broken on the position of resistance: This is the concern and the duty of the front line infantry divisions. The defense of this position will therefore be conducted as a continuous defense, without any break in its continuity, by the main bodies of the front line divisions reinforced, if need be, at certain important points, by elements detached from second line divisions." The second-line divisions were to be deployed not only to support the first-line divisions but also to "pass to the counteroffensive, either locally to reestablish the integrity of the position of resistance or in a general movement involving the whole army launched in an attack to regain lost ground after the main body of the enemy forces has been checked by the resistance of the front line divisions." This "counteroffensive," it should be noted, referred not to the offensive that would take place on July 18 but to the operations to restore the Marne line that would take place on July 16–17.⁷

In practice, Pétain gave his army commanders significant leeway in deciding how to deploy their forces to meet the initial enemy attack. French army and corps commanders were, like the Germans, deeply divided on the issue of whether to defend rigidly from the front or in depth. East of Reims, General Henri Gouraud, commanding the French Fourth Army (which included the US 42d Division and the US 93d Division's 369th Regiment), famously elected to employ a flexible defense in his sector of the Champagne region west of the Argonne Forest. There, first-line defenses would be held with a minimum of force to avoid excessive casualties from the initial German barrage. The main infantry forces would wait farther back and launch a counterstroke once the German assault, pummeled by French artillery, lost its initial momentum. Berthelot imposed a somewhat less elastic system on his Fifth Army, as did Degoutte on his Sixth Army and its component US 2d, 26th, and 28th Divisions. However, there would be some nuance to Degoutte's system, resulting in the employment of different tactics by its French and American formations.⁸

Montdésir prescribed a rigid defensive system for his XXXVIII Corps. On July 6 he announced to its component US 3d and French 39th Divisions (the latter containing the US 28th Division's 56th Brigade): "It is on the Marne itself that it is easiest for us to halt the enemy because he can cross it only by small fractions in boats, or by columns on the foot bridges, and because he approaches or reaches the River, necessarily disorganized. Our outposts on the Marne should therefore be firm and there can be no question of their withdrawing." Degoutte reinforced this recipe for defense during personal visits to division headquarters. On July 11 he appeared at 3d Division headquarters and insisted, as Dickman recalled, "that the Marne 'must be defended with one foot in the water,' and ordered heavy reinforcement of our front line." Unfortunately for the Americans, the same system would not be used in the adjoining French III Corps to the east, where the 125th Division defended the Jaulgonne Bend. This lack of coordination at the corps and division levels would have unhappy results.⁹

In his memoirs, Dickman notes that he viewed Degoutte's demand for a rigid defense as "a violation of fundamental principles and utterly erroneous." Seeking sympathy from his corps commander—an odd approach, given the specific orders issued for XXXVIII Corps on July 6—Dickman bluntly suggested to Montdésir that they simply disobey the army commander. Instead of a rigid defense, Dickman claimed that he proposed to Montdésir "an offer to let 10,000 Germans come across to the railroad unmolested, so confident were we of [our] ability to destroy them on the plain more than one mile deep between the railroad and the aqueduct, and long before they could reach our main line on the crest of the plateau." If Dickman actually made this suggestion to the corps commander, he should not have wasted his time. Montdésir—whom Dickman's chief of staff later denounced as a "fussy old woman" with little tactical understanding and a tendency to alternate between wild optimism and halfheartedness—rejected the proposal. The defense would be conducted in the first line.[10]

There is, however, reason to doubt at least some aspects of Dickman's version of events. Colonel Conrad Lanza, an artilleryman who conducted a thorough review of the Marne Defensive's operations just after they occurred and would later serve as the army artillery chief of operations for the US First Army, provided a profoundly different perspective in a 1937 article. According to him, it was not Montdésir but Dickman who insisted on a rigid defense on the river line. Lanza's account is worth quoting at length:

> General de Montdésir . . . had several conversations with General Dickman. . . . General de Montdésir believed that the enemy would try to force a crossing in the double bends of the Marne between Gland and Passy-sur-Marne, covering this crossing with heavy concentrations of artillery fire from the Bois de Barbillon and the Foret de Ris. He saw no particular advantage in attempting to hold the foreground against such an attack. He was prepared to see his infantry evacuate the forward area at the first sign of a hostile attack, and retire behind the rear line of defense south of St. Agnan. Most of the artillery would also be back of this line. In fact, all of the French Divisions [in French III Corps] east of the 3d Division were to fall back. He assumed that the American troops would do the same, and would not hold their front positions, and that the Germans would probably succeed in seizing the bend and occupying Crezancy. He thought the two bretelle lines meeting near Bochage Farm [and blocking the Surmelin Valley] would contain the enemy and hold him.
>
> The foregoing statements, advanced by the corps commander as suggestions, did not please 3d Division headquarters. They were still further shocked when the liaison officer with the French 125th Division, on their right, advised that it really was true that that command was preparing to evacuate its present positions, and fall back, maybe 5 to 6 kilometers, at the first signs of a hostile attack. And he added that the other French divisions further east were apparently going to do the very same thing.

Montdésir, Lanza continued, "had orders from the Sixth Army not to oppose the enemy's crossing of the Marne too strenuously, but to stop them on his rear line." The primary object was not to stop the enemy in his tracks but to "hold the enemy along the Marne, slightly south of it if possible, but without incurring serious losses. With the exception of army commanders, no one knew that a counterattack between Soissons and Château-Thierry was contemplated by the C-in-C. The 3d and 28th Divisions did not suspect it. They did not connect the intent to withdraw from advance positions with any proposed later operations."[11]

Lanza's account suggests a dangerous level of dysfunctionality in Franco-American military liaison. This came to light in a situation that arose briefly on July 15, when the 3d Division's right flank was left in the air, and the four companies of the US 28th Division accompanying the French 125th Division were left isolated. According to Lanza, it was not the French but the Americans who insisted that "a stubborn defense was to be made at the most advanced line and was to be continued by each unit, however small, even though the enemy succeeded in advancing on both sides and in rear of the unit." No thorough record exists of the conversations between Dickman and Montdésir, and Lanza's account is unsourced. Montdésir's orders of July 6—issued two days before the French 125th Division was shifted over to Lebrun's III Corps—prescribed a rigid defense along the Marne. But it is equally true that the conduct of the 125th Division on July 15—and of the French divisions in III Corps to its immediate east—bears all the hallmarks of a planned withdrawal. After all, the Jaulgonne Bend possessed no profound military value and was easily cut off, so abandoning it under pressure made sound military sense. And although the behavior of the 3d Division and the four front-line companies of the 28th Division on July 15 suggest that the Americans thought they were supposed to hold fast, there is also evidence that Dickman and the commander of his 38th Regiment knew very well that the 125th Division would abandon the Jaulgonne Bend. If so, it seems inconceivable that neither the French nor Dickman's staff warned 28th Division headquarters so that it could instruct its companies to pull back along with the French. Whatever the source of the disconnect, it suggests an absence of firm control at the level of Degoutte's Sixth Army and, more significantly, an almost total lack of clear communication and coordination between the French and the Americans—and, strangely, between the US 3d and 28th Divisions—at all levels.[12]

American and French defensive dispositions in the XXXVIII and III Corps sectors were incomplete—perhaps reflecting an intention to advance, from the American perspective, or an intention to withdraw, from the French perspective. As the 3d Division's operations report explained, "The defensive works constructed were in a rather elemental stage, due to several circumstances, the most important of which were the more or less open character of the recent fighting, the lack of engineer personnel, and the constant shifting of units in the early stages of organization, and the continual changes in sector limits, occasioned by the army corps organizations and reorganization." Dickman's division had all four of its regiments in line. On the left, the 5th Brigade was commanded by Brigadier General Fred W. Sladen; on the right, the 6th Brigade was commanded by Brigadier General Charles Crawford. The 4th Regiment (Colonel Halstead Dorey) held ground from east of Château-Thierry to just east of Blesmes. The 7th Regiment (Colonel T. M. Anderson) was deployed from there to Le Rû Chailly Farm. The 30th Regiment (Colonel Cromwell Stacey) held ground from that point to Mézy, where it linked up with the 38th Regiment (Colonel Ulysses Grant McAlexander), which extended to the boundary with the French 125th Division northeast of Moulins.[13]

The 3d Division's defensive dispositions included an outpost zone with observation posts along the Marne and strongpoints along the railroad track. These posts were not supposed to be held indefinitely. Instead, the infantrymen occupying them were expected to delay the enemy briefly before pulling back to the Aqueduct Line to their rear (although in the event, most of the forward platoons did not withdraw). The Aqueduct Line roughly followed the course of an old aqueduct on the northern slopes of hills overlooking the river. Behind it, the Woods Line ran through Janvier Ferme, Le Souvrien Ferme, Le Rocq Ferme-et-Château, and Fontaine aux Charmes. The Aqueduct Line was the main line of defense, and the Woods Line was a support position. American and French division and corps field artillery—mostly 75s, but with a smattering of 105s and 155s—stood in support. This was Degoutte's preference, based on the "theory that the primary function of artillery was to protect line of support in second positions and it should be located far enough back to do this at convenient range and not be in danger of capture in a suddenly successful rush on second line." The 8th Machine Gun Battalion was arrayed in support of the infantry, along with the 6th Engineers; the 7th Machine Gun Battalion lay in corps reserve. Farther back, the French 73d Division occupied close reserve positions, in preparation for its likely use in the counterattack. Behind it, the Sixth Army busily organized another line of defense in case of emergency.[14]

The bulk of the American infantry was ordered to stand firm on the first line of defense. Division chief of staff Colonel Robert H. C. Kelton summarized the division's orders, which were based (according to Kelton

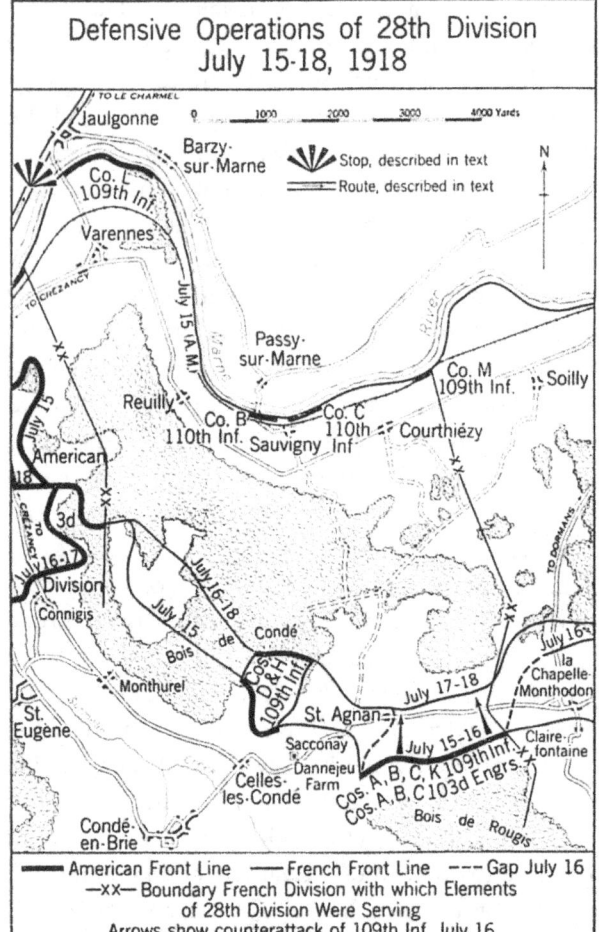

Defensive dispositions of the 28th Division, July 15–18, 1918. (*American Armies and Battlefields in Europe*, 65)

and Dickman) on French XXXVIII Corps orders: "Division orders outlining the plan of defense prescribed that all units hold the ground entrusted to them and that lost ground be immediately regained by counterattack. Pursuant to corps orders it was directed that this stubborn defense begin at the most advanced line and be continued by each unit, however small, even though the enemy succeeded in gaining ground to both sides and in rear of the unit." Regimental commanders were thus given to understand that they would hold the Aqueduct Line in strength and consider it the primary line of defense. No specific orders were issued on the disposition of French flank units, although in the event, the 38th Regiment's commander would take some precautions on his own.[15]

★ ★ ★

The US 28th Division had been organized in August 1917 from the Pennsylvania National Guard. Like other AEF divisions, its regional designation was purely nominal, since it contained men from all over the country, including draftees. Major General Charles H. Muir, popularly known as "Uncle Charley," commanded the division. Born in Michigan in 1860, he had graduated from West Point in 1885. He was a combat veteran and had been decorated with the Distinguished Service Cross for his conduct as a sharpshooter during the Spanish-American War; he had also served during the Philippine insurrection and the Chinese Boxer Rebellion. Though well liked, Muir was a stubborn, inflexible commander who was prone to dismiss obstacles in his determination to get things done. Obviously, such a personality could work to the detriment or benefit of his men, depending on the circumstances.

The 28th Division was as yet substantially unbloodied, having arrived in France in mid-May and trained with the British for a month. The division's artillery was sent elsewhere and did not rejoin its parent formation until August. In early June the division was transferred to French command. The 55th Brigade under Brigadier General Thomas Darrah, consisting of the 109th and 110th Regiments, was attached to the French 125th Division, which, at the time, was part of French XXXVIII Corps. The 56th Brigade under Brigadier General William Weigel, consisting of the 111th and 112th Regiments, was attached to the French 39th Division, part of French III Corps. On June 28 these French divisions were moved to the Château-Thierry sector. Both American brigades were placed in the second line of defense, where they were gradually introduced to front-line conditions. Unfortunately, this entailed breaking down battalions to the company and even platoon level for service under French command, and this was how the Americans got their first taste of combat. On July 1 two platoons from the 111th Regiment joined the French 153d Regiment in assaulting Hill 204—unsuccessfully—in conjunction with the US 2d Division's attack on Vaux; from July 6 to 9 some sections of its infantry joined the French in fighting in the Bois de Courteau, east of Hill 204.[16]

As the Germans' final offensive of the war approached, the 56th Brigade was deployed for defense with the French 39th Division, but it would not be tested in the operations of July 15–17. Elements of the 55th Brigade, attached to the French 125th Division, would see some combat, however. Most of this brigade occupied second-line positions along six kilometers of frontage from west of Bois de Rougis to north of Coufremaux, with the US 3d Division to its left and the French 51st Division to its right. On July 9 three American companies were moved into the front lines along the Marne as part of the French 113th Regiment. Company M of the 3/109th Regiment was deployed northeast of Courthiezy, and Companies B and C of the 1/110th Regiment were placed west and east of Sauvigny, respectively. Two days later, Company L of the 3/109th was attached to the French 131st Regiment and was sent to help guard the Marne north of Varennes. These four companies were fully interspersed with the French. Platoons occupied outposts on high ground along the river's south bank. In accordance with what they understood to be Montdésir's orders for a rigid line of resistance, they believed they were tasked with preventing the enemy from crossing the river. They were to hold their line of resistance "at all costs" and to fight on, even if surrounded. It seems that none of the platoon commanders were aware that their French counterparts had different ideas.[17]

The deployment of these three companies with the 125th Division seemed inauspicious, for it was a somewhat shaky formation. The line strength of its three infantry regiments on July 14 was only 4,868 men plus 228 engineers, along with seventy-two 75mm and nineteen 155mm artillery pieces—weak even by the 1918 standards of the French army. Dickman later claimed that the French division's trenches were "sadly deficient," reflecting an attitude of "why dig elaborate trenches if you don't intend to defend them?" Kelton, his chief of staff, later asserted that he thought the 55th Brigade had been placed behind the 125th Division "to catch the pieces after the front line busted." Dickman's and Kelton's ex post facto disparagement of the French notwithstanding, the 125th Division's commander, General Diebold, informed at least some Americans that he intended to evacuate the Jaulgonne Bend and pull back to support positions as soon as the anticipated German attack took place. A few days before the attack, the commander of the 38th Regiment, Colonel McAlexander, ordered trenches dug on his right for flank defense after learning that the French would withdraw "as soon as a serious attack developed." This would prove to be prescient, but despite the fact that others must have been privy to this knowledge, no other precautions were taken.[18]

Both the 3d and 28th Divisions, then, would experience the consequences of divided and detached command—and both would become examples of how much could go wrong with the compromise pseudo-amalgamation arrangements foisted on Pershing. Dickman's crew had already been through the mill. Called up to defend the Marne River crossings in the emergency following the German Chemin des Dames offensive of May 27, the 3d Division had been dispersed in detachments along the river under French command. And although the division had officially received command of the Château-Thierry sector on June 6 and maintained responsibility for that sector in July, some of its regiments had served elsewhere. Elements of the 30th Regiment fought alongside the French on Hill 204, and the 7th Regiment relieved the marines for a week in Belleau Wood. Even though the 30th Regiment's experiences were generally positive, both deployments left lingering resentments that would hinder functional tactical cooperation.

At the level of French and American general headquarters, the arrangements for command and liaison under mixed deployments seemed reasonably clear. On June 19 Pétain had issued orders aimed at clarifying "the prerogatives of French commanders of divisions or divisional infantry with respect to American units allotted to French divisions." Since Pershing's GHQ had "reserved to itself the right to regroup its divisions at some future time," these units would continue to report there "on the subjects of promotion, interior economy, administration and the exercise of military jurisdiction." American provisions for training would also be taken into careful consideration. However, "insofar as concerns tactical employment and administrative measures connected therewith (routes of march, shelter, supplies, etc.), the American regiments are entirely under the orders of the French division command."[19] And therein lay the rub. Responsible French officers could be trusted to ease the Americans into the fighting intelligently, but others could not. The 3d and 28th Divisions had both sent detachments to fight alongside the French on Hill 204, and in both cases the collaboration seems to have gone reasonably well. During the Marne Defensive, though, any positive lessons learned from those earlier deployments were tossed aside. Despite the presence of American and French liaison officers who had been given ample opportunity to get acquainted with their counterparts, the lack of communication was almost total.

The experiences of the other two American divisions that would participate in the Marne Defensive demonstrate that Franco-American liaison could work effectively under the right circumstances—and especially with well-intentioned officers in charge. The US 42d Division—the third National Guard formation to arrive at the front—was one of the more colorful units in the AEF. It was an amalgam of National Guard units assembled from twenty-six states plus the District of Columbia, inspiring the moniker the Rainbow Division. Major General Charles T. Menoher commanded the division. Born in Pennsylvania in 1862, he had graduated from West Point in 1886. An artilleryman, Menoher had served in the Spanish-American War and in the Philippines. His brigade commanders were Brigadier General Michael Lenihan (83d Brigade) and Brigadier General Douglas MacArthur

(84th Brigade). The division had arrived in Europe in November 1917 and spent several months training in quiet sectors; it therefore had more time to prepare and to acclimate to French command than many other American formations did. It moved to the Champagne region on July 3, where it was assigned to Gouraud's Fourth Army and served in General Naulin's French XXI Corps' reserve line of defense near St. Hilaire. Elements of the 165th, 166th, and 167th Regiments were deployed there on the night of July 14–15. In the Fourth Army—unlike in Degoutte's Sixth—Franco-American liaison worked efficiently. Gouraud, who had lost an arm at Gallipoli, was a flamboyant but amiable man. He treated the Americans respectfully, and they held him in some degree of awe. In addition, as officers of a National Guard outfit, the 42d Division's staff felt undervalued by GHQ, and the fact that Gouraud placed them in a relatively important sector of the front—albeit in a secondary line of defense—soothed their resentment.[20]

Also serving happily under Gouraud was the 369th Regiment of the African American US 93d Division. It was posted in the VIII Corps' second line of defense between Hans and La Neuville. Once the 15th New York Regiment, what would come to be known as the Harlem Rattlers (more popularly, the "Hell Fighters") had once lobbied to become part of the Rainbow Division but had allegedly been told that "black was not one of the colors of the rainbow." That was only one, relatively minor episode of the racism the regiment would face before being assigned to combat duty. Commanded by Colonel William Hayward and other (mostly) white officers, the regiment had endured standard AEF training, leavened with a heavy dose of racist mistreatment, in South Carolina and New Jersey before sailing for Europe and arriving in France on New Year's Day 1918. Five days later, Harbord, then AEF chief of staff, wrote to Pershing to suggest that the 369th and three other "Negro" regiments be turned over to the French in fulfillment of a proposal made by Pétain. "Their retention in the Interior presents problems familiar to those who know the negro in his southern environment," Harbord explained. "They are nevertheless an asset in man-power which the Allies cannot disdain or discard [and] the French have no race prejudice." Under French command, they would be trained in areas where the civilian population had been largely withdrawn. In addition, shedding the 369th Regiment presented an opportunity to strike a blow against amalgamation. "I believe," Harbord continued, that "General Pétain will either be glad to accept these regiments or will be obliged to cease pressing his idea fixe [sic] of getting our regiments trained in French divisions." So the 369th Regiment trained with the French, and quite successfully. In fact, on June 19 André Tardieu, the French high commissioner in the United States, asked that eight new African American regiments be formed and sent to serve with the French. In his response of June 25, however, Pershing politely but firmly declined. The Harlem Rattlers would get their first opportunity to demonstrate what black troops could do in extended combat on the Marne River.[21]

Apparent proof that the anticipated German offensive was imminent arrived on the evening of July 14 in the form of confessions taken from twenty-seven prisoners captured during a French raid. The attack, they said, would take place early the next morning. Countermeasures, including a heavy counterbarrage, had been prepared in advance and were put in place at the army and corps levels. Not until 2340, however, did the 3d Division receive word from XXXVIII Corps about the prisoners' revelation that the attack would commence the next morning—or that the counterbarrage would begin in five minutes! Consequently, despite indications earlier that evening that something was brewing, many American officers remained skeptical that anything would happen that night. "As there had been several previous warnings as to the enemy attacking," recalled Lanza, "the men in line were not at all certain that this might not be again a false alarm." Therefore, the American units "went right along with" their plans to relieve units in the front line—meaning that, in the event, both relievers and relieved would be jumbled together when the German bombardment and assault came just after midnight.[22]

French and American artillery began their counterbarrage at 2345 on July 14, inflicting serious damage on the German attack formations. Despite obvious evidence that the cat was out of the bag, the German artillery opened up its own bombardment on schedule at 0010 on July 15 all along the line. Both high explosives and gas were used against infantry front-line and support positions and against artillery emplacements. The 3d Division was hit the hardest among American formations, but the 42d Division also received its share. Lieutenant Hugh S. Thompson with the 168th Regiment described the shelling's impact:

> We groped forward through the roaring, flashing thunder. Men stumbled over each other in the trench bottoms. The darkness was now violet and now splotched with green, yellow, and red flames of fire. Gravel rained on our helmets, trees fell, we choked in swirls of dust. We tripped over a figure, whose piercing screams sounded muffled in the terrifying din. Now shadowy, now vivid forms huddled against the

walls of the fire trench. . . . Flashing detonations filled the woods, the whine of shells half-obscured by the thundering noise. We staggered through stretches of trench and crawled around a series of erupting bayous. Stretcher-bearers stumbled by in the choking dust, their yelling, "Gangway, gangway," soft under the blanket of fearful, volcanic sound.[23]

The 3d Division suffered the worst shelling along the riverbank, where its unfortunate platoons were deployed to defend the river from shore; the 30th Regiment's commander later discovered "shell holes every five feet in the front line." The Americans along the Marne suffered additional casualties because of their flimsy emplacements, as well as because the relief of infantry units was under way at the time. But the German guns, which included calibers up to 210mm, reached as far as ten kilometers back, hitting artillery and supply positions. All wired communications with the front were cut within ten minutes, forcing officers to rely on couriers on foot, horseback, or motorcycle. American and French artillery also took serious casualties and were badly disorganized. At dawn the Germans laid smoke shells, as well as sneezing and tear gas, along the river while their troops prepared boat ferries and their engineers built pontoons. As the crossing began under cover of smoke and fog, more high-explosive shells rained down on the slopes and heights south of the river. Here, the Germans delivered "enormous quantities" of lethal gas, especially between Mézy and the Jaulgonne Bend. But American gas discipline was "excellent," demonstrating the "results of careful training," and casualties from gas were insignificant. This marked a significant change from earlier experiences, but because the troops had to wear their masks for several hours, the effects were still enervating.[24]

German plans envisaged an advance of up to two kilometers in the 3d Division's sector on the first day. Three German divisions played a role in the attack. The 10th Landwehr Division was ordered to hold the river line in front of the Americans while the jaded but more potent 10th and 36th Divisions—the former returned from a month's rest after tangling with the marines near Belleau Wood—crossed the Marne to attack. Each of these divisions contained only about 5,000 combat-effectives. After the bombardment commenced at 0010, the German troops were to begin the quick construction of bridges and ferries at 0150; then, following a rolling barrage that would start along the railroad at 0350, they would advance. The 10th Division was tasked with crossing the river in front of Mézy and Le Rû Chailly Farm, outflanking Fossoy from the east, and attacking the

Bois d'Aigremont. The 36th Division, deployed farther east along the Surmelin River valley, was to cross east of Courtemont-Vorennes and attack in a southeasterly direction. The Germans' primary objective was to drive along that valley and its stream measuring thirty to forty yards wide, which formed "the best inroad to the south and east between Château-Thierry and Rheims, from either a tactical or strategical point of view."[25]

Dawn came at 0400 and revealed the Marne wreathed in fog and smoke. Not until 0520 did word arrive at regimental headquarters that German troops had reached the south bank at multiple points. As soon as this became apparent, orders arrived from brigade and division headquarters for the preparation and execution of immediate counterattacks, but these took time to organize. On the American left, the German 10th Division's 398th Regiment crossed the Marne on boat ferries and drove southeast. Above Fossoy, the 1/398th—which had been severely damaged by the previous night's counterbarrage—plowed into forward elements of the American 2/7th and 3/7th Battalions. Platoons of Companies F, L, and I held the American front along the railroad embankment west and northwest of Fossoy. Upslope to their rear, more American infantry occupied trenches along the village's northern outskirts and in the woods flanking it on either side. The Americans were no longer green, having been tested a few weeks earlier in Belleau Wood, but their forward positions were not easy to defend.[26]

The Germans stormed the embankment, breaking through at multiple points and isolating two platoons of Companies F and I. Instead of withdrawing, as they were supposed to, these platoons fought fiercely, killing a number of Germans before being eliminated. Pushing upslope north of Fossoy, the Germans again faced tenacious resistance from American infantry and machine guns around Le Rû Chailly Farm. Farther east, however, the 2/398th and 3/398th had made progress against the 30th Regiment. Colonel Anderson struggled to maintain liaison between his 7th Regiment's right flank and the 30th Regiment's left flank around Crézancy. In his postbattle report, Anderson noted that his own "gallant regiment, whose right was gravely exposed by the withdrawal of the 30th Infantry on its right, reached out and held the sector left vacant by such withdrawal. All other regiments from our right on were either forced back or withdrew up to the gates of Rheims." Meanwhile, on Anderson's left, the 1/398th surged eastward from the embankment between Fossoy and the farm just after 0500, driving across a road leading north from the village. With this move, they isolated the farm's defenders, who fought until they were destroyed—a fight that "was settled by the use of hand grenades, of which the enemy had many and the Americans none." Pressed on both flanks, elements of

Companies E, F, and I had to fall back to the immediate outskirts of Fossoy and "Fall Woods" to its east, where they halted the German advance by 0900, roughly along the road leading east to Crézancy.[27]

Meanwhile, just northeast of Le Rû Chailly Farm, the 2/398th and 3/398th had attacked positions held by the American 1/30th Battalion, with the 3/30th Battalion in support. Here too, forward elements—in this case, platoons of B and C Companies, along with detachments of the machine gun company—occupied trenches and dugouts along the river and along and just behind the railway embankment. These forward detachments inflicted casualties on the Germans as they attempted to land. First Lieutenant James R. Kingery, who stood up to hurl grenades at the enemy boats, was among the many who distinguished themselves. The Germans nevertheless overran these positions—although isolated parties fought on—and pushed up the bluff jutting north between Fossoy and Crézancy. Lieutenant William Ryan watched them approach:

> Directly in front of us and down by the railroad I could see German infantrymen, wearing overcoats, coming straight toward us in approach formation, similar to that used by our army. As they approached up the hill they dropped out of sight until they drew close to us. The German infantry and machine gunners came on at a slow walk, as steady as though on a drill ground. An officer at the head of them was swinging a walking stick.[28]

The Americans opened fire, and Ryan heard the "chauchats rattle like machine guns." But the Germans pressed their attack, and unfortunately, Companies A, D, and K did not respond well. The commanding officer of the 1/30th Battalion, Major Fred L. Walker, concluded that his frontline platoons were "a total loss" and requested an SOS barrage (which was fired) on the former front line of defense. He then "decided that the French idea as to abandoning forward areas to the enemy, and resisting on a rear line, was just about the right thing to do. He thereupon issued orders to withdraw, and personally going to the rear, ordered his two leading companies to follow." As Brigadier General Charles Crawford detailed in his after-action report, some platoons reacted too late to the penetration on their flanks, and when they withdrew, "it was not controlled and many of the troops went back along the east slopes of the Bois d'Aigremont woods until stopped by 38th Infantry officers in the vicinity of Le Chauet, where they were reformed." Reaching the bluff's 145-meter crest against uneven resistance, the Germans cautiously probed southwest, south, and southeast. Some patrols penetrated the Aqueduct Line, reaching woods half a kilometer south of Fossoy; others advanced toward Crézancy.²⁹

Farther east, the remainder of the 1/30th Battalion's C Company faced assaults from two regiments—the 47th Infantry and 6th Grenadiers of the German 10th Division. Though heavily outnumbered, the Americans held stoutly. Below Mont St. Père, the Germans constructed a pontoon bridge where a river island made the passage easier. Sergeant Edward J. Radcliffe, a scout with the 28th Division's 3/109th Battalion, had ventured near the front at this point and watched them cross "at dawn on their courdoroy bridges which they rolled down the north bank of the river and quickly stept over, sometimes with machine guns on litters borne by huns with red crosses on their arms." Here, the 1/47th Battalion crossed at 0400, only to come under heavy fire in the wheat fields between the riverbank and the railroad. The attack immediately bogged down, according to a German report:

> On account of the high wheat, the troops could fire only in the standing position; whoever showed his face over the ears was almost always hit. All six machine guns immediately assumed the highest possible firing position and opened fire. Since the enemy (Americans) was apparently well dug in and probably sitting on trees as well [in a copse behind the railway embankment], and the wheat being too high even for the highest firing position of the machine guns, no effect was obtained despite the concentrated fire and the ample use of ammunition.... The attack of the battalion therefore came to a standstill, since the men were hit, by the enemy riflemen sitting on the trees, even when crawling. Whoever of the battalion could crawl back, did so and took up a position on the northern bank of the Marne.

Meanwhile, the 3/47th Battalion attempted to cross the river by boat ferries west of Mézy, only to be shattered by American machine gun fire and driven back in disorder across the Marne. Both battalions left behind about 200 prisoners, including officers. Here, at least, the doctrine of the forward defense was seemingly vindicated.³⁰

But the Germans weren't done yet. At 0845 the German 2/47th Battalion crossed the Marne at the pontoon bridge and pushed across the wheat fields to the railroad embankment. The men of C Company remained feisty enough, but now the 398th Regiment fired on the Americans from atop the bluff to their left rear (from where Major Walker had withdrawn), and inaccurate American artillery (or possibly the SOS barrage requested by Walker) sealed the insult with a stiff dose of friendly fire. C Company withdrew, except for an infantry and mortar platoon in Mézy. This village, defended jointly with G Company of the neighboring 38th Regiment, had come under attack earlier that morning from the German 6th Grenadier Regiment. East of Mézy, the 3/6th Grenadiers crossed the Marne by boat ferries and reached the railroad embankment before G Company threw them back across the river by 0500, despite losing two platoons in forward positions that were surrounded and wiped out. West of Mézy, the 1/6th and 2/6th Grenadiers took severe casualties but held on, and as the 2/47th Battalion drove back the rest of C Company, the grenadiers attempted to take the village.[31]

Holding Mézy required cooperation and improvisation. Captain Jesse Walton Woolridge, commanding Company G, assembled about forty men from the two platoons of the 30th Regiment's Company C; a couple dozen unwounded men from his own company; a trench mortar battery that had run out of ammunition; and a motley assemblage of cooks, clerks, and runners to establish defensive positions in the village. Woolridge's ersatz company repelled numerous German assaults supported by machine guns and aircraft. As the grenadiers prepared to launch their final attack at around 1030, Woolridge preempted them with a counterattack of his own. Astonishingly, the 6th Grenadiers imploded under the pressure of Woolridge's attack. The Americans claimed they captured 400 prisoners. "It's God's truth," the captain exulted, "that one Company of American soldiers beat and routed a full regiment of picked shock troops of the German Army."[32]

The stubborn defense of Mézy helped prevent the Germans from taking advantage of dangerous confusion occurring farther back at the 30th Regiment's positions along the Aqueduct Line. After the repulse of the initial assault by the 1/47th and 3/47th Battalions, and while the 2/398th and 3/398th Battalions were moving up the bluff between Fossoy and Crézancy, Major Walker's three companies of the 30th Regiment abruptly abandoned their positions and pulled back to the Woods Line, along the northern edge of the Bois d'Aigremont. An aggressive German advance might have exploited this opportunity to devastating advantage, but continuing resistance from Fossoy and Mézy on either flank (probably combined with exhaustion) held them back. They could not even push in force beyond the Fossoy-Crézancy road.

The 38th Regiment, engaged with the 6th Grenadier Regiment at Mézy, also faced a crossing by the 5th Grenadier Regiment (36th Division) farther east, near the juncture with the French 125th Division. Unlike the 7th and

30th Regiments, the 38th Regiment had seen no significant action in the war. It was deployed with the 2/38th Battalion in front, and Companies G, H, and E were in line along the riverbank and railroad from Mézy to where the Marne bent northward, northeast of Moulins. The 1/38th Battalion stood in support positions along the banks of Surmelin Creek, while the 3/38th Battalion was farther back in reserve, on the Woods Line above Connigis. To the 38th Regiment's right stood the French 125th Division, along with its four companies from the US 28th Division. The French occupied a vulnerable salient—the Jaulgonne Bend—where the Marne turned north above Moulins, continued east past Varennes, and then bent sharply southward past Courtemont-Varennes and Reuilly. The French enjoyed the advantage of occupying the wooded 231-meter bluff of Moulins Ridge, crested by Moulins Ruiné Signal (a ruined mill), which roughly followed the river's contours; however, they remained vulnerable to being cut off by a concentric enemy attack. As Colonel McAlexander knew, Diebold's officers had no intention of holding on for long.[33]

The previous night's allied counterbarrage had caused enough damage to the German 36th Division to weaken its initial assaults, in conjunction with the problems caused by assembling at the riverside in the dark. However, the Germans' preparatory barrage had also fallen heavily on the Jaulgonne Bend sector, demoralizing some men of the 38th Regiment (by the Americans' own admission) and forcing the defenders to don gas masks. As the barrage continued through the early-morning hours, frequent phone messages from the 3d Division, 6th Brigade, and 38th Regiment to Diebold's headquarters sought information and repeatedly asked for French liaison officers to maintain contact. As the rolling barrage moved back over Moulins Ridge and along the Surmelin Valley, German troops began to cross the Marne at three points, in just the sort of concentric attack the French had no doubt anticipated. The 5th Grenadier Regiment crossed at the Franco-American divisional boundary above Moulins, the 175th Regiment crossed on boat ferries between Barzy and Varennes, and the 128th Regiment struck deep into the French right rear by crossing between Passy and Reuilly. Nevertheless, Company E of the 1/38th initially had little trouble repelling the German grenadiers attempting to cross west of the mouth of the Surmelin, thanks in part to the Germans' heavy casualties and severe disorganization caused by the early-morning artillery barrage. However, by 0400, the Germans were pushing into Company E's right rear by advancing southwest along the road at the foot of the bluff between Varennes and Moulins. Company F launched what XXXVIII Corps' war diary described as a "brilliant" counterattack from its support position at 0430 and succeeded in pushing the Germans back. But the 38th Regiment's right flank remained in danger.[34]

Farther east, the 125th Division's four American companies were in deep trouble. The Americans, who had been deployed with the French "for purposes of instruction," occupied shallow, "partially completed trenches" that had been casually constructed by Italian labor gangs with "no dug-outs and practically no splinter-proofs." The trenches occupied by their French neighbors were in a similar condition. The Americans were deployed, from left to right, as follows: Company L had two platoons along the railroad south of Jaulgonne and Barzy sur Marne and two platoons at the edge of the woods near the crest of a hill to the south. Companies B and C each had two platoons west and east, respectively, of the wrecked river bridge south of Passy and two more at the edge of some woods a kilometer to the south. Company M had two platoons along the railroad east of Company C and two more in an orchard on the slope of a hill just to the south. Relief had been in progress when the German bombardment opened, so front-line and support platoons were to some extent intermingled. Moreover, both American and French positions were dispersed and poorly interconnected, allowing easy flank penetration. And as an American postbattle study showed, the green troops of the 28th Division took no steps to protect their flanks anyway.[35]

The Germans crossed the river and landed in small, twenty-man boats; in addition, some horses were pulled across by ropes. As this was happening, American and French machine guns kept up a steady fire. But as the enemy began ascending Moulins Ridge in files, the French infantry "backed up," as if it had been ordered to do so. The American liaison officer with the division later reported that "the headquarters packed up and sent to the rear, or destroyed, all records and property, commencing at the very beginning of the artillery preparation." French machine gunners hung on for a little longer, but then they too began to pull out. The American companies, obeying what they thought were French orders to "resist to the utmost," and not sensing the danger the German thrust from Reuilly posed to their rear, fought on. As daybreak approached, the German 175th Regiment took Varennes and Courtemont-Varennes and pushed over the crest of Moulins Ridge toward Moulins Ruiné Signal, while the German 128th Regiment advanced rapidly south and southwest from Reuilly. At 0700 Brigadier General Crawford's 6th Brigade headquarters phoned Diebold to tell him that French troops were falling back from the 38th Regiment's right. Fifteen minutes later, 3d Division headquarters phoned the 125th Division to complain about the lack of support on the right, but Diebold was on another phone discussing plans to withdraw his artillery. As indicated by subsequent reports to the French, the 3d Division continued to hold, but Diebold apparently dismissed the Americans from his mind. At 0720, 55th Brigade headquarters learned from its own sources that the Germans had "forced the principal line of resistance" of the 125th Division. Soon thereafter, retreating French infantry appeared in the second-line positions held by the American brigade. At 0805 a report from Colonel Millard Brown of the 109th Regiment indicated "that the French are pouring back through his front line and he is making an effort, with the assistance of the French detachment assigned to the 109th Inf. to stop the French and form them up in his rear." Attempts to rally the French were fruitless. An American officer posted as an observer with the French reported at 0830 that a French colonel, "after making every effort to stop his men from retreating, mounted and rode to the rear with his staff."[36]

Although the Americans interpreted the withdrawal as a rout, neither Lebrun nor Diebold showed undue concern. Indeed, the French III Corps' war diary described the German advance in the Jaulgonne Bend as unimportant. Although Diebold's officers had evidently warned Colonel McAlexander of their plans ahead of time, the French apparently made no attempt to inform the four companies of the US 28th Division that they should pull back as well. A detailed chronology of phone messages to and from Diebold's headquarters through the morning contains no mention of these companies. The chronology records numerous requests for information from 3d Division, but Diebold was primarily worried about the French 51st Division's withdrawal on his right, and he made little effort to keep the Americans up to date. Nor did Diebold alert the 55th Brigade to his rear in a timely fashion (0920) that it might encounter enemy infantry that had penetrated the lines via "infiltration." Such conflicting messages and lack of communication amounted to a liaison failure of the highest order, and the Americans paid the price. Companies B and C of the 1/110th and Companies L and M of the 3/109th fought until 0800, at which time their isolation became apparent and they tried to force their way out to the south. They had little chance, and some men panicked. Company M on the extreme right managed to force its way back through the woods and reach French lines north of Conde en Brie with 150 men. According to one account, "the other three companies held their ground, the forward platoons being almost to a man either killed or captured, while the support platoons held their ground until outflanked or surrounded. But a small percentage of these three companies succeeded in reaching our lines." Another study, however, indicated that Company L "appears to have broken up and to have retreated in considerable disorder to Regimental Headquarters at Grande Fontaine, seven kilometers in direct line from where the fight took place."[37]

Meanwhile, the Germans followed up the French retreat, and by 0915—five minutes before Diebold phoned the 55th Brigade and told it to prepare to face the enemy—they had pushed to a line running east of Connigis. There was no organized French resistance in this sector, and the 109th and 110th Regiments held the front line for a while. The Americans were so shocked at the appearance of Germans that at first they did not open fire, wondering whether they might be French or Americans. Soon, though, their machine guns engaged the enemy at a range of 1,500 yards. Tension built as fleeing French infantry streamed to the rear. Some elements of the US 10th Field Artillery got caught up in the retreat and fled with them, abandoning their guns—seventy-five stragglers would eventually be rounded up and sent back to their batteries. Diebold ordered the two American regiments to hold their positions "at any cost," and they dug in to await the anticipated German attack. Brigadier General Darrah phoned at 1135 and told the 109th's commander, Colonel Brown, to "let the men in the line know that their job today is to hold the line and that when this help arrives they will push the enemy back over the river."[38]

Sergeant Radcliffe of the 3/109th had rejoined his regiment and found the men jumpy. As they waited, an American came crashing through the woods yelling that the Germans were coming. Radcliffe ordered his men to drop and fire on the first "strange uniform" they saw. Unfortunately, that uniform belonged to a French officer standing in the woods to their right, cradling a white poodle in his arms. One of Radcliffe's scouts opened fire on the Frenchman and shot him in the back; the poodle evidently scurried away unharmed. The scout later explained that he thought the officer "was a spy" and had "acted suspiciously." Like others, he had heard stories of Germans wearing French or American uniforms, and the officer had made some motion that convinced the scout he was signaling to the German artillery—or perhaps the scout simply didn't like Frenchmen. "Right or wrong he got a blighty," Radcliffe quipped. German artillery did hit the allied line in the early afternoon, but after a brief consultation, the German infantry decided not to attack. Ultimately, although some German patrols managed to infiltrate the American lines and had to be rounded up, the American positions were not seriously tested. By 1445 the Germans rested on a line from La Chapelle to Monthodon, St. Agnan, point 223, Grange aux Bois, and Hill 231.[39]

The fate of the American companies left behind was not apparent at 55th Brigade headquarters. At 1305 General Diebold remarked that he had "expended the two American companies that were on the switch." But it was worse than that. At 2000 hours a lieutenant and a few of his men from L Company arrived at brigade headquarters, exhausted and looking for food. When they were able to speak, they reported that they were all that remained of their company. Companies B and C of the 110th were effectively eliminated. Captain Aulanier, a French liaison officer with the 28th Division, later reported with profound understatement that although the beleaguered companies had "conducted themselves splendidly," the "liaison during the withdrawal between the French and American elements was not perfect. Some American detachments, not reached by the orders to fall back, interpreted unfavorably the withdrawal of the 125th Division (already tired when it entered the sector). The 4 companies in line in the sector of the 125th Division suffered extremely heavy losses." In fact, the 109th had an estimated 561 casualties on that day, and the 110th lost 371, most of them from the isolated companies.[40]

While the 55th Brigade was dealing with its own crisis, the 38th Regiment worked to eliminate the danger to its right. Following up the French retreat, the German 175th Regiment passed over Moulins Ridge east of the signal and emerged from the woods northeast and east of Paroy at about 0515. Although this grave threat to the 38th Regiment's flank was not immediately obvious to units closer to the river, the supporting 1/38th Battalion deployed B and D Companies south of Launay. The trenches McAlexander had ordered dug a few days earlier now came in handy. At 0555 McAlexander ordered the two companies to attack northeast, with the objective of restoring the Aqueduct Line between Moulins and Moulins Ruiné Signal. The companies moved swiftly and effectively, attacking at 0700, passing through Paroy, and driving the Germans back up the ridge. While they established a perimeter along the ridge between Moulins and the ruined mill, the 3/38th moved up from the Woods Line at Connigis and drove back some Germans who had penetrated into a ravine east of Launay. Only then did units along the river awake to the danger that—for now—had been averted. A message from XXXVIII Corps to Dickman at 0745 demanded that the American "main line of resistance be held at all costs"; five minutes later, a runner from the 9th Machine Gun Battalion informed division headquarters that the "French on right have pulled out and left our right in the air." Major Guy Rowe, commanding the 2/38th, then informed headquarters that he had been outflanked and would have to pull back. At 1000 hours, however, a more confident McAlexander phoned Diebold to tell him that the Americans were "solidly" holding their lines. By 1030, the German 175th Regiment had been pushed back to the central and eastern portions of Moulins Ridge, but the German 128th Regiment continued to advance southwest of Reuilly, and reserves were on the way.[41]

The 38th Regiment briefly seemed to be in danger on both flanks. On the left, the German 398th Regiment had advanced between Fossoy and Crézancy, but by 1100, the Germans had already decided to halt and consolidate their positions. Reinforcements in the form of companies lent from the 4th Regiment arrived around noon and strengthened counterattacks by the US 7th and 30th Regiments in the afternoon. Initial assaults were broken up by German artillery, but at dusk the American infantry regained full control of Fossoy and Crézancy and hustled the Germans back toward the railroad embankment. There the refugees joined the German 2/47th Battalion, which had gained a foothold south of the river but now had to refuse its left flank, thanks to the 6th Grenadiers' disintegration at the hands of Captain Woolridge in Mézy. Some German detachments stayed behind, and the Americans would spend the remainder of the evening and part of the next day clearing them out. Otherwise, the only German-held point south of the railway embankment and west of Mézy was Le Rû Chailly Farm, where the Germans had dug in a few machine guns. The 38th Regiment's left was safe.[42]

On the right, east and southeast of Mézy and Moulins, the breach was not closed so easily. Although counterattacks by the 38th Regiment's reserve battalions had restored the Aqueduct Line as far as Moulins Ridge, the departure of the French 125th Division created a predicament that Dickman's division could not resolve on its own. The 38th Regiment accordingly pulled back its right flank from Moulins Ridge to occupy the bretelle line (a reserve strongpoint constructed as a rallying point for defense and eventual counterattack in the event of an enemy breakthrough), blocking the Surmelin Valley below Connigis. At 1000 the commander of the French 73d Division (in reserve) phoned Diebold to assure him that his troops would come up to plug the gap between the US 3d Division and the French 125th Division. Not until 1245, however, did Montdésir formally order the 73d Division, supported by tanks, to counterattack in a northeasterly direction from its position along Le Surmelin Ruisseau, between Connigis and Monthurel. In so doing, it would hopefully restore the line lost by the 125th Division, which had fallen back some three kilometers, all the way into the Bois de Condé just northeast of Monthurel. The 73d Division would also, Montdésir told Dickman, "free your right completely."[43]

It took several hours for the 73d Division to deploy, however—to the annoyance of the 3d Division's officers, who thought it moved much too slowly. In the meantime, the Americans had to hold off the Germans on their right as best they could. Sensing an opportunity to pry the Americans back from the Marne and force a significant breach in Sixth Army's defenses, the German 36th Division deployed its reserves immediately. All three battalions of the 175th Regiment were brought to the front, while the 10th Landwehr Division's 372d Regiment crossed the Marne at Passy and drove west from Reuilly over Moulins Ridge to assist the 175th in breaching the American defenses between Moulins and Launay. But the German attacks failed. The American defenses held true, even on the extreme right of the 38th Regiment's line, where Company M maintained tenuous contact with the French 125th Division at Les Etangs Farm southeast of Launay. When the French abandoned the farm that afternoon, Company M banded together with Company L, situated to its left in the ravine east of Launay, to repulse repeated German attacks.[44]

The solid defensive efforts of Companies L and M blocked the last German opportunity to force a breakthrough. At 1930 the French 73d Division launched its counterattack, and although it made slow progress, the French managed to retake Les Etangs Farm and establish full contact with the 38th Regiment. Despite their early success along Moulins Ridge, the Germans in this sector had shot their bolt. An order for them to resume the attack at 2130 was canceled, and while the 36th Division organized its modest gains for defense, the remnants of the 10th Division were pulled back across the Marne altogether. The Marne Defensive was not yet over, but the crisis had passed.[45]

Though tired, the 3d Division's doughboys retained a stolid determination to hold the line in the face of renewed enemy attacks. As Lieutenant H. L. White of the 7th Regiment reported:

> We have been under heavy shell fire from the Boche ever since the night of the 14th, and have had nothing to eat or drink, nor have we had any sleep since that time. My men were exhausted and they sat down, not being able to stand longer, with their bayonets toward the Boche and said: "Let them come." . . . [But] they have been put on the front line and won't move back at any cost.[46]

The riverbank was littered with heaps of dead Germans, as multiple reports attested all along the line, and hundreds more were already on their way to prisoner of war camps in the rear. With this knowledge came the dawning realization of victory. Despite adverse circumstances and what seemed to be French cowardice in the Jaulgonne Bend, the 3d Division had held the Marne River line and stopped a major German offensive dead in its tracks.

German efforts elsewhere on July 15 had been almost equally disastrous, despite some promising early signs. Gouraud's flexible defense proved to be a brilliant success for his Fourth Army, as German attacks in its sector made practically no progress but resulted in exceptionally heavy German casualties. In the center, Berthelot's Fifth Army struggled to withstand the German assault after the initial enemy barrage ravaged the French first line of resistance. Pétain was deeply concerned for a time, and he even considered removing the US 2d Division from its position with Mangin's Tenth Army to reinforce Berthelot's weakening front. Foch, however, refused to countenance the weakening of Tenth Army, and in the event, Fifth Army was able to hold after some initial reverses. At most, the Germans gained five kilometers.[47]

The other American divisions in the line had not been severely tested. The 26th Division was bombarded but not attacked. In the 42d Division's sector north of Chalons, the Germans attacked at 0350, initially against the lightly held first position and then against the intermediate positions held by the French 13th and 170th Divisions. As elsewhere in Fourth Army, the attackers wasted their initial momentum on Gouraud's so-called false front, and in most places, the French were able to hurl the Germans back on their own. In a few spots, however, German forces were able to penetrate French positions, only to be thwarted by alert and strongly defended American positions. Later in the morning on July 15, XXI Corps commander General Naulin called on battalion- and company-size elements of the 165th, 167th, and 168th Regiments to help shore up his intermediate line. The Americans fought minor defensive engagements—sometimes against the ubiquitous Germans in French uniforms—and at one point, two American companies of the 167th cooperated with two French companies in a successful local counterattack. American artillery and machine gunners of the 150th and 151st Machine Gun Battalions also played a part.[48]

Overall, combat in this sector demonstrated how effectively the Americans and French could collaborate on the small-unit level when they were getting along. Father Francis Duffy, chaplain of the 165th Regiment, was impressed by the French. He noted that when the first German soldiers appeared opposite his men, "A few wise old French soldiers stood by to restrain them from firing too soon, for in the half lights it is hard for an unaccustomed eye to discern the difference between the Poilu's faded-coat-of-blue and the field gray of the Germans." The French liaison officer with the 42d Division summarized the Americans' conduct: "The conduct of the

American troops has been perfect and has been greatly admired by French officers and men. Calm and perfect bearing under artillery fire, endurance of fatigue and privations, tenacity in defense, eagerness in counterattack, willingness to engage in hand-to-hand fighting—such are the qualities that have been reported to me by all the French officers I have seen." Although the Americans gained some valuable if fleeting combat experience, the 42d Division—and its relationship with the French—had not yet been placed under serious pressure.[49]

The 369th Regiment also performed well. Occupying the second line of defense in VIII Corps behind the French 16th Division, it was not hit by the first German assault, although American runners braved intense shell fire to maintain liaison with the front. After the initial attack faded, the 369th was ordered to shift six kilometers to the left and enter the intermediate line to reinforce the French 161st Division. "Officers and men were tired almost to the point of utter exhaustion," reported the regimental commander, Colonel William Hayward, as "they had been hours without food or water; nevertheless they executed this order, moved into and occupied their assigned positions and took up the combat cheerfully and without complaint." The 3/369th Battalion relieved a Moroccan battalion at the front and helped fend off last-gasp German efforts to break through that evening and the following day.[50]

The morning of July 16 found some elements of the US 3d Division in rough shape—particularly the 30th Regiment. The men were exhausted, hungry, and thirsty, their provisions having been spoiled by gas. The 28th Division's 2/111th Battalion was dispatched to shore up the line in this sector. At 0930 Montdésir surveyed XXXVIII Corps' situation and noted that while things seemed stable on the left, on the right, "the 125th D.I. [division d'infanterie] appears to have withdrawn considerably as well from North to South as from East to West. A grave danger exists for the C.A. [corps d'armée], namely, the possession of the western edges of the woods by the Germans." He ordered Dickman's division to "bar at any cost the bend at Charteves in front of Fossoy-Crezancy" and to "bar the Valley of Surmelin," while eliminating any German outposts that remained below the Marne in its sector. The task of regaining the 125th Division's positions in the Jaulgonne Bend, however, was the primary task of the French 73d Division. That unit would continue its counterattack in conjunction with the French 18th and 77th Divisions to its right.[51]

Although Corps Kathen ordered its elements south of the Marne to begin withdrawing to the north bank on the evening of July 15, it took the French and Americans two days to restore their entire position. By noon, the 3d Division could report that the situation had "cleared up entirely satisfactorily west of Surmelin Valley." East of that, the French continued their counterattack, with some support from the 28th Division's 1/109th Battalion and two other American companies. Unfortunately for the Americans, they jumped off twenty minutes late, thanks to the language barrier and some other difficulties. As a result, they fell behind the French rolling barrage and came under heavy German fire from Moulins Ridge. Captain Aulanier thought the 1/109th "behaved very well, attacking even with spirit. Unfortunately some undamaged machine guns checked its dash. It was obliged to return to the trench from which it had jumped off, after suffering heavy losses." Since the French made limited progress, the attack had to be continued on July 17. That day started inauspiciously at 0900, when a German spoiling attack on the 73d Division briefly pushed it back and temporarily routed two American companies that were caught eating breakfast. Lanza described the scene:

> [After departing from their trenches because of friendly fire] the men reassembled at the company kitchens, in the St. Agnan ravine. As the artillery fire ceased an assumption was made that there would be nothing more doing, at least for some time, so arms were laid aside, and locating their mess kits, the men lined up for breakfast. Everybody was hungry, and the breakfast looked good. Nobody suspected any danger. In the midst of the general contentment, hostile infantry suddenly appeared, making a counterattack of their own. Neither side recognized the other until they were about 100 meters apart. The Germans opened a hot fire. Abandoning all equipment, the men of the 109th who were not casualties jumped down into the ravine and fled in all directions. The enemy ate the breakfast, after which he retired.

Shortly thereafter the French advance resumed, and by the end of the day, the Jaulgonne Bend had been restored. Likewise, in the Fourth and Fifth Armies' sectors, July 17 found the Germans right back where they had started two days earlier.[52]

The Marne Defensive had resulted in a crushing allied victory—no less so for the Americans than for the French. Among the captured documents was an account from a German adjutant of the 5th Grenadiers. He called the battle, as Dickman proudly recounted it, "the heaviest defeat of the war! It was only necessary to go down the northern slopes of the Marne. Never have I seen so many dead men, never such frightful battle scenes.

The Americans . . . shot practically all of them down in heaps. This enemy had nerve; we must give him credit for that; but he also displayed a savage roughness. 'The Americans kill everybody!' was the cry of terror of July 15th." From July 15 to 18, the Americans lost 678 casualties in the 7th Regiment, 595 casualties in the 30th Regiment, 596 casualties in the 38th Regiment, 561 casualties in the 109th Regiment, and 371 casualties in the 110th Regiment. Crown Prince Wilhelm was despondent when he realized that the offensive had failed totally; Ludendorff, verging on the delusional, still hoped to resume the offensive at some future date.[53]

Remarkably, this splendidly successful defensive effort left behind a legacy of bitterness. Even as the Marne Defensive concluded and the counter-offensive began, Kelton wrote to Conner to complain that the official AEF communiqué issued on July 18 failed to acknowledge that his division had "saved the day on the Marne and made it possible for the French Command to start the counter-attack which is now apparently succeeding." Talk of the 3d Division regaining its positions was ridiculous, he said, because the men had never left them. "We did not drive the Boche back; we killed him by the thousands and those that we did not kill we took prisoners. We killed them before they crossed the river; we killed them in the river and we killed them on the south bank as fast as the machine guns and rifles could pump lead into them."[54]

The grievances expressed by Dickman and his staff extended in multiple directions. Of the air services, including the US 1st Pursuit Group (with forty-one Nieuports and one Spad), which made 115 sorties on July 15 and 95 on July 16, Kelton had this to say:

> Throughout the battle south of the Marne, and the advance toward the north, hostile aircraft flew over our troops with impunity, observing for the enemy artillery, bombing, and firing upon all concentrations with machine guns. Many of our casualties were due to the work of these planes. In spite of all the work made by the division staff and repeated requests of the division commander, our planes put in their appearance only very tardily and never for any extensive period of time. It is absolutely necessary from a tactical standpoint and from that of morale that our air forces attain and maintain supremacy over those of the enemy.

Recriminations also flew from Colonel Anderson's 7th Regiment about the alleged misconduct of the 30th Regiment on its right. For his part, Dickman blasted Anderson in official reports, even though he later wrote in his memoirs that Anderson had "ably" commanded his regiment. Meanwhile, Kelton and Crawford discovered that they strongly disliked each other: Crawford suspected Kelton of power grabbing, and Kelton considered Crawford "slow, weak, and unresponsive to orders."[55]

Most of the bad feeling, of course, was reserved for the French. Although Robert Bruce has argued that "the French and Americans made a formidable team along the Marne" and cooperated efficiently, this was certainly not the case in Sixth Army. In fact, their relationship was seriously dysfunctional. The 125th Division's withdrawal was a particular source of bitterness. Kelton, never shy when it came to denouncing others (he even privately savaged Dickman for napping while his staff worked), went so far as to amass evidence against the French for possible use in the future. A few days after the battle, Kelton perused aerial photos allegedly demonstrating that German artillery had registered almost no hits on French positions in the Jaulgonne Bend, supposedly indicating that the French could have held if they wanted to (but taking no note of German infantry thrusts deep into the French right rear). Kelton passed this evidence on to his G-2 with instructions "to keep that set of photographs absolutely for future record." This conduct appears in an even worse light if one considers the possibility that 3d Division headquarters knew all along that the French division planned to withdraw.[56]

By the end of the defensive, Kelton—whom Dickman aptly described as "a highly efficient officer as well as a forceful character"—was utterly fed up with serving under French command. On July 20 he appealed to Conner to do something about "the subject which I have most at heart; namely, to get American units out from under French control." A major source of irritation was the XXXVIII Corps' chief of staff, whom Dickman described as "a cross-grained little Frenchman, known to his comrades as L'Ours, or the Bear. By causing frequent changes in the stations of our troops, and in various other ways, he made life a burden to the American 'shavetail.'" On the afternoon of July 20, Kelton complained, the Bear summoned him and gave him minute instructions—which Kelton took as patronizing to the point of insulting—on how to cross the Marne in pursuit of the by-then withdrawing Germans:

> When he began to tell me where to place companies, I lost patience, and, through an interpreter, I told him in damned straight language that whatever he wanted done with the 3d Division all he had to do was say so in ten words and that "how to do it" was my business

and he didn't need to waste his breath on that subject. He looked a little startled and then thoughtful for perhaps thirty seconds and then shrugged his shoulders and [said] that the idea was good, and went in and told his Corps Commander that his orders would be carried out.

Unsatisfied, Kelton charged over and gave the Frenchman another earful about excessive oversight. His adversary replied that he would be glad to step back if he could be sure the 3d Division "would do the right thing." By now utterly furious, Kelton barked back that "he could go on that basis so far as the American troops were concerned and he would have to do so, so far as the 3d Division was concerned." Ten days later Kelton was livid again, this time about the "stinking mean" billet assignments the division had received from the French, and he threatened to resign unless Dickman worked up the "courage" to demand better quarters for his men. "Don't ever expect me to agree with J. J. P[ershing] and his 50/50 theories about the French," Kelton huffed.[57]

Despite Kelton's insinuations about his lack of forcefulness, Dickman was no happier with the French than his chief of staff was. Nor did he entertain a high opinion of Montdésir, who "was very much elated over the unexpected outcome of the battle. He went into ecstasies over the wonderful physical vigor and enthusiasm of the young American soldier. He failed to mention their bravery, fighting spirit, initiative, endurance, discipline, or skill with weapons of all kinds. It was faint praise, but in the excitement of the moment he probably forgot about the other factors contributing to the victory." Dickman was also conscious of the growing resentment among his staff over the division's employment "as a tactical unit for over a month—until a few days before the battle." He went on:

> Our administrative and supply staff were at times in disagreement with the French, and it required constant watching on my part and conversations with the corps commander to mitigate the annoyances and keep peace in the family. As our officers gained in experience they began to understand the things which caused the trouble. The French, on the other hand, must have realized the growing superiority of the American soldier, and that their own prestige was slipping; this did not tend to improve their temper. . . . The days of tutelage, patronage and condescension had passed. . . . The psychological moment had arrived for release of the division from intimate association with a French command.

But the Americans were not the only ones who thought the time had come to escape from French tutelage. Captain Aulanier, the French liaison officer with the 28th Division, believed that "the offensive spirit of the command and the troops is unquestionable. Undoubtedly, their training is far from being complete, but this frequent parceling out hampers all efforts to train either the staff or the troops. I consider that it is important to place the American 28th Division in sector" so that its officers and men can hurt Germans and "perfect their knowledge of combined arms."[58]

All the bickering by Kelton, Dickman, and others exposed serious command problems at US 3d Division headquarters, and the poor Franco-American relationship reflected not just national differences but also deficiencies in French army and corps command. Still, in most respects, the American soldiers had conducted themselves well. Their courage—in both defense and attack—had sometimes landed the doughboys in hot water, such as when platoons and companies failed to withdraw and were instead surrounded and destroyed. The French, by contrast, had been quick to abandon unimportant territory and thus avoid casualties—albeit leaving their American comrades in the lurch. There had been some instances of American shakiness, but no more than would be expected with green divisions containing a significant number of draftees. At multiple important points, the Americans had endured cruel artillery and gas bombardments and then held firm in the face of strong German infantry attacks. And although a couple of battalion commanders had bungled once or twice, and artillery-infantry liaison had been poor, on the whole, officers from platoon to regimental level had performed effectively. Yet, in addition to crediting the Americans' fine conduct, attention must be given to the Germans' dismal performance. The once formidable 10th and 36th Divisions simply had no staying power. The 10th—supposedly a "crack" division and "one of the best in the Imperial German Army"—was a mere shell of its former self, thanks in part to the drubbing it had received near Belleau Wood. The 36th Division was likewise shabby. Moreover, the German infantry was well aware that its crossing was anticipated, and the men therefore lacked confidence in their prospects for success even before the attack began.[59]

The Americans—this time, the army—had been well and truly blooded. Artillery officer Frederick Trevenen Edwards, on the way to the front to join the 3d Division in mid-July, passed a trainload of returning Americans wounded during the Marne Defensive. "American troops, wounded, made me know, as never before, what it all meant," he wrote home to his father. "My heart went out to the poor fellows! It was a sweltering afternoon and they lay with their faces pressed against the sashes, panting for fresh air; drawn, tired youngsters, with the rattling, jarring train to open their wounds." For the Germans, the experience of defeat had been crushing. Lieutenant Herbert Sulzbach of the 9th Division had looked forward to the offensive with confidence: "You are so sure of your ground," he had mused in his diary on July 15, "that you are convinced that everything is going to succeed—the barrage, and the infantry assault, and the victory!" The next day he wrote, "Our morale is quite terrible. . . . We hear that our attack has in fact been repulsed by the French in this sector, with heavy losses. We feel really desperate." The initiative had passed firmly to the allies. The time had come to turn the tables.[60]

14

"Deal the Enemy a Crushing Blow"
Soissons, July 18–22, 1918

With the crushing failure of Operation Marneschutz-Reims, the time had come for Foch's counterstroke—what would be known as the Second Battle of the Marne. For several hours on July 15, it had looked like no counteroffensive would be possible. Pétain, worried by early German gains against Fifth Army, had wanted to draw heavily on the reserves—including the US 2d Division—assembled for the counteroffensive, which would have meant delaying or even canceling it. Fortunately, Foch intervened. His offensive, aimed at cutting the Soissons-Paris railway and road and interdicting another supply route the Germans had constructed east of town, would go forward as planned on July 18. If successful, it would force the Germans to abandon the entire Marne salient they had shed so much blood capturing in the spring and summer.[1]

The attack on the salient would be concentric and roughly simultaneous, but Mangin's Tenth Army would conduct the primary offensive. His army consisted of four corps, from left to right: I Corps, XX Corps, XXX Corps, and XI Corps. The French II Cavalry Corps stood in reserve, ready to exploit any breakthrough. Spearheading XX Corps under Major General Pierre Berdoulat were the US 1st Division, the crack Moroccan 1st Division, and the US 2d Division; two more French divisions stood in XX Corps' reserve. Berdoulat's mission, as specified in orders issued by Mangin on July 14, would be to drive eastward, parallel to the Aisne River south of Pommiers; capture Chaudun and Vierzy; cross the Soissons–Château-Thierry highway; and then seize the high ground east of that road and south of Soissons. The occupation of this ground—provided Tenth Army's other corps did their

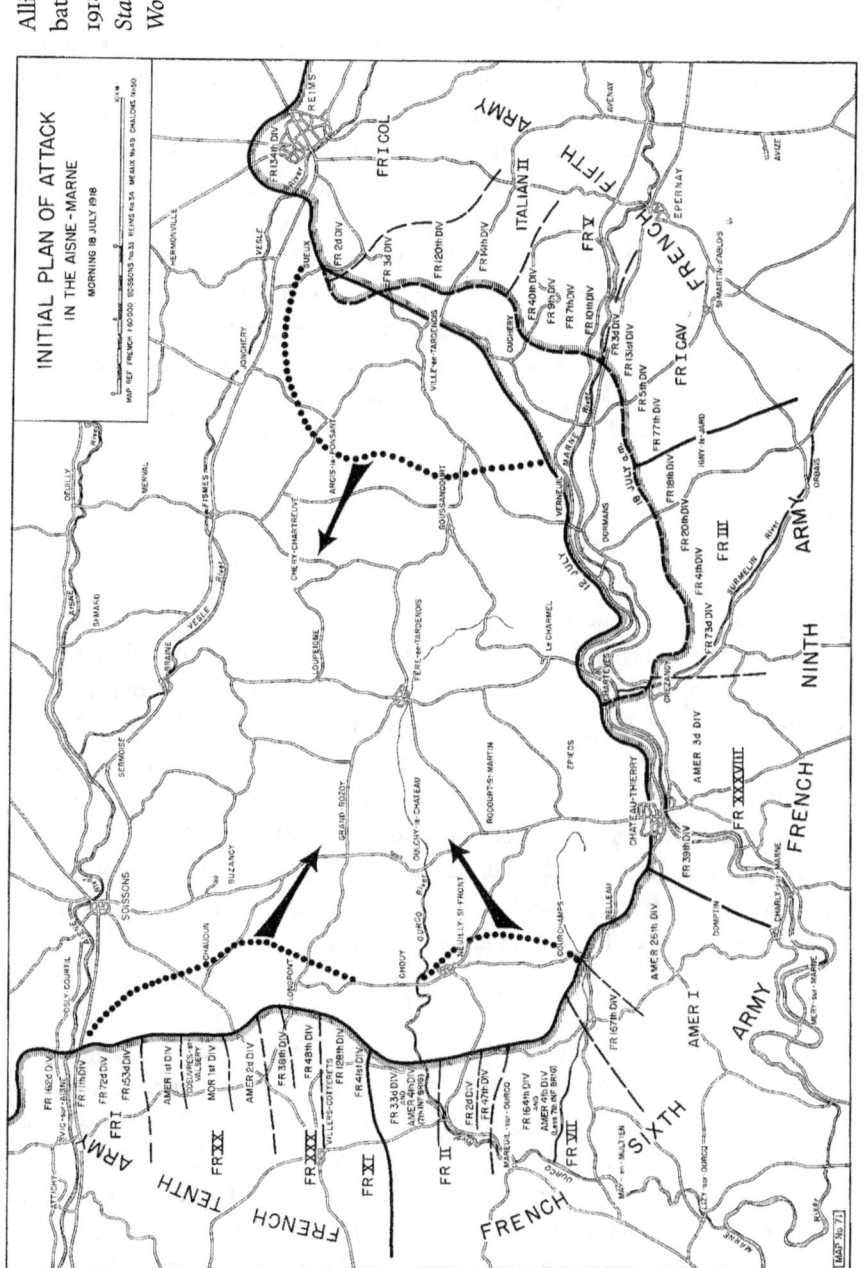

Allied order of battle, July 18, 1918. (*United States Army in the World War*, 5:231)

job—would endanger and possibly even cut communications and supply lines to the entire Marne salient and its forty German divisions. To add punch to his drive, Mangin possessed ample artillery; 324 Schneider, St. Chamond, and Renault tanks (156 of them with XX Corps); and forty squadrons of the French 1st Air Division.[2]

It would not be an easy task, but the potential for glory and prestige was great. Despite claims that they had already saved France on numerous occasions, the truth was that the Americans had participated only in secondary operations of minor to moderate tactical importance. More often than not, they had done so on the company to battalion level and under French command. And although American divisions had occasionally stood side by side or in close proximity, they had never had the opportunity to conduct significant operations in tandem. The Soissons offensive would mark the first time that intact American divisions would participate together in a major operation under the same corps command—albeit with a Moroccan division in the line between them. Success would not be just a point of pride; it would demonstrate the viability of an American army as an intact unit on the western front.

Meanwhile, the American military presence was also increasing elsewhere, albeit with maddening slowness. While XX Corps conducted the primary attack south of Soissons, the French Sixth, Ninth, and Fifth Armies would conduct secondary operations against the southwestern, southern, and southeastern faces of the Marne salient. Sixth Army included brigade detachments of the US 4th Division in the French II and VII Corps, as well as General Hunter Liggett's US I Corps with the US 26th Division. French Ninth Army (Henri de Mitry), which would conduct primarily holding operations along the Marne, now included the US 3d Division—its officers no doubt delighted to be released from Degoutte's control. Four more American divisions, the 28th, 32d, 42d, and 77th, lay in reserve and would be deployed during the campaign to reduce the salient—the so-called Aisne-Marne offensive—which would last until August 6.[3]

Unfortunately for the Americans of XX Corps, theirs had been a last-minute assignment. The 1st Division was ordered to join Tenth Army on July 11. Over the next few days, it had to move more than 100 kilometers—from Froisy to near Dammartin-en-Goële, northeast of Paris. There, most of the soldiers boarded trucks (some unlucky outfits remained on foot) and moved by night toward Mortefontaine, about 20 kilometers west of Soissons. The movement was hectic and poorly organized. The trucks drove 30 to 45 kilometers per night. Horses drew the artillery at first, but the animals moved too slowly, so the guns were unhitched from the horses and hitched to whatever trucks were available to tow them. They would not arrive at the front until the very last minute on the night of July 17–18. The infantry, machine gunners, and engineers arrived a little sooner, on the night of July 15–16, in the forest of Compiègne near Pierrefonds. Division headquarters was established at Mortefontaine while heavy rain drenched the officers and men.[4]

The 2d Division was resting and training about ten kilometers behind Château-Thierry on July 14 when orders arrived assigning it to Mangin's Tenth Army. The division's artillery immediately began moving toward the new front southwest of Soissons, but trucks did not arrive for the soldiers and marines until two days later. The division's report of operations recounted that the "Annamese drove the camions through clouds of dust, which covered all with a monotonous gray coat. Each Asiatic, with eye fixed on the camion ahead, seemed to have one thought, that of following at the regulation distance." After an overnight dash, the troops debarked at Taillefontaine—about seven kilometers behind the assigned jumping-off positions at Montgobert—on July 17. From there, it was a matter of scrambling toward the front in time to carry out the attack on the following day, even as division headquarters prepared and issued the attack orders. Needless to say, neither officers nor men got any rest.[5]

Major changes were under way at the headquarters of both divisions as the officers and staff scrambled to undertake the largest American operation in the war up to this point. On July 15 the 1st Division learned of its assignment to XX Corps. On the following day, while officers and staff unloaded their baggage at Mortefontaine, General Charles P. Summerall replaced General Bullard as division commander. Bullard was reassigned to command US III Corps, which would exercise administrative but not tactical control over the 1st and 2d Divisions in the coming operations. After Cantigny, Pershing had told Summerall, who had presided over the artillery in that battle: "Summerall, I am going to make you a major general, and I want you to learn to handle infantry as well as you handle artillery." Summerall replied, "General, all I know about artillery I learned from the study of infantry and how artillery could serve it." Born in Florida in 1867, Summerall had graduated from West Point in 1892 and served as an artillery officer in the Spanish-American War, the Philippines, and the Chinese Boxer Rebellion. He had also taught artillery tactics for several years at West Point and was an advocate of the importance of firepower at GHQ. Summerall was a difficult man to like: vain, overbearing, and tough on subordinates. But he had drive and aggressiveness, qualities that would quickly be impressed on his hard-charging division. He would also benefit from the culture of aggressiveness cultivated by Bullard.[6]

The 2d Division was far from recovered from its ordeal in Belleau Wood, which had ended just a few weeks earlier. And it was undergoing change as well. Bundy, who had proved ineffective as a division commander, had left to take command of US VI Corps, which would soon begin planning for Saint-Mihiel and future operations. Harbord—who had managed to escape criticism for his failures at Belleau Wood—learned on July 11 that he would take over as division commander, and he did so at 0900 on July 15. Wendell Neville was promoted to brigadier general and took Harbord's place in command of the 4th Brigade. He was a marked improvement over Harbord, and his men were pleased to have a marine back in command. The 3d Brigade, which was still essentially green, despite the walkover at Vaux, also underwent a change in command: the nettlesome Hanson Ely was brought over from the 1st Division and promoted to brigadier general to replace Lewis, who took command of the 30th Division in Flanders. As they assumed their new commands, these officers had to scramble to prepare attack orders while pandemonium reigned around them. No allowance would be made for failure, even under the frantic circumstances leading up to the Soissons offensive.[7]

The tactical deficiencies of the Americans would hinder the 1st Moroccan Division under General Dogan from doing its job effectively. This was a shame, because the division was a superb formation. Comprising North African, Senegalese, and French Foreign Legion troops, the 1st Moroccan Division was led by men of a special caliber. Lieutenant Joseph Patch of the 18th Regiment, which would advance alongside a French Foreign Legion battalion, was impressed by its commanding officer, who was typical of his fellow officers:

> He was a big, fierce-looking French officer with a big black mustache and wore a Croix de Guerre with a long ribbon stretching almost from his shoulder to his waist, on which there were so many palm leaves that it was hard to count them. . . . He gave me a drink of their "eau de vie" which was "white lightning" and about 120 proof. We had a nice visit and he said he hoped it would be sunny on the morrow, as it was much better weather for killing Germans, and that he was looking forward to it. He looked as if he meant it, too.[8]

With such fearsome divisions marked out on the maps at Mangin's headquarters, Berdoulat's XX Corps seemed to be ready to fulfill its decisive role in the offensive. It was deployed facing east on a roughly eight-kilometer front between Cutry and Longpont, with the US 1st Division on the left, the 1st Moroccan Division in the center, and the US 2d Division on the right. The Americans were deployed in columns of battalions. The US 1st Division had the 28th, 26th, 16th, and 18th Regiments in line from left to right, and the help of forty-eight Schneider tanks. The 1st Moroccan Division was led by its 1st Brigade of Foreign Legion (left) and Senegalese (right) troops, also supported by forty-eight Schneider tanks. Finally, the US 2d Division would attack with its 5th Marine, 9th, and 23d Regiments in front, from left to right, and the 6th Marines in reserve, accompanied by seventy-five to eighty St. Chamond tanks.[9]

Berdoulat's orders for the attack, issued to his division commanders on July 16, envisioned the three divisions advancing toward their objectives on "J day" in a "first rush" and "second rush," after which they would "progress ... with their available elements" toward a line from Hill 166 to Chaudun and Vierzy—roughly five to six kilometers from their starting positions. There would be no preparatory barrage—just a rolling barrage to maintain surprise. Berdoulat's orders included no specific instructions on terrain, perhaps on the assumption that divisional and regimental officers would work out such problems on their own—a fatuous assumption, because the two American divisions would be arriving at their jumping-off positions immediately before the attack began. XX Corps' path of advance lay over the Dommiers plateau, which was bisected by a number of north-south ravines that favored the defenders. Woods, villages and farms with fortifiable stone buildings, quarries, and caves completed the terrain features that could be put to effective use by a clever defender. The uneven nature of these features almost guaranteed an uneven pace of advance. Terrain posed problems for liaison as well, particularly between the 1st Moroccan and the US 2d Divisions, as their boundary would lay in the midst of thick woods for the first kilometer of the advance. Yet because numerous enemy strongpoints lay along divisional and regimental boundaries, interunit and interallied cooperation would be crucial.[10]

The Germans enjoyed substantial terrain advantages, but their forces were in tatters. Two German armies, the Ninth on the German right and the Seventh on the left, would face the allied attack on July 18. The brunt of Mangin's assault would fall on Ninth Army (after it was "almost completely shattered," the left part of its frontage would be turned over to Seventh Army at 2100 on July 18). Two corps of Ninth Army stood in Mangin's primary zone of attack: XXXIX Reserve Corps (or Corps Staabs, named after its commander, General Hermann von Staabs) on the German right, and XIII Corps (or Corps Watter, for General Theodor Freiherr von Watter) on the German left. Corps Staabs consisted of the 53d Division on the right, well outside XX Corps' zone; the 241st Division in the center, facing the French from the Pernant ravine to the northwest; and the 11th Bavarian Division, deployed primarily in the Missy ravine above Missy-aux-Bois. These units would face the French 153d Division and the US 1st Division's 2d Brigade. Corps Watter consisted of the 42d Division on the right, covering the area from Missy-aux-Bois to Chaudun; the 14th Reserve Division and elements of the 47th Reserve Division in the center, between Chaudun and Vierzy; and the 115th Division on the left, from Vierzy to the Bois de Mauloy. These units would face the US 1st Division's 1st Brigade, the 1st Moroccan Division, the US 2d Division, and part of the French 38th Division. Other German divisions, including the 28th, which had been shredded by the marines at Belleau Wood, remained in corps or army group reserve and would be drawn into combat on the first day.[11]

The German Ninth and Seventh Armies were supposed to consider the line from Soissons to Hartennes, Latilly, and Château-Thierry as the "line of last resistance which must be held under all circumstances." "The guiding principle of the defense," noted US 2d Division historian John W. Thomason, "was a deep, elastic forward zone, support battalions located for prompt local counterattacks, and reserve battalions in position of absorption." Whether they could accomplish this mission was doubtful, for the Germans suffered from several serious handicaps. First, the opposing Franco-American positions within the dense Forest of Retz made German ground reconnaissance "absolutely out of the question" and air reconnaissance "almost so"; in other words, it was easy for XX Corps to assemble in secret and assault with the element of surprise. And although the German formations currently in place had held their positions since mid-June, they were all so worn out and exhausted that they had been unable to fortify their positions properly—usually a German specialty. Food supplies were poor, and troops who routinely broke ranks to plunder local farms and fields for food were disciplined by rear-area officers, stoking resentment. Field officers were in such short supply—the 47th Reserve Division, for example, had a whopping 127 officer vacancies—that some battalions were commanded by lieutenants. German assessments of the 6,500-man 11th Bavarian Division on July 16–17 noted that the men were barely trained, exhausted, sick, and infested with lice. The "lack of smoking material," the division reported to corps, was "especially hard to endure." Overall, the division regarded itself as "suitable only for position warfare as it is below strength and lacks sufficient training." The 42d, 14th Reserve, and 115th Divisions could barely scrape together enough soldiers to man their primary lines of defense; the 14th Reserve had an average company strength of only forty men. Along the front as a whole, the Germans would fight at a 5:3 disadvantage in infantry and artillery. Of this the Americans were not unaware. A 1st Division intelligence report issued on July 16 noted that "the enemy's morale is not believed to be high. He has suffered heavy losses, is now greatly fatigued, and has, it is believed, suffered also from the prevailing epidemic of Grippe."[12]

Under such circumstances, the Germans had hoped against hope that Operation Marneschutz-Reims would mask their own weaknesses and keep the French fixated on defending Paris. With its failure, it was clear they would be unable to hold the salient for long should the French place it under heavy pressure. Contingency planning for evacuating the salient began on July 17. If an evacuation became necessary, though, it was imperative that the territory be held long enough to allow for a withdrawal in easy stages. The critical point was not Soissons itself or the roads and railway leading to it from the south—which allied artillery had already made nearly unusable—but the curve of the railroad the Germans had built six kilometers east of Soissons to maintain an unhindered supply for the troops in the salient. If this fell or was made unusable by a swift enemy advance, the situation of the kaiser's troops in the salient would become desperate.[13]

The night of July 17–18 was a severe ordeal for the American and French infantry, artillery, and support formations that were attempting to reach their jumping-off positions at the last moment. They had to move forward in the pitch-dark and pouring rain that reached "tropical violence." The circumstances were not well suited to the promotion of interallied comity, and sometimes the bonds of comradeship broke down. Sergeant Gus Gulberg of the 6th Marines remembered:

> At last we came on the main road. It was jammed. The air was full of cursing and grinding noises, as the drivers fought their way through. There was light artillery, heavy artillery, tanks, trucks, water wagons, field kitchens, supply trains, motor-cycles, and in the ditches on both sides were endless columns of American infantry, staggering along, faint from loss of sleep, hunger and thirst. We were desperately thirsty and took to robbing the French water wagons. The drivers

slashed at us with their whips and cursed us in French, but we didn't mind. Anything for water.

Closer to the front, the Americans found themselves dependent on French or Moroccan guides. Men in the 1st Division's 28th Regiment were being led by Moroccans; they approached their designated positions in single file, each soldier gripping the shoulder or pack of the man in front of him so as not to get lost. Lieutenant Joseph D. Patch of the 1st Division's 1/18th Battalion heard about a conversation between two of his soldiers as they trudged toward the front:

> The first one said that it was a hell of a thing to be led by officers who didn't know what they were up to. The second replied that they knew exactly what they were doing; they were getting the men in a frame of mind to fight; this he said they accomplished by denying them chow and sleep, and marching them with loaded packs, and as far as he was concerned, they had succeeded. He said he couldn't take it out on them, but that he could take it out on the Germans, and they had conditioned him to kill the first dozen he ran into.

For many men, griping was the only outlet for venting their frustration at what was beginning to look like a tangled mess.[14]

Despite the precautions of moving at night and the cover offered by the rain and dense woods, Mangin's preparations did not go unnoticed. German patrols observed the presence of additional French and American infantry and artillery at and behind the front. On July 17 the "unusually" quiet nature of the front led General Watter to believe that something was afoot, so he frantically began assembling a "mobile reserve" of artillery and ammunition stockpiles to address emergencies. That night, the Germans heard enemy tanks moving up toward the front, and two French deserters came over to warn the 11th Bavarian Division of the offensive just minutes before it began. Ninth Army consequently ordered an immediate stand-to, and its artillery opened fire, inflicting some casualties on support formations. Unfortunately for the Germans, the rainstorms that tormented the attackers on the night of July 17–18 also ruined the effectiveness of the "generous" quantities of gas the Germans included in their barrage.[15]

Foch's grand offensive would open at 0435 with a massive rolling barrage and the forward movement of thousands of French and American infantry, accompanied by many varieties of tanks. Despite the warning and last-moment preparations, the Germans would be amazed at the size and

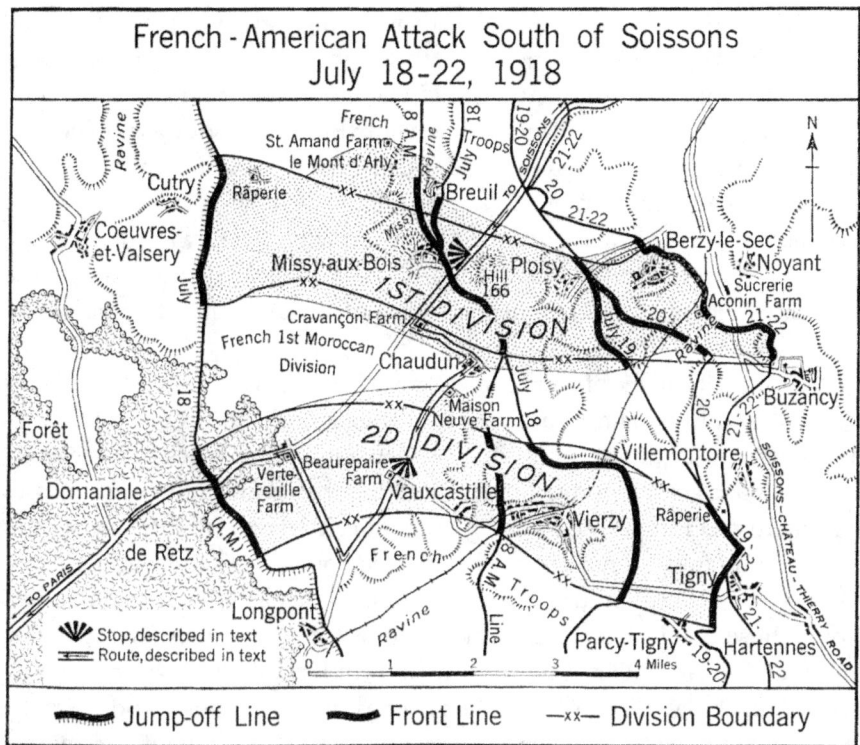

French XX Corps at Soissons, July 18–22, 1918. (*American Armies and Battlefields in Europe*, 83)

force of the attack. Lieutenant Herbert Sulzbach, whose 9th Division was rushed forward to reinforce Seventh Army as the attack began, wrote in his diary, "It looks as though we are being thrown into the largest enemy offensive of all time—and it was supposed to be *our* offensive! We couldn't even have dreamed that this would happen—ever." But while the force was overwhelming, allied coordination left something to be desired.[16]

Remarkably, all of the 1st Division's infantry would reach their jumping-off positions in time for the attack, which began shortly after the rain stopped. They would attack on a frontage of 2,800 meters. The village of Cutry and the eastern edge of the Coeuvres ravine lay just behind the American lines. That soggy ravine and the nearby shell holes were filled with water that had been impregnated with mustard gas and caused severe burns, as the waiting troops painfully discovered. Ahead lay about three kilometers of open, gently rolling farmland with waist-high grain. Beyond that, the troops—particularly the 28th and 26th Regiments of General Beaumont Buck's 2d Brigade on the left—would encounter the craggy and swampy Missy ravine, with the village of Missy-aux-Bois at its southern edge. Beyond lay another two kilometers of open land, followed in swift succession (again, primarily in front of the 2d Brigade) by the village of Ploisy with its ravine, and Berzy-le-Sec with the Chazelle ravine. Next was the swampy Crise valley, the primary road leading south from Soissons, and finally the ultimate objective—the 120-meter heights of Buzancy that dominated the battlefield.[17]

Summerall and his officers conferred with Mangin at corps headquarters at 1300 on July 17, and two hours later, the brigade and regimental commanders met at division headquarters. Around them trucks and wagons bearing guns and equipment roared forward, surrounded by dense masses of infantry. During these meetings, the officers learned that in addition to the French tanks—which could navigate the open farmland easily but not the ravines—they would be assisted by the French 42d Aero Recon Squadron, whose planes had buzzed overhead at Cantigny; divisional machine guns; divisional artillery (the 5th, 6th, and 7th Field Artillery) reinforced by three French battalions of 75s and batteries of 105mm guns; and a French balloon company to assist with observation. The American infantry would have one-pounders and Stokes mortars accompanying assault and support battalions, and one company of engineers per brigade.[18]

The infantry would be pressed to move fast. Summerall's orders, following Berdoulat's guidelines, set Route 2, the road leading southwest from Soissons to Paris—just beyond the Missy ravine—and ground north of Chaudun on the right divisional boundary as the first day's objectives. The rolling barrage would move forward at a rate of fifty meters per minute until it hit the first objective (an unimproved road leading northeast from Dommiers). It would stand there for twenty minutes, then continue forward to the second objective (along the eastern edge of the Missy ravine); finally, it would continue at a rate of twenty-five meters per minute until it reached the last objective east of Chaudun. Heavy artillery, including 155mm howitzers, would fire on the Missy ravine—an expected strongpoint—until it was reported subdued. On the left, the French 153d Division—another colonial outfit, albeit not as effective as the 1st Moroccan—was expected to keep pace with the American advance and help capture the Missy ravine.[19]

Buck's 2d Brigade had its 28th and 26th Regiments in front from left to right. The 28th, in typical AEF fashion, had undergone a change of command just a day before the assault. It was now led by Colonel Conrad Stanton Babcock; he replaced Hanson Ely, who was put in command of the 2d Division's 3d Brigade. Babcock's background was with the cavalry, after which he held a number of staff positions and briefly commanded the AEF Tank Corps' training center at Bovington. The 2/28th (Major Clarence Huebner) would lead, with the 3/28th (Major Willis Tack) in support and the 1/28th (Major George Rozelle) in reserve. The 26th Regiment, commanded by Colonel Hamilton Smith, was led by the 2/26th Battalion (Major James McCloud), with the 3/26th (Captain Walter R. McClure) in support and the 1/26th (Major Theodore Roosevelt) in reserve.[20]

The 2d Brigade's attack started out well. Huebner's 2/28th moved forward swiftly, overrunning the 11th Bavarian Division's first line of defense. The doughboys collaborated with the French tanks—which included a company of light Renaults that the Germans had trouble seeing in the tall wheat—to wipe out enemy machine guns ensconced in pits and trenches. The 2/26th advanced rapidly as well, and by 0530, both battalions were on their first objectives. "All going well," Roosevelt reported to Buck as the Germans hurried up what reserves they could muster. But worrying signs were already present for the Americans. Inexperienced company and battalion commanders lost their bearings and became disoriented, veering beyond their prescribed zones of advance. As the Americans approached the Missy ravine, the more methodical French 153d Division on the left fell somewhat behind, and Huebner's men began taking fire from German machine guns around St. Amand Farm. This farm lay on the western edge of the ravine and 900 yards north of the divisional boundary. Huebner nevertheless sent part of his battalion northeast to assault the farm, which the Americans did successfully by 0700. Meanwhile, to Huebner's right, the 2/26th had also come up to the western edge of the ravine.[21]

Just a few hours into the fighting, the combat was already severe. Among the attackers that morning was Private Dan Edwards of the 2d Brigade's 3d Machine Gun Battalion. Though seriously wounded at Cantigny, he had gone AWOL from the hospital and rejoined his unit in time for the Battle of Soissons. During the advance, his right arm was shattered by a German shell, so he crawled into a German trench clutching a pistol in his left hand. There, he killed four Germans and took four more prisoner. While returning with the prisoners, another German shell landed nearby, killing one of the Germans and destroying Edwards's legs. For his courage and sacrifice, Edwards would receive the Medal of Honor. Many others who demonstrated courage that day would not be individually recognized—but they were legion.[22]

By the time it reached the Missy ravine, the 2d Brigade had already taken serious casualties and was beginning to lose cohesion. Although part of the blame can be ascribed to flanking fire from German machine guns to the north and northeast and to enemy artillery firing from and across the ravine, German and French accounts make it clear that poor American tactics were largely at fault. The doughboys were aggressive, but without method. An NCO of the German 3d Bavarian Regiment holding the southern rim of the Missy ravine wrote, "The uninterrupted advance of the enemy gradually produced a sense of the weird; it seemed as if the enemy was not at all sensitive to his losses and we came to the conclusion that the enemy must be drunk." Other Germans made similar observations, including machine gunners who fired at the Americans until their water boiled. As for the French—allegedly dilatory in their approach to the Missy ravine—an officer of the German 13th Regiment on the 3d Bavarian Regiment's right got the impression that "the French paved the way while the British or Americans merely followed in the terrain which had been gained, and did not participate in the action until later." The German 22d Regiment, engaged largely with the French on the 13th Regiment's right, noted that the French were slowed down by casualties to a greater extent than the Americans but attacked with forcefulness and efficiency, despite serious losses. And so far as the French were concerned, their attack was perfectly *rapidement* as they cleared the Pernant ravine, shattering the left wing of the German 241st Division and hurling it back against the Aisne. Their advance paused only when their main forces came up against the Missy ravine, not far behind the Americans.[23]

This ravine posed a significant obstacle to both the French and the Americans. Half a mile wide, its bushy banks were at a steep sixty-degree angle; a 600-meter-wide marsh lay at the bottom, with a narrow but deep stream. Corduroy roads snaked through the marsh, but these had been preregistered by the German artillery, in expectation that the attackers would use them. German machine guns and field artillery, the latter including a battery of 150s and many 77s, were plentiful in the ravine. They were concentrated on the eastern bank and around the primary center of resistance at Saconin-et-Breuil in the French zone, just northeast of St. Amand Farm. The defenders also made ample use of caves and deep dugouts in the sides of the ravine.

Once the American and French forward elements began the assault, a bitter fight ensued. Twice Huebner sent his battalion across. The troops scrambled down the banks and plunged into the morass, only to come under heavy enemy fire and return after advancing 200 to 300 yards. In the second attack, five French tanks gamely attempted to enter the ravine, but three were knocked out, and the other two bottomed out in the swamp. By now, the 2/28th had incurred about 50 percent casualties. The 2/26th to the south had better luck, entering the ravine at about 0715 and immediately encountering sections of German infantry and machine guns. The Americans successfully broke through, and after hand-to-hand fighting with the crews of some 77mm field guns, they and troops of the 16th Regiment captured the village of Missy-aux-Bois by 0900, along with a nice haul of artillery pieces, machine guns, and prisoners.[24]

The capture of Missy-aux-Bois breached the Germans' main line of defense. The 11th Bavarian Division had not done well so far. Poor infantry-artillery liaison and the inexperienced gunners' deployment too close to the line meant that the field pieces often fired blindly, sometimes into their own troops. Machine gunners and infantry were also confused, and although they inflicted casualties on the Americans, the Germans failed to maintain a cohesive defense and were broken into fragments that fought without coordination. Now they struggled to hold on to the remainder of the Missy ravine. Meanwhile, a reserve regiment of the 11th Bavarian Division and two more regiments of the German 34th Division moved forward to occupy the last-ditch position running southwest behind Route 2, from Soissons and Vauxbuin to Hill 166. These forces were, the Germans realized, "very weak," but they were ordered to "hold to the last man." If the allies could break through the Missy ravine quickly and in good order, there was a good chance they could penetrate the Vauxbuin position and clear the path to Soissons.[25]

For Huebner, cooperation and improvisation would be the key to success. Tack's 3/28th, damaged by the German prebombardment but still relatively fresh, had come up, and the two officers decided to swing it around to the right so the two battalions could carry out the assault together instead of continuing in a column of battalions, as the orders had dictated. The French 153d Division was also fully engaged on the left and cooperating to some degree with the Americans. The French stormed the ravine successfully, capturing Saconin and advancing 300 meters past the ravine's eastern edge. Meanwhile, one of Huebner's companies assisted the French in assaulting the village of Le Mont d'Arly on the ravine's western rim; it then swung northeast across the ravine to capture the heights south of Saconin-et-Breuil. Another two American companies attacked across the ravine to the north of Breuil, while the rest of Huebner's and Tack's infantry attacked toward that village and the area between it and Missy-aux-Bois.

Wading across the swamp and avoiding footbridges that had been preregistered by the enemy, the Americans moved effectively across the ravine.

But there were grim encounters. "On one occasion," recorded the regimental history, "a high ranking German officer buried himself in the mud and water until his head and arms were exposed and continued firing upon the slowly advancing Americans until he was killed and trampled into the mud by the infuriated soldiers." Artillery crews fired at the attackers over open sights and abandoned or blew up their guns at the last moment before surrendering or fleeing. In the end, the Americans not only stormed the ravine's eastern ridge by 0900—simultaneous with the French east of Saconin—but also destroyed two German regiments and bottled up an entire German infantry battalion with 24 officers and 580 men in a cave to their rear. A dose of grenades eventually convinced the Germans to surrender, after which there emerged "a column of Huns with their hands over their heads and at the rear of the column was a German Colonel, walking with a military step and bearing common to Prussian officers."[26]

The capture of the Missy ravine left the Germans reeling. Except for a few remnants that escaped the inferno, the 11th Bavarian Division fell apart, having committed the last of its scanty reserves to no purpose and losing a whopping 4,000 men out of its prebattle strength of 6,500. Its remaining infantry fled, streaming heedlessly past raging German officers who threatened to—and sometimes did—shoot them. The fugitives reached the Vauxbuin position and dubious sanctuary. There, the Germans had managed to assemble a thin line of infantry, but the soldiers were short of small-arms ammunition and lacked artillery support because of the loss of so many field guns in the Missy ravine. Something close to panic set in as the US 3/26th Battalion passed through the 2/26th at Missy-aux-Bois, crossed Route 2, and captured Hill 166, establishing a lodgment in the final German line of defense. Some tanks accompanied them, and had the 28th Regiment and the French erupted quickly from the Missy ravine, all might have been lost for the Germans. The 3/26th's surge was unsupported from the north, however, largely because of the confusion and weakness resulting from the 28th Regiment's earlier move into the French zone and its consequent entanglement in the ravine. The German 28th Division's 109th Regiment appeared just in time to push the Americans back from Hill 166. German machine guns took the Americans under fire while field artillery—including dug-in 77mm field pieces and converted antiaircraft guns that had been unlimbered in the wheat fields east of the road and to the north just as the American attack began—opened fire point-blank. The guns set the French tanks afire and forced the American battalion to withdraw across the road. By 1100, the first crisis had passed.[27]

For the Americans, success had come at the cost of high casualties—all the company officers in the 2/28th had been killed or wounded—as well as significant confusion and disorganization. Instead of advancing to the third objective specified in the attack orders, the battalion would have to spend the rest of the day reorganizing and disentangling itself from its neighbors. The 2/26th and 3/26th had, to some extent, become intermingled, and so had the 2/28th and 3/28th. Worse, by blundering into the French 153d Division's zone on its left, the 2/28th had tripped up the poilus and interfered with their route of advance.

Not that any apologies were forthcoming. In the official summary of operations that Summerall ordered prepared, his chief of staff, Colonel Campbell King, blamed the French for the 2d Brigade's inability to advance further: "The failure of the 2d Brigade to advance was occasioned by very heavy enfilading machine-gun fire from machine-gun nests to the north and northeast. The 153d Inf. Div. on the left was unable to capture these nests, which lay in its zone, and the fire for the time being held up our attack." In his memoirs, Summerall recalled incorrectly that the French had "never tried to advance and left our flank entirely exposed." Buck was angry too. According to his memoirs, practically every hindrance the Americans suffered was the fault of the French; because of the dilatoriness of the poilus, he claimed, the 2d Brigade had to "spread out into the sector of the French Division on our left and captured the fortified places he was expected to capture." A divisional G-3 conference ten days later concluded, "It is certain that had the French, on the 1st Division's left, been able to advance, or had advanced at the same rate as the 1st Division, that the latter could have gone certainly as far as the high-road on the first day's fight." There was, of course, no consideration of what might have happened if the Americans had advanced at the same rate as the French. Babcock, visiting the front late that morning, spoke with the commander of the French regiment on his left, who reported that "he has lost heavily and his men are tired." The "attack seems to have stopped," Babcock complained, "because *Allies* were exhausted."[28]

Yet as the French 153d Division's "Historique des Faits" makes clear, its mission was a difficult one. Its route of advance traversed powerful German defensive works, an additional ravine forking south from Pernant on the left, and the strongest part of the Missy ravine at Saconin. As it advanced, the division had to continually refuse its left in order to maintain contact with the French division there (which played a supporting role and advanced only slightly) and protect the northern rim of the salient. In the process, the 153d Division had to endure severe flanking fire from the north and northeast—some of which undoubtedly hit the Americans as well. Despite this, French tanks and infantry had provided tangible support for the 28th Regiment's attacks into the Missy ravine—as Huebner could attest, but unbeknownst to division and brigade headquarters. That the Americans had strayed into their divisional zone was not the poilus' fault, but the French nevertheless advanced quickly, according to their standards. The French division commander, General Goubeau, moved toward the front quickly and established his command post about 1.5 kilometers west of St. Amand Farm at 1130. Assessing the situation, he decided that the time was ripe to continue the assault toward the prescribed third objective at 1730. The commander of what remained of the 11th Bavarian Division was certain that an attack on the Vauxbuin position would break through, provided the enemy could muster up some tanks. Unfortunately, after consulting with the Americans, Goubeau found them exhausted, disorganized, and uncertain of their positions and thus unable to coordinate effectively. The attack was canceled, and the battered 2/28th pulled out of the line so the French could resume full responsibility for the sector originally assigned to them.[29]

As General Goubeau had discovered, the 2d Brigade's confusion at the front was enhanced by serious command and liaison difficulties. Anticipating that deficiencies in these areas might create problems, Summerall had sent his brigade commanders a memo the night before the attack, emphasizing the importance of maintaining order, command control, and liaison. "Forward units," he ordered, "must keep higher authority constantly advised by frequent reports as to the progress of the attack and the state of the fight" via communications centers established at regiment, brigade, and division headquarters. None of this would do much good, however, if general officers were nowhere to be found. Colonel Babcock, the 28th Regiment's commander, had chosen to remain at headquarters until it became evident at 1100 that he needed to visit the front to separate his mingled battalions and reinforce liaison with the French. Buck had spent much of the day whizzing about the battlefields, with no obvious purpose other than to see what a real war looked like. This might have been excusable in the short term, but the fact that he continued to do so for days signifies some neglect of his command responsibilities. "I wanted," he argued in his memoirs, "to see my men in action and to be able to judge from first hand knowledge what was best for them, and what they could, and what they could not do. Their lives were in my keeping. I would expend them grudgingly except to deal the enemy a crushing blow." No benefit was immediately apparent, however—men's lives were expended with prodigality all the same—and Buck's repeated absences from headquarters would soon lead to many more bad consequences.[30]

★ ★ ★

Brigadier General John L. Hines's 1st Brigade had an easier time that morning than 2d Brigade did, but liaison problems would dog it as well. Attacking on schedule and preceded by French tanks, the first battalion of Colonel Frank Bamford's 16th Regiment on the left and the third battalion of Colonel Frank Parker's 18th Regiment on the right moved rapidly across the wheat fields. The troops were confident—one group of the 16th even opened fire (and missed) when a rabbit scampered across the field ahead of them. The Americans' quickness stunned the defenders of the German first line, which collapsed in short order. What one German referred to as the "absolute apathy" of the German regiment responsible for defending this sector was a contributing factor. The tanks had a positive impact for the attackers, but as the Germans observed, they could be both a blessing and a curse:

> The enemy felt so safe behind these long rows of battle machines rolling forward that he did not have his assault infantry follow in thin formations which modern combat demands, but led his assault infantry forward shoulder to shoulder in long lines, followed by heavy columns closed up. This method gave him the advantage of being able to penetrate our front immediately with strong forces, the disadvantage that his losses necessarily increased out of the ordinary [once the tanks fell out of the line and the German artillery and machine guns grew increasingly effective].[31]

As they continued, the Americans began to receive significant machine gun fire from three sides. These nests held out more firmly, and the standard dirty tricks—false surrenders and the like—came into play as the guns were knocked out one at a time. The 1st Brigade passed Coeuvres and approached Route 2, where the rolling barrage had paused for forty minutes. This road and its border of tall trees (now partially shattered) were also easily registered by the German artillery, and as the French tanks crossed it, two of them were knocked out. One "took its last toll of the enemy just as it floundered in a final move after being hit. It came down with a crash on a group of Germans in position by the side of the road and crushed them into a mass of mangled bone and flesh." The infantry followed, taking some casualties from enemy fire but crossing by 0830. By 0900, they were moving on to their second objective, having advanced up to six kilometers.[32]

In the process of the advance, though, company commanders had done a poor job of maintaining direction. As a result, companies became jumbled together with units on either side of them. As the 1/18th passed through the 3/18th and the 2/16th passed through the 1/16th—both prescribed moves—the intermingling of units became even worse. On the left, the 16th Regiment had moved ahead faster than the 26th and 28th, which were still battling for the Missy ravine. German machine guns east of Missy-aux-Bois were soon shredding the 16th's left, which had to be refused to maintain liaison with the 26th. Moreover, the 18th had outstripped the carefully paced advance of the Moroccans on the right. There, liaison was nearly nonexistent. Some German guns in an old French trench were irritating the doughboys, so once again, the Americans strayed into their allies' zone of advance to deal with the troublesome enemy nests. The 18th Regiment swerved 500 yards to the south, took the trench and Cravancon Farm, and then attacked Chaudun, even though the Moroccans were responsible for taking that heavily fortified town. The upshot was that, although the 1st Brigade achieved its objectives, it allowed dangerous gaps to open on both sides; by the afternoon, it was taking severe flanking fire from the north and south.[33]

The Moroccans, primarily facing the German 42d Division, had overcome stubborn opposition in the Dommiers ravine, the Bois de Quesnoy, Dommiers, and Glaux Farm. They paced themselves in an advance that slowed as the troops progressed and allowed the leading brigade commander to halt where necessary to clear his flanks; they also cooperated effectively with the four dozen Schneider tanks at their disposal (some sporting searchlights). In this manner, the Foreign Legion and Senegalese troops approached Chaudun. Their advance was certainly fast enough for their foes, who claimed they had no time to assemble counterattacks. At Chaudun, the Moroccans encountered a seething melee as mixed groups of American soldiers and marines assaulted the town from multiple directions. The unlucky defenders—also from a mélange of units that included the 42d, 14th Reserve, and 28th Divisions—had been thrown into Chaudun as a stopgap. Yet they fought hard, mowing down Americans and swaths of Senegalese, who were often wasted with astonishing recklessness by their French officers. The Germans also noted with satisfaction that their fire—which included small quantities of armor-piercing bullets, along with high explosives and *minenwerfers* firing at flat trajectories—caused some of the French tankers to ditch their mechanical monsters when the shells fell too close. In the village the fighting was bitter and replete with hand-to-hand combat, but the defenders were enveloped on three sides. The final indignity came when they were bombarded by their own artillery and the infantry broke at 0930. The Germans were closely pursued, and their attempt to hold some trenches east of town failed. A number of German batteries that had already been wrecked by the preliminary barrage were captured during this operation. The enemy retreated to high ground between Chaudun and the Chazelle ravine and dug in as the Americans began extricating themselves from the Moroccan zone of advance.[34]

As the sun climbed toward noon, the 1st Brigade had advanced a kilometer farther than the 2d Brigade on its left and the Moroccan division on its right. As a result, Hines's men were badly exposed. Machine gun fire raked them from three directions, artillery pounded them, and enemy aircraft bombed and strafed them. Their losses, according to the division history, were nothing less than "staggering." The 2/16th was effectively wiped out and fell under the command of a sergeant. Artillery fire cut off the Americans from food and water, and they had to scrounge whatever they could.[35]

The Americans' exhaustion and disorganization were especially unfortunate because the Germans opposite them were in desperate straits. As the 11th Bavarian Division's resistance "collapsed completely" and its remnants fled east to Vauxbuin, Corps Watter's elements were hurled back from Chaudun. Large gaps opened in the German defenses between Vauxbuin and Buzancy, and the Germans had no reserves immediately available to fill them. Two regiments of the half-shattered German 241st Division were still holding northwest of Pernant and could fire into the Franco-American left flank; however, the collapse of the German front southeast of there posed a dire threat to the entire salient. Anticipating the possibility of a rapid Franco-American thrust to the northeast, some reserves were even dispatched to Soissons—but not enough, the Germans realized, to hold it against a determined enemy attack. The overall situation for both Ninth and Seventh Armies was "critical," as even the "slightest success" by the allies would lead to the loss of the Soissons railroad that supplied German troops throughout the salient, thus putting them in the "gravest danger." Stopping the enemy southwest of Soissons now became of "primary importance"; the Germans knew the salient was lost, but they still hoped to abandon it in stages while inflicting casualties on a persistent enemy attacking "in dense skirmish lines and columns."[36]

Summerall, whose division had suffered 1,500 casualties during the day (probably an understatement), cautiously advised his brigadiers to prepare their positions thoroughly against a possible counterattack. But he also sensed the shakiness of the enemy and was more than a little unhappy that the advance could not be extended immediately. At 1820 he ordered Buck, "As soon as your regiments are reorganized, . . . advance this evening to the crest overlooking the Ploissy ravine [Hill 166], in order to enable you to cover any attack coming up that ravine." But the brigade commander refused, replying at 2135, "Gen. Buck will make no further advance tonight." In truth, the best any of his men could do was try to get themselves reorganized for a renewal of their drive on the following day. They had done well: mostly destroying the 11th Bavarian Division, capturing 1,500 prisoners and thirty field pieces, advancing up to six kilometers, and tearing a hole in the enemy lines that was big enough to cause the Germans to fear for the security of Soissons. But the 1st Division's transition from a semigreen to a veteran formation had been traumatic. Stragglers were common in the rear areas; a lieutenant colonel of the 28th Regiment reported at 1750 that he had seen "many men" drifting back with fishy stories of having been relieved or sent on errands. For those who stuck it out, "the cries of the many wounded who had not been evacuated, were heard through the night." That Summerall's officers and men were able to pick themselves up and carry on for three more days would be an astonishing accomplishment in itself.[37]

If anything, the 2d Division's rush to the front on the night of July 17–18 was even more hectic than that of the 1st Division. The circumstances generated further ill will toward the French. In an account published in the *Cavalry Journal* in 1925, Berdoulat painted a misleading picture of bonhomie. According to Berdoulat, Harbord arrived at corps headquarters hungry and unhappy about the difficulties his troops were experiencing. Before allowing him to continue, the Frenchman graciously responded, "First of all you are going to have your dinner served you, during which time affairs will take shape." But a bitter memorandum prepared five years later—apparently under Harbord's direction—accused the French of peremptorily snatching the 2d Division from its rest positions and directing it "to points unknown" on foot and by truck. Berdoulat "and his staff were unable to state the points at which the Second Division would be debussed or where orders could reach it which would enable it to be moved promptly and swiftly to its assigned attack position. This within thirty hours of a decisive battle." Instead of helping him, the memorandum claimed, the French just showered Harbord with maps and corps attack orders and told him to get going.[38]

That night, Harbord rushed to Taillefontaine, where US III Corps was posted to observe the coming battle but had no control over its course. There he found Bullard and his chief of staff, Brigadier General A. W. Bjornstad, poring over stacks of papers; with them was Colonel Preston Brown, who helped Harbord begin drawing up the 2d Division's attack orders.

While they were working, a French staff officer, Major Albert Bertier de Sauvigny, arrived. A stereotypical French soldier-aristocrat, he had fought in the area earlier in the war and gave Harbord a brief memorandum on the nature of the ground he would encounter. "This short memorandum," commented the postwar report, "was the sole intelligence material furnished or available for use in writing the division attack order." However, division historian John W. Thomason Jr. found an extensively detailed plan of attack (in 1st Moroccan Division files) that the French evidently offered to Harbord upon his arrival, but he either rejected or ignored it. It included careful instructions for the Americans to pace their advance methodically, in close synchronization with the French. For the Americans, disregarding these instructions would have bloody consequences.[39]

Just after dawn on July 17, Harbord and his staff rushed off to find his division and distribute maps and attack orders. They found the roads "congested with traffic to a degree hitherto undreamed of." In part, the author of the postwar memorandum asserted, this traffic jam occurred because the 2d Division had been directed to a deployment area fit only for the much smaller European divisions. As marines and soldiers crowded toward the front, the French 38th Division, which they were relieving, attempted to pull back, congesting the roads even more. Establishing contact with all the brigade and regiment commanders took all day, and everywhere he went, Harbord heard bitter complaints about how the trucks had dropped off the infantry willy-nilly, without specific directions where to go: "they had no maps, they were not told where to go, and could only follow the instinct of the American soldier and walk to the front." In one example of the confusion, the Marine Brigade's machine guns were unceremoniously dumped near Pierrefonds without transport, and the gunners had to carry them on foot through mud and congested roads more than twelve miles to the front; they did not make it in time for the attack. The tanks were also late to arrive.[40]

The circumstances for the men were appalling. Trucks jammed to bursting with soldiers jounced over poor roads at breakneck speed. Upon arrival, the men virtually had to start running as soon as the trucks stopped and their feet hit the ground. No provisions were made for food, let alone sleep. The best they could hope for was a few moments to fill their canteens. Water was plentiful—it was pouring rain. As they finally cleared the rear-area congestion and found their way toward the front, some companies had to march double-time to reach their jumping-off positions at the prescribed hour. Field officers lacked guides, maps, or proper directions, but they tried to bring some order to the chaos and make sense of the hurried attack orders passed down from division. By the time the offensive began, both officers and men were drunk with fatigue. Yet for many, deep down, it was like a repeat of the early days of June. For Lieutenant Elliott D. Cooke of the 2/5th, it was "symbolic of America in the war. Weary Frenchmen coming out: determined Yanks going in to take over."[41]

Under such circumstances, it is perhaps understandable that Harbord's attack orders for the 2d Division—Field Order No. 15, issued at 0430 on July 17—lacked sophistication (although his attack orders for the Marine Brigade at Belleau Wood had been no better). As he had a month earlier, Harbord simply ordered a frontal attack at a constant rate of advance. His orders took no account of the troops' need for rest, the necessity of filtering fresh battalions into the line, the terrain, or enemy dispositions. Summerall's 1st Division, with a slightly less hasty deployment, had considered some of these things. The 1st Moroccan Division, which had held its positions for many days, issued orders for a methodical advance according to standards now prevalent in the French army. The Moroccans also benefited from an understanding of the terrain that the Americans—by force of circumstances and Berdoulat's neglect to issue specific orders—lacked.[42]

Harbord ordered a rate of advance of fifty meters per minute, with only "short" pauses at intermediate objectives until the primary objective on a line from Chaudun (in the French zone) to Vierzy (in the 2d Division's right zone) had been reached. To conform with the movements of the divisions on either flank, all of Harbord's regiments would have to undertake a tricky change of direction from the northeast to the southeast after reaching the intermediate objective—difficult at any time, and especially so with tired and poorly informed men. Reflecting Berdoulat's specifications in the corps orders, Harbord included careful instructions for liaison between the two US brigades and with the French divisions on either flank, with a company and a machine gun platoon being provided at each point. Harbord also issued directions for coordination with the French tanks, which would be employed here in numbers the Americans had not seen before. Infantrymen were told that if they wanted the tanks to destroy an objective, an officer or NCO should tie a handkerchief to the end of his rifle, point in the direction of the objective, and raise or lower his rifle several times. For their part, the tankers would place red and white panels on the rear of their tanks to indicate to the infantry that the way was clear and they should follow. Infantrymen were further instructed not to halt when tanks were incapacitated (as was frequently the case) and not to be afraid to fire on the tanks if the Germans surrounded them, since the machines were bulletproof. However, Harbord included no specific prescriptions for the use of machine guns, mortars, or one-pounders in support. As Grotelueschen has argued, "More than any other AEF attack of the war, this battle became a test of the offensive power of the rifle and the bayonet." Equally unfortunately, the hasty rate of advance set by Harbord, despite the more methodical approach proposed by the French, would make liaison with French units on either flank next to impossible and ensure German pressure from either direction as the Americans moved ahead.[43]

The 5th Marines, now commanded by Colonel Logan Feland after Neville's promotion, faced possibly the most daunting prospect of any American regiment on July 18. The regiment, attacking on a frontage more appropriate for a brigade, would have to advance northeast through partially wooded territory, roughly paralleling Route 2. Entering open terrain, and with Chaudun in view, the marines would have to turn right, *away* from that tantalizing target—offering any Germans their left flank if the Moroccans had not showed up yet—and then veer southeast toward the rough ground around Vierzy. The marines would have to execute this maneuver without significant machine gun or tank support, which had not yet arrived. Whether Feland (whose headquarters personnel had disappeared into the maelstrom of congestion behind the front) or his battalion commanders understood this route of attack is doubtful. Neville had not had time to issue written orders from brigade headquarters, and there were no guides to direct them. Moreover, the marines had been forced to detruck twelve miles behind the lines on the previous evening and rush to the front, double-timing the last few miles. Most of them made it to their jumping-off positions literally as the rolling barrage started forward, and they had to attack without a pause. Finally, as the flank regiment, the 5th Marines would be expected to maintain liaison with the Moroccans on their left—difficult in the best of circumstances, and impossible in the conditions of July 18. Adding insult to injury, the 6th Marines had been placed in corps rather than division reserve, and it could be called on for support only with the permission of Berdoulat and Mangin.[44]

The wide attack frontage forced Feland to deploy two battalions abreast with one in support, rather than in the standard column of three battalions: Major Julius S. Turrill's 1/5th Marines on the left, Major Ralph S. Keyser's 2/5th Marines on the right, and Major Maurice Shearer's 3/5th, still well understrength after Belleau Wood, in support. The 1/5th arrived at the front just as the rolling barrage began and immediately rushed forward; some of the companies of the 2/5th did not arrive on time and had to deploy piecemeal as they reached the front. Feland had no real control of his battalions after they moved forward, and the battalion commanders did not exercise much authority either. Junior officers and NCOs exercised command. For marines who had been in Belleau Wood, where the fighting was largely on the platoon and even the individual level, such circumstances may have seemed natural and even comfortable. But in the mostly open terrain now facing them, where the route of attack called for complicated maneuvers and liaison was all-important, the loss of command control was a recipe for mass confusion.[45]

No one expected a cakewalk. The night before the attack, Keyser had shocked his junior officers by announcing that each company would leave one officer and twenty men behind "as a nucleus to build new companies after the attack." Fear, exhaustion, and confusion about the route of attack caused no hesitation. The marines moved forward decisively, but unfortunately, their decisions were often not well informed. Turrill's 1/5th, 20 percent of which never reached the front, moved northeast, as directed, through the woods. German snipers caused the marines some casualties as they pushed along Route 2, but resistance was disorganized. Some of the defenders, dazed by sulfur fumes from the Franco-American bombardment, had donned gas masks and could barely see in the fog- and smoke-choked woods. Emerging from the trees to open ground southwest of Chaudun, the Americans encountered another road leading northeast to that village. "All I knew was what I could see," recalled Cooke. "Behind us was a forest. In front, a road bordered by trees at regular intervals, cut through rolling fields of wheat. On the horizon was a town of white stone houses with red tiled roofs." Up the road, before it reached Chaudun but in the French zone, was Maison-Neuve Farm. German machine guns at the farm and in and around Chaudun were active, inflicting serious casualties on the marines. First Lieutenant Samuel Cumming watched his men being "mowed down like wheat. A whiz bang (high explosive shell) hit on my right and an automatic team which was there a moment ago disappeared, while men on the right and left were armless, legless or tearing at their faces."[46]

The Americans were supposed to execute a right turn here and proceed to the southeast, but in the heat of the moment, it seemed much more logical to turn left and wipe out their tormentors at the farm and village. That is what most of the marines did. As Turrill's companies advanced on the village, elements of the 2/5th Marines and the 9th Regiment fell in alongside. Meanwhile, Senegalese troops moved up stolidly on the left, and elements of the US 1st Division's 18th Infantry swooped in from the north. German machine guns took a heavy toll on the dense formations (better described as clumps) of American soldiers and marines. Even so, the defenders didn't stand a chance. They fought desperately, however, and the capture of the village took almost an hour. Turrill witnessed and approved of the attack on Chaudun—though he gave scant credit to the Senegalese for its capture—saying that doing so was necessary to continue the advance. After it was over, though, his battalion was scattered and without direction. For the rest of the morning, Turrill knew next to nothing about what was going on—he later complained that information from the front was "meagre." In the resulting pandemonium, the 1/5th Marines scattered; only 150 men would be located by battalion headquarters at the end of the day.[47]

The jumble at Chaudun and the need to pause there for the rest of the afternoon to sort out the lines also squandered an opportunity to accomplish a full and dangerous penetration of the German defenses in this sector. According to the German 42d Division's 65th Brigade, which was responsible for this area, a "prompt and sharp pursuit" by the Moroccans and Americans immediately after capturing Chaudun would have pushed the Germans back much farther. The Germans regarded this as a "failure" of leadership on the part of their enemies; they estimated that, by noon, "a reckless continuation of the assault would probably have enabled him to gain the road: Soissons-Hartennes the very first day." But since the Americans did not advance, the Germans were able to bring up reserves by evening and plug the line. Had the Americans been more patient and allowed the Moroccans to set the pace—a quick one, at that—the results might have been different.[48]

Keyser's 2/5th Marines, moving northeast in disconnected companies, captured Verte Feuille Ferme thanks in part to "remarkable" assistance by the tanks. The battalion then split, with some platoons following the 1/5th Marines to Chaudun and others properly executing the change of direction to the southeast. In doing so, they took the German defenders—echeloned in this sector from southwest to northeast—in the northern flank and rolled them up. The marines and 9th Regiment soldiers, though not blending cheerfully, made good progress toward Vauxcastille ravine. This place, the Americans quickly discovered, was packed with German artillery "camouflaged by nets and shocks of wheat," along with some infantry of the 14th Reserve and 47th Reserve Divisions. Lieutenant Cooke, who had ended up here with elements of his 2/5th Marines, remembered that "the gunners were caught by surprise but still managed to blast out a brace of shells into our charging ranks. The belch of the cannon licked out like a hot breath. I thought a couple of boilers had blown up in my face. Water welled into my eyes and my helmet jerked back against its chin strap.

The shells had screamed past before I could duck but, half blinded, I hit the deck anyhow." Elements of the German 3d Reserve and 28th Divisions had been ordered forward to reinforce the ravine, but thanks to the increasing confusion behind the German front, they did not arrive in time to aid the exposed batteries and their supporting infantry. The Americans captured these units as they cleared the ravine, bottling up an entire battalion of the German 47th Reserve Division.[49]

The Americans moved on to gain a lodgment on the slopes above Vierzy—which was situated in a ravine—by around 0700. Despite all their confusion, the marines and soldiers were already close to the day's third and final objective in their sector. Opposite them, the German front was crumbling fast. Officers in staff cars and on horseback crisscrossed the battlefield along with weary messenger dogs, but communications broke down almost entirely. The 14th Reserve Division fell to pieces, with many of its troops throwing down their weapons and fleeing in disorder. Their flight left the 115th Division around Vierzy with its right flank in the air. At 0830 Corps Watter faced reality and directed what remained of its front-line formations to retire to a line running from Chaudun to Vierzy and the Bois de Mauloy, effectively abandoning its forward lines of defense. At the same time, the German 3d Reserve Division was ordered to relieve the collapsing 115th Division around Vierzy, even as the marines pressed their attack—always a vulnerable moment for the defenders. The French 38th Division on the 3d Brigade's right was also doing well, putting heavy pressure on the Germans below Vierzy. Nor would the defenders have the benefit of much artillery support, thanks to the loss of a number of field batteries, chaos behind the front, and a lack of ammunition, despite Watter's last-minute precautions to form a "mobile reserve." For Private William A. Francis, whose company of the 2/5th had not been in the leading wave, the attack had been "nothing but a hike" so far, and the good luck seemed set to continue.[50]

As the Americans approached Vierzy, however, German resistance stiffened considerably, owing to the timely appearance of two regiments of the relieving 3d Reserve Division. The Americans attacked doggedly if not always in unison, for marine and army officers fell to arguing over tactics. "Pull your go'damn Marines out of here!" screamed one army major at Cooke. "Get over on the left where you belong and protect my flank!" But Cooke refused to obey. They reached the edge of the town by 0930. "We finally noticed that they were firing from the top of the buildings and we dislodged them, and also got one out of a tree," Francis recalled. The Americans' strength was spent, however, and they had to pull back without taking the village. To the north, meanwhile, the Moroccans had consolidated

Chaudun by 1100—capturing German holdouts and shooing away milling groups of American marines and soldiers—and pushed forward to some trenches on that village's eastern outskirts.[51]

The 3d Brigade began the attack on a frontage of only 1,000 meters, allowing its constituent regiments to advance in the columns of battalions to which they were accustomed. On the left, Colonel LeRoy Upton commanded the 9th Regiment, which would move forward with the 1/9th (Captain Charles Speer) in the first wave, the 2/9th (Major Arthur E. Bouton) in support, and the 3/9th (Captain Henry H. Worthington) in reserve. Upton's men were tired, but they had at least managed to get to the front with a couple of hours to spare. Unfortunately, the soldiers lacked grenades and ammunition for automatic rifles and had only thirty rifle rounds per man. Upton— whom Ely had rebuked before the battle for excessive complaining about being passed over for promotion—was in an "electric and terse mood" as he assembled his officers before the attack. The 2d Division, he told them, was about to deliver a "smashing blow" to the enemy that would be the "turning point of the war." It was, recalled First Lieutenant Ladislav Janda, "a deadly serious talk, brutally to the point, that left everyone with the feeling of we-may-get-it-but-who-cares." If the men ran out of ammunition, Upton told his officers, they were to continue forward with their bayonets. That was it—no written orders, no set objectives, no food. The few maps that were available were impossible to read in the dark. The men would just go forward when the rolling barrage began (no one knew when) and hope for the best. As for food, the men begged for scraps from any passing Frenchmen they encountered.[52]

German signal flares rocketed skyward in a bewildering variety of colors as the soldiers commenced their attack behind the rolling barrage. It was, remembered Janda, a "hot sultry morning," with mixed fog and smoke adding to the confusion as the soldiers moved forward. The French tanks came up just in time to contribute. Upton gleefully watched them "swatting every Boche machine gun that they could find." Other machine gunners were dealt with by the American infantrymen, who were in a deadly mood. In one incident of a sort that would be repeated countless times in this war, Private Willie McMullen of the regimental headquarters company joined a group of five Americans who managed to outflank and surprise a German machine gunner who had already killed many of their comrades. When they approached, the German leaped up, yelling *"Kamerad!"* But he received no mercy. "We all closed in on the German machine-gunner who stood with his hands as high as he could reach. The man on my left said, 'no shoot'm son-o-bitch—no shoot'm son-o-bitch, killum son-o-bitch' and with that he lunged past me thrusting his bayonet through the German's stomach. The German crumpled into a pile of human flesh and bone behind the gun he had used in knocking down many Americans."[53]

The 1/9th advanced quickly, rushing Beaurepaire Farm and capturing some Germans, but it took casualties from German machine guns hidden among the wheat fields to the left, since the 2/5th Marines had not yet come up in significant numbers. Fire from Verte Feuille Farm pulled the soldiers north even before the marines arrived in enough strength to take the place. From there, the 2/5th Marines and 1/9th Battalion advanced side by side until Chaudun came into view. At that point, most of the soldiers and marines headed north, taking Maison-Neuve Farm and capturing some German artillery before moving on to Chaudun. Most of the supporting 2/9th simply followed in their path. Only the reserve 3/9th, in which Janda commanded M Company, took the right turn after the officers paused to consult their maps. By that time, unfortunately, companies had taken what Janda estimated to be 40 to 50 percent casualties from German artillery and machine gun fire.[54]

M Company approached Vauxcastille ravine and found it strongly defended by a battery of field artillery well covered by a machine gun—one of a number of German batteries in the ravine that American soldiers and marines would overrun that morning. Like the German infantry, the artillerymen were exhausted even before the attack began. The commander of one field artillery battalion reported on July 14 that his men had grown prone to "fainting spells." Others were drunk on the morning of July 18, having broken into the division's commissary stores, and they spent the day riding around the battlefield "without rhyme or reason." For the most part, however, they would defend their guns to the last.

The commander of Janda's 3/9th Battalion, Captain Worthington, was nowhere to be found. Janda therefore took charge and deployed his men to attack. As the men took their positions, a salvo of tear gas landed among them. If the gas was intended to disperse them, it worked; but instead of fleeing rearward, the soldiers charged into the ravine. Remembered Janda: "Almost without orders what remained of the men literally plunged down the slope, with eyes streaming and cursing a blue streak. This is no attempt at heroics but the actual fact." The sight of a crowd of Americans barreling across the ravine was too much for the German artillerymen. They fled, abandoning their guns, and would subsequently join with bands of infantry. Coming to their senses and realizing that they had captured the ravine—except for one German battalion still holding out in a cave—Janda and his men paused momentarily to survey their haul of booty—weapons, equipment, and a brand new keg of sauerkraut. Though parched with thirst, the men were also hungry, so they broke open the keg, and each man grabbed a handful of sauerkraut before taking his place in the skirmish line. Exiting the ravine, they "moved out thru the wheatfield, each man with a rifle in one hand, eating sauerkraut out of the other."[55]

Scattered groups of soldiers and marines were approaching Vierzy from multiple directions when Janda's group ran into heavy fire from a German blockhouse to their left front and from machine guns in the rugged ground around the village. Realizing that their numbers were too few to take on the enemy—M Company, which had started the day with 230 men, now had 35—Janda ordered his men to drop into the wheat and await support. It was a long, tense wait. At one point, about twenty brightly colored German planes dove down, strafing and bombing Janda's little group and dropping grenades out of their cockpits, but miraculously, no one was hurt. A more serious threat came in the form of a counterattack by German infantry, which approached cautiously through the wheat, unable to see Janda's men. When the Germans were within 300 yards, Janda ordered his widely spaced men to open fire. The Germans had no stomach for a fight and quickly retired, but as the afternoon began, Janda's men were still pinned down and desperately awaiting help.[56]

Colonel Paul Malone's 23d Regiment was the rightmost regiment on the 2d Division's front, next to the French 38th Division. It attacked with the 2/23d (Major D'Arly Fechet) in front, the 1/23d (Major Edmund Waddill) in support, and the 3/23d (Major Charles Elliott) in reserve. Unlike the 9th Regiment, the 23d arrived at the front just in time to participate in the battle, after double-timing to the line. A good number of Malone's men got lost on the way as they dodged obstacles in the dark and staggered toward the front. Second Lieutenant Robert Kean, on duty at Malone's headquarters, watched as French infantry scrambled out of the line to avoid the inevitable counterbarrage as the panting Americans arrived. Some French tanks were there too, and their commanding officer could not get anyone to tell him when the attack would begin. Unable to find anyone else in a position of authority, Kean told the bewildered Frenchman to move out at 0435. The tanks' support was especially welcome because the infantry would have to move forward without machine guns, one-pounders, mortars, or grenades of any kind.[57]

Despite their exhausting and chaotic approach to the front, the soldiers did a good job of executing the attack. Fortunately, they did not initially encounter any significant terrain obstacles. The 2/23d managed to drive 1,000 yards in the first fifteen minutes and, for the most part, effected the right turn to the southeast as planned, although some men did drift left to join the 9th Regiment. Liaison with the French 38th Division was lost almost immediately, however, and as the troops approached the Vauxcastille ravine, the formations began losing cohesion. The 1/23d drifted out of support and moved up to Fechet's right, and two companies of the 3/23d independently moved up from reserve to the front. Lieutenant Kean, serving as an artillery liaison officer, tried to get information from Malone on his troops' location, but the colonel had no idea. Kean therefore followed the infantry, only to find the commander of one of the leading battalions "very rattled":

> He only had one or two runners, had completely lost control over his battalion and did not, in fact, know where his own troops were. Isolated platoons were attacking the ravine on the right, but there seemed no control nor liaison by regimental or battalion commanders. It was a case of the enlisted men and platoon leaders continuing forward with utmost bravery, with the higher officers incapable of controlling them. These platoon leaders were inexperienced, had no maps, did not know exactly what was expected of them, and isolated groups of enlisted men were wandering around asking only to be led, completely at a loss as to what they should do next.

"Liaison inside the 23d Infantry," Kean concluded, "had broken down completely."[58]

The mixed battalions of the 23d Regiment nevertheless managed to reach and cross the Vauxcastille ravine at roughly the same time as the forces to their north. Beyond this north-south ravine, which the French tanks could not pass, they encountered the east-west ravine containing the village of Vierzy. The lack of supporting infantry weapons proved crippling to the attackers, who were unable to penetrate the enemy defenses (which didn't amount to much, since many of the defenders had fled that morning) despite uncoordinated attacks against the town by the mob of 9th Regiment troops and marines from the north. Major Bertier de Sauvigny, the French staff officer who had provided Harbord with information about the terrain in this sector, scoffed in his journal that the whole 2d Division was being stopped at Vierzy "by a few enemy platoons." But there was nothing anyone could do. The division had run out of gas—and the doors were falling off too.[59]

At XX Corps headquarters early that afternoon, as Berdoulat later recounted, the mood was cheery, with Bullard supposedly exulting, "Oh General! What a fine attack!" The attack had indeed been delivered with great courage and overwhelming force, and the Germans had been battered badly all along XX Corps' front. But Summerall and Harbord were like a couple of hunters who had just fired their loads of buckshot and now had to pick up all the pellets and reload. As the 2d Division historian put it, the Americans had "lost formation but retained so much individual energy that the German formations on their front were destroyed or rendered incapable." Although the front of Ninth Army had been "clearly breached," and Seventh Army was also in a bad way, penetrating much farther before enemy reinforcements arrived was going to be next to impossible.[60]

Berdoulat was nevertheless willing to give it a try. After learning of the capture of Chaudun, he announced at 1100 that the day's objectives had been reached and declared the beginning of the exploitation phase beyond the Soissons–Château-Thierry highway. The 1st Division, as we have seen, ultimately did not continue its advance beyond the Missy ravine. Harbord, however, issued his attack orders at 1330 after receiving orders from XX Corps and then left his command post for the front to personally ensure that the attack moved forward. Ely also moved toward the front and established contact with Upton and Malone. Communications remained poor, however, and despite their closer proximity to the front, commanders at the division, brigade, and regiment levels exercised next to no control over their units. Officers' tendency to crowd their units toward the front made control even more difficult and increased the casualties incurred from enemy fire.[61]

While Harbord and his officers attempted to sort out their formations and get a full-scale attack under way, small-unit fighting crackled at the front throughout the afternoon. In the Vauxcastille ravine, the trapped German battalion of the 47th Reserve Division's 218th Regiment continued to hold out. The battalion's de facto commander, Second Lieutenant Nohlen, sent a messenger dog to regimental headquarters to report his desperate situation; the dog returned an hour later with the message that the regimental headquarters had disappeared without a trace, along with all the dog handlers. Nohlen nevertheless kept trying to venture out of the cave and establish a perimeter around its entrance. What he called a "desperate game" persisted all afternoon as American and French troops attacked his perimeter and tried to push him back in. His machine guns continued to inflict losses on American troops passing through the ravine to the north and south, but as more German stragglers took shelter in the cave, water supplies dwindled and the machine guns ran out of ammunition; the end was clearly near. Finally, a detachment of Moroccans broke through to the cave's mouth at 1815, and Nohlen's few remaining perimeter guards fled into the cave in panic. The Moroccans accepted the Germans' subsequent surrender and handed them over to the Americans for interrogation and internment. The ravine would be filled that day with dead, wounded, and all the detritus of war.[62]

For Lieutenant Ladislav Janda and the remnants of the 3/9th Battalion's M Company, which had been pinned down for hours in the wheat fields above Vierzy, help came around noon in the form of a French St. Chamond tank that lumbered into view from the left. Janda signaled according to Harbord's instructions—with a handkerchief tied to the end of a rifle—and to his pleasant surprise, the tankers paid attention. The Americans pointed to the blockhouse, and the tank swerved in that direction: "Ploughing up to within fifty yards of this thorn in our side, it let loose three seventy-fives and down came the structure." Further advance was impossible, however. Three French tanks rumbled toward Vierzy at 1400, but two of them were blown up by German 77s, and the third retired. A group of French cavalry appeared briefly and then withdrew after taking some casualties. Finally, at 1530, a group of sixty Moroccans and three Schneiders—apparently strays from an attack toward Lechelle that was taking place at this time in the French zone—moved up through the wheat, ignoring the Americans even as they passed stoically among them. German artillery and machine gun fire swept through the Moroccans, wiping them out, driving back the tanks, and hitting many of the Americans, including Janda, who took a bullet in the knee.[63]

The main attack began much later than Berdoulat or Harbord had hoped, but under the circumstances, it is remarkable that it got under way at all. Division headquarters issued attack orders almost immediately after receiving orders from corps, and it specified that the primary attack would be made by the 3d Brigade. Ely, who was given overall command of the attack, did not issue his own orders until 1630, and he directed that the attack would go forth at 1800. In the event, the soldiers did not start out until 1915. In theory, the plan was for the 2/5th Marines to provide support on the left while the 2/9th, 1/23d, and 2/23d Battalions led the primary assault on Vierzy, backed up by the 3/9th, 1/9th, and 3/23d Battalions. In reality, the battalions were so jumbled together that field officers just gathered any men they could find and led them forward.[64]

The attack, Ely wryly observed, was "launched in a rather ragged manner." Official records suggest an intricate series of movements by intact army and marine battalions north and east of Vierzy and into the village itself. But the formations were organized only on paper. Six tanks that advanced with the infantry only drew fire on the vulnerable doughboys and marines, and four of the tanks were knocked out. Leaders were at a premium. Upton's arrival at the front in a staff car made a big difference in getting the men moving, but he needed help. Upton therefore shanghaied Kean, the artillery observer, to deliver messages to soldiers and marines who were advancing through the wheat in short rushes. "As I moved forward," Kean recalled, "a half dozen infantrymen would get behind me in Indian-file so that my body would protect them from German machine-gun bullets. If I swung to the left they would swing behind me to the left; if I went to the right, they would swing behind me to the right." Near Vierzy, Kean ended up commanding infantry for a time because no other officers were present; eventually, to his immense relief, a marine officer showed up and took over. Upton later followed the men forward on foot.[65]

German resistance stiffened at Vierzy, where there was more or less a free-for-all as mixed Moroccan and American forces—the latter primarily of the 23d Regiment, but with a good number of marines and 9th Regiment soldiers—stormed the village. The German 28th Division's 110th Grenadier Regiment helped stiffen the defenders, who were also a jumble of units, including elements of the 3d Reserve, 47th Reserve, and 115th Divisions. Watter ordered that the line in and around Vierzy be held "to the last man." German artillery had also found its voice after the morning's turmoil and lent direct support. Nevertheless, thanks in part to Ely, who directed the assault, and to successful attacks by the French 38th Division on the right that outflanked the village, the Americans captured Vierzy and established a loose perimeter to the east by 2100. Active tactical cooperation between soldiers and marines was out of the question, however—the mutual contempt was too strong. Private Elton Mackin of the 1/5th Marines was unlucky enough to find himself the target of an angry army colonel: "One could easily picture someplace where we gyrenes had stolen glory and a fair share of the news from this old soldier's own good army outfit." Still, working separately, the Americans got the job done. Later on, officers who had not been present at the taking of Vierzy fought over who should receive credit. Feland claimed the 1/5th Marines had captured the village, barely mentioning the 2/5th Marines and ignoring the army altogether. Keyser graciously gave partial credit to the 1/5th Marines but demanded an equal share of glory for the 2/5th Marines—and also ignored the army. Upton and Malone naturally did not take kindly to this slight and protested loudly that their soldiers had done the work.[66]

Meanwhile, marines and soldiers collapsed on the ground and fell instantly asleep or scrounged desperately for food and drinkable water. French soldiers were better supplied and willing to help when they could, but there were limits to what they could provide. Upton helped organize the defensive perimeter. Rest was scarce, though, as they had to fend off a number of small counterattacks the Germans mounted during the night. The two army regimental commanders were not shy about letting brigade and division headquarters know that the men had reached their limit. Upton told Harbord that because the men had been without sleep for three nights and without food and water for two days, it was "necessary" for the entire division to "be relieved tonight and allowed to have food, water and rest. . . . Officers and men are dead on their feet. Losses fairly heavy." Malone said his men were "utterly exhausted." Other 3d Brigade officers thought "it would be better to shove on a new division beyond where they are." Harbord replied that he was aware of the exhaustion, but he pointed out that the Germans were in "disorder"—which they were—and wondered whether his men had the spirit to push on.[67]

Thus ended the first day of the Battle of Soissons. From one perspective, the attack had been a resounding success. XX Corps' attack had shattered the German Ninth Army's left. Four German divisions—the 11th Bavarian, 14th Reserve, 47th Reserve, and 115th—had effectively ceased to exist, while a fourth (the 42d) had been badly thrashed. Altogether, the French and Americans had captured some 20,000 Germans, along with 518 artillery pieces and 3,000 machine guns. Mangin's Tenth Army posed an especially serious problem for the Germans. Recognizing the threat not only to Soissons but also to lines of communication to the south, Corps Watter was transferred to Seventh Army's control. While trying to bring order to Corps Watter, which had already absorbed the 3d Reserve and 28th Divisions into its front and was now being reinforced by the 40th Reserve and 20th Divisions (the latter boasting "full combat power" at a strength of 6,336 men), Seventh Army formed Combat Group (later Corps) Etzel behind the front. This group, consisting of the 10th and 19th Ersatz Divisions plus other hastily assembled troops, would be used as a mobile reserve to shore up the front in Corps Watter's zone and the area to its south. Though impressive on paper, these were desperate measures. The Germans had little reserve strength to call on, and their morale was plummeting fast. At 1145 on July 18, Ludendorff ordered Army Group Crown Prince to "make preparations to withdraw the fighting troops in the line south of the Marne." The troops there would be pulled back across the river on the night of July 19–20, marking the first stages of the salient's evacuation.[68]

For Mangin's troops, the plan for July 19 seemed clear. With the Germans tottering, XX Corps must push ahead boldly to cut enemy supplies routed to the Marne salient. Yet there was cause for disquiet. In both the 1st and 2d Divisions, especially the latter, command control had been almost absent. This was partly a result of circumstances and the hasty deployment. But liaison and communications had also been dismal, and at all stages, "positions were carelessly and inadequately organized and consolidated." There was no reason to expect these problems to be cured overnight. Janda, brought back to an aid station at Beaurepaire Farm, found "it was a bloody mess. All of the wounded seemed to be clearing from there and the doctors were having a frantic time trying to pick out and temporarily patch the emergency cases. Even the sides of the buildings were bloody." Despite problems of interallied cooperation, one image would stay with Kean: On returning from the battle around Vierzy, "an old Frenchman (he looked at least 50) in a tattered blue uniform was walking slowly down the road carrying on his back, towards the dressing station, a wounded American Doughboy. Every time I have felt annoyed since then at France, this picture comes to my mind and my anger softens."[69]

Tenth Army's ability to exploit the successes achieved by XX Corps on July 18 resulted in part from communications issued from the top downward. Berdoulat issued exploitation orders for XX Corps as early as 1100 on July 18, but nothing came of these orders, except for the 2d Division's seizure (with French help) of Vierzy and the final clearing of the Vauxcastille ravine. The French 6th Cavalry Division made some hesitant movements redolent of a possible intention to exploit, but after a few horsemen were dumped from their saddles by German machine guns, the cavalry withdrew. At 2000 hours on July 18, Mangin at Tenth Army headquarters issued orders for renewal of the attack at 0400 on July 19, but once again, the trickle-down process was slow, and the 1st Division did not issue its own attack orders until 0135. Astonishingly, these orders did not even begin to reach units in the line until 0300, and some did not arrive until minutes before the attack was set to begin. Fire orders likewise did not reach the artillery until just before the attack, and they did not reflect true conditions on the ground. The rolling bombardment on July 19 would be based on the presumption that all the previous day's objectives had been reached, but such was not the case.⁷⁰

Berdoulat continued to have high expectations for the Americans, noting that the previous day's losses "do not seem excessive. They seem to have been more marked in the Moroccan Div. than in the two Allied Divisions." Despite the corps commander's belief that the day's objectives had "bright prospects," they proved difficult to attain, given the actual state of the American divisions. On the left, I Corps' French 153d Division was to drive southeast from the Missy ravine and take Vauxbuin, Courmelles, and Berzy-le-Sec. The 1st Division, advancing in the same direction, was to attain a line from Berzy-le-Sec to Buzancy, which was to be taken by the Moroccans, along with Villemontoire. Recognizing that the French 153d and US 1st Divisions occupied the northern edge of what was a growing salient and could expect pressure on their left, Berdoulat specified that after seizing its objectives, Summerall's division was to be "faced to the northeast, in strong contact on its left with the right of the French 153d Inf. Div., in the vicinity of Berzy-le-Sec." Finally, the nearly defunct US 2d Division was to capture Tigny and push on to Hartennes, in conjunction with the hard-charging (by 1918 standards) French 38th Division on its right.⁷¹

The soldiers assessed the day's prospects with resolve but without optimism. "Very few received any rest during the night," remembered Captain Harry Bennett of the 26th Regiment:

> A few slept when and where they could. Reorganizing kept every one busy. A German counterattack was expected. The shock and strain of the day [July 18] had told on all, and greater than all, everyone knew that with dawn, the attack would be continued. All night long the Germans could be heard digging and pounding. They were making more emplacements for their machine guns. This provided food for thought. In front of the regiment, the Germans still held the high ground.

Bennett's trepidation would prove justified.⁷²

For the US 1st Division, things began to look bad within minutes after the attack got under way at about 0430. In the zone of the 2d Brigade—again leaderless, since Buck had departed brigade headquarters for distant points of the battlefield as soon as the attack began—Babcock's 2/28th and 3/28th Battalions attacked together in line on the left. Their immediate goal was to cross Route 2, capture Hill 166, and reach the Ploisy ravine. Beyond lay Berzy-le-Sec in the French sector. Unfortunately, to their left stood a heavy concentration of German machine guns in the rough ground around Vauxbuin. The French were supposed to take this, but they did not; the artillery was supposed to suppress the machine guns, but it did not; and the almost complete absence of American machine guns to provide covering fire left the soldiers exposed and unable to advance. The infantry had to deal with machine guns in their zone as best they could, for the tanks were much fewer in number this day and ineffective. By midmorning, enervated and parched in the growing midsummer heat and feeling helpless after taking serious casualties, the regiment sat down on its haunches and waited for somebody to do something.[73]

The 26th Regiment attacked with its 2d and 3d Battalions in line from left to right and Major Theodore Roosevelt's 1/26th following in support. Some companies started late because orders had not reached them; a regimental staff officer was still hurrying along the line at 0450, yelling at company commanders to move out independently. As the leading battalions crossed the Route 2 embankment and attempted to advance upslope toward Hill 166—conspicuous for the wrecked French tanks at its crest—Roosevelt sent a message to brigade headquarters that he thought the attack was "progressing well." But he was mistaken. As soon as they left the shelter of the road embankment, the Americans and their accompanying tanks came under devastating fire from artillery and machine guns. There was a machine gun in one of the wrecked French tanks; others were situated in nests among the wheat fields or in the Ploisy ravine to their left. "From what seemed like hundreds of machine guns came a fire that was deadly in its significance," remembered Captain Bennett. "Officers dashed to the front of their men and with shouts and gestures they led their units straight into the successive lines of machine guns." The tanks were blown up, and men fell in large numbers, but the survivors pressed on and tried to make it over the crest. Some succeeded—Major James McCloud crossed over the hill with the remnants of the 2/26th and disappeared from view—but the remainder fell back to the tree-lined embankment, which provided the only cover. Roosevelt, arriving at the road with his battalion, attempted to push east, but he too was pinned down after going about 200 yards. At 0730 he sent a message to Buck (not realizing he had already departed), reporting that he had found Captain Walter McClure with the "remnants of 3rd Bn. much cut up," and he was "pushing forward [with a] small detachment and trying to establish connection with McCloud which has been lost." But McCloud was dead, and shortly after sending the message, Roosevelt was wounded in the knee.[74]

By the time Buck arrived at the road embankment later that morning,

Roosevelt had been evacuated—much against his will. On his way there, Buck would have passed a regimental medical corps post just southeast of Breuil. The post commander, Lieutenant Norman Vann, was likely unaware of Buck's proximity and was frantically pleading with brigade headquarters: "For God's sake if you possibly can send me 2 wagons or carts or anything I can send wounded away in. I have fifty men here, badly wounded, and they are shelling the place and have already killed 3 of my wounded. . . . The field ahead is covered with wounded and I must get these out. The old Battalion is giving them Hell, but is almost finished." At the road, meanwhile, Buck looked with interest at four field guns that had been pushed up to the embankment but could not be operated because of enemy fire, and he noted the burning French tanks dotting the field ahead. There is no record that Buck imparted any directions to McClure or to the regimental commander, Colonel Hamilton Smith, before he left for more sightseeing. "I roamed all over the battle field that day and the next day," he later recalled. "I wanted to see and judge the troops and the fighting." By then, his brigade was a spent force.[75]

The French were much despised, then and subsequently, for their inability to keep up and relieve the pressure from the Americans' left. Summerall was furious, and so was Babcock. Bullard later wrote, "The ill feeling . . . which I found existing between the French and the Americans . . . in the remainder of the Aisne-Marne campaign was due very largely to the Americans' belief that the French would not stand beside them in the face of the enemy." Little to no attempt was made to discover why the French had failed to keep up. But as the 153d Division's records make clear, that unit suffered from the communications problems emanating from Tenth Army and I Corps even more so than the Americans in XX Corps. Attack orders did not reach the 153d Division's front-line units until ten minutes *after* the advance was supposed to begin, and after the rolling barrage had left the infantry far behind. Even so, the French advanced *rapidement* and reached Route 2 just west of Vauxbuin at 0600. There, however, they paused under heavy German machine gun fire from Vauxbuin and from the unchallenged German-held ridges to the northeast. Instead of plunging forward and allowing his men to be slaughtered—a common enough action until the Nivelle offensive in 1917—General Goubeau proceeded in the methodical manner that had become standard in Pétain's divisions by 1918: he assembled his support arms, brought up reinforcements, and sought to secure his vulnerable left flank before continuing the attack.[76]

While the French girded their loins for another advance, the American 2d Brigade, which *had* attempted to plunge forward and paid a high price for it, was severely bloodied, exhausted, and disorganized. A divisional narrative of events concluded, with some understatement: "Considerable confusion arose along the front line [during the morning], so that the remainder of the morning and the afternoon were consumed in reorganizing, and in re-establishing contact between the various units, and with the 153d French Division." There could be no question of the brigade attacking again until much later that afternoon, if at all.[77]

The 1st Brigade had done a little better. On the left, the 1/16th Battalion led the assault, supported by the 3/16th (the 2/16th, now commanded by a sergeant, was fit for nothing but recuperation). On the right, the 1/18th and 3/18th Battalions—totaling the typical strength of about half a battalion—led the assault, while the 2/18th waited in division reserve. Partially sheltered from the German machine guns around Vauxbuin by Hill 166 and the Ploisy ravine—a luxury the 2d Brigade did not enjoy—and supported by the rapid advance of the Moroccans to their right, the two regiments were able to make decent progress for about 1.5 kilometers, getting as far as the ground between the Ploisy and Chazelle ravines. Tanks there were initially effective against machine guns to the brigade's front, but they were soon knocked out by German artillery. German planes bombed and strafed the advancing troops. Faced with stiffening resistance and the strain of maintaining contact with the shattered 2d Brigade on the left, 1st Brigade's advance also ground to a halt.[78]

A lull settled over the battlefield in the afternoon as XX Corps issued orders for the French 153d Division to resume the attack at 1730 in conjunction with the Americans. Summerall accordingly issued orders to the 2d Brigade to attack in conjunction with the French, while the 1st Brigade advanced to follow up the Germans who had started pulling back from its front. Because Babcock's 2/28th and 3/28th were incapable of further exertion—they would be merged into a combined battalion led by Lieutenant Samuel I. Parker—that regiment's assault would be led by Major George Rozelle's intact 1/28th. The objective was to reach the Ploisy ravine's western edge, while the 26th Regiment pushed forward to the south. Babcock did not like the orders, however, and he phoned Summerall to protest that the general was ordering him to capture open ground below Vauxbuin in the French zone. His demurral was not well received. Summerall ordered Babcock to allow his brigade commanders (actually, just Rozelle) to carry out the attack orders without standing in their way. Babcock had "showed himself unsuited to be a combat regimental commander," Summerall later wrote, while Buck was "too worn out and mentally confused to force the attack."[79]

The rolling barrage commenced at 1730 on the dot, while 155s pounded enemy concentrations in the Ploisy ravine and American machine guns in the 26th Regiment's zone fired into the Germans' left flank. Rozelle's battalion dashed off to attack in conjunction with the French on his left and the 2/26th and 1/26th Battalions on his right. Rozelle's assault was exceptionally bold and costly, for "the wheatfields and depressions in the rolling ground seemed alive with German machine guns." Within two hours, the Americans had entered the Ploisy ravine, and after another hour of fighting, sometimes hand to hand, they secured the village it sheltered. Rozelle had worked up such a surge of energy that he charged ahead with two officers and four runners until he reached the outskirts of Berzy-le-Sec, only to find that he had lost contact with the rest of his battalion and had to withdraw. Yet the 2d Brigade's attack was a success, not because of the infantry tactics employed, which were unremarkable, but because of the courage of the officers and men who carried it out against tenacious resistance. Active and efficient support from artillery and machine guns also played a role. At the cost of devastating casualties—about 3,000 on this day alone—the 2d Brigade had advanced up to three kilometers, captured 1,000 Germans and about twenty artillery pieces, and secured a firm lodgment in the Ploisy ravine.[80]

To the left, the French 153d Division had spent much of the afternoon grappling with attacks and counterattacks by the German 241st Division and elements of the 6th, 11th Bavarian, and 34th Divisions on the heights above the heavily defended Vauxbuin ravine. In what the Germans characterized as "bitter fighting"—some of the most serious they encountered that day, and occurring during raging thunderstorms—control of the heights seesawed back and forth. It was a true slugfest, and German operations reports indicate that the French came close to winning as the defenders' ammunition and manpower dwindled. Finally, however, the Germans seized firm control in midafternoon. In the 1730 attack, the French tried again. In the wheat fields below Vauxbuin, French tanks and infantry pushed hard and almost broke through toward Courmelles, threatening to outflank the German strongpoint from the south. At one point, a tank knocked out a German field gun with a direct hit and surged through the defenders' lines, followed by two more tanks and some infantry. The tanks' rampage continued for thirty minutes as they swung north toward Vauxbuin. One was knocked out by a field piece, but the others continued until the defending troops of the German 34th Division began to break and flee. Luckily for the Germans, "at the critical moment," one of the tanks was set on fire by artillery, and the other was immobilized by heavy machine gun fire. The defenders warily filtered back into their positions and held back the now-scattered French infantry. The French nevertheless managed to advance to the northern tip of the Ploisy ravine on their right. The 153d Division's gallant attacks on the heavily defended Vauxbuin strongpoint, however, collapsed amid much slaughter. After taking very heavy losses that reduced its regiments to an average of 700 men and forced the merger of some battalions, the French collapsed in exhaustion. No one could justly say they hadn't given it their best. But because of the 153d Division's failure, the 2d Brigade's left flank remained open to enemy fire.[81]

The 1st Brigade was able to keep pace with the attack, with the 1/16th, 3/16th, and 3/18th advancing to the high ground between the Ploisy and Chazelle ravines. The Germans had pulled back about a kilometer from their front, so the Americans took only artillery fire during their advance, which took place in solid liaison with the Moroccans on their right. When the men of the 3/18th tried to push their luck and outpace the Moroccans by advancing farther toward Buzancy, however, they had to pull back to the Chazelle ravine after taking casualties from "unendurable" flank fire.[82]

According to the war diary of the German Ninth Army, which had been so badly battered on July 18 that Corps Watter had been removed from its control, the events of July 19 would force the "decision" of whether the Marne salient could be evacuated methodically. "The events of the day," the diary concluded, "removed our greatest danger," thanks to the "bloody collapse of enemy mass attacks." The records of the German divisions facing the French 153d Division and the US 1st Division reveal the near fatalism with which they began the day and the sense of shocked but pleasant surprise with which they ended it. German morale was correspondingly improved by the "splendid repulse" of the enemy. So far as they were concerned, the enemy had lost a major opportunity to force a hasty and costly evacuation of the salient (such as the one achieved by the American First Army at Saint-Mihiel in September). In this sector, unfortunately, the French 153d Division maintained cohesion but lacked punch, and although the US 1st Division still had punch in spite of its losses, it lacked cohesion. While the Moroccans and the French 38th Division farther south performed very well on this day, the US 2d Division would prove unable to make up the difference.[83]

In June the 2d Division had spent three weeks in the line in Belleau Wood. At Soissons, it lasted two days before collapsing in exhaustion and having to be withdrawn. The writing was already on the wall by the morning of July 19. Like the 1st Division, the 2d Division had endured a harrowing move to the front, heavy casualties, and serious disorganization on the day of the attack. Unlike the 1st Division, the 2d Division was still in the early stages of recovery from Belleau Wood. It simply couldn't take much more. The 5th Marines and the 9th and 23d Regiments were in shambles.

Harbord had one last resource to call on: the 6th Marines. This regiment was in corps reserve and thus technically not available without permission from Berdoulat and Mangin, but Harbord apparently called it up on the night of July 18–19 without seeking their authority, and no French protests were forthcoming. XX Corps attack orders reached Harbord's headquarters at Beaurepaire Farm at 0200, and he passed them on to the 6th Marines' commander, Lieutenant Colonel Harry Lee, an hour later. Recognizing that there was no chance of executing Berdoulat's attack order by 0400, Harbord told Lee to be ready to attack at 0700; this was later delayed to 0800, 0815, and then 0900. Unfortunately, there was little effort to keep the artillery up to date on the postponements.[84]

The 6th Marines' orders were to pass through the 5th Marines' frontage east of Vierzy and push beyond Tigny to cut the north-south Soissons-Paris road. It would be supported by the 6th Machine Gun Regiment and twenty-eight French tanks that had been scraped together from the previous day's remnants. It is hard to imagine how anyone could have believed that Lee's one regiment could succeed, against improved defenses, where three had failed the previous day. The ground between Vierzy and Tigny was open and dominated by the heights of Buzancy to the northeast and other high ground to the east. Moreover, the Germans had brought in fresh infantry—particularly the seasoned 10th and 20th Divisions on the US 2d Division's front, which also faced a veritable salad of other cobbled-together German formations—and had improved their machine gun and artillery defenses.[85]

The artillery opened its barrage to shield the marines at 0630. Unfortunately, Lee did not issue deployment orders from his headquarters in Vierzy until 0815, partly to give his supporting battalion time to close up to the front. And because the marines had two kilometers to cover until they reached the front line, they did not actually begin their attack until 0900. By then, their supporting barrage was long gone. And they had already endured casualties, thanks to poor liaison between the infantry and tanks. As Private Albert J. Campbell of the 2/6th Marines recalled:

> The men had been ordered to lay down in a wheat field in wave formation and await further orders. About 300 yards to the rear were four small French tanks which started moving forward, not aware that

the Marines were in the wheat field [again, poor liaison]. The Germans opened up immediately with artillery and machine guns, and the tanks were out of action in short order. Since the Marines had not dug in, they could only lay there and take everything the Germans threw at them. The men had to lay there for an hour before the orders were given to start the advance. . . . The loss of the four supporting tanks, plus the heavy machine gun fire, surely took a toll on the morale of the men.[86]

The attack was led by the 1/6th Marines (Major John A. Hughes) on the right and the 2/6th Marines (Major Thomas Holcomb) on the left, with the 3/6th Marines (Major Berton Sibley) in support. Advancing in four lines in "perfect alignment," they had barely passed through the front lines and commenced their assault before the wheat fields erupted in a cloud of steel and flame. Some doughboys called out to the marines to take cover as they entered the inferno, but the leathernecks refused. Recalled Private Warren Jackson of the 1/6th Marines:

Frequent sprays of machine-gun bullets nipped the wheat about us. One shell after another fell in quick succession. Many of the shells came from artillery on the hillside not more than a mile away and were fired *point blank* into our ranks. So many shells were in the air at once that the ear was unable to detect the course of each separate shell: a terrific explosion a few steps to the right or left, in front or behind, was the first knowledge of the coming of these fiendish missiles. . . . Two or three shells, like insuperable demons from hell, would fall appallingly close, bursting almost simultaneously. As we tried to dodge from one or more shells here, our ears would still be ringing when we almost ran into the path of more, to have the earth shaken under us by terrific explosions that every moment threatened to hurl us into eternity. The senses ceased to function normally. Only in a vague sort of way did I comprehend that the ranks to the left were being shot to pieces. However, as my eyes chanced to be in that direction, something caught my gaze with an almost paralyzing reality. A shell made a direct hit on the line, and a pack and helmet went spinning high into the air. Yet there were minutes such that had all the world, more than a dozen steps away, ceased to exist, we would not have realized it.

Private Carl Brannen of the 2/6th had a similar experience:

> We formed our lines in a road through a cut or ravine and came out for a charge across a sugar beet field. The tanks were leading, with our lines right behind them. . . . The Germans turned loose everything they had. . . . Just ahead of me, a few men grouped and started down a ditch. My training told me to keep out of groups, for a shell could kill several at one time. I leaped some barbed wire to the right of them as a shell hit, making a clean sweep. One of the men near me was shot through the shoulder; another had a finger shot off his hand. . . . By this time, all of the tanks had been crippled or stopped and all the men around me shot down. . . . In thirty or forty minutes, our regiment had been almost annihilated. The field which had been recently crossed was strewn with dead and dying. Their cries for water and help got weaker as the hot July day wore on.

In the attack, the marines reverted to prewar form. Insofar as lessons learned, it was as if June 6, 1918, had never occurred at all.[87]

Within thirty minutes, dangerous gaps had appeared in the marines' front, forcing Sibley to detach his companies, including his headquarters company, one at a time to fill them. According to a report by a defending battalion, the Americans nevertheless managed to penetrate the German forward positions because "of the reckless employment, again and again, of new waves of infantrymen, who suffered the heaviest losses possible." By 1000 hours, some American detachments had secured a toehold in the Bois de Tigny, just over a kilometer from the point of advance, driving shell-shocked troops of the German 3d and 14th Reserve Divisions and elements of the 28th Division out of their trenches. A few marine remnants attempted to probe farther east and northeast before being forced to fall back. Recalled Campbell:

> The Company moved out in two waves, about fifty yards between waves. It was about 1000 yards to the German lines, and as the men started forward the Germans concentrated their artillery fire about 160 yards in front of their own lines. Men were going down all around due to the shell fire, machine gun, and rifle fire. When they did reach the German lines they were able to fall into a series of foxholes that had been abandoned by the Germans. . . . This advance to the German positions had not taken long, approximately two hours, but the remainder of the day was spent under heavy shell fire, plus machine gun and rifle fire. . . . The Germans had been forced to pull back, but not from any pressure put on them by the Marines.[88]

That was the best the marines could do. At 1145 Lee reported to Harbord that the attack had been halted with 30 percent casualties. Actually, they were much higher: 1,300 of the 2,450 men who had started the attack were now casualties. German aircraft soared above and strafed the beleaguered Americans with virtual impunity, as they did throughout the Soissons battle. They also directed the accurate German artillery. Extended and under heavy pressure, the marines were extremely vulnerable at that point to counterattack from three sides.[89]

Fortunately for them, the French did a good job of shielding the Americans. To the left, the 1st Moroccan Division (with tanks) attacked the German 42d Division and elements (or remnants) of the 14th Reserve and 28th Divisions at 0430. The positions held by the 14th Reserve Division quickly fell apart, and by 1110, Germans were retreating "in droves" across the hill between Villemontaire and Buzancy before the victorious Moroccans—forcing German officers to ride up on horseback to stem the rout. German artillery hit some tanks but also shelled its own troops. Intrepid French field officers ventured close to the front—one of them was "picked off" at Chazelle by a German lieutenant, who secured his papers and the car. Fortunately for the Germans, the 42d and 28th Divisions managed to stop the Moroccans at the Lechelle ravine, deep in the Americans' left rear. The Moroccans successfully repulsed a German counterattack there late in the morning, however, and because of French pressure, Corps Watter ordered its troops to pull back to ground northeast of Charantigny at 1200. The Moroccans followed up quickly and linked up with the 6th Marines' left, forcing some of the German defenders opposite the marines to pull back to avoid being outflanked.[90]

To the marines' right, meanwhile, the French 38th Division shattered the remains of the German 115th Division east of Blanzy; routed elements of the 3d Reserve Division, which fled in disorder beyond Hartennes; and hit the newly inserted German Corps Etzel hard, pushing northeast toward Tigny. In so doing, the French were able to come abreast of the marines near Parcy-Tigny and shield their right. Thanks to the (needless to say, uncredited) French successes on either flank, by the time the German 20th Division mounted a counterattack west of Villemontaire that evening, on the marines' left flank, the Americans were well secured and able to assist the Moroccans in stopping the Germans in their tracks. Unlike the Americans, however, who essentially lay prostrate after the fighting ended, the Moroccans engaged the German 20th and 42d Divisions in fighting that lasted until midnight—providing additional cover for the worn-out marines.[91]

To his credit, unlike Bundy at Belleau Wood, Harbord made no bones about the 2d Division's need for immediate relief, and he placed no restrictions on whether an American or French division took over. The Marine Brigade was little more than a blasted hulk. Even the Army Brigade—not seriously tested in Belleau Wood—was in bad shape. Mangin, anticipating the division's exhaustion and perhaps intending to allow the Americans to save face, had released the French 58th Division at 0545 on July 19 to relieve the US 2d Division, rather than waiting for an American cry for help. This permitted Harbord to claim, bombastically and untruthfully, that the French had ordered the Americans out of the line because the Yanks had outrun both their artillery and their neighbors, who were still panting to catch up. "Victorious troops, they marched out conscious of their achievement."[92]

As relief began that night, remembered Brannen, "The surviving marines who left the battle line were a terrible looking bunch of people. They looked more like animals. They had almost a week's growth of beard and were dirty and ragged. Their eyes were sunk back in their heads. There had been very little sleep or rest for four days and no food. . . . The boys were more despondent than I ever saw them after this last battle, and no wonder." In two days the division had captured 66 German officers and 2,810 enlisted men. But it had also suffered 4,180 casualties in its two brigades, 2,289 of those in the 3d Brigade. Upton's 9th Regiment was especially hard hit—on July 19 he reported only 334 officers and men fit for duty, not counting stragglers—but all four regiments had been severely punished.[93]

The 2d Division's short sojourn in the lines at Soissons put the lie to the American "blockbuster division" concept. Though twice the size (at least) of nearby French divisions, it lacked their staying power. Part of this, as already noted, was the legacy of Belleau Wood. Some of the division's travails were attributable to the French, who, because of Foch's last-minute dispositions, had once again rushed the Americans to the front and thrown them into battle without preparation. However, just like at Belleau Wood, much of the trouble could be blamed on faulty American tactics. Ignoring French advice for a measured pace of assault, Harbord had ordered a pell-mell, straight-ahead advance that took no account of terrain, fatigue, or the inevitably slower movements of the French on either flank and made no provisions for machine gun support. As occurred so often during this war, the men had performed bravely, and the field officers and NCOs had done well overall under difficult circumstances and with little to no direction from above.

A more subtle and beneficial outcome of the 2d Division's experiences in June and July was that French and colonial troops had begun to accept the Americans as tested warriors rather than callow newcomers. On their way to the front in late May and early June, marines and soldiers had been welcomed with taunts by veteran poilus and doubts about whether they would fight. Now many Americans and French mixed freely as comrades and equals. While Private William Carter of the 6th Marines was preparing for relief by the French on July 19–20, he and some other marines ended up "mingling" with a group of Algerians:

> Before we moved out the Algerians gave us their only mascot, Dodo, a genuine African monkey that had been through every battle with them, and his antics contributed many a happy hour to the arduous days and nights that followed. He was a Simian Militarist to the tip of his tail. The sight of a person not in uniform would throw him into a rage and whenever civilians appeared they were in danger of being routed.

It was, of course, a different story elsewhere, especially among French and American staff officers. But such ground-level bonhomie was at least a start.[94]

With the 2d Division out of the line, after July 20 the 1st Division would carry the American flag for what remained of XX Corps' Soissons offensive. Though scarcely less tired than the 2d Division, the 1st Division was also given increased responsibilities—perhaps to Summerall's relief, given the alleged dilatoriness of the French 153d Division on the left. XX Corps' northern boundary was extended to include Berzy-le-Sec, and Berdoulat promptly issued orders for the 1st Division to take that place in an attack beginning at 0445. Summerall ordered his brigades to attack after a two-hour artillery barrage. Success would be a matter of pride, especially given the earlier finger-pointing at the French for their inability to advance in that sector previously. What the boundary change did not solve, however, was the problem of Vauxbuin, which would continue to be a German strongpoint and a Franco-American sore point.[95]

Berzy-le-Sec, observed Bennett, "presented a forbidding task. [It] stood on a prominent knoll almost surrounded by ravines and it flanked the line of advance of the division." It had also been an exceptionally important position when the Soissons offensive began, as the 153-meter eminence dominated at its rear both the north-south Soissons-Paris road and the Soissons-Paris railroad. With the first stages of the German withdrawal from the Marne salient already under way, however, its importance had vastly diminished. This would be the 2d Brigade's target. The 1st Brigade, meanwhile, would have to attack into the heart of the "deep and precipitous Chazelle Ravine, the valley of the Crise, with its boggy sloughs and thick brush, and the heights of Buzancy, from which the enemy commanded every foot of the ground with artillery and machine guns." The Crise valley "contained a fairly deep stream, and its bottom was marshy and interspersed with treacherous sloughs or overrun with rank vegetation." While taking on these objectives, both brigades would have to endure flanking fire from their left: the 2d Brigade from the vicinity of Courmelles and Vauxbuin, where the French would be unlikely to advance far, and the 1st Brigade from Berzy-le-Sec until the 2d Brigade could take it. Neither brigade would have it easy.[96]

The 1st Division's attack was uncoordinated for reasons that remain unclear. Summerall's orders called for a two-hour preparatory barrage followed by a rolling barrage, and although his official report (which made no mention of the 1st Brigade) claimed that such a barrage was delivered, other records and eyewitness accounts indicate that it was not—or at least not everywhere. Tenth Army orders had called for XX Corps to attack at 0445. The 1st Brigade attacked at 0830 in conjunction with the Moroccans, but the 2d Brigade did not begin its own attack until 1400. The difficulties involved in gradually relieving the French 153d Division with the French 69th Division in the Vauxbuin area, while still expecting both divisions to attack, were one reason for the delay. Poor liaison at all levels is the most obvious explanation for the lack of coordination between brigades or with the artillery.[97]

The 1st Brigade attacked with mixed elements of the 1/16th and 3/16th on the left and the 1/18th and 3/18th on the right. Moving rapidly and successfully in coordination with the Moroccans, who had shattered resistance to their front above Villemontaire, the Americans met little opposition until, after advancing more than a kilometer, they entered some woods and then scrambled down a bluff to the Soissons-Paris railroad. There the Americans came under heavy German artillery and machine gun fire from multiple directions and took shelter behind the railroad embankment and in the Bois de Gérard to its east. This penetration caused a temporary withdrawal of two regiments of the German 28th Division posted in the area, leaving a dangerous gap in the lines that lasted until nightfall but was undetected by the Americans. Fortunately, the Americans were in firm contact with the Moroccans on their right, and later that afternoon, elements of the 1/26th were able to reach forward and make contact with the 2d Brigade on their left. Although the heights of Buzancy had not been attained, the railroad had been cut (as it had been in the Moroccan zone as well). But in the process, both of Hines's regiments had been reduced to almost nothing. The 1/16th, which had entered the campaign with 1,100 men, now had no more than 40 present and accounted for. Later on July 20, Colonel Frank Parker complained to Summerall about the condition of his 18th Regiment: "General," he said, "my regiment has lost 60 percent of its officers, nearly all of its old noncommissioned officers, and most of its men, and I don't think that is the way to treat a regiment." Summerall retorted: "Colonel, I did not come here to have you criticize my orders or to tell me of your losses. I know them as well as you do. I came to tell you that the Germans recrossed the Marne last night and are in full retreat and you will attack tomorrow morning at 4:30."[98]

If it was any consolation to Hines, Buck knew what the 1st Brigade was going through. That morning, Buck had gone "riding off into the blue" in a motorcycle sidecar and ended up in the 1st Brigade's sector. He spent the rest of the morning chatting with Parker and Colonel Frank Bamford of the 16th Regiment before returning to his own brigade around noon. Meanwhile, the 2d Brigade was preparing to attack, and Babcock of the 28th Regiment was once again unhappy. Not informed until 1315 that his regiment was scheduled to attack at 1400, Babcock was also surprised to learn that the 2d Brigade would receive little if any artillery support. He protested that casualties were bound to be unendurably heavy under such conditions, but Summerall and Buck overruled him. Interestingly, instead of ordering his troops forward against Berzy-le-Sec frontally, Babcock and Rozelle of the 1/28th put Lieutenant Soren C. Sorensen in charge of three sixteen-man squads charged with infiltrating the Ploisy ravine in a northeasterly direction and attempting to enter the village from the north. If successful, more men would filter through behind them until the entire battalion had slipped in.[99]

Meanwhile, the 26th Regiment, led by the 3/26th and supported by remnants of the other two battalions, attacked on schedule at 1400 against positions now held mostly by the German 42d Division and a few stray shards of the 11th Bavarian Division. An observer near Chaudun watched the assault battalion form in a column about a kilometer long and 300 meters wide; it then turned and marched in a "slow and stately" manner toward its objective. The observer also witnessed what happened next on this scorching, sunny day:

> Our leading waves now appeared approaching the crest of the ridge above Berzy-le-Sec, following the barrage. Each individual soldier in

the attack was distinctly visible against the grassy hillsides. The whole mass was proceeding with the utmost regularity and precision. As the leading elements reached the crest of the ridge, a single battery of enemy 150-mm. howitzers opened fire with time shell, obviously with observed fire on the target. This battery was followed almost at once by many other batteries of 150-mm. and 105-mm. howitzers, all firing time shell. The accuracy of preparation of this fire was such that practically no adjustment was required, and, almost immediately, our infantry was shrouded in smoke and dust. Great gaps were left in the ranks as the shells crashed among them. Nevertheless, the advance continued in the most orderly way. It was noticed that the enemy's artillery diminished its range as our infantry advanced.

Many of our infantry passed out of sight over the ridge, accompanied by the devastating fire of the enemy's artillery. Men struck by the enemy's fire either disappeared or ran aimlessly about and toppled over.

Then began to be heard also the rattle of the enemy's machine guns. The attack had met the resistance of a strong position occupied in great force by the enemy. It could not be taken at this time by our worn soldiers, and, after this advance, they could go no further. The thin lines lay down in shell holes, while long files of wounded hobbled painfully back.

Then appeared a sight which at first seemed inexplicable. Individual men and groups of twos and threes began to wander about all over the field. They were the unit leaders, reorganizing their groups against counter-attack.

As the observer described, the attack was a disaster. The 26th Regiment cleared part of the plateau before Berzy-le-Sec and maintained tenuous liaison with the 1st Brigade, but nothing more—and at the cost of brutal casualties. Lieutenant Sorensen, meanwhile, reached the outskirts of Berzy-le-Sec but decided it was impracticable to enter the village until after dark. Babcock duly planned for an attack at 2300, but after learning that allied artillery was going to bombard the place at 0445 the next morning, he called off the attack. While all this was going on, Buck was somewhere behind the 2d Brigade's lines trying to organize stragglers and had no contact with his regimental commanders.[100]

Sometime after the collapse of the 2d Brigade's attack, Mangin visited the 1st Division. Summerall soon learned that Bullard and Pershing would follow. Possibly anticipating a grilling for his inability to take Berzy-le-Sec,

Summerall departed to visit the front and did not return until 0100 on July 21. According to an account prepared many years later, when Summerall reached the 26th Regiment command post, he found Colonel Smith "exhausted. He was sullen and defiant. I asked him why his regiment had not attacked. He replied: 'The order was impossible, and I did not try to obey it.' I could have relieved him, but it was evident that he was overwrought and scarcely responsible. The strain had been too great for him." Summerall temporarily relieved Smith with his second in command, Lieutenant Colonel Clark R. Elliott, and moved on. Later accounts by men who did not actually witness the exchange, such as Lieutenant Joseph Patch of the 1/18th, claimed that Summerall had questioned Smith's courage and ordered him to stick closer to the front. Whatever actually happened, Smith went so far as to personally direct a pointless attack on a German machine gun emplacement while the division was in the process of relief on July 22, and he was killed. Claimed Patch: "The men of the 26th never forgave Summerall for this."[101]

Though benefiting from having the Moroccans on the right, the 1st Division once again received scant support on the left from the gutted French 153d Division, which had been given the impossible objective of attacking in conjunction with the French 69th Division as the latter was relieving it. This was a cause for further recriminations in that quarter. During his tour of the lines, Summerall also found men who promised to take Berzy-le-Sec on July 21, but only if American guns supported them, as "they did not like the French artillery." To a large degree, however, and as German records indicate, much of the artillery and machine gun fire that plagued the Americans also tormented the French because it came from north of the Aisne.[102]

By now, the Germans felt entirely secure in their plans to withdraw from the Marne salient on their own timetable. The German Seventh Army war diary crowed:

> [July 20 was a] major combat day for the Seventh Army and brought a complete defensive victory. . . . As has so often been the case on the occasion of major offensives the enemy either did not know how or else did not dare to judge correctly and to exploit the success of his first assault. . . . There were no forces worth mentioning which could have opposed his advance against the Conde area on the 18th and even on the 19th the new front was just in the making and might easily have faltered again. But on the 20th the front of the Seventh Army again was solid. The most difficult crisis had passed.

Crown Prince Wilhelm offered his thanks with a special commendation for the German 42d Division, which had stood stoutly against the Americans and Moroccans while other units around it crumbled.[103]

The chance for a breakthrough had ended, and the 1st Division was getting ready for relief (the brave Moroccans were relieved on the night of July 20–21 by the French 87th Division, and the French 153d Division was relieved by the French 69th Division). Still, Summerall was determined to make one more lunge toward Berzy-le-Sec. This time, no one would have cause to complain about a lack of artillery support, even though American artillerymen such as Sergeant Joseph J. Gleeson had reached a state of near-total exhaustion and despair. He wrote in his diary:

> Impossible for me to describe the doings of these terrible days. Dead, dead and more dead. Will probably be the next. We opened up at 4, fired for a few hours and advanced. We were in an open field and oh such a scene. Able was hurt seriously. Several more killed and about 1/3 of the boys wounded. I was stunned by a burst but wasn't hurt. We have to go back for men.

The gunners still fired, however, and the Germans felt the consequences. What Corps Watter described as "the heaviest kind of drum fire" fell all along the front at 0430, followed by a powerful rolling barrage. Lieutenant Herbert Sulzbach, a veteran newly arrived at this front with the German 9th Division, was impressed: "I don't know the word indicating the difference in degree required to describe the wholly crazy artillery fire which the French turn on for the attack in the morning. The word 'hell' expresses something tender and peaceful compared to what is starting here and now."[104]

As on the previous day, the 1st Brigade got started first, with the infantry beginning to move forward at 0445 and the assault starting at 0600. The attack was led by the 2/18th and 1/16th, which were the only semi-intact battalions the brigade could muster; mixed remnants of other battalions followed in support, while the French 87th Division attacked alongside the Americans on the right. On the left, the 16th Regiment assaulted and seized Aconin Farm, crossed the Soissons road, and pushed up the heights northwest of Buzancy, despite the need to continually bend back its left to maintain contact with the 2d Brigade. On the right, the 18th Regiment crossed the boggy Crise ravine and the road and surged all the way up to the heights of Buzancy, where it captured the château and 200 Germans who had taken shelter in a "deep cavern." The German defenders, sensing that the Americans opposite them were "noticeably weak," launched desperate counterattacks but could muster little punch from their shadow formations. Although some soldiers from the US 18th Regiment surrendered when German infantry of the 46th Reserve Division recaptured the ruined château, the remaining Americans grimly held on to the heights. On the whole, Hines's men had done surprisingly well.[105]

The 2d Brigade's attack was delayed until 0830 because the commander of the French 69th Division on the left insisted that he needed extra time for the artillery to get into position and prepare its support—a sensible precaution. Although battalion designations were somewhat blurry at this point, given the overall wastage and disorganization, on paper, the attack was supposed to be led by the 1/28th on the left and the 3/26th on the right, with support from a mixture of elements. The regiments would have to advance over the plateau crest where they had suffered so heavily the previous day, descend into the valley, cross the railroad, and then cross the Soissons road. Beyond the road, the 28th was to take Berzy while the 26th captured an abandoned sugar factory south of the village.

In this, the 1st Division's final major assault in the Battle of Soissons, Summerall's gamble paid off. Thanks in part to "crushing" artillery fire laid that morning on Berzy-le-Sec, the 28th Regiment—its first wave under the command of Second Lieutenant John R. D. Cleland, who was wounded—was able to storm the knoll of Berzy-le-Sec in two forward rushes. They captured a good number of enemy machine guns and even a battery of 77s that had fired on the Americans point-blank. They seized the village and established a defensive perimeter on the other side by 1015—albeit with only 280 men present and accounted for in the entire regiment. The 26th Regiment took heavy fire, as anticipated, as it surged over the plateau into the valley, but after a pause as units intermingled, the regiment managed to reach and take the sugar factory. German counterattacks recaptured the factory but failed to push the Americans back any further. They remained as one thin line under German artillery fire for the rest of the day (the 26th would retake the factory on July 22—one of its final acts before leaving the lines). And all this was accomplished despite the fact that the French 69th Division was unable to make significant progress owing to devastating flank fire from German artillery north of the Aisne. However, the French 87th Division on the right did manage to capture Buzancy temporarily.[106]

Success resulted from a number of factors, with the resolve of the attackers being first and foremost. Artillery support was crucial. Unlike on previous days, Buck was present where it mattered, moving forward with the support troops to urge the attack waves onward. The tongue-lashing he had likely received from Summerall may have caused him to do so, but because both regimental commanders, Babcock and Smith, were out of favor at division, Buck's guidance of the remaining field officers and men was all the more necessary. However, Buck's self-congratulatory depiction of his conduct in the day's events, calling himself an officer who "must throw personal safety to the winds, must show himself to his men, and encourage them by his example," should be considered with caution, even though he subsequently received the Legion of Honor and a promotion to major general.[107]

On the other side, the Germans were surprised by the ferocity of the day's assault in both the American and French sectors, but they were not unduly troubled by its consequences, since strong reinforcements were on hand and the opening moves of the withdrawal from the Marne salient were already under way. Lieutenant Sulzbach wrote in his diary:

> I don't see how the French have managed *this*—first bringing our offensive of 15 July to an unsuccessful halt, and then, completely unobserved by us, preparing and carrying out an attack on a huge scale, with such quantities of troops and equipment. The Americans must be very strongly represented here, especially with artillery and infantry. It is also a fact that in the War and because of it, the French have grown hugely in strength, energy and morale; they have got tough and developed very considerable endurance.[108]

Along the 1st Division's front, the sudden German collapse had taken place among severely depleted shadow formations, such as battalions of the once-proud 28th Division, along with the 3d Reserve and 46th Reserve Divisions. But the 20th and 42d Divisions had been drubbed too—by American formations that were also wasted and tired—and attempts at counterattack that evening by the newly arrived 5th Division made little progress. The most accurate conclusion seems to be the simplest and most straightforward one: the Americans were becoming more effective, and the Germans were becoming less so.[109]

Though pride had been satisfied, by this point, the capture of Berzy-le-Sec and Buzancy had little meaning in the absence of sufficient Franco-American strength to force a breakthrough, which Mangin's weary formations lacked. South of XX Corps, German Corps Winckler, Schoeler, and Kathen successfully concluded the first stages of their withdrawals on July 21, so the French in their sectors lunged forward against "nothing." But none of this mattered much to the men of the 1st Division. Without a doubt, they had passed through the crucible and become veterans. Relief began on the evening of July 21–22 and would be completed the following night. On their final day in the line, July 22, the doughboys gathered up their dead and wounded, rounded up stragglers, and tried to reassemble their units. Many men came in with letters from officers of the 1st Moroccan Division or the French 153d Division attesting that they had inadvertently wandered into adjoining zones and "done their bit where they found it" for days—no doubt resulting in some tantalizing stories of Franco-American cooperation that they likely shared with their comrades but have not filtered down to the present day.[110]

On the night of July 22, the men that remained marched rearward. Captain Bennett of the 26th Regiment remembered how "small groups, the remnants of companies, gathered about the kitchens. Little was said. Men were pale, wan and disheveled. Shock from loss of many friends seemed to be a great thought." The regiment had entered the line with 96 officers and 3,100 enlisted men; its casualties numbered 62 officers (64 percent), including 20 dead, and 1,560 enlisted men (more than 50 percent of the prebattle total). The regiment's colonel, lieutenant colonel, operations officer, and one major had been killed, and the two other majors were wounded. The 16th and 18th Regiments lost all their officers except their colonels, and the relatively fortunate 28th lost two of its field officers. Overall, the division incurred about 7,317 casualties, including 60 percent of its officers and 75 percent of its field officers.[111]

The Battle of Soissons was both a success and a missed opportunity. Although it is tempting to dwell on the latter, it is important to emphasize that Mangin's Tenth Army did in fact achieve an important strategic victory. His troops—specifically, Berdoulat's XX Corps—inflicted serious damage on the German Ninth and Seventh Armies and forced Ludendorff to order, on July 19, a gradual abandonment of the Marne salient. At Pétain's GHQ, French staff officers cavorted delightedly, congratulating the American liaison officer there, Colonel Paul H. Clark, and telling him, "Without the Americans this would never have been possible. We owe it all to you." The achievements of the US 1st and 2d Divisions and the French 1st Moroccan Division were indeed significant; to a lesser extent, so were those of adjoining formations such as the French 38th and 153d Divisions. Americans and French (and Senegalese) fought courageously, shattering whole German divisions and throwing them into panic on numerous occasions. Tanks and artillery often played important roles in fostering the infantry's success. While it is true that XX Corps did not achieve a breakthrough, conditions on the western front in World War I made breakthroughs almost impossible to accomplish. In addition, the absence of sufficient infantry force (the cavalry was useless) to XX Corps' left and right to widen the breach on July 18 and protect Berdoulat's flanks made a major penetration unfeasible. All that being said, however, more could have been accomplished.[112]

The Americans' continuing tactical deficiencies were made apparent in multiple reports prepared after the battle. First Lieutenant M. M. Andrews of the 26th Regiment gave his broad impressions:

> Lack of liaison between units, particularly from front to rear. The signal Corps fell down completely. . . . Very noticeable lack of distinct attack orders, lack of defining objectives and great lack of time given the infantry company before attacking. . . . Noticeable tendency for men in both front and rear waves of the attacking group to "bunch." . . . During the last two days of the action, trench warfare tactics were used instead of open warfare tactics.

Junior officers, he said, were not well directed from above, and sergeants lacked adequate training as platoon commanders. Captain P. N. Starlings of the same unit reported: "After the second day there was a continuous stream of men going to the rear whose place was at the front. The Military Police should have stopped this, but they failed. The result was that our front was weakened and the men who did remain had to do double work."[113]

Poor internal liaison generated bad feelings between machine gun and infantry officers. The 1st Division's machine gun officer issued a blistering report on August 5, charging that the infantry had next to no understanding of how to employ machine guns during the offensive; he also outlined the overall miserable liaison with machine gun units. Drawing on that memo, Summerall noted that his infantry battalion commanders had issued practically no orders to machine gun units, except to tell them to accompany the advance. As a result, these units "followed the infantry blindly and almost without exception were lost from the units to which assigned." During the battle, infantry gave no orders to the machine gunners at all: "it appears that the Battalion commander, not knowing just what to do with his machine guns, let them follow with a view to utilizing them as the necessity arose." Liaison was "practically nil," so in practice, the machine guns were deployed almost at random, sometimes in the front and sometimes in the rear or on the flanks. And when the guns ran short of ammunition, no one seemed to know where the dumps were located.[114]

Captain Harry Bennett, who participated in the offensive with the 26th Regiment and later compiled a study for the Command and General Staff College at Fort Leavenworth, remarked that the 1st Division as a whole had failed to apply "the principles of Economy of Force and of Mass" by directing its main effort toward certain critical areas ("mass in a main effort") rather than attacking equally everywhere. Infantry units, he noted, had a tendency to reach their objectives and then dig in, instead of maintaining pressure on the enemy with active probes, patrols, and so on—something the Moroccans excelled in throughout the battle, as German records noted. Even supplies of food and munitions were poorly maintained "due to a lack of aggressiveness on the part of supply personnel."[115]

Tactically speaking, the 2d Division did not make the same mistakes caused by inexperience that plagued the 1st Division. But it had ample problems of its own. In Belleau Wood the previous month, the 5th and 6th Marines in particular had learned the importance of on-the-field improvisation and individual initiative. Yet ironically, small-unit initiative sometimes played a negative role at Soissons. Faced with the almost total breakdown of command and control, which left them well outside the orbit of regimental and even battalion supervision, junior officers, NCOs, and men just followed their impulses. Chaos was often the result. Internally and externally, a spirit of collaboration was in exceptionally short supply. Growing mistrust and even hatred between army and marine officers and men cost lives as they argued and refused to cooperate at places like Vierzy. Even worse was the Americans' inability or unwillingness to work closely with the French.

A French summary of action for Soissons prepared on July 22 noted the following:

[The American] offensive spirit is indisputable . . . [but] it is to this ardor that one must attribute the heavy proportion of loss suffered. In his desire to come immediately into a hand to hand fight, the American officer as well as soldier often loses sight of the precautions necessary to avoid useless loss. The attack troop is not scattered enough. Evidently they are still somewhat lacking in experience. The necessary liaison practice has not been acquired either for the work outside or in the Division itself.[116]

For their part, American observers did not condescend to pay enough attention to French tactics to critique them. Often, they were not even aware of the numerical designations of French units attacking alongside them. Instead, Summerall, Harbord, and their officers delivered long litanies of complaints about French slowness or their failure to advance, blaming them for the Americans' defeats. American officers paid scant attention to the difficulties their neighbors faced and almost never credited their bravery—such as the 153d Division's gallant and self-sacrificing (if ultimately futile) attempts to storm the German stronghold at Vauxbuin.

The frequent American transgression of divisional boundaries, especially on July 18, proved a distinct nuisance to the 1st Moroccan Division. But no self-criticism was expressed in either American division for this clumsiness, which slowed the entire XX Corps. Instead, American reports praised the bravery of officers who abandoned their own objectives in favor of ad-libbing in the French zone—such as the marines' "bold attack" on Chaudun on July 18. From the point of view of platoon and company commanders who had been given little opportunity to learn their orders and the overall lay of the land, such improvisations made perfect sense. Below Chaudun, for example, the marines were taking deadly fire from their flank and saw no obvious signs that the Moroccans—who were actually only minutes behind—were prepared to deal with it. So, with a decisiveness and courage that would have been laudable under most circumstances, the marines and soldiers who followed them decided to deal with the problem themselves. At the same time, Summerall, Harbord, and their officers all encouraged the natural tendency at lower levels to hurry the advance, even at the cost of disorganization. This tendency was understandable, given the troops' general eagerness to prove themselves and given their training, which had inculcated the aggressive pursuit of open warfare. But this was a fundamental error. Harbord did not even have the excuse of not knowing the pace at which his neighbors intended to advance, since the staff of the Moroccan division had tried in vain to provide clear instructions on how to pace his advance with theirs. And it is hard to conceive that Summerall, who had somewhat more time to prepare, did not know French intentions either. Instead, both American divisions found it more convenient to simply charge ahead at their own pace and blame the French for falling behind. It is remarkable that neither here at Soissons nor in any other sector during the war was this problem of differing rates of advance addressed thoroughly at the command level. Pride may have played a role, as well as the hope that someday soon American units would no longer have to fight alongside the French.[117]

Despite these failings, Americans in both divisions looked back on Soissons with pride. A classified report titled "The American Military Factor in the War," prepared for Pershing by the Historical Section of the General Staff on January 14, 1919, commented, "It was only the conspicuous fighting power of our divisions that enabled the Allied forces to register a success that may well be called the turning point of the campaign." Recalled Summerall: "There can be no doubt that during the Battle of Soissons the heroic advance of the First Division, in spite of unprecedented losses and the most determined resistance of elements of eight German divisions, turned the fate of the war." In his official report he specified that his division had advanced eleven kilometers, moving at least as far as any other unit, and "came out depleted but still a fighting unit." The 2d Division's official report concluded, "This attack, a complete and overwhelming surprise, was a stunning blow to the German High Command. . . . Four hundred thousand Huns were packed there [in the salient] waiting to break through the Allied lines and to smash on to Paris. . . . This attack relieved the tremendous enemy pressure on Paris," forcing the evacuation of the salient and freeing the allies to "deliver hammer blows" all along the front. At the same time, Summerall was cognizant of the cost to his troops on their way out of the line: "All were pitifully worn, hollow cheeked, dazed, and exhausted. . . . All companies were mere skeletons of the well-filled ranks that entered the battle." Many years later, Captain Jeremiah Evarts of the 18th Regiment summed up his perspective on Soissons: "Hundreds of our men were just blown to pieces. It was a nightmare! The miracle was not only that any of us survived but that we could keep moving."[118]

15

Reducing the Marne Salient
US Troops in the Aisne-Marne Campaign, July 18–August 6, 1918

The stated German objective for the next phase of operations in the Marne salient was to "retire step by step, save our precious war material from the clutches of the enemy, and withdraw in good order to a new line of defense which nature offered us in the Aisne-Vesle sector." In essence, it was to be a delaying action on the Germans' part, against the steady application of pressure along a broad front by the French and Americans. After Soissons, there was no question of forcing a breakthrough at the shoulders of the salient and cutting off significant numbers of the kaiser's troops. For the American divisions involved in compressing the salient, the next few weeks would be a matter of occupying territory that was already won, disrupting Ludendorff's timetable as much as possible, and gaining valuable experience that could be put to good use in the more important battles to come. The process for the newly arrived formations would be much the same as it had been for American divisions entering the lines earlier. Perhaps the most astonishing aspect of the so-called Aisne-Marne offensive would be the tendency of green divisions to repeat the same mistakes, without applying any of the lessons supposedly learned by the AEF in June and the first half of July. Another characteristic of the Aisne-Marne offensive—disturbing but unsurprising at this point—would be the increasingly intractable dysfunctionality of the Franco-American military relationship. This relationship would reach its nadir under the much-loathed Degoutte at Fismes and Fismette in August.[1]

Four American divisions occupied frontage on the Marne salient with the French Sixth Army (to Tenth Army's right) at the time Mangin began his attack below Soissons on July 18. Starting from the left, the US 4th Division had its 7th Brigade (39th and 47th Regiments) attached to French II Corps between the Ourcq River and the Ruisseau d'Alland. This corps would make Sixth Army's primary attack on July 18. The 4th Division's 8th Brigade (58th and 59th Regiments) was stationed with the adjacent French VII Corps from the Ruisseau d'Alland to the Clignon River. Next to that was Liggett's US I Corps, consisting of the French 167th Division and the US 26th Division. Gouraud's French Fourth Army continued to command the US 93d Division's 369th Regiment—the "Harlem Rattlers"—attached to the French 161st Division. These were the only American units that would take part in the initial fighting from July 18 to 21. Subsequently, as the campaign to follow up the German withdrawal from the Marne salient continued, the US 3d and 28th Divisions would enter the fight with French XXXVIII Corps, followed by other US divisions introduced to the front at various points.

The 4th Division had initially been organized in December 1917, primarily from Regular Army units stationed on the American West Coast. In February 1918 it received an influx of volunteers, and the following month it was rounded out with draftees. It arrived at various ports in Europe in May and trained with the British before being sent for additional training (in detachments) with the French Sixth Army in June. Its constituent elements were assigned to the French II and VII Corps on July 1, and they were placed in second-line positions a few days later. By the time the Soissons offensive began on July 18, the 4th Division had not yet been assembled as a complete unit. Major General George H. Cameron had commanded the division since its creation. Born in Illinois in 1861, he had graduated from West Point in 1883 and was a cavalryman through and through. His cavalry assignments lasted until the late summer of 1917, when he was assigned to the infantry (it had been decided that the cavalry would have to stay home during the coming war). For such a high-ranking officer, Cameron is an obscure figure. After his not especially distinguished command of V Corps during the Meuse-Argonne campaign, he disappears from the military record. His command of the 4th Division during the Aisne-Marne campaign was likewise unremarkable.[2]

At dawn on July 18, the 7th Brigade's 39th Regiment was attached to the French 33d Division in French II Corps. Assigned a subsidiary role in the morning's events, the Americans initially watched as elements of the French 41st Division on their left and the 33d Division on their right moved forward to the attack at 0435. The regiment's three battalions then attacked concurrently. The 1/39th on the left moved out at 0745 and slowly but efficiently crossed the narrow but deep and marsh-lined Saviere River on jerry-rigged

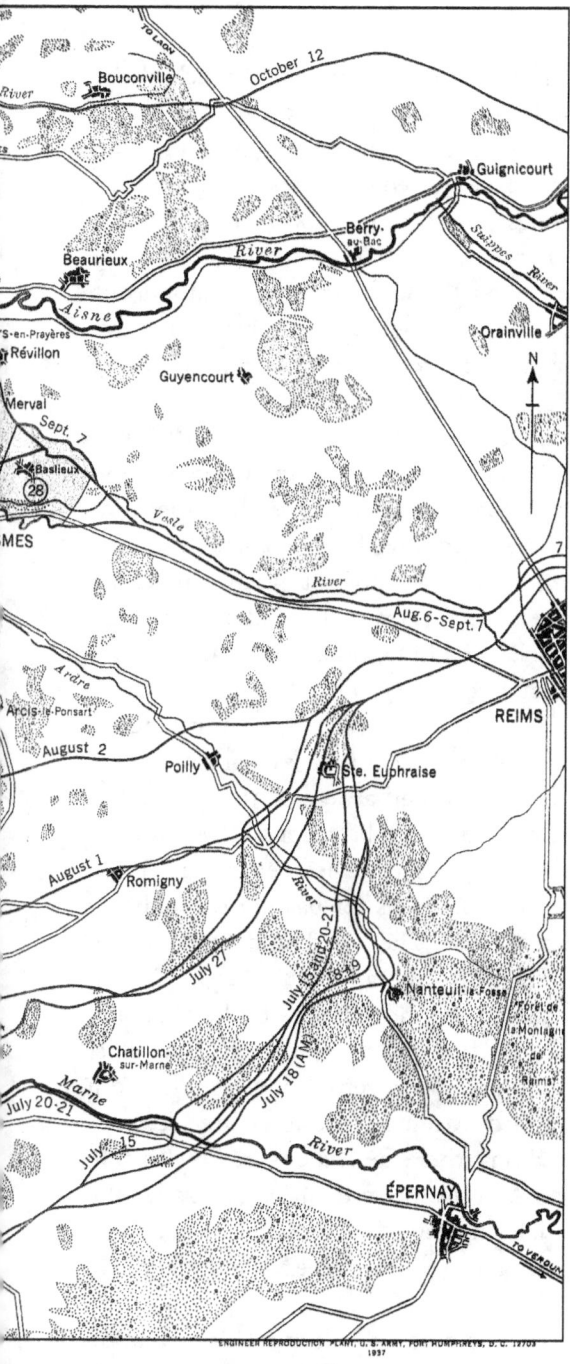

Reducing the Aisne-Marne salient, July 18–August 6, 1918. (Fold-out map, *American Armies and Battlefields in Europe*, 120)

footbridges. The battalion spent the rest of the morning and much of the afternoon establishing itself in the Buisson de Cresnes, "a large thicket on a hill" that the Germans had not fortified. A few machine guns and about 100 Germans were captured. The 3/39th followed up at 0900 and pushed its lines alongside the Buisson de Cresnes; later that afternoon it responded to a French call for assistance and participated in the capture of Noroy while the 2/39th drew up behind. These were all modest advances in support of what was essentially a French operation, but they were conducted successfully. American eagerness to enter the battle was on full display, as was the tendency for battalions to intermingle and crowd to the front.[3]

The 8th Brigade had a similarly promising start in French VII Corps, attached to the French 164th Division. Here again, the Americans were in a subsidiary role. The French commander elected to deploy the Americans in a novel manner, forming his division into three groups, each with three French battalions and one American battalion of the 58th Regiment, along with French and American machine gun companies. Instead of advancing toward their objectives near Sommelans within rigid zones of action, "the commander of each was to take ground or give ground on his inside flank, in favor of the other group, as might be made necessary by circumstances." The attack began at 0400 with no artillery preparation except for smoke. The Germans responded with a heavy counterbarrage of their own, but French liaison officers attached to the American battalions proved invaluable: "Marching with the battalion commanders, these experienced veterans indicated to the majors the best methods for passing through the German barrage with a minimum of loss." The 1/58th and 2/58th maintained cohesion alongside the French, performing mop-up duty in the village of Hautevesnes and helping to capture the villages of Chevillon and Courchamps. However, at around 1000 hours, the 2/58th, which had lost touch with its French neighbors and possibly received poor service from its liaison officer, surged ahead toward extremely strong enemy defenses in the Bois de l'Orme. Unsupported on either side and unsure how to take on the well-entrenched enemy, the Americans were hurled back after the battalion had been all but shattered, losing 609 of its 1,281 officers and men. Elements of the 59th Regiment were released from reserve and moved up during the evening.[4]

The pressures were greater in the adjoining US I Corps. This formation had taken tactical command of the French III Corps' sector east of Château-Thierry on July 4, marking what Liggett described as "the beginning of the first tactical operation of an American army corps since the Civil War." At his disposal on July 18 were the French 167th Division, which had fought alongside the US 2d Division the previous month, and the US 26th Division, which was yearning for an opportunity to redeem its reputation since the fiasco at Seicheprey. As a mixed command under an American general, I Corps was predisposed to some serious friction, but it never developed. This was thanks in large part to Liggett. He was born in Reading, Pennsylvania, in 1857 and graduated from West Point in 1879, after which he saw brief combat service in the Spanish-American War and the Philippines. He also served as president of the Army War College. Liggett was the quintessential manager. Intelligent, levelheaded, and confident, he balanced strong opinions and a willingness to state them openly with a remarkable sense of tact.

Liggett's qualities impressed the French, and he got along well with both his superior Degoutte and his subordinate Schmidt of the 167th Division. Unlike many other American generals, Liggett possessed an easy self-confidence that precluded the need (typically born of insecurity) to denigrate his battle-tested allies. "As always," Liggett remembered, "we found the French good comrades and good soldiers." Liggett—whose corpulent physique betrayed his fondness for good food—described his technique for forging a strong bond with Degoutte and his staff:

> Our staff had been working since June 22 with the corresponding heads of the French staffs with whom we were associated, but we continued to give every spare moment to getting better acquainted; you can't know too well the man you are fighting beside. I had with me a cook I was willing to compare with the best *cordon-bleu chef* of France, a Greek candy merchant from Seattle who had been cook of the headquarters company of the Forty-first Division, and I entertained Degoutte and his corps commanders and staffs as often as possible to that end. My headquarters was a pleasant château, the country home of a Paris business man, and it permitted a hospitality not always practical in war. The owner traveled up from Paris several times to inspect it and complimented us on the care we gave it.

One should not underestimate the diplomatic benefits of a little taste for good living. As for Schmidt, Liggett found him to be "as easy as a fellow American to work with. He told me, in fact, that he preferred to serve under American command; that his own corps commanders were too inclined to annoy him with petty details. The French . . . are a suave race."[5]

Unfortunately, Liggett's relationship with Edwards was not as smooth. As already noted, Pershing and his staff at GHQ had it in for Edwards for various reasons. Liggett's concern about the Yankee Division commander seems to have been devoid of any prejudice. Instead, he repeatedly—and probably rightly—expressed concern at the sense of carelessness at Yankee Division headquarters, which hindered efficient military operations to the detriment of learning and at the cost of lives. Edwards's response to the issuance of orders on the evening of July 17 for the coming Aisne-Marne offensive did nothing to encourage Liggett. Seeking to apply lessons learned by other divisions, Liggett explained I Corps orders and calmly exhorted Edwards "not to crowd men too much in the front line to take shell fire and not to let the attack run away beyond the objective, where further orders from the corps will determine the next move." However, Edwards "did not seem to grasp his responsibilities in the matter or to have a clear idea of his mission." He and his division would be watched closely.[6]

The Yankees occupied a gruesome zone of operations that ran approximately from Givry and Torcy on the left to Vaux on the right. In the rear were the foul and haunted ruins of Belleau Wood. When the 26th Division arrived in this sector on July 14, Private Connell Albertine was horrified at what he saw—and smelled:

> What sights we saw! This part of the woods was literally covered with dead Boches and Marines. The stench from these bodies was sickening, and again many of us vomited. There was no protection here at all. . . . There was no time to bury the dead, because the Boches shelled the woods continually, as we discovered when making the relief. . . . We stayed here for two days and two nights without a wink of sleep, with death staring us in the face every minute. . . . We were wishing to God that we would receive orders to go ahead or get out, for this sure was a hell hole if ever there was one.[7]

Moving forward was the best means of obtaining release from this charnel zone. Division attack orders issued at 0030 on July 18 directed the 52d Brigade (Brigadier General Charles H. Cole), with the 3/103d, 3/104th, and 2/103d Battalions in line from left to right, to attack and capture Torcy, Givry, Belleau, and the railroad above Bouresches.[8]

The night before the attack, the same line of thunderstorms that drenched Mangin's XX Corps hit Liggett's I Corps. Major Frank Sibley remembered that the "worst thunderstorm of our whole stay in France broke with astounding fury" on the long lines of traffic and supply parties snaking forward on roads to the front. German shells fell too. For Albertine:

It wasn't enough that we had the terrific noise of the bursting shells all around us; the thunder and lightning made it worse. How much is a human being supposed to take? Soon all these fox-holes were filled with water; nothing one could do but stay put, for shrapnel and tree splinters were flying in all directions, and if we ventured out we would be killed. Because we couldn't stand up in these shallow fox-holes, we just had to lie flat and keep our heads up so we could breathe.

The rain stopped by 0330, followed by "a clear, rosy dawn; happily, as the light grew and the warm wind sprang up, a fine, thick mist began to drift up from the meadows." This mist provided cover for the advance, but the troops were still drenched and exhausted from their grueling journey to the front, and they were in no mood to compliment the weather as the attack began. The Germans, primarily of the 87th Division in this sector, would soon make them feel much worse.[9]

Corporal Horatio Rogers of the 101st Field Artillery had ideal ground from which to watch the attack go forward. He also observed how his opposite numbers among the German artillery responded to the assault:

Below our rising ground was a sunken road from which our infantry were trying to attack a low plateau, and on the plateau a company of German machine gunners were setting up their guns in shell holes. The whole thing was in plain sight from our hill. I could see the German officer giving directions and pointing with a cane as groups of men moved about in the field. Our guns were firing by direct observation and were making hit after hit, but what Germans were left kept doggedly at their job.

The Germans had good reasons to stick to their guns. They were finding plenty of targets.[10]

The assault proceeded most successfully on the left, where the 3/103d advanced in conjunction with the French 167th Division. Following the rolling barrage, the battalion left the woods and moved downhill across cratered wheat fields to Torcy and the railroad behind it, at the foot of Hill 193. The Americans captured the village without much opposition. In the center, Captain James H. McDade commanding the 3/104th balked at moving forward with the rolling barrage because two of his companies had gotten lost in the night and his machine gunners had not received their ammunition. Furious, Brigadier General Cole relieved McDade and replaced him with

Major Roy L. Hanson, but since Hanson was unfamiliar with the ground over which he was supposed to advance, McDade led the attack anyway when it went forward at 0820. Despite the delay, the battalion captured Belleau, but at the cost of serious casualties. Private Harry G. Wright, a platoon runner with Company L, wrote in his diary of the "living hell" he and his comrades experienced as they moved forward under artillery and machine gun fire that took down men all around him. Wright watched in shock as his sergeant and lieutenant fell simultaneously to his left and right. The private bent down to lift up the lieutenant and speak with him, only to find that the officer was dead, with a bullet between his eyes. Stunned and moving his lips silently, "possibly in prayer," Wright put down the lieutenant and ran off to catch up with his comrades in front. After a pause the battalion moved forward again to capture Givry and advance partway up Hill 193. Following hand-to-hand combat with the Germans defending that eminence, the battalion found itself too exposed and had to pull back. On the right, finally, the 2/103d successfully stormed the railroad embankment above Bouresches. When it attempted to keep moving forward, however, the battalion came under withering fire from the front and Hill 193 to the left and had to pull back. Brave but foolhardy attempts by some platoons to charge German machine guns frontally had predictable results.[11]

The aftermath of the day's attacks was gruesome for the men who were seeing combat on a large scale for the first time. Earl Yeomans of the 102d Regiment was impressed at the number of American dead who lay scattered through the wheat fields. Engineers later appeared and "combed through the wheat fields, and when bodies were located, rifles were stuck in the ground in an inverted position with the butt sticking up over the wheat. Standing on an elevated ground, thousands of these rifles could be seen, grim sentinels watching over the dead." Albertine responded to the spectacle with anger, especially after finding wounded Americans who had been bayoneted by the Germans: "We all vowed revenge, and we did not take a prisoner but let all the Boches we came in contact with have it, the same as they killed our Buddies," he recalled. The same fate would be meted out to all varieties of Germans, whether they were the "cruel and vicious" Prussians or the "yellow and cowardly" Bavarians.[12]

On July 19 the 26th Division's attack plans were canceled, allegedly because of the French 167th Division's failure to move forward. The US 4th Division's separated brigades did attack, however. The 39th Regiment, attached to the French 33d Division, attacked at 0400 north of the Ourcq River, with its 1st and 2d Battalions in front from left to right and the 3d Battalion in support. Unfortunately, the Americans moved out before orders postponing the attack could reach them. As a result, the beginning of a French rolling barrage fell at 0430 on the advancing American troops. Even so, the Americans doggedly continued onward, overcoming stiff resistance despite casualties and severe disorganization caused by rough ground and enemy fire. They captured the abandoned and burning village of Chouy and then marched on to take their third objective near the Moulin des Croutes. Hammered to the tune of 283 casualties but a little wiser, the regiment was withdrawn from the lines that night and returned to the 7th Brigade in preparation for the division's reassembly.[13]

The US 58th and 59th Regiments, attached to the French 164th Division, also encountered heavier fighting than they had the previous day. The three battalions of the 59th Regiment attacked between 0435 and 0500 in conjunction with the French 13th Chasseurs and supported by a good number of French tanks. As each battalion attempted to cross the Courchamps-Priez road, however, invisible German artillery and machine gunners set the tanks afire and felled the attacking infantry: "The men began to fall, first singly, then in groups. From all sides came the cries of the wounded. Forward they lunged, firing as they went, usually without aim. All they wanted was to see their opponents, to get at close quarters with them. They paid the price." Commented a French officer: "Had I not seen it with my own eyes, I would never have believed that green troops would advance under such fire." But it was to no purpose, as the French and American infantry were driven back. The 1/58th endured similar experiences in support of the French 133d Regiment. Ardor was not enough. On July 20 elements of both regiments participated in further advances with limited success, driving well forward at one point only to be driven back by a German counterattack. With that, to the Americans' relief, the experiment ended; all their regiments were withdrawn from the front pursuant to the full reconstitution of the 4th Division. After spending just a few days in the line, the 4th Division had taken 2,333 casualties. Although its first operations under French tutelage on July 18 had gone well, it subsequently reverted all too quickly to the standard errors committed by green American formations.[14]

The 26th Division leaped back into action on July 20, partly because the successes of Mangin's Tenth Army were having a visible effect on the Germans, who began obvious preparations for withdrawal. Degoutte consequently ordered Liggett's corps to push forward all along the line. In the 26th Division's zone of action, that meant advancing with both brigades and all four regiments in front from Givry to Vaux, led by the 3/104th, 1/104th, 3/102d, and 3/101st from left to right. There was uneven artillery preparation. And despite Liggett's prescriptions—reinforced to some extent by Edwards—for infantry commanders to advance carefully, the tactics employed were exceedingly clumsy. As the attack went forward at 1500, the men of the 3/102d "entered Bouresches wood, going like hell. . . . The advance across the open country to Bois de Bouresches was rapidly made, the men moving on the run and throwing off their packs which hindered their speed. The abandoning of the packs caused much subsequent hardship because of the loss of all protective covering and reserve rations." But the Germans, supposedly in retreat, were waiting. All four American battalions suffered severe casualties from German machine guns, with minimal gain. Here too, the problem of liaison and rates of advance reared its ugly head as the relatively slow advance of the French 167th Division caused the Americans to take enfilading fire from their flank. Liggett was an involved corps commander, providing Edwards with regular instructions on how to conduct his advance, but he could do nothing to either slow down the Americans or speed up the French; for both, their pace was a matter of habit if not instinct. However, when he visited division headquarters at the end of the day, Liggett was unhappy to learn that Edwards and his chief of staff did not know where all their units were. There would be repercussions.[15]

With the German withdrawal now clearly under way, the two American divisions in French XXXVIII Corps entered the fray along the Marne. Unfortunately for them, the Germans in this sector had succeeded in secretly evacuating their bridgeheads, directly under their enemies' noses. On July 19, unaware of the impending German withdrawal, Montdésir had told Dickman that the 3d Division's immediate objectives would be limited. "It is a question," he wrote, "for the 3d Division of re-establishing itself at Moulin Ruine and all along the edge of the wood, so that the enemy may no longer have observation posts hanging directly over, and at arms' length, from the troops in the valley and in the bend of Charteves." The next morning the French discovered that the Germans had left during the night, and they ordered the 3d Division to cross the Marne forthwith. The 38th Regiment did so after 0900 in conjunction with the French 73d Division, capturing Varennes while the other American regiments prepared to follow. The French likewise ordered the 28th Division forward, complained the 3d Division's chief of staff R. H. C. Kelton, with "an intense amount of insurrecto boom-boom only to find that Mr. Boche had pulled his freight at midnight." Instead of capturing 15,000 prisoners, which they would have done if they had properly anticipated the German withdrawal, Kelton groused, the Americans captured only about 100 stragglers.[16]

By July 21 the allied advance was in full swing, with the US 26th and 3d

Divisions in the forefront and ordered to press on without regard to their flanks. Edwards expressed some trepidation to Liggett as the Yankee Division's attack began, because his outfit had suffered 1,752 casualties in the previous three days and the men were tired. Fortunately, though, the Germans had withdrawn overnight. The Yankees, with both brigades in the van, advanced nine kilometers and suffered few casualties, except at the end of the day as German resistance stiffened below Épieds and Trugny. However, continued confusion at division headquarters regarding the location of troops and the direction of advance increasingly worried Liggett. The 3d Division, meanwhile, experienced some trouble from German rear guards who fired on their attempts to bridge the Marne. By afternoon, though, the division was almost fully across and had advanced to capture Brasles, Chartèves, and, best of all, Château-Thierry.[17]

July 22 was not a happy day for the Yankee Division. On the previous night, some confusion in the corps and division chain of command—for which both Liggett and Edwards were apparently to blame—had led to a left sideslip by some units that intermingled them with the French 167th Division. In addition, Épieds and Trugny—"little villages in a broad valley, with gentle slopes back of them, and a wood that had been jammed full of machine guns"—formed elements of the first of four German defensive systems before the Aisne and were not easily taken. An attempt to outflank Trugny, where the defenders supposedly had one machine gun for every seven yards of front, failed, so the Americans attacked frontally, with harrowing results. Remembered Captain Daniel Strickland of the 102d Regiment:

> The new men became demoralized by the withering fire and constantly sought cover without orders. This checked the rush of the advance and it became necessary for squad leaders to drive their men forward in some cases by force. Greenhorns in the rear tried to fire through the ranks ahead and increased the casualties. It developed that morning that the last batch of replacements sent up could not even load a rifle, much less fire it.

According to the Germans, "The Americans charged forward in dense crowds accompanied by numerous tanks, and were caught by our artillery and machine gun fire." Eventually, the Yankees took both villages, but a German counterattack threw them out of Épieds and netted 130 doughboy prisoners. Hit by sudden salvos of gas, some American companies pulled back with fishy stories that they had been ordered to do so, while other company commanders had to drive platoons back to the front at gunpoint. Edwards was horrified by what was happening to his men and sent Liggett "an urgent request for immediate reinforcement, in view of the exhausted condition of his troops and the casualties sustained." Liggett lacked reserves of his own and, to his embarrassment, had to relay the request to Degoutte. The army commander complied by moving up the 28th Division's 56th Brigade. Liggett no doubt expressed his growing annoyance to Pershing, who was passing by that day and visited 26th Division headquarters, where he gave an impromptu speech to the officers, praising their work. But to their subsequent frustration, the division was not mentioned in AEF dispatches. Pershing would not visit the division again while Edwards was in command.[18]

The 3d Division, meanwhile, was still struggling to get the remainder of its formations across the Marne and move forward. Enemy resistance was spotty but effective, and thanks to poor liaison with French forces on either flank, the Americans could do no more than capture Jaulgonne just across the river. Numerous excuses were offered for the slow advance. Said Colonel McAlexander of the 38th Regiment regarding July 21–22: "Our troops had been subjected to severe shelling and constant machine gun fire. In addition, enemy aeroplanes continually swooped down across our lines, raking them with machine guns. Considering the strong opposition of the enemy, the lack of food and sleep of our own men and the nature of the terrain crossed, the advance made on the first day was indeed a remarkable one." The division would only inch forward on July 23 as well, capturing a few farms but unable to overcome feisty German resistance.[19]

On July 23, despite frantic orders from Degoutte to "push, push, push . . . to the limit of endurance," the Yankee Division, led by its 101st Regiment, again made scant progress, notwithstanding a strong and precise artillery barrage planned by Edwards. Private Fred Wilder of that regiment vividly described how his company assaulted the woods between Épieds and Trugny. Moving out that morning during a violent rainstorm, the waves of American infantry were soon surrounded by a cacophony of whizzing bullets and exploding shells. Soon "incessant fire, coming from shell holes, dugouts, and from behind clumps of bushes, held us at bay," and the men took cover. They could not stay down all day, however, so Wilder's company commander ordered a charge:

> We were eagerly responsive, and more than willing to obey the command. Advancing, we combed the woods and shouted like a pack of wild Indians. High up in a tree I saw an object which caused me to

stop and look for signs of motion. After a brief interval it moved, and I could see that it was a German sniper. I was not long in placing my rifle to my shoulder and firing. The enemy sniper came down like a porcupine, and for a moment I was reminded of my hunting days in the Maine woods. But by the time I had reached him, the others had rifled him of souvenirs.

The Americans successfully cleared the woods and reached a road where, lacking picks and spades, they used bayonets and mess kit covers to dig shelters as German shells, bullets, and gas descended on them. Shortly thereafter, some "rather formidable" looking Germans were observed working their way down the road from the right. Seeing the Americans, the Germans plunged into the woods opposite the road, and a savage firefight ensued. "Within two minutes," Wilder remembered, "each faction was doing its best to annihilate the other. Men fell on both sides, and it was hard to tell who the next victim would be." In a blur, Wilder saw a soldier rise up on the other side in an American uniform and cry, "Don't shoot, we're Americans." Silence descended for a moment as the Yanks gaped in bewilderment, but soon the Germans opened fire again, having gained some initiative and a sense of the Yankee positions. Recalled Wilder:

> Any attempt of mine to describe that battle would be futile. In my mind's eye I can see the whole panorama, as freshly and as vividly as though I was passing through the same ordeal again, and your mind's eye, the imagination, must supply the touches which my words cannot convey. Two bodies of soldiers facing each other with the resolve to kill or conquer, each employing deadly weapons with deadliest earnestness; men praying, cursing, laughing, some even crying, while others are frantic with excitement.

Eventually, the Germans withdrew. Wilder's section found itself isolated, and the Americans pulled back too. The day's gain had been exactly nothing. Since July 21, the division had suffered another 1,861 casualties. Morale, as Liggett observed, was increasingly poor.[20]

On July 24 Foch called a meeting of the Supreme War Council at Bombon. The slow deflation of the Marne salient currently under way was all very well, but it would not end the war any sooner. Instead, Foch proposed to launch "a series of well ordered actions" to maintain pressure on the enemy, retain the initiative, and prepare for more decisive actions later on. From Pershing's point of view, the best part of Foch's plan was that it finally envisaged the creation of an American army with its own front and objective: reduction of the Saint-Mihiel salient. With a pleasure that can easily be imagined, Pershing issued orders for the creation of American First Army, to take place on August 10. The multifarious tasks related to organizing that army now became paramount. It is unsurprising that, in this context, Pershing and the GHQ staff had little time to think about the American divisions following the German withdrawal to the Aisne.[21]

While the generals met at Bombon, the German positions in front of the US 26th and 3d Divisions finally loosened up a bit. The previous night, Liggett had ordered an attack at dawn, but Edwards had balked, and Brigadier General George H. Shelton of the 51st Brigade had "strongly advised against the attack." Fortunately for them, the Germans had already withdrawn, and when the 28th Division's 111th and 112th Regiments (operating under Yankee Division control) moved forward, they were able to advance more than five kilometers in a northeasterly direction as far as Beards. There, German fire brought them to a halt. The Yankee Division troops who followed up the Pennsylvanians were utterly exhausted. During a pause, Private Wilder had a moment of weakness: he "decided to stay there awhile and rest and then go back of the lines as a gassed or shell-shocked victim. Others had done it, and so why shouldn't I? . . . But I finally decided that as long as I had stuck it out so far, I could go awhile longer, so when the column started I gathered myself and started along with the rest." That night the 26th Division, which had advanced seventeen kilometers but taken 5,080 casualties since the beginning of July, would finally be relieved by the US 42d Division.[22]

The Yankee Division departed the lines under a cloud. Liggett was furious with Edwards and just about all his staff and field officers, all the way down to the regimental level. Summarizing his complaints in a memo to GHQ on August 13, Liggett castigated the divisional staff's "tendency to question orders" from corps. He also pointed to the lack of "a spirit of implicit and prompt obedience" and a "spirit of endurance and determination in the officers." As a result, Liggett "observed a hesitation and lack of keenness in the execution of orders for the pursuit" and intolerably clumsy movements in and out of combat. Liggett's whip fell particularly hard on the 52d Brigade, and he believed that both its commanding officer (Brigadier General Cole) and the regimental commanders should be relieved of duty. Liggett concluded:

It is my belief that the usefulness of the 26th Division as a dependable fighting unit can be restored only after a period of thorough basic training and reconstruction, together with such readjustment or substitution among the officers of higher command as will insure a correction and eradication of the faults above mentioned, together with the instilling of a spirit of obedience and obliteration of personal complaints. It is fair to state, such basic training has never been given this division.

There were signs that the division was becoming what Grotelueschen calls "doctrinally heretical" as well, although Liggett was neither an open-warfare fanatic nor a Francophobe. In any event, the Yankee Division would not return to the front until the Saint-Mihiel offensive in September. Edwards would be relieved of duty on October 23.[23]

Farther east, and moving in a converging line of advance with I Corps, the 3d Division followed up the withdrawing Germans on July 24 as far as Le Charmel. The next day the Americans managed to capture Le Charmel but were unable to advance much further. By that point, they were still more than three kilometers north of Jaulgonne. For once, the French were in a position to criticize the Americans' slow rate of advance. This seemed to be the result of not just German resistance but also faulty American command control and tactics. Montdésir acidly took full advantage of the opportunity to chide the Americans in a letter he wrote to Dickman at 1200 on July 25:

> There is on the front of your Division a density of troops greater than the mission to be fulfilled requires. . . . In the present situation, it is not yet a question of breaking a strong enemy resistance; it is only necessary to bring about by maneuver and by infiltration the fall of the line of machine guns by which the enemy covers his retreat. For this purpose there is required a small effective in troops in order to diminish the loss, but light and ship-shape to be able to out flank rapidly the machine guns which are uncovered. . . . It would be sufficient to put in line one Brigade, the other Brigade, being in reserve and resting. The first line Brigade does not need more than two Battalions in first line. . . . In this manner, the losses would be diminished and it would be possible to allow the troops a little rest, having them relieve each other for the 1st line service. . . . This is the method which the experience of four years of war has caused the French Divisions to adopt;

this permits them to last for a long time in the fight although they have effectives infinitely smaller than those of the American Divisions and although they are composed of older men.

Though his criticisms were well placed, Montdésir's patronizing tone was not well received. Relations between the French and Americans under XXXVIII Corps command were rapidly deteriorating.[24]

On July 25–26 I Corps changed its horses midstream. The US 26th Division and the US 28th Division's 56th Brigade pulled out, as did the French 167th Division. In their place, the US 42d Division took over the entire corps front—a novel arrangement made possible as the overall frontage shrank because of converging zones of advance. Brigadier General Douglas MacArthur's 84th Brigade made its presence felt at 1650 on July 26 by attacking Red Cross Farm, a well-prepared position with a superb field of fire that bristled with enemy machine guns. No effort was made to coordinate with the French on the left. Attacking with the 1/167th and 3/167th on the left and the 2/168th on the right, the Americans suffered "heavy losses from machine-gun fire" as they attacked in what the defenders thought were thick lines. The first assault failed, and the doughboys were pinned down. Subsequent assaults at around 1800 were more successful as the attackers spread out more thinly, firing as they advanced; they then overcame the Germans at close quarters, capturing the farm. According to MacArthur, "We reverted to tactics I had seen so often in the Indian wars of my frontier days. Crawling forward in twos and threes against each stubborn nest of enemy guns, we closed in with the bayonet and the hand grenade. It was savage and there was no quarter asked or given." Individuals improvising with machine guns and one-pounders made a significant difference, although their actions were uncoordinated. Red Cross Farm had been captured at the cost of more than 1,000 American casualties.[25]

For the 3d Division farther east—now almost adjacent to US I Corps, with only the French 39th Division in between—July 26 brought more frustration tempered by hope of relief. At 1000 hours French XXXVIII Corps ordered an attack that afternoon by the French 39th Division and two battalions of the US 5th Brigade's 4th and 7th Regiments, aimed at capturing some farm buildings and possibly seizing Le Charmel. Brigadier General Fred Sladen, commanding the 5th Brigade, was pessimistic about the prospects for success and was proved correct. The attack went forward at 1650, but the 39th Division advanced slowly. The American battalions reached Le

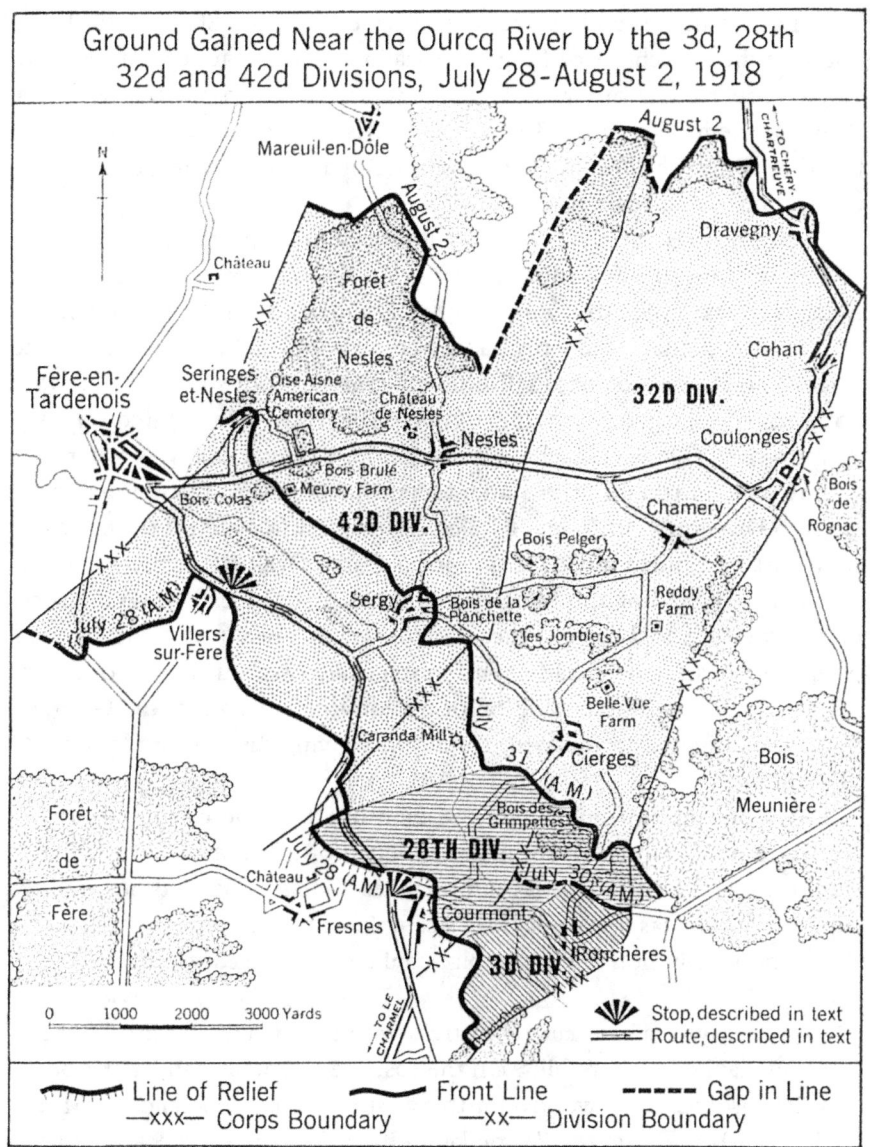

Clearing the line of the Ourcq, July 28–August 2, 1918. (*American Armies and Battlefields in Europe*, 68)

Charmel but had to pull back under heavy enemy fire. Sladen bitterly denounced the French for rushing his battalions into the attack without providing proper direction or intelligence and for failing to protect his flanks. Plans for the following day, fortunately, envisaged the 3d Division taking a breather while the US 28th Division's 55th Brigade passed through to attack toward the Ourcq River.[26]

The next phase of the German withdrawal took place on the night of July 26–27. Liggett's and Montdésir's orders for the US 42d and 28th Divisions to attack on the morning of July 27 were just being executed when it was discovered that the enemy had withdrawn overnight to the Ourcq, and a pursuit was ordered instead. Pushing northeast about six kilometers with both brigades in line, the Rainbow Division reached the Ourcq opposite Sergy, where German machine guns announced that this was where the enemy would make his next stand. Meanwhile, the US 3d Division and the US 28th Division's 55th Brigade followed up a few kilometers to the Ourcq southeast of Courmont. At this point, I Corps faced the far southern tip of what remained of the Marne salient. Deep advances by French forces on the western and eastern faces of the salient meant that the German positions on the Ourcq had been "strategically outflanked," according to Liggett. Yet in the finest tradition of a dedicated rear guard, the Germans here would fight vigorously for some time, giving their comrades time to pull out.[27]

Faced on the morning of July 28 by a line that the enemy clearly intended to hold in force for some time, Liggett ordered Menoher's 42d Division to force the Ourcq with both brigades abreast—but without artillery support, which was not available in strength. Unfortunately, the vista facing the Rainbow Division did not inspire confidence in an easy victory:

> The enemy was in a natural fortress with the village of Sergy in the valley flanked by bare hills. On the east the Germans had a flank position protected by woods, on the west a small creek called the Ru du Pont Brule. Meurcy Ferme lay in the valley of this creek near its junction with the Ourcq, and farther up the creek was the village of Nesles. Farther to the west the village of Seringes gave a commanding position over Meurcy Ferme.

It was, in other words, a natural bottleneck that would funnel the attackers into ready-made killing grounds. In the early stages of their advance, the men of the Rainbow Division forced the Ourcq, which did not pose a significant obstacle, but there followed a series of uncoordinated battalion-strength attacks that resulted in what Liggett called "as desperate fighting as we had encountered in the war." Martin Hogan of the 3/165th, the "Shamrock Battalion," recalled:

> [It seemed like] the enemy had a machine gun behind every tree, and he was working these frantically. One felt a queer uneasy sensation in the pit of the stomach as one ran to think of the myriads of steel needles streaming through the air around him, and one felt from minute to minute that the end could only be a matter of the next step or so. The air was alive with death and the mocking rat-a-tat and crackle of death.... Men plunged to earth to the right and left of me. Almost at every stride some comrade fell, stumbling forward lifeless, or falling to wind and rock for a while through the first disordering sting of a fatal wound. Others just slipped down and lay low and still, too badly wounded and spent to go on with the advance, but most of them to be saved by the rapidly working mercy service of the American army. I saw these incidents, little nightmare incidents, flashed upon the screen of my vision in jumbled, jerky fashion, and I ran on feeling that the whole thing was just a dream, stopping to aim and fire as some chance gray uniform showed, and then blindly running on.

While both the 83d and 84th Brigades established bridgeheads across the river at multiple points, each battalion suffered severely from flanking fire, thanks in part to spotty liaison with other battalions and with adjoining French and US 28th Division units. The German strongpoint at Sergy changed hands multiple times as the German 4th Guards Division counterattacked, and combat surged back and forth through the town. Surveying the aftermath, Father Duffy was dismayed at how men's lives had been wasted in a bayonet charge across open ground in what was properly "an artillery job."[28]

To the east, meanwhile, XXXVIII Corps had become a jumble. The US 28th Division's 55th Brigade would carry out the primary attack on July 28 along a 2.5-kilometer front taken over from the French 39th Division, which was now pulled out of the line. To the 55th Brigade's right, the US 3d Division's 5th Brigade remained in the line at least temporarily, with the objective of assisting passage of the Ourcq. Moving up behind was the US 32d Division—designated to relieve both the 28th and 3d Divisions, but not yet. Attempts to manage these simultaneous attacks and reliefs would cause significant confusion.

The 55th Brigade faced a difficult prospect. The German-held ground north of the Ourcq in this sector was, said Colonel Conrad Lanza, "one of the finest positions for the defense that could have been selected." German rifle pits and machine gun nests on Hill 188 and along the edge of the Bois des Grimpettes and surrounding areas provided them with a superb field of fire over the wheat fields the Americans would have to cross. German positions in Cierges and on Hill 212, southeast of Sergy to the Americans' left, were also formidable and gave the defenders good artillery observation. Brigadier General Thomas Darrah, commanding the 55th Brigade, chose this inauspicious moment to remove Colonel George E. Kemp, commanding the attacking 110th Regiment, for general inefficiency (Darrah himself would later be removed for inefficiency during the Meuse-Argonne campaign). He also declined the proffered services of sixteen British armored cars that arrived at Fresnes that morning and could have been used creatively to strike the enemy flanks. Despite minute and largely useless attack orders that Darrah supplied to Kemp's successor, Major Edward Martin, the attack lacked artillery support and stood little chance of success.

The 2/110th and 3/110th attacked at daybreak and moved hesitantly downslope over exposed ground toward the riverbank, under fire from German artillery and machine guns. At noon the Americans finally reached the river—its bed was twenty feet wide, with banks six to seven feet high, but the water was only six feet wide and one foot deep. The Americans tried to take cover there from enemy fire during the afternoon, but shelter was scant and they continued to take casualties. Montdésir ordered a renewal of the attack at 1630, with the US 3d Division's 5th Brigade on the right providing support for a thrust toward enemy-held high ground in the Bois des Grimpettes, but to little avail. Still unsupported by artillery—which had not yet come up after the German withdrawal the preceding day—the 5th Brigade got just a few hundred meters north of Ronchères before being driven back by enemy machine guns. The 110th Regiment was likewise stopped cold and forced back to the river, where it spent the night.[29]

Further attacks on July 29 at first accomplished little. The 42d Division attacked on a two-brigade frontage again that morning, but aside from securing Sergy and pushing the line forward a little here and there, the Americans were unable to breach the German defenses. Command confusion again caused units to intermingle, and the commanders of two companies of the 166th Regiment gave the major commanding the 2/167th a little hell for it. The major claimed they "used vile and profane language at him at this time," the officers later reported, "but as we were never given to profanity, we are of the opinion that the excitement of combat caused him to imagine this." The 55th Brigade had similar problems. Although its attack orders puzzlingly assumed that the enemy was in full flight and set attack objectives twelve kilometers north of the Ourcq, artillery support was lacking, and the 110th Regiment continued to make little progress. Finally, at 1600, two companies of the 42d Division's 2/166th Battalion on the far left came up from reserve and, despite "desperate resistance," were able to occupy Seringes-et-Nesles by 1800. Captain John A. Stevenson, commanding one of the companies, later recalled that the job was done with a bit of on-the-spot improvisation by men who were learning their trade against a canny enemy:

> Our companies were halted in an orchard and most of the men were taking refuge back of an old stone wall. I hurried toward E Co. and met [Lieutenant] Herman [Doellinger] on the way to find me. We hurriedly decided that E Co. would swing to the right and attack the village from the right flank while F Co. would proceed to the road directly ahead and attack in the general direction of the road. We moved forward in approach formation until it was necessary to halt to wait for our guns to lift fire. I remember we were not greatly impressed with our barrage and I do not believe more than one battery was firing on the village.
>
> After a minute or so the barrage lifted and we moved forward, this time by squad rushes and later by individuals. It was a relief to be in action again as we were losing men fast from the plunging machine gun fire from directly ahead and the enfilading fire from the hill to our right.
>
> We entered the village without engaging the enemy in hand to hand encounter, but at a terrible cost. The Boche machine gunners were well posted and well concealed and they fired up to the last minute before retiring to the crest of the hill overlooking the village from the northwest. . . . Mopping up parties were quickly organized and sent from house to house. But the enemy had completely withdrawn, leaving the village in our possession. Platoons were posted in strategic positions and the terrible suspense began. The enemy were now on three sides of our positions; on the left and directly ahead the machine gunners were from seventy-five to three hundred yards distant; on the right the enemy was nearly a kilometer from the village, but from his position across the valley he had excellent observation of our movements. We soon discovered that from the attics of two or three of the houses that still remained standing, we could look directly into the trenches and pits of the Boche gunners. An observer was kept

posted with strict orders under no consideration to fire; this post later proved to be invaluable.

With the tenuous capture of the village, claimed Menoher, "the backbone of the enemy's resistance on the heights north of the Ourcq [was] broken." The Germans saw fit to disagree.[30]

By July 30 Liggett was under increasing pressure from Sixth Army to move his corps forward as quickly as possible. However, the lack of American and French progress on either flank had left the Rainbow Division "sticking out like a sore thumb across the river," and Liggett had to detail elements of the US 4th Division to provide flank support. "Degoutte tried to persuade me to push my corps still farther ahead," the American recalled, "but I declined until the French got up on our right and left—my only disagreement with Degoutte, and that soon forgotten." In some respects the urge to move forward was moot anyway, since the 42d Division made no significant progress in repeated attacks that day. Despite the overall futility, acts of bravery were common—none more so than those of Sergeant Richard O'Neill of the 165th Regiment's D Company, who attacked a detachment of twenty-five Germans with only his pistol, received multiple wounds in subsequent hand-to-hand fighting, and nevertheless remained in command of his men all day. For these acts he would be awarded the Medal of Honor.[31]

It was the 28th Division's turn to enjoy a little success, supported by the now-arriving 32d Division and with the 42d Division's 168th Regiment on its left. Thankfully, the big guns had finally come up. Following an artillery preparation that was "short and violent on points of resistance," the 110th Regiment attacked at 0340 and was able to get a substantial toehold in the Bois des Grimpettes before increasing enemy fire forced it back. Another attack at 1430, again well supported by artillery, made greater progress as the 110th slowly but steadily pushed through the woods and finally cleared them, seizing the high ground north of Cierges. Although a German prisoner from the 216th Division later told his interrogators that the defenders had removed their machine guns because "there was no intention of holding the wood," the Germans attempted to counterattack, only to be driven back by the timely arrival of support from the 32d Division's 127th Regiment, which came up on the Pennsylvanians' right. It was a nice reward, as the 28th Division was pulled out of the line that night, along with the remaining elements of the US 3d Division.[32]

From this point forward, the primary American effort on the lower tip of the Marne salient would be carried out by the newly arrived US 32d Division. Organized in August 1917 from the Michigan and Wisconsin National Guard and leavened with a heavy infusion of draftees, this division was shipped to France in packets in January–March 1918. For a month it suffered the indignity of serving as a replacement division, but in May the unit was reassembled and sent to train in a quiet sector near Belfort. The 32d Division remained there until it was transferred to the vicinity of Château-Thierry in late July. Major General William Haan—born in Indiana in 1863 and graduated from West Point in 1889—took command of the division in December 1917 after Pershing decided that his predecessor, Major General James Parker (born in 1854), was too old. Haan was stolid, dependable, and popular with his men, who affectionately called him "Bunker," a sobriquet he had earned during his West Point days. Haan "ruled by love" and "commanded confidence," remembered a West Point classmate, and he "never shared the sentiment of the stay-at-homes that hostilities stopped too soon" in November 1918. "I did not," Haan said after the armistice, "want to see another of those wonderful lads jeopardized needlessly." For such a man, the learning experiences endured by the 32d Division in the Aisne-Marne must have been particularly painful.[33]

As previously noted, the 127th Regiment arrived at the front on July 30. In this case, the Americans' eagerness—typical among units entering the line for the first time—proved beneficial. The 2/127th attacked that morning without waiting for division orders and made enough progress in subsequent afternoon attacks to come up on the 110th Regiment's flank just in time to fend off a German counterattack. This led the Germans to take another step backward to a line north of Goussancourt and Cierges. But despite the 127th Regiment's success, it suffered from the disorganization and confusion common to green American formations. Companies wandered off at divergent axes and crossed into adjacent zones of advance, to the detriment of all. However, each in his own way, the individual soldiers became acclimated to the front. Sergeant Lyle S. Cole of the 125th Regiment's Company I entered the woods below Cierges that night and tried to dig a foxhole in the dark so he could get some sleep:

> Too many roots. Try a new spot, more roots. After the third try I found a place that was easier digging, got down about a foot and found more roots. I reached down to pull the roots out and the bark came off in my hand. It was so dark I could not see what I had in my hand, but from the odor I knew I had run into a Dutchman and what I had in my hand was the skin off his fingers. He was just getting ripe.

I said, "To hell with it," curled up in my blanket on the ground and went to sleep.

The hardest lessons, though, would be learned in combat.[34]

The dawn of the last day of July found the Germans clearly making preparations for a final withdrawal, but the Americans were unable to take advantage of the opportunity to strike the enemy off balance. The 42d Division did not advance at all, despite a few demonstrations on its front. The 32d Division did not get very far until Haan ordered at 1200 an advance by both his brigades "as soon as possible." The attack began just after 1400, and although the Americans made steady progress, the Germans made them pay for every step. As Sergeant Cole attacked up Hill 212 northwest of Cierges:

> Sergeant Wojezechowski, over on my left, called to me, "Let's give them hell Cole." I shouted back, "I'm with you, we will show them." The next time I looked back Wojezechowski threw up his hands, dropped his rifle, whirled around, and fell to the ground. He was a good friend of mine. . . . It made me so mad all I could think of was getting to the top and getting at those Dutch bastards. It was a sight I have dreamed of many, many times.

He would never get the opportunity to mete out revenge, however. Reaching the top of the hill with just a few other soldiers, Cole was shot in the foot by a machine gun bullet and would later be evacuated. The remaining infantrymen pushed on, and Cierges fell into American hands, but the Germans saturated it with gas. Unable to advance another step beyond the town, the doughboys abandoned their gains and pulled back. Complained the French liaison officer with the 32d Division:

> Sometimes the fighting was more in the manner of cavalry than of infantry. I mean the troops advance with dash, then fall back. For instance, the 63rd Brigade had taken Cierges. The village being then drenched with gas, the brigade evacuated it; but instead of advancing beyond the village, which is in a hollow, it withdrew to the rear, far more exposed to the view of the enemy and his fire.

Montdésir ordered the division to make a nighttime attack, but the Americans were too exhausted. Haan, meanwhile, seethed at the apparent dilatoriness of the French 4th Division on his right (which in turn blamed its shortcomings on the even slower French 18th Division to *its* right).[35]

The Germans held the line north of the Ourcq for one more day. On August 1 the US 42d and 32d Divisions attacked side by side and made next to no progress. Haan, growing increasingly irritated with the French as his casualty count climbed, claimed that Montdésir was squashing his brigades onto a frontage that was too small for them. But the primary problem was his officers' tactical inefficiency. One company of the 128th Regiment, for example, attacked directly uphill against a German machine gun. In "15 minutes of fighting the company melted away and for four days was lost as a unit of the regiment. It started 200 strong and when it was reorganized a few days later only 65 men remained." The next company that attacked the German gun was cautioned "not to rush into German machine guns out there with the whole company" but to flank the enemy position by platoons; it did so, in the process taking "only" 50 percent casualties. The division managed to capture Hill 230 and Bellevue Farm at heavy cost, but, the official 32d Division history notwithstanding, this was hardly the "key to [the] Ourcq."[36]

The French 4th Division adjacent to the Americans refused to assist the 32d Division's attack on Hill 230, on the grounds that the French had no orders to do so. Their intransigence led Colonel Glenn Garlock of the 127th Regiment to wish "a hundred times that day that those Frenchmen were ten miles away." During the battle, he blamed the French for the casualties he suffered, and after it ended, he confronted General Haan to ask why the French had not been ordered to support him. Haan replied that the "Allied High Command" had told Bullard, "Your new divisions must prove themselves before you can organize American Corps and Armies and operate independently."

> For this reason, said General Haan, General Bullard was storming up and down my room at le Charmel Château [on August 1] insisting that the 32nd Division must take Hill 230 and prove its fighting ability. If it was unequal to the task he, General Bullard, might not be allowed to take command of the Third American Corps and General Pershing might not be permitted to organize the First American Army. General Haan told Bullard the 32nd would camp on Hill 230 that night.

Regardless of whether this account is accurate, the perception that the Americans had to prove they could take objectives on their own was genuine and widespread.[37]

Though tired, the German defenders were moving back exactly on schedule, despite pressure from a fresh—though green—American division. Any time the Americans made a forward lodgment, the Germans would counterattack and, if not actually drive them back, at least set them on their heels. Instead of advancing aggressively forward, at 1910 on August 1 Haan ordered his men to take up defensive positions in anticipation of a major German counterattack supported by tanks. Corporal John D. McDaniels and his fellows in Company H of the 126th Regiment gladly spent the evening digging deep holes in the limestone hills to provide good protection. For once, they thought, the roles of attackers and defenders would be reversed, allowing them to inflict some casualties on their tormentors. Instead of attacking, though, the Germans began their grand withdrawal to the Vesle River that night.[38]

The German withdrawal to the Vesle was a model of efficiency. In Liggett's I Corps, it caught the 42d Division in the middle of preparations for relief by the US 4th Division. Brigadier General MacArthur nevertheless ordered his infantry and artillery to postpone relief operations and "advance with audacity." Colonel George Leach of the 151st Field Artillery tried to barrel through Seringes-et-Nesles in a Dodge truck with three flat tires, only to find the place choked with dead and nearly impassable: "The town is a smoking ruin and the fields covered with dead. There are dead Americans and Germans in every house. I counted 18 German machine guns in one field with the gun squads all dead at their posts. We had to remove the dead from the road before we could progress and picked our way through the shell holes." Relief could hardly be conducted on the run, however, so the Rainbow Division advanced only a short distance before stopping to allow the 4th "Ivy" Division to take over. Meanwhile, Montdésir ordered the 32d Division to "push back the enemy, [making] progress without halting so as not to allow the enemy to make a stand." The first attempts to move forward that morning were hindered by diehard German machine gunners who had remained behind to induce hesitancy in the American advance. In this they succeeded. Corporal Samuel Kent of Company K, 128th Regiment, was hit hard by his company's first casualty that morning as the Americans stormed a German machine gun nest in a steeple near Reddy Farm. A sergeant had barely raised his head to tell another man to stay down when a German bullet shot him dead. The farm soon fell, and the Americans resumed their advance that afternoon under a fine, steady rain. They advanced six kilometers but moved cautiously because of severe German gas shelling that, like the machine gunners, was intended to hold them back. The Americans were unable to catch up with any large bodies of German troops before the enemy pulled back across the Vesle that evening.[39]

By this time, the campaign was all but over. Soissons had fallen, and the Marne salient was no more. In the central sector where American troops were active, the Germans had established a strong line behind the Vesle and were busily preparing a second line of defense along the Aisne, twenty kilometers farther north. There were, however, a few dramas remaining to be played out. One—not the type generally noted by historians keen to chronicle the movements of battalions and regiments—occurred as Father Francis Duffy watched the remains of the Rainbow Division pull back from the lines after its ordeal of the past two weeks:

Back came our decimated battalions along the way they had already traveled. They marched in wearied silence until they came to the slopes around Meurcy Farm. Then from end to end of the line came the sound of dry, suppressed sobs. They were marching among the bodies of their unburied dead. In the stress of battle there had been but little time to think of them—all minds had been turned on victory. But the men who lay there were dearer to them than kindred, dearer than life; and these strong warriors paid their bashful involuntary tribute to the ties of love and long regret that bind brave men to the memory of their departed comrades.[40]

The 4th Division had relieved the 42d and resumed the advance on August 3 as far as Chéry-Chartreuve, but orders to attack again after dark and push the line fully five kilometers north of the Vesle came to nothing when the 59th Brigade lost its way in the dark and managed only to establish some outposts south of the river. The 32d Division also made it to the south bank of the Vesle, advancing another seven kilometers past burning enemy supply dumps that provided indications of what seemed to be a precipitate retreat. However, as Haan noted, "From this point forward, a very considerable resistance was met, so much that the advance elements were withdrawn to keep them from heavy losses due to a nearly continuous fire of artillery and machine guns." Corporal Kent was encouraged by the sight of French peasants moving back into their liberated villages with their wheelbarrows full of possessions, calling out to the Americans, "'Boche, capoot—Allemand, par bon' . . . to which we respond, lustily, 'yah, yah, and oui, oui' much to their amusement." Rain, however, made the doughboys wet and miserable. Many of them were falling sick from dysentery after sipping water out of shell holes as they moved forward. As Haan's division approached Fismes on the south bank of the Vesle, he hesitated to make preparations to cross the river with the help of engineers, despite urgent prodding from

Montdésir. "The town of Fismes," Haan reported, "is located in the valley and undoubtedly will be heavily shelled as soon as occupied by our troops." No further advance would be made this day.[41]

August 4 brought the US 4th Division up to the Vesle on the left and the 32d Division to the outskirts of Fismes on the right. This village—which, with Fismette, its smaller twin on the north bank, would become the scene of savage fighting over the next month—posed a major obstacle. The Vesle River was about six feet deep and thirty-five feet wide here, choked with debris, and its bridges were partially wrecked. Both Fismes and the low ground adjoining it were under full observation from enemy guns on the north bank, making it "an almost invincible barrier." As Haan had predicted, the Germans shelled Fismes and its outskirts vigorously with high explosives and gas as the Americans—now under the command of US III Corps (Bullard), but with Montdésir's earlier orders to force the Vesle still in place—worked their way into the town. Haan had recovered his confidence, deciding after a personal view of Fismes that his men could both take the town and cross the river. "It is my opinion that we can throw bridges across the river tonight and cross a force over without much difficulty," he reported. The 3/127th and 2/126th penetrated the village in rushes. Despite serious casualties inflicted by roving German patrols and well-placed machine guns, the doughboys occupied most of the place by nightfall. However, because "we were having a considerable number of casualties [from enemy artillery and machine guns] without accomplishing anything, during the day time," Haan told his brigade commanders to "hold the front with [a] very thin line of combat troops" and prepare for a river crossing that night. Only a few patrols were able to make it across, however, before the Germans drove them back. An escaped French prisoner told the Americans that the Germans had organized strong defenses north of the river, especially around Fismette. Nevertheless, at 2245 Bullard announced, "It is not believed that the enemy intends to make a serious resistance between the Vesle and the Aisne Rivers, but probably proposes to re-establish himself north of the Aisne."[42]

After a few minor movements on August 5 under pouring rain, and while German artillery stepped up its efforts to obliterate Fismes from the face of the earth, the campaign to reduce the Marne salient officially ended on August 6. In broad terms, the Americans had successfully aided French forces in following up the German withdrawal necessitated by the Soissons offensive and the actions preceding it. The Germans, however, had fulfilled their objectives by pulling back in good order and on their own schedule, while severely bloodying the units opposing them. The 32d Division, relieved on

August 6–7 by the 28th Division, had suffered 4,701 casualties. Haan's doughboys thought they had achieved elite status. Wrote Corporal Kent: "We feel as tho we are now veterans and are ready and fit for any job—in fact, I understand we are designated as 'shock troops'"—allegedly, the French called them *"Soldats le Terrible."* The men of the 28th Division, meanwhile—now fully assembled as a division at the front, after many dispiriting weeks of being detached by everything from companies to brigades—looked forward to showing what they could do on the Vesle.[43]

The so-called Aisne-Marne campaign (perhaps more accurately denoted the Vesle-Marne campaign, since American forces did not reach the Aisne until September) figures hardly at all in the annals of modern American military history. Though regrettable, the neglect is understandable in light of the fact that US forces accomplished nothing tangible that had not already been decided at Soissons and earlier. Most evaluations of the campaign point to the intangibles. For example, the campaign supposedly marked the beginning of a period of greater Franco-American cooperation, constituted the final precursor to a more important American role on the western front, and demonstrated how American forces were providing a significant boost to French morale. The divisions involved relearned many of the lessons that had supposedly been learned earlier, and this time those lessons were taking hold. "The AEF was now making its presence felt in a decisive way," comments Pershing biographer Donald Smythe. The 270,000 American troops that contributed in those late summer days "had a salutary effect on the morale of the Allied forces," says David Trask. But the lessons were not all positive.[44]

The 369th Regiment, attached to the French 161st Division with Gouraud's Fourth Army, entered the front lines in battalion detachments at various points during the offensive. Although they learned some tough lessons—particularly with respect to gas—the African American doughboys conducted themselves well under bombardments and during patrols. They were not given assignments involving any great responsibility, however, and under the pressure of intense German shelling, some of the men began to suspect that the French "were using them up to spare the lives of their countrymen." That concern was mild, however, compared with the insult delivered by Pershing's GHQ in late July when orders arrived—while the regiment was in combat at the Butte du Mesnil—that all its black officers would be transferred and replaced by white officers. Even under French command, the Harlem Rattlers were not immune from American racism.[45]

More broadly speaking, as both American and French staff officers realized, the performance of units such as the US 26th, 32d, and 42d Divisions, though creditable, pointed to problems in the AEF that could only be regarded as endemic. On August 7 Pershing issued his "Notes on Recent Operations No. 1" and ordered it disseminated down to the company level. Incorporating observations made at Soissons and in the Aisne-Marne campaign, it highlighted the usual problems. Attack formations were sloppy, and units intermingled during the advance. Infantry seemed incapable of practicing basic tenets of fire and maneuver against enemy machine guns. Rifles and automatic rifles were not used to provide covering fire, and the doughboys all too often discarded their frustrating but valuable Chauchats in favor of rifles picked up from the dead and wounded. Grenades were poorly supplied and not used properly when available. Stokes mortars and one-pounders were not employed effectively. Machine guns (as widely reported) were too often neglected or badly used in the attack. Written instructions and maps were not widely distributed. The list went on and on.[46]

Liggett, as already noted, was highly critical of the performance of the 26th Division. And while he damned that division with faint praise in his postwar memoirs, he waxed relatively lyrical in the same work about the performance of the Rainbow Division. As his report on the service of I Corps with French Sixth Army from July 4 to August 14 pointed out, however, General Edwards's many faults were also applicable to other units in the AEF. To make his point, Liggett drew a stark comparison between General Schmidt's French 167th Division, which had fought under his command, and the Americans. "The endurance of the 167th Division as a small unit continuously in action, is worthy of note," he stated. Numbering at most 9,000 men with only about 5,000 "rifles," the division had been in action continuously from June 20 to July 26—frequently attacking. The 26th Division (and the 42d and 32d, though Liggett did not make the comparison), by contrast, endured only a fraction of that time. Moreover, the command problems evident in the 26th Division had "demonstrated clearly the necessity for supervision by the higher command of the use of infantry battalions and a well-organized system of maneuver to prevent smaller units escaping from divisional control." Liggett was a stickler for command control, and his annoyance with Edwards was by now common knowledge. As any thinking observer could deduce, however, the failings he pointed out in the 26th Division had been experienced to greater or lesser degrees in every other American division that had gone into the line—including the vaunted 1st and 2d Divisions. And in late July and early August, well after the Yankee

Division had departed I Corps, continuing clumsy American tactics led Liggett to issue "Tactical Instructions—Means for Overcoming the Enemy's Machine Gun Defense" for attacks along the Ourcq and Vesle.[47]

The French, of course, observed many of the same problems, but their views were not as welcome at American headquarters. Colonel De Poumayrac, French liaison officer to Dickman's 3d Division, wrote a blistering report on August 1 about that division's performance from July 19 to 29. In sum, the report is nothing less than astonishing. De Poumayrac's many complaints about the Americans included the following: poor dissemination of attack orders, poor internal liaison, command posts set too far back, insufficient reports from front-line officers, poor infantry-artillery liaison, and poor use of machine guns and infantry support guns. At times, American infantry made inadequate use of cover and infiltration tactics:

> This method would have reduced the losses considerably. Too much importance has been attached to the maintenance of "a line." . . . The advance of certain units has been too often delayed in order to wait for the neighbours on the right and left. . . . The American platoon seems to be rather heavy. The combat group of the French army (1/2 platoon) is less visible, more flexible and more appropriate for infiltration. When advancing in line of one, the American platoon forms a long caterpillar which is too easily sighted by enemy artillery. The men walk too close to each other; they should be ten paces apart, or behind the other. The columns should have between them a space of 30 to 40 yards, to escape being hit by the same shell.

One imagines the French colonel pausing to draw a deep breath before continuing in the same vein. The American infantry carried too much equipment, he groused, and the "food supply has generally not been very satisfactory. Some companies have had no hot meal for several days." The men ate their iron rations too early. Officers didn't give their men enough rest. Stretcher bearers carried the wounded too far back in the rear. There were not enough reserve officers. Resting troops failed to use camouflage to conceal their positions. There was poor traffic management. American engineers were slow to repair roads. Dead horses and men were not buried quickly enough. As if this were not enough, De Poumayrac issued another long, hectoring report on August 3, further dissecting American tactics and comparing them unfavorably with the French. Compliments were scarce. Though undoubtedly accurate in many if not all respects, De Poumayrac's reports help explain the dismal state of Franco-American relations at US 3d Division headquarters and elsewhere. Dickman's annoyance at reading these reports is easy to imagine.[48]

German prisoners captured by French Sixth Army reinforced impressions of American tactical inefficiency and the pointless wastage of manpower:

> The Americans sacrifice their troops needlessly by close formation, by needless headlong rushes at machine-gun nests, and by insufficient attention of soldiers to their shelter from German fire. . . . One prisoner declared: "I am sure that my company without casualties on one occasion mowed down three American companies." . . . An enemy officer declared: "The Americans advance in close formation. They attack slowly without paying attention to bullets instead of going forward by jumps and seeking occasional cover."

French officers pointedly relayed these reports to the Americans. Despite Liggett's professed attempts to get the message through to his troops, however, such admonitions had little effect.[49]

Once these disparaging comparisons between the French and the Americans got going, they were hard to stop. Of course, not all evaluations were negative. Mangin's summary of the performance of the American troops with his Tenth Army from July 16 to August 5, transmitted through US liaison officer Captain David Gray to Chief of Staff James McAndrew at GHQ on August 16, concluded that the Americans "as troops [were] potentially of the first order. He considers them primarily as troops of attack." Confessed Mangin (as explained by Gray):

> [French effectiveness] was increased not only by the physical aid of the American troops under his command but by their effect on the general morale. . . . The effect of friendly international rivalry is valuable. . . . The presence in line of American troops made for increased confidence and elan, as the French troops had visual evidence of the presence and aid of their allies. . . . He reports throughout the operation a most satisfactory relation between American and French personnel of all grades.[50]

After the war ended, however, Major General Robert L. Howze, commander of the US 3d Division, provided GHQ with a "frank statement" based on wartime reports and testimony. According to Howze, Franco-

American relations at 3d Division headquarters remained intact (barely) because of "the generosity and whole-hearted forbearance of the Americans when any conflict of opinion arose." Howze's sources indicated that American soldiers conducted better patrols than the French and that, during the Aisne-Marne campaign, "the American troops showed themselves far superior to the French, who did not seem to have the dash and vim so necessary to the successful and continual carrying-on of an offensive action." Bad feelings toward the French still persisted one month after the armistice, in part because "the opinion prevails among all ranks of the Division that the French assigned the meanest and most difficult sectors to the American troops." In conclusion, Howze argued that the Americans had shown themselves "quicker to think, resourceful, philosophical, of excellent physique, and, above all, [more] practical" than the French, who even practiced poor traffic control! Brigadier General Sladen backed up Howze's report with one of his own, arguing that the Americans were much more efficient than the French.[51]

Internally, some Americans were willing to look more honestly at American operations in the Aisne-Marne campaign and make more objective comparisons with the French, although their opinions were not always well received. "Study Showing Accomplishments of American Divisions which Attacked under Command of the French or British," found in the G-3 correspondence files in the National Archives, includes an undated report by Lieutenant Colonel X. H. Price titled "Operations of the 26th, 3rd, 42nd, 32nd, 4th and 28th Divisions in Connection with the Reduction of the Aisne-Marne Salient." In it, Price concluded:

> These operations do not prove that "no advance was made by the Allies until our troops got in." . . . There is no question but what our troops put morale in the French troops. . . . [But] it is interesting to note that American divisions state that the American divisions alongside of them were behind as much as they state the French divisions were. In other words our proof that the French divisions were behind is all on one side and, of course, taken from one of our divisional reports.

Blasphemously, Price suggested that the French and British were already doing well when the Americans arrived and that, on the whole, the Americans had done better during the war when fighting alongside the French and British than when fighting in conjunction with other American units: "When our divisions attacked with the French and British they practically always did better than the average division in the attack and in a majority of cases did the best," he opined. A handwritten note at the end of Price's report perhaps needlessly points out that the opinions are his own "and have never been accepted by higher authority."[52]

Liggett's I Corps is notable with respect to the cordiality maintained between its staff officers and the French at all levels. With Liggett, Degoutte never experienced the problems he had with other American commanders. In his I Corps report, Liggett stated that he enjoyed "cordial relations with the 6th French Army, the French corps and divisions":

> General Degoutte took a close personal interest in the work of the 1st Corps. By almost daily visits to Corps headquarters he maintained an intimate contact with affairs that prevented the possibility of a misunderstanding. His staff as a unit and the individual officers with whom the Corps came into contact exemplified the spirit which ruled in all operations with French units—cordial personal relations and service to the troops the keynote of all action.

Appendices by Liggett's staff further praised the French and did not always credit the Americans. Lieutenant Colonel Noble B. Judah, assistant chief of staff in G-2, reiterated that relations with the French were "at all times close and cordial, without any conditions arising that suggested a strain." Contradicting complaints about slow French neighbors and the open American flanks that plagued the Aisne-Marne (just as they had other battles), Judah remarked that while the Americans may have been a little more effective, this was often "owing to their characteristics of advancing regardless of losses while the French showed a tendency to conserve their strength in view of the relatively slight importance of the operation [a minor attack around Vaux]." Judah also admitted that, with respect to American troops, "The characteristic . . . of getting there, whatever it cost, took them ahead faster, but at the same time it exhausted them much more quickly. As a result the American Divisions had to be relieved oftener than the French. . . . [Thus, all things considered] the French troops were at least as efficient as the Americans."[53]

Such reports provided obvious lessons. Put simply, the Americans were courageous and had much to learn, and the French were courageous and had much to teach. And given that the Germans were still more than capable of inflicting pain, much work remained to be done. Lives depended on it. Yet while Liggett's command provided a shining example of how the Franco-American relationship could work effectively and with mutual respect, Dickman's 3d Division was an object lesson in how much could go wrong when understanding was absent on both sides. Of these lessons, however, Pershing's command seems to have been largely oblivious. Of all the American units on the western front in August 1918, the US 3d and 28th Divisions probably had the most reason to be displeased with the French, with grievances dating back to the Marne Defensive of July 15 and beyond. But instead of being rested preparatory to assignment to the US First Army, the "Rock of the Marne" division was unceremoniously broken up yet again on August 2, and its 6th Brigade was assigned to French III Corps along the Vesle. That assignment would not go well. Nor would that of the 28th Division. Though fighting as part of US III Corps under Bullard's command, the 28th was subjected to a whim of Degoutte's that would place it out on a limb at Fismes-Fismette and vulnerable to German counterattack. The flame-drenched end to the 28th Division's ordeal at Fismette on August 27 nearly doomed any hope of continued Franco-American tactical cooperation in World War I.

16

Tragedy at Fismette

Travails of the 28th Division, August 1918

The Second Battle of the Marne, of which the Soissons and Aisne-Marne campaigns were components, inflicted a crushing defeat on the German army. In the course of destroying the salient, the French and Americans captured 29,000 German soldiers, more than 3,000 machine guns, and several hundred cannon. As French and American forces drew up along the Vesle in early August, Foch implemented plans for operations to clear out the major German salient remaining in French territory, after which it was hoped that hammer blows in the autumn would wreck the kaiser's forces and end the war by 1919. The first of these operations, launched by the British and French (with some American help) against the Montdidier-Amiens salient on August 8, was devastatingly successful, leading Ludendorff to call it the "black day" of the German army. The allies captured 29,000 Germans in the offensive's first four days, and they would double that number as the offensive continued through the end of the month. The next step, delegated to the Americans, would be to eliminate the Saint-Mihiel salient below Verdun.[1]

By comparison, the fighting along the Vesle and Aisne Rivers, which would carry on through August and into September, looked like a sideshow. Pershing and his staff at GHQ, preoccupied with organizing US First Army and planning for the big offensive at Saint-Mihiel, had little time to spare for troops on the Vesle. To some extent, they were right to set their sights on bigger things. Although the Germans had established a defensive line along the Vesle that they clearly intended to hold, no one had any illusions that a campaign to force them back to the Aisne would win the

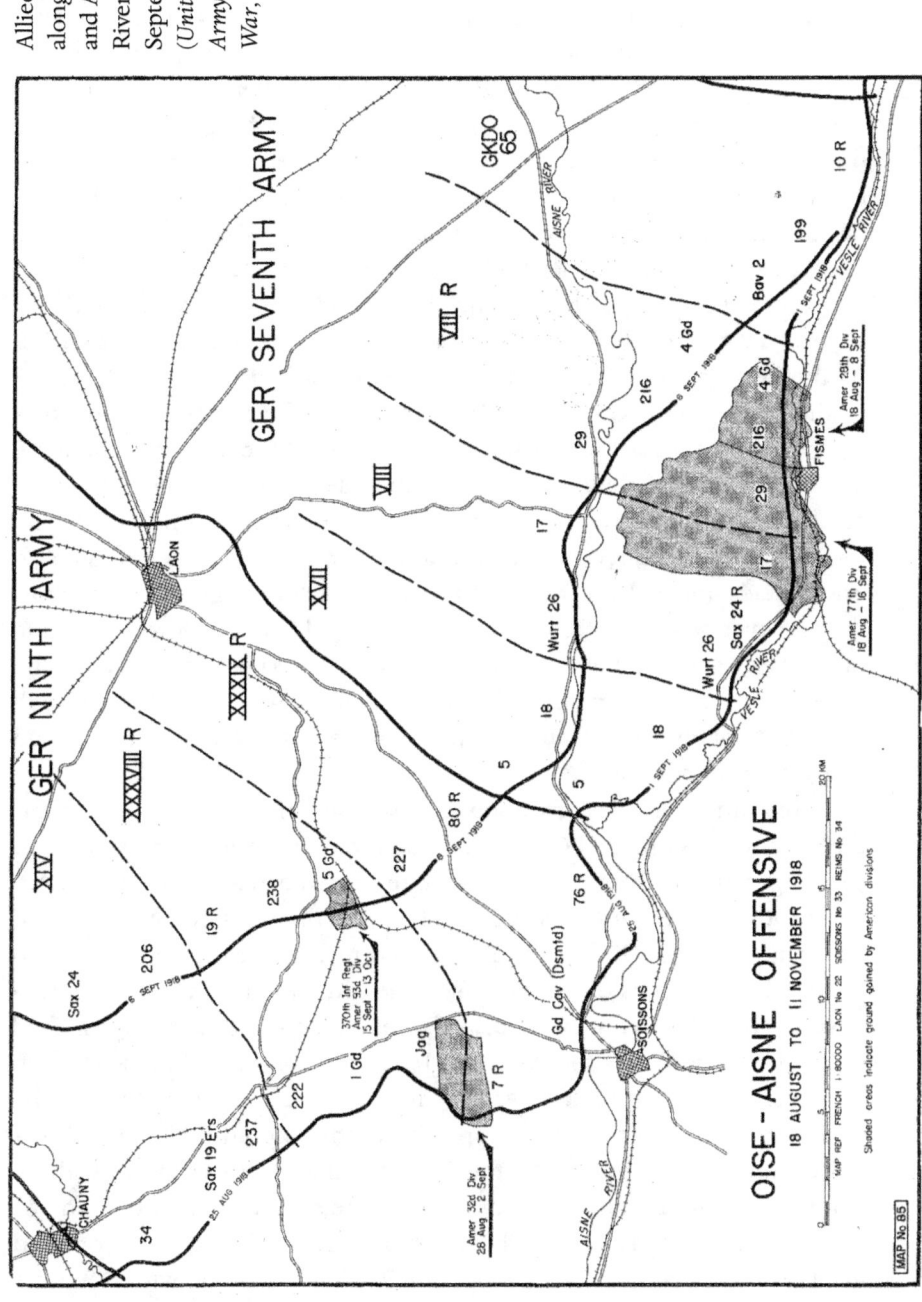

Allied positions along the Vesle and Aisne Rivers, August–September 1918. (*United States Army in the World War*, 6:203)

war. And for much of August, such a campaign seemed a long way off. To the men of the American divisions in US III Corps and other American units still fighting under French command, however, the final bloody acts of that summer would encapsulate everything that was wrong with the amalgamation idea and reinforce the necessity of uniting the AEF under a single American command.

In announcing the closing of the Aisne-Marne offensive at 2035 on August 6, Pétain stated, "The enemy seems to be establishing himself strongly on the Vesle. A decisive action with powerful means is necessary to dislodge him." He subsequently ordered that all bridgeheads north of the river be "preserved, widened, and reinforced," with a view to preparing for the "decisive blow" toward the Aisne that would take place at some future, unspecified time. No such bridgeheads existed in the area of US III Corps or in adjacent areas, but Degoutte warned on August 6 that "this situation on the Vesle is not to last any longer," and he ordered the "establishment of the bridgeheads north of the Vesle to permit the construction of footbridges across the river for the later continuation of the offensive." Multiple attempts would be made to comply with this directive at different points, but the most aggressive were undertaken by Bullard's US III Corps. Following Degoutte's directive, Bullard ordered the 28th Division to establish bridgeheads north of the Vesle. At 2230 on August 6, Muir issued Field Order 14, which stated: "A General attack by the 3rd Corps to force a crossing of the Vesle and to establish bridgeheads for the purpose of protecting the crossing of our main bodies will be made tomorrow. . . . This advance will be made towards the plateau 4 km. north of Fismes in two main bodies and one secondary column."[2]

Three American divisions stood abreast along the Vesle. On the left was the US 4th Division (US I Corps). This division, primarily with its 47th and 59th Regiments in front, would cross to the north bank of the Vesle on August 7, but despite numerous attempts between then and August 11, when it was relieved by the US 77th Division, it was unable to storm the heights to the north and take its objective at Bazoches. In the center was the US 28th Division (US III Corps), with dispositions at Fismes-Fismette (described later). To its right was the unlucky US 3d Division's 6th Brigade (French III Corps). Although Bullard was not in charge of Dickman's brigade, he met with him and other American officers throughout the area and was a little surprised at how testy the Franco-American relationship had become. He found Dickman and his staff "quite critical and fault-finding of the French command under which they had been serving." Harbord and his staff in the US 2d Division, which had fought under and with Degoutte in June, were "equally critical of the French command," and "in both cases French commanders had fully reciprocated, severely criticizing especially the chiefs-of-staff of these American divisions but somewhat passing over the division commanders." Sensing a real problem, Bullard "thought fit to caution the commanders of both American divisions to be more careful with the French."[3]

Unfortunately, the 6th Brigade's experiences over the next few days would only make things worse. This brigade arrived at the Vesle on August 7 and made numerous unsuccessful attempts to force the river until it was relieved by the French 164th Division on August 10. These failures caused more friction between the 3d Division and the French. Dickman later related with some bitterness how the 6th Brigade's commander, Brigadier General Charles Crawford, had been "reprimanded by a French general" for failures that resulted, in Dickman's opinion, from factors beyond his control and unrealistic attack orders. "One of the French generals, known as 'the Butcher' [in fact, Mangin, not Degoutte, was known by this name]," Dickman recalled, "was quite free with orders imposing conditions of service and setting tasks for American troops which he knew were out of the question with his own veterans. . . . The young American soldiers had no inclination to hold back, and were not skillful in evading orders." Bullard described the friction with somewhat greater nuance:

> Just relieved from the front lines for rest, this brigade was ordered back to reinforce a weak French corps. In returning under trying conditions of fatigue, darkness, and ill-known roads, its orders were changed by the French commander, causing (for no good reason, said the general and his officers) further fatigue and confusion. It was this very thing—this changing of orders—which the 3d Division had been criticizing in the French command. The brigade apparently became stubborn and the orders were but ill, or not at all, executed. . . . Preceding and succeeding this were other failures of the same brigade to meet higher commanders' expectations as to promptness, vigour, and energy, against the enemy. Altogether these things resulted shortly in the general's losing his brigade.

Of course, Crawford's shortcomings were not acknowledged to the French.[4]

The 28th Division, standing initially between the US 4th and 3d Divisions, entered the lines below the Vesle with its left roughly at Mont St. Martin, Perles (exclusive), and Blanzy-les-Fismes and its right at Fismes, Baslieux (exclusive), and Glennes. The 56th Brigade held the front, with the 112th Reg-

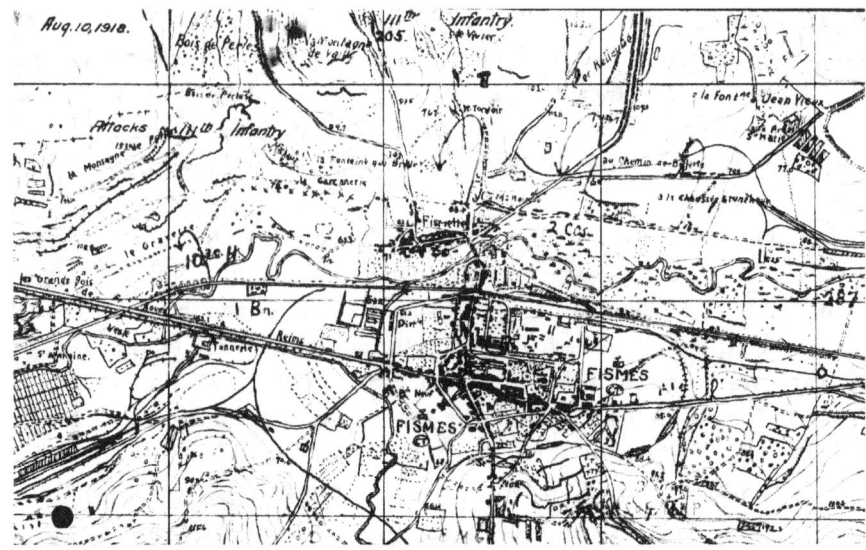

Fismes-Fismette, August 1918. (Contemporary map, courtesy National Archives)

iment in and around Fismes. It was supported by the 109th Machine Gun Battalion stationed mainly on heights overlooking Fismes from the southwest. The 111th Regiment was in support, while the 55th Brigade remained in reserve. For better or worse, this division would carry the primary burden of Degoutte's directive to take and hold bridgeheads north of the Vesle.

Nineteen-year-old Corporal Harold Pierce of Company A, 1/112th, was not unduly impressed as he approached Fismes for the first time from the valley below: "A white cloud of gas and smoke hovers over the town but otherwise it looks peaceful enough," he observed. That changed on the evening of August 7, when his company moved past an old mill and railroad track into Fismes, where two large fires burned "lustily in the town sending a red glow into the sky." Shells began to fall as the doughboys ran past a wrecked Dodge staff car, smaller fires crackling with exploding cartridges, and corpses; the "streets [were] littered with fallen buildings, shell holes, poles, wires and other debris." It got worse. Despite claims that the departing 32d Division had "captured" Fismes, the place was still full of German snipers who had either filtered back into town from the north bank or never been dealt with in the first place.[5]

The cross-shaped town of Fismes was about three times the size of its smaller twin, Fismette, which lay across the Vesle to the north. Many buildings were clustered along the west-east Rouen-Reims road that paralleled the river. However, most of Fismes's buildings lined another road that en-

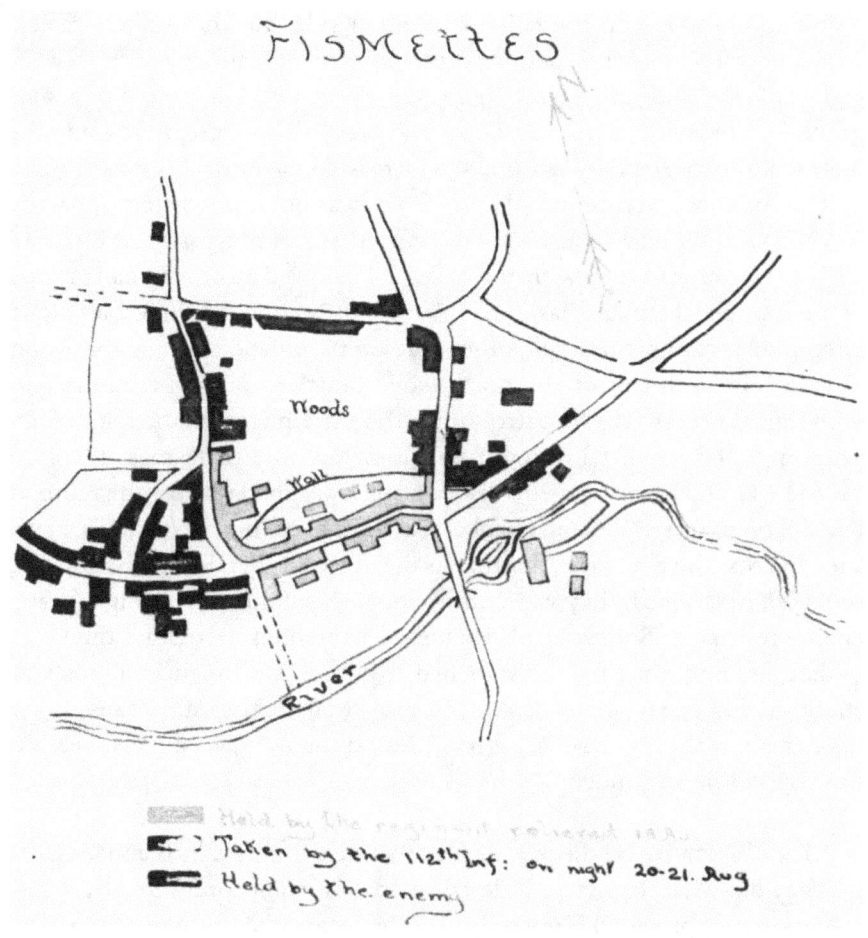

Fismette, August 1918. (Contemporary map, courtesy National Archives)

tered the Vesle valley from the south, traversed the town, crossed the river on a (partially wrecked) bridge, entered Fismette, and, after taking a sharp right turn, climbed the heights to the north. Just east of the bridge was an old wagon ford that allowed better (and safer) access across the river, but since most of the doughboys didn't know about it, they crossed on the bridge. A west-east railroad also passed through Fismes close to the riverbank. Across the Vesle, Fismette's stone buildings lay primarily on a west-east axis, mostly along a road that branched west from where the main road from Fismes turned northeast and headed up the heights. Farther west, another road—the "Rue Cervante"—plunged directly down the heights into Fismette, providing a natural avenue of penetration for any attackers from the north. Nestled in the bottom of the valley, both villages were clearly visible to observers on the heights to either side, but the well-concealed German defenders were better served by artillery amply stocked with high-explosive and gas shells. There was about two kilometers of rising ground dotted with farms, haystacks, and orchards and bisected by numerous ravines between Fismette and the plateau to the north.[6]

The Americans' tenuous hold on Fismes was not immediately apparent to Muir, who at Bullard's instructions ordered a prompt crossing of the river by "small groups of men with auto rifles . . . followed by other small groups of men in checkerboard fashion." The 112th Regiment's three battalions attempted to comply multiple times that afternoon and evening, following a weak bombardment of the north bank, but they did so hesitantly and with slight success. At 1230 patrols from the 3/112th crossed the river on an impromptu bridge of fallen logs two kilometers west of Fismes at a place called Le Grand Savart and established a weak perimeter below the railroad embankment near "Château Diable." Companies of the 1/112th and 2/112th tried to cross the river later, but thanks in part to the detailed but confusing orders they received, they were unsure how to counter surprisingly heavy enemy resistance. Some patrols wandered around Fismette for a time, but by late evening, they had all returned to Fismes. In his incisive postwar study of this engagement, Colonel Lanza thought the Americans might have made real progress if they had pressed their attacks aggressively on this day, but he concluded:

> Lack of initiative on the part of subordinate commanders is apparent. They did what they were ordered to do, but when confronted by situations not provided for in orders, stood by and did nothing. Companies making attacks were followed by troops who watched the failure of those in front, without serious effort to come to their assistance. This is a defect due to lack of training and lack of confidence, and was general throughout the American forces at this time.[7]

While these halting attacks were under way, Muir came up to visit the headquarters of the 112th Regiment, which was commanded by Colonel George Rickards. There, Muir gathered information firsthand, none of it pleasant. The Vesle, he discovered, was unfordable in the thirty yards directly between Fismes and Fismette. This meant the attackers would have to either charge directly over a rickety plank footbridge the American pioneers had set up next to the half-ruined bridge or cross elsewhere and approach Fismette obliquely from the west or east. Worse, the general learned that Fismette and the slopes above were "filled with Boche," and those slopes held numerous ideal spots for concealing batteries and machine guns. From these, the Germans could easily hold Fismes and Fismette in enfilade, making a real advance up the heights above Fismette impossible unless units were supported in strength simultaneously on both flanks. Perhaps most troubling, Muir—like Corporal Pierce—learned that Fismes was still polluted not only with enemy snipers but also with German machine gun nests. Muir thereupon contacted Bullard and told him, "It would be suicidal to attempt the crossing as first contemplated in division order." He suggested postponing further operations until the following morning so that he could fully secure Fismes and gather more intelligence about Fismette. Muir ordered Rickards to clear Fismes; thus began what the colonel called a "quiet search" for Germans in the town. "One sniper," Rickards reported, "fastened to a tree in the wood on the left flank, was shot out, but remained hanging by the foot, head down, from a seat in the tree."[8]

With Fismes at last firmly under American control, Colonel Rickards consulted with the officers of the 2/112th at midnight and decided to ask permission to attack Fismette again in the morning. Muir, who by now was satisfied that the crossing would be difficult but not impossible, granted permission and secured some artillery support. The guns opened up on the north bank at 0400, and an hour later the Americans hotfooted it across the footbridge and into Fismette. They were able to hold on there for only a short time before converging machine gun and artillery fire—some of the latter, Corporal Pierce claimed, coming from American guns—drove them back. After another bombardment lasting two and a half hours, the 2/112th attacked again at 1330, this time more carefully and following a rolling barrage that ripped through Fismette. Fighting desperately, they were able to gain footholds in the southern and eastern parts of the village and took forty prisoners. It wasn't much, but at least they had made a start. Overnight the infantry worked its way forward to take most of the village, including its west-east thoroughfare. American artillery worked hard that evening and night to degrade German defenses above the village, but the enemy retaliated in kind.[9]

August 9 dawned with the Americans in Fismette just trying to hold on. "Very intense" German artillery fire, including gas, descended on the village all day, making relief difficult. Harold Pierce and his brother Hugh were among those who had to make the dash across the footbridge in daylight that afternoon, at their captain's direct orders:

> He commands to go and we start as fast as our legs can go, over the bridge past a big dud aerial bomb. I see my brother Hugh fall and I

think he is shot but he has only jumped into a hole in the bridge and we all follow him in to get our wind. Two dead men are lying half in the water. We climb out again and run to the end of the bridge and turn quickly to the left into the houses. Near the first house an American is lying so covered with rock dust he looks like a marble man.

Pierce found some doughboys in a house; they were sniping at Germans and cutting notches in their barrels to count the kills. The men were out of cigarettes and so desperate that they had been smoking leaves. Pierce didn't smoke, so he "hand[ed] out packs of Camels and Chesterfields and know how the Good Samaritan felt. I am a hero, a saint, a philanthropist in their eyes. . . . They inhale and relax." Beyond, he found houses filled with wounded and killed—the doughboys had been too afraid to carry them back to Fismes. Pierce, his brother, and the others were then sent to join the doughboys behind a stone wall along the north end of Fismette's west-east street. The Americans behind the wall fired uphill into an orchard, where they heard but did not see a gun firing, ignoring their officer's admonitions to conserve their ammunition:

> Hugh claims it is an American gun and does not get down although it is firing steady now and the crack of its bullets are plain now over our heads. I yell at him to get down but he laughs and fires another shot. I jump and grab him around the neck and shoulders and throw him to the ground heavily and light on top of him. Just then a leaf comes tumbling out of the peach branches cut by a bullet not over a foot over his head. He is willing to admit I am right. . . . [Later], the men open fire together as if the whole German army are marching down the streets. Quickly I shift my Springfield to the right to get in a shot. As I shoot a man from "F" Company next to me drops to the ground as if dead. I had the muzzle about six inches from his ear. He is out for a few seconds, then rolls onto his back, stares to the sky and asks me where he is hit. A sergeant next to him, whose ear drums were almost broken, curses at me but the one who was knocked out says "Never mind buddy." I settle back of the wall ashamed but then my intentions were good.[10]

Lieutenant Bob Hoffman of the 111th Regiment, just moving in to relieve the 112th Regiment, also spent time exploring Fismette, walking behind the trigger-happy doughboys along the stone wall and taking a moment to peer up the Rue Cervante that entered from the north:

I could see the famous Rue Cervante, which I came to know so well. For the next five days that was to be the scene of my worst battle of the war. . . . It was one of the most futile, most horrible experiences of the American army. German soldiers were lying the entire way up this street. There was a barricade part-way up, behind which either the French troops long before, or the Americans, had made their stand. The Germans had come down the street under cover of machine gun fire and artillery fire from the hills, as they were to do several times during our occupancy of the city, only to be stopped by our troops at the barricade.

Multiple German attempts to attack down that street, including a vigorous effort to storm the village at 1620 on August 9, were turned back by Americans at the barricade and behind the stone wall. The attackers—members of the German 4th Guards Division—would be back. Meanwhile, all that afternoon and evening the Germans filtered snipers and machine gunners into Fismette to undermine American control of the town.[11]

On the night of August 9–10, Hoffman's 1/111th Battalion entered Fismette to relieve the 1/112th and 2/112th. For many of the doughboys with the newly arrived battalion, the next few hours would be something akin to hell and would scar them for the rest of their lives. More than fifty years later, Private Duncan Kemerer of Company B, 1/111th, would remember racing desperately across the shell-torn bridge, down the west-east main street in Fismette, and into an abandoned building with part of his platoon. Some of the doughboys took up positions on the first or second floor, but Kemerer went into the basement, where his buddy found a French magazine and read it with his feet propped up on a stove. Nervous, Kemerer looked outside and saw a German barrage closing in—the enemy had seen the Americans enter the building. In a near panic, Kemerer decided that the doorway was the safest place to take shelter. And sure enough, two shells hit the building directly, killing eight men, including his buddy in the basement, and hurling Kemerer twenty feet into the street. He climbed to his feet without helmet, rifle, or gas mask, his uniform in shreds, and his back covered with his own blood from a head wound.

In pain and terror-stricken, Kemerer raced toward the river, but a soldier grabbed him and pulled him into a dugout containing an aid station. Still in a daze, Kemerer docilely waited in line until only one wounded soldier remained between him and the doctor. Suddenly, yet another shell landed in the dugout entrance, blowing to pieces the wounded man in front of Kemerer. Overwhelmed, and having gone without food or water for two to three days, he fainted. When he recovered consciousness, Kemerer was lying on the dugout's dirt floor, and more shells were pounding the ceiling overhead. His mind cracked. Screaming desperately, Kemerer scrabbled to dig a hole in the floor for protection—and mercifully lost consciousness again. He recovered awareness briefly some hours later as he was being evacuated through Fismes and eventually ended up as a shell-shock patient at a hospital in Chaumont. In the ward, if someone so much as dropped a spoon on the floor, Kemerer would shriek and dive under the covers—but only three weeks later, the doctors deemed him fully recovered and sent him back to the front.[12]

Back in Fismette, the trials were just beginning. According to Bullard, the always aggressive Degoutte was "demonstrating great impatience at not being allowed to push the enemy hard." In addition, the Frenchman was allegedly fearful that his army would be dissolved in upcoming consolidations, and he wanted to show what he could do. Thus Degoutte "was constantly insisting upon raids from these small points with a view to enlarging his 'bridgeheads.'" Although Bullard apparently did not demur at the time, he later wrote in his memoirs, "These small operations seemed to me to offer no chance worth the risk and loss of life"—especially in view of the fact that neighboring French corps were not being asked to take such an aggressive posture. In any event, Bullard ordered Muir to attempt to expand the primary bridgehead to strengthen the lodgment and wipe out at least some of the enemy machine guns tormenting the village. Following an artillery bombardment, the 1/111th would attack uphill to capture a spur northwest of Fismette and, if that operation was successful, capture another spur to the northeast. To the west, meanwhile, the 2/111th, which had taken over the tiny bridgehead established by the 3/112th below the railroad at Grand Savart, would seek to seize the aptly named and well-fortified Château Diable. The attacks would commence at dawn.[13]

This would be no reckless frontal assault by doughboys moving in thick waves. Following Bullard's instructions that he was not to launch a general attack but send out "strong reconnoitering parties" to first probe the strength of enemy defenses, Muir specified that his companies would carefully follow a creeping barrage, advancing at about 100 meters every five minutes in small squads supported by automatic riflemen and using infiltration tactics to penetrate enemy positions. Once reached, the "final objective will be held, consolidated and reinforced," Muir ordered, "thus enlarging our bridgehead for the crossing of the main body." To the west, the 2/111th successfully stormed the Château Diable and captured about thirty enemy machine guns, although it proved unable to reach the plateau above. In

Fismette, the 1/111th managed to consolidate its hold over the remainder of the village, but leaving the shelter of the stone wall to advance up the open slopes was essentially impossible. Lieutenant Hoffman was with the attackers as they made the attempt:

> We were going over, right into the rain of death which was coming from in front and to the left of us. We couldn't see much—just the ruined house and outbuildings, the haystack, and the wagons. But they were out there somewhere, for from this apparent void was coming a veritable hail of death. We were so close to the guns that we no longer heard the zst-zst-zst of their searching fingers—just the wicked crack they made as they went past our ears. There must have been a battalion of machine gunners in front of us. . . . The noise they made was not unlike hundreds of riveting machines such as can be heard in building a skyscraper in New York or some other large city. . . . We advanced fifty yards. There was absolutely no place to advance to. . . . We had to fall back to our lines. There was nothing else we could do. We left some of our men dead and wounded in the orchards and fields.[14]

The Germans retaliated. Sometime after the doughboys' final lunge had fizzled, German infantry began making obvious preparations to storm down its favorite avenue of attack into Fismette—the Rue Cervante. Hoffman noticed the enemy preparations and quickly deployed his tired men in a block of ruined houses linked together with strongpoints and even tunnels. The doughboys had just finished setting up, pushing their rifles through holes in the battered stone wall, when the Germans charged down the street. The image of their clumsy but intimidating approach would stay with Hoffman for many years: "Clumpety-clump, they were going, with their high boots and huge coal bucket helmets. I can see them coming yet— bent over, rifle in one hand, potato-masher grenade in the other; husky, red-faced young fellows, their eyes almost popping out of their heads as they dashed down the street, their necks red and perspiring." The Americans had positioned themselves well. As the fifty or so Germans entered the village, they unwittingly ventured into presited kill zones before the doughboys' barricade and started to fall under a hail of bullets. As the fighting raged, a young German breathlessly dodged into the doorway of the house where Hoffman was sheltered. Standing in the semidarkness of the ruined house, Hoffman briefly hesitated. Should he shoot the German, yell at him to turn around and fight, or just bayonet him in the back? The last seemed simplest and safest, so Hoffman lunged. After a gasp of surprise, the German died spitted on his bayonet. The enemy raiders were killed almost to a man.[15]

The events of August 10 proved that enemy resistance above Fismette was much stronger than Bullard had hoped. That fact dictated a balanced policy of activity tempered with caution. Regular patrols should project confidence and secure regular and accurate knowledge of the enemy, but no general attack should be undertaken lest it expose American weakness and provoke a full-scale enemy counterattack that would endanger the bridgehead. That evening Bullard laid out the policy he wanted Muir to pursue:

> In order to conserve our strength and at the same time keep that close contact with the enemy which is necessary, we should hold on our front strong bridgeheads. From these bridgeheads we should push forward strong aggressive patrols covered by box barrages. If these patrols (strength 1 company or less) reach their selected objectives with little or no opposition, we have the evidence that we are looking for, and the broadening of the bridgehead then becomes our duty. If on the contrary the opposition is strong, it is evidence that the enemy still holds the plateau with some strength and determination and the situation then demands a general attack, which will not be undertaken by us until the army commander so directs. Therefore each aggressive patrol sent out by you is authorized and expected to feel the enemy's line with determination but not to attack with determination if the enemy is holding strongly, but to retire to the bridgehead. A succession of such strong patrols, each afforded adequate artillery support, must be carried out at various points and at various times.

It was a sensible policy (barring abandonment of the bridgehead, which Degoutte would not have allowed), fully in keeping with the policies Bullard had followed with the US 1st Division following the Seicheprey raid back in 1917. Much later, Bullard would blame Degoutte for suggesting this aggressive stance, which in this case had sad consequences. However, Bullard himself clearly believed as a matter of principle that an inert bunker mentality—simply holding territory without constantly testing the enemy—only invited reprisal.[16]

Colonel Edward C. Shannon, commanding the 111th, hewed closely to the aggressive policy mandated by Bullard. Conception was one thing, however, and execution another. That afternoon, Shannon ordered two combat patrols of the 3/111th, now up from reserve, to set out from Fismette and test the German defenses on the slopes above the village. One patrol would follow the western edge of the spur northeast of town, while the other followed its eastern edge. To many of the shell-bedeviled doughboys and their officers, the idea of sending patrols up those slopes seemed insane. To Lieutenant Hervey Allen, "it was a frightful order, murder." Incredulous that anyone would even think of such a thing, he begged Major Alan Donnelly, commanding the 3/111th, to reconsider. Donnelly naturally refused, given that he was under orders to send the patrols. The word "murder" also floated through Hoffman's mind as he watched the patrols assemble, but he said nothing. Thankfully, neither Allen nor Hoffman would have to join them.[17]

Artillery supported the patrols, but the German guns quickly retaliated, and the hillside erupted in flames. Watching from a building in Fismette, Allen was sickened by the sight of the "ugly nose of a machine gun" in a haystack, "from which went up a faint blue haze." That gun was one of many mowing down the combat patrols. Soon Fismette was caught up in the inferno:

> The whole hill seemed to be alive with machine guns and artillery. Such a barrage fell on Fismette that we were instantly driven from our posts into the dugout. In the yard beside us shell after shell smashed. We closed the iron door to our cave to keep out the fragments, but the choking gas and the smell of high explosives came in. Above all the roar suddenly sounded, seemingly right above our heads, the sharp bark of our own single machine gun. Brave lads, they were still sticking to it in the garret. We knew they had only one box of ammunition left. Houses along the street were blown up and disappeared inwardly in a cloud of dust and a sliding noise. I hopped out once to see major Donnely [sic] at the big cave.
>
> "Hang on," he said.
>
> After what seemed an eternity, some one came and said our men were coming back—then our own barrage fell. It was the greatest we had thrown around there. The hillside was tossed about for an hour and the German shells had ceased. As always, when it lifted, there followed the silence of the dead. We were all breathing in relief when what was left of the other companies returned. It was a miserable remnant. The loss had been terrific. Some of the companies were down to a few men.

III Corps' operations report for the day stated simply: "Both patrols met severe resistance from machine guns, although the raid was preceded by artillery. Heavy casualties." Unfortunately, as Colonel Shannon reported, the heavy shelling made the evacuation of casualties in the daytime next to impossible.[18]

Worse was to come. German artillery shells rained on Fismette all night, inflicting casualties and making sleep impossible. The shelling intensified toward dawn and then fell silent as sunlight struggled to break through the clouds of smoke and dust. "This," Allen knew, "meant only one thing." In as much of a panic as his dazed condition would allow, he ordered every man who could stand to get out of the dugout and pushed them toward the stone wall. "They are all dead up there along the wall, lieutenant," someone cried. Hoffman, nearby and heading for the same wall, thought the same. "Everywhere I looked were dead men. There seemed to be no live men around to man the guns." Then someone shouted, "Here they come." Beyond the wall, Allen watched a puff of smoke roll forward, along with a spout of yellow flame. Men curled up like leaves in self-protection as smoke and flames rolled over them, and another flash engulfed some nearby houses. In a scene that would always haunt Allen and that became the climactic end to his superb war memoir, one doughboy leaped up and whirled to face the young lieutenant, his body outlined against the flames. "Oh! My God!" he screamed, staring terror-stricken into Allen's face. "Oh! God!"[19]

Hoffman's stomach twisted with the same terror that Allen experienced as German soldiers bearing tanks on their backs surged forward, their hoses spewing liquid flames up to fifty yards. Heat scorched his body as billowing clouds of smoke wafted through the village and barricades, walls, houses, and men were engulfed in flames. Yet the doughboys held, opening fire on the attackers from behind the wall and along the village perimeter. Naturally concentrating on the flamethrowers, the Americans' hearts leaped whenever they scored a hit. One by one the flamethrowers were eliminated or driven back. German infantrymen continued the attack, however, blasting their way into several houses with rifles and grenades, and even penetrating between the village and the river at some points. Eventually, their momentum was spent and, for the most part, they pulled out, leaving a few emplacements behind.[20]

The ten days that followed witnessed a steady grind of attrition. On August 13–14 the 109th Regiment relieved the 111th in Fismette and patrolled aggressively while also working to pry out the few machine gun emplacements the Germans had managed to establish on the northeastern and western edges of the village. It was a frustrating battle. As soon as one nest was identified and pummeled with artillery, American patrols would move forward only to discover that the Germans had pulled out and reestablished themselves elsewhere. The 1/112th entered Fismette in relief of the 109th on August 18, and the 3/112th had its turn on August 22. Constant low-grade but savage fighting raged in and around the village as the opponents sought weaknesses and grappled for control. By then, the place had become, in the words of Corporal Pierce, "a city of the dead":

> At every turn and corner they lie, some now only bony skeletons. Germans and Americans side by side, on top of the ground and half buried by the debris. A few have been buried but hundreds have not. The stench is sickening, flies and yellow jackets everywhere and men must live here. Buildings are leveled much more than when I was here before. The entire atmosphere is dismal and terrifying, surely the Valley of Death.[21]

As the days passed, Muir pondered his options for both offense and defense—anything seemed better than just sitting and taking it. Surveying his position, the general detected some hopeful signs. The green but fresh 77th Division had come into the line on his left on August 11–12, taking over the small 28th Division bridgehead at the Château Diable and eventually merging into Bullard's III Corps. And on August 18 the French had opened their Oise-Aisne offensive sixty kilometers northwest of Fismes at Noyon. If successful, they would force the Germans to abandon the line of the Vesle and retreat to the Aisne, releasing the 28th Division from its predicament at Fismette. Buoyed by these events, Muir considered the possibility that, "following up the success of the troops of the 56th Brigade in establishing bridgehead at Fismette, the 55th Brigade will attack, at an hour to be designated later, in the general direction of Baslieux." In case the Germans did not relent, Muir prepared a "plan of defense" in which he optimistically claimed that "the enemy is not holding the area between the Vesle river and the Aisne river with any considerable force. He has established well selected machine gun, minnewerfer [sic] and light artillery positions along the south edge of the plateau without any permanent concentration of infantry." Muir conceded the possibility of a "serious" attack on Fismette, but in that case, he thought it reasonable to insist that the bridgehead be held "at all costs." Support troops, he predicted, would shore up the perimeter and regain any ground lost by counterattack.[22]

West of Fismette, the bridgehead at Château Diable—which the 28th Division had occupied on August 7 and the 4th Division had subsequently failed to expand to include Bazoches—had been occupied by troops of the green US 77th Division. Captain Robert Patterson, future undersecretary of war who would help manage US mobilization in World War II, spent several days in the bridgehead and described what it amounted to:

> It was along the railroad tracks half a mile west of Bazoches, a village on the north bank of the Vesle. The Vesle was two or three hundred yards in the rear; the railroad tracks were in a deep cut here, and the main line of defense was in the cut. North of the tracks there was a wide, level field. The advance posts were in little shallow trenches in this field, some three hundred yards beyond the tracks. South of the tracks lay a lagoon, with a patch of woods just behind it. The company headquarters was in a little dugout between the lagoon and the tracks and connected with the lagoon by a short communication trench two or three feet deep.

Holding on to this bridgehead was almost as nerve-racking as fighting in Fismette, for dead German and American bodies were everywhere, and enemy outposts were very close on all sides. Raids and patrols were frequent. During one of them on August 14, Patterson inadvertently found himself behind enemy lines, and after killing a number of Germans in a protracted running fight, he finally escaped by feigning death and returning to the bridgehead after dark. Fortunately, Patterson's company was relieved from the bridgehead before the next phase. On August 22, in an operation wryly code-named Amerika, the Germans assaulted the tiny bridgehead and destroyed it, capturing thirty-three Americans and throwing the rest of the doughboys back across the river. It was a worrying sign that here, regardless of the Oise-Aisne offensive at Noyon, the Germans remained very aggressive indeed. Anyone reading the signs might conclude that Fismette would be next on the enemy's list.[23]

On August 23 Bullard visited 56th Brigade headquarters and suggested shoring up Fismette's defenses by placing combat groups with Chauchats and machine guns within several hundred yards of the footbridge over Vesle and using heavy artillery, one-pounders, and trench mortars against German trench mortar emplacements to keep them at bay. But despite these precautions, events were rapidly moving toward a violent denouement. The 77th Division's 308th Regiment attacked across the Vesle on August 23 and, after severe fighting, was able to retake the Château Diable, but two days later, the 3/110th's attempt to expand the Fismette bridgehead and push back enemy patrols that had moved *south* of the river collapsed in failure.[24]

Bullard later claimed that around August 18—just as the French began the Oise-Aisne offensive and while Muir was making plans based on assumptions that the German forces north of the Aisne were nothing to worry about—he tried to order the evacuation of Fismette. But as we have seen, Degoutte's aggressive policy of launching regular patrols against the enemy was fully in agreement with Bullard's command philosophy, and there is no compelling reason to believe that he did not endorse it at the time. Nevertheless, it is only fair to consider Bullard's explanation of his conduct, as stated in his memoirs:

> It was evident that whenever the enemy desired he could wipe out the company [sic] on the north bank of the Vesle. After its failure in the raid ordered by General Degoutte, I ordered that company withdrawn to the south bank of the Vesle man by man at night. My chief-of-staff, who was very much in favour of the French general's idea of "bridgeheads," knew of the order which I was going to give. When I returned from Fismes late in the afternoon, I found the French general at my corps headquarters and learned that my chief-of-staff had informed him of my order to withdraw the company. The French army commander ordered me at once to replace it. This was done.

A letter of disavowal that Bullard wrote to Pershing on August 28, obviously intended for the public record, presented events a little differently:

> I . . . began to withdraw the garrison of Fismette some 300 metres back across the Vesle River into Fismes. Before this was finished, the French general commanding the Sixth Army, to which I belong, arrived at my headquarters and, learning of my orders for withdrawal from Fismette, himself, in person, directed me to continue to hold Fismette and how to hold it. My orders were changed in his presence and his orders were obeyed.

Later on, Bullard claimed that he met with Pershing, who asked him irritably: "Why did you not disobey the order given by General Degoutte?" There is no way of knowing the truth. The chain of events as described by Bullard would have left no paper trail.[25]

Colonel Rickards, interestingly, said nothing to battalion historian James A. Murrin about an attempt to withdraw from Fismette. Rickards did, however, give Murrin an account that, though not exculpating Degoutte, places Bullard's and Muir's roles in a somewhat less sympathetic light:

On the afternoon of August 26th, General Robert Bullard, then in command of the Army [sic] of which the 28th Division was a part, accompanied Major-General Muir to the advance regimental P.C. of the 112th, and Colonel Rickards explained the Fismette situation to both, asking for permission to withdraw unless attacks could be made on the flanks, thus strengthening the bridgehead. General Bullard left, promising to see what he could do.

If Bullard's claim is accurate—that he had already tried to pull the garrison out of Fismette but was overruled by Degoutte—his promise to Rickards to "see what he could do" seems curious. There would have been nothing he could do. And twelve hours later, it was too late.[26]

On the night of August 26–27, the 2/112th relieved the 3/112th in Fismette and Fismes. Companies G and H—236 men, all largely unfamiliar with their new surroundings—took up positions in Fismette early on the morning of August 27. Over the past few days, there had been continued fighting and patrolling around Fismette and along the river on either side. Nevertheless, divisional intelligence reports contained no warnings of anything unusual in the offing, least of all a major enemy attack. What was coming would be a complete surprise.

At 0400 on August 27, German artillery opened fire along the Vesle. There were 77s, 150s, and 210s—heavy stuff. Muir heard the barrage and went outside to see what was going on, but as no reports had arrived at division headquarters, he assumed the firing was taking place in an adjoining zone and went back inside. Regimental and even battalion headquarters in Fismes had no idea what was happening either. But it was a German box barrage—a standard precursor to an attack—and it was cutting off Fismette. The shells fell for twenty minutes, and then German infantry in approximately battalion strength—members of the 4th Guards Division's 5th Grenadier Regiment in "excellent" spirits—stormed the village.

Previous attacks had come down the Rue Cervante. This time, however, the Germans sent only a light diversionary patrol down that well-trod avenue while simultaneously attacking the American positions on both flanks with flamethrowers, machine guns, and grenades. The defenders were stunned. To the east, they fought well and managed to keep the enemy at bay. To the west, it was a different story. There the Germans broke through at some points and began to squeeze between the defenders and the river. According to a special report prepared shortly after the battle at Bullard's demand, Lieutenant Milton W. Fridenburg decided that all was lost and called on his fellow defenders to surrender. Most did not listen to him at first, deciding instead to keep fighting or to swim the river to the south bank. Still, the act was evidently jarring enough to break the last wisp of coherence in the defenders' cordon. A "cowardly soldier"—nobody ever identified him, and some claimed he was a crafty German—raced down the street saying that the lieutenant had called for surrender. Also under attack from bombing and strafing enemy aircraft, the garrison collapsed in minutes, with 75 killed, 127 prisoners including 4 lieutenants (their captains had remained in Fismes during the attack), and 34 survivors who splashed across the Vesle. Commented the report:

> It is apparent that the combat groups on the west were not as well led as they might have been and it is not believed that they fought with the same amount of skill and valor as the troops on the east of town. . . . And it is believed [they] became panic stricken and lost confidence in their officers, which, it is believed at this office, was in a great measure responsible for the failure of the defense.

Muir defended Fridenburg's reputation as a good soldier, saying that the surrender call may have been a German ruse. But in any event, he thought it "aided largely in weakening the resistance in Fismette."[27]

Other elements of the report indicate that blame for the initial surprise and subsequent collapse of Fismette lay squarely at the door of division headquarters, if not higher up. Oddly enough, during the attack, no signal was given for a counterbarrage, and no call was made for reinforcements or other help. The reason was that officers in Fismette had been told to handle any attacks themselves and that higher command would consider any calls for help to be signs of panic or incompetence. Muir explained in his report: "The belief had become quite general that the German line facing us was composed mainly of machine gunners with a large force of artillery fairly well back, and that a vigorous attack would cause this line to collapse. The sharing of this belief is what caused the instruction to avoid useless calls for 'barrage' to be issued." The general said nothing of his own role in promoting this belief, which contributed both to the initial surprise and to the failure to call for assistance before it was too late. Instead of issuing a mea culpa, Muir blamed his own junior officers for their "culpable negligence" in not calling for a barrage, even though they had been warned not to do so needlessly. He also cited their "doubtless faulty" defensive dispositions, which made no allowance for possible flank attacks, and their "feeble resistance" against their attackers. Yet he was convinced that they had not made a "useless sacrifice," since they had inflicted what he thought were heavy casualties on the attackers. The testimony of a German prisoner, though, claimed that the attackers had suffered only slight losses.[28]

Incredibly, the scale of the disaster, and even the fact that the garrison had been defeated, was not fully understood for days, even though regimental headquarters stood just across the Vesle in Fismes. The division's operations report covering the period up to noon on August 27 claimed that the 112th had scored a defensive "success" in Fismette against "strong raiding parties," although there were "heavy casualties" and some men taken prisoner. The journal of operations echoed this confident claim, and on August 28 it recorded that "reports on the final outcome of the Fismette situation are still vague," although "it is possible the number taken prisoners is greater than at first reports." Part of the problem was that the area had become such a hornet's nest that scouts could not even get near the river, as Harold Pierce discovered.[29]

Sometime after the German attack, Pierce's captain ordered him and two other men to dodge through shell-torn Fismes to the riverbank and, if possible, cross over into Fismette to find out what had happened. To minimize the harm should he be captured, Pierce first had to relinquish his rifle, pistol, and papers. As he handed them over, the captain's aide looked at him sorrowfully and said, "Goodbye Pierce." As he approached Fismes and contemplated rushing through the enemy shell fire, Pierce's mind grew confused:

> I have time for a short prayer but my prayer is so mixed up with a dirty little song about the private life of a woman named Lulu that I am afraid it does no good. All day long this song has been running through my mind so much that I cannot get my mind on my prayer. The next shell is whining in our direction, flat on the ground we dig in our feet to start as soon as its pieces have whizzed by us. "Crumph," it goes, the pieces whistle over us, we are up and away, a hundred yard dash in which I never tried harder for speed, ready to dive, equipment banging and breath coming hard. "My Lulu was arrested." We reach the protection of the sunken road yet we do not stop. We slow down at the old mill, then cross the railroad tracks. A 77 shell comes toward us, we flatten out till it bursts, then on again. Lulu is humming through my head and I try and switch to "Jesus, Savior, Pilot Me." Another shell, we slide on the ground as it bursts. I come up with Lulu and run on again. I roll into another depression to let the next shell burst, then on again, up and down, cross that shell-swept field, a few yards, diving, on again, up and down, up and down between shell bursts, trying to get rid of that dirty little song as I do not want to die

with it on my mind, frantic, scared, panting and sweating, between trees and through bushes, over and into shell holes, by dead men and horses, till at last we have passed through the shell fire unhurt but exhausted.

At the riverbank, finally, someone told Pierce what had happened in Fismette. He looked through his field glasses across the river and could see piles of mostly American dead and the Germans firmly in possession. Later he spoke with some exhausted survivors, who told of their ordeal before collapsing: "These men could not stay awake long, they went to sleep in exhaustion in all sorts of grotesque positions." Over the next few days, the Germans heavily reinforced their river defenses to prevent another American crossing, including installing searchlights to keep an eye on the ruined bridge and the river.[30]

Fismette was lost, but there remained a few final acts in this performance before the curtain would open on the first major American offensive of the war at Saint-Mihiel. West of Fismette, the US 77th Division would continue to hold on to the tiny bridgehead around Château Diable, fending off local counterattacks and making abortive attempts to expand the bridgehead until the Germans' withdrawal to the Aisne began on September 4. The division would spend the next ten days following up the German advance and then establishing positions along the Aisne, sometimes attacking and overcoming local German strongpoints. The 77th Division had taken 1,475 casualties from August 18 to September 3, and it took another 1,738 between September 4 and 16.[31]

The US 32d Division had rested in III Corps reserve for the first half of August and was there when the Oisne-Aisne offensive opened on August 18. It was attached to French XXX Corps on August 25, and on the night of August 27–28 it relieved the French 127th Division west of Juvigny. From there, with the French 64th Division on the left and the French 59th Division (French I Corps) on the right, the 32d Division would participate in events that, though fought on the Aisne, would eventually prod the Germans to abandon the Vesle along with Fismette. The division's immediate objective was the high ground west of the town of Juvigny, which was regarded as a hinge of the remaining Vesle salient.

The American 126th Regiment attacked at 0700 on August 28, over chalky ground pitted with caves that the defenders had dug to shelter their artillery. The first thrust was successful in forcing the Germans back to the railroad and netting ninety-two prisoners. The American assault groups lost direction and became entangled, however; this also opened gaps, and the 125th Regiment was forced to move up and plug them. German artillery then pounded the attackers, and a counterattack at 1100 hit both the Americans and their French neighbors. According to Corporal John McDaniels, the Americans fought back as if they were at a target range: "Some of the fellows stood up to fire, others were kneeling, while still others lay prone. Whatever his position, everyone fired just as rapidly as possible. Gradually the German lines became thinner but kept coming forward. Our rifle fire got too hot and the Germans retreated." The French 59th Division was pushed back, however, forcing the Americans to refuse their right and take additional casualties from that direction.[32]

Tanks supported the attack that went forward at 0525 the next morning. Unfortunately, mechanical problems held them back—annoying McDaniels, who was advancing behind them as they constantly stalled—and they attracted German shell fire that killed Americans who got too close. The attacks were "smothered" by enemy artillery and machine gun fire and made no progress whatsoever. The Americans were taking so many casualties, especially on their line along the railroad, which was subject to enemy enfilade, that Haan visited the front personally and ordered his officers to thin their troops in the front line. Fortunately, they would not have to endure much more. On August 30 the Germans, having determined that their Aisne line was secure and that the withdrawal from the Vesle could begin, withdrew from the 32d Division's front. The Americans followed up to capture Juvigny that evening. They would spend another two days in the line, sparring intermittently with the slowly withdrawing Germans, until they were pulled out of the line on September 1. During its brief but intense stay since August 28, the 32d Division had taken 2,646 casualties.[33]

Haan put a positive spin on his outfit's final run in the lines under French command. He had seen better initiative by junior officers, more effective use of machine guns, and better liaison and supply than he had in July. The division's machine gun officer backed this up by noting the doughboys' deft use of captured enemy machine guns and *minenwerfers* against the Germans. Officers had suffered heavy losses, but Haan thought both they and their men remained eager for battle. He even had praise for the French liaison officers serving with the division. Lieutenant Colonel X. H. Price, whose earlier report on the Aisne-Marne had tended to back up French criticisms of the Americans, also saw improvement in the 32d Division's "very creditable" performance around Juvigny. He concluded that "this operation is an example of the fact that when American divisions attacked alongside of French divisions, they generally led," albeit at the price of additional casualties.[34]

Even now, at the end of a long summer but before the really large American operations got under way in the fall, there were signs of exhaustion among some American units, the 32d among them. One of Haan's staff officers remarked on September 18, "after several weeks of observation of the command," that the division's officers had become negativistic complainers:

> [He] found many of them continually talking about their losses, seemingly overwhelmed by their losses in a series of fine, hard fights in the greatest campaign in history. That is a time when the born soldier is most on his toes, most cheerful and stimulating and ready and willing for the next fight, and making every provision for it—instead of showing himself worn out, anxious for rest, talking about going home and complaining about the minor hardships of the best life on earth. Every officer must remember that his feelings, bearing and talk at once communicate themselves to his men, just as the temper and nervousness of a rider at once affect and cause his horse to react like a nervous brute instead of playing up to the light hand of a good horseman.[35]

The same was even truer of the hard-pressed 28th Division. That unit was still licking its wounds from the Fismette fiasco—which had chewed up a lot of companies, in addition to the ones destroyed at the end—when the Germans began withdrawing from its front on September 4. The Pennsylvanians followed up across the Vesle, retaking Fismette and moving uphill to Baslieux and to just south of Glennes. The Germans pulled back slowly, continually inflicting casualties until the 28th Division was finally pulled out of the line on September 7, having taken a whopping 8,772 casualties during the Aisne-Marne and Vesle River campaigns. Harold Pierce was not on the casualty lists, but he was one of the wounded just the same. Describing his state of mind under bombardment at the end of August, he later wrote:

> I am soon a nervous wreck. I lose control as the bombardment wears on into hours. The strain of the last week with this added is too much. I cannot lie still. I want to scream and run and throw myself. My gas mask irritates me and I am on the verge of tearing it off, gas or no gas. My throat is dry and cracked from the mask but the saliva runs from my mouth and swishes around on my face. When I hear the whistle of an approaching shell I dig my toes into the ground and push on the walls of the dugout, trembling when it bursts, then in agony waiting

for the next shell. My body is trembling all over like St Vitus dance, tense when they come, rolling and turning between shells, moaning and groaning. . . . I am licked [he imagines Germans exulting over their tormenting of him]. . . . Back in my brain just a slight sense of reason keeps me from running upright into the fire and tearing my mask off. I know that my best hope is to stay as far down in that hole as possible. My brother and the other man watch over me to keep me from doing anything rash, yelling words of encouragement and saying that it would soon be over.

After midnight the shelling tapered off, allowing Pierce and his fellows to remove their masks. He had time for a brief prayer before he passed into unconsciousness.[36]

By the beginning of September 1918, the talk at Pershing's GHQ was all about the future. July and August had been brutal months for the German army. The so-called Second Battle of the Marne had turned the tide with the Soissons offensive and the Germans' slow withdrawal to the Vesle and the Aisne; after that had come the shattering allied victory at Amiens. The AEF had done its tour of duty under French and British tutelage—although certain units, such as the 27th and 30th Divisions in Flanders and the 36th and 93d Divisions in Champagne, would remain unheralded under foreign command—and the AEF seemed to have come of age. French efforts to continue to instruct American soldiers were brushed off with an easy confidence that conveyed the Yanks' belief that they had learned the ropes. Pershing's chief of staff, James McAndrew, issued a memorandum to AEF officers stating that all training and instruction would now be conducted under American command and according to American principles. Noting that the French had sneakily tried to send some American officers to French training schools—and been firmly rebuffed—McAndrew declared that AEF commanders should "courteously decline to comply" with all future French attempts to teach their allies. Big things were in store. The Saint-Mihiel salient came first, but after that, even greater offensives were possible, maybe even a drive toward the heart of Germany via Metz. Whatever happened, the Americans were determined to move ahead on their own.[37]

Behind the scenes, however, there was a great deal of self-examination and recrimination going on. For many French and Americans, with the notable exception of those associated with Liggett's I Corps, the events of the summer left bitter memories. Signs of discord had been growing, and word of this discord not only reached Pershing's GHQ but also traveled all the way across the ocean to the United States. From there, the army's adjutant general, Brigadier General Henry McCain, cabled Pershing on July 24, 1918: "Report being spread that French require Americans to pay rent for trenches occupied. Request statement of facts and explanation." At the same time, complaints began swirling that the French were cavalierly issuing movement orders to American units under their command, without bothering to inform GHQ. This led to a formal complaint on July 28 from McAndrew to Andre Tardieu, chief of the French Military Mission.[38]

On August 11 McCain brought even more troubling accusations to Pershing's attention:

> An assistant to this office just returned from Soissons Sector reports that greatest discord between French and American divisions at front was scarcity of dead behind American lines and quantity behind French [one reason being that French companies were smaller and had less time for burial details]. General Degoutte stated only criticism he had on United States troops was their poor food or its lack of proper cooking . . . also close lining up of men for rations which attracts aeroplanes, and their close order in going into action which increases potency of enemy shell fire. He considers United States Companies are too large as officers cannot efficiently handle so many men. One French Division, of which he spoke, had been in line sixty days, twenty days of which was active fighting. United States division next to it was relieved three times; reason being Germans concentrated their attacks against Americans hoping for weakness and to reduce morale, and stability was slightly less than French. General Degoutte cannot even now relieve this particular division having no other to replace it showing scarcity of French reserves. He spoke strongly against poor American mail service which was depressing and affecting the moral of our troops.

Pershing shrugged off the information, responding on August 15, "There is no discord between French and American Divisions due to cause stated nor to any other cause. Our troops are efficient in the police of the battlefield and scarcity of dead behind advancing American lines is the best testimony to that fact. Criticism as to the food is away wide of the mark." He also said that Degoutte must have been misquoted in saying that American companies were too large or that they spent little time in the lines before being relieved. The "entire report," he concluded, "was evidently made by inexperienced officer who could not deduce facts from casual conversation."[39]

But the complaints were worse than Pershing let on. From the French perspective, in fact, the Americans had shown admirable courage but little else during the summer campaign. Their tactics in particular were execrable and showed little improvement over time. A lengthy French memorandum of August 28, translated by G-5 at Pershing's GHQ, is worth quoting in detail. "The formations adopted [were] *much too dense*. The units are close together, *rigid*, heavy in maneuvering, and *insufficiently echeloned in depth*," the memorandum reported (emphasis in the original). The Americans also employed mixed units too often, it continued:

> At the time of the first attacks, a few units still used the lines of skirmishers, almost *elbow to elbow* and were supported by columns of squads *without sufficient intervals*; this disposition proceeded straight ahead; the losses were heavy. *During the pursuit*, the advance guards remained close to the main body, not pushing their light reconnaissance elements far enough ahead. . . . On the roads and in the villages there was considerable assembling of troops which attracted the attention of the hostile aviation and drew murderous bombardments. . . . The heaviness of formations, the lack of experience in utilization of the terrain and in maneuvering made this pursuit very slow. Example: A large U.S. unit pushes through a breach in the line: a stop is made to wait until the infantry and artillery have passed through before the advance is continued, instead of there having been light elements sent forward to maintain contact and cover the operation. The hostile machine gun nests have repeatedly checked the advance of the American troops. With a courage which is beyond all praise, some units attacked these nests from the front and were decimated. A machine gun is never attacked from the front, whatever may be the strength of the infantry at hand. The machine gun is neutralized from the front by the heaviest fire which can be directed on it and attempt is made to get it on the flank or from the rear, use being made of the terrain. Finally, the reserves do not move in thin enough formations. . . . Owing to the little confidence many American units have in the automatic rifle, the machine guns were brought together in the first wave, decreasing the nimbleness and mobility of the latter and rendering it more vulnerable. In general, the first wave is not the proper place for the machine gun.

So far, the French critique had not significantly diverged from American self-critiques, although it was delivered more ruthlessly. But as it continued, the memorandum took swipes at some of the very principles that Pershing and others had emphasized as the new, superior style of warfare the AEF was bringing to the western front. In particular, it stated that the Americans' aggressiveness—which the Yanks championed, in contrast to the alleged dilatoriness if not cowardice of the French—was counterproductive, and so was their dependence on their rifles: "In the course of the attack, the dash and splendid offensive spirit of the Americans often led them to exceed the rate of speed fixed. Entire units found themselves under the fire of our 75's." Infantry officers got lost and their units became intermingled not because the French were too lazy to supply them with maps (as many Americans complained) but because "most of the infantry officers do not know how to use the *compass* or the *map*, or else do not bring any along." As a result, "the units coming up on their objectives were more or less in disorder, and, generally too dense." The consequence was heavy losses from German counterattacks and artillery fire. The memorandum continued:

> Finally, and this is a highly important point, no one thinks of work of digging in. Scorn of the entrenching tool should be driven from the minds of the American officers. Even on the offensive, it is necessary, as soon as a stop is made, to work the shovel and pick, to start work on an organization, shelter the personnel to as great an extent as possible, in a word, execute the orders of the plan of occupation and organization of the conquered terrain, as if no further advance were to be made. Here again is manifested the lack of initiative of the subaltern officers and platoon commanders.

Lines of occupation were almost never marked. "The little marking that was done was executed very often only after express and repeated requests from adjacent French units or from the aviation (when they were able to be in liaison with the U.S. units—which happened but very rarely)."

Even the Yanks' much-touted proclivity with rifles (recall American accounts' many secondhand quotations from French observers expressing admiration at the doughboys' marksmanship) was not necessarily an asset. "It should be noted first of all that the American infantryman is an excellent shot, that he loves his rifle, has an unshakeable confidence in it," the memorandum stated, "which fact often causes him wrongfully to scorn the use of the automatic rifle and the machine gun. Automatic arms (the automatic rifle and the machine gun) are the infantry's most effective means of action." Combined-arms opportunities disappeared because many Americans ditched their automatic rifles as they advanced. There was poor liaison between machine gun units and infantry, between artillery and infantry, and between aviation and infantry. One-pounders and Stokes mortars were rarely and ineffectively used. "Some Stokes batteries did not follow the infantry, giving as a reason that their horses might have been killed!!!"

Finally, there was the matter of supply. Images of muscular, well-dressed, well-fed Yankees parading through war-torn Europe belie the fact that, near the front, the doughboys were practically reduced to the status of beggars, compared with their relatively well-supplied French and British counterparts. As the French memorandum laid it out:

> The supplying of food during the battle was wholly insufficient. The men suffered terribly from hunger and thirst. One division [perhaps the US 2d Division at Soissons] was exhausted at the end of 36 hours, solely through the lack of food and drink. During the pursuit, some units had almost nothing to eat for 48 hours. . . . On the other hand, the French infantry never lacked anything; supplying of food was carried on every day in a normal manner, or almost so.

This failure was attributable in part to "the American officer, whose activity is remarkable," but he "generally evinces a fair degree of indifference for the feeding of his troops, appearing to forget that soldiers who fight, must eat." American soldiers were careless as well, failing to preserve food and water for the advance and suffering for their neglect as the supply services failed to bring up reserves during the action. Men were sent into battle with full packs, which they quickly tossed aside, leaving them with nothing. In conclusion, despite the Americans' emphasis on individual initiative, "The officer exposes himself too much; he does not think enough of details. . . . The company commanders, below the rank of captain, greatly lack initiative."[40]

This brutal dissection of AEF tactics must have raised hackles. Major F. W. Manley, 3d Division G-3, subsequently submitted a report to Fox Conner titled "Notes on Report Submitted by French High Command at Washington to War Department Direct." In it, Manley paraded a list of 3d Division grievances dating back to the Marne Defensive of July 15 and expanded on them with the bitter memories of other American units that had been forced to spend the summer under French command. Quoting an extract of a letter from 3d Division chief of staff Colonel Robert Kelton to Conner, Manley reminded him of the actions of the French 125th Division:

> [The division] absolutely melted and disappeared into thin air. There is not today a single unit of the Division in line, except its Division Commander and his Staff and I think they have been canned. This 125th Division had assigned to it a battalion from one of the regiments of the 28th Division and its companies were placed along the front to prove to the French that we were there, and the French left them there and less than one-half of them ever got out of it. They did all they could but they were overwhelmed.

The French deserted their positions and abandoned emplacements, even though they had endured practically no German artillery fire. They left the 28th Division's elements alone in the front line, without intelligence of any kind. The French artillerymen also abandoned guns that the advancing Germans then turned on the Americans. Manley went on to note that American supply problems often resulted from French negligence. At Soissons, "The Second Division was completely in the hands of the French as far as transportation was concerned, and the failure of the organizations to reach their proper positions before H-hour was due entirely to the French and not because orders were delayed."[41]

Such was the state of the Franco-American alliance as the end of summer approached and the US First Army prepared for its big test at Saint-Mihiel. Looking back to the experiences they had shared since November 1917, the officers and men of the AEF—at least those in battle-tested formations—had reason to conclude that they had seen enough to consider themselves veterans who knew how to take on and overcome an adversary. From the early embarrassing raids at Bathelémont and Seicheprey to the minor victory at Cantigny, the bloodbath at Belleau Wood, the successful defense of the Marne, the chaotic but victorious Battle of Soissons, and the triumphant race to the Vesle and advance to the Aisne, the Americans had shown that they could have a tangible impact on military events. If the French did not appreciate their qualities, that was just too bad; the Americans had their own army and sector of the front, and there was no turning back. Next stop: Saint-Mihiel. After that: Berlin.

Conclusion

The Road to Saint-Mihiel, September 1918

Even as the summer operations wrapped up on the Aisne and the Vesle, preparations for the Saint-Mihiel offensive, and particularly for what would come afterward, were fully under way. Saint-Mihiel was an attractive prospect. It occupied the apex of a 200-square-mile salient that had been created as part of the Germans' attempt to seize Verdun in the early months of the war. Its elimination, therefore, would not just roll back German gains from the spring of 1918 but also announce to the world that the tide had truly turned with the liberation of a swath of France that had been subjected to enemy domination for four long years. Capturing the salient would also symbolically peel back a potential threat to the famous fortress of Verdun. Of course, the fact that the Americans would be accomplishing this largely on their own was a source of particular pride.[1]

Yet the reduction of just another German salient was not enough. Something more decisive seemed to be in order. Behind the salient's base lay the strategically vital Briey Iron Basin and the coal-producing Saar region, near the fortress city of Metz. What would be more natural than continuing the Saint-Mihiel offensive with a drive toward Metz—only thirty-six miles away—and a triumphant march into Germany? The prospect was tantalizing—but also rather obvious. To draw German attention away from Saint-Mihiel and any future operations in that region, Pershing and his GHQ staff decided on an elaborate ruse in which Major General Omar Bundy, the undistinguished former commander of the 2d Division at Belleau Wood, would be the unwitting pawn.

Bundy spent two weeks in command of US VI Corps—a purely purely paper formation—from August 26 to September 12. On August 28, just as he was about to enjoy dinner with his staff, Bundy received a dispatch from Fox Conner at GHQ, writing on Pershing's behalf and ordering Bundy to begin laying out plans for an offensive into the Belfort region of upper Alsace and possibly into Germany. "In preparing these plans," Conner specified, "you will consider the front of attack as extending from Altkirch to Thann. The objective is Mulhouse and the line of heights extending to the southeast from that place. It is intended by the occupation of this line to insure the destruction of the Rhine bridges and eventually to establish our line along the river itself."

The plan sounded fantastic—and indeed, it was. But Bundy took his job seriously, compiling exceptionally detailed reports on the proposed thrust into Germany. He thought the chances for success were good. On September 3 he reported to Pershing that "a successful offensive can be conducted in this sector and that the present time is the most favorable that could be chosen for the purpose." The enemy had strong entrenchments, but Bundy thought they were "weakly held" with deep wire that was old and overgrown with grass and weeds, since this front had not changed since 1914. In confronting these entrenchments, "the solution to this problem is believed to be found in the employment of tanks on as liberal a scale as they may be available for this purpose. . . . The progress of the advance should be methodical. . . . The enemy lines average about five kilometers in depth. After they are crossed the fighting will be in the open and progress will be rapid." Although the French were skeptical that tanks could negotiate this terrain, Bundy thought it fully "suitable for the employment of tanks." The offensive, he insisted, could be carried as far as the Rhine and Colmar. The attack frontage would be twenty-four kilometers from Cernay to Altkirch, and the line of attack would proceed slightly north of due east. Because a tank was needed for every fifty meters of front, that would require 400 tanks total. Strong artillery would also be needed to cut the enemy wire. Bundy envisaged seven US divisions in the first line, with possibly five US divisions and a few French in support. The attacking divisions—all entirely green, although Bundy said nothing of that—would be the US 35th, 78th, 91st, 36th, 80th, 29th, and 79th.

Thus, Bundy's plan was for green American divisions, utilizing crude frontal assault tactics, to attack in a region where the French had suffered hundreds of thousands killed in the Battle of the Frontiers in 1914. Fortunately, the idea came to nothing. On September 4 Conner informed Bundy that the proposed operation had been postponed but that planning should proceed "in as active a manner as possible."

> The Commander-in-Chief also directs that your studies be extended in scope so as to include the possibility of the entry into section of divisions to the north and also the method of employing divisions for exploiting the success. It is believed that your plans should provide for the successive entry into action of divisions at least as far north as the pass east of Gerardmer. The plans should also definitely select the bridge-heads on the Rhine which it would be advantageous to secure.

Bundy responded by submitting an exceptionally detailed report on September 12, his final day in command of VI Corps. In it, he scaled back the level of artillery support, proposing instead that the tanks—now numbering 450, light and heavy—handle the task of flattening the enemy wire. And so the dreaming continued.[2]

Such grandiose scheming—which may have validated Pershing's decision to relieve Bundy from involvement in any operations involving actual flesh and blood—ignored the many limitations in American military capacity exposed in the events of the previous few months, especially since Cantigny and Belleau Wood. The French certainly knew it, and so, probably, did the Germans. Conner's assistant, A. L. Conger, warned GHQ that the Germans were unlikely "to be deceived by any mere paperwork demonstration or reconnaissance of officers unaccompanied by actual preparations of guns, munitions, material and sustenance." He added, "The French staffs have been very polite and helpful, but have given me the impression by their attitude of feeling: 'You Americans are very simple minded indeed if you think you can fool either us or the Germans by any such game as this.'" There is no evidence, in fact, that the Belfort ruse had any effect. If so, its failure resulted not just from clumsy implementation but also from the AEF's manifest incapacity to launch any operation on such a scale (though Pershing would have denied this).[3]

The AEF had learned some real lessons. Though battered, the 1st, 2d, 3d, 4th, 26th, 28th, 32d, 42d, and 77th Divisions (as well as the 369th Regiment) were savvier and more tactically proficient in early September 1918 than they had been before. Bad officers had been winnowed out to some extent at all levels, and their replacements were learning the ropes. The AEF even had two capable corps commanders in Bullard and Liggett. Unfortunately, though, each American division, whether it began fighting in May or in August, had to learn the hard lessons of modern warfare essentially on its own. Officers like Liggett issued copious memos to newly arriving units pointing out basic tenets, such as the need to avoid crowding the front lines and to pace advances carefully. Early on, Liggett pointed out:

> On numerous occasions [French] forces failed to keep abreast of our younger and fresher troops, usually due to the fact that the French preferred to take a position in half a day at small cost, where the impatient young men from afar carried it in fifteen minutes and paid the price. . . . The American Army endlessly took chances that no French soldier in his right mind would have chanced; nor would our men had they been fighting since 1914.

But his efforts to correct these mistakes did little good. To fight effectively and avoid useless casualties, green troops needed extensive training under seasoned officers. And for that, there was simply no time. Untested formations that attacked the Germans in the Meuse-Argonne in September and October would employ exactly the same clumsy and bloody tactics used in May through August, despite the passage of time and opportunities to transmit these lessons across the AEF.[4]

Accepting instruction from allied officers was one possibility, but most American officers had an ingrained resistance to taking advice from the French. In a curiously schizophrenic outlook, Americans both craved French praise—witness the plethora of prideful references in American unit histories to French medals and citations for AEF formations—and lost no opportunity to disparage or even slander the French for alleged cowardice. Resentment against patronizing French and British attitudes toward US troops and pressures for amalgamation provoked an evident need among Americans to prove that they fought better than the French and were better off on their own than under any allied tutelage. This need would reach a crescendo after the war ended and American officers began to look back on the lessons learned on the western front.

On April 2, 1919, Fox Conner submitted a memo to the AEF chief of staff titled "Comparison of Casualties Suffered by American Troops under French and under American Command." Going division by division, he concluded that the US 1st Division had lost 900 men per day under French command but only 507 men per day under American command. "The losses while with [the] French," Conner concluded, "were unnecessarily great, as American divisions were always in the lead, the neighboring French units failing to keep up. Americans subjected to flank fire." The 2d Division fought through the entire Château-Thierry and Belleau Wood period under French command, "during a month [of] principally defensive work with counter-attacks. . . . Result: German advance to Paris checked. Americans bore the brunt of fighting." At Soissons in July there were "unnecessary sacrifices . . . owing to failure of neighboring French divisions to keep up . . . subjecting division to heavy enfilade fire." Conner's conclusion: the 2d "Division [was] incomparably better handled by Americans." For the 28th Division, Conner focused on the Marne Defensive and the painful memories of the French 125th Division's withdrawal, resulting in American casualties. "The inefficiency of the 125th French Div. with which the 109th Regiment was brigaded," Conner pointed out, "was the direct cause of the above casualties." Summing up, Conner stated, "In the defense no American division lost ground entrusted to it except locally and then only for a few hours, and no American division failed in attack. No other nation has such a record."[5]

By the time Conner wrote his report, Germany was occupied, and Franco-American tensions had reached a crescendo. The stress was so bad that Captain Stuart Benson, serving as a liaison officer with the French Army of Occupation, submitted to GHQ on February 3, 1919, a special report on the "strained relations" between the Americans and the French. He focused on disputes in the army of occupation but conceded that "American resentment against the French, which may have existed in embryo before, was brought to a critical point the middle of December 1918." Anti-French feeling, once primarily confined to staff and command, now permeated all levels. Benson found that "the almost hatred of the enlisted man for the French" had been exacerbated by their bad experiences with French civilians during the war. Along the Rhine, the Yanks got along much better with the Germans than they did with the French. In fairness, Benson pointed out that the Americans failed to understand that the war's direct impact on French civilians in the war zone was much greater than its impact on the Germans. French common soldiers were more willing to be friendly to the Americans than vice versa, Benson thought, and German propaganda was taking advantage of the prevailing Francophobic feelings.[6]

Evidence of this strong mutual mistrust between the French and the Americans during and after the war seems to contradict previous research suggesting widespread good feelings, but it must be kept in context. Many experiences were positive. Liggett's I Corps and its officers coexisted nicely with General Degoutte and his French Sixth Army, despite tensions elsewhere. Officers such as Colonel Paul H. Clark, Pershing's liaison officer at French army headquarters, seemed to get along well with the French. So did Major Robert H. Lewis, who served as the US 1st Division's liaison officer with the French. Lewis was less worried about Franco-American tensions than about Anglo-French tensions, which he thought came close to threatening the war effort. Writing to Conner on May 8, 1918, Lewis fretted:

> One of the most striking things I noticed is the open way in which the French and the British are beginning to criticize each other to me. It does not look good to me at all. The French say that the British soldier is magnificent but that his staffs are rotten and that they won't learn. The British say that the French are piddlers and do not live up to their agreements as to furnishing reserves and relieving worn out British troops in the line.[7]

At the tactical level, Franco-American relations and operations were mixed. Often the most positive experiences took place when small American formations entered combat under French command for the first time. The US 30th Regiment did well with the French on Hill 204 in June, as did elements of the US 4th and 42d Divisions in the advance against the Marne salient in July. The 28th Division's experiences on Hill 204 and during the Marne Defensive were not so positive. There appears to be no correlation, however, between how much time American companies and battalions spent under French tutelage and how well they performed later. Despite its successes on Hill 204, the 30th Regiment was distinctly tottery under American divisional control during the Marne Defensive on July 15. Units of the 4th Division that did well fighting alongside the French one day would be decimated when they tried to launch massed frontal attacks on the next. And units that had reason to rue their experiences with the French, such as the battalions of the 28th Division, generally performed well when released to American care. In short, there is no hard evidence to either prove or disprove the effectiveness of amalgamation, given the luxury of time to implement it.

It all came down to training. Mark Grotelueschen has amply demonstrated the uneven application of Pershing's "open-warfare" doctrine throughout the AEF and the willingness of brigade and division commanders to ditch this doctrine in favor of European ideas when the latter seemed better suited to their needs. Closer to the ground, Richard S. Faulkner has pointed out the persistence of junior leaders' tactical deficiencies as a result of the short and often misguided instructions they received in camp. In practice, many if not most American officers and men simply freelanced. Numerous American accounts attest that green troops began by advancing under fire in dense waves but then quickly and instinctively adopted open,

"Indian-style" tactics they remembered from books read and war games played during childhood. But there was no steady arc of improvement. The 5th and 6th Marines learned many tough lessons in Belleau Wood. Officers and men both learned how to improvise effectively on the fly in smoke- and gas-choked woods where visibility was limited to a couple of dozen feet. In the open at Soissons, however, these same marines improvised, and the result was chaos. And on July 19 the 6th Marines went back to attacking in dense waves, just as they had on the first day at Belleau Wood, with equally tragic results. As for their commander, General Harbord, the lessons he supposedly learned in early June about the importance of firepower would quickly be discarded if he thought he needed to maintain the element of surprise. Nor were lessons about the use of supporting arms such as machine guns, or fire and maneuver learned very quickly. The Americans improved gradually over time in many respects, but for every two steps forward, they took one step back.

Readers of military history might grow tired of litanies of American deficiencies in the First World War. The impression that the doughboys and their officers were "brave but stupid," as one individual commented to me with evident outrage, is no more satisfying than the oft-quoted mantra that the British were "lions led by donkeys." Accounts that emphasize the stories of individual heroes—of which there were many—or those that focus on the human elements of small-unit achievements and interactions seem much more appealing. It is worth remembering, however, that the doughboys of World War I were thrown into the fire exceptionally quickly. Most American divisions that entered the fight in 1918 did so only a few months after their arrival in France, and only about seventeen to eighteen months passed between American entry into World War I and the AEF's first grand-scale military operations in the Saint-Mihiel and Meuse-Argonne campaigns. By contrast, the first comparable American military operation in World War II did not occur until June 6, 1944. Considered in that context, the doughboys performed extraordinarily well. They had nothing to hang their heads about.

As American and French artillery opened fire along the Saint-Mihiel salient's perimeter on the night of September 11–12, 1918, the waiting doughboys and marines felt a mixture of trepidation and confidence. Most of the nine divisions in the first line of attack were seasoned, filled with veterans who had seen the worst the Germans had to offer. Hearing the guns and watching the flames erupt in the German trenches, one 2d Division doughboy shouted exultantly into a friend's ear, "Say, boy, some Fourth of July we're having!" Finally, after months of waiting, the true test had come. As Pershing watched the bombardment, his thoughts might have wandered back to all the effort expended just to get to this point. His doughboys were ready to show the world what they could do. But they still had a lot to learn. And the Germans were waiting to teach them.[8]

NOTES

Abbreviations

ABMC	American Battle Monuments Commission, *Summary of Operations in the World War* [by division] (Washington, D.C.: Government Printing Office, 1944)
CARL	Combined Arms Research Library, Fort Leavenworth, Kans.
FO	Field Order
France MDLD	French unit war diaries, 26N, Service Historique de la Défense, Département de l'Armée de Terre, Château de Vincennes
NARA	National Archives and Records Administration, College Park, Md.
RG	Record Group
USAHEC	United States Army Heritage and Education Center, Carlisle, Pa.
USAWW	*United States Army in the World War, 1917–1919*, 17 vols. (Washington, D.C.: Center for Military History, 1988–1992)
WWIR	*World War Records, First Division, AEF, Regular*, 25 vols. (Washington, D.C.: n.p., 1928–1930)
WWIR German	*World War Records, First Division, AEF, Regular: German Documents*, 5 vols. (Washington, D.C.: n.p., 1930–1933)

Introduction: Approaches to Study of the AEF at War, 1917–1918

1. Robert L. Bullard, *Personalities and Reminiscences of the War* (Garden City, N.Y.: Doubleday, Page, 1925), 236.

2. Hervey Allen, *Toward the Flame: A Memoir of World War I* (Lincoln: University of Nebraska Press, 2003), 249–250.

3. Frank Whelton to Hervey Allen, January 10, 1937, transcription provided courtesy of Clark Whelton.

4. The United States was an associated power or cobelligerent with Great Britain and France rather than a formal ally. However, for ease of reading and to avoid convoluted verbal gymnastics, the Americans, British, and French are generally referred to as "allies" in this book.

Chapter 1. Setting the Stage

1. Mark E. Grotelueschen, *The AEF Way of War: The American Army and Combat in World War I* (Cambridge: Cambridge University Press, 2007), 11.

2. Ibid., 14ff.

3. Richard S. Faulkner, *The School of Hard Knocks: Combat Leadership in the American Expeditionary Forces* (College Station: Texas A&M University Press, 2012), 6.

4. Edward M. Coffman, *The War to End All Wars: The American Military Experience in World War I* (Madison: University of Wisconsin Press, 1986), 55–56; Jennifer Keene, *World War I* (Westport, Conn.: Greenwood Press, 2006), 48.

5. Grotelueschen, *AEF Way of War*, 32, 39; Keene, *World War I*, 54.

6. Quoted in Grotelueschen, *AEF Way of War*, 44; Jeffrey Lamonica, "Infantry Tactics in the Meuse-Argonne," in *A Companion to the Meuse-Argonne Campaign*, ed. Edward G. Lengel (London: Wiley-Blackwell, 2014), 357–373.

7. Grotelueschen, *AEF Way of War*, 44; Alexander Stewart, *A Very Unimportant Officer: Life and Death on the Somme and at Passchendaele*, ed. Cameron Stewart (London: Hodder & Stoughton, 2008), 26.

8. Grotelueschen, *AEF Way of War*, 348.

9. Ibid., 60; Faulkner, *School of Hard Knocks*, 67.

10. Grotelueschen, *AEF Way of War*, 146.

11. George B. Clark, ed., *Devil Dogs Chronicle: Voices of the 4th Marine Brigade in World War I* (Lawrence: University Press of Kansas, 2013), 2–3.

12. Ibid., 32.

13. Ibid., 35–36.

14. Ibid., 60.

15. Brian F. Neumann, "Preparations," in Lengel, *Companion to the Meuse-Argonne*, 21–35.

16. Donald Smythe, *Pershing: General of the Armies* (Bloomington: Indiana University Press, 1986), 12.

17. James G. Harbord, *Leaves from a War Diary* (New York: Dodd, Mead, 1925), 277.

18. Coffman, *War to End All Wars*, 134.

19. Faulkner, *School of Hard Knocks*, 146–147; Sibert to Pershing, October 8, 1917, and November 27, 1918, in WWIR, vol. 12.

20. Grotelueschen, *AEF Way of War*, 147–149; Pétain to Pershing, December 28, 1917, NARA, RG 120, entry 11, G-5 Secret & Confidential Files, box 1385, folder 15703.

21. Malone to Harbord, January 3, 1918; Conner to Harbord, January 3, 1918; NARA, RG 120, entry 267, G-3 General Correspondence, box 3114, folder 693.

Chapter 2. Into the Line: November 1917–April 1918

1. Charles H. Abels, *The Last of the Fighting Four* (New York: Vantage Press, 1968), 75; Mark E. Grotelueschen, *The AEF Way of War: The American Army and Combat in World War I* (Cambridge: Cambridge University Press, 2007), 60–62.

2. Beaumont B. Buck, *Memories of Peace and War* (San Antonio, Tex.: Naylor, 1935), 161.

3. James H. Hallas, ed., *Doughboy War: The American Expeditionary Force in World War I* (Mechanicsburg, Pa.: Stackpole Books, 2000), 68–69.

4. Lt. Willis Comfort report, WWIR, vol. 12; Board of Officers report, November 14, 1918, WWIR, vol. 12.

5. George C. Marshall report to 1st Division Chief of Staff, November 3, 1917, WWIR, vol. 12; German prisoner interrogation, November 3, 1917, ibid.; Comfort report; Board of Officers report; Hallas, *Doughboy War*, 68–69.

6. Ibid.

7. ABMC, *1st Division*, 5–6; *History of the First Division during the World War, 1917–1919* (Philadelphia: John C. Winston, 1931), 30–31; David Bonk, *Château Thierry &*

Belleau Wood 1918: America's Baptism of Fire on the Marne (Oxford: Osprey, 2007), 26; Joseph Dorst Patch, *A Soldier's War: The First Infantry Division A.E.F. (1917–1918)* (Corpus Christi, Tex.: Mission Press, 1966), 58–59; Marshall report.

8. Marshall interview, tape 6M, April 5, 1957, George C. Marshall Foundation; Marshall report.

9. Marshall interview. Marshall's memoirs significantly downplay the tension between himself and General Bordeaux, and historian Robert Bruce omits this tension from his account of the affair. See George C. Marshall, *Memoirs of My Services in the World War, 1917–1919* (Boston: Houghton Mifflin, 1976), 45–50; Robert B. Bruce, *A Fraternity of Arms: America and France in the Great War* (Lawrence: University Press of Kansas, 2003), 140–142; Marshall report.

10. Marshall interview; Marshall, *Memoirs of My Services*, 48–50; John J. Pershing, *My Experiences in the World War*, 2 vols. (New York: Frederick A. Stokes, 1931), 1:218; William C. Levere, *My Hut: A Memoir of a YMCA Volunteer in World War One*, ed. Jenny Thompson (Lincoln, Neb.: iUniverse, 2006), 115–116; Marshall to Sibley, November 5, 1917, *WWIR*, vol. 12. In the course of his speech, General Bordeaux called for the monument's inscription to read: "Here lie the first soldiers of the famous United States Republic to fall on the soil of France, for Justice and Liberty." After it was constructed in 1918, the inscription read: "As worthy sons of this great and noble Nation, they have fought for Justice, Liberty and Civilization against German Imperialism, the scourge of mankind." The dead Americans were repatriated after the war, but invading German troops, likely annoyed by the reference to "German Imperialism," destroyed the monument in 1940. A new monument constructed at the site after World War II bears no such contentious remarks. See "Lorraine Will Build Monument to First Americans Killed," *New York Times*, May 26, 1918; *History of the First Division*, 226; Patch, *Soldier's War*, 58–59; speech transcript in *WWIR*, vol. 12.

11. Marshall report; Bordeaux report to 1st Division Chief of Staff, November 3, 1917, *WWIR*, vol. 12.

12. Board of Officers report; Conner to Eltinge, January 7, 1918, NARA, RG 120, entry 267, G-3 General Correspondence, box 3120, folder 730; Edward M. Coffman, *The War to End All Wars: The American Military Experience in World War I* (Madison: University of Wisconsin Press, 1986), 139–140; Bonk, *Château Thierry & Belleau Wood*, 26; Marshall, *Memoirs of My Services*, 51–52. Roosevelt would receive the Silver Star for his gallantry at Cantigny.

13. Grotelueschen, *AEF Way of War*, 63–71.

14. *History of the First Division*, 42–66; undated telegram; Bullard report, March 1, 1918; King to Eltinge, March 2, 1918, all in *WWIR*, vol. 12. Bullard demanded thorough reports of the numerous small raids and patrols, which also appear in *WWIR*, vol. 12.

15. Rexmond C. Cochrane, *The 1st Division at Ansauville, January–April 1918* (Army Chemical Center, Md.: US Army Chemical Corps Historical Office, 1958); Bonk, *Château Thierry & Belleau Wood*, 27. *WWIR*, vol. 12, contains numerous reports of gas attacks; see, for example, Bullard's report to the commander of XXXIII Corps, February 27, 1918.

16. Cochrane, *1st Division at Ansauville*; *History of the First Division*, 42–66.

17. David T. Zabecki, *The German 1918 Offensives: A Case Study in the Operational Level of War* (London: Routledge, 2006), 113–161.

18. Donald Smythe, *Pershing: General of the Armies* (Bloomington: Indiana University Press, 1986), 101–102; David F. Trask, *The AEF and Coalition Warmaking, 1917–1918* (Lawrence: University Press of Kansas, 1993), 53–55.

19. Trask, *AEF and Coalition Warmaking*, 59; Zabecki, *German 1918 Offensives*, 198–199.

20. Michael E. Shay, *The Yankee Division in the First World War: In the Highest Tradition* (College Station: Texas A&M University Press, 2008), 3; ABMC, *26th Division*, 4.

21. Shay, *Yankee Division*, 64–66; Grotelueschen, *AEF Way of War*, 152.

22. Earl Yeomans (no rank given), 102d Infantry, 26th Division, WWI Survey, USAHEC; ABMC, *26th Division*, 4.

23. Frank P. Sibley, *With the Yankee Division in France* (Boston: Little, Brown, 1919), 54–63; Shay, *Yankee Division*, 46–63.

24. Shay, *Yankee Division*, 69–70.

25. Sibley, *With the Yankee Division*, 111–119; Shay, *Yankee Division*, 46–63; Grotelueschen, *AEF Way of War*, 155–156.

26. Henry Berry, *Make the Kaiser Dance* (New York: Doubleday, 1978), 177.

27. Shay praises the "initiative and flexibility" of Parker and Traub for "taking steps to prepare for" the German attack, but aside from placing a company of engineers behind Seicheprey, it is unclear what they accomplished (Shay, *Yankee Division*, 79, 89).

28. Sibley, *With the Yankee Division*, 140–41; Sebastian Laudan, "Landsknechte v. Sportsmen: Operation Kirschblüte—Seicheprey, 20 April 1918," *Stand To!* 92 (September 2011): 4–13.

29. Laudan, "Landsknechte v. Sportsmen," 4–13.

30. Sibley, *With the Yankee Division*, 142–156; Laudan, "Landsknechte v. Sportsmen," 4–13.

31. NARA, RG 120, entry 267, G-3 General Correspondence, box 3227, folder 2174.

32. Laudan, "Landsknechte v. Sportsmen," 4–13; Richard Hunt (no rank given), 51st Brigade headquarters, 26th Division, WWI Survey, USAHEC.

33. Sibley, *With the Yankee Division*, 146–156, 357–360.

34. NARA, RG 120, entry 267, G-3 General Correspondence, box 3227, folder 2177; Hunt, WWI Survey; Sibley, *With the Yankee Division*, 139.

35. NARA, RG 120, entry 267, G-3 General Correspondence, box 3227, folder 2174.

36. Robert H. Ferrell, ed., *In the Company of Generals: The World War I Diary of Pierpont L. Stackpole* (Columbia: University of Missouri Press, 2009), 51.

37. NARA, RG 120, entry 267, G-3 General Correspondence, box 3227, folder 2178.

38. Craig to Eltinge, February 7, 1919, NARA, RG 120, entry 267, G-3 General Correspondence, box 3227, folder 2178; Shay, *Yankee Division*, 88. The exaggeration continued well after the war. Edwards provided an account, faithfully recorded in the division history, that the Germans had attacked in overwhelming numbers

and suffered about 1,200 casualties (double the size of the actual attacking force). "The Boches worked thirty-six hours with twenty-six pairs of litter bearers taking away their wounded," he claimed. He also insisted that the Germans had obviously intended to take and hold Seicheprey but had fled in terror as soon as they discovered that the Americans were about to counterattack (Harry A. Benwell, *A History of the Yankee Division* [Boston: Cornhill, 1919], 74). Sibley admitted to only 130 Americans captured and insisted that the Germans had suffered up to 75 percent casualties (Sibley, *With the Yankee Division*, 139). Modern sources continue to vastly overestimate the number of German troops participating and the extent of their casualties (Bonk, *Château Thierry & Belleau Wood*, 29–30; Shay, *Yankee Division*, 89). Grotelueschen, citing immediate after-action reports and German documents allegedly captured by the Americans, also characterizes Seicheprey as something like an American success (Grotelueschen, *AEF Way of War*, 157–158). The actual scale of German casualties is uncertain.

39. Sibley, *With the Yankee Division*, 160–162.

40. NARA, RG 120, entry 267, G-3 General Correspondence, box 3114, folder 693; Shay, *Yankee Division*, 89, 253; Ferrell, *In the Company of Generals*, 51; Smythe, *Pershing*, 108.

41. Quoted in Trask, *AEF and Coalition Warmaking*, 59.

Chapter 3. Cantigny: May 1918

1. Donald Smythe, *Pershing: General of the Armies* (Bloomington: Indiana University Press, 1986), 109–110; David F. Trask, *The AEF and Coalition Warmaking, 1917–1918* (Lawrence: University Press of Kansas, 1993), 61–62.

2. Smythe, *Pershing*, 111–119; Trask, *AEF and Coalition Warmaking*, 63–65.

3. *USAWW*, 4:260; Smythe, *Pershing*, 106–107.

4. Charles H. Abels, *The Last of the Fighting Four* (New York: Vantage Press, 1968), 59; Mark E. Grotelueschen, *The AEF Way of War: The American Army and Combat in World War I* (Cambridge: Cambridge University Press, 2007), 72; Ben-Hur Chastaine, *History of the 18th U.S. Infantry First Division 1812–1919* (New York: Hymans, n.d.), 48; Lewis to Conner, May 2, 1918, WWIR, vol. 12.

5. Rexmond C. Cochrane, *The 1st Division at Cantigny, May 1918* (Army Chemical Center, Md.: US Army Chemical Corps Historical Office, 1958), 10; Robert Lee Bullard, *Personalities and Reminiscences of the War* (Garden City, N.Y.: Doubleday, Page, 1925), 192–193; John J. Pershing, *My Experiences in the World War*, 2 vols. (New York: Frederick A. Stokes, 1931), 2:59.

6. Cochrane, *1st Division at Cantigny*, 2, 10, 12, 29; *History of the First Division during the World War, 1917–1919* (Philadelphia: John C. Winston, 1931), 74–75; *USAWW*, 4:266; Lewis to Conner, May 5, 1918, WWIR, vol. 12.

7. Cochrane, *1st Division at Cantigny*, 18–23; Bullard, *Personalities and Reminiscences*, 159, 193–194.

8. Cochrane, *1st Division at Cantigny*, 13–16; Abels, *Last of the Fighting Four*, 58.

9. Cochrane, *1st Division at Cantigny*, 8; Allan R. Millett, *Well Planned, Splendidly Executed: The Battle of Cantigny, May 28–31, 1918* (Chicago: Cantigny First Division Foundation, 2010), 25–26; *History of the First Division*, 77.

10. Cochrane, *1st Division at Cantigny*, 1, 27; Millett, *Well Planned*, 30; *USAWW*, 4:270, 275; Lewis to Conner, May 17, 1918, *WWIR*, vol. 12.

11. Beaumont B. Buck, *Memories of Peace and War* (San Antonio, Tex.: Naylor, 1935), 171; Grotelueschen, *AEF Way of War*, 74; Cochrane, *1st Division at Cantigny*, 1; Pershing, *My Experiences*, 2:55; Jennings C. Wise, *The Turn of the Tide: American Operations at Cantigny, Château-Thierry, and the Second Battle of the Marne* (New York: Henry Holt, 1920), 11.

12. FO 18, May 20, 1918, *WWIR*, vol. 1; *USAWW*, 4:281–284; Douglas V. Johnson and Rolfe L. Hillman Jr., *Soissons 1918* (College Station: Texas A&M University Press, 1999), 60; ABMC, *1st Division*, 12–15; Millett, *Well Planned*, 30–32; Grotelueschen, *AEF Way of War*, 74; Buck, *Memories of Peace and War*, 172.

13. *History of the First Division*, 78–79; Leonard B. Gallagher, "A Study of the Employment of the 1st Engineers in the A.E.F.," memorandum for the Command and General Staff School, Fort Leavenworth, Kans., n.d., 4, CARL; memorandum re FO 18, May 18, 1918, *WWIR*, vol. 1.

14. Cochrane, *1st Division at Cantigny*, 35; Millett, *Well Planned*, 37–38.

15. *USAWW*, 4:296.

16. Ibid., 295, 338–340; *History of the First Division*, 80; Paul B. Harm, *Cantigny Operation: Documents Pertaining to German Raids (May 27, 1918) and American Attack and Capture of Cantigny (May 28, 1918)* (typescript, n.d.), 4–7, 39, 52, CARL; Wise, *Turn of the Tide*, 20; Bullard to Pershing, May 27, 1918, and Lewis to Conner, May 27, 1918, *WWIR*, vol. 12.

17. Cochrane, *1st Division at Cantigny*, 5, 29; *History of the First Division*, 79–82; Millett, *Well Planned*, 29. Grotelueschen provides somewhat different figures, indicating that 234 artillery pieces supported the attack (Grotelueschen, *AEF Way of War*, 76). Another source indicates that French artillery support included 132 75mm, 35 155mm, and 16 220mm and 280mm guns and howitzers, along with 24 58mm, 6 150mm, and 4 240mm mortars (Wise, *Turn of the Tide*, 18).

18. *USAWW*, 4:321; Lowell Thomas, *This Side of Hell: Dan Edwards, Adventurer* (New York: P. F. Collier & Son, 1932), 202; Harm, *Cantigny Operation*, 8; Buck, *Memories of Peace and War*, 177.

19. Grotelueschen, *AEF Way of War*, 76; *History of the First Division*, 82; James H. Hallas, ed., *Doughboy War: The American Expeditionary Force in World War I* (Mechanicsburg, Pa.: Stackpole Books, 2000), 80; annex #7 to FO 18, May 23, 1918; G-3 memorandum, "Cooperation of Adjacent Divisions," May 25, 1918, *WWIR*, vol. 1; report by commander on the "Forsanz Groupment of Tanks," May 28, 1918, *WWIR*, vol. 12. Beaumont Buck later claimed, falsely, that all the French tanks had been knocked out by enemy artillery and left behind, playing no role in the attack (Buck, *Memories of Peace and War*, 174).

20. *USAWW*, 4:341–344; Harm, *Cantigny Operation*, 57, 72; Thomas, *This Side of Hell*, 203–205.

21. *USAWW*, 4:291–301, 322; Cochrane, *1st Division at Cantigny*, 40, 48; *History of the First Division*, 83–84; Harm, *Cantigny Operation*, 8, 56; David Bonk, *Château-Thierry & Belleau Wood 1918: America's Baptism of Fire on the Marne* (Oxford: Osprey, 2007), 34; Paul Herbert, "The Battle of Cantigny and the Dawn of the Modern

American Army," *On Point: The Journal of Army History* 13, 4 (Spring 2008): 12; Vandenberg report, May 29, 1918, *WWIR*, vol. 12 (see numerous reports on the operation in the same source).

22. In keeping with the meticulous preparations for this operation, plans for the establishment of the defensive perimeter had been carefully laid out days before. Annex 3 to FO 18, May 24, 1918, *WWIR*, vol. 1; Gallagher, "Study of the Employment of 1st Engineers," 4; Bonk, *Château-Thierry & Belleau Wood*, 34; Cochrane, *1st Division at Cantigny*, 40; Millett, *Well Planned*, 42–43; Herbert, "Battle of Cantigny," 12.

23. Lewis reported to Conner from X Corps headquarters on May 29: "Our success in this small operation is very much over shadowed by the gravity of the situation on the Aisne. Everybody here is very much worried and says that the situation is even graver than that of the 21st of March and that no one knows what may happen" (*WWIR*, vol. 12). Ongoing Franco-British bickering had Lewis concerned that the Entente was in trouble. Cochrane, *1st Division at Cantigny*, 41–42; *History of the First Division*, 85; Harm, *Cantigny Operation*, 18.

24. Harm, *Cantigny Operation*, 8; *USAWW*, 4:343–344; *The Story of the Twenty-Eighth Infantry in the Great War, American Expeditionary Forces* (n.p., 1919), 17–20; 2d Brigade operations report for May 28, dated May 29, 1918, *WWIR*, vol. 13.

25. Thomas, *This Side of Hell*, 209–212.

26. Field message 1800 hours, May 28, 1918, *WWIR*, vol. 15.

27. 2d Brigade field messages, *WWIR*, vol. 15; 28th Regiment operations reports, *WWIR*, vol. 13. See the especially detailed reports provided by front-line officers in the latter source; reports of fleeing infantry, sometimes with NCOs and junior officers, were numerous. Maxey's replacement, Captain Clarence R. Huebner, would later command the division in 1944 as it landed at Omaha Beach.

28. Hallas, *Doughboy War*, 81–82.

29. *History of the First Division*, 85; Cochrane, *1st Division at Cantigny*, 43–51; Harm, *Cantigny Operation*, 7–8, 19, 39–40, 48, 67; Bonk, *Château-Thierry & Belleau Wood*, 35; *USAWW*, 4:305–309; Millett, *Well Planned*, 44–45. Division-level reports show no knowledge of the gravity of the situation—or Bullard's reluctance to admit it to outsiders (*WWIR*, vol. 12); but see 2d Brigade field messages, May 28, 1918, *WWIR*, vol. 15.

30. Accounts of German tank support are dubious, although Edwards claimed that he encountered and dispatched a German tank with the help of a "big tank grenade" (Thomas, *This Side of Hell*, 224).

31. 18th Regiment field messages, Campbell's report to commanding officer of 2/18th, July 5, 1918, *WWIR*, vol. 13; Cochrane, *1st Division at Cantigny*, 45.

32. Cochrane, *1st Division at Cantigny*, 45, 47; *USAWW*, 4:316–319; *History of the First Division*, 85; Harm, *Cantigny Operation*, 10–12, 20–21, 40, 67, 149–150; 2d Brigade field messages, May 27–30, 1918, *WWIR*, vol. 15.

33. Cochrane, *1st Division at Cantigny*, 51–52; Harm, *Cantigny Operation*, 12–13, 22, 42, 93.

34. Cochrane, *1st Division at Cantigny*, 2, 27, 51, 67, 69, 75–76; Harm, *Cantigny Operation*, 9, 148; *USAWW*, 4:342; *History of the First Division*, 86.

35. Bullard, *Personalities and Reminiscences*, 198; Herbert, "Battle of Cantigny," 13;

Trask, *AEF and Coalition Warmaking*, 68; Grotelueschen, *AEF Way of War*, 73, 80–82. Grotelueschen admits that bunching before and during the attack led to unnecessary American casualties, but he does not discuss the problems faced in defending the village.

36. Pershing, *My Experiences*, 2:60; *USAWW*, 4:342.

37. Harm, *Cantigny Operation*, 8, 42, 47, 52; Cochrane, *1st Division at Cantigny*, 54; Harm, *Cantigny Operation*, 8, 42, 52.

Chapter 4. Château-Thierry: May 1918

1. David T. Zabecki, *The German 1918 Offensives: A Case Study in the Operational Level of War* (London: Routledge, 2006), 43.

2. Ibid., 47.

3. Ibid., 47–48.

4. ABMC, *3d Division*, 1–4; NARA, RG 120, entry 267, G-3 General Correspondence, box 3093, folder 312. See also *USAWW*, 4:172–173.

5. ABMC, *3d Division*, 13; *USAWW*, 4:167–171.

6. ABMC, *3d Division*, 13; *USAWW*, 4:174–176; David Bonk, *Château Thierry & Belleau Wood 1918: America's Baptism of Fire on the Marne* (Oxford: Osprey, 2007), 41; John R. Mendenhall, "The Fist in the Dyke," *Coast Artillery Journal* 79, 1 (January–February 1936): 13.

7. John Lewis Barkley, *Scarlet Fields: The Combat Memoir of a World War I Medal of Honor Hero*, ed. Steven Trout (Lawrence: University Press of Kansas, 2012), 63.

8. Jennings C. Wise, *The Turn of the Tide: American Operations at Cantigny, Château-Thierry, and the Second Battle of the Marne* (New York: Henry Holt, 1920), 54.

9. Ibid., 56–57.

10. *USAWW*, 4:211–213; Bonk, *Château Thierry & Belleau Wood*, 41; NARA, RG 120, entry 1241, 3d Division Records, 7th Machine Gun Battalion, box 34, file 203.33.6.

11. Corps Conta War Diary, May 31–June 1, 1918, and 231st Division War Diary, May 31–June 1, 1918, in Cylburn O. Mattfeldt, ed., *Translations: War Diaries of German Units Opposed to the Second Division (Regular), 1918*, 9 vols. (Washington, D.C.: Army War College, 1930–1935), 1/2, 4/2 (citations indicate vol./pt.). General Marchand, in praising the Americans, reported that French counterattacks on the evening of May 31 had been "vigorously supported by the American Machine Guns" ("Action of the 7th MG Bn. at Château Thierry," NARA, RG 120, entry 1241, 3d Division Records, 7th Machine Gun Battalion, box 34, file 203.33.6). Evidently, this is a mistaken reference to action on the evening of June 1. According to Captain Mendenhall's account, generally not prone to understatement, the Americans did not open fire until after daybreak on June 1, and American records do not indicate any action before this time (Mendenhall, "Fist in the Dyke," 16).

12. *USAWW*, 4:182–184, 187; Wise, *Turn of the Tide*, 59–60.

13. 231st Division War Diary, in Mattfeldt, *Translations*, 4/2. Mendenhall slanderously accuses the French colonials of being pressured into "out-and-out flight" across the river by evening, but German records indicate that they continued to fight heroically, despite some inevitable straggling (Mendenhall, "Fist in the Dyke,"

18). Barkley's account has massed columns of Germans attempting to surge across the bridges, only to be mowed down in droves by the American machine guns, but no such action took place (Barkley, *Scarlet Fields*, 65).

14. The after-action report of June 12 indicates that Bissell withdrew at "about 1 a.m.," but as he thought he had discovered Germans occupying the stone bridge, it is likely he began his withdrawal around the same time Captain Wilhelmy assaulted the bridge (*USAWW*, 4:211–213). Mendenhall has Bissell beginning his withdrawal at 2100 (Mendenhall, "Fist in the Dyke," 19).

15. 231st Division War Diary and 442d Regiment War Diary, in Mattfeldt, *Translations*, 4/2; "Action of the 7th MG Bn. at Château Thierry"; Mendenhall, "Fist in the Dyke," 18.

16. *USAWW*, 4:211–213. Bissell apparently brought about 30 French and American soldiers with him across the bridge. In recommending Bissell for the Medal of Honor on June 4, Major James Taylor multiplied that by 10, claiming that Bissell had escorted 300 French soldiers to safety—an impossibly large number, especially given that the French had no intention of withdrawing and defended their positions to the last. Bissell, who received the Silver Star for his conduct in Château-Thierry, would have a distinguished military career in World War II (NARA, RG 120, entry 1241, 3d Division Records, 7th Machine Gun Battalion, box 34, file 203.33.6).

17. *USAWW*, 4:212.

18. United States Infantry School, *Infantry in Battle*, 2d ed. (Washington, D.C.: Infantry School, 1939), 201–202. Mendenhall's subsequently published account provides a substantially different narrative of events that absolves him of blame for the mix-up (Mendenhall, "Fist in the Dyke," 19–20).

19. Mendenhall's claim that he turned back a German attack just in time sounds like a disingenuous attempt at self-redemption. See US Infantry School, *Infantry in Battle*, 203; Mendenhall, "Fist in the Dyke," 19–20; 231st Division War Diary, in Mattfeldt, *Translations*, 4/2.

20. US Infantry School, *Infantry in Battle*, 203. The major's disavowal of knowledge of the retreat seems to indicate either that Mendenhall had not informed him or that Taylor had no interest in informing the lieutenants of their captain's mistake.

21. 442d Regiment War Diary, in Mattfeldt, *Translations*, 4/2. Mendenhall ("Fist in the Dyke," 19) conveys the distrust and discomfort felt by Americans who had to fight next to the black Senegalese:

> These Senegalese, recruited in the French Congo and speaking an unintelligible patois, were little more than savages and had earned a reputation for ruthless cruelty. They were an uncomfortable crew to have around, for one was never sure just what they intended to do. At times they seemed to have real difficulty distinguishing between Germans and Americans, and the latter had an uneasy feeling that a few honest mistakes would not lie heavily on the Senegalese conscience. Thus their value at any particular moment was one of those things on which you pay your money and take your choice.

22. 231st Division War Diary, in Mattfeldt, *Translations*, 4/2; Bonk, *Château Thierry & Belleau Wood*, 42; Frederic Vinton Hemenway, *History of the Third Division United States Army in the World War for the Period December 1, 1917 to January 1, 1919* (Anderbach-on-the-Rhine, n.p., 1919), 3; "Action of the 7th MG Bn. at Château Thierry."

23. *USAWW*, 4:213; "Action of the 7th MG Bn. at Château Thierry," NARA, RG 120, entry 1241, 3d Division Records, 7th Machine Gun Battalion, box 34, file 203.33.6, and box 18, file 203.33.6, folder 61; Hemenway, *History of the Third Division*, 268–269; George B. Clark, *Devil Dogs: Fighting Marines of World War I* (Novato, Calif.: Presidio Press, 1999), 65.

Chapter 5. The 2d Division Enters the Lines: May 31–June 5, 1918

1. In theory, if not always in practice, each of the six machine gun companies per brigade was assigned to an infantry battalion. Thus, in the 4th Brigade, they were distributed as follows: 1/5th (8th Company), 2/5th (23d Company), 3/5th (77th Company), 1/6th (73d Company), 2/6th (81st Company), and 3/6th (15th company). L. W. T. Waller, "Machine Guns of the Fourth Brigade," Marine Corps Gazette 5, 1 (March 1920): 2–4.

2. John W. Thomason Jr., "The Marine Brigade," U.S. Naval Institute Proceedings 54, 11 (November 1928): 964–965; Edwin N. McClellan, "A Brief History of the Fourth Brigade of Marines," Marine Corps Gazette 4 (December 1919): 345–347.

3. Mark E. Grotelueschen, *The AEF Way of War: The American Army and Combat in World War I* (Cambridge: Cambridge University Press, 2007), 206.

4. H. W. Edwards, "Harbord and Lejeune: A Command Precedent," Marine Corps Gazette 37, 7 (July 1953): 12–13; Douglas V. Johnson and Rolfe L. Hillman Jr., *Soissons 1918* (College Station: Texas A&M University Press, 1999), 58; quoted in Edwin N. McClellan, "Capture of Hill 142, Battle of Belleau Wood, and Capture of Bouresches," Marine Corps Gazette 5, 3–4 (September–December 1920): 280; James G. Harbord, *Leaves from a War Diary* (New York: Dodd, Mead, 1925), 299.

5. John W. Thomason Jr., "History of the 2d Division in World War I" (typescript, 1918, CARL), 22–37; David Bonk, *Château Thierry & Belleau Wood 1918: America's Baptism of Fire on the Marne* (Oxford: Osprey, 2007), 28–29. The Germans claimed losses of thirty-nine killed, eighty-three wounded, and none captured; they maintained that they captured twenty-nine prisoners.

6. Thomason, "History of the 2d Division," 37–38.

7. ABMC, *2d Division*, 5–6; Bonk, *Château Thierry & Belleau Wood*, 42; A. W. Catlin, *"With the Help of God and a Few Marines"* (Garden City, N.Y.: Doubleday, Page, 1919), 80–81.

8. Hunter Liggett, *AEF: Ten Years Ago in France* (New York: Dodd, Mead, 1928), 129; Jennings C. Wise, *The Turn of the Tide: American Operations at Cantigny, Château-Thierry, and the Second Battle of the Marne* (New York: Henry Holt, 1920), 64–65.

9. Bonk, *Château Thierry & Belleau Wood*, 45–46; George B. Clark, *Devil Dogs: Fighting Marines of World War I* (Novato, Calif.: Presidio Press, 1999), 71; Catlin, *"With the Help of God,"* 82; Wise, *Turn of the Tide*, 64. Although Degoutte and other French generals are frequently criticized in American accounts for either their ti-

midity or their bloody-minded aggressiveness, their praise was highly sought after. This was true of Degoutte, even though he commanded American troops in multiple capacities throughout the summer and was widely hated; his proclamation of August 9, 1918, praising the "glorious . . . ardor and gallantry" of the Yanks is often quoted in American accounts. See, for example, Bert Ford, *The Fighting Yankees Overseas* (Boston: Norman E. McPhail, 1919), 43.

10. Warren R. Jackson, *His Time in Hell. A Texas Marine in France: The World War I Memoir of Warren R. Jackson*, ed. George B. Clark (Novato, Calif.: Presidio Press, 2001), 87–88; Harbord, *Leaves from a War Diary*, 288–289; Clark, *Devil Dogs*, 68–69; Catlin, "With the Help of God," 70, 87. Postwar German accounts likewise found it convenient, particularly in the virulently anti-French atmosphere of the 1920s, to highlight alleged French defeatism and claim that the Germans had been stopped only by the fresh Americans. See Ernst Otto, "The Battles for the Possession of Belleau Woods, June 1918," *U.S. Naval Institute Proceedings* 54, 11 (November 1928): 940–941. Otto's assertion that Degoutte's faulty tactics were to blame for the heavy American casualties on the first day of Belleau Wood made even Harbord balk; see ibid., 946–947.

11. Edwin N. McClellan, "Operations of the Fourth Brigade of Marines in the Aisne Defensive," *Marine Corps Gazette* 5, 2 (June 1920): 189; NARA, RG 120, entry 267, G-3 General Correspondence, box 3114, folder 694.

12. ABMC, *2d Division*, 7–10; Bonk, *Château Thierry & Belleau Wood*, 42–43, 46–52; Catlin, "With the Help of God," 80–81; 2d Division Journal of Operations, in Cylburn O. Mattfeldt, ed., *Records of the Second Division (Regular)*, 10 vols. (Washington, D.C.: Army War College, 1924–1929), 6/1; Tom FitzPatrick, *Tidewater Warrior: The World War I Years: General Lemuel C. Shepherd, Jr., USMC, Twentieth Commandant* (Fairfax, Va.: Tom FitzPatrick, 2010), 224; Levi E. Hemrick, *Once a Marine* (New York: Carlton Press, 1968), 99.

13. Cylburn O. Mattfeldt, ed., *Translations: War Diaries of German Units Opposed to the Second Division (Regular), 1918*, 9 vols. (Washington, D.C.: Army War College, 1930–1935), 1/2; Otto, "Battles for the Possession of Belleau Woods," 940–941.

14. Clark, *Devil Dogs*, 74; Von Conta orders 2000h, May 31, 1918, 197th Division War Diary, in Mattfeldt, *Translations*, 1/2, 4/1. The 197th Division took 395 casualties on June 1, 252 on June 2, and 195 on June 3. George B. Clark claims that the only significant defensive fire on June 1 "emanated from the American lines" and that French artillery was "more effective" in hitting American positions "than against the Boche" (Clark, *Devil Dogs*, 75). German sources amply contradict such assertions.

15. French 43d Division War Diary, France MDLD; FitzPatrick, *Tidewater Warrior*, 224–225.

16. Henry Berry, *Make the Kaiser Dance* (New York: Doubleday, 1978), 78; Clark, *Devil Dogs*, 76; FitzPatrick, *Tidewater Warrior*, 227–229; Bonk, *Château Thierry & Belleau Wood*, 47.

17. 6th Machine Gun Battalion War Diary, in Mattfeldt, *Records of the Second Division*, 8/2.

18. 4th Brigade Report, in Mattfeldt, *Records of the Second Division*, 6/2; French

43d Division War Diary, France MDLD; Clark, *Devil Dogs*, 81. The 2d Division's journal of operations, based on information supplied by 4th Brigade headquarters, claimed that "the 6th Machine Gun Battalion stopped the German advance several times" (Mattfeldt, *Records of the Second Division*, 6/1). Peter F. Owen, drawing on this journal and a personal account given in 1979, says that the American machine guns and French artillery combined to "rip apart the thick waves of advancing infantry. The long-range fire forced the Germans to slow down and creep ahead by short rushes of smaller groups. The [American] Hotchkiss guns cut down more enemy soldiers as they attempted to dash through the wheat. Holcomb's riflemen picked off a few diehards when they popped up close to the marine positions" (Peter F. Owen, *To the Limit of Endurance: A Battalion of Marines in the Great War* [College Station: Texas A&M University Press, 2007], 68–69). It is unlikely that the Germans pushed their advance to that extent, however, given that the 10th Division was under orders to take up defensive positions after capturing Bouresches (which it did) (Otto, "Battles for the Possession of Belleau Woods," 942).

19. Corps Conta War Diary, 197th Division War Diary, in Mattfeldt, *Translations*, 1/2, 4/1; French 43d Division War Diary, France MDLD; FitzPatrick, *Tidewater Warrior*, 225. Contrast these facts to George B. Clark's unattributed assertion that the Germans faced only "a minimum of resistance from the defending French" at this time (Clark, *Devil Dogs*, 80).

20. 2d Division Journal of Operations, 5th and 6th Marines field messages, in Mattfeldt, *Records of the Second Division*, 4/2, 5/2, 6/1; French 43d Division War Diary, France MDLD. Later American accounts would blame this confusion on poor French maps, although sheer stubbornness on the part of Major Maurice E. Shearer of the 1/6th and Wise may have played a role as well (Clark, *Devil Dogs*, 86–87).

21. Mattfeldt, *Records of the Second Division*, 5/1; Von Conta Corps orders June 3, 1918, 10th Division War Diary, in Mattfeldt, *Translations*, 1/2.

22. Clark, *Devil Dogs*, 88; Mattfeldt, *Translations*, 4/1; French 43d Division War Diary, France MDLD.

23. *USAWW*, 4:133; 4th Reserve Corps orders, June 3, 1918, 237th Division War Diary, in Mattfeldt, *Translations*, 1/2, 4/3. Works giving the Americans primary credit for halting the Germans between June 1 and 4 include Clark, *Devil Dogs*, and Robert B. Asprey, *At Belleau Wood* (Denton: University of North Texas Press, 1996). William E. Moore is more charitable: "The French line opposing the Germans was so thin it had to give way. It was retreating, but the retirement was slow. It was under orders. It was not so disorderly as has often been pictured" (William E. Moore, "The 'Bloody Angle' of the A.E.F.," *American Legion Weekly*, February 24, 1922, 15–17). The Germans briefly considered resuming the advance a few days later to attain positions deemed more suitable for defense, but the 2d Division's assault on Belleau Wood and the exhaustion of the German front-line divisions put an end to such plans.

24. Asprey, *At Belleau Wood*, 119–120; Alan Axelrod, *Miracle at Belleau Wood: The Birth of the Modern U.S. Marine Corps* (Guilford, Conn.: Lyons Press, 2007), 85–86; Mattfeldt, *Records of the Second Division*, 5/2; Bonk, *Château-Thierry & Belleau Wood*,

49; George B. Clark, *The Second Infantry Division in World War I: A History of the American Expeditionary Force Regulars, 1917–1919* (Jefferson, N.C.: McFarland, 2007), 49; Daniel E. Morgan, *When the World Went Mad: A Thrilling Story of the Late War, Told in the Language of the Trenches* (Boston: Christopher Publishing House, 1931), 28. Whether Williams—who was subsequently killed in action—ever uttered these famous words is now impossible to say. George B. Clark argues that "most everyone in attendance agreed that Williams was the man" to make the statement, but this author has found no eyewitness accounts to that effect (Clark, *Second Infantry Division*, 49). Postwar discussions of the origin of the legend sometimes boiled down to the question of which marine officer on the spot would have been more acquainted with "cussing" and thus more likely to use strong language in response to the French order (Moore, "'Bloody Angle' of the A.E.F.").

Colonel Frederic Wise laid claim, probably falsely, to the quotation in his memoir. His account is replete with de rigueur tales of cowardly French troops who abandoned the Americans to defend Les Mares Farm on their own. That the fleeing men were black probably reinforced the believability of his story in many readers' minds. "A battalion of French Senegalese troops came rushing toward the rear through my extreme left," he wrote. "Only a few of them had kept their rifles. The bulk of them, weapons thrown away, were in a panic of retreat. The way those niggers were running I thought maybe the English Channel might stop them when they got there, but nothing less" (Frederic M. Wise, *A Marine Tells It to You* [New York: J. H. Sears, 1919], 202).

25. Shepherd took credit for the decision to occupy the knoll, but other sources indicate that Captain Blanchfield ordered him to establish the outpost. See Moore, "'Bloody Angle' of the A.E.F."; FitzPatrick, *Tidewater Warrior*, 233; McClellan, "Operations of the Fourth Brigade," 194.

26. Catlin, *"With the Help of God,"* 99; Mattfeldt, *Translations*, 4/1.

27. McClellan, "Operations of the Fourth Brigade," 194; FitzPatrick, *Tidewater Warrior*, 232–237; Berry, *Make the Kaiser Dance*, 79–80; Moore, "'Bloody Angle' of the A.E.F." Sources, both contemporary and postwar, disagree about the date of the attack at Les Mares Farm; some claim the German assault took place on June 3, and others have it occurring on June 4 or even June 5. Allowing for hyperbole, it is probable that a number of small engagements in and around Les Mares Farm have become blurred. However, the preponderance of evidence from both German and American sources suggests that the initial contact took place on the evening of June 3, with several small engagements occurring on June 4 and possibly June 5. According to Berry, Shepherd recalls that the event took place on June 5 (Berry, *Make the Kaiser Dance*, 80).

28. Shepherd's postwar testimony to Berry that he was wounded before ever reaching the outpost, while leaning against a tree under artillery fire, contradicts articles by McClellan and Moore, as well as testimony in FitzPatrick that he continued to the outpost and calmly directed fire against the advancing Germans. See McClellan, "Operations of the Fourth Brigade," 194; Asprey, *At Belleau Wood*, 121–124; FitzPatrick, *Tidewater Warrior*, 232–237; Moore, "'Bloody Angle' of the A.E.F." Asprey also draws on McClellan and Moore in an account that Shepherd later praised

in a letter written on April 2, 1975, to Charles F. Rinker. Rinker had served in the 55th Company's 4th Platoon and testified that his company had "stopped the Germans dead" at Les Mares Farm, saving Paris (Charles F. Rinker, 2d Division, WWI Survey, USAHEC).

29. Catlin, *"With the Help of God,"* 92–96.

30. Ibid., 95. Just as many marine accounts provide nearly identical descriptions of French soldiers fleeing the front and shouting that Paris was lost, "eyewitness" depictions of the Les Mares Farm affair are suspiciously similar—and often implausible. Thus, Corporal Joe Rendinell, a battalion intelligence officer in the 3/6th Marines (a unit that did not directly participate in the fighting on June 3, although it may have helped repel a German attack the next morning), writes:

> On June third, about 5 o'clock, the enemy attacked again & then we were ordered to open fire. 'Make every shot count, men. Pass the word on down the line. Do not waste ammunition.' It was machine-gun & rifle fire. How we raked the German ranks. We all took careful aim before every shot. My gun got so hot I could not touch it, so I crawled over & took one of my buddies rifles for he was done for and I used both guns, alterinating [sic] as they got too hot. The Germans kept a-coming though. Then they would stop and seemed wondering what kind of fighting is this, anyhow? At last they broke and started to beat it. A French observer reported he had never seen such accurate shooting as what we did.

Rendinell also takes credit for slaughtering an entire German patrol that evening (Joseph Edward Rendinell, *One Man's War: The Diary of a Leatherneck* [New York: J. H. Sears, 1928], 93–95).

War correspondent Floyd Gibbons, not an eyewitness but a relentless marine publicist, echoed—or perhaps initiated—these accounts with his tales of how each American artillery burst left a "circle of German dead"; how French aircraft signaled "bravos" at the American shooting and "the French marveled at the deliberateness and accuracy of our riflemen"; and how the Germans, in their "flush of victory" on the road to Paris, "encountered the Marines' stone wall and reeled back in surprise" (Floyd Phillips Gibbons, *"And They Thought We Wouldn't Fight"* [New York: George H. Doran, 1918], 294–295).

Wise, commander of the 2/5th, later claimed that he had commanded the defense of Les Mares Farm from the front, although his presence there is not mentioned by other alleged eyewitnesses. His description of the German assault somewhat contradicts those offered by other marines. "It was about mid-afternoon," he recalled:

> There we were, a single line of Marines in fox holes, stretched over two and a half miles of front. A few more than nine hundred men. Nothing to protect our flanks. Paris behind us. The victorious German army in front of us. Shells falling all around us. Our allies had vanished. . . . The German attack was coming. A long way off over those grain fields I could see thin lines of in-

fantry advancing.... It wasn't the mass formation I had expected to see after what I had heard of German attacks. Those lines were well extended. At least six or seven paces of open space were between the men. There seemed to be four or five lines, about twenty-five yards apart. They wore the "coal-scuttle" helmet. Their rifles, bayonets fixed, were at the ready. They advanced slowly and steadily. I couldn't distinguish any leaders.... When the German front line was about a hundred yards from us, we opened up. Up and down the line I could see my men working their rifle bolts. I looked for the front line of the Germans. There wasn't any! Killed and wounded, they had crumpled and vanished in the grain. Their second line moved steadily forward. Their rifles were at their shoulders. They were shooting as they came. Suddenly they, too, crumpled and vanished.... That deadly rifle fire seemed to take the heart out of the Germans who were still on their feet. Suddenly they broke ranks and ran. Back through the grain fields they retreated raggedly and vanished in the distance.

According to Wise, the marines had broken the German attack by "trained German veterans of the Twenty-sixth Division [sic]—splendid troops"—solely by rifle fire (Wise, *A Marine Tells It to You*, 203–204).

31. Bonk, *Château-Thierry & Belleau Wood*, 49–50; Clark, *Devil Dogs*, 91–92. McClellan, perhaps tellingly, makes no reference to gigantic heaps of German dead, stating more modestly: "It is believed that a number of German casualties resulted and that the fire of the Marines surprised and confused them" (McClellan, "Operations of the Fourth Brigade," 194–195).

32. Clark, *Second Infantry Division*, 51–52; telephone report, 0830h, June 4, 1918, from Maj. Millet to Capt. Le Bleu, translated by G-3, NARA, RG 120, entry 267, G-3 General Correspondence, box 3114, folder 694; Bonk, *Château-Thierry & Belleau Wood*, 50. Division historian John W. Thomason, perhaps tellingly, sums up the day's events as follows: "American Infantry and Marines, lying in their lines, noted movements of the enemy on their front; they saw him on the Clignon crests, from one to three kilometers away. A few bursts of machine gun fire were gotten off at him, where the target was tempting and in front of Les Mares Farm men tried long-range rifle shots." Thomason mentions no other American-German engagements on this date, although he does describe the patrol on June 4 that netted a few German prisoners (John W. Thomason Jr., *The United States Army Second Division Northwest of Château Thierry in World War I*, ed. George B. Clark [Jefferson, N.C.: McFarland, 2006], 68–69). Ernst Otto's 1928 article, which generally plays up the American contribution while denigrating the French, makes no reference to this encounter in describing the events of June 2–4 (Otto, "Battles for the Possession of Belleau Woods," 942–943).

33. FitzPatrick, *Tidewater Warrior*, 227–237; Catlin, "With the Help of God," 100; Amos N. Wilder, *Armageddon Revisited: A World War I Journal* (New Haven, Conn.: Yale University Press, 1994), 101; ABMC, *2d Division*, 10; 2d Division Journal of Operations, June 4, 1918, 4th Brigade Daily Report, June 4, 19198, in Mattfeldt, *Records of the Second Division*, 6/1.

34. Asprey, *At Belleau Wood*, 125–126; ABMC, *2d Division*, 10; Mattfeldt, *Records of the Second Division*, 6/2; Mattfeldt, *Translations*, 4/1; Martin Gus Gulberg, *A War Diary* (Chicago: Drake Press, 1927), 26. Whether by "the third day" Gulberg meant their third day in the line or the third day of June is unclear; George B. Clark makes the latter assumption and attributes this account to June 3 (Clark, *Devil Dogs*, 90).

35. Some accounts have this episode occurring on June 5 or being directed against a German patrol rather than a machine gun nest. See 2d Division Report of Operations, in Mattfeldt, *Records of the Second Division*, 6/1; "Château-Thierry–Belleau Woods Operation 2nd Division Intelligence Reports April 10th May 10th & June 5th 1918," WWI Survey, USAHEC; FitzPatrick, *Tidewater Warrior*, 237–240. George B. Clark claims that the Americans took out a "thirty-man raiding group," of which "only five Germans escaped to their lines in safety" (Clark, *Devil Dogs*, 96).

36. McClellan, "Operations of the Fourth Brigade," 193, 213.

37. FitzPatrick, *Tidewater Warrior*, 240; American Battle Monuments Commission, *American Armies and Battlefields in Europe* (1938; reprint, Washington, D.C.: US Army Center of Military History, 1992), 46; William J. Mowry, "The Greatest Day," *Marine Corps Gazette* 47, 7 (July 1963): 36; George B. Clark, introduction to Elton E. Mackin, *Suddenly We Didn't Want to Die: Memoirs of a World War I Marine* (Novato, Calif.: Presidio, 1993), 6; Axelrod, *Miracle at Belleau Wood*, 94; Bonk, *Château-Thierry & Belleau Wood*, 50.

38. Mattfeldt, *Translations*, 1/2.

39. Ibid.; David T. Zabecki, *The German 1918 Offensives: A Case Study in the Operational Level of War* (London: Routledge, 2006), 48–49; Asprey, *At Belleau Wood*, 133.

40. Mattfeldt, *Translations*, 1/2.

Chapter 6. Into the Woods: June 6, 1918

1. 2d Division Journal of Operations, 4th Brigade War Diary, in Cylburn O. Mattfeldt, ed., *Records of the Second Division (Regular)*, 10 vols. (Washington, D.C.: Army War College, 1924–1929), 6/1, 6/2; ABMC, *2d Division*, 10–11; Joseph J. Gleeson, *A Soldier's Story: A Daily Account of World War I by Sergeant Joseph J. Gleeson, January 1918 to March 1919* (privately printed, 1999), 28; *USAWW*, 4:131, 137–139. Catlin claims that Berry's 3/5th Battalion attacked at 0300 on this date in conjunction with a French battalion and captured Hill 165, driving the Germans back about 1.5 kilometers toward Torcy and capturing many guns, but there is no record of this action elsewhere (A. W. Catlin, "*With the Help of God and a Few Marines*" [Garden City, N.Y.: Doubleday, Page, 1919], 103). The French, meanwhile, apparently abandoned Les Mares Farm—which they may have viewed as untenable—to the Germans, at least temporarily. On the night of June 4–5, according to German records, the 197th Division took the farm, and the 237th Division occupied the remainder of Belleau Wood and advanced to the foot of Hill 142 (197th and 237th Divisions War Diaries, in Cylburn O. Mattfeldt, ed., *Translations: War Diaries of German Units Opposed to the Second Division [Regular], 1918*, 9 vols. [Washington, D.C.: Army War College, 1930–1935], 1/2).

2. David Bonk, *Château-Thierry & Belleau Wood 1918: America's Baptism of Fire on*

the Marne (Oxford: Osprey, 2007), 52; Warren R. Jackson, *His Time in Hell. A Texas Marine in France: The World War I Memoir of Warren R. Jackson*, ed. George B. Clark (Novato, Calif.: Presidio Press, 2001), 97; Robert Winthrop Kean, *Dear Marraine (1917–1919)* (privately printed, 1969), 96–97.

3. *USAWW*, 4:135. Robert Asprey has criticized Degoutte's decision as premature. "A commander cannot switch from the defense to the offense with the ease of turning a water tap on or off," he writes, arguing that the Americans were unprepared for quick action (Robert B. Asprey, *At Belleau Wood* [Denton: University of North Texas Press, 1996], 139–141). The Marine Brigade's confusion on the night before the attack lends support to this conclusion. Nevertheless, Degoutte's desire to move before the Germans—who were clearly exhausted after their long advance—had time to dig in and bring up their heavy artillery seems justified in retrospect. Given more time to dig in, the German positions in Belleau Wood might have been impossible to overcome, instead of just extremely challenging for the green Americans. However, the lack of proper intelligence would contribute to the high casualty toll, as Harbord continued to heed inaccurate French and American reports suggesting that the Germans held the woods only lightly. Ultimately, the disastrous results of the battle's first days can be attributed to both hasty preparation and poor tactics. Whether the Americans would have employed better tactics given another day or two to prepare is debatable. Bundy later wrote that "General Degoutte . . . saw the importance of Belleau Wood, and was in full accord with our desire to take it as soon as possible," suggesting that the primary impetus for a quick attack came not from the French but from the Americans (Edwin N. McClellan, "Capture of Hill 142, Battle of Belleau Wood, and Capture of Bouresches," *Marine Corps Gazette* 5, 3–4 [September–December 1920]: 286).

4. *USAWW*, 4:143–145.

5. Ibid., 150, 353; Bonk, *Château-Thierry & Belleau Wood*, 53.

6. George B. Clark, *Devil Dogs: Fighting Marines of World War I* (Novato, Calif.: Presidio Press, 1999), 97–98; Asprey, *At Belleau Wood*, 140; 4th Brigade field messages, in Mattfeldt, *Records of the Second Division*, 4/2; Bonk, *Château-Thierry & Belleau Wood*, 53.

7. Clark, *Devil Dogs*, 99–102; Bonk, *Château-Thierry & Belleau Wood*, 54.

8. Gleeson, *Soldier's Story*, 28; Clark, *Devil Dogs*, 101.

9. Mark E. Grotelueschen, *The AEF Way of War: The American Army and Combat in World War I* (Cambridge: Cambridge University Press, 2007), 211; Bonk, *Château-Thierry & Belleau Wood*, 54–55; Clark, *Devil Dogs*, 100–101. John W. Thomason Jr., in his draft history of the 2d Division, blames the absence of these two companies on French troops that allegedly came late to relieve them. George B. Clark comments, rightly, that this "looks like a cover-up, possibly brought about by the 2nd Division history project leadership" (John W. Thomason Jr., *The United States Army Second Division Northwest of Château-Thierry in World War I*, ed. George B. Clark [Jefferson, N.C.: McFarland, 2006], 83).

10. Clark, *Devil Dogs*, 102–106; Thomason, *United States Army Second Division*, 84–85.

11. Thomason, *United States Army Second Division*, 84–85; Bonk, *Château-Thierry & Belleau Wood*, 55. Hamilton's account appears in Mattfeldt, *Records of the Second Division*, 5/2; see also Clark, *Devil Dogs*, 110–112.

12. Mattfeldt, *Records of the Second Division*, 5/2; see also Clark, *Devil Dogs*, 110–112. A few of Hamilton's men even managed to make it into Torcy itself, where they were killed. Their bodies were not discovered until 1927, tumbled into a common grave with two dead Germans (Thomason, *United States Army Second Division*, 85).

13. 4th Brigade War Diary, 4th Brigade field messages, in Mattfeldt, *Records of the Second Division*, 4/1, 6/2; French 167th Division War Diary, France MDLD; US-AWW, 4:359–360; quoted in Clark, *Devil Dogs*, 108.

14. Thomason, *United States Army Second Division*, 85–89.

15. Mattfeldt, *Records of the Second Division*, 5/2; Clark, *Devil Dogs*, 110–112; French 167th Division War Diary, France MDLD; Thomason, *United States Army Second Division*, 88–89.

16. Bonk, *Château-Thierry & Belleau Wood*, 58.

17. German 197th Division War Diary, in Mattfeldt, *Translations*, 4/1; USAWW, 4:354.

18. 17th Company field messages, in Mattfeldt, *Records of the Second Division*, 5/2; Thomason, *United States Army Second Division*, 90–91; Bonk, *Château-Thierry & Belleau Wood*, 56–58; Clark, *Devil Dogs*, 106, 110.

19. Catlin, "With the Help of God," 104–105.

20. Thomason, *United States Army Second Division*, 98–99.

21. USAWW, 4:364–365; Bonk, *Château-Thierry & Belleau Wood*, 60–61.

22. Clark, *Devil Dogs*, 113–117.

23. Bonk, *Château-Thierry & Belleau Wood*, 60–61; Catlin, "With the Help of God," 108–112.

24. Hartlieb report to Jacobi, June 17, 1918, in Mattfeldt, *Translations*, 4/3; US-AWW, 4:383; Bonk, *Château-Thierry & Belleau Wood*, 59–60.

25. Catlin, "With the Help of God," 112; Hartlieb to Jacobi, June 17, in Mattfeldt, *Translations*, 4/3.

26. George B. Clark, *The Second Infantry Division in World War I: A History of the American Expeditionary Force Regulars, 1917–1919* (Jefferson, N.C.: McFarland, 2007), 58; George B. Clark, ed., *Devil Dogs Chronicle: Voices of the 4th Marine Brigade in World War I* (Lawrence: University Press of Kansas, 2013), 160; Ernst Otto, "The Battles for the Possession of Belleau Woods, June 1918," *U.S. Naval Institute Proceedings* 54, 11 (November 1928): 948; Bonk, *Château-Thierry & Belleau Wood*, 61–62.

27. USAWW, 4:392; Floyd Phillips Gibbons, *"And They Thought We Wouldn't Fight"* (New York: George H. Doran, 1918), 304; J. D. Wilmeth, "Bois de la Brigade de Marine," *Marine Corps Gazette* 23, 1 (March 1939): 28. Just five pages later, Gibbons contradicts this account in another description of the same attack: "And then we went over. There are really no heroics about it. There is no bugle call, no sword waving, no dramatic enunciation of catchy commands, no theatricalism—it's just plain get up and go over. And it is done just the same as one would walk across a peaceful wheat field out in Iowa" (Gibbons, *"And They Thought We Wouldn't Fight,"* 309).

28. 4th Brigade War Diary and field messages, in Mattfeldt, *Records of the Second*

Division, 4/2, 6/2; *USAWW*, 4:367; Clark, *Second Infantry Division*, 58–59; Gibbons, "And They Thought We Wouldn't Fight," 311–315; Bonk, *Château-Thierry & Belleau Wood*, 62–63.

29. Catlin, "With the Help of God," 114–115; *USAWW*, 4:392–393; Bonk, *Château-Thierry & Belleau Wood*, 63; Clark, *Devil Dogs*, 119–121; Thomason, *United States Army Second Division*, 99–100.

30. Clark, *Devil Dogs Chronicle*, 169.

31. Catlin, "With the Help of God," 118–119.

32. Clark, *Devil Dogs Chronicle*, 171; Peter F. Owen, *To the Limit of Endurance: A Battalion of Marines in the Great War* (College Station: Texas A&M University Press, 2007), 74.

33. 398th Regiment War Diary, in Mattfeldt, *Translations*, 1/2. Peter F. Owen, agreeing with American accounts, has the marines advancing in skirmish lines (Owen, *To the Limit of Endurance*, 75, 80–81).

34. *USAWW*, 4:392–393; Bonk, *Château-Thierry & Belleau Wood*, 64; Clark, *Second Infantry Division*, 60–61; Clark, *Devil Dogs*, 121–123; Thomason, *United States Army Second Division*, 106–108.

35. *USAWW*, 4:368; 4th Brigade War Diary and field messages, in Mattfeldt, *Records of the Second Division*, 4/2, 6/2.

36. 4th Brigade War Diary, in Mattfeldt, *Records of the Second Division*, 6/2; Thomason, *United States Army Second Division*, 102; *USAWW*, 4:372–373; French 167th Division War Diary, France MDLD. It is unclear whether any French troops were actually supposed to be to the right of the Marine Brigade, where the US 23d Regiment was deployed.

37. *USAWW*, 4:371, 376; Mattfeldt, *Records of the Second Division*, 5/2.

38. *USAWW*, 4:392–393; Mattfeldt, *Records of the Second Division*, 6/2; Bonk, *Château-Thierry & Belleau Wood*, 66; Clark, *Devil Dogs*, 128–129.

39. *USAWW*, 4:569; Corps Conta War Diary, 237th Division War Diary, in Mattfeldt, *Translations*, 1/2, 4/3.

40. Bischoff and Hartlieb reports, in Mattfeldt, *Translations*, 4/3.

41. Thomason, *United States Army Second Division*, 113.

42. 10th Division, 398th and 47th Regiment reports, June 4, 1918, in Mattfeldt, *Translations*, 1/2.

43. Mattfeldt, *Records of the Second Division*, 7/1; *USAWW*, 4:378–379; Thomason, *United States Army Second Division*, 113–114; Douglas V. Johnson and Rolfe L. Hillman Jr., *Soissons 1918* (College Station: Texas A&M University Press, 1999), 73.

44. *USAWW*, 4: 378–382; Thomason, *United States Army Second Division*, 113–114.

45. Mattfeldt, *Records of the Second Division*, 5/1; 47th Regiment War Diary, in Mattfeldt, *Translations*, 1/2; *USAWW*, 4:373, 378–379, 382.

46. 3d Brigade field messages, in Mattfeldt, *Records of the Second Division*, 4/1, 4/2; *USAWW*, 4:378–379.

47. 47th and 398th Regiments War Diaries, in Mattfeldt, *Translations*, 1/2.

48. *USAWW*, 4:378–379, 389; 47th and 398th Regiments War Diaries, in Mattfeldt, *Translations*, 1/2; Corp. Frank L. Faulkner, 23d Regiment, WWI Survey, USAHEC.

49. ABMC, *2d Division*, 11–14.

50. Grotelueschen, *AEF Way of War*, 213; Otto, "Battles for the Possession of Belleau Woods," 949.

Chapter 7. "Sporting Soldiers": Belleau Wood, June 7–8, 1918

1. *USAWW*, 4:401; Cylburn O. Mattfeldt, ed., *Records of the Second Division (Regular)*, 10 vols. (Washington, D.C.: Army War College, 1924–1929), 5/1; David Bonk, *Château-Thierry & Belleau Wood 1918: America's Baptism of Fire on the Marne* (Oxford: Osprey, 2007), 66–67; George B. Clark, *The Second Infantry Division in World War I: A History of the American Expeditionary Force Regulars, 1917–1919* (Jefferson, N.C.: McFarland, 2007), 64–65.

2. Mattfeldt, *Records of the Second Division*, 4/1; *USAWW*, 4:398, 403; Bonk, *Château-Thierry & Belleau Wood*, 67.

3. The 197th Division had taken 650 casualties on June 6 (more than twice the casualties suffered by the 237th or 10th Division facing the Americans that day) and another 413 on June 7. 197th Division War Diary, 5th Guards War Diary and field messages, in Cylburn O. Mattfeldt, ed., *Translations: War Diaries of German Units Opposed to the Second Division (Regular), 1918*, 9 vols. (Washington, D.C.: Army War College, 1930–1935), 1/2, 4/1; French 167th Division War Diary, France MDLD.

4. German 28th Division field messages, June 7–8 (latter 2130h), 237th Division War Diary, in Mattfeldt, *Translations*, 2/1, 4/2, 4/3; John W. Thomason Jr., *The United States Army Second Division Northwest of Château Thierry in World War I*, ed. George B. Clark (Jefferson, N.C.: McFarland, 2006), 122–123.

5. Jacobi report to IV Corps, June 18, 1918; Bischoff to Jacobi, June 17, 1918; 461st Regiment reports and field messages, in Mattfeldt, *Translations*, 4/3.

6. Mattfeldt, *Translations*, 2/1.

7. Robert C. Hoffman, *I Remember the Last War* (York, Pa.: Strength & Health, 1940), 92.

8. 442d Regiment War Diary, in Mattfeldt, *Translations*, 4/2; ABMC, *3d Division*, 17–18; Frederic Vinton Hemenway, *History of the Third Division United States Army in the World War for the Period December 1, 1917 to January 1, 1919* (Anderbach-on-the-Rhine: n.p., 1919), 135–136.

9. *USAWW*, 4:402, 581; Mattfeldt, *Records of the Second Division*, 4/1; Mattfeldt, *Translations*, 1/2; Bonk, *Château-Thierry & Belleau Wood*, 70. The unsuccessful counterattacks against the Germans are not mentioned in American sources.

10. Thomason, *United States Army Second Division*, 125–126; George B. Clark, *Devil Dogs: Fighting Marines of World War I* (Novato, Calif.: Presidio Press, 1999), 135; *USAWW*, 4:405; Harbord to Bundy, 0625h and other field messages, in Mattfeldt, *Records of the Second Division*, 4/1, 5/2.

11. *USAWW*, 4:406; Sibley to Harbord, 1205h, in Mattfeldt, *Records of the Second Division*, 4/2.

12. 237th Division War Diary, in Mattfeldt, *Translations*, 4/3; 4th Brigade field messages, in Mattfeldt, *Records of the Second Division*, 4/1; Ernst Otto, "The Battles for the Possession of Belleau Woods, June 1918," *U.S. Naval Institute Proceedings* 54, 11 (November 1928): 950.

13. Mattfeldt, *Records of the Second Division*, 5/2, 4/2.

14. *USAWW*, 4:413.
15. Mattfeldt, *Translations*, 4/2; Hemenway, *History of the Third Division*, 135–136.
16. *USAWW*, 4:411; Mattfeldt, *Records of the Second Division*, 4/2; Mark E. Grotelueschen, *The AEF Way of War: The American Army and Combat in World War I* (Cambridge: Cambridge University Press, 2007), 216.
17. Mattfeldt, *Translations*, 4/3.
18. 28th Division field messages and daily reports, June 8, 1918, in Mattfeldt, *Translations*, 2/1, 2/2; Otto, "Battles for the Possession of Belleau Woods," 961; Bonk, *Château-Thierry & Belleau Wood*, 71.
19. Mattfeldt, *Translations*, 1/2; *USAWW*, 4:579–580. 2d Division intelligence denoted the 5th Guards a "first class division" with "special training in open warfare" and noted that it was closer to full strength than perhaps any other in Von Conta's arsenal (*USAWW*, 4:421–422).

Chapter 8. "We Want the Damn Woods": Belleau Wood, June 9–10, 1918

1. Donald Smythe, *Pershing: General of the Armies* (Bloomington: Indiana University Press, 1986), 133–137; David F. Trask, *The AEF and Coalition Warmaking, 1917–1918* (Lawrence: University Press of Kansas, 1993), 73–77; David Bonk, *Château-Thierry & Belleau Wood 1918: America's Baptism of Fire on the Marne* (Oxford: Osprey, 2007), 71.
2. *USAWW*, 4:416, 422–423; 2d Division Journal of Operations, 4th Brigade field messages, in Cylburn O. Mattfeldt, ed., *Records of the Second Division (Regular)*, 10 vols. (Washington, D.C.: Army War College, 1924–1929), 4/1, 6/1; 237th Division War Diary, in Cylburn O. Mattfeldt, ed., *Translations: War Diaries of German Units Opposed to the Second Division (Regular), 1918*, 9 vols. (Washington, D.C.: Army War College, 1930–1935), 4/3; George B. Clark, *Devil Dogs: Fighting Marines of World War I* (Novato, Calif.: Presidio Press, 1999), 138–139.
3. *USAWW*, 4:423, 583–584; German 5th Guards and 237th Divisions field messages, 237th Division War Diary, in Mattfeldt, *Translations*, 1/2, 4/3; French 167th Division War Diary, France MDLD; Ernst Otto, "The Battles for the Possession of Belleau Woods, June 1918," *U.S. Naval Institute Proceedings* 54, 11 (November 1928): 950–951.
4. 231st Division field messages, in Mattfeldt, *Translations*, 4/2.
5. Hughes to Harbord, in Mattfeldt, *Records of the Second Division*, 4/1; *USAWW*, 4:425–426, 434; Joseph J. Gleeson, *A Soldier's Story: A Daily Account of World War I by Sergeant Joseph J. Gleeson, January 1918 to March 1919* (privately printed, 1999), 29; Warren R. Jackson, *His Time in Hell. A Texas Marine in France: The World War I Memoir of Warren R. Jackson*, ed. George B. Clark (Novato, Calif.: Presidio Press, 2001), 101.
6. 28th Division and 40th Fusilier Regiment War Diaries, in Mattfeldt, *Translations*, 2/1; 4th Brigade field messages, in Mattfeldt, *Records of the Second Division*, 4/2, 5/2; Clark, *Devil Dogs*, 141. Capt. H. E. Major and then Capt. George H. Osterhout Jr. commanded the 6th Machine Gun Battalion until June 20, when Maj. L. W. T. Waller took command (Edwin N. McClellan, "A Brief History of the Fourth Brigade of Marines," *Marine Corps Gazette* 4 [December 1919]: 352). Grotelueschen

depicts the June 10 operation as a success because of the relatively slight casualties incurred by the marines, but it is worth emphasizing that the Americans captured no objectives of note (Mark E. Grotelueschen, *The AEF Way of War: The American Army and Combat in World War I* [Cambridge: Cambridge University Press, 2007], 217).

7. 4th Brigade field messages, in Mattfeldt, *Records of the Second Division*, 4/2; Bonk, *Château-Thierry & Belleau Wood*, 73.

8. Frederic M. Wise, *A Marine Tells It to You* (New York: J. H. Sears, 1919), 215; *USAWW*, 4:432.

9. Wise, *A Marine Tells It to You*, 217. George B. Clark, citing unnamed "German records," claims that the sector of the woods targeted by Wise, north of Hill 169, was poorly defended (Clark, *Devil Dogs*, 144).

10. *USAWW*, 4:587; 231st Division, 442d and 444th Regiments War Diaries, in Mattfeldt, *Translations*, 1/2, 4/2.

Chapter 9. "No Idea of Tactical Principles": Belleau Wood, June 11–12, 1918

1. George B. Clark, *Devil Dogs: Fighting Marines of World War I* (Novato, Calif.: Presidio Press, 1999), 146; George B. Clark, ed., *Devil Dogs Chronicle: Voices of the 4th Marine Brigade in World War I* (Lawrence: University Press of Kansas, 2013), 194.

2. Clark, *Devil Dogs Chronicle*, 194; Frederic M. Wise, *A Marine Tells It to You* (New York: J. H. Sears, 1919), 219.

3. John W. Thomason Jr., *The United States Army Second Division Northwest of Château-Thierry in World War I*, ed. George B. Clark (Jefferson, N.C.: McFarland, 2006), 136–137. For some reason, Wise remained convinced after the war that his men had faced here—just as at Les Mares Farm—"the Twenty-Sixth Jaeger Division, veteran Alpine troops" (Wise, *A Marine Tells It to You*, 220).

4. Clark, *Devil Dogs Chronicle*, 195–196.

5. 28th and 237th Division field messages, Bischoff to Jacobi, June 17, 1918, in Cylburn O. Mattfeldt, ed., *Translations: War Diaries of German Units Opposed to the Second Division (Regular), 1918*, 9 vols. (Washington, D.C.: Army War College, 1930–1935), 4/3; Wise, *A Marine Tells It to You*, 220. A translator's note to the German survivor's account reads: "The American 'marching fire' was unheard of, and the word-forms here used to describe it show that it was considered a new departure."

6. 237th Division and 461st Regiment War Diaries and field messages, in Mattfeldt, *Translations*, 4/3; *USAWW*, 4:592. Bischoff's version of events is uncritically accepted by most American commentators.

7. 28th Division and 40th Regiment War Diaries and field messages, in Mattfeldt, *Translations*, 2/1. Marines in Bouresches initially thought that formations of German infantry gathering north of the village were preparing to attack them, but in fact, they were elements of the 40th Fusiliers and 110th Grenadiers preparing to reinforce and later counterattack the Americans in Belleau Wood. The success with which American artillery broke up these formations testifies to improved infantry-artillery liaison (4th Brigade field messages, in Cylburn O. Mattfeldt, ed.,

Records of the Second Division [Regular], 10 vols. [Washington, D.C.: Army War College, 1924–1929], 4/1; *USAWW*, 4:435–436).

8. 28th Division and 40th Regiment War Diaries and field messages, in Mattfeldt, *Translations*, 2/1, 3/1. In a message to Von Conta on this date, Böhm angrily denied any suggestion that the Americans had broken the 40th Fusiliers frontally and then "rolled up the 461st Inf from the south. This assertion is wrong. Actually the enemy entered through the stream bed which runs through the middle of the Bois de Belleau, in northeast direction" and attacked the 40th on the flank and rear, forcing it back out of the woods. Over the following weeks, Böhm and members of his staff worked relentlessly to gather information supporting this interpretation of events, blaming the 461st Regiment for not taking control of a ravine that was supposed to be in its sector (Mattfeldt, *Translations*, 2/1).

9. *USAWW*, 4:437, 439.

10. Ibid., 438–439; Clark, *Devil Dogs*, 154; Thomason, *United States Army Second Division*, 139–140.

11. 28th and 237th Divisions and 461st Regiment War Diaries and field messages, in Mattfeldt, *Translations*, 2/1, 2/2, 3/1.

12. 4th Brigade reports and field messages, Harbord to Wise, 1145, in Mattfeldt, *Records of the Second Division*, 4/2, 6/1; *USAWW*, 4:431–433, 453; Thomason, *United States Army Second Division*, 137, 140–141.

13. Thomason, *United States Army Second Division*, 142; Ernst Otto, "The Battles for the Possession of Belleau Woods, June 1918," *U.S. Naval Institute Proceedings* 54, 11 (November 1928): 954–955.

14. Mattfeldt, *Translations*, 1/2.

15. Mattfeldt, *Records of the Second Division*, 4/2; Clark, *Devil Dogs Chronicle*, 197.

16. *USAWW*, 4:427–430, 438; Mattfeldt, *Records of the Second Division*, 6/1.

17. 237th Division and 40th and 110th Regiments War Diaries and field messages, in Mattfeldt, *Translations*, 2/2, 4/3.

18. Clark, *Devil Dogs Chronicle*, 183; *USAWW*, 4:445; Private William A. Francis, WWI survey, USAHEC.

19. Wise, *A Marine Tells It to You*, 225.

20. 237th Division reports and field messages, in Mattfeldt, *Translations*, 4/3; Mark E. Grotelueschen, *The AEF Way of War: The American Army and Combat in World War I* (Cambridge: Cambridge University Press, 2007), 218.

21. 237th Division and 40th and 110th Regiments reports and field messages, 461st Regiment War Diary, Bischoff to Jacobi, June 17, 1918, in Mattfeldt, *Translations*, 2/2, 3/1, 4/3; *USAWW*, 4:453; David Bonk, *Château-Thierry & Belleau Wood 1918: America's Baptism of Fire on the Marne* (Oxford: Osprey, 2007), 79–81. Just as on June 11, the two German divisions would blame each other for their defeat.

22. Warren R. Jackson, *His Time in Hell. A Texas Marine in France: The World War I Memoir of Warren R. Jackson*, ed. George B. Clark (Novato, Calif.: Presidio Press, 2001), 107; Wise to Bundy, June 18, 1918, in Mattfeldt, *Records of the Second Division*, 7/1; *USAWW*, 4:447, 452; Thomason, *United States Army Second Division*, 152–153.

23. Hughes to Lee, June 13, 1918, in Mattfeldt, *Records of the Second Division*, 5/2.

24. *USAWW*, 4:448–449, 453; Mattfeldt, *Records of the Second Division*, 6/1.

25. *USAWW*, 4:450–451.

26. Malone to Harbord, June 12, 1918, in Mattfeldt, *Records of the Second Division*, 4/2; *USAWW*, 4:447–448.

27. *USAWW*, 4:594; Corps Conta orders, 28th Division orders, June 13, 1918, in Mattfeldt, *Translations*, 1/2, 2/1.

Chapter 10. Gas and Exhaustion: Belleau Wood, June 13–15, 1918

1. Hartlieb report, 28th Division field reports, in Cylburn O. Mattfeldt, ed., *Translations: War Diaries of German Units Opposed to the Second Division (Regular), 1918*, 9 vols. (Washington, D.C.: Army War College, 1930–1935), 2/2, 3/1, 4/3; Ernst Otto, "The Battles for the Possession of Belleau Woods, June 1918," *U.S. Naval Institute Proceedings* 54, 11 (November 1928): 957.

2. 237th Division and 109th Regiment War Diaries, in Mattfeldt, *Translations*, 2/1, 4/3.

3. *USAWW*, 4:457, 599; 4th Brigade field messages and Bundy to Harbord, 0505, in Cylburn O. Mattfeldt, ed., *Records of the Second Division (Regular)*, 10 vols. (Washington, D.C.: Army War College, 1924–1929), 4/1, 4/2; 28th Division field messages, 109th Regiment War Diary, in Mattfeldt, *Translations*, 2/1, 2/2, 3/1.

4. *USAWW*, 4:598; Mattfeldt, *Translations*, 4/3.

5. Mattfeldt, *Records of the Second Division*, 4/1.

6. *USAWW*, 4:464–467.

7. Ibid., 600.

8. Rexmond C. Cochrane, *Gas Warfare at Belleau Wood, June 1918* (Army Chemical Center, Md.: US Army Chemical Corps Historical Office, 1957), 10–11.

9. Ibid., 32–34; Peter F. Owen, *To the Limit of Endurance: A Battalion of Marines in the Great War* (College Station: Texas A&M University Press, 2007), 93–96.

10. *USAWW*, 4:490; Cochrane, *Gas Warfare at Belleau Wood*, 34–35.

11. Cochrane, *Gas Warfare at Belleau Wood*, 36.

12. Mattfeldt, *Records of the Second Division*, 4/2.

13. *USAWW*, 4:471, 490; Mattfeldt, *Records of the Second Division*, 4/2, 6/2.

14. Joseph J. Gleeson, *A Soldier's Story: A Daily Account of World War I by Sergeant Joseph J. Gleeson, January 1918 to March 1919* (privately printed, 1999), 29; George B. Clark, *The Second Infantry Division in World War I: A History of the American Expeditionary Force Regulars, 1917–1919* (Jefferson, N.C.: McFarland, 2007), 75; John W. Thomason Jr., *The United States Army Second Division Northwest of Château-Thierry in World War I*, ed. George B. Clark (Jefferson, N.C.: McFarland, 2006), 160–161.

15. *USAWW*, 4:491; Cochrane, *Gas Warfare at Belleau Wood*, 1, 28, 38. Division historian John W. Thomason Jr. concurred: "It is hard to see how 2/5 extended in a thin line along the eastern edge [of the woods], could have avoided a disaster if the German tactics had been aggressive" (Thomason, *United States Army Second Division*, 162).

16. Thomason, *United States Army Second Division*, 166; *USAWW*, 4:468–469, 476–477, 485–486.

17. 237th Division and 109th Regiment War Diaries, Bischoff to Jacobi, June 17, 1918, in Mattfeldt, *Translations*, 1/2, 2/1, 4/3; Mattfeldt, *Records of the Second Di-*

vision, 4/1. The man was probably a leftover from the now-defunct "Russian Legion," which had been attached for a time to the French 10th Colonial Division. The Germans were also busy rounding them up by the dozen as they wandered aimlessly about the countryside (Mattfeldt, *Translations*, 1/2).

18. Mattfeldt, *Translations*, 2/1; Cochrane, *Gas Warfare at Belleau Wood*, 40.

19. Mattfeldt, *Records of the Second Division*, 4/1, 5/2; David Bonk, *Château-Thierry & Belleau Wood 1918: America's Baptism of Fire on the Marne* (Oxford: Osprey, 2007), 84.

20. Neville to Harbord, 0820, in Mattfeldt, *Records of the Second Division*, 4/2; *USAWW*, 4:492; 237th and 28th Divisions War Diaries, in Mattfeldt, *Translations*, 1/2, 2/1; George B. Clark, *Devil Dogs: Fighting Marines of World War I* (Novato, Calif.: Presidio Press, 1999), 182–183; Bonk, *Château-Thierry & Belleau Wood*, 85.

21. *USAWW*, 4:478–479.

Chapter 11. Enter the US Army: Belleau Wood, June 16–21, 1918

1. Frederic M. Wise, *A Marine Tells It to You* (New York: J. H. Sears, 1919), 237; John W. Thomason Jr., *The United States Army Second Division Northwest of Château-Thierry in World War I*, ed. George B. Clark (Jefferson, N.C.: McFarland, 2006), 169.

2. Wise, *A Marine Tells It to You*, 237–238.

3. *USAWW*, 4:495–498.

4. Ibid., 607–608; Cylburn O. Mattfeldt, ed., *Translations: War Diaries of German Units Opposed to the Second Division (Regular), 1918*, 9 vols. (Washington, D.C.: Army War College, 1930–1935), 1/2.

5. Mattfeldt, *Translations*, 2/1.

6. *USAWW*, 4:604; 87th Division and IV Corps field messages, in Mattfeldt, *Translations*, 1/2, 3/2; David Bonk, *Château-Thierry & Belleau Wood 1918: America's Baptism of Fire on the Marne* (Oxford: Osprey, 2007), 85.

7. *USAWW*, 4:492, 498, 508; Cylburn O. Mattfeldt, ed., *Records of the Second Division (Regular)*, 10 vols. (Washington, D.C.: Army War College, 1924–1929), 4/1; 109th Regiment War Diary and field messages, in Mattfeldt, *Translations*, 2/1.

8. Mattfeldt, *Records of the Second Division*, 6/1.

9. *USAWW*, 4:503–504.

10. Frederic Vinton Hemenway, *History of the Third Division United States Army in the World War for the Period December 1, 1917 to January 1, 1919* (Anderbach-on-the-Rhine: n.p., 1919), 89; 87th Division War Diary and field messages, in Mattfeldt, *Translations*, 1/2, 3/2. The date of the second attack has been questioned, with some contemporary sources placing it on June 19 and others on June 20 (Thomason, *United States Army Second Division*, 170).

11. 87th Division War Diary and field messages, in Mattfeldt, *Translations*, 2/1, 3/2; *USAWW*, 4:612.

12. *USAWW*, 4:515, 518, 521; Mattfeldt, *Records of the Second Division*, 6/2.

13. *USAWW*, 4:515–517.

14. Mattfeldt, *Records of the Second Division*, 5/1; Hemenway, *History of the Third Division*, 90; *USAWW*, 4:521; 87th Division War Diary, in Mattfeldt, *Translations*, 2/1.

15. *USAWW*, 4:522; Mattfeldt, *Records of the Second Division*, 6/2.

16. 2/347th Battalion War Diary, in Mattfeldt, *Translations*, 3/2; Mattfeldt, *Records of the Second Division*, 6/2; *USAWW*, 4:525–526. The 2d Division's journal of operations and other reports recount numerous alleged instances of Germans wearing American or even French uniforms. On this same day, Col. Malone of the 23d Regiment reported that a "suspicious character" in the uniform of a field artillery lieutenant colonel had been seen moving toward the front, and he ordered increased security (Mattfeldt, *Records of the Second Division*, 5/1, 6/1).

17. *USAWW*, 4:538.

18. Mattfeldt, *Records of the Second Division*, 5/2.

19. *USAWW*, 4:537. Capt. P. J. Hurley, commanding the 2/7th Battalion, reported burying "eight Marines, whose bodies had been rifled by the Germans and no mark of identity remained" (*USAWW*, 4:537). Soldiers of the US 26th and 28th Divisions, who passed through the area later in June and July, reported seeing dead marines scattered throughout the woods, but it is impossible to determine whether these casualties resulted from the fighting before June 16 or after June 23. First Lt. Clifton Cates recorded that he "felt sorry" for the "poor Army boys that have not been under fire before" as they came in to relieve his outfit (Robert B. Asprey, *At Belleau Wood* [Denton: University of North Texas Press, 1996], 306–307). This author has found no recorded instances of marine officers stopping to instruct the "poor Army boys" on how to cope with the conditions they would face in the woods.

20. *USAWW*, 4:537.

21. Joseph T. Dickman, *The Great Crusade: A Narrative of the World War* (New York: D. Appleton, 1927), 52, 56, 70. Asprey calls the deployment of the 7th Regiment "a sad mistake" (Asprey, *At Belleau Wood*, 305).

22. George B. Clark, *The Second Infantry Division in World War I: A History of the American Expeditionary Force Regulars, 1917–1919* (Jefferson, N.C.: McFarland, 2007), 81.

23. Mattfeldt, *Records of the Second Division*, 4/1, 5/1.

24. Ibid., 5/1.

25. *USAWW*, 4:516–517.

26. Mattfeldt, *Records of the Second Division*, 5/1.

Chapter 12. Finishing the Job: June 22–July 2, 1918

1. 2d Division Journal of Operations, June 22, 1918, in Cylburn O. Mattfeldt, ed., *Records of the Second Division (Regular)*, 10 vols. (Washington, D.C.: Army War College, 1924–1929), 6/2; *USAWW*, 4:531.

2. *USAWW*, 4:531, 535.

3. 1/347th Battalion War Diary, in Cylburn O. Mattfeldt, ed., *Translations: War Diaries of German Units Opposed to the Second Division (Regular), 1918*, 9 vols. (Washington, D.C.: Army War College, 1930–1935), 2/1, 3/2; George B. Clark, ed., *Devil Dogs Chronicle: Voices of the 4th Marine Brigade in World War I* (Lawrence: University Press of Kansas, 2013), 207–208.

4. *USAWW*, 4:538–539; Mattfeldt, *Records of the Second Division*, 5/2; 1/347th Battalion War Diary, in Mattfeldt, *Translations*, 3/2.

5. Mattfeldt, *Records of the Second Division*, 4/1, 4/2, 6/1.

6. 87th Division War Diary, in Mattfeldt, *Translations*, 3/2; *USAWW*, 4:500–502; Mattfeldt, *Records of the Second Division*, 4/1, 4/2; Rexmond C. Cochrane, *Gas Warfare at Belleau Wood, June 1918* (Army Chemical Center, Md.: US Army Chemical Corps Historical Office, 1957), 52–53.

7. Mattfeldt, *Translations*, 2/1.

8. Ibid., 2/1, 2/2.

9. Mattfeldt, *Records of the Second Division*, 5/1.

10. *USAWW*, 4:542; George B. Clark, *The Second Infantry Division in World War I: A History of the American Expeditionary Force Regulars, 1917–1919* (Jefferson, N.C.: McFarland, 2007), 84; 87th Division War Diary, in Mattfeldt, *Translations*, 3/2.

11. These Americans wearing German uniforms—which had probably been liberated from prisoners of the 109th Grenadiers captured days earlier—were reported by too many witnesses to refute. See German 87th Division War Diary and field messages, in Mattfeldt, *Translations*, 3/2; *USAWW*, 4:622.

12. 1/347th Battalion, 347th Regiment, and 87th Division War Diaries, in Mattfeldt, *Translations*, 3/2. The list of decorations was long; see George B. Clark, *Devil Dogs: Fighting Marines of World War I* (Novato, Calif.: Presidio Press, 1999), 199–201.

13. Mattfeldt, *Records of the Second Division*, 4/1; *USAWW*, 4:553, 556–558.

14. Mattfeldt, *Records of the Second Division*, 6/1; Mattfeldt, *Translations*, 2/1. Although the 87th Division consciously sought to conduct a defense in depth, an army group postmortem sent to Ludendorff on July 8 claimed that the defenders had not done so. Instead, stated the report, "the engagement in Belleau Wood is a typical example proving that the rigid unyielding holding of terrain, particularly in unfortified positions, always means a beginning accompanied by heaviest casualties and generally terminating in failure" (Mattfeldt, *Translations*, 3/2).

15. *USAWW*, 4:546–547.

16. Ibid., 633–639; Robert B. Asprey, *At Belleau Wood* (Denton: University of North Texas Press, 1996), 330–331; Mark E. Grotelueschen, *The AEF Way of War: The American Army and Combat in World War I* (Cambridge: Cambridge University Press, 2007), 221.

17. *USAWW*, 4:641–646, 652–656; Clark, *Second Infantry Division*, 87–88.

18. 402d Regiment War Diary, in Mattfeldt, *Translations*, 3/3; *USAWW*, 4:663, 668; Robert Winthrop Kean, *Dear Marraine (1917–1919)* (privately printed, 1969), 126; Grotelueschen, *AEF Way of War*, 222.

19. *USAWW*, 4:666–670; William Brown, *The Adventures of an American Doughboy* (Tacoma, Wash.: Smith-Kinney, 1919), 47; Cochrane, *Gas Warfare at Belleau Wood*, 57–58; David Bonk, *Château-Thierry & Belleau Wood 1918: America's Baptism of Fire on the Marne* (Oxford: Osprey, 2007), 90.

20. Robert C. Hoffman, *I Remember the Last War* (York, Pa.: Strength & Health, 1940), 96, 101, 104–105.

21. Ibid., 108–119.

22. 402d Regiment War Diary, in Mattfeldt, *Translations*, 3/3; *USAWW*, 4:669; Cochrane, *Gas Warfare at Belleau Wood*, 59–60. Overall, 78 percent of the 2d Division's wartime gas casualties were suffered in June 1918, and 32 percent of its total casualties for June 1918 resulted from gas. The division's total casualties for this

period were 217 officers and 9,560 men (4th Brigade, 126 officers and 5,073 men; 3d Brigade, 68 officers and 3,184 men). Of these, 41 officers and 3,111 men had been gassed (Cochrane, *Gas Warfare at Belleau Wood*, 65–66).

23. NARA, RG 120, entry 268, G-3 Secret Correspondence, box 3154, folder 1092.

24. James G. Harbord, *Leaves from a War Diary* (New York: Dodd, Mead, 1925), 293–294. In his diary and in his memoirs, Harbord expresses his indignation at the French "vandalism" of the house he chose as his headquarters (James G. Harbord, *The American Army in France, 1917–1919* [Boston: Little, Brown, 1936], 274). Postwar German accounts later found it convenient to repeat the myth of French cowardice, particularly in the context of the French occupation of the Ruhr in 1923. On March 2, 1923, the German minister of defense declared in the *New York Times*, "In the summer of 1918 France was saved only by the fact than an American division revived the fighting, and at the last moment prevented the taking of Paris" (quoted in Clark, *Second Infantry Division*, 92–93). Robert Bruce suggests that American references to the French during this period were only slightly patronizing, but in fact, the disdain, contempt, and positive refusal to grant credit where it was due permeate American contemporary records and postwar accounts (Robert B. Bruce, *A Fraternity of Arms: America and France in the Great War* [Lawrence: University Press of Kansas, 2003], 206–218).

25. NARA, RG 120, entry 11, G-5 Secret & Confidential Files, box 1392, folders 16875–16877.

26. Harbord, *American Army in France*, 290; Asprey, *At Belleau Wood*, 346; Clark, *Devil Dogs Chronicle*, 211. At dinner with Pershing after the battle, Bullard said to him:

> "General, I see that the 2nd Marines," (emphasizing the 2nd as though that division was all Marines) "have won the war at Belleau Wood." "Yes," he answered dryly, "and I stopped it yesterday as I passed there." But had he? He stopped only what was yet to come, not what had already gone forth. That he could not stop, and it was, I say, enough to convince all good enthusiastic Americans that at Belleau Wood there was nothing but Marines and, of course, dead Germans, their victims and theirs alone. (Robert L. Bullard, *Personalities and Reminiscences of the War* [Garden City, N.Y.: Doubleday, Page, 1925], 209)

Harbord and many others have made the excuse that censorship regulations did not permit the media to refer to specific units, only to service branches. Thus the marines—by an oversight, Harbord claims—received overwhelming and disproportionate credit because, in their case, the whole active service branch in France amounted to only two regiments (Harbord, *American Army in France*, 290–291).

27. James G. Harbord, "A Month in Belleau Wood in 1918," *Leatherneck* 11, 6 (June 1928): 10–12, 54; Clark, *Second Infantry Division*, 93–94; Richard Rubin, "Where the Americans Turned the Tide," *New York Times*, October 26, 2014.

28. Bruce, *Fraternity of Arms*, 210; Price's "Montdidier-Noyon Offensive," NARA, RG 120, entry 267, G-3 General Correspondence, box 3158, folder 1136.

29. Although Degoutte's longer-term objectives depended partly on the occupa-

tion of Belleau Wood for flank protection, his plans had no strategic repercussions and could have been pushed back almost indefinitely. The attack on Vaux, intended to follow the occupation of Belleau Wood, was eventually pushed back until July 1; even then, it was launched not because of some overarching imperative but because it offered an opportunity to straighten the lines and showcase the 3d Brigade's abilities. The defeat of the French 39th Division on Hill 204—a more important point than Vaux or the territory to the west—provoked no obvious consternation at French headquarters.

30. Harbord, *Leaves from a War Diary*, 294.

Chapter 13. Rock of the Marne: The Marne River Defense, July 15–17, 1918

1. Donald Smythe, *Pershing: General of the Armies* (Bloomington: Indiana University Press, 1986), 146–147; David F. Trask, *The AEF and Coalition Warmaking, 1917–1918* (Lawrence: University Press of Kansas, 1993), 78.

2. David T. Zabecki, *The German 1918 Offensives: A Case Study in the Operational Level of War* (London: Routledge, 2006), 246–253.

3. Michael S. Neiberg, *The Second Battle of the Marne* (Bloomington: Indiana University Press, 2008), 72–77, 88–90.

4. Robert A. Doughty, *Pyrrhic Victory: French Strategy and Operations in the Great War* (Cambridge, Mass.: Harvard University Press, 2005), 465–468; Neiberg, *Second Battle of the Marne*, 81.

5. Conrad H. Lanza, "The German XXIII Reserve Corps Crosses the Marne," *Field Artillery Journal* 27, 4 (July–August 1937): 306. Another American division, the 26th, had occupied the 2d Division's old front and now formed part of the American I Corps under Major General Hunter Liggett. Though under Degoutte's command in Sixth Army, it stood west of the planned German offensive and engaged in only minor operations over the next few days. Much of its time was spent burying German and American dead left behind in Belleau Wood (Frank P. Sibley, *With the Yankee Division in France* [Boston: Little, Brown, 1919], 197–198). Liggett's command included the French 167th Division—a nice reversal of seniority for the Americans. Liggett proudly remarked that this was the first time Americans had commanded foreign troops since the Revolutionary War (Hunter Liggett, *Commanding an American Army: Recollections of the World War* [Boston: Houghton Mifflin, 1925], 31).

6. Conrad H. Lanza, "Bridgeheads of the Marne," *Field Artillery Journal* 27, 3 (May–June 1937): 206; J. S. Switzer Jr., "The Champagne-Marne Defensive," *Infantry Journal* 20 (January–June 1922): 37.

7. Neiberg, *Second Battle of the Marne*, 107–108; USAWW, 5:3.

8. Walter C. Short, "The A.E.F. in the World War: The Champagne-Marne Defensive" (typescript, n.d.), 6, CARL.

9. NARA, RG 120, entry 1241, 3d Division Records, box 17, file 203.32.7; Joseph T. Dickman, *The Great Crusade: A Narrative of the World War* (New York: D. Appleton, 1927), 73–74.

10. Dickman, *Great Crusade*, 73–74; Kelton to Conner, July 20, 1918, NARA, RG 120, entry 1241, 3d Division records, box 18, file 203.33.6.

11. Lanza, "Bridgeheads of the Marne," 209–210.

12. Ibid., 211. Extensive research in French archives—not within the purview of this study—would help delineate the lines of command and communications within Sixth Army, XXXVIII Corps, and III Corps and perhaps clarify the respective intentions of Montdésir and Lebrun. The French war diaries are not illuminating on these points.

13. *USAWW*, 5:101; NARA, RG 120, entry 1241, 3d Division records, box 18, file 203.33.6.

14. Lanza, "Bridgeheads of the Marne," 207; Switzer, "Champagne-Marne Defensive," 184; Robert H. Ferrell, ed., *In the Company of Generals: The World War I Diary of Pierpont L. Stackpole* (Columbia: University of Missouri Press, 2009), 97; ABMC, *3d Division*, 22–23.

15. *USAWW*, 5:102; NARA, RG 120, entry 1241, 3d Division records, box 18, file 203.33.6.

16. ABMC, *28th Division*, 1–10.

17. Ibid., 8–9.

18. Dickman, *Great Crusade*, 72; Kelton to Conner, July 20, 1918, NARA, RG 120, entry 1241, 3d Division records, box 18, file 203.33.6; Short, "A.E.F. in the World War," 12; Lanza, "Bridgeheads of the Marne," 229; French 125th Division War Diary, France MDLD. If, as Lanza suggests, Dickman knew the French were going to withdraw and simply refused to pull back in conjunction with them, it was in his interest to deny previous knowledge of the French withdrawal from the Jaulgonne Bend and present it as an unexpected rout. But this still begs the question of why the four companies of the US 28th Division were taken by surprise by the withdrawal.

19. *USAWW*, 4:511–512.

20. ABMC, *42d Division*, 1–11; James J. Cooke, *The Rainbow Division in the Great War, 1917–1919* (Westport, Conn.: Praeger, 1994), 97–98; Robert B. Bruce, *A Fraternity of Arms: America and France in the Great War* (Lawrence: University Press of Kansas, 2003), 227–228.

21. Arthur W. Little, *From Harlem to the Rhine: The Story of New York's Colored Volunteers* (New York: Covici Friede, 1936), 46; NARA, RG 120, entry 11, G-5 Secret & Confidential Files, box 1385, folder 15703; NARA, RG 120, entry 267, G-3 General Correspondence, box 3114, folder 694. For a thorough study of the 369th Regiment, including its training and deployments, see Jeffrey T. Sammons and John H. Morrow Jr., *Harlem's Rattlers and the Great War: The Undaunted 369th Regiment and the African American Quest for Equality* (Lawrence: University Press of Kansas, 2014).

22. NARA, RG 120, entry 1241, 3d Division records, box 18, file 203.33.6; Lanza, "Bridgeheads of the Marne," 211.

23. Hugh S. Thompson, *Trench Knives and Mustard Gas: With the 42d Rainbow Division in France*, ed. Robert H. Ferrell (College Station: Texas A&M University Press, 2004), 124.

24. *USAWW*, 5:72–74, 78, 90–91; NARA, RG 120, entry 1241, 3d Division records, box 18, file 203.33.6; Lanza, "Bridgeheads of the Marne," 213.

25. ABMC, *3d Division*, 23–24; Short, "A.E.F. in the World War," 8; Lanza, "Bridge-

heads of the Marne," 229; Lanza, "German XXIII Reserve Corps," 307; Switzer, "Champagne-Marne Defensive," 38.

26. ABMC, *3d Division*, 25–26; Lanza, "Bridgeheads of the Marne," 214; Lanza, "German XXIII Reserve Corps," 311.

27. ABMC, *3d Division*, 26–27; Dickman, *Great Crusade*, 87–88; Frederic Vinton Hemenway, *History of the Third Division United States Army in the World War for the Period December 1, 1917 to January 1, 1919* (Anderbach-on-the-Rhine: n.p., 1919), 95–96; NARA, RG 120, entry 1241, 3d Division records, box 18, file 203.33.6, folder 65; Lanza, "Bridgeheads of the Marne," 227.

28. James H. Hallas, ed., *Doughboy War: The American Expeditionary Force in World War I* (Mechanicsburg, Pa.: Stackpole Books, 2000), 103.

29. ABMC, *3d Division*, 26–27; Hemenway, *History of the Third Division*, 137–138; NARA, RG 120, entry 1241, 3d Division records, box 18, file 203.33.6, folder 65; Lanza, "Bridgeheads of the Marne," 229; United States Infantry School, *Infantry in Battle*, 2d ed. (Washington, D.C.: Infantry School, 1939), 126–127. Kingery received the Silver Star for gallantry.

30. Sgt. Edward J. Radcliffe, 28th Division, 3/109th Battalion, WWI Survey, USAHEC; Dickman, *Great Crusade*, 92–93; *USAWW*, 5:77.

31. ABMC, *3d Division*, 25–29; Conrad H. Lanza, "The German XXIII Reserve Corps Crosses the Marne," *Field Artillery Journal* 27, 5 (September–October 1937): 372–373.

32. *USAWW*, 5:81, 94; Hemenway, *History of the Third Division*, 159; http://www.worldwar1.com/dbc/2marne.htm. Woolridge received the Distinguished Service Cross and the Distinguished Service Medal for this action.

33. Hemenway, *History of the Third Division*, 155–157.

34. ABMC, *3d Division*, 27–29; Lanza, "German XXIII Reserve Corps," 311–313; French XXXVIII Corps, 125th Division War Diaries, France MDLD.

35. Report by Brig. Gen. Richardson, December 15, 1918, NARA, RG 120, entry 1241, 28th Division records, box 8, file 228.33.6; battle map, ibid., box 12, file 228.32.2; Lanza study, ibid., box 14, file 228.18.2.

36. *USAWW*, 5:91, 107–109; ABMC, *28th Division*, 24–25; Richardson report, December 15, 1918; 28th Division Report of Operations, February 12, 1919, NARA, RG 120, entry 1241, 28th Division records, box 3263, folder 1; Dickman interview with Lt. W. M. R. Crossman of Company L, 28th Division, July 16, 1918, ibid., 3d Division records, box 18, file 203.33.6; Lanza, "Bridgeheads of the Marne," 218, 229; French 125th Division War Diary, France MDLD.

37. The language used by the III Corps war diary to describe the German advance in the Jaulgonne Bend is as follows: "Dans le Secteur de gauche, la progression [of the Germans] est moins rapide et moins importante" than German attacks further east (with the French 125th Division War Diary, France MDLD). Richardson report, December 15, 1918; Lanza study; Lanza, "Bridgeheads of the Marne," 215–216.

38. 28th Division Report of Operations, February 12, 1919.

39. Radcliffe, WWI Survey, USAHEC; *USAWW*, 5:107–109; ABMC, *28th Division*, 12–13; Lanza, "Bridgeheads of the Marne," 383. On July 23 General Muir ordered the

publication of a memorandum claiming that, during the attack of July 15, the Germans infiltrated groups of retreating stragglers with agents wearing French and American uniforms. Some of these disguised Germans penetrated lines of defense and set up machine guns in the rear to fire on American forces. Others masqueraded as NCOs and handed out bogus retreat orders (NARA, RG 120, entry 1241, 28th Division records, box 6, file 228.32.15).

40. *USAWW*, 5:18, 113, 122–123; NARA, RG 120, entry 1241, 28th Division records, box 8, file 228.33.6.

41. ABMC, *3d Division*, 24–25; NARA, RG 120, entry 1241, 3d Division records, box 18, file 203.33.6.

42. ABMC, *3d Division*, 28–32; Lanza, "Bridgeheads of the Marne," 217, 222; Lanza, "German XXIII Reserve Corps," 381.

43. *USAWW*, 5:60–61; French 125th Division War Diary, France MDLD.

44. ABMC, *3d Division*, 29; NARA, RG 120, entry 1241, 3d Division records, box 18, file 203.33.6, folder 65.

45. *USAWW*, 5:64; Lanza claims that the French division's attack was postponed until the following day (Lanza, "Bridgeheads of the Marne," 226–227).

46. NARA, RG 120, entry 1241, 3d Division records, box 18, file 203.33.6, folder 65.

47. Doughty, *Pyrrhic Victory*, 469–470.

48. American accounts of the Rainbow Division in the Marne Defensive ignore the French and give the doughboys the leading role in hurling back the attackers. Thus, Capt. R. M. Cheseldine, who commanded a supply company of the 166th Regiment located well in the rear on July 15, described alleged German frontal attacks on Rainbow Division positions that morning:

> Doggedly, and bravely, he came on! Behind him thousands pushing forward. No man could turn back. On they came, and in spite of all that were killed, their bodies piled before the American wire, thousands more were there to take the places of the dead. It was impossible to kill them all, and some gained a foothold in the trenches. Then arose the American fighting man, and with bayonet, trench knife, grenades, clubbed rifle or clenched fist, threw himself upon his enemy and killed—killed a-plenty, until they had their fill! (R. M. Cheseldine, *Ohio in the Rainbow: Official Story of the 166th Infantry 42nd Division in the World War* [Columbus, Ohio: F. J. Heer, 1924], 165–166)

Historian James J. Cooke, relying largely on postwar American memoirs, credits the French but vastly overstates the "massive" German assault against Rainbow Division positions that ended in "horrible slaughter," with mountainous heaps of German dead (Cooke, *Rainbow Division*, 106–112).

49. Francis P. Duffy, *Father Duffy's Story: A Tale of Humor and Heroism, of Life and Death with the Fighting Sixty-Ninth* (New York: George H. Doran, 1919), 133; *USAWW*, 5:155, 167, 171.

50. *USAWW*, 5:172–174.

51. Ibid., 77; NARA, RG 120, entry 1241, 3d Division records, box 17, file 203.32.7; ABMC, *28th Division*, 32–33.

52. Lanza described why the 1/109th started late on July 16:

> The officer commanding this battalion received a copy of the attack order. It was written in French, with which language he was unfamiliar. So, after looking at the order from several directions, he decided it was unintelligible, and marked it file. Later he received a short message, also in French, the body of which read "H est dix," or H hour is 10:00 AM. This meant nothing to our commander, so he made an assumption that it was unimportant, and added it to the file (pocket in OD shirt). He then forgot about these French papers.

Lanza continued: Later, "the barrage started to roll. Our commander watched it; he hoped to see some delayed infantry hastening to catch up. None appeared. Our commander was certain that somebody was AWOL on an extremely important occasion. He hoped it was a Frenchman; it did not occur to him that it might be himself. He felt sorry for him, whoever he might be" (Lanza, "Bridgeheads of the Marne," 232–234). *USAWW*, 5:123, 180–181; ABMC, *28th Division*, 15; NARA, RG 120, entry 1241, 3d Division records, box 18, file 203.33.1; Richardson report, December 15, 1918; 28th Division Report of Operations, February 12,1919.

53. Dickman, *Great Crusade*, 112; Lanza, "Bridgeheads of the Marne," 236; Neiberg, *Second Battle of the Marne*, 115–116.

54. Kelton to Conner, July 18, 1918, NARA, RG 120, entry 1241, 3d Division records, box 18, file 203.33.6.

55. *USAWW*, 5:44–47, 103–104; operations report, July 4–August 14, 1918, NARA, RG 120, entry 1241, 3d Division records, box 18, file 203.33.6; Dickman, *Great Crusade*, 89; Timothy K. Nenninger, "'Unsystematic as a Mode of Command': Commanders and the Process of Command in the American Expeditionary Forces, 1917–1918," *Journal of Military History* 64, 3 (July 2000): 758.

56. Bruce, *Fraternity of Arms*, 236; Kelton to Conner, July 20 and 30, 1918, NARA, RG 120, entry 1241, 3d Division records, box 18, file 203.33.6. Bruce takes no account of any Franco-American disharmony in the Marne defensive.

57. Kelton to Conner, July 18 and 30, 1918, NARA, RG 120, entry 1241, 3d Division records, box 18, file 203.33.6; Dickman, *Great Crusade*, 117–118.

58. Dickman, *Great Crusade*, 110, 117–118; *USAWW*, 5:123.

59. Bruce, *Fraternity of Arms*, 235; Lanza, "German XXIII Reserve Corps," 309, 389.

60. Herbert Sulzbach, *With the German Guns: Four Years on the Western Front 1914–1918* (Hamden, Conn.: Archon Books, 1981), 201–202; Frederick Trevenen Edwards, *Fort Sheridan to Montfaucon: The War Letters of Frederick Trevenen Edwards* (DeLand, Fla.: E. O. Painter, 1954), 235.

Chapter 14. "Deal the Enemy a Crushing Blow": Soissons, July 18–22, 1918

1. Robert A. Doughty, *Pyrrhic Victory: French Strategy and Operations in the Great War* (Cambridge, Mass.: Harvard University Press, 2005), 469–471; Donald Smythe, *Pershing: General of the Armies* (Bloomington: Indiana University Press, 1986), 152.

2. *USAWW*, 5:235–237, 276–277; ABMC, *1st Division*, 20; Douglas V. Johnson and Rolfe L. Hillman Jr., *Soissons 1918* (College Station: Texas A&M University Press, 1999), 11–12, 39.

3. Michael S. Neiberg, *The Second Battle of the Marne* (Bloomington: Indiana University Press, 2008), 123–124. These American deployments are discussed in chapter 15.

4. *History of the First Division during the World War, 1917–1919* (Philadelphia: John C. Winston, 1931), 100–102.

5. ABMC, *2d Division*, 26; Edwin N. McClellan, "The Aisne-Marne Offensive," *Marine Corps Gazette* 6, 1–2 (March–June 1921): 76.

6. Charles Pelot Summerall, *The Way of Duty, Honor, Country: The Memoir of Charles Pelot Summerall*, ed. Timothy K. Nenninger (Lexington: University Press of Kentucky, 2010), 123.

7. Johnson and Hillman, *Soissons 1918*, 58; *Soissons Operations* (typescript compilation), 8, USAHEC. Pershing had written in his diary on June 9, "Gen. Bundy disappoints me. He lacks the grasp. I shall relieve him at the first opportunity" (quoted in Mark E. Grotelueschen, *The AEF Way of War: The American Army and Combat in World War I* [Cambridge: Cambridge University Press, 2007], 226).

8. Joseph Dorst Patch, *A Soldier's War: The First Infantry Division A.E.F. (1917–1918)* (Corpus Christi, Tex.: Mission Press, 1966), 125–127.

9. *USAWW*, 5:278; John W. Thomason Jr., "Soissons" (US Army War College monograph), 56, CARL; Johnson and Hillman, *Soissons 1918*, 39–40.

10. *USAWW*, 5:290–292; Johnson and Hillman, *Soissons 1918*, 39–41.

11. Ninth Army situation map and reports, July 18, 1918, Cylburn O. Mattfeldt, ed., *Translations: War Diaries of German Units Opposed to the Second Division (Regular), 1918*, 9 vols. (Washington, D.C.: Army War College, 1930–1935), 5/1; Thomason, "Soissons," 33–34.

12. Thomason, "Soissons," 36; *WWIR*, vol. 4; German Seventh Army War Diary, 11th Division reports, July 16–17, 1918, *WWIR German*, 2/1; Ninth Army orders, 1200, July 18, 1918; Corps Watter report, August 6, 1918; 14th Reserve Division War Diary and divisional report; 47th Reserve Division War Diary, in Mattfeldt, *Translations*, 5/1, 5/2; "Narrative Account of the July 18th Attack by the 1st and 2nd Divisions in the Aisne-Marne Offensive," in *Soissons Operations*, 5; David T. Zabecki, *The German 1918 Offensives: A Case Study in the Operational Level of War* (London: Routledge, 2006), 265–267.

13. German Ninth Army and Corps Staabs War Diaries, *WWIR German*, 2/1.

14. Harry L. Bennett, *Operations of the Twenty Sixth Infantry, First Division, 17–23 July 1918* (Fort Leavenworth, Kans.: Command and General Staff School, 1931), 5, CARL; Martin Gus Gulberg, *A War Diary* (Chicago: Drake Press, 1927), 34; *The Story of the Twenty-Eighth Infantry in the Great War, American Expeditionary Forces* (n.p., 1919), 21–23; Patch, *Soldier's War*, 128.

15. ABMC, *1st Division*, 22; Johnson and Hillman, *Soissons 1918*, 42–44; *History of the First Division*, 111; Ninth Army and XXXIX Corps War Diaries, *WWIR German*, 2/1; Corps Watter report, August 6, 1918, in Mattfeldt, *Translations*, 5/1.

16. German Seventh Army War Diary, *WWIR German*, 2/1; Herbert Sulzbach, *With the German Guns: Four Years on the Western Front 1914–1918* (Hamden, Conn.: Archon Books, 1981), 204.

17. *History of the First Division*, 103–104. Summerall warned his officers about the mustard-filled shell holes and ravine; FO 27, *WWIR*, vol. 2.

18. G-3 memo, "Meeting on July 17," July 17, 1918, *WWIR*, vol. 2.

19. FO 27, July 16, 1918, *WWIR*, vol. 2; *History of the First Division*, 104–105, 110–112; *USAWW*, 5:312; ABMC, *1st Division*, 20–22.

20. Johnson and Hillman, *Soissons 1918*, 44.

21. Babcock report, July 26, 1918, 28th Regiment operations reports, *WWIR*, vol. 13; Johnson and Hillman, *Soissons 1918*, 45–46; *USAWW*, 5:325; ABMC, *1st Division*, 22; Bennett, *Operations of the Twenty Sixth Infantry*, 7–9; *Story of the Twenty-Eighth*, 21–23; 2d Brigade field messages, *WWIR*, vol. 15; German 11th Division War Diary, *WWIR German*, 2/1; German 3d and 13th Regiments War Diaries, *WWIR German*, 2/2.

22. Though Edwards clearly merited the Medal of Honor he later received for this exploit, the account of this action portrayed by Lowell Thomas is unreliable (Lowell Thomas, *This Side of Hell: Dan Edwards, Adventurer* [New York: P. F. Collier & Son, 1932], 268).

23. 11th Division War Diary and July 18 divisional report, *WWIR German*, 2/1; 3d, 13th, and 22d Regiments War Diaries and records, *WWIR German*, 2/2; French 153d Division War Diary, France MDLD.

24. Huebner report for July 18–21, 1918; Babcock report, July 26, 1918; 28th Regiment operations reports, *WWIR*, vol. 13; Bennett, *Operations of the Twenty Sixth Infantry*, 10–11; Johnson and Hillman, *Soissons 1918*, 45–47, 50–51; Charles B. Fullerton, *The Twenty-Sixth Infantry in France* (privately printed, 1919), 37; *History of the First Division*, 113; 2d Brigade and 28th Regiment field messages, *WWIR*, vol. 15.

25. German 11th Division War Diary; July 18 divisional report; *WWIR German*, 2/1.

26. Huebner report; Babcock report; 28th Regiment operations reports, *WWIR*, vol. 13; Johnson and Hillman, *Soissons 1918*, 47–51; ABMC, *1st Division*, 24–25; *Story of the Twenty-Eighth*, 21–23; 11th Division, 3d Regiment War Diaries, *WWIR German*, 2/1, 2/2; French 153d Division War Diary, France MDLD.

27. Huebner report; Babcock report; 28th Regiment operations reports, *WWIR*, vol. 13; Bennett, *Operations of the Twenty Sixth Infantry*, 11–12; Johnson and Hillman, *Soissons 1918*, 47–51; Fullerton, *Twenty-Sixth Infantry in France*, 37; *History of the First Division*, 114–117; ABMC, *1st Division*, 24–25; *Story of the Twenty-Eighth*, 21–23; Ninth Army, Corps Staabs, 11th Division, 13th Regiment War Diaries, *WWIR German*, 2/1, 2/2; 109th Regiment War Diary, in Mattfeldt, *Translations*, 5/3. An 11th Division postmortem on July 18 called that day "the most trying day of the war" for the unit (*WWIR German*, 2/1). But the German artillery was deadly effective: Harry Bennett, inspecting the ground afterward, counted eleven hits on one French tank alone.

28. 1st Division G-3 conference notes, July 28, 1918; Summerall report, July 27,

1918, *WWIR*, vol. 12; *USAWW*, 5:323–327; Johnson and Hillman, *Soissons 1918*, 47–48; Summerall, *Way of Duty*, 128; Beaumont B. Buck, *Memories of Peace and War* (San Antonio, Tex.: Naylor, 1935), 194; *Soissons Operations*, 12.

29. French 153d Division War Diary, France MDLD; ABMC, *1st Division*, 24–25; *History of the First Division*, 114–117; *Story of the Twenty-Eighth*, 21–23; Babcock to Buck, 1325, 2d Brigade and 28th Regiment field messages, *WWIR*, vol. 15; German 11th Division War Diary, *WWIR German*, 2/1.

30. Babcock to Buck, 1325, 2d Brigade and 28th Regiment field messages, *WWIR*, vol. 15; G-3 memo to brigade commanders, July 17, 1918, *WWIR*, vol. 2; Buck, *Memories of Peace and War*, 194–197. Johnson and Hillman, *Soissons 1918*, 100–101, dwells at length on Buck's "patently aberrant behavior," which certainly cost lives.

31. Operations report, 1st Brigade, July 16–23, 1918, Hines to Summerall, August 4, 1918, *WWIR*, vol. 13; German Ninth and Seventh Armies, Corps Staabs and Watter, 3d Regiment War Diaries, *WWIR German*, 2/1, 2/2.

32. Operations report, 1st Brigade, July 16–23, Hines to Summerall, August 4, *WWIR*, vol. 13; ABMC, *1st Division*, 23; Ben-Hur Chastaine, *History of the 18th U.S. Infantry First Division 1812–1919* (New York: Hymans, n.d.), 63; Johnson and Hillman, *Soissons 1918*, 52–53; *The Story of the Sixteenth Infantry in France* (Montabaur, Germany: Martin Flock, 1919), n.p.

33. Operations report, 1st Brigade, July 16–23, Hines to Summerall, August 4, *WWIR*, vol. 13; ABMC, *1st Division*, 23; Chastaine, *History of the 18th U.S. Infantry*, 63–64; Johnson and Hillman, *Soissons 1918*, 52–53.

34. Thomason, "Soissons," 57; Corps Watter report, August 6, 1918; 14th Reserve Division War Diary; 42d Division War Diary; 65th Brigade report, in Mattfeldt, *Translations*, 5/1, 5/2; *History of the First Division*, 117–118; Chastaine, *History of the 18th U.S. Infantry*, 64; Johnson and Hillman, *Soissons 1918*, 54–55; Operations report, 1st Brigade, July 16–23, Hines to Summerall, August 4, *WWIR*, vol. 13. The 65th Brigade report commented that enemy snipers commonly occupied knocked-out tanks and inflicted damage from there, and French crews who had abandoned their vehicles reentered them after dark and resumed operations.

35. *History of the First Division*, 118–120; *Story of the Sixteenth Infantry*, n.p.; Johnson and Hillman, *Soissons 1918*, 75.

36. Ninth Army and Corps Staabs War Diaries, *WWIR German*, 2/1.

37. 2d Brigade and 28th Regiment field messages, *WWIR*, vol. 15; *History of the First Division*, 121; *Soissons Operations*, 12; Bennett, *Operations of the Twenty Sixth Infantry*, 13; Grotelueschen, *AEF Way of War*, 92.

38. Pierre Emile Berdoulat, "The First and Second American Divisions in the Offensive of July [1]8, 1918," *Cavalry Journal* 34, 141 (October 1925): 407; memorandum to Harbord, March 28, 1923, Hillman Papers, Major Ladislav Janda Subcollection, box 10, USAHEC. Hillman believed that Col. Preston Brown prepared the memorandum for Harbord to use in his postwar memoirs.

39. The existence of these orders turns on its head the Americans' supposition that they suffered casualties because of French failures to advance (Thomason, "Soissons," 58).

40. Memorandum to Harbord, USAHEC; Johnson and Hillman, *Soissons 1918*,

59; ABMC, *2d Division*, 27. According to Berdoulat, the staff at 2d Division headquarters responded to the news that their machine guns would not arrive in time with a cheery quip: "All right, we'll take the Boche machine-guns" (Berdoulat, "First and Second American Divisions," 408). More likely they used somewhat choicer language.

41. Johnson and Hillman, *Soissons 1918*, 61; George B. Clark, ed., *Devil Dogs Chronicle: Voices of the 4th Marine Brigade in World War I* (Lawrence: University Press of Kansas, 2013), 221.

42. Attack orders, July 17, 1918, in Cylburn O. Mattfeldt, ed., *Records of the Second Division (Regular)*, 10 vols. (Washington, D.C.: Army War College, 1924–1929), 1; *USAWW*, 5:328–329; Johnson and Hillman, *Soissons 1918*, 59.

43. Attack orders, July 17, 1918, in Mattfeldt, *Records of the Second Division*, 1; *USAWW*, 5:290–292, 328–329; Thomason, "Soissons," 58; Grotelueschen, *AEF Way of War*, 228. Ironically, one German division commander reported after the battle that the constant American changes of direction—many of which reflected confusion rather than Harbord's orders—took his men off guard as formations were suddenly sidestepped and caught in the flank, helping to undermine the defense (14th Reserve Division report, July 18, 1918, in Mattfeldt, *Translations*, 5/1).

44. 5th Marines field reports and messages, in Mattfeldt, *Records of the Second Division*, 7/1; Johnson and Hillman, *Soissons 1918*, 62–63; George B. Clark, *The Second Infantry Division in World War I: A History of the American Expeditionary Force Regulars, 1917–1919* (Jefferson, N.C.: McFarland, 2007), 98–100; George B. Clark, *Devil Dogs: Fighting Marines of World War I* (Novato, Calif.: Presidio Press, 1999), 225–229.

45. Johnson and Hillman, *Soissons 1918*, 62–63; ABMC, *2d Division*, 27.

46. Turrill report in McClellan, "Aisne-Marne Offensive," 79, 199; 40th Reserve Regiment combat report, 115th Division, in Mattfeldt, *Translations*, 5/2; James H. Hallas, ed., *Doughboy War: The American Expeditionary Force in World War I* (Mechanicsburg, Pa.: Stackpole Books, 2000), 106, 109; Clark, *Devil Dogs Chronicle*, 226.

47. Turrill report in McClellan, "Aisne-Marne Offensive," 79, 199; Corps Watter report, August 6, 1918; 14th Reserve Division battalion reports, in Mattfeldt, *Translations*, 5/1; ABMC, *2d Division*, 28–29; Johnson and Hillman, *Soissons 1918*, 65; Clark, *Second Infantry Division*, 100–101; Clark, *Devil Dogs*, 228–231.

48. German 65th Brigade reports, July 18 and 28, 1918, in Mattfeldt, *Translations*, 5/2.

49. Thomason, "Soissons," 36.

50. Private William A. Francis, 5th Marines, WWI Survey, USAHEC.

51. 5th Marines field reports and messages, in Mattfeldt, *Records of the Second Division*, 7/1; Francis, WWI Survey; Corps Watter report, August 6, 1918, Corps Watter War Diary, 14th Reserve Division War Diary and divisional report, July 18, 1918; 115th Division War Diary; 3d Reserve Division War Diary, in Mattfeldt, *Translations*, 5/1, 5/2, 5/3; Thomason, "Soissons," 88–92; ABMC, *2d Division*, 28–29; Johnson and Hillman, *Soissons 1918*, 66, 75; Clark, *Devil Dogs*, 231–238; Keyser report in McClellan, "Aisne-Marne Offensive," 80; Clark, *Devil Dogs Chronicle*, 227–229.

52. Company reports, 9th Regiment, in Mattfeldt, *Records of the Second Division*, 7/1; 1st Lt. Ladislav T. Janda, 9th Regiment, WWI Survey, USAHEC; *The Ninth U.S.*

Infantry in the World War (n.p., 1919), 14; Johnson and Hillman, *Soissons 1918*, 67; Pvt. Willie McMullen, 9th Regiment, WWI Survey, USAHEC.

53. Quoted in Johnson and Hillman, *Soissons 1918*, 68; McMullen, WWI Survey.

54. Ely 3d Brigade report, July 18, 1918; company reports, 9th Regiment, in Mattfeldt, *Records of the Second Division*, 6/2, 7/1; ABMC, *2d Division*, 28; *Ninth U.S. Infantry*, 14; Janda, WWI Survey.

55. Janda, WWI Survey; 14th Reserve Division field artillery reports, in Mattfeldt, *Translations*, 5/1. Upton later found the ravine littered with abandoned German artillery pieces (report of July 18, in Mattfeldt, *Records of the Second Division*, 7/1).

56. Thomason, "Soissons," 83–86; Janda, WWI Survey.

57. Malone report, July 18, 1918; company reports, 23d Infantry, in Mattfeldt, *Records of the Second Division*, 7/1; ABMC, *2d Division*, 26–27; Robert Winthrop Kean, *Dear Marraine (1917–1919)* (privately printed, 1969), 147; Johnson and Hillman, *Soissons 1918*, 73.

58. Ely 3d Brigade report, July 18; company reports, 23d Regiment, in Mattfeldt, *Records of the Second Division*, 6/2, 7/1; ABMC, *2d Division*, 28; Johnson and Hillman, *Soissons 1918*, 73; Kean, *Dear Marraine*, 148–150.

59. Company reports, 23d Regiment, in Mattfeldt, *Records of the Second Division*, 7/1; Thomason, "Soissons," 78–82, 103; ABMC, *2d Division*, 28; "Journal Kept by Commandant Bertier," in *Soissons Operations*, 3.

60. Berdoulat, "First and Second American Division," 408; Thomason, "Soissons," 77.

61. *USAWW*, 5:296–297, 333; Johnson and Hillman, *Soissons 1918*, 76–78.

62. 47th Reserve Division regimental and battalion reports, in Mattfeldt, *Translations*, 5/2.

63. Janda, WWI Survey; Johnson and Hillman, *Soissons 1918*, 79. Lt. Cooke also attested to the presence of the Moroccans and to strafing attacks around Vierzy by German planes (Clark, *Devil Dogs Chronicle*, 230–231). The Moroccans had evidently decided to join the free-for-all that ignored unit boundaries, or they simply elected to help out their American allies, perhaps in response to a request for assistance.

64. ABMC, *2d Division*, 29–30.

65. Ely 3d Brigade report, July 18, in Mattfeldt, *Records of the Second Division*, 6/2; reports in McClellan, "Aisne-Marne Offensive," 78, 82, 201; Thomason, "Soissons," 98–102; Kean, *Dear Marraine*, 155–156; Johnson and Hillman, *Soissons 1918*, 81–82.

66. Ely 3d Brigade report, July 18, in Mattfeldt, *Records of the Second Division*, 6/2; Corps Watter report, August 6, 1918; 47th Reserve Division regimental and battalion reports, in Mattfeldt, *Translations*, 5/1, 5/2; reports in McClellan, "Aisne-Marne Offensive," 78, 82, 201; ABMC, *2d Division*, 29–30; Clark, *Devil Dogs Chronicle*, 233; Johnson and Hillman, *Soissons 1918*, 81–84. Clark insists that Vierzy was taken "by many Marines and some Doughboys"; Thomason more evenhandedly awards the town equally to both (Clark, *Devil Dogs Chronicle*, 234; Thomason, "Soissons," 105).

67. Upton to Harbord, 1315, July 18; Malone to Harbord, 2025, July 18; brigade and regimental reports, in Mattfeldt, *Records of the Second Division*, 4/1; Johnson and Hillman, *Soissons 1918*, 81–82; ABMC, *2d Division*, 30–31.

68. Neiberg, *Second Battle of the Marne*, 130; Corps Watter reports and war diary,

July 18, 1918; US report on German 20th Division, November 7, 1922, in Mattfeldt, *Translations*, 5/1, 5/3; quoted in Grotelueschen, *AEF Way of War*, 93; Doughty, *Pyrrhic Victory*, 472. To Corps Watter's left stood the XXV Reserve Corps (Corps Winckler), consisting from right to left of the 40th, 10th Bavarian, 45th Reserve, 51st Reserve, and 78th Reserve Divisions.

69. Janda, WWI Survey; *Soissons Operations*, 15; Kean, *Dear Marraine*, 158.

70. *USAWW*, 5:249–250, 296–297; Johnson and Hillman, *Soissons 1918*, 89–93. Johnson and Hillman attribute these problems to a "systemic rigidity in American thinking," although French army and corps commands were likely also to blame.

71. *USAWW*, 5:297–299. Berdoulat's misleading impression of the previous day's casualty rate may have reflected the more effective reporting mechanisms in the 1st Moroccan Division compared with the two American divisions.

72. Bennett, *Operations of the Twenty Sixth Infantry*, 14.

73. Summerall report, July 19, 1918, *WWIR*, vol. 12; Babcock report, July 26, 1918, 28th Regiment operations reports, *WWIR*, vol. 13; Johnson and Hillman, *Soissons 1918*, 93–95; ABMC, *1st Division*, 26; *History of the First Division*, 123–124; *Story of the Twenty-Eighth*, 24; Buck, *Memories of Peace and War*, 197.

74. Field messages, 2d Brigade, July 19, 1918, *WWIR*, vol. 15; Bennett, *Operations of the Twenty Sixth Infantry*, 15; *History of the First Division*, 123; Fullerton, *Twenty-Sixth Infantry in France*, 38; Johnson and Hillman, *Soissons 1918*, 99. Bennett, who was posted with the regimental combat train, was "instructed to deliver medical supplies at all costs to the advance first-aid station, and after all means of transportation had failed, Captain Bennett secured a wheel litter which he packed with medical supplies, then filled his arms and started forward under heavy artillery bombardment. He delivered the supplies as directed after having passed through the intense hostile counter barrage and aided in saving the lives of many wounded men" (Distinguished Service Cross citation).

75. 2d Brigade and 26th Regiment field messages, July 19, 1918, *WWIR*, vol. 15; Buck, *Memories of Peace and War*, 198.

76. Robert L. Bullard, *Personalities and Reminiscences of the War* (Garden City, N.Y.: Doubleday, Page, 1925), 243–244; French 153d Division War Diary, France MDLD; Summerall report of July 20, in *Soissons Operations*, 16–17.

77. *Soissons Operations*, 16–17.

78. Johnson and Hillman, *Soissons 1918*, 99–102; Chastaine, *History of the 18th U.S. Infantry*, 64; *History of the First Division*, 122–123; *Story of the Sixteenth Infantry*, n.p.

79. Field messages, 1st Division, *WWIR*, vol. 15; Babcock report, July 26; 28th Regiment operations reports, *WWIR*, vol. 13; Johnson and Hillman, *Soissons 1918*, 96–97. Summerall commented, "I found that the colonel's connections were such that it would be best not to relieve him, but after the battle he was transferred out of the division" (Summerall, *Way of Duty*, 128).

80. 2d Brigade operations reports and field messages; Babcock report, July 26; 28th Regiment operations reports, *WWIR*, vol. 13; Summerall report, July 27, *WWIR*, vol. 12; Bennett, *Operations of the Twenty Sixth Infantry*, 18–19; ABMC, *1st Division*, 27; Johnson and Hillman, *Soissons 1918*, 96–102; Fullerton, *Twenty-Sixth Infantry in France*, 38; *Soissons Operations*, 16–17; *History of the First Division*, 124–127;

Story of the Twenty-Eighth, 24. By the end of the attack, Babcock's 28th Regiment had only eight officers remaining in the line. Johnson and Hillman praise Babcock for doing a "remarkable job against terrible opposition to his left front and ignorant prejudice to his rear. His brigade commander, Brigadier General Buck, who should have been the connecting link between Babcock and division, was off gallivanting around the battlefield. And Major General Summerall . . . merely frothed in ignorance, failing to make the necessary effort to understand the situation adequately" (Johnson and Hillman, *Soissons 1918*, 102).

81. French 153d Division War Diary, France MDLD; German Ninth Army, Corps Staabs, 11th Bavarian Division, and 34th Division War Diaries and operations reports, *WWIR German*, 2/1, 2/2.

82. Operations report, 1st Brigade, July 19; Hines to Summerall, August 4, *WWIR*, vol. 13; ABMC, *1st Division*, 26–27; Chastaine, *History of the 18th U.S. Infantry*, 64–65.

83. German Ninth Army, 1/145th Battalion War Diaries, *WWIR German*, 2/1, 2/2.

84. Thomason, "Soissons," 114–115; Johnson and Hillman, *Soissons 1918*, 103–104.

85. Thomason, "Soissons," 114–117; Johnson and Hillman, *Soissons 1918*, 105. Two other German divisions, the 5th and the 9th, were on their way up (Seventh Army orders, 0130, in Mattfeldt, *Translations*, 5/1).

86. Peter F. Owen, *To the Limit of Endurance: A Battalion of Marines in the Great War* (College Station: Texas A&M University Press, 2007), 118; Clark, *Devil Dogs Chronicle*, 235; McClellan, "Aisne-Marne Offensive," 205.

87. Owen, *To the Limit of Endurance*, 119; Johnson and Hillman, *Soissons 1918*, 107; Warren R. Jackson, *His Time in Hell. A Texas Marine in France: The World War I Memoir of Warren R. Jackson*, ed. George B. Clark (Novato, Calif.: Presidio Press, 2001), 142; Carl Edward Brannen, *Over There: A Marine in the Great War*, ed. Rolfe L. Hillman Jr. and Peter F. Owen (College Station: Texas A&M University Press, 1996), 31–32.

88. Thomason, "Soissons," 114–117; ABMC, *2d Division*, 31; Clark, *Devil Dogs Chronicle*, 235; German 28th Division War Diary and operations reports, in Mattfeldt, *Translations*, 5/3; Owen, *To the Limit of Endurance*, 121–122. The Americans did manage to eviscerate the already wobbly 3d Reserve Division, which began the day with an average battalion strength of 514 but suffered up to 50 percent casualties; by evening, it was "no longer fit for action" and "urgently" in need of rest (3d Reserve Division War Diary and operations reports, in Mattfeldt, *Translations*, 5/1).

89. 6th Marines War Diary, in Mattfeldt, *Records of the Second Division*, 6/1; Thomason, "Soissons," 115–117; McClellan, "Aisne-Marne Offensive," 211–213; ABMC, *2d Division*, 31–32; Johnson and Hillman, *Soissons 1918*, 103, 107–111; Grotelueschen, *AEF Way of War*, 233.

90. Corps Watter, 14th Reserve Division, 42d Division, 3d Reserve Division, and 28th Division War Diaries and operations reports, in Mattfeldt, *Translations*, 5/1, 5/2, 5/3. By the end of the day, the German 42d Division, which had been repeatedly savaged by the Moroccans and Americans, was thoroughly demoralized and down to a combat strength of only forty men per regiment (Mattfeldt, *Translations*, 5/2).

91. Corps Watter, Corps Etzel, 115th Division, 3d Reserve Division, and 20th

Division War Diaries and operations reports, in Mattfeldt, *Translations*, 5/1, 5/2, 5/3. Peter F. Owen, misidentifying the flanking French unit as the "20th Moroccan Division," follows the gist of most American reports by blaming the French for the flanking fire the marines received; however, it is clear that far from hindering the Americans, the French provided substantial security against German counterattacks on both flanks (Owen, *To the Limit of Endurance*, 121).

92. Thomason, "Soissons," 139–140; *USAWW*, 5:281, 299; memo for Harbord, March 28, 1923, Hillman Papers, Janda Subcollection, box 10, USAHEC; Johnson and Hillman, *Soissons 1918*, 111–114; James G. Harbord, *Leaves from a War Diary* (New York: Dodd, Mead, 1925), 327–328.

93. Brannen, *Over There*, 33–34; Thomason, "Soissons," 142–143; Upton to Harbord, July 19, and Malone to Harbord, July 20, in Mattfeldt, *Records of the Second Division*, 5/1; Johnson and Hillman, *Soissons 1918*, 114.

94. William A. Carter, *The Tale of a Devil Dog* (Washington, D.C.: Canteen Press, 1920), 59–60. The Germans increasingly respected the US 2d Division as well, with the German 20th Division referring to the Americans as "elite" in a war diary entry for July 20 (Mattfeldt, *Translations*, 5/3).

95. Summerall report, July 27, *WWIR*, vol. 12; ABMC, *1st Division*, 28.

96. Bennett, *Operations of the Twenty Sixth Infantry*, 20; *History of the First Division*, 128, 134; Johnson and Hillman, *Soissons 1918*, 116–117; Summerall report, July 27, *WWIR*, vol. 12.

97. Summerall report, July 27, *WWIR*, vol. 12; *USAWW*, 5:319, 326; Johnson and Hillman, *Soissons 1918*, 119–120.

98. Hines to Summerall, August 4, *WWIR*, vol. 13; Corps Watter, 42d Division, 28th Division War Diaries, in Mattfeldt, *Translations*, 5/1, 5/2, 5/3; ABMC, *1st Division*, 28–29; *History of the First Division*, 129; *Story of the Sixteenth Infantry*, n.p.; Summerall, *Way of Duty*, 127; Johnson and Hillman, *Soissons 1918*, 126–133.

99. Babcock report, July 26, 28th Regiment operations reports, *WWIR*, vol. 13; Johnson and Hillman, *Soissons 1918*, 117–120.

100. *History of the First Division*, 129–132; Summerall report, July 27, *WWIR*, vol. 13; Babcock report, July 26, 28th Regiment operations reports, *WWIR*, vol. 13; Bennett, *Operations of the Twenty Sixth Infantry*, 20–21; ABMC, *1st Division*, 28–29; Johnson and Hillman, *Soissons 1918*, 118–120. Johnson and Hillman say of Buck: "The smell of cowardice is faintly present. If not that, then of considerable mental confusion" (Johnson and Hillman, *Soissons 1918*, 118). Although the suggestion of cowardice is unjustified, it is hard to account for Buck's behavior during the first three days of the Soissons offensive. His memoirs for this period present disjointed impressions of various scenes of ruins, cavalry, aid stations, bombardments, airplanes, and other goings-on behind the front—almost as if he were a child eager to see the action without actually participating in it or taking responsibility for what would happen (Buck, *Memories of Peace and War*, 200–201).

101. Summerall, *Way of Duty*, 126–127; Johnson and Hillman, *Soissons 1918*, 121–125; Patch, *Soldier's War*, 39.

102. Summerall, *Way of Duty*, 126–127; *Soissons Operations*, 19; German Ninth Army War Diary, *WWIR German*, 2/1.

103. German Ninth Army War Diary, *WWIR German*, 2/1; German Seventh Army War Diary, in Mattfeldt, *Translations*, 2/1.

104. Joseph J. Gleeson, *A Soldier's Story: A Daily Account of World War I by Sergeant Joseph J. Gleeson, January 1918 to March 1919* (privately printed, 1999), 49; Corps Watter War Diary, in Mattfeldt, *Translations*, 5/1; Sulzbach, *With the German Guns*, 206.

105. 1st Brigade operations report, Hines to Summerall, August 4, *WWIR*, vol. 13; German Corps Watter, 42d Division War Diaries and combat reports, in Mattfeldt, *Translations*, 5/1, 5/2; ABMC, *1st Division*, 30; Chastaine, *History of the 18th U.S. Infantry*, 66; *History of the First Division*, 134–135; Johnson and Hillman, *Soissons 1918*, 129–130.

106. Summerall report, July 27, *WWIR*, vol. 12; Babcock report, July 26, 28th Regiment operations reports, *WWIR*, vol. 13; 2d Brigade operations reports, *WWIR*, vol. 13; Ninth Army, Corps Staabs War Diaries, *WWIR German*, 2/1; ABMC, *1st Division*, 30–31; *History of the First Division*, 135–137; *Story of the Twenty-Eighth*, 25; Johnson and Hillman, *Soissons 1918*, 129–130. Summerall's official report—as always, highly critical of the French—and subsequent American accounts refer to the French division on the 1st Division's left as the 153d Division, even though that division had been replaced by the 69th. One wonders whether the error reflects a dismissive attitude toward the French in general.

107. Johnson and Hillman, *Soissons 1918*, 131–133; Buck, *Memories of Peace and War*, 202–206.

108. Sulzbach, *With the German Guns*, 206.

109. Ibid.; German Seventh Army, Corps Watter War Diaries, in Mattfeldt, *Translations*, 5/1. War diaries and combat reports for all German divisions engaged on this day constantly report being shelled by their own artillery. The after-action report of the German 20th Division was especially outspoken in denouncing the artillery and its officers, who were accused of hiding in their dugouts and making no attempt to assess conditions at the front (Mattfeldt, *Translations*, 5/3).

110. German Seventh Army War Diary, in Mattfeldt, *Translations*, 5/1; Bennett, *Operations of the Twenty Sixth Infantry*, 28–30. In any event, the quality of the French formations that replaced the US 2d Division and entered the line nearby was apparently quite poor. Units of the German 3d Reserve Division still fighting around Tigny on July 24 scoffed that the French troops opposite them attacked only when they possessed overwhelming numerical superiority and after severe artillery fire, and they followed their tanks "hesitatingly" and pulled back as soon as the machines were destroyed; in addition, "effective MG fire causes him to put up his hands," and "any determined attack will put him to flight" (German 3d Reserve Division War Diary, in Mattfeldt, *Translations*, 5/3).

111. Bennett, *Operations of the Twenty Sixth Infantry*, 28–30; Summerall report, July 27, *WWIR*, vol. 12; *History of the First Division*, 141.

112. Smythe, *Pershing*, 158.

113. 26th Regiment field messages, reports dated August 3, 1918, *WWIR*, vol. 13.

114. NARA, RG 120, entry 267, G-3 General Correspondence, box 3225, folder 2145; Campbell King memo, August 5, 1918, *WWIR*, vol. 12.

115. Bennett, *Operations of the Twenty Sixth Infantry*, 31–33.

116. Berdoulat, "First and Second American Divisions," 411–412.

117. McClellan, "Aisne-Marne Offensive," 193.

118. NARA, RG 120, entry 268, G-3 Secret Correspondence, box 3154, folder 1092; Summerall, *Way of Duty*, 126, 131; Summerall report, July 27, *WWIR*, vol. 12; McClellan, "Aisne-Marne Offensive," 214; Henry Berry, *Make the Kaiser Dance* (New York: Doubleday, 1978), 59. Johnson and Hillman conclude that, despite "his huge ego and bluster, [Summerall] was the proper man at Soissons"—which is surely damning with faint praise. They also slam Summerall's "personal insecurities" and conclude that "while he seems to have made more correct than bad decisions in combat, his ridiculous blathering and evident fear of any challenge to his authority made his performance as army chief of staff poor" (Johnson and Hillman, *Soissons 1918*, 139, 155).

Chapter 15. Reducing the Marne Salient: US Troops in the Aisne-Marne Campaign, July 18–August 6, 1918

1. Quoted in David F. Trask, *The AEF and Coalition Warmaking, 1917–1918* (Lawrence: University Press of Kansas, 1993), 90.

2. ABMC, *4th Division*, 1–6.

3. Christian A. Bach and Henry Noble Hall, *The Fourth Division: Its Services and Achievements in the World War Gathered from the Records of the Division* (Garden City, N.Y.: Christian A. Bach, 1920), 71–73; ABMC, *4th Division*, 15–21.

4. *USAWW*, 5:496; Bach and Hall, *Fourth Division*, 76–80; ABMC, *4th Division*, 10–11.

5. Hunter Liggett, *AEF: Ten Years Ago in France* (New York: Dodd, Mead, 1928), 86–88.

6. Robert H. Ferrell, ed., *In the Company of Generals: The World War I Diary of Pierpont L. Stackpole* (Columbia: University of Missouri Press, 2009), 101; Mark E. Grotelueschen, *The AEF Way of War: The American Army and Combat in World War I* (Cambridge: Cambridge University Press, 2007), 159.

7. Connell Albertine, *The Yankee Doughboy* (Boston: Branden Press, 1968), 152–153.

8. *USAWW*, 5:415–416.

9. *USAWW*, 5:424, 501; Frank P. Sibley, *With the Yankee Division in France* (Boston: Little, Brown, 1919), 206–207; Albertine, *Yankee Doughboy*, 154.

10. Horatio Rogers, *World War I through My Sights* (San Rafael, Calif.: Presidio Press, 1976), 169.

11. *USAWW*, 5:418; ABMC, *26th Division*, 11–12; Sibley, *With the Yankee Division*, 208–211; Pvt. Harry G. Wright, 3/104th Battalion, WWI Survey, USAHEC.

12. Earl Yeomans, WWI Survey USAHEC; Albertine, *Yankee Doughboy*, 155–156.

13. Bach and Hall, *Fourth Division*, 73–75; ABMC, *4th Division*, 22–23.

14. Bach and Hall, *Fourth Division*, 82–87; ABMC, *4th Division*, 12–14.

15. *USAWW*, 4:425–426; Grotelueschen, *AEF Way of War*, 164–165; Rexmond C. Cochrane, *The 26th Division in the Aisne-Marne Campaign, July 1918* (Army Chemical Center, Md.: US Army Chemical Corps Historical Office, 1957), 24; Michael E. Shay, *The Yankee Division in the First World War: In the Highest Tradition* (College Station: Texas A&M University Press, 2008), 118–122; ABMC, *26th Division*, 14.

16. Montdésir to Dickman, July 19, 1918; Kelton to Conner, July 20, 1918, NARA, RG 120, entry 1241, 3d Division records box 17, file 203.32.7. Of the Americans' equal responsibility for evaluating German intentions through the use of scouts and patrols, Kelton had nothing to say.

17. *USAWW*, 5:427, 430–431, 480–481; ABMC, *26th Division*, 16–17; Sibley, *With the Yankee Division*, 215; Shay, *Yankee Division*, 123–126; ABMC, *3d Division*, 36–38.

18. James H. Hallas, ed., *Doughboy War: The American Expeditionary Force in World War I* (Mechanicsburg, Pa.: Stackpole Books, 2000), 122; *USAWW*, 5:478; ABMC, *26th Division*, 17–18; Cochrane, *26th Division in the Aisne-Marne Campaign*, 29–33; Sibley, *With the Yankee Division*, 215–220; Shay, *Yankee Division*, 126–130; Grotelueschen, *AEF Way of War*, 166–167.

19. *USAWW*, 5:600–601; Frederic Vinton Hemenway, *History of the Third Division United States Army in the World War for the Period December 1, 1917 to January 1, 1919* (Anderbach-on-the-Rhine: n.p., 1919), 160–162; ABMC, *3d Division*, 38–41.

20. Fred Calvin Wilder, *War Experiences of F. C. Wilder* (Belchertown, Mass.: Lewis H. Blackmer, 1926), 84–87; Shay, *Yankee Division*, 130–131; Grotelueschen, *AEF Way of War*, 170.

21. Trask, *AEF and Coalition Warmaking*, 93–94; Donald Smythe, *Pershing: General of the Armies* (Bloomington: Indiana University Press, 1986), 161.

22. Shay, *Yankee Division*, 132; Wilder, *War Experiences*, 88; Cochrane, *26th Division in the Aisne-Marne Campaign*, 3; ABMC, *26th Division*, 19–21.

23. *USAWW*, 5:477–479; Grotelueschen, *AEF Way of War*, 170. Edwards's relief is controversial. There is no doubt that he and his staff made multiple mistakes, but some have questioned whether their errors were more plentiful or more important than those of any other division headquarters at this awkward time in the history of American military administration. Rivalry between the Regular Army and the National Guard, in which Pershing and Edwards fell on opposite sides, undoubtedly played a role in the friction between 26th Division headquarters and GHQ. For a discussion of Edwards's relief and a summary of his qualities as a division commander, see Shay, *Yankee Division*, 181–187, 223–233.

24. NARA, RG 120, entry 1241, 3d Division records, box 17, file 203.32.7.

25. *USAWW*, 5:520, 529; ABMC, *42d Division*, 18–21; Liggett, *AEF*, 126; Douglas MacArthur, *Reminiscences* (New York: McGraw-Hill, 1964), 59; "The Battle of Croix Rouge Farm," Croix Rouge Farm Memorial Foundation, http://croixrougefarm.org/history-battle/ (accessed April 24, 2014); James J. Cooke, *The Rainbow Division in the Great War, 1917–1919* (Westport, Conn.: Praeger, 1994), 122.

26. Sladen report on 5th Brigade, NARA, RG 120, entry 1241, 3d Division records, box 18, file 203.33.6; ABMC, *3d Division*, 43–44.

27. Hunter Liggett, *Commanding an American Army: Recollections of the World War* (Boston: Houghton Mifflin, 1925), 41–42; ABMC, *42d Division*, 22–23.

28. R. M. Cheseldine, *Ohio in the Rainbow: Official Story of the 166th Infantry 42nd Division in the World War* (Columbus, Ohio: F. J. Heer, 1924), 195; *USAWW*, 5:521, 529–531; Liggett, *AEF*, 126–127; Martin J. Hogan, *The Shamrock Battalion in the Great War*, ed. James J. Cooke (Columbia: University of Missouri Press, 2007), 79–80; Francis P. Duffy, *Father Duffy's Story: A Tale of Humor and Heroism, of Life and Death*

with the Fighting Sixty-Ninth (New York: George H. Doran, 1919), 179; ABMC, *42d Division*, 24–25.

29. Col. Conrad H. Lanza, "The Passage of the Ourcq by the 28th Division," NARA, RG 120, entry 1241, 28th Division records, box 2, file 228-18.2; ABMC, *3d Division*, 44–45.

30. Cheseldine, *Ohio in the Rainbow*, 201–202, 207; *USAWW*, 5:524; Lanza, "Passage of the Ourcq"; ABMC, *42d Division*, 26–27; ABMC, *28th Division*, 20–21.

31. Liggett, *AEF*, 127; ABMC, *42d Division*, 28; Henry Berry, *Make the Kaiser Dance* (New York: Doubleday, 1978), 335–337.

32. ABMC, *28th Division*, 22–23; NARA, RG 120, entry 1241, 28th Division records, box 4, file 228.22.3; ABMC, *3d Division*, 46–47. Lanza's postmortem noted that although the 28th Division's attack orders sometimes envisaged it advancing sixteen kilometers in one day, it actually managed one kilometer in three days. Divisional leadership, he thought, unfairly blamed the men for not giving their all, when in fact they had. He also noted that a single regiment, the 110th, had been ordered to attack repeatedly on a two-kilometer front that was too large for it, while unemployed reserves—an entire brigade, in fact—lay close at hand. Finally, Lanza critiqued the lack of personal observation of conditions on the line by higher officers, as well as the lack of artillery support (Lanza, "Passage of the Ourcq").

33. ABMC, *32d Division*, 1–5; Edward M. Coffman, *The War to End All Wars: The American Military Experience in World War I* (Madison: University of Wisconsin Press, 1986), 259; *Fifty-Seventh Annual Report of the Association of Graduates of the United States Military Academy* (Saginaw, Mich.: Seemann & Peters, 1926), 103–109.

34. ABMC, *32d Division*, 10–11; 32d Division report of operations, NARA, RG 120, entry 1241, 32d Division records, box 1396, file 16931.6; Sgt. Lyle S. Cole, 125th Regiment, WWI Survey, USAHEC.

35. Rexmond C. Cochrane, *The 32nd Division Advances to Fismes, August 1918* (Army Chemical Center, Md.: US Army Chemical Corps Historical Office, 1960), 22; *USAWW*, 5:643; Cole, WWI Survey; ABMC, *42d Division*, 28–29; ABMC, *32d Division*, 12–13; 32d Division report of operations.

36. Glenn Garlock, *Tales of the Thirty-Second* (West Salem, Wis.: Badger Publishing Company, 1927), 108–111; *The 32nd Division in the World War 1917–1919* (Madison: Wisconsin War History Commission, 1920), 62.

37. Garlock, *Tales of the Thirty-Second*, 102, 115.

38. *USAWW*, 5:647; ABMC, *42d Division*, 29–30; ABMC, *32d Division*, 14–15; 32d Division report of operations; Corp. John D. McDaniels, 126th Regiment, "Corporal Tanglefoot's Diary," WWI Survey, USAHEC.

39. ABMC, *42d Division*, 30–32; Corp. Samuel Kent, 128th Regiment, WWI Survey, USAHEC; George E. Leach, *War Diary* (n.p., 1923), 107; Cochrane, *32nd Division Advances to Fismes*, 31; ABMC, *32d Division*, 16–17; 32d Division report of operations.

40. Duffy, *Father Duffy's Story*, 206.

41. ABMC, *4th Division*, 26–27; ABMC, *32d Division*, 17–19; 32d Division report of operations; Kent and McDaniels, WWI Surveys.

42. Cochrane, *32nd Division Advances to Fismes*, 36; ABMC, *4th Division*, 27–28; ABMC, *32d Division*, 19–20; 32d Division report of operations.

43. Cochrane, *32nd Division Advances to Fismes*, 59; ABMC, *4th Division*, 28–30; 32d Division report of operations; Kent, WWI Survey.

44. Smythe, *Pershing*, 159; Trask, *AEF and Coalition Warmaking*, 91; Robert B. Bruce, *A Fraternity of Arms: America and France in the Great War* (Lawrence: University Press of Kansas, 2003), 245–246.

45. Richard Slotkin, *Lost Battalions: The Great War and the Crisis of American Nationality* (New York: Henry Holt, 2005), 180–190.

46. NARA, RG 120, entry 267, G-3 General Correspondence, box 3226, folder 2158.

47. "Report of Operations of the 1st Army Corps, while Serving under the 6th French Army, July 4 to Aug. 14, 1918," NARA, RG 120, entry 1241, 3d Division records, box 18, file 203.33.6.

48. NARA, RG 120, entry 1241, 3d Division records, box 18, file 203.33.6, folder 69. Earlier reports in this file are in folder 73.

49. Cochrane, *26th Division in the Aisne-Marne Campaign*, 59.

50. NARA, RG 120, entry 267, G-3 General Correspondence, box 3120, folder 730.

51. Report dated December 19, 1918, NARA, RG 120, entry 1241, 3d Division records, box 18, file 203.33.6, folder 61.

52. NARA, RG 120, entry 267, G-3 General Correspondence, box 3158, folder 1135.

53. "Report of Operations of the 1st Army Corps." The same report and its annexes praised the French supply system—"not the slightest interruption occurred of any kind"—and claimed that even translation was never an issue. Rexmond Cochrane's study concluded that the 26th Division suffered 4,093 casualties from all causes from July 18 to 28, while the adjacent French 167th Division suffered only 1,156 during the same period (Cochrane, *26th Division in the Aisne-Marne Campaign*, 64).

Chapter 16. Tragedy at Fismette: Travails of the 28th Division, August 1918

1. Robert A. Doughty, *Pyrrhic Victory: French Strategy and Operations in the Great War* (Cambridge, Mass.: Harvard University Press, 2005), 473–478.

2. *USAWW*, 5:274–275, 395, 398; 28th Division reports of operations, August 11, 1918, and April 10, 1919, NARA, RG 120, entry 1241, 28th Division records, box 3263, folder 2.

3. Robert L. Bullard, *Personalities and Reminiscences of the War* (Garden City, N.Y.: Doubleday, Page, 1925), 227.

4. ABMC, *4th Division*, 25–31; Christian A. Bach and Henry Noble Hall, *The Fourth Division: Its Services and Achievements in the World War Gathered from the Records of the Division* (Garden City, N.Y.: Christian A. Bach, 1920), 119–126; ABMC, *3d Division*, 46–51; Joseph T. Dickman, *The Great Crusade: A Narrative of the World War* (New York: D. Appleton, 1927), 129–130; Bullard, *Personalities and Reminiscences*, 227–228.

5. Corp. Harold Pierce, 112th Regiment, WWI Survey, USAHEC.

6. Report by "Second Section G.S.," in Maj. John W. Foos Papers, 109th Machine Gun Battalion, WWI Survey, USAHEC. Col. Conrad Lanza conducted a detailed investigation of German positions above and around Fismette on April 9, 1919. He discovered German strongpoints in Les Grands Bois (north) and Château Diable

(southwest), along the road leading west from Fismes after it crossed the Vesle; there were also German trenches along the hill north and northwest of Fismette on the Montagne de Vailly and along an unimproved road leading west from Fismette to the lower slopes of the Montagne de Perles. Lanza took a photo from the top of the Montagne de Vailly toward Fismes; in it, German trenches are evident there and along the high road leading southwest toward Fismette and Fismes (NARA, RG 120, entry 1241, 28th Division records, box 13, file 228.33.1).

7. 28th Division reports of operations, August 11, 1918, and April 10, 1919; NARA, RG 120, entry 1241, 28th Division records, box 13, file 228.33.1; Charles M. Clement, ed., *Pennsylvania in the World War; An Illustrated History of the Twenty-Eighth Division*, 2 vols. (Pittsburgh: State Publications Society, 1921), 1:178–180; ABMC, *28th Division*, 25–26.

8. 28th Division reports of operations, August 11, 1918, and April 10, 1919; *USAWW*, 6:114–116.

9. 28th Division reports of operations, August 11, 1918, and April 10, 1919; ABMC, *28th Division*, 26–27.

10. Pierce, WWI Survey.

11. Robert C. Hoffman, *I Remember the Last War* (York, Pa.: Strength & Health, 1940), 212.

12. Pvt. Duncan Kemerer, 111th Regiment, WWI Survey, USAHEC.

13. 28th Division reports of operations, August 11, 1918, and April 10, 1919; NARA, RG 120, entry 1241, 28th Division records, box 3, file 228-20.1; *USAWW*, 6:80, 117–118; Bullard, *Personalities and Reminiscences*, 229, 235; ABMC, *28th Division*, 27–28.

14. NARA, RG 120, entry 1241, 28th Division records, box 5, file 228.32.1; *USAWW*, 6:117–118; Clement, *Pennsylvania in the World War*, 1:182–183; Hoffman, *I Remember the Last War*, 220–221.

15. Hoffman, *I Remember the Last War*, 284–285.

16. *USAWW*, 6:118–119.

17. George W. Cooper, *Our Second Battalion: The Accurate and Authentic History of the Second Battalion 111th Infantry* (Pittsburgh: Second Battalion Book Company, 1920), 231; Hervey Allen, *Toward the Flame: A Memoir of World War I* (Lincoln: University of Nebraska Press, 2003), 269.

18. Allen, *Toward the Flame*, 271–272; Cooper, *Our Second Battalion*, 231. According to the divisional summary of intelligence, at one point, the raiders managed to drive some Germans into the open and then mow them down with captured machine guns (summaries of intelligence, NARA, RG 120, entry 1241, 28th Division records, box 3, file 228-20.1).

19. Allen, *Toward the Flame*, 276–277; Hoffman, *I Remember the Last War*, 312–320.

20. Hoffman, *I Remember the Last War*, 312–320; summaries of intelligence, NARA, RG 120, entry 1241, 28th Division records, box 3, file 228-20.1; ABMC, *28th Division*, 28–29.

21. Clement, *Pennsylvania in the World War*, 1:184–188; ABMC, *28th Division*, 27–29; Pierce, WWI Survey.

22. NARA, RG 120, entry 1241, 28th Division records, box 5, file 228.32.1; ibid., box 7, file 228.32.8; Foos Papers, USAHEC.

23. Robert B. Patterson, *The World War I Memoirs of Robert B. Patterson: A Captain in the Great War* (Knoxville: University of Tennessee Press, 2012), 36–44; Rexmond C. Cochrane, *The End of the Aisne-Marne Campaign, August–September 1918* (Army Chemical Center, Md.: US Army Chemical Corps Historical Office, 1960), 23; ABMC, *77th Division*, 10.

24. NARA, RG 120, entry 1241, 28th Division records, box 7, file 228.32.8.

25. Bullard, *Personalities and Reminiscences*, 235–238.

26. James A. Murrin, *With the 112th in France: A Doughboy's Story of the War* (Philadelphia: J. B. Lippincott, 1919), 193–194.

27. Although Muir's initial report of August 29 conceded that the man running down the street may have been an American, another memo he compiled on September 1 asserted, "It is known that a man, dressed in American uniform, ran along the street shouting out words calculated to bring about a surrender of the American soldiers. There is every reason to believe that this man was a German dressed in the American uniform" (NARA, RG 120, entry 1241, 28th Division records, box 6, file 228.32.15). Fridenburg was not disciplined for his role in this affair. However, he and Lt. Edward Schmelzer were interrogated about the event after their release from German prisoner-of-war camps after the end of the war. By that time, Fridenburg had been promoted to captain (NARA, RG 120, entry 1241, 28th Division records, box 15, file 228.11.4). The Germans claimed to have captured 144 American soldiers and 2 officers (Cochrane, *End of the Aisne-Marne Campaign*, 24).

28. 56th Brigade report to Muir, August 29, 1918, Muir and Rickards reports and associated files, NARA, RG 120, entry 1241, 28th Division records, box 8, file 228.33.6; 28th Division report of operations, April 10, 1919; German prisoner interrogation, September 6, NARA, RG 120, entry 1241, 28th Division records, box 4, file 228.22.3.

29. NARA, RG 120, entry 1241, 28th Division records, box 7, file 228.33.1; ibid., box 8, file 228.33.3. Pershing's communiqués about the 28th Division, based on reports from that formation, barely mentioned this affair. The communiqué of August 28 quoted a division report of that morning: "Strong enemy raiding party attacked Fismette at 4:20 A.M., August 27th. Last reports indicate we still have troops in the town." No other official mention was made of the Fismette disaster (ibid., box 4, file 228.20.3).

30. Pierce, WWI Survey; 28th Division report of operations, April 10, 1919.

31. ABMC, *77th Division*, 20–21.

32. ABMC, *32d Division*, 24–26; 32d Division report of operations, NARA, RG 120, entry 1241, 32d Division records, box 3265, folder 2; Corp. John D. McDaniels, 126th Regiment, "Corporal Tanglefoot's Diary," WWI Survey, USAHEC.

33. ABMC, *32d Division*, 27–31; 32d Division report of operations; McDaniels, WWI Survey.

34. 32d Division report of operations; Lt. Col. X. H. Price, "Operations of the 32nd Division North of Soissons with the X French Army" (undated), NARA, RG 120, entry 267, G-3 General Correspondence, box 3160, folder 1148.

35. NARA, RG 120, entry 11, G-5 Secret & Confidential Files, box 1392, folder 16883.

36. Pierce, WWI Survey; ABMC, *28th Division*, 33–36.

37. Memorandum, August 20, 1918, NARA, RG 120, entry 11, G-5 Secret & Confidential Files, box 1385, folder 15703.

38. NARA, RG 120, entry 267, G-3 General Correspondence, box 3105, folder 591; ibid., box 3114, folder 694.

39. NARA, RG 120, entry 267, G-3 General Correspondence, box 3105, folder 591.

40. NARA, RG 120, entry 11, G-5 Secret & Confidential Files, box 1397, folder 16937-1.

41. Report dated December 5, 1918, NARA, RG 120, entry 267, G-3 General Correspondence, box 3114, folder 695.

Conclusion: The Road to Saint-Mihiel, September 1918

1. James H. Hallas, *Squandered Victory: The American First Army at St. Mihiel* (Westport, Conn.: Praeger, 1995), 2.

2. "Operations in Upper Alsace. Study by General Bundy," NARA, RG 120, entry 267, G-3 General Correspondence, box 3160, folders 1150–1157; Hallas, *Squandered Victory*, 44–45.

3. Quoted in Hallas, *Squandered Victory*, 46.

4. Hunter Liggett, *AEF: Ten Years Ago in France* (New York: Dodd, Mead, 1928), 129–130.

5. NARA, RG 120, entry 268, G-3 Secret Correspondence, box 3143, folder 994.

6. NARA, RG 120, entry 267, G-3 General Correspondence, box 3107, folder 620.

7. *WWIR*, vol. 12.

8. William Brown, *The Adventures of an American Doughboy* (Tacoma, Wash.: Smith-Kinney, 1919), 63.

BIBLIOGRAPHY

Unpublished Works and Repositories

Combined Arms Research Library (CARL), Fort Leavenworth, Kans.
French unit war diaries, 26N, Service Historique de la Défense, Département de l'Armée de Terre, Château de Vincennes. http://www.memoiredeshommes.sga.defense.gouv.fr/fr/article.php?larub=2&titre=journaux-des-unites-engagees-dans-la-premiere-guerre-mondiale.
George C. Marshall Foundation, Lexington, Va. George C. Marshall interview tapes.
National Archives and Records Administration, College Park, Md. Record Group 120, Records of the American Expeditionary Forces, 1917–1923.
US Army Heritage and Education Center (USAHEC), US Army War College, Carlisle, Pa. World War I Veterans Survey.

Published Works and Typescripts

Abels, Charles H. *The Last of the Fighting Four.* New York: Vantage Press, 1968.
Albertine, Connell. *The Yankee Doughboy.* Boston: Branden Press, 1968.
Allen, Hervey. *Toward the Flame: A Memoir of World War I.* 1926, 1934. Reprint, Lincoln: University of Nebraska Press, 2003.
American Battle Monuments Commission. *American Armies and Battlefields in Europe.* 1938. Reprint, Washington, D.C.: US Army Center of Military History, 1992.
———. *1st Division Summary of Operations in the World War.* Washington, D.C.: Government Printing Office, 1944.
———. *2d Division Summary of Operations in the World War.* Washington, D.C.: Government Printing Office, 1944.
———. *3d Division Summary of Operations in the World War.* Washington, D.C.: Government Printing Office, 1944.
———. *4th Division Summary of Operations in the World War.* Washington, D.C.: Government Printing Office, 1944.
———. *26th Division Summary of Operations in the World War.* Washington, D.C.: Government Printing Office, 1944.
———. *28th Division Summary of Operations in the World War.* Washington, D.C.: Government Printing Office, 1944.
———. *32d Division Summary of Operations in the World War.* Washington, D.C.: Government Printing Office, 1944.
———. *42d Division Summary of Operations in the World War.* Washington, D.C.: Government Printing Office, 1944.
———. *77th Division Summary of Operations in the World War.* Washington, D.C.: Government Printing Office, 1944.

———. *93d Division Summary of Operations in the World War*. Washington, D.C.: Government Printing Office, 1944.
Asprey, Robert B. *At Belleau Wood*. Denton: University of North Texas Press, 1996.
Axelrod, Alan. *Miracle at Belleau Wood: The Birth of the Modern U.S. Marine Corps*. Guilford, Conn.: Lyons Press, 2007.
Bach, Christian A., and Henry Noble Hall. *The Fourth Division: Its Services and Achievements in the World War Gathered from the Records of the Division*. Garden City, N.Y.: Christian A. Bach, 1920.
Barkley, John Lewis. *Scarlet Fields: The Combat Memoir of a World War I Medal of Honor Hero*, ed. Steven Trout. Lawrence: University Press of Kansas, 2012.
Bennett, Harry L. *Operations of the Twenty Sixth Infantry, First Division, 17–23 July 1918*. Fort Leavenworth, Kans.: Command and General Staff School, 1931, CARL.
Benwell, Harry A. *A History of the Yankee Division*. Boston: Cornhill, 1919.
Berdoulat, Pierre Emile. "The First and Second American Divisions in the Offensive of July [1]8, 1918." *Cavalry Journal* 34, 141 (October 1925): 407–412.
Berry, Henry. *Make the Kaiser Dance*. New York: Doubleday, 1978.
Boff, Jonathan. *Winning and Losing on the Western Front: The British Third Army and the Defeat of Germany in 1918*. Cambridge: Cambridge University Press, 2012.
Bonk, David. *Château-Thierry & Belleau Wood 1918: America's Baptism of Fire on the Marne*. Oxford: Osprey, 2007.
Brannen, Carl Edward. *Over There: A Marine in the Great War*, ed. Rolfe L. Hillman Jr. and Peter F. Owen. College Station: Texas A&M University Press, 1996.
Brown, William. *The Adventures of an American Doughboy*. Tacoma, Wash.: Smith-Kinney, 1919.
Bruce, Robert B. *A Fraternity of Arms: America and France in the Great War*. Lawrence: University Press of Kansas, 2003.
Buck, Beaumont B. *Memories of Peace and War*. San Antonio, Tex.: Naylor, 1935.
Bullard, Robert Lee. *Personalities and Reminiscences of the War*. Garden City, N.Y.: Doubleday, Page, 1925.
Camp, Dick. *The Devil Dogs at Belleau Wood: U.S. Marines in World War I*. Minneapolis: Zenith Press, 2008.
Carter, William A. *The Tale of a Devil Dog*. Washington, D.C.: Canteen Press, 1920.
Catlin, A. W. *"With the Help of God and a Few Marines."* Garden City, N.Y.: Doubleday, Page, 1919.
Chastaine, Ben-Hur. *History of the 18th U.S. Infantry First Division 1812–1919*. New York: Hymans, n.d.
Cheseldine, R. M. *Ohio in the Rainbow: Official Story of the 166th Infantry 42nd Division in the World War*. Columbus, Ohio: F. J. Heer, 1924.
Clark, George B. *Devil Dogs: Fighting Marines of World War I*. Novato, Calif.: Presidio Press, 1999.
———. *The Second Infantry Division in World War I: A History of the American Expeditionary Force Regulars, 1917–1919*. Jefferson, N.C.: McFarland, 2007.
———, ed. *Devil Dogs Chronicle: Voices of the 4th Marine Brigade in World War I*. Lawrence: University Press of Kansas, 2013.

Clement, Charles M., ed. *Pennsylvania in the World War: An Illustrated History of the Twenty-Eighth Division*. 2 vols. Pittsburgh: State Publications Society, 1921.

Cochrane, Rexmond C. *The End of the Aisne-Marne Campaign, August–September 1918*. Army Chemical Center, Md.: US Army Chemical Corps Historical Office, 1960.

———. *The 1st Division at Ansauville, January–April 1918*. Army Chemical Center, Md.: US Army Chemical Corps Historical Office, 1958.

———. *The 1st Division at Cantigny, May 1918*. Army Chemical Center, Md.: US Army Chemical Corps Historical Office, 1958.

———. *Gas Warfare at Belleau Wood, June 1918*. Army Chemical Center, Md.: US Army Chemical Corps Historical Office, 1957.

———. *Gas Warfare at Château-Thierry, June 1918*. Army Chemical Center, Md.: US Army Chemical Corps Historical Office, 1956.

———. *The 32nd Division Advances to Fismes, August 1918*. Army Chemical Center, Md.: US Army Chemical Corps Historical Office, 1960.

———. *The 26th Division in the Aisne-Marne Campaign, July 1918*. Army Chemical Center, Md.: US Army Chemical Corps Historical Office, 1957.

Coffman, Edward M. *The War to End All Wars: The American Military Experience in World War I*. Madison: University of Wisconsin Press, 1986.

Cooke, Elliot D. "We Attack." *Infantry Journal* 45, 1 (January–February 1938): 41–47.

———. "We Can Take It." *Infantry Journal* 44, 3 (May–June 1937): 205–212.

Cooke, James J. *The Rainbow Division in the Great War, 1917–1919*. Westport, Conn.: Praeger, 1994.

Cooper, George W. *Our Second Battalion: The Accurate and Authentic History of the Second Battalion 111th Infantry*. Pittsburgh: Second Battalion Book Company, 1920.

Dalessandro, Robert J. *American Lions: The 332nd Infantry Regiment in Italy in World War I*. Atglen, Pa.: Schiffer, 2010.

Dickman, Joseph T. *The Great Crusade: A Narrative of the World War*. New York: D. Appleton, 1927.

Doughty, Robert A. *Pyrrhic Victory: French Strategy and Operations in the Great War*. Cambridge, Mass.: Harvard University Press, 2005.

Duffy, Francis P. *Father Duffy's Story: A Tale of Humor and Heroism, of Life and Death with the Fighting Sixty-Ninth*. New York: George H. Doran, 1919.

Edwards, Frederick Trevenen. *Fort Sheridan to Montfaucon: The War Letters of Frederick Trevenen Edwards*. DeLand, Fla.: E. O. Painter, 1954.

Edwards, H. W. "Harbord and Lejeune: A Command Precedent." *Marine Corps Gazette* 37, 7 (July 1953): 12–15.

Evarts, Jeremiah M. *Cantigny: A Corner of the War*. Privately printed, 1938.

Faulkner, Richard S. *The School of Hard Knocks: Combat Leadership in the American Expeditionary Forces*. College Station: Texas A&M University Press, 2012.

Ferrell, Robert H., ed. *In the Company of Generals: The World War I Diary of Pierpont L. Stackpole*. Columbia: University of Missouri Press, 2009.

Fifty-Seventh Annual Report of the Association of Graduates of the United States Military Academy. Saginaw, Mich.: Seemann & Peters, 1926.

FitzPatrick, Tom. *Tidewater Warrior: The World War I Years: General Lemuel C. Shepherd, Jr., USMC, Twentieth Commandant*. Fairfax, Va.: Tom FitzPatrick, 2010.
Ford, Bert. *The Fighting Yankees Overseas*. Boston: Norman E. McPhail, 1919.
Fullerton, Charles B. *The Twenty-Sixth Infantry in France*. Privately printed, 1919.
Gallagher, Leonard B. "A Study of the Employment of the 1st Engineers in the A.E.F." Memorandum for the Command and General Staff School, Fort Leavenworth, Kans., n.d., CARL.
Garlock, Glenn. *Tales of the Thirty-Second*. West Salem, Wis.: Badger Publishing Company, 1927.
Gibbons, Floyd Phillips. *"And They Thought We Wouldn't Fight."* New York: George H. Doran, 1918.
Gleeson, Joseph J. *A Soldier's Story: A Daily Account of World War I by Sergeant Joseph J. Gleeson, January 1918 to March 1919*. Privately printed, 1999.
Graham, William J. *Hell's Observer: The Epic Wartime Journal of William J. Graham, American Expeditionary Forces*, ed. C. Stephen Badgley and Bruce A. Jarvis. Canal Winchester, Ohio: Badgley Publishing, 2012.
Greenhalgh, Elizabeth. *Foch in Command: The Forging of a First World War General*. Cambridge: Cambridge University Press, 2011.
Grotelueschen, Mark E. *The AEF Way of War: The American Army and Combat in World War I*. Cambridge: Cambridge University Press, 2007.
Gulberg, Martin Gus. *A War Diary*. Chicago: Drake Press, 1927.
Hallas, James H., ed. *Doughboy War: The American Expeditionary Force in World War I*. Mechanicsburg, Pa.: Stackpole Books, 2000.
———. *Squandered Victory: The American First Army at St. Mihiel*. Westport, Conn.: Praeger, 1995.
Harbord, James G. *The American Army in France, 1917–1919*. Boston: Little, Brown, 1936.
———. *Leaves from a War Diary*. New York: Dodd, Mead, 1925.
———. "A Month in Belleau Wood in 1918." *Leatherneck* 11, 6 (June 1928): 10–12, 54.
Harm, Paul B. *Cantigny Operation: Documents Pertaining to German Raids (May 27, 1918) and American Attack and Capture of Cantigny (May 28, 1918)*. Typescript, n.d., CARL.
Hemenway, Frederic Vinton. *History of the Third Division United States Army in the World War for the Period December 1, 1917 to January 1, 1919*. Anderbach-on-the-Rhine, n.p., 1919.
Hemrick, Levi E. *Once a Marine*. New York: Carlton Press, 1968.
Herbert, Paul. "The Battle of Cantigny and the Dawn of the Modern American Army." *On Point: The Journal of Army History* 13, 4 (Spring 2008): 5–13.
History of the First Division during the World War, 1917–1919. Philadelphia: John C. Winston, 1931.
Hoffman, Robert C. *I Remember the Last War*. York, Pa.: Strength & Health, 1940.
Hogan, Martin J. *The Shamrock Battalion in the Great War*, ed. James J. Cooke. Columbia: University of Missouri Press, 2007.
Jackson, Warren R. *His Time in Hell. A Texas Marine in France: The World War I*

Memoir of Warren R. Jackson, ed. George B. Clark. Novato, Calif.: Presidio Press, 2001.

Johnson, Douglas V., and Rolfe L. Hillman Jr. *Soissons 1918*. College Station: Texas A&M University Press, 1999.

Kean, Robert Winthrop. *Dear Marraine (1917–1919)*. Privately printed, 1969.

Keene, Jennifer. *World War I*. Westport, Conn: Greenwood Press, 2006.

Langille, Leslie. *Men of the Rainbow*. Chicago: O'Sullivan Publishing House, 1933.

Lanza, Conrad H. "Bridgeheads of the Marne." *Field Artillery Journal* 27, 3 (May–June 1937): 205–238.

———. "The German XXIII Reserve Corps Crosses the Marne." *Field Artillery Journal* 27, 4 (July–August 1937): 305–316; 27, 5 (September–October 1937): 371–389.

Laudan, Sebastian. "Landsknechte v. Sportsmen: Operation Kirschblüte—Seicheprey, 20 April 1918." *Stand To!* 92 (September 2011): 4–13.

Leach, George E. *War Diary*. N.p., 1923.

Lengel, Edward G., ed. *A Companion to the Meuse-Argonne Campaign*. London: Wiley-Blackwell, 2014.

Levere, William C. *My Hut: A Memoir of a YMCA Volunteer in World War One*, ed. Jenny Thompson. Lincoln, Neb.: iUniverse, 2006.

Liggett, Hunter. *AEF: Ten Years Ago in France*. New York: Dodd, Mead, 1928.

———. *Commanding an American Army: Recollections of the World War*. Boston: Houghton Mifflin, 1925.

Little, Arthur W. *From Harlem to the Rhine: The Story of New York's Colored Volunteers*. New York: Covici Friede, 1936.

MacArthur, Douglas. *Reminiscences*. New York: McGraw-Hill, 1964.

Mackin, Elton E. *Suddenly We Didn't Want to Die: Memoirs of a World War I Marine*. Novato, Calif.: Presidio, 1993.

Marshall, George C. *Memoirs of My Services in the World War, 1917–1919*. Boston: Houghton Mifflin, 1976.

Mattfeldt, Cylburn O., ed. *Records of the Second Division (Regular)*. 10 vols. Washington, D.C.: Army War College, 1924–1929.

———. *Translations: War Diaries of German Units Opposed to the Second Division (Regular), 1918*. 9 vols. Washington, D.C.: Army War College, 1930–1935.

Maverick, Maury. *A Maverick American*. New York: Covici Friede, 1937.

McClellan, Edwin N. "The Aisne-Marne Offensive." *Marine Corps Gazette* 6, 1 (March 1921): 66–84; 6, 2 (June 1921): 188–227.

———. "A Brief History of the Fourth Brigade of Marines." *Marine Corps Gazette* 4 (December 1919): 342–368.

———. "Capture of Hill 142, Battle of Belleau Wood, and Capture of Bouresches." *Marine Corps Gazette* 5, 3–4 (September–December 1920): 277–313, 371–405.

———. "Marines Stop Germans at Les Mares Farm, Point Nearest Paris Reached by Enemy in 1918." In *The United States Navy in the World War: Official Pictures*, by James C. Russell and William E. Moore, 262. Washington, D.C.: Pictorial Bureau, 1921.

———. "Operations of the Fourth Brigade of Marines in the Aisne Defensive." *Marine Corps Gazette* 5, 2 (June 1920): 182–214.
Mendenhall, John R. "The Fist in the Dyke." *Coast Artillery Journal* 79, 1 (January–February 1936): 13–20.
Millett, Allan R. *Well Planned, Splendidly Executed: The Battle of Cantigny, May 28–31, 1918*. Chicago: Cantigny First Division Foundation, 2010.
Moore, William E. "The 'Bloody Angle' of the A.E.F." *American Legion Weekly*, February 24, 1922, 15–17.
Morgan, Daniel E. *When the World Went Mad: A Thrilling Story of the Late War, Told in the Language of the Trenches*. Boston: Christopher Publishing House, 1931.
Mowry, William J. "The Greatest Day." *Marine Corps Gazette* 47, 7 (July 1963): 32–36.
Murrin, James A. *With the 112th in France: A Doughboy's Story of the War*. Philadelphia: J. B. Lippincott, 1919.
Neiberg, Michael S. *The Second Battle of the Marne*. Bloomington: Indiana University Press, 2008.
Nenninger, Timothy K. "'Unsystematic as a Mode of Command': Commanders and the Process of Command in the American Expeditionary Forces, 1917–1918." *Journal of Military History* 64, 3 (July 2000): 739–768.
The Ninth U.S. Infantry in the World War. N.p., 1919.
Otto, Ernst. "The Battles for the Possession of Belleau Woods, June 1918." *U.S. Naval Institute Proceedings* 54, 11 (November 1928): 941–962.
Owen, Peter F. *To the Limit of Endurance: A Battalion of Marines in the Great War*. College Station: Texas A&M University Press, 2007.
Patch, Joseph Dorst. *A Soldier's War: The First Infantry Division A.E.F. (1917–1918)*. Corpus Christi, Tex.: Mission Press, 1966.
Patterson, Robert B. *The World War I Memoirs of Robert B. Patterson: A Captain in the Great War*. Knoxville: University of Tennessee Press, 2012.
Pershing, John J. *My Experiences in the World War*. 2 vols. New York: Frederick A. Stokes, 1931.
Rendinell, Joseph Edward. *One Man's War: The Diary of a Leatherneck*. New York: J. H. Sears, 1928.
Rogers, Horatio. *World War I through My Sights*. San Rafael, Calif.: Presidio Press, 1976.
Sammons, Jeffrey T., and John H. Morrow Jr. *Harlem's Rattlers and the Great War: The Undaunted 369th Regiment and the African American Quest for Equality*. Lawrence: University Press of Kansas, 2014.
Shay, Michael E. *The Yankee Division in the First World War: In the Highest Tradition*. College Station: Texas A&M University Press, 2008.
Short, Walter C. "The A.E.F. in the World War: The Champagne-Marne Defensive." Typescript, n.d., CARL.
Sibley, Frank P. *With the Yankee Division in France*. Boston: Little, Brown, 1919.
Slotkin, Richard. *Lost Battalions: The Great War and the Crisis of American Nationality*. New York: Henry Holt, 2005.

Smythe, Donald. *Pershing: General of the Armies*. Bloomington: Indiana University Press, 1986.
Soissons Operations. Typescript compilation, USAHEC.
Stewart, Alexander. *A Very Unimportant Officer: Life and Death on the Somme and at Passchendaele*, ed. Cameron Stewart. London: Hodder & Stoughton, 2008.
The Story of the Sixteenth Infantry in France. Montabaur, Germany: Martin Flock, 1919.
The Story of the Twenty-Eighth Infantry in the Great War, American Expeditionary Forces. N.p., 1919.
Sulzbach, Herbert. *With the German Guns: Four Years on the Western Front 1914–1918*. Hamden, Conn.: Archon Books, 1981.
Summerall, Charles Pelot. *The Way of Duty, Honor, Country: The Memoir of Charles Pelot Summerall*, ed. Timothy K. Nenninger. Lexington: University Press of Kentucky, 2010.
Switzer, J. S., Jr. "The Champagne-Marne Defensive." *Infantry Journal* 19 (July–December 1921): 653–658; 20 (January–June 1922): 34–40, 184–191, 263–269, 401–407, 526–531, 653–659.
The 32nd Division in the World War 1917–1919. Madison: Wisconsin War History Commission, 1920.
Thomas, Lowell. *This Side of Hell: Dan Edwards, Adventurer*. New York: P. F. Collier & Son, 1932.
Thomason, John W., Jr. *Fix Bayonets!* New York: Charles Scribner's Sons, 1926.
———. "History of the 2d Division in World War I." Typescript, 1918, CARL.
———. "The Marine Brigade." *U.S. Naval Institute Proceedings* 54, 11 (November 1928): 963–968.
———. "Soissons." US Army War College monograph, CARL.
———. *The United States Army Second Division Northwest of Château-Thierry in World War I*, ed. George B. Clark. Jefferson, N.C.: McFarland, 2006.
Thompson, Hugh S. *Trench Knives and Mustard Gas: With the 42d Rainbow Division in France*, ed. Robert H. Ferrell. College Station: Texas A&M University Press, 2004.
Trask, David F. *The AEF and Coalition Warmaking, 1917–1918*. Lawrence: University Press of Kansas, 1993.
United States Army in the World War, 1917–1919. 17 vols. Washington, D.C.: Center for Military History, 1988–1992.
United States Infantry School. *Infantry in Battle*. 2d ed. Washington, D.C.: Infantry School, 1939.
Waller, L. W. T. "Machine Guns of the Fourth Brigade." *Marine Corps Gazette* 5, 1 (March 1920): 1–31.
Wilder, Amos N. *Armageddon Revisited: A World War I Journal*. New Haven, Conn.: Yale University Press, 1994.
Wilder, Fred Calvin. *War Experiences of F. C. Wilder*. Belchertown, Mass.: Lewis H. Blackmer, 1926.
Wilmeth, J. D. "Bois de la Brigade de Marine." *Marine Corps Gazette* 23, 1 (March 1939): 26–29, 58.

Wise, Frederic M. *A Marine Tells It to You*. New York: J. H. Sears, 1919.
Wise, Jennings C. *The Turn of the Tide: American Operations at Cantigny, Château-Thierry, and the Second Battle of the Marne*. New York: Henry Holt, 1920.
World War Records, First Division, A.E.F., Regular. 25 vols. Washington, D.C.: n.p., 1928–1930.
World War Records, First Division, A.E.F., Regular: German Documents. 5 vols. Washington, D.C.: n.p., 1930–1933.
Yockelson, Mitchell. *Borrowed Soldiers: Americans under British Command, 1918*. Norman: University of Oklahoma Press, 2008.
Zabecki, David T. *The German 1918 Offensives: A Case Study in the Operational Level of War*. London: Routledge, 2006.
———. "The U.S. Marines' Mythic Fight at Belleau Wood: Piercing the Fog of War to Separate Legend from Fact." *Military History* 28, 6 (March 2012): 40–49.

INDEX

1st Air Division, 244
First Army (French), 46
First Army (US), 207, 213, 327, 337
   creation of, 316
   Saint-Mihiel and, 8–9, 283, 338, 367
1st Artillery Brigade, 49
1st Battalion, 84, 180
1st Brigade (Foreign Legion), 247
1st Brigade (US), 260, 261, 283, 291, 294
   advance of, 281
   Berzy-le-Sec and, 292
   Chazelle ravine and, 290
   Coeuvres and, 259
   Second Marne and, 248
I Corps (French), 359
I Corps (US), 37, 42, 280, 308, 320, 328, 336, 359, 362, 372, 405n5
   26th Division and, 332–333
   153d Division and, 278
   advance of, 317
   changes for, 318
   Marne salient and, 303
   pressures for, 306–307
   Second Marne and, 242, 244
1st Division, 17, 21, 26, 34, 36, 57, 58, 244, 246, 257, 266, 277, 278, 283–284, 292, 299, 372–373
   XX Corps and, 245
   XXXII Corps and, 33
   Ansauville sector and, 37
   attack by, 158 (photo)
   Cantigny and, 6, 16, 45 (map), 48, 61, 62, 64 (map), 136
   casualties for, 49, 60
   Château-Thierry and, 74
   cohesion/strength for, 283
   funeral for soldiers of, 157 (photo)
   inspection of, 157 (photo)
   Manfred and, 51
   Missy ravine and, 273
   Montdidier and, 48
   morale and, 249
   Moroccans and, 250
   performance of, 262
   regiments of, 247
   relief for, 294, 297
   Second Marne and, 242, 248, 251
   Seicheprey and, 350
   Soissons and, 7, 295, 297, 301
   Sommerviller and, 27
   support for, 293
   training for, 23, 31
1st Engineers, 50, 55
1st Field Artillery Brigade, 33
1st Moroccan Division, 246, 247, 252, 263, 264, 278, 287, 300
   Second Marne and, 242, 248
   Soissons and, 297
1st Pursuit Group, sorties by, 237
2d Brigade, 56, 248, 259, 261, 278, 280–281, 292, 294
   attack by, 253, 257, 282, 290, 291, 295
   Missy ravine and, 252, 253–254
   problems for, 258, 283
II Corps, 303
2d Division, 9, 16, 18, 21, 25, 65, 76, 77, 81, 86, 133, 149, 154, 164, 170, 212, 246, 247, 253, 269, 271, 277, 278, 283–284, 299, 332, 340, 367, 368, 374–375
   10th Colonial Division and, 128
   arrival of, 75 (map), 83 (map), 96
   attack orders for, 262–263, 264
   Belleau Wood and, 7, 72, 91, 92, 100, 107, 122, 125, 128, 135, 136, 138, 165, 172, 174 (map), 194, 199, 200, 202–203, 205, 206, 283, 284, 388n23
   Blanc Mont and, 205
   Cantigny and, 64
   casualties for, 206, 403n22
   Château-Thierry and, 74, 245
   Chemin des Dames and, 6
   deployment of, 80, 82
   fighting by, 289, 371–372
   Franco-American relations and, 8, 288–289
   gas attacks and, 166, 169

[435]

2d Division, *continued*
   German offensive and, 79
   handling of, 372
   Hill 142 and, 87, 100
   individual initiative of, 273
   Les Mares Farm and, 94
   Marne salient and, 307
   performance of, 79, 98, 202–203, 417n94
   rating for, 176–177, 205
   relief of, 288, 418n110
   Second Marne and, 242, 248
   Soissons and, 7, 283, 297, 301, 366
   support for, 178
   training for, 23, 78–79
   Vaux and, 217
   Vierzy and, 177, 272–273
2d Engineers, 84, 147
2d Field Artillery Brigade, 92, 108
2d Machine Gun Company, 193
Third Army, 42, 307
3d Battalion, 93, 119, 181, 279, 310
3d Bavarian Regiment, Missy Ravine and, 254
3d Brigade, 17, 18, 77, 99, 149, 153–154, 205, 253, 274, 276, 288, 404n22, 405n29
   advance by, 74, 122
   attack by, 194, 269
   attack on, 178
   Bouresches and, 148, 165, 178
   problems for, 76, 186, 202
   support by, 184
   Vaux and, 195, 198, 246
   Vierzy and, 268
III Corps (French), 194, 195, 212, 213, 217, 229, 306, 337, 340, 406n12, 407n37
   6th Brigade and, 337
   defensive by, 210, 214–215
III Corps (US), 16, 245, 330, 337, 353, 359
   39th Division and, 195
   Fismes and, 340
   Fismette and, 351–352
   Taillefontaine and, 262
3d Division (Rock of the Marne), 35, 181, 199, 212, 214, 215, 217, 235, 238, 312–313, 316, 318, 322, 324
   XXXVIII Corps and, 221
   125th Division and, 228–229, 232
   advance of, 317

   attack on, 221–222, 233
   Belleau Wood and, 128, 173, 177
   Cantigny and, 64
   Château-Thierry and, 6, 65, 74, 79, 170
   command of, 218–219, 240
   criticism of, 65, 239
   defensive by, 210
   evaluation of, 177
   formation of, 66
   Franco-American relations and, 8, 67, 334–335, 341
   French command and, 337
   grievances of, 366–367
   Hill 204 and, 128, 219
   Marne River and, 69, 215, 234, 237, 314
   Marne salient and, 303, 312
   Moulin Ruiné and, 312
   nickname of, 7
   organization of, 66
   performance of, 333
   relief by, 173
   relief of, 320, 321, 324
   Second Marne and, 244
   Surmelin Valley and, 236
   Vesle and, 341
   Viels-Maisons and, 69
3d Ersatz Regiments, 190
3d Machine Gun Battalion, 253
3d Reserve Division, 276, 286, 416n88
   collapse of, 296
   Hartennes and, 287
   Tigny and, 418n110
   Vierzy and, 268, 275
Fourth Army, 209, 212, 236, 331
   defensive by, 234
   Franco-American liaison and, 220
   Marne Defensive and, 210
   Marne salient and, 303
4th Brigade, 74, 82, 85, 93, 115, 122, 147, 154, 172, 194, 246
   formation of, 18, 76
   Hill 142 and, 179
   Les Mares Farm and, 99
4th Division (Ivy Division), 17, 149, 154, 310, 324, 326, 328, 340, 353, 373
   casualties for, 311
   Hill 230 and, 327
   Marne salient and, 303
   relief of, 329

Second Marne and, 244
Vesle and, 330, 341
4th Ersatz Division, health issues for, 192
4th Guards Division, 4–5, 321, 347, 356
4th Regiment, 67, 69, 215, 232, 318
4th Reserve Corps. *See* Corps Conta
Fifth Army, 209, 210, 212, 236, 242
  defensive by, 234
  reserves of, 234
  Second Marne and, 244
5th Battalion, 108, 148, 171, 193
  attack by, 392n1
  Belleau Wood and, 189
5th Brigade, 215, 318, 321, 322
V Corps, 303
5th Division, advance by, 296
5th Field Artillery, 52, 57, 252
5th Grenadier Regiment, 226, 227, 236, 356
5th Groupe Char d'Assaut Schneider, 50, 52
5th Guards Division, 82, 95, 125, 134–135, 164, 397n19
  167th Division and, 137
  Belleau Wood and, 141, 204
  health issues for, 192
  withdrawal of, 154
5th Machine Gun Battalion, 84
5th Marines, 18, 21, 74, 76, 83, 84, 86, 87, 92, 95, 115, 116, 131, 151, 153, 183, 190, 193, 205, 247, 264, 265, 266, 268, 270, 276, 284
  Belleau Wood and, 99, 100–101, 102, 104, 105, 107, 137, 139, 140, 143, 146, 167, 170, 187, 374
  Bouresches and, 168
  Chaudun and, 267
  gas attacks and, 168
  Hill 133 and, 108
  Hill 142 and, 106, 117
  individual initiative by, 299
  La Thiolet and, 124
  relief of, 173
  Vierzy and, 274, 275
Sixth Army, 37, 66, 79, 91, 172, 209, 210, 212, 214, 238, 324, 332, 334, 372
  Marne Defensive and, 233
  Marne salient and, 302, 303
  Second Marne and, 244
6th Battalion, 112, 138, 143
6th Brigade, 215, 228, 337, 341

6th Cavalry Division, 277
VI Corps, 46, 47, 246, 369, 370
6th Division, 215, 282
6th Engineers, 35, 65, 215
6th Field Artillery, 252
6th Grenadier Regiment, 225, 226, 232
6th Machine Gun Battalion, 82, 84, 92, 102, 139, 388n18, 397n6
6th Machine Gun Regiment, 284
6th Marines, 18, 74, 76, 80, 82, 84, 85, 86, 90, 92, 93, 95, 99, 101, 114, 118, 147, 152, 205, 206, 249, 287
  advance of, 119, 146, 153, 284
  Algerians and, 289
  assembling of, 76
  attack by, 145, 285
  attack on, 124, 126
  Belleau Wood and, 107, 108, 126, 130, 131, 137, 138–139, 153, 164, 167, 168, 170, 183, 187, 374
  casualties for, 117
  gas attacks and, 166
  individual initiative by, 299
  Lucy and, 87
  Medical Detachment, soldier of, 159 (photo)
  Moroccans and, 287
  relief by, 168
  relief of, 173
  in reserve, 247, 265, 284
  training for, 19
Seventh Army, 82, 95, 96, 207, 210, 261
  attack on, 273
  Corps Watter and, 276
  damage to, 297
  defensive for, 293
  offensive by, 166
  Second Marne and, 247, 248, 251
7th Battalion, 179, 182, 183, 223, 402n19
  Belleau Wood and, 187
  casualties for, 181
  relief by, 173
7th Bavarian Landwehr Regiment, 28
VII Corps, 79
  Marne salient and, 303, 306
  Second Marne and, 244
  Soissons and, 64–65
7th Field Artillery, 252

INDEX [437]

7th Machine Gun Battalion, 71, 73, 215
  casualties for, 72
  Château-Thierry and, 66–67, 72
7th Regiment, 69, 171, 172, 173, 178, 180, 188, 189, 191, 206, 215, 223, 226, 232
  Belleau Wood and, 172, 183, 184, 205, 219
  casualties for, 237
  criticism of, 182–183, 184, 202
  deployment of, 402n21
  Le Charmel and, 318
  lessons for, 176
  orders for, 183–184
Eighth Army, 37, 43
8th Brigade, Marne salient and, 303, 306
VIII Corps, 192, 220, 235
8th Machine Gun Battalion, 215
8th Machine Gun Company, 84, 171
Ninth Army, 261, 283
  attack on, 273, 297
  collapse of, 276
  Second Marne and, 244, 247, 248, 250
9th Battalion, 77, 198, 270
  attack on, 78
  casualties for, 78
  Vaux and, 196
  Vierzy and, 274
IX Corps, 27
9th Division, 241, 251, 294
9th Machine Gun Battalion, 66, 231
9th Regiment, 74, 76, 77, 82, 86, 92, 95, 99, 195, 247, 266, 267, 271, 272, 284, 288
  attack by, 196, 269, 270
  Beaurepaire Farm and, 270
  Belleau Wood and, 120, 122, 126, 130
  Hill 192 and, 128
  mustard gas and, 191
  repulse of, 124
  Vierzy and, 275
Tenth Army, 209, 245, 280, 290, 311, 334
  XX Corps and, 277
  Second Marne and, 242, 244, 302
  Soissons and, 297
10th Bavarian Division, 82, 126, 415n68
10th Colonial Division, 66, 67, 92, 96, 122, 148, 149, 154, 195, 200
  2d Division and, 128
  Belleau Wood and, 204
  Hill 204 and, 128, 129–130, 135, 204

X Corps, 46
10th Division, 82, 85, 95, 119, 225, 284
  Bouresches and, 86, 87, 117, 125, 388n18
  casualties for, 86, 123, 396n3
  Château-Thierry and, 68
  defensive by, 87, 125, 126
  performance of, 240
  task for, 222–223
  withdrawal of, 233
10th Ersatz Division, reinforcement by, 276
10th Field Artillery, 230
10th Landwehr Division, 222, 233
11th Bavarian Division, 253, 282, 291
  collapse of, 256, 261, 262, 276
  performance of, 255
  Second Marne and, 248, 250
XI Corps, 37, 242
12th Field Artillery, 115
13th Chasseurs, 311
XIII Corps, Second Marne and, 248
13th Division, 234
14th Reserve Division, 248, 267, 286, 287
  Chaudun and, 260
  collapse of, 268, 276
  strength of, 249
15th Field Artillery, 99, 196
15th New York Regiment (Harlem Rattlers), 220, 221, 303, 331
16th Battalion, 29, 32, 281
16th Division, 235
16th Regiment, 26, 27, 32, 59, 247, 259, 260, 290, 291, 297
  Aconin Farm and, 294
  advance of, 283
  destruction of, 261
  Missy-aux-Bois and, 255
17th Field Artillery, 92
Eighteenth Army, 50, 51
18th Division, 27, 29, 235, 326
18th Regiment, 26, 33, 49, 246, 247, 266
  advance of, 259, 283
  attack on, 58
  Buzancy and, 294
  casualties for, 47, 291, 297
  Chaudun and, 260
  relief by, 58
  relief of, 50
  Soissons and, 301

[438]   INDEX

surrender of, 295
Villers-Tournelle and, 46–47
19th Ersatz Division, reinforcement by, 278
20th Company, 110, 138–139, 190
  casualties for, 11
XX Corps, 246–247, 273, 290, 296, 300, 308
  1st Division and, 245
  153d Division and, 281
  attack by, 276, 284, 298
  Second Marne and, 242, 248, 277
  Soissons and, 244, 289, 297
20th Division, 284, 418n109
  counterattack by, 287
  mauling of, 296
  strength of, 276
20th Moroccan Division, 417n91
XXI Corps, 79, 135, 153, 172, 210, 220, 234
  Belleau Wood and, 154
  map of, 75
23d Battalion, 183, 186, 195, 274
23d Regiment, 74, 77, 83, 87, 92, 95, 101,
    119, 120, 121, 167, 170, 184, 195, 247,
    271, 284
  advance of, 206, 272
  attack orders for, 196
  Belleau Wood and, 122, 126, 130,
    154–155, 167
  Bouresches and, 166, 169
  Brumetz and, 84, 86
  deployment of, 395n36
  Hill 192 and, 128
  mustard gas and, 191
  panic by, 164
  relief of, 186–187
  repulse of, 124
  training for, 76
  Vierzy and, 275
XXIII Reserve Corps, 210
XXV Reserve Corps, 415n68
25th Reserve Division, 51, 52, 56
26th Battalion, 253, 256, 282
26th Division (Yankee Division), 7, 16, 17,
    21, 24, 38, 45, 212, 307–308, 311, 312,
    314, 316–317
  I Corps and, 332–333
  attack plans by, 310
  bombardment of, 234
  casualties for, 313, 316, 422n53
  formation of, 36

Marne salient and, 303, 307
  problems for, 313, 332
  Saint-Mihiel offensive and, 317
  Second Marne and, 244
  Seicheprey and, 43, 44
  service for, 37
  training for, 23, 25
  usefulness of, 317
  withdrawal of, 318
26th Jäger Battalion, 105
26th Jäger Division, 398n3
26th Regiment, 26, 32, 247, 253, 278, 282,
    290, 291, 297, 298, 299
  attack by, 279, 295
  attack on, 58
  Berzy-le-Sec and, 292
  casualties for, 255
  intermingling of units of, 257
  Missy ravine and, 252, 260
XXVI Reserve Corps, 51
26th Reserve Jäger Battalion, 88, 93
27th Division, 362
28th Brigade, 295
28th Division (German), 82, 148, 151, 164,
    171, 192, 204, 286, 287
  Belleau Wood and, 126, 127, 128, 135,
    138, 140, 163, 166, 171, 177, 204, 206
  casualties for, 361
  Chaudun and, 260
  collapse of, 152, 296
  defensive position of, 216 (map)
  Hill 166 and, 256
  reinforcement by, 268, 275, 276
  Second Marne and, 248
  withdrawal of, 290
28th Division (US), 16, 17, 21, 95, 154,
    195–196, 210, 212, 214, 225, 229, 231,
    235, 236, 255, 278, 318, 335, 356, 367
  advance by, 312, 314, 316
  attack orders for, 421n32
  casualties for, 331
  Château Diable and, 353
  command of, 218
  courage of, 163
  Fismes and, 340
  Fismette and, 1, 5, 7, 337, 361
  French command and, 337
  Hill 204 and, 128, 197, 219, 373
  Jaulgonne Bend and, 211, 227

INDEX [439]

28th Division (US), *continued*
   lessons for, 228
   Marne salient and, 303
   organization of, 217
   Ourcq River and, 320
   Pershing and, 424n29
   praise for, 240
   relief of, 321
   Second Marne and, 244
   success for, 12–13, 324
   Vesle and, 340, 341
28th Ersatz Infantry, Veuilly-la-Poterie and, 87
28th Regiment, 27, 49–50, 58–59, 247, 256, 262, 291, 416n80
   attack by, 327
   attack on, 58
   Berzy-le-Sec and, 295
   Cantigny and, 52, 54, 56, 61
   casualties for, 60, 255, 257
   intermingling of units of, 257
   Missy ravine and, 258, 260
   Moroccans and, 250
   support for, 258
   weaponry for, 351
29th Division, 369
30th Battalion, 224, 225
XXX Corps, 242, 359
30th Division, 77, 246, 362
30th Regiment, 69, 138, 148, 149, 215, 222, 223, 226, 232, 235, 373
   Belleau Wood and, 128, 129, 204
   casualties for, 237
   conduct of, 237
   Hill 204 and, 154, 179, 195, 219
   Vaux and, 132
XXXII Corps, 33, 37, 41, 43
32d Division, 17, 21, 326, 328, 359, 361
   Aisne-Marne and, 325
   casualties for, 330–331, 360
   Château-Thierry and, 325
   Fismes and, 330, 342
   Hill 230 and, 327
   Juvigny and, 360
   Ourcq River and, 327
   performance of, 332, 360
   relief by, 321
   Second Marne and, 244
   support from, 324–325
   Vesle and, 329
33d Division, 303, 310
34th Division, 255, 282
35th Division, 369
36th Division, 223, 226, 233, 240, 369
XXXVIII Corps, 66, 69, 135, 212, 216, 217, 227, 231, 235, 238, 406n12
   3d Division and, 221
   defensive by, 210, 214–215
   Franco-American relations and, 318
   Hill 204 and, 128
   Marne salient and, 303, 312
   problems for, 321
38th Division, 263, 271, 272, 275, 278, 287, 297
   Second Marne and, 248
   Vierzy and, 268
38th Regiment, 69, 215, 216, 218, 224, 226, 227, 228, 231, 232, 312, 314
   casualties for, 237
   Les Etangs Farm and, 233
39th Division, 210, 212, 217
   III Corps and, 195
   Hill 204 and, 405n29
   Le Charmel and, 318
   relief of, 321
39th Regiment, 303, 306, 310
XXXIX Reserve Corps, Second Marne and, 248
40th Fusilier Regiment, 127, 130, 144, 145, 149, 150, 151, 152, 164, 172, 398n7
   Belleau Wood and, 126, 128, 138, 140, 143, 192
   counterattack by, 146–148
40th Reserve Division, 276, 415n68
41st Division, 303, 307
42d Aero Recon Squadron, 252
42d Division (German), 248, 267, 287, 291
   attack by, 322
   Chaudun and, 260
   defensive by, 294
   mauling of, 296
   strength of, 249
42d Division (Rainbow Division), 17, 21, 25, 149, 170, 212, 323, 324, 326, 332, 373
   attack on, 221, 234, 408n48, 416n90
   Franco-American relations and, 235
   Harlem Rattlers and, 220

Marne Defensive and, 210
National Guard and, 219
Ourcq River and, 320, 327
performance of, 7, 234–235, 332
relief by, 316, 318
relief of, 328, 329
Second Marne and, 244
training for, 23
43d Company, 84, 142, 143
43d Division, 79, 82, 84, 85, 98
  Bois des Mares and, 87
  withdrawal by, 92, 203
45th Company, 104, 107, 109, 116
  casualties for, 111
  Hill 142 and, 108
45th Division, 46
45th Reserve Division, 415n68
46th Reserve Division, 295, 296
47th Battalion, 225, 226, 232
47th Company, casualties for, 111
47th Regiment, 119, 120, 121, 225, 303
47th Reserve Division, 248, 267, 268, 273
  collapse of, 277
  Vierzy and, 275
49th Company, 102, 171
51st Brigade, 39, 316
51st Company, 84, 88, 142, 143
51st Division, 210, 217
51st Reserve Division, 415n68
52d Brigade, 308, 316
53d Division, Second Marne and, 248
55th Brigade, 151, 210, 217, 218, 229, 230, 231, 353
  attack by, 321
  Fismes and, 342
  Ourcq River and, 320
  problems for, 322–323
  prospects for, 321–322
55th Company, 84, 89, 91, 390n28
  Belleau Wood and, 142, 143
56th Brigade, 210, 212, 217, 314, 341, 354
  withdrawal of, 318
58th Division, relief by, 288
58th Regiment, 303, 306, 311
59th Division, 359, 360
59th Regiment, 303, 306, 311
63d Brigade, Cierges and, 326
64th Division, 359
65th Brigade, 267, 412n34

66th Company, 102, 104, 171
67th Company, 102, 103
69th Division, 290, 293, 294, 295, 418n106
73d Division, 125, 215, 312
  attack on, 236
  deployment of, 232–233
  Jaulgonne Bend and, 235
77th Division, 16, 340, 353, 354, 359
  Jaulgonne Bend and, 235
  Second Marne and, 244
77th Machine Gun Company, 108
78th Division, 369
78th Reserve Division, 39, 415n68
79th Company, 114, 115
79th Division, 369
80th Division, 369
82d Company, 112, 130, 131
82d Reserve Division, 48, 51, 56, 78
83d Brigade, 219, 321
83d Company, 112, 130
84th Brigade, 220, 318, 321
84th Company, 112, 113
87th Division, 179, 309, 403n14
  Belleau Wood and, 171, 178, 206
  Buzancy and, 295
  relief by, 165, 166, 171, 294
87th Ersatz Division, health issues for, 192
91st Division, 369
93d Division, 212, 220, 303, 362
96th Company, 114, 117, 120
97th Company, 112, 113
101st Field Artillery, 309
101st Machine Gun Battalion, 38
102d Regiment, 38, 39, 310, 312, 313
103d Battalion, 308, 310
104th Battalion, 38, 308, 309
109th Battalion, 225, 229, 230, 236
  casualties for, 231
109th Grenadiers, 127, 164, 170, 171–172, 178, 193
  Belleau Wood and, 126
  liberation of, 403n11
109th Machine Gun Battalion, Fismes and, 342
109th Regiment, 164, 218, 229, 256, 372, 409n52
  casualties for, 237
  deployment of, 126

109th Regiment, *continued*
  Fismette and, 352
  relief of, 353
110th Battalion, 147, 149, 229, 231
110th Grenadiers, 149, 151, 172, 275, 398n7
  counterattack by, 146–147
110th Regiment, 150, 152, 230, 322, 325, 421n32
  Bois des Grimpettes and, 324
  casualties for, 237
  Fismette and, 354
  health conditions for, 192
  Sauvigny and, 218
  strength of, 164
111th Battalion, 235, 347
111th Regiment, 128, 316, 346, 348, 350
  Fismes and, 342
  Fismette and, 349
  Hill 204 and, 217
  relief of, 352
112th Regiment, 5, 217, 316, 341–342, 346, 348, 355, 356
  Fismes and, 342, 344
  Fismette and, 5, 345, 347, 353
115th Division, 287
  collapse of, 277
  Second Marne and, 248
  strength of, 249
  Vierzy and, 268, 275
116th Infantry Regiment, Les Mares Farm and, 99
125th Division, 210, 213, 215, 217, 218, 226, 227, 229, 238
  3d Division and, 232
  casualties for, 231
  Jaulgonne Bend and, 211, 214, 235
  Les Etangs Farm and, 233
  problems for, 228, 232, 367
  withdrawal of, 235, 372
125th Regiment, 325–326, 360
126th Regiment, 328, 330, 359
127th Division, 327, 359
127th Regiment, 324, 325, 330
128th Regiment, 227, 228, 232, 327, 328
133d Division, support for, 311
150th Machine Gun Battalion, 234
151st Field Artillery, Seringes-et-Nesles and, 328
151st Machine Gun Battalion, 234

152d Division, 52
153d Division, 248, 252, 253, 278, 281, 282, 289, 290, 293, 297, 418n106
  28th Regiment and, 257
  cohesion/strength for, 283
  communications problems for, 280
  failure of, 283
  history of, 257
  relief of, 294
  Saconin and, 255
  sacrifice by, 300
153d Regiment, Hill 204 and, 217
161st Division, 235, 303, 331
162d Division, 39, 46
164th Division, 79, 82, 306, 311, 341
165th Battalion (Shamrock Battalion), 321
165th Regiment, 220, 234, 324
166th Regiment, 220, 322, 408n48
167th Division, 98, 100, 115, 122, 125, 135, 154, 200, 309, 312, 313, 332, 405n5
  5th Guards and, 137
  advance of, 105
  Belleau Wood and, 204
  casualties for, 422n53
  Hautevesnes and, 134, 178
  Marne salient and, 303, 306–307
  withdrawal of, 318
167th Regiment, 220, 234, 318, 322
168th Regiment, 221–222, 234, 318, 324
170th Division, 234
175th Regiment, 227, 228, 231, 232, 233
197th Division, 82, 88, 89, 93, 95, 102, 105, 115–116, 137
  attack on, 85
  casualties for, 83, 387n14, 396n3
  effort by, 86–87
  Les Mares Farm and, 392n1
  loss of, 125
  Marigny and, 87
201st Division, 141, 195, 198
201st Ersatz Division, health issues for, 192
216th Division, 324
231st Division, 82, 95, 135, 137–138
  Château-Thierry and, 68, 72
  counterattack by, 132
  defensive by, 138
  Hill 204 and, 126, 141, 149
237th Division, 82, 95, 102, 105, 117, 125–126, 135, 150, 151, 164, 178, 179

Belleau Wood and, 87, 109, 127, 128, 131, 140, 237, 392n1
    casualties for, 86, 123, 396n3
    Clignon Creek and, 141
    courage of, 163
    defensive by, 87
    Hill 142 and, 125, 137
    relief of, 165, 166, 171
241st Division, 248, 254, 261, 282
244th Brigade, 127
270th Reserve Regiment, 59–60
271st Reserve Regiment, 51, 53
272d Reserve Regiment, 51, 78
273d Regiment, 105, 106
304th Pioneer Company, 68–69
347th Battalion, 182, 193, 194
347th Ersatz Regiment, 190
347th Regiment, 179
369th Regiment, 212, 331, 406n21
    Marne Defensive and, 210
    Marne salient and, 303
    performance of, 235
    training for, 220
398th Regiment, 114, 119, 121, 223, 224, 225, 232
442d Battalion, 129, 138
442d Regiment, 69, 72, 204
444th Battalion, Hill 204 and, 141
444th Regiment, 68, 69
460th Regiment, 102, 105
461st Battalion, 143, 144, 145, 151–152
461st Regiment, 147, 150, 163, 165, 177, 182, 399n8
    advance of, 152
    Belleau Wood and, 109, 126, 127, 128, 130, 131, 140, 143, 144
462d Battalion, 137, 144, 152

Abbeville agreement, 44
Abels, Charles H., 26, 46
Adams, John P., 173, 180, 181
AEF. *See* American Expeditionary Forces
AEF Tank Corps, 253
AEF Way of War: The American Army and Combat in World War I, The (Grotelueschen), 5
African American regiments, 220–221, 331

Aisne-Marne offensive, 6, 244, 280, 302, 308, 325, 331, 332, 335, 336, 338, 340, 360, 361
    map of, 243
Aisne-Marne salient, reducing, 304–305 (map)
Aisne River, 242, 254, 313, 330, 338, 359, 362, 367, 368
    advance on, 331
    defense along, 329
    map of, 339
Albertine, Connell, 310
    recollection of, 308–309
Allen, Hervey, 4, 351, 352
    recollections of, 1–2
Amalgamation, 6, 8, 14, 21, 22, 45, 49, 218, 219, 220, 340, 371, 373
American Armies and Battlefields in Europe (FitzPatrick), 94
American Expeditionary Forces (AEF), 11, 22, 24, 35, 36, 47, 60, 147, 169
    adaptation by, 16
    development of, 7
    doctrine of, 14, 15, 123
    French critique of, 364–366
    hopes of, 19–20
    lessons for, 331, 370–371
    Marine Corps and, 17
    military impact of, 9, 209
    necessities for, 12
    preparedness of, 10
    scholarship on, 5–6
    staff of, 20–21
    tactics of, 15, 366
    training by, 220
    travails of, 19–20, 332, 370
American Legion Weekly, 94
American Lions: The 332nd Infantry Regiment in Italy in World War I (Dalessandro), 6
"American Military Factor in the War, The" (General Staff Historical Section), 199, 301
Anderson, Thomas M., Jr., 172, 173, 180, 215, 223
    Harbord and, 182
    praise for, 238
    recriminations from, 237
Andrews, M. M., 298

Ansauville sector, 33, 34, 36, 37, 45
Anthoine, François Paul, 65
Aqueduct Line, 215, 216, 225, 226, 231, 232
Army Group Crown Prince, Marne salient and, 277
Army Staff College, 20
Asprey, Robert B., 6, 90, 201, 393n3, 402n21
At Belleau Wood (Asprey), 6
Aulanier, Captain, 231, 236, 240
Axelrod, Alan, on Corps Contra, 94

Babcock, Conrad Stanton, 252–253, 257, 258, 278, 280, 296, 416n80
    28th Regiment and, 291
    Summerall and, 281
Baker, Joseph M., 103
Baker, Newton D., 21, 35, 44
Bamford, Frank, 259, 291
Barbed Wire Entanglements (Malone), 119
Barkley, John Lewis (Jack), 67, 385n13
Barnett, George, 17–18, 74
Bathelémont, 6, 27, 31, 33, 39, 62, 147, 367
Battle of the Frontiers, 369
Beaurepaire Farm, 270, 277, 284
BEF. *See* British Expeditionary Force
Belfort, 325, 369, 370
Belleau, 100, 125
    capture of, 86, 308, 310
Belleau Wood, 15, 18, 72, 76, 82, 85, 91, 93, 96, 97, 98, 99, 110, 113, 115, 121–122, 125, 126, 128, 129, 132, 133, 139, 140, 141, 142, 148, 151, 168, 170, 171, 177, 179, 180, 188, 202
    capture of, 87, 100, 112, 116, 117, 118, 119, 146–147, 155, 179, 189 (map), 194, 204, 207
    casualties in, 405n5
    counterattack in, 398n7
    defending, 9, 126, 127, 134, 135, 140, 189
    deployment in, 174 (map)
    described, 106–107, 193
    fighting in, 6–7, 16, 101, 102, 117, 126, 130–131, 133, 135, 136, 137, 144, 146, 148, 149, 150, 153, 154, 163, 164–165, 189, 192, 201, 202–203, 204, 205
    Franco-American relations and, 77
    gas attacks in, 166, 167
    lessons from, 8
    recovery from, 284
    tactics at, 12
    withdrawal from, 86
Bellevue Farm, capture of, 327
Bennett, Harry, 279, 289, 299, 411n27, 415n74
    recollections of, 278, 297
Benson, Stuart, 372
Berdoulat, Pierre, 246, 262, 264, 265, 274, 278, 284, 289, 298, 413n40
    attack orders from, 247, 252
    Bullard and, 273
    impression of, 415n71
    Second Marne and, 242
    Soissons and, 297
Berry, Major, 101, 113, 131, 140, 142, 205, 389n28, 392n1
    5th Marines and, 105, 108, 124
    attack by, 115
    Belleau Wood and, 107, 108–109
    on Shepherd, 389n27
    wounding of, 111–112, 116
Berthelot, Henri-Mathias, 209, 212, 234
Bertier de Sauvigny, Albert, 263, 272
Berzy-le-Sec, 252, 278, 282, 289, 290, 292–293, 296
    advance on, 291
    capture of, 295
Bischoff, Josef, 109, 118, 144, 147, 150, 152, 163, 177, 206, 398n6
    Belleau Wood and, 117, 126, 127, 143
    report by, 165
Bissell, John T., 68, 69, 385n16
    Mendenhall and, 70, 385n14
Bjornstad, A. W., 262
Blanchfield, John, 84, 89, 91, 389n25
    death of, 93
Bliss, Tasker, 35
"'Bloody Angle' of the A. E. F., The" (Moore), 94
Böhm, Gustav, 126, 127, 133, 138, 150, 154, 155, 399n8
    Belleau Wood and, 135, 146–147, 148, 204
    Bouresches and, 140
    planning by, 134
Böhn, Hans von, 82
Bois de Clerembauts, 82, 99, 119, 154
Bois de la Morette, 86, 92, 99
Bois des Mares, 87, 89, 100, 104

Bois de Tigny, toehold in, 286
Bois de Veuilly, 84, 87, 92, 100
Bombon, 207, 315, 316
Bonk, David, 91, 94
Bordeaux, Paul, 29, 30–31, 32, 379nn9–10
Borrowed Soldiers: Americans under British Command, 1918 (Yockelson), 6
Bouresches, 99, 107, 112, 113, 118, 119, 124, 125, 126, 127, 137, 138, 165, 166, 167, 168, 171, 178, 184, 186, 187, 195, 308, 310
    attack on, 85, 87, 101, 108, 114, 116, 120, 135, 140, 312
    Belleau Wood and, 117
    capture of, 86, 115, 116, 388n18
    fighting at, 130, 143, 145, 148, 149, 155
    problems in, 164, 185
Bouton, Arthur E., 198, 269
Brannen, Carl, recollections of, 284–286, 288
British Expeditionary Force (BEF), 10, 12, 17
Brown, Millard, 229, 230
Brown, Preston, 79–80, 101, 115, 143, 167, 172, 262, 412n38
    Belleau Wood and, 153, 194
    Bundy and, 170
    on French rations, 185
    Pershing and, 153
Brown, William, 196
Bruce, Robert B., 8, 203, 379n9, 404n24, 409n56
    on Franco-American relations, 238
Buck, Beaumont Bonaparte, 58, 257, 258, 262, 278, 279, 280, 281, 416n80
    1st Brigade and, 291
    2d Brigade and, 252
    behavior of, 412n30
    on French, 27
    Hill 166 and, 261
    leadership of, 296
    Second Marne and, 252
    Soissons and, 417n100
Bullard, Robert Lee, 46, 48, 49, 51, 56, 58, 292, 330, 370
    1st Division and, 16
    on 2d Marines, 404n26
    III Corps and, 337, 340, 353
    28th Division and, 356
    56th Brigade and, 354
    aggressiveness and, 246
    attack orders by, 348
    Berdoulat and, 273
    Cantigny and, 60, 61
    Degoutte and, 201, 340, 348, 350
    Fismette and, 1, 5, 355
    Franco-American relations and, 280, 341
    gas attacks and, 47
    Haan and, 327
    Muir and, 344, 345, 348, 350
    Pershing and, 355
    photo of, 157
    role of, 33, 355
    Sibert and, 33
    Summerall and, 245
    Taillefontaine and, 262
    trench conditions and, 38
Bundy, Omar, 85, 89, 100, 106, 107, 115, 119, 146, 154, 165, 167, 171, 180, 184, 188, 200, 246, 287, 368
    2d Division and, 88, 98
    advance by, 204
    Belleau Wood and, 77, 122, 130, 135, 136, 194, 204
    Brown and, 170
    Conner and, 369–370
    criticism of, 76, 207
    on Degoutte's corps, 79–80, 81
    Franco-American relations and, 77
    Harbord and, 77, 125, 149, 169, 202
    Malone and, 121, 186
    Pershing and, 147, 149, 191, 194, 369
    plan by, 369
    Wise and, 152
Bussiares, 85, 86, 87, 88, 89, 95, 99, 100, 101, 105, 106, 137, 154
Buy, Lieutenant von, on 2d Division, 176–177
Buzancy, 252, 261, 278, 283, 284, 287, 290, 294, 296
    capture of, 295

Cameron, George H., 303
Campbell, Albert J., recollection of, 284–285, 286
Campbell, S. D., 58, 59

Cantigny, 6, 55, 57, 59, 136, 245, 252, 253, 367, 370
   1st Division and, 45 (map)
   artillery in, 46
   attack on, 48–49, 50, 51, 53, 56, 58, 61–62, 64 (map)
   casualties at, 60
   defending, 56, 61
   described, 52
Carson, William P., on French, 23
Carter, William, recollections of, 289
Casualties, 36, 105–106, 115, 144, 146, 152, 155
   French, 240, 360
   gas, 34, 60, 168, 171, 198, 403n22
   German, 41, 42, 83, 86, 111, 250, 261, 288, 381n38
   US, 6, 7, 29, 35, 37, 38, 43, 47, 48, 49, 50, 51, 54, 118, 123, 191, 193, 254, 256–257, 315, 316, 318, 330, 360
Cates, Clifton B., 114–115, 402n19
Catlin, Albertus, 76, 80, 90, 91, 93, 108–109, 110, 112, 113, 115, 205
   5th Marines and, 109
   on Belleau Wood, 106–107
   on French, 81
   Harbord and, 88
Cavalry Journal, 262
Central Army Group, 209
Chaffee, Adna, 66
Champillon, 82, 84, 85, 86, 87, 88, 98, 99, 100
Château Diable, 344, 348, 353, 354, 359, 422–423n6
Château-Thierry, 8, 63, 64, 65, 66, 82, 95, 96, 98, 128, 135, 141, 170, 184, 195, 199, 210, 214, 215, 217, 219, 223
   defending, 126, 202, 203
   described, 67–68
   fighting at, 69, 70, 72, 73, 74, 79
Chateauvillain Training Area, 66
Chaudun, 242, 247, 248, 252, 260, 261, 264, 265, 266, 267, 268, 269, 270, 291, 300
   capture of, 273
Chazelle ravine, 252, 261, 281, 283, 287, 290
Chemin des Dames, 6, 50, 55, 61, 63, 218
   described, 37
Cheseldine, R. M., 408n48
Chicago Tribune, Gibbons and, 111

Clark, George B., 6, 87, 91, 102, 202, 387n14, 388n19, 389n24, 392nn34–35, 393n9
   on 2d Division, 201
   on Château-Thierry, 73
   on Les Mares Farm, 94
Clark, Paul H., 149, 203, 297, 372
Cleland, John R. D., 295
Clemenceau, Georges, 21, 34, 200
Clignon Creek, 86, 100, 104, 122, 124, 125, 135, 137, 141, 154, 303
Cochrane, Rexmond, 169, 422n53
Coffman, Edward M., 6
Cole, Charles H., 308, 309–310, 316
Cole, Edward, 82, 113, 115, 116, 139
Cole, Lyle S., recollections of, 325–326
Comfort, Willis E., 27, 28, 29, 32
"Comparison of Casualties Suffered by American Troops under French and under American Command" (Conner), 371
Compiègne, 65, 96, 245
Conachy, Peter, 45th Company and, 109
Conger, Arthur L., 195, 370
Conner, Fox, 32, 42, 153, 166, 366, 367
   on 2d Division, 372
   Bundy and, 369–370
   Clark and, 149
   Dickman and, 66
   Grant and, 88
   Harbord and, 25
   Kelton and, 237, 238
   Lewis and, 373, 383n23
   memo from, 371
   service of, 20
Cooke, Elliot D., 142, 143, 149, 264, 266, 414n63
   recollections of, 267–268
Cooke, James J., 408n48
Cooperation, 53, 61, 118, 219, 226, 255
   Franco-American, 247, 277, 297, 331, 337
   tactical, 275, 337
Corbin, William O., 88
Corps Conta, 82, 95, 96, 176, 203
   advance by, 83
   Château-Thierry and, 65
   defense by, 128
   disbandment of, 192
   mauling of, 94

Corps Etzel, 276, 287
Corps Kathen, 235–236, 296
Corps Schoeler, 192, 296
Corps Staabs, Second Marne and, 248
Corps Watter, 248, 268, 283, 287, 294, 415n68
    Chaudun and, 261
    Second Marne and, 248
    transfer of, 276
Corps Winckler, 296, 415n68
Courmelles, 278, 282, 290
Courtemont-Varennes, 223, 227, 228
Craig, Malin, 42
Crawford, Charles, 215, 224, 228
    criticism of, 341
    Franco-American relations and, 341
    Kelton and, 238
Crezancy, 213, 223, 224, 225, 226, 232
Crise ravine, 252, 290, 294
Crowther, Orlando, 102, 103
Cumming, Samuel, 266

Dalessandro, Robert J., 6, 9
Darrah, Thomas, 217, 230, 322
Debeney, Marie-Eugène, 48, 49
Degoutte, Jean-Marie, 80, 135, 170, 179, 209, 212, 214, 215, 220, 311, 314, 324, 342, 355, 356, 372
    2d Division and, 98, 100, 107, 122, 124
    3d Brigade and, 194
    Sixth Army and, 172
    XXI Corps and, 79
    28th Division and, 337
    Belleau Wood and, 107, 122, 129, 153, 154, 201
    Bullard and, 340, 348, 350
    Bundy and, 81
    criticism of, 8, 203–204, 206, 340–341, 348, 363, 386–387n9
    Fismes/Fismette and, 302, 355
    Harbord and, 165, 201
    Hill 142 and, 106
    Liggett and, 307, 366
    Otto and, 387n10
    Pershing and, 201
    Second Marne and, 244
    Upton and, 79
De Mitry, Henri, Second Marne and, 244
De Poumayrac, Colonel, report by, 333–334

De Saza, Nick, Fismette and, 2–4
D'Espèrey, Franchet, 66, 209
Detachment Mencke, 149, 150
Detroit Bond Club, Harbord at, 202
Dickman, Joseph T., 16, 69, 214, 216, 218, 231, 312, 406n8
    3d Division and, 66, 215, 333, 337
    Château-Thierry and, 72, 184
    Conner and, 66
    criticism of, 184, 238
    Degoutte and, 201
    Franco-American relations and, 334, 340, 341
    grievances of, 237
    Hill 204 and, 129
    Kelton and, 238, 239, 240
    on Mangin, 341
    on Marne Defensive, 212, 236
    military career of, 66
    Montdésir and, 212–213, 235, 317–318
    on Pershing/French, 239
    photo of, 159
    problems for, 232
Diebold, General, 227, 228, 230–231
    3d Division and, 229
    55th Brigade and, 230
    125th Division and, 218
    McAlexander and, 231–232
Dockx, Francis J., 93
Doellinger, Herman, 323
Dogan, General, 246
Donnelly, Alan, 351
Dorey, Halstead, 215
Doyen, Charles A., 76
Duchêsne, Denis, 81
Duffy, Francis, 234, 321
    recollections of, 329
Duncan, Donald, 114

Edwards, Clarence, 24, 25, 312, 332, 370n38, 383n30
    casualties for, 43
    criticism of, 332
    Harbord and, 37
    Liggett and, 307–308, 313, 314, 316
    medal for, 411n22
    Pershing and, 36, 42–43, 307–308, 314, 420n23
    personality of, 36–37

Edwards, Clarence, *continued*
   relief of, 317, 420n23
   Traub and, 40, 41, 43
   trench conditions and, 38
Edwards, Dan
   on Cantigny, 52
   recollections of, 53–54, 56
   wounding of, 253
Edwards, Frederick Trevenen, 240
Elliott, Charles B., 185, 271
   La Thiolet and, 124
   Malone and, 120–121, 185
   Moore and, 186
   Waddill and, 119
Elliott, Clark R., 293
Eltinge, LeRoy, 32, 42
Ely, Hanson, 55, 56, 58, 59, 253, 274
   3d Brigade and, 246
   defensive perimeter of, 57
   described, 49–50
   on Vierzy, 275
Enright, Thomas F., 31
Ettighoffer, P. C., 39, 41
Evarts, Jeremiah, 301

Faulkner, Frank L., on Belleau Wood, 121–122
Faulkner, Richard S., 5, 6, 12, 13, 373
Feland, Logan, 173, 179, 205, 275
   5th Marines and, 265
   Belleau Wood and, 205
   Neville and, 180, 183
   problems for, 266
   Turrill and, 108
   Wise and, 171
Field Service Regulations, 15
Fiske, Harold B., 200
Fismes, 1, 2, 4, 302, 337, 341, 348, 355, 356, 423n6
   capture of, 330, 342
   defending, 344, 345
   described, 342–343
   map of, 342
   photo of, 161, 162
Fismette, 8, 161, 302, 330, 337, 344, 356, 359
   battle at, 345, 346, 347, 348, 349, 350–352, 353, 354
   defending, 330, 345, 350, 357
   described, 2, 342–343

   disaster at, 1, 4, 361, 424n29
   map of, 342, 343
   photo of, 162
   success in, 358, 368
FitzPatrick, Tom, 94, 389n28
Foch, Ferdinand, 6, 35, 45, 49, 64, 136, 169–170
   Tenth Army and, 234
   Abbeville agreement and, 44
   appointment of, 36
   attack orders by, 315–316
   counterstroke by, 209–210, 242
   German offensives and, 48, 209
   Haig and, 21
   Pershing and, 8, 207, 316
   Second Marne and, 242, 250–251
Foreign Legion, 246, 247, 260
Fossoy, 222, 223, 224, 225, 226, 232
Francis, William A., 150, 268
Franco-American command, 9, 45, 297, 331, 337
Franco-American relations, 132, 219, 220, 235, 238, 280, 300, 302, 307, 327, 334–335, 336–337, 340, 373
   generalizations about, 8
   trials of, 76, 318, 362–363, 364–366
Fraternity of Arms: America and France in the Great War, A (Bruce), 8
French, John, 10
French Army of Occupation, 372
French Military Mission, 169, 363
Fridenburg, Milton W., 356, 357, 424n27

Gallant, John J., 41
Garlock, Glenn, on French, 327
Gas attacks, 1, 34, 37, 38, 166, 167, 168, 169, 171, 191–192, 198, 250–251, 315, 344
   defense against, 47–48, 50, 347
Gas masks, 50, 347
   training with, 47–48, 156 (photo)
Geer, Corporal, 103
General Orders No. 8 (1917), 20
General Orders No. 31 (1918), 20
General Staff Historical Section, 199, 301
German High Command, 199, 301
Gibbons, Floyd, 111–112, 390n30, 394n27
Givry, capture of, 308, 310, 311
Gleeson, Joseph J., 98, 138, 169
   recollections of, 102, 294

Glückert, Lieutenant, Hill 192 and, 121
Goubeau, General, 258, 280
Gouraud, Henri, 209, 212, 220, 331
    defense of, 234
    false front and, 234
    Marne salient and, 303
Grant, W. S., 153, 165, 167
    Conner and, 88
    investigation by, 42
    report by, 166
Gray, David, 334
Gresham, James B., 28–29, 31
Grotelueschen, Mark E., 5, 6, 265, 373, 381n38, 382n17, 384n35
    on 26th Division, 317
    American army/deficiencies and, 11
    on artillery support, 123
    on Cantigny, 60
    on infantry commanders, 16
Group of Armies of the North, 66, 79
Group of Armies of the Reserve, 79
Gulberg, Martin Gus, 392n34
    recollections of, 92–93, 249–250

Haan, William, 325, 328, 331, 360, 361
    32d Division and, 326
    Allied High Command and, 327
    Bullard and, 327
    Fismes and, 329, 330
Haig, Douglas, 6, 21, 36, 44, 64, 136
Haldane Reforms (1907), 10
Hallas, James H., 6
Halyburton, Ed, 27, 28
Hamilton, George, 102, 103, 104, 394nn11–12
    on counterattacks, 105
    Turrill and, 105
Hammersmith, Philip, on Parker, 38
Hanson, Roy L., 310
Harbord, James G., 21, 89, 98, 100, 102, 104, 106, 109, 124, 133, 164, 167, 178, 179, 180, 220, 276, 374, 387n10, 393n3, 404n24, 404nn26–27, 412n38
    2d Division and, 287–288
    2d Field Artillery Brigade and, 108
    6th Marines and, 284
    7th Regiment and, 183–184
    advance by, 204, 288
    on Allies, 22
    Anderson and, 182
    artillery support by, 150
    attack orders by, 262–263, 264, 265, 273
    Belleau Wood and, 16, 77, 122, 129, 131–132, 136, 140, 141, 142, 148–149, 153, 154, 171, 184, 188, 189, 194, 204
    Berry and, 111
    Bundy and, 77, 125, 130, 149, 169, 202
    casualties and, 86
    Catlin and, 88
    Cole and, 115
    Conner and, 25
    criticism by, 340–341
    criticism of, 101, 206
    defensive and, 85
    Degoutte and, 165, 201
    Edwards and, 37
    field orders and, 107, 140
    Franco-American relations and, 200, 300
    grenades and, 190
    on Helms, 181
    Hill 204 and, 132
    Hughes and, 138, 139
    Janda and, 274
    Lee and, 116, 284, 287
    Malone and, 154
    memo for, 24, 263
    Neville and, 116, 168, 191, 194, 246
    Pershing and, 20
    photo of, 158
    plan by, 141, 143
    on recognition, 76–77
    on reconnaissance, 188
    refugees and, 80
    service of, 19–20
    Sibley and, 131
    Taillefontaine and, 262
    Wise and, 139, 146, 147, 150, 153, 189, 205
Harlem Rattlers, 220, 221, 303, 331
Hartlieb, Hans von, 109, 118, 144, 147, 151, 163, 170, 206
Hautevesnes, 125, 134, 135, 178, 306
Hay, Merle D., 31
Hayward, William, 220, 235
Health issues, 192, 193, 249
Hell, Emil, 192
    28th Division and, 164
    on Americans, 194

Hell, Emil, *continued*
   Belleau Wood and, 204
   divisional order of, 170–171
   offensive and, 166
Helms, Captain, cowardice of, 181
Hemrick, Levi, 82, 113
Hill 104, 56
   capture of, 48, 61
Hill 126, 85–86, 87, 108, 135
Hill 133, 107, 108, 140
Hill 142, 84, 86, 87, 99, 102, 103, 105, 118, 122, 124, 126, 128, 137, 170, 179
   battle for, 93, 107, 108, 142
   capture of, 116, 117
   defending, 104, 125
   described, 101
Hill 165, 86–87, 89, 95, 100, 106
   capture of, 392n1
Hill 166, 247, 255, 256, 261, 281
   capture of, 166, 278, 279
Hill 169, 86, 107, 138, 142, 147, 148, 168, 398n9
Hill 181, 107, 112, 126, 127, 142, 147, 148, 168
Hill 192, 119, 154, 179, 184
   advance on, 120, 128
   capture of, 121, 124
Hill 193, 309, 310
Hill 204, 95, 99, 119, 122, 148, 149, 154, 166, 195, 204, 373
   attack on, 68, 128–129, 137–138, 197, 217, 219
   capture of, 129–130, 405n29
   defending, 126, 135, 141
   described, 128
   Franco-American operations on, 132
   operation and, 198
   tactics on, 132–133
Hill 230, capture of, 327
Hill 326, attack on, 326
Hillman, Rolfe L., 412n38, 415n70
   on Buck, 417n100
   Soissons and, 6
   on Summerall, 419n118
Hines, John L., 259, 261, 291, 295
Hoffman, Bob, 198, 346, 350, 351, 352
   Fismette and, 347
   Hill 204 and, 128, 197

   recollections of, 349
Hoffman, Charles F., 105
Hogan, Martin, recollections of, 321
Holcomb, Thomas, 82, 84, 85, 101, 108, 130, 153, 168, 205, 285, 388n18
   6th Marines and, 114
   Bouresches and, 115
   relief of, 137
Howze, Robert L., on Franco-American relations, 334–335
Huebner, Clarence R., 253, 254, 383n27
   improvisation by, 255
   Missy ravine and, 258
Hughes, Bill, 146
Hughes, John A., 131, 151, 206, 285
   gas attacks and, 168
   Harbord and, 138, 139
   Wise and, 152, 153, 171
Hurley, P. J., 183, 184, 402n19
Hutier, Von, 51

Individual initiative, 8, 11, 273, 299, 380n27
Instructors, French, 156 (photo)
Interpreters, problems with, 23

Jackson, Warren R., 138, 152
   on French, 80
   recollections of, 99, 150, 285
Jacobi, Lieutenant General von, 127
Jacobs, Frank, 190
Janda, Ladislav, 269, 270, 271, 277
   Harbord and, 274
   wounding of, 274
Jaulgonne Bend, 211, 218, 222, 227, 228, 229, 234, 236, 238, 317, 407n47
   capture of, 314
   withdrawal from, 214, 406n18
Johnson, Douglas V., 415n70
   on Buck, 417n100
   Soissons and, 6
   on Summerall, 419n118
   on training, 15
Judah, Noble B., 336

Kathen, Hugo von, 210
Kean, Robert, 100, 196, 271, 275, 277
   on 23d Infantry, 272
   French and, 99

Kelton, Robert H. C., 215–216, 218, 312, 367, 420n16
   Conner and, 237, 238
   Crawford and, 238
   criticism by, 238, 239
   Dickman and, 238, 239, 240
Kemerer, Duncan, 347, 348
Kemp, George E., 322
Kent, Samuel, 328, 329, 331
Keyser, Ralph S., 189, 205, 265, 275–276
   Verte Feuille Ferme and, 267
King, Campbell, 47, 257
Kingery, James R., 224
Krulewitch, Melvin, on boot camp, 18

Lanza, Conrad, 221, 236, 322, 406n18, 408n45, 423n6
   on 109th Regiment, 409n52
   critique by, 344, 421n32
   investigation by, 422n6
   Marne Defensive and, 213
Lay, Harry, 115
Leach, George, 328
Leatherneck, 94
Lebrun, General, 210, 214, 229, 406n12
Lee, Harry, 115, 138–139
   6th Marines and, 284
   Harbord and, 116, 284, 287
   Neville and, 205
   Vizery and, 284
Lenihan, Michael, 219
Le Rû Chailly Farm, 215, 222, 223, 224, 232
Les Mares Farm, 84, 87, 88, 89, 91, 96, 99, 105, 389n27, 391n32, 398n3
   abandoning, 392n1
   defending, 203, 389n24, 390n28, 390n30
   fighting at, 92, 93, 94–95
   Hill 165 and, 106
Lewis, Edward M., 120, 121, 148, 149, 195, 205
   3d Brigade and, 77
   30th Division and, 246
   Belleau Wood and, 122
   Pershing and, 77
Lewis, Robert H., 372–373
   on casualties, 47
   Conner and, 373, 383n23
   Franco-American relations and, 46
Liggett, Hunter, 79, 306, 311–312, 320, 321, 324, 333, 334, 362, 370, 372, 405n5
   I Corps and, 42, 308, 336
   26th Division and, 316–317, 332
   Degoutte and, 307, 336
   Edwards and, 307–308, 313, 314, 316
   Franco-American relations and, 307, 336–337
   on French forces, 371
   Marne salient and, 303
   morale and, 314
   open warfare and, 317
   Pershing and, 37, 314
   Schmidt and, 307
   Second Marne and, 244
Lines of communication, 21, 39, 276
Lloyd George, David, 21, 43
Lucy-le-Bocage, 82, 84, 95, 99, 107, 109, 112, 113, 167
Ludendorff, Erich von, 50, 72, 94, 276–277, 403n14
   "black day" and, 338
   Marne salient and, 297
   morale and, 209
   offensive by, 34–35, 36, 63, 136, 207–208, 237
   Prince Wilhelm and, 95
   Soissons and, 302
   strategy of, 134, 135

MacArthur, Douglas, 219–220, 318, 328
Mach, Lieutenant von, 164
Machine gun crew, German, 162 (photo)
Mackin, Elton E., 275
Major, H. E., 397n6
Malone, Paul B., 24, 77, 84, 124, 184, 195, 271, 273, 276, 402n16
   Bouresches and, 185
   Bundy and, 121, 186
   controversy for, 119–120
   defeat for, 121
   Elliott and, 120–121, 185
   gas attacks and, 198
   Harbord and, 154
   Moore and, 186
Mangin, Charles, 177, 246, 247, 288, 292, 296, 308, 341
   Tenth Army and, 209, 234, 242, 245, 276, 277, 297, 311
   artillery for, 244

Mangin, Charles, *continued*
  assault by, 247–248
  Berdoulat and, 265, 284
  on French effectiveness, 334
  Second Marne and, 250
  Soissons and, 297, 302
  Summerall and, 252
Manley, F. W., 366, 367
Marchand, Jean-Baptiste, 67, 68, 70, 73, 384n11
Mare Island, training at, 18
Marigny, 83, 84, 86, 87, 88, 89, 95
Marine Brigade, 76, 116, 195, 202, 263
  achievement of, 205
  Belleau Wood and, 188, 203, 264
  casualties for, 123
  relief of, 169–170
  strength of, 19, 288
Marine Corps Gazette, 93, 94
Marine Corps Historical Section, 93
Marne Defensive, 6, 135, 210, 212, 213, 233, 240, 337, 366, 372, 373
  counterattack following, 237
  Franco-American liaison and, 219
  impact of, 236–237
Marne River, 66, 68, 79, 213, 222, 223, 227, 235
  crossing, 65, 67, 69, 70, 71, 72–73, 82, 214, 233, 238, 313, 314
  defending, 209, 210, 211, 212, 217–218, 221, 225, 234
Marne salient, 209, 242, 244, 276, 277, 289, 320, 330
  occupation of, 302–303, 315, 324–325, 329
  withdrawal from, 293–294, 296, 297, 302
Marshall, George C., 29–30, 49
  on American forces, 30
  Bordeaux and, 30–31, 32, 379n9
  French and, 30–31
  on Roosevelt, 33
  Sibert and, 31
Martin, Edward, 322
Maxey, Robert, 54, 383n27
McAlexander, Ulysses Grant, 215, 218, 227, 229
  Diebold and, 231–232
  recollections of, 314
McAndrew, James, 334, 362, 363

McCain, Henry, 363
McClellan, Edwin N., 93, 389n28, 391n31
McCloskey, Colonel, 115
McCloud, James, 253, 279
McClure, Walter R., 253, 279, 280
McDade, James H., 309–310
McDaniels, John D., 328, 360
McLaughlin, Lieutenant, 27–28, 29, 30
McMullen, Willie, 269
Mendenhall, John R., 71, 384n11, 384n13, 385n19
  Bissell and, 70, 385n14
  Taylor and, 385n20
  withdrawal by, 72
Menoher, Charles T., 219, 320, 324
Meuse-Argonne campaign, 6, 303, 322, 371, 374
  American infantry operations from, 12
Mézy, 210, 215, 222, 225, 226, 227, 232
Michigan National Guard, 325
Millett, Allan R., Cantigny and, 6
Missy-aux-Bois, 248, 252, 255, 256, 260
Missy ravine, 248, 252, 253–254, 255, 256, 257, 260, 273, 278
  attack into, 258
Montdésir, Jean de, 135, 210, 214, 218, 235, 312, 322, 326, 327, 330
  32d Division and, 328
  XXXVIII Corps and, 69, 236
  criticism of, 239, 318
  defensive by, 212
  Dickman and, 212–213, 235, 317–318
Montdidier-Amiens salient, 338
Moore, Charles E., 185, 186, 193
Moore, William E., 98, 388n23, 389n28
Morale, 9, 22, 25, 34, 76, 134, 331
  AEF, 61
  French, 85, 125, 203, 296, 331, 335
  German, 83, 92, 104, 192, 209, 211, 241, 249, 276, 283
  US, 49, 96, 149, 153, 169, 201, 205, 237, 285, 315, 334, 363
Morgan, Daniel E., 89
Moulins, 215, 227, 231, 232, 233
Moulins Ridge, 227, 228, 231, 232, 233, 236
Moulins Ruiné Signal, 227, 228, 231, 312
Muir, Charles H., 344, 353, 356, 424n28
  28th Division and, 217
  Bullard and, 344, 345, 348, 350

Fismette and, 5
Fridenburg and, 357
photo of, 160
report by, 424n27
Rickards and, 345
role of, 355
Murrin, James A., 355
Mustard gas, 34, 47, 48, 50, 166, 168, 171, 185, 191, 198, 211, 251

National Defense Act (1916), 17
National Guard, 13, 18, 36, 37, 220, 420n23
42d Division and, 219
division numerals for, 17
officers of, 17
Regular Army and, 17
size of, 10
training of, 17
Naulin, Stanislaus, 170, 172, 178, 210, 220, 234
Neiberg, Michael S., 211
Neville, Wendell, 76, 84, 104, 130, 133, 152, 173, 180, 183, 265
Harbord and, 116, 168, 191, 194, 246
Lee and, 205
promotion for, 246
Turrill and, 105
Wise and, 175
New York Times, 202, 404n24
Nivelle offensive, 26, 280
Nohlen, Lieutenant, 273–274
Nolan, Dennis E., 20
Noscereau, Emile, 52
"Notes on Recent Operations No. 1" (Pershing), 332
"Notes on Report Submitted by French High Command at Washington to War Department Direct" (Manley), 366

Oberlin, A. F., 41–42
Oise-Aisne offensive, 6, 354, 355, 359
O'Neill, Richard, 324
Open warfare, 15, 27, 101, 317, 373
training for, 76
trench warfare and, 14
Operation Amerika, 354
Operation Baden, 134
Operation Blücher, 63, 95

Operation Georgette, 36, 63
Operation Gneisenau, 96, 136
Operation *Kirschblüte*, 39
Operation Manfred, 51
Operation Marneschutz-Reims, 207, 242, 249
Operation Michael, 34–35, 63
"Operations of the 26th, 3rd, 42nd, 32nd, 4th, and 28th Divisions in Connection with the Reduction of the Aisne-Marne Salient" (Price), 335
Operation Tannenberg, 51
Operation Tarnopol, 51
"Orders for Gas Defense," issuing of, 119
Osterhout, George H., Jr., 397n6
Otto, Ernst, 148, 387n10, 391n32
Ourcq River, 303, 310, 323, 324, 327
advance on, 321, 322
clearing line of, 319 (map)
Owen, Peter F., 388n18, 395n33, 417n91

Parker, Frank, 259, 291
Parker, James, 325
Parker, John A., artillery/machine guns and, 14
Parker, John H. "Machine Gun," 14, 39, 40, 42, 143
criticism of, 38
initiative/flexibility of, 380n27
Parker, Samuel I., 281
Parris Island, training at, 18
Passaga, Fénelon, 41, 43
Patch, Joseph D., 246, 293
recollections of, 250
Patterson, Robert B., 354
Paysley, Lieutenant, 182
Pennsylvania National Guard, 217
Pernant ravine, 248, 254, 257, 261
Pershing, John J., 25, 26, 31, 33, 48, 74, 90, 100, 169, 219, 292, 327, 331, 332, 368, 370, 375
1st Division and, 36, 45
28th Division and, 424n29
Abbeville agreement and, 44
AEF and, 21–22
African American regiments and, 221
amalgamation and, 6, 22, 49, 218, 220
Baker and, 21
Belleau Wood and, 136

Pershing, John J., *continued*
    Brown and, 153
    Buck on, 27
    Bullard and, 355
    Bundy and, 147, 149, 191, 194, 369
    Cantigny and, 61
    cobelligerents and, 21
    controversy over, 19
    decisions by, 207
    declaration by, 35
    Edwards and, 36, 42–43, 307–308, 314, 420n23
    experience for, 11
    Foch and, 8, 207, 316
    French command and, 30, 239, 337
    French critique and, 362, 363, 364, 365–366
    on German bombardment, 46
    Harbord and, 20
    individual initiative and, 8
    Lewis and, 77
    Liggett and, 37, 314
    memorandum by, 44
    open warfare and, 15, 76, 373
    Parker and, 325
    Pétain and, 24
    photo of, 157
    report for, 199, 301
    resourcefulness and, 15
    Saint-Mihiel and, 338
    Seicheprey and, 43
    self-reliance and, 14, 15
    Sibert and, 23, 24
    staff of, 19
    Summerall and, 245
    tactical theories of, 14, 15
    training and, 23
Pétain, Henri-Philippe, 63, 65, 67, 212, 219, 242, 280, 297
    2d Division and, 234
    on Aisne-Marne offensive, 340
    appointment of, 26
    Directive No. 4 and, 211
    German offensives and, 209
    Pershing and, 24
    proposal by, 25, 220
Pierce, Harold
    Fismes and, 342, 346, 358
    Fismette and, 345, 359
    recollection of, 353, 361–362

Pierce, Hugh, 345, 346
Ploisy ravine, 252, 261, 279, 281, 282, 283, 291
Pohlmann, Georg, 127
Price, X. H., 335, 336, 360
Prisoners
    American, 34, 35, 39, 40, 51, 123, 177
    described, 192
    German, 34, 262, 334

Quantico, 19, 76

Radcliffe, Edward J., 225, 230
Rageneau, Camille M., 169, 170
Regular Army, 13, 15, 65, 303, 420n23
    National Guard and, 17
    officers of, 17
    size of, 10
Renault tanks, 244, 253
Rendinell, Joseph Edward, 390n30
Reuilly, 227, 228, 233
Richardson, Robert C., 153–154, 166
Rickards, George, 5, 344, 356, 424n28
    Fismette and, 345, 355
    Muir and, 345
Rinker, Charles F., 390n28
Robertson, James F., 114
Rogers, Horatio, recollections of, 309
Roosevelt, Archie, 32
Roosevelt, Theodore, Jr., 32, 33, 253
    wounding of, 279–280
Root, Elihu, 11
Route 2, 252, 255, 256, 259, 265, 266, 278, 279, 280
Rowe, Guy, 231
Rozelle, George, 253, 281, 282, 291
Rubin, Richard, 202
Rue-Cervante, 343, 346, 349, 356
Russian Legion, 401n17
Ryan, William, 224

Saconin, 254, 255, 256, 257
Saint-Mihiel, 6, 33, 246, 283, 338, 359, 362, 367, 374
Saint-Mihiel offensive, 7, 9, 316, 317, 368
Sargent, Daniel, 52, 57, 59
Schmelzer, Edward, 424n27
Schmidt, General, 307, 332
Schneider tanks, 50, 244, 247, 260, 274

School of Hard Knocks: Combat Leadership in the American Expeditionary Forces, The (Faulkner), 5
Seicheprey, 6, 33, 36, 39, 43, 44–45, 62, 350, 367, 380n27, 381n38
    assault at, 38
    defeat at, 41, 307
    resistance at, 40
Seller, James McBrayer, on training, 19
Senegalese, 72, 246, 247, 260, 266, 297, 385n21
Shannon, Edward C., 350, 352
Shay, Michael E., 36, 380n27
Shearer, Maurice E., 131, 191, 194, 205, 265, 388n20
    Belleau Wood and, 143, 189
    Bouresches and, 166, 168
    casualties for, 193
    grenades and, 190
Shelton, George H., 316
Shepherd, Lemuel, 84–85, 89, 93, 94, 389n25, 389nn27–28
    Asprey and, 90
    wounding of, 90
Sibert, William S., 26, 30, 31, 33
    on interpreters, 23
    Pershing and, 23, 24
Sibley, Berton, 108, 115, 133, 138, 205, 285, 286, 381n38
    6th Marines and, 101, 107, 112, 137
    Bouresches and, 114, 116
    casualties for, 116
    French Command and, 113
    Harbord and, 131
    problems for, 130
Sibley, Frank, 308
Silverthorn, Merwin, 110, 111
Sladen, Fred W., 215, 318, 320, 335
Smith, Hamilton, 253, 280, 293, 296
Smythe, Donald, 22, 331
Soissons, 82, 160, 209, 214, 242, 244, 245, 248, 249, 252, 255, 261, 262, 276, 277, 287, 288
    Buck and, 417n100
    capture of, 64–65, 329
    Summerall and, 419n118
Soissons offensive, 6, 7, 8, 244, 246, 253, 295, 302, 303, 330, 332, 338, 362
    beginning of, 12, 289

    individual initiative in, 299
    map of, 251
    summation of, 297, 299, 300, 301
Soissons railroad, 242, 289, 290
    loss of, 261
Sorensen, Soren C., 291, 292
"Special Memorandum Relating to the Guarding of the Marne Crossings" (memo), 65
Speer, Charles, 269
St. Agnan ravine, 69, 213, 230, 236
St. Chamond tanks, 244, 247, 274
Staabs, Hermann von, 248
Stabenau, Marksman, 193
Stacey, Cromwell, 215
Stackpole, Pierpont L., 42
Starlings, P. N., 298
Stevenson, John A., recollections of, 323–324
Stewart, Alexander, resourcefulness and, 15
Strickland, Daniel, recollections of, 313
"Study Showing Accomplishments of American Divisions which Attacked under Command of the French or British," 335
Sulzbach, Herbert, 241, 251
    recollections of, 294, 296
Summerall, Charles P., 16, 49, 258, 262, 264, 273, 278, 280, 289, 290, 296, 298, 411n17, 415n79, 416n80
    artillery/machine guns and, 14
    Babcock and, 281
    Berzy-le-Sec and, 294
    Bullard and, 245
    casualties for, 261
    command for, 33
    Franco-American relations and, 300
    Mangin and, 252
    Pershing and, 245
    Smith and, 293
    Soissons and, 295, 301, 419n118
    summary of operations and, 257
Supreme War Council, 136, 315
Surmelin Valley, 23, 210, 213, 227, 233, 235, 236

Tack, Willis, 253, 255
"Tactical Instructions—Means for Overcoming the Enemy's Machine Gun Defense" (Liggett), 333

Tank Battalion 5, 53
Tardieu, André, 220–221, 363
Taylor, James, 66, 71, 385n16
Thomas, Lowell, 56, 411n22
Thomason, John W., Jr., 76, 94, 248, 263, 391n32, 393n9, 400n15
   Belleau Wood and, 107
Thompson, Hugh S., recollections of, 221–222
Torcy, 99, 100, 101, 104, 105, 108, 115, 124, 125, 177, 194
   abandonment of, 86
   capture of, 308, 309
Training, 5, 31, 34, 37, 220, 222, 300
   advanced, 18–19
   basic, 13, 19
   British, 201
   deficiency in, 13, 15, 27
   in France, 22–23, 25, 201
   gas mask, 47–48, 156 (photo)
   officer, 13–14, 17
   open warfare, 76
   rifle, 18
   stages of, 25
Trask, David F., 6, 331
Traub, Peter E., 42
   countermeasures by, 40–41
   Edwards and, 40, 41, 43
   initiative/flexibility of, 380n27
   Parker and, 39, 40
Trench warfare, 23, 27, 37, 110
   open warfare and, 14
   phases of, 24
   relying on, 132–133
Triangle, 82, 84, 95, 99, 119, 130, 179, 194, 195
Triangle Wood, 115, 118–119
Turrill, Julius S., 84, 100, 101, 102, 103, 109, 115, 265
   Chaudun and, 266, 267
   Feland and, 108
   Hamilton and, 105
   Hill 126 and, 108
   Hill 142 and, 104, 106
   Neville and, 105

Upton, LeRoy, 77, 195, 269, 273, 275, 276, 288, 414n55
   Degoutte and, 79

US Marine Corps, 6, 74, 102, 192
   AEF and, 17
   boot camp for, 18
   courage/audacity of, 163
   size of, 10
   training, 156 (photo)

Valentine, Captain, 185
Vandenberg, Charles A., 48–49, 54
Vann, Norma, 280
Varennes, 218, 227, 228, 312
Vaux, 87, 119, 128, 129, 135, 137, 154, 179, 194, 246, 308, 311, 336
   attack on, 132, 171, 206, 217, 405n29
   capture of, 6, 86, 195, 198
Vauxbuin, 255, 256, 261, 279, 280, 281, 282, 290
   advance on, 300
   defending, 283
Vauxcastille ravine, 267, 270, 272, 273, 277
Verdun, 27, 127, 368
Vesle River, 1, 16, 329, 330, 331, 333, 337, 338, 343, 344, 353, 354, 355, 356, 357, 358
   advance on, 63, 340, 341, 342
   footbridge at, 161 (photo)
   map of, 339
   salient, 359
   withdrawal to, 328
Veuilly-la-Poterie, 86, 87, 88, 100, 104, 122, 125, 135, 203
   evacuation of, 106
Vierzy, 242, 247, 248, 264, 265, 268, 271, 272–273, 284, 299, 414n63
   advance on, 274
   fighting at, 275–276, 277
Villa, Pancho, 20
Von Conta, 82, 83, 95, 96, 127, 206, 397n19, 399n8
   87th Division and, 165
   attack by, 88, 148–149, 177–178
   attack on, 94
   Belleau Wood and, 137, 141, 154, 204
   defensive by, 98, 135, 138
   offensive and, 166, 169
   orders from, 95
   responsibilities of, 134

Wackerine, Georges, 68

Waddill, Edmund C., 119, 120, 271
Walker, Fred L., 224, 225, 226
Waller, L. W. T., 397n6
War Department, National Guard formations and, 17
Watter, Theodor Freiherr von, 248, 250, 268, 275
Weigel, William, 217
Well Planned, Splendidly Executed: The Battle of Cantigny, May 28–31, 1918 (Millett), 6
Whelton, Frank, 2–3, 4
White, H. L., on 3d Division, 233
Wilder, Amos N., 17th Field Artillery and, 92
Wilder, Fred Calvin, 316
   recollections of, 314–315
Wilhelm, Crown Prince, 209, 294
   Ludendorff and, 95
   offensive and, 237
Wilhelm II, Kaiser, 10
Wilhelmy, Captain, 69, 70, 385n14
Williams, Lloyd, 88, 389n24
Wilson, Woodrow, 14
Winans, Roswell, 171
Wisconsin National Guard, 325

Wise, Frederic, 89, 140–141, 147, 151, 170, 181, 183, 206, 388n20, 389n24, 398n3
   5th Marines and, 84, 124, 390n30
   Belleau Wood and, 142–143
   Bundy and, 152
   Feland and, 171
   Harbord and, 139, 146, 147, 150, 153, 189, 205
   Hughes and, 152, 153, 171
   intelligence and, 175
   losses for, 176
   mistakes by, 176
   Neville and, 175
   plan by, 141
   recollections of, 390–391n30
   relief for, 168, 173
Wise, Jennings C., 49, 67
Woods Line, 215, 226, 227, 231
Wooldridge, Jesse Walton, 226, 232
Worthington, Henry H., 269, 270
Wright, Harry G., 310

Yeomans, Earl, 310
Yockelson, Mitchell, 6, 9

Zane, Randolph T., 114, 130